AT THE
PULPIT

AT THE PULPIT

185 YEARS OF DISCOURSES BY LATTER-DAY SAINT WOMEN

EDITED BY
Jennifer Reeder and Kate Holbrook

THE CHURCH HISTORIAN'S PRESS

The Church Historian's Press is an imprint of the Church History Department of The Church of Jesus Christ of Latter-day Saints, Salt Lake City, Utah, and a trademark of Intellectual Reserve, Inc.

www.churchhistorianspress.org

Art direction: Richard Erickson.
Cover and jacket design: Riley M. Lorimer and Heather G. Ward. Interior design: Heather G. Ward.
Typography: Expand Business Solutions, Inc., Salt Lake City, Utah, and Riley M. Lorimer.

Library of Congress Cataloging-in-Publication Data

Names: Reeder, Jennifer, editor. | Holbrook, Kate, editor.
Title: At the Pulpit: 185 Years of Discourses by Latter-day Saint Women / Jennifer Reeder and Kate Holbrook.
Description: Salt Lake City: The Church Historian's Press, [2017] | Includes bibliographical references and index.
Identifiers: LCCN 2016027869 | ISBN 9781629722825 (hardbound: alk. paper)
Subjects: LCSH: Mormon Church—Doctrines. | Church of Jesus Christ of Latter-day Saints—Doctrines. | LCGFT: Speeches.

Classification: LCC BX8639.A1 A8 2016 | DDC 230/.9332—dc23

LC record available at http://lccn.loc.gov/2016027869

Printed in the United States of America on acid-free paper.
10 9 8 7 6 5 4 3 2

CONTENTS

◇◇◇

ILLUSTRATIONS

◇◇◇

INTRODUCTION

◇◇◇

SARAH STURTEVANT LEAVITT could scarcely express the depth of her conviction after her baptism as a Latter-day Saint in the 1830s. "I had some[thing] of more importance that was shut up like fire in my bones," she wrote. Leavitt shared her message in local taverns, speaking earnestly to anyone who would listen. At one visit to a sick neighbor, where a large group had gathered, Leavitt remembered, "The Lord gave me great liberty of speech. I prayed with the Spirit and with understanding, also to him be the glory."[1]

From the earliest days of the Church of Jesus Christ of Latter-day Saints, women and men have participated in religious discussion, shared the gospel message with family and friends, given testimonies, and spoken in meetings. In the two centuries since the church's founding, church members have recorded the testimonies and teachings of thousands of women. Many of these records are difficult to access today, forgotten in old minute books and obscure newspapers. By contrast, the public teaching and preaching done by men, particularly church leaders, was much more likely to be preserved in historical records and published for a wide audience. For this and other reasons, the voices and experiences of men are much more commonly the subject of scholarly investigation and contemporary teaching and preaching in the church than are those of women. Nevertheless, the available records powerfully demonstrate that women have contributed to Latter-day Saint devotion through sermons, speeches, prayers, songs, and stories.

This volume showcases the tradition of Latter-day Saint women's discourses with fifty-four speeches given from 1831 to 2016. Introductions and annotation provide insight into the biographical, historical, theological, and cultural context of each talk. In addition to being a scholarly history, this book provides a resource for contemporary church members as they study, speak, teach, and lead.

Elizabeth Ann Whitney, Emmeline B. Wells, and Eliza R. Snow. Circa 1876. Whitney (left) and Snow (right) were members of the Nauvoo Relief Society and served together when the general board of the Relief Society was organized in 1880. Emmeline B. Wells (center) edited the *Woman's Exponent* and worked as the general secretary and then general president of the Relief Society in later years. These three women traveled often to speak to different congregations. Photograph by Charles R. Savage. (Church History Library, Salt Lake City.)

"This Is My Voice unto All": A History of Mormon Women Speaking in an American Context

In early July 1830, Emma Hale Smith received a revelation through her husband, Joseph Smith, about her position and responsibilities in the new Church of Christ. Recorded in the voice of God, the revelation (now known as section 25 of the Doctrine and Covenants) described Emma Smith as an "elect lady" and charged her "to expound scriptures and exhort the church according as it shall be given thee by my spirit." The responsibilities were weighty—in expounding, Emma Smith was by definition tasked to "explain, to lay open the meaning, to clear of obscurity, to interpret," while in exhorting, she was to "encourage, to embolden, to cheer, to advise, to excite or to give strength, spirit, or courage."[2] The revelation contained specific counsel for Smith, but its charge to teach and preach can be interpreted as universal—"this is my voice unto all," it concluded.[3] While there are no surviving records of her preaching publicly in the roughly twelve years following the revelation, Emma Smith worked alongside her husband during those years in ministering to the Saints.[4]

In March 1842, Emma Smith and a small group of Latter-day Saint women worked with Joseph Smith to organize the Female Relief Society of Nauvoo. In that body, she developed her voice, promoting unity and teaching the women that it was their duty as Relief Society members to "seek out and relieve the distressed."[5] In the first meeting of the organization, Joseph Smith read aloud the 1830 revelation directed to Emma Smith, explaining that "she was ordained at the time the revelation was given to expound the scriptures to all; and to teach the female part of [the] community." He further stated that "not she alone, but others, may attain to the same blessings."[6] In the meetings of the Nauvoo Relief Society, women preached, discussed, and endeavored "not only to relieve the poor, but to save souls," as they had been charged by Joseph Smith.[7]

The Relief Society was founded in an era when women's speaking and preaching in church were contentious issues, even though women composed the majority in most Christian churches in eighteenth- and early-nineteenth-century America. Indeed, many Christian denominations at the time held that women should be "silent" in church.[8] Female speaking in formal religious settings was the subject of lively and bitter debates—and yet women did speak.[9] In the 1630s in Boston, Massachusetts Bay Colony, Anne Hutchinson had taught groups of women and men in her home, encouraging them to pray, to teach their children, and to attend religious services. "The elder women should instruct the young," she wrote, paraphrasing the New Testament injunction.[10] Viewed as dangerous because of her teaching and for other reasons, Hutchinson was expelled from the colony.

In the two centuries between Hutchinson's expulsion and the revelation to Emma Smith, many churches became more open to public speaking by women. In the eighteenth century, the Great Awakening and American Revolution transformed the spiritual and political landscape. That transformation opened possibilities for women's teaching and preaching, in part by emphasizing leadership by common people and encouraging personal expression. From that period of religious enthusiasm and ideological evolution to the early 1800s, many churches that were viewed as radical—from Quakers and Methodists to Shakers and Freewill Baptists—gave women the opportunity to speak publicly and even act as religious leaders.[11]

The Second Great Awakening in the early nineteenth century further encouraged ideals of equality and democracy within religious organizations, leading more women to preach in churches. Like many other people of faith, Latter-day Saints asserted the importance of everyday members instructing one another.[12] Both Lucy Mack Smith and Elizabeth Ann Whitney, whose words are featured in this volume, demonstrated this type of religious expression as they gave extemporaneous voice to their faith.[13] Following the Second Great Awakening, however, some churches reemphasized male authority and decreased the number of opportunities for women to preach.[14] American Methodism, for example, allowed female preachers in the late eighteenth and early nineteenth centuries but then returned to a system of primarily male preaching.[15]

During the early and mid-1800s, women speaking before mixed-gender audiences often provoked suspicion and hostility in the broader culture. As such, many religious women, including Latter-day Saints, spoke primarily in women's meetings. The Relief Society provided an institutional pulpit for Latter-day Saint women from 1842 to 1844, but it was disbanded before the migration of the Latter-day Saints to the American West. Small, informal groups of women gathered often while crossing the plains and in the early days in the Salt Lake Valley, speaking and experiencing spiritual manifestations together.[16] The exercise of spiritual gifts was an important part of public speaking for many early Mormon women, who spoke in tongues, gave blessings of health or comfort, and related dreams, visions, and revelations.[17] After short-lived attempts to reestablish local Relief Societies in the 1850s, the Relief Society was permanently reorganized on a congregational level in the late 1860s.[18] Organizations led by women and intended for young women (Young Ladies' Mutual Improvement Association, later known as Young Women) and children (Primary) followed in the next decade. In the late nineteenth and early twentieth centuries, these organizations—along with groups promoting suffrage, silk production, women's health, and other causes—provided more venues in which Latter-day Saint women could speak. Leaders including

Eliza R. Snow, Zina D. H. Young, and Mary Isabella Horne traveled to local wards and trained women to run local organizations.[19] And in 1889, the Relief Society began holding semiannual conferences, where general leaders trained and preached to members and leaders from local societies.[20] Most of the discourses included in this volume were delivered in meetings of official church organizations for women.

The creation of secular women's organizations in nineteenth-century America gave women access to nonreligious lecterns in addition to the pulpits they commanded in their churches. Through benevolent associations, women sought social and moral reform.[21] Starting in the 1820s, for instance, Catharine Beecher opened a female seminary and organized petitions and held public meetings to protest the removal of American Indians from their traditional lands in the eastern United States. Quakers Sarah and Angelica Grimké gained oratory experience in church meetings and then promoted abolition on lecture circuits in the 1830s.[22] The Grimkés and other women used their public speaking opportunities to fuel the development of the women's rights movement.[23]

Like women elsewhere in the United States, Latter-day Saint women claimed a role in the political process. In part because of cultural backlash against the practice of plural marriage, contemporary writers often derided Latter-day Saint women as weak and mindless. Mormon women therefore had particular motivation to demonstrate their eloquence and strength, which they did in "mass meetings" where they defended their faith and sought the right to vote.[24] They also participated actively in national women's groups and by the late 1800s were regular speakers at national conferences of women's organizations; several such orations are included in this volume.[25]

Gradually, female speakers before mixed-gender audiences became more common both in Latter-day Saint meetings and in other religious and social movements. In the 1800s, Mormon women spoke at meetings where church members met together while fasting to share extemporaneous testimonies. With the exception of those meetings, women seldom spoke in sacrament meetings during the nineteenth century; men with leadership callings were the primary speakers, and attendance at these meetings was sometimes sporadic.[26] Women did speak in cottage meetings, prayer meetings, and other informal gatherings from the early days of the church.[27] By 1896, the general leaders of the Young Ladies' Mutual Improvement Association began holding annual training meetings with their counterparts in the Young Men's Mutual Improvement Association, with both men and women training leaders of both sexes.[28] Additional opportunities came in 1898, when single female missionaries were called for the first time and began to preach publicly on behalf of the church.[29]

The twentieth century saw an overall expansion of women's participation in the public life of many denominations—both in the United States and throughout the world—including the ordination of women by United Methodists, Presbyterians, Reform Jews, and others.[30] Catholic, evangelical, and Jewish laywomen often spoke in women's groups, advocacy groups, and women's homes rather than at a formal pulpit.[31] Latter-day Saint women in the twentieth century preached and taught in small, single-gender settings as their nineteenth-century counterparts had done—in weekly meetings of the Relief Society, Sunday School, Young Women, and Primary organizations.[32] But in the early twentieth century, missionaries of both genders and representatives of auxiliary organizations—including the Relief Society and Young Women—occasionally organized and participated in their congregations' sacrament meetings, which provided more opportunities for women to address audiences of women and men.[33] The 1944 church *Handbook of Instructions,* however, ended auxiliary-sponsored sacrament meetings, specifying that "the sacrament meeting should be like a family gathering where as many as possible may participate in the exercises and all worship in love, reverence, and fellowship."[34]

Nevertheless, Latter-day Saint women's opportunities to speak in church meetings of both men and women at all levels of the church have increased in number and visibility over time. Mormons believe that members are to learn from each other and that any woman can enlighten those around her. During the 1900s, women leaders spoke on a churchwide level in Mutual Improvement Association June conferences, general Relief Society conferences, Primary conferences, and Sunday School conferences.[35] With the end of auxiliary general conferences in 1975, firesides became a popular venue for women to speak in.[36] For instance, the Relief Society held a churchwide fireside in 1978, and the Young Women organization sponsored one in 1980.[37] Brigham Young University's weekly devotionals—religious lectures meant to unify and strengthen the student body—started in the late nineteenth century. Rose Marie Reid was the first woman to speak at a BYU devotional, in July 1953.[38] In 1976, the university began hosting an annual women's conference, where women gathered both to teach and to be taught.[39]

Women began speaking consistently at the church's semiannual general conferences in the 1980s,[40] around the same time the Relief Society resumed holding an annual general meeting for all its members.[41] Soon after, young women twelve and older were invited to join them for the general women's meeting,[42] and Primary girls ten and older began attending that meeting in 1983. This meeting continued to be held until the fall of 1993, when the Relief Society began holding an annual general meeting for adult women in the fall; the Young Women organization began holding its own annual meeting starting the following spring.[43]

Brigham Young University Women's Conference. 2016. The Marriott Center holds plenary sessions of BYU Women's Conference, which began in 1976. The image of Sandra Rogers, international vice president of BYU, appears on the large screen. Photograph by Maddi Driggs. (Courtesy *Daily Universe* [Provo, UT].)

Beginning in 2014, the Relief Society and Young Women discontinued their individual meetings, and all girls and women ages eight and older began again to meet for a general women's meeting on the Saturday before general conference.[44] Later that same year, church leaders officially designated that meeting the general women's session and announced that it would be considered the opening session of general conference. Ordinarily, speakers at the general women's session are members of the general presidencies of the Relief Society, Young Women, or Primary organizations, along with one member of the First Presidency.[45]

"Have Something to Say": Overcoming Obstacles and Speaking with Authority

Notwithstanding the tradition of Mormon women's discourses, many Latter-day Saint women have been reluctant to speak or preach publicly for a variety of reasons, both cultural and personal. Even Zina D. H. Young—who became a prominent leader and celebrated speaker in later life—was initially hesitant at the prospect of addressing an audience. "I am not accustomed to public speaking," Young said as she began her 1869 speech to the Lehi Relief Society, "but pleased to look upon the faces of my sisters."[46] Many early Latter-day Saint converts came from religious traditions that discouraged women from speaking in formal religious settings. The broader nineteenth-century cultural debates about the appropriateness of women speaking in public, particularly before audiences of both men and women, also contributed to Mormon women's reluctance to speak from the pulpit.

To counteract this reticence, both male and female church leaders have encouraged women to speak and participate in church gatherings. In 1879, Eliza R. Snow, who became Relief Society general president the following year, told the women of Morgan, Utah, that "it was necessary that the sisters should stand up and speak to and bear their testimony to each other, as it would fit them to fill any position they might be called upon to fill with self-possession and dignity."[47] A decade later, apostle Franklin D. Richards spoke to the Weber Stake Relief Society, urging women to participate in public work even though they might feel timid or worry about appearing presumptuous. He also spoke against influences that contributed to women feeling insecure about their efforts, rebuking men who either taunted women speakers or viewed their public work with jealousy. "I think the brethren, by hindering them, withhold blessings from themselves," he said.[48]

Eliza R. Snow also instructed women to be prepared when assignments or opportunities to speak came to them. Emily Richards remembered how Snow helped her learn to speak in public: "The first time [she] asked me to speak in meeting, I could not, and she said, 'Never mind, but when you are asked to speak again, try and have something to say,' and I did."[49] Years later, Richards spoke at a meeting of the National Woman Suffrage Association in Washington DC, and a journalist described her on that occasion as "trembling slightly under the scrutinizing gaze of the multitude, yet reserved, self-possessed, dignified, and as pure and sweet as an angel."[50] Snow's urging was echoed by later church leaders, who likewise encouraged women to increase their public participation. At a Relief Society conference meeting for officers in 1958, Joseph Fielding Smith, a member of the Quorum of the Twelve Apostles, spoke of women's authority to bear witness and to perform work necessary for salvation. "You can speak with authority, because the Lord has placed authority upon you," he proclaimed.[51]

Women throughout the church's history, including those whose words appear in this volume, have seen their authority to speak as coming not only from official positions within the church but also by virtue of their expertise, their personal experience and conviction, and the witness of the Holy Spirit. Often multiple sources of authority, entwined together, reinforce their common strength.

A discourse by Lucy Mack Smith in this volume exemplifies these braided sources of authority. She spoke in April 1831 on the deck of a steamboat at the mouth of Buffalo Harbor on the frozen Erie Canal. Before embarking on their move to Kirtland, Ohio, the company of Saints from Fayette, New York, had given her leadership over the group. When they reached Buffalo, the ice made it impossible for them to continue. Others had waited for weeks for a thaw that would allow them to cross Lake Erie. Though Smith did not have a formal appointment in the young church, her position as the mother of founding prophet Joseph Smith bolstered her authority to lead and preach. With the authority of her faith, Smith proclaimed, "Brethren and sisters, if you will all of you raise your desires to heaven that the ice may give way before us and we be set at liberty to go on our way, as sure as the Lord lives it shall be done." When she documented this incident in the 1840s, Smith reported that immediately after her speech, the ice cracked and parted, making a narrow pathway for the boat to cross.[52]

Women receive explicit authority with official positions in the Church of Jesus Christ of Latter-day Saints.[53] When Elaine L. Jack addressed the students, faculty, administration, and staff of Brigham Young University in 1993, she did so as general president of the Relief Society. Prior to her service in that position, she had worked for twelve years overseeing Relief Society curriculum and served as a member of the Young Women general presidency. She had concentrated on the elements of human development and had been responsible for helping women flourish from adolescence through adulthood. With the authority of her position, she interpreted the stories of people in the scriptures. She compared her vantage point to that of Moses, saying, "My dear brothers and sisters, like Moses, I stand watching you, the young adults of the church, prepare to cross into many lands of promise. Tonight I repeat Moses's words and ask you to choose life."[54]

Many women who speak in these pages do so from the authority of personal experience and conviction. Jane H. Neyman spoke with this kind of authority at a Relief Society meeting in 1869. Her initial petition to join the Nauvoo Relief Society was rejected in 1842 because of community gossip about her daughters. In 1869, six months after completing a term as ward Relief Society president, she encouraged "all to be forbearing and forgiving; refraining as much as possible from scrutinizing the conduct of our neighbors, remembering always that we are human and must therefore err." She spoke as a former victim of neighbors' scrutiny and as one who had forgiven ostracism from church members and stood by both the church and the Relief Society.[55]

More than a century later, Irina Kratzer, a convert to the church from Russia, likewise spoke from the authority of her personal conviction. She remarked, "I know how it is to live without the gospel. I lived that way for thirty years." Kratzer said that she did not think about God before investigating the church but felt pain over her poor choices. She later came to believe that pain had been the Light of Christ, directing her to distinguish between right and wrong. As she read the Book of Mormon, she began to see a gap between Christ's teaching and the way she lived, and she felt that discrepancy was the reason for her misery. She wanted to change. This is the background from which she declared her understanding of how to live and how to achieve happiness: "I have learned that almost every miracle I have experienced since my baptism has come as a result of prayer and effort. God requires effort and faith on our part."[56]

Ultimately, Latter-day Saints believe that the Holy Spirit both prompts speakers to address topics of divine importance and confirms to listeners the authority of a speaker who preaches by genuine inspiration. Russell M. Nelson, president of the Quorum of the Twelve Apostles, emphasized that speaking with inspiration is not exclusive to leaders: "My dear sisters, whatever your calling, whatever your circumstances, we need your impressions, your insights, and your inspiration. . . . Married or single, you sisters possess distinctive capabilities and special intuition you have received as gifts from God."[57] Regardless of their church positions, members generally feel an obligation to try to speak in concert with the Holy Spirit. For example, Carol F. McConkie, first counselor in the Young Women general presidency, prayed and studied in preparation for a general conference talk and knew what she wanted to speak about. But when her husband, Oscar, asked about her topic, she found herself telling him something different from what she had prepared. She changed her talk during subsequent weeks, wrestling, praying, fasting, and writing. She clearly remembered kneeling to pray to ask God whether this talk was the right one: "My heart and mind and entire being filled with absolute assurance and a peace that gave me the confidence to submit the talk," she said. The talks that preceded hers in the Sunday morning session of general conference coordinated with hers and convinced her that God had directed her efforts. "I knew," she said, "that the words of the talk I had written were from God."[58]

Throughout the church's history, Latter-day Saint women have sought to fulfill the revelatory charge to "expound scriptures and exhort the church"—to give voice to the "fire in [the] bones" described by Sarah Sturtevant Leavitt.[59] In the October 2015 general conference, apostle Russell M. Nelson declared, "The kingdom of God is not and cannot be complete without women who make sacred covenants and then keep them, women who can speak with the power and authority of God! . . . We need you to speak up and speak out."[60] The discourses in this volume allow readers to hear the historical and contemporary voices of women who have spoken up and spoken out. Their words serve as a testament to the idea that each individual's witness strengthens the whole, as former Relief Society general president Julie B. Beck described. "The real power in this great worldwide sisterhood lies within each woman," she said. "We all share a noble heritage and can develop a faith that is equal to that of the remarkable, faithful women who have gone before us."[61]

FINDING, SELECTING, AND PRESENTING THE DISCOURSES

◇◇◇

THIS VOLUME PRESENTS transcripts of fifty-four discourses given by Latter-day Saint women from 1831 to 2016. In selecting addresses for this volume, the editors took a broad view of the idea of *discourse*. The discourses included here encompass everything from discussions at early Relief Society meetings to formal remarks at Latter-day Saint general conferences. While many types of "pulpits" exist in Latter-day Saint culture, the discourses in this volume were delivered primarily in institutional church settings, and many of the talks were reprinted in church magazines and conference reports. With their selections, the editors tried to represent many of the varied ways that Mormon women have addressed public audiences.

Even within institutional settings, the formats in which Latter-day Saint women speak have changed over time, and those changes are reflected in the discourses that were selected for this volume. In the early years of the church, Mormon women's public speaking was sometimes tied to the exercise of spiritual gifts, such as speaking in tongues and administering blessings of health or comfort.[1] For instance, Elizabeth Ann Whitney's discourse in chapter 2 is a song she sang by the gift of tongues in the partially constructed temple in Kirtland, Ohio. Early Mormon women also recited poetry, read personal essays, and offered public prayers. Chapter 20 demonstrates one of these forms of public expression with Elvira S. Barney's 1889 invocation at a meeting of the Utah Woman Suffrage Association, which reads like a detailed sermon. Women's speeches changed as their meetings and public gatherings became more formal. Members of early Relief Societies most often spoke through discussion, but regular meetings gave rise to extemporaneous speeches, which in turn gave way to increasingly formal and polished discourses, as evident in the latter part of this volume.

Finding the Discourses

Locating discourses delivered in such varied venues and formats over 185 years requires a historian's proclivity to excavate old sources. While women's discourses can be found throughout the Latter-day Saint historical record, these sources are often difficult to access. Some of the earliest talks by Latter-day Saint women were preserved in personal reminiscences, like those of Lucy Mack Smith. Minute books of women's organizations are a particularly valuable source for women's discourses. Female secretaries typically kept minutes of meetings, but the accuracy of these minutes depended on the individual secretaries. Some took meticulous notes, while others provided only summaries, and many female secretaries recorded the discourses of men in more detail than they did the speeches of women. Around 1915, church organizations replaced handwritten minute books with standardized forms, which recorded the names of speakers but little else.[2] As a result, the historical record lost many spontaneous utterances of everyday members in their regular meetings.

Newspapers and magazines often distributed speeches to a wider readership, though women's words were typically summarized rather than reproduced in full, especially in the nineteenth century. The *Woman's Exponent* (1872–1914) was written, edited, printed, and distributed by women and included reports of women's meetings, often submitted by local organizations' secretaries. Women's speeches also appeared in the *Millennial Star* (1840–1970) and the *Young Woman's Journal* (1889–1929). In the twentieth century, the *Relief Society Magazine* (1915–1970) published women's discourses, as did Relief Society, Mutual Improvement Association, and Young Women conference reports. General conference reports and transcripts of Brigham Young University (BYU) devotionals—especially in the late twentieth and early twenty-first centuries—provide a rich collection of discourses given by women. Talks from the BYU Women's Conference are available in published collections, the first of which was released in 1980.[3] By the close of the twentieth century, Mormon women's discourses were available in the *Ensign* and *Liahona,* in printed books, on television broadcasts, and on the Internet.

The advent of recording technology vastly increased the number of women's discourses that were preserved, and as a result, the editors of this volume had far more speeches to choose from in the later decades of church history than they did in the early years. Later talks were captured with more detail and precision, and the average length of recorded discourses increased over time. Most of the later talks come from published sources, while most of the early talks were found in newspapers or minute books.

The available sources are heavily weighted toward discourses given in Utah, and the selection in this book does not adequately represent non-American voices. Nevertheless, the voices of international women do appear in this book. They include a nineteenth-century address given in England by Elicia A. Grist and several discourses by English and Scottish immigrants who converted to the church and joined the Latter-day Saints in Utah. Church growth in international areas accelerated rapidly in the second half of the twentieth century, and discourses by women from Germany, Russia, South Africa, Mexico, and Kenya represent in some small degree the international composition of the modern church. Non-American voices are found in 1970s Area Conference Reports, including the speech of Lucrecia Suárez de Juárez, a Mexican Latter-day Saint. When Carol Lee Hawkins coordinated the BYU Women's Conference during the early 1990s, she made a point of inviting speakers who lived their formative years outside of the United States, and her efforts yielded a number of talks, including that of Jutta B. Busche in this volume.[4] More work remains to be done by both scholars and church members in preserving the spoken insights of Latter-day Saint women outside the United States.

Selecting the Discourses

After collecting and reviewing hundreds of discourses, the editors chose engaging talks that focused on doctrinal themes, rather than talks that recounted or represented historically significant moments. The editors prioritized speeches that were well written, that contained theological analysis, and that illustrated women's faith throughout the years since the church's founding in 1830. Some women featured in this volume were well known in their day, and some of them are known to today's readers. Others were, until now, obscure and largely forgotten. The discourses are arranged in chronological order by creation date, with two exceptions: Lucy Mack Smith's discourse in chapter 1 and Elizabeth Ann Whitney's song in chapter 2 are placed at the time those discourses were originally delivered, though they were recorded or printed years after the fact.

The editors have usually selected the earliest known extant version of a given discourse for inclusion in this volume. Generally the entire speech is reproduced, but on occasion material not relevant to the main topic of the address has been omitted. Where this occurs at the beginning of a speech, the material has been omitted silently; where the omission is made within the text of the talk, the deletion is marked with ellipses. A source note at the end of each transcript provides information on the source used and the repository where the source material is held.

Presenting the Discourses

Rules of Transcription

To ensure accuracy in representing the texts, transcripts were verified three times against either the original documents or digital images, each time by a different reader or pair of readers.

Most of the earlier talks were found in reminiscences or minute books and did not receive the benefit of professional editing. To provide a more uniform reading experience across the chapters, the editors of this volume corrected errors of spelling and punctuation. Quotations included in the chapter introductions or the endnotes were corrected in the same manner. Most of the later talks came from published sources and did not require such corrections. Editors also standardized capitalization, paragraphing, and indention. These changes were made silently, without the use of editorial brackets or *sic.* Two different readers reviewed these corrections. In rare instances, the editors have added words to enhance clarity; such additions are enclosed in brackets.

Discourse Titles

The original records of these discourses did not always provide formal titles. If the original address had a title, that same title was used in the volume. If the original did not have a title or had a title that was simply a label (for example, "Address of Mrs. Mattie Horne Tingey"), the editors created a title that reflected the content of the discourse. Where the editors supplied titles, that fact is noted in the source note at the end of the discourse.

Annotation Conventions

The editors have included introductions and endnotes to provide background and context for these discourses. The introduction to each chapter describes aspects of the speaker's life experiences that most relate to the content of her discourse, as well as the place and time in which she spoke. This context helps readers more accurately interpret speakers' assertions and interpretations. The speaker's full name—including maiden name and all subsequent surnames—appears at the beginning of the introduction. The byline for each chapter gives the name the speaker was known by at the time she delivered her discourse.

Common initialisms are used throughout the text. The first time organizations are listed in chapter introductions, their names are fully spelled out, followed by the initialism. Common initialisms include the following: Mutual Improvement Association (MIA), Young Ladies' Mutual Improvement Association (YLMIA), Young Men's Mutual Improvement Association (YMMIA), Young Women's Mutual Improvement Association (YWMIA), and Brigham Young University (BYU).

Many terms with specialized meaning appear in the texts and annotation. While some of the terms may be explained or defined in this volume, a working familiarity with much of the terminology has been assumed. Researchers seeking additional information on Mormon terminology can consult the glossary on josephsmithpapers.org and the *Encyclopedia of Mormonism,* online at eom.byu.edu.

Many individual names appear in these documents. Biographical information is included in the annotation for some of these people, but no attempt has been made to be exhaustive. Many names from the earlier period appear in the biographical directory for *The First Fifty Years of Relief Society,* online at churchhistorianspress.org, or in the biographical sketches on josephsmithpapers.org.

AT THE PULPIT

185 YEARS OF DISCOURSES BY LATTER-DAY SAINT WOMEN

1

WHERE IS YOUR CONFIDENCE IN GOD?

◇◇◇

LUCY MACK SMITH

Gathering of Emigrating Saints at Lake Erie
Buffalo, New York
May 1831

Lucy Mack Smith (1775–1856) was the mother of Joseph and Hyrum Smith and nine other children, and she was a strong voice in the early church. Her son William Smith remembered, "My mother, who was a very pious woman and much interested in the welfare of her children, both here and hereafter, made use of every means which her parental love could suggest, to get us engaged in seeking for our souls' salvation, or (as the term then was) 'in getting religion.'"[1] In her own search for religion, Smith studied the Bible, prayed, discussed dreams and visions, and attended religious meetings and revivals sponsored by various denominations.[2] She was baptized a Latter-day Saint soon after her son Joseph organized the Church of Christ on April 6, 1830.[3]

In early May 1831, Smith was part of a company of approximately eighty church members from the Fayette, New York, area who were traveling to join the larger group of Latter-day Saints in Kirtland, Ohio. They hoped that the warm spring weather would allow them to travel along the waterways from New York to Ohio, rather than overland.[4] According to her later account of the journey, both Solomon Humphrey, the oldest member of the church at the time, and Hiram Page, one of the Eight Witnesses of the Book of Mormon, refused leadership of the group, instead deferring to Smith. Her later history records that the entire congregation agreed: "'Yes,' responded they all together, 'just as Mother Smith says, so we will do.'" Smith recalled that before leaving, "I called them all round me. 'Now,' said I, 'brothers and sisters, we have set out just as Father Lehi did to travel by the commandment of the Lord to a land that the Lord will show unto us if we are faithful, and I want you all to be solemn and lift your hearts to God in prayer continually that we may be prospered." While traveling along the Cayuga-Seneca Canal and the Erie Canal, as she remembered it, Smith led the company in song and prayer and took charge of some of the finances, the food, and the lodging.[5]

The journey proved less than ideal: adverse weather, suspicion on the part of local townspeople, and unprepared travelers with few supplies and unruly children created tension within the group. Five days after departure, the Fayette group arrived at Buffalo, where they met another group of Saints from Colesville, New York, who had been waiting for a week for the ice to break in Buffalo Harbor and allow boats to get through.[6] According to Smith, the Colesville party encouraged the Fayette company to wait quietly for the weather to change without admitting their religious identity to the local population, which might incite prejudice that would prevent them from securing local lodging and transportation. Instead, Smith stood on the deck of the steamboat where her company was gathered and boldly proclaimed her Mormon beliefs to gathered townspeople.

After testifying to local spectators, Smith observed what she considered inappropriate behavior among the Saints on the boat, including debating, complaining, and flirting. Smith worried that the sight of unruly behavior would undermine her earlier public witness, and she turned to speak to the Saints as recorded in the discourse featured here. Just as she finished speaking, she recounted, "a noise was heard like bursting thunder, and the captain cried out, 'Every man to his post!' and the ice parted, leaving barely a pathway for the boat."[7] They crossed safely and quickly to Fairport Harbor in Ohio, about twelve miles northeast of Kirtland, and arrived around May 11, 1831.[8] This exhortation was recorded by Lucy Mack Smith in her own words about thirteen years later and demonstrates the authority she exercised as "Mother Smith," a respected matriarch of the church.

"BRETHREN AND SISTERS," said I, "we call ourselves Latter-day Saints and profess to have come out from among the world for the purpose of serving God with a determination to serve him with our whole might, mind, and strength at the expense of all earthly things, and will you suffer yourselves to begin at the very first sacrifice of comfort to complain and murmur like the children of Israel? And even worse, for here are my sisters fretting for the want of their rocking chairs![9] And brethren, from you I expected assistance and looked for some firmness in you, but instead of that you are complaining that you have left a good house and now you have no home to go to and do not know as you shall have one when you get to the end of your journey, and more than all, you do not know but you will all starve before you get away from Buffalo. Who in the company has been hungry? Who has lacked anything to make them comfortable, as our circumstances would admit of? Have I not set food before you every day and made you all as welcome as my own children, that those who had not provided for yourselves might lack nothing?[10]

"And even if this were not the case, where is your faith?[11] Where is your confidence in God? Do you know that all things are in his hands? He made all things and still rules over them, and how easy a thing it would be with God if every Saint here would just lift their desires to him in prayer that the way might be opened before us. How easy would it be for God to cause the ice to break away, and in a moment's time we could be off on our journey; but how can you expect the Lord to prosper you when you are continually murmuring against him?"

Just then a man cried out from the shore, "Is the Book of Mormon true?" "That book," said I, "was brought forth by the power of God and translated by the same power. And if I could make my voice to sound as loud as the trumpet of Michael the Archangel, I would declare the truth from land to land and from sea to sea, and it would echo from isle to isle until not one should remain of the whole family of man but that was left without excuse. For all should hear the truth of the gospel of the Son of God, and I would sound it in every ear that he has again revealed himself to man in these last days and set his hand to gather his people together upon a goodly land, and if they will fear him and walk uprightly before him it shall be unto them for an inheritance; but if they rebel against his law, his hand will be against them, to scatter them abroad and cut them off from the face of the earth. For God is now going to do a work upon the earth, and man cannot hinder a work which is for the salvation of all who will believe it unto the uttermost, even all who call on him; and it will prove unto everyone who stands here this day a savior of life unto life or of death unto death: a savior of life unto life if ye will receive it, but of death unto death if ye reject the counsel of God unto your own condemnation.[12] For every man shall have the desires of his heart. If he desires this truth, the way is open to all and if he will, he may hear and live;[13] whereas if they treat the truth with contempt and trample upon the simplicity of the word of God, they will shut the gate of heaven against themselves. And now, brethren and sisters, if you will, all of you, raise your desires to heaven that the ice may give way before us and we be set at liberty to go on our way, as sure as the Lord lives it shall be done."

Lucy Mack Smith, History, 1844–1845, book 11, p. [12]–book 12, p. [2], CHL. Handwriting of Martha Jane Knowlton Coray and Howard Coray. Title supplied by the editors.

2

ADAM-ONDI-AHMAN

◇◇◇

ELIZABETH ANN WHITNEY

Patriarchal Blessing Meeting
House of the Lord, Kirtland, Ohio
September 14, 1835

It would not have been unusual for Elizabeth Ann Smith Whitney (1800–1882) to express herself through music in the temple in Kirtland, Ohio. She grew up in Connecticut in a cultured family, enjoying singing and dancing; she was known throughout her life for her vocal talent.[1] Though she and her husband, Newel K. Whitney, did not belong to any religious denomination before 1830, she nevertheless described herself as "naturally religious," with a desire to explore different churches.[2] She remembered, "We had been praying to know from the Lord how we could obtain the gift of the Holy Ghost. . . . We were seeking to know how to obtain the Spirit and the gifts bestowed upon the ancient Saints." Whitney stated that in response to their prayers, they felt the presence of the Spirit of the Lord, experienced a vision of a heavenly cloud, and heard a voice commanding them to prepare to receive the truth.[3] The Whitneys learned about the Church of Christ, as it was then known, from the missionary Parley P. Pratt in Kirtland in late 1830, and they were baptized that November.[4]

Believing that the spiritual gifts of the New Testament were available in their time, many people in the nineteenth century described experiences with dreams, visions, healings, and speaking in tongues.[5] In the early Mormon tradition, both men and women spoke and sang in tongues and translated for each other in public and private settings.[6] On September 14, 1835, Whitney gathered with many others, most likely in the partially completed Kirtland temple, to receive a patriarchal blessing from Joseph Smith Sr., the church's patriarch. Whitney remembered the "great manifestations of power" at such meetings.[7] Pratt commented that during this same time period "many persons were carried away in the visions of the Spirit and saw and heard unspeakable things; and many enjoyed the ministering of angels, and the gift of healing and of speaking in tongues."[8] In the blessing given to Whitney, Joseph Smith Sr. promised her "the gift of singing inspirationally." Joseph Smith Jr. told her that she would never lose this gift if she used it wisely.[9] After Whitney received her blessing, she stood and sang in tongues; her song was interpreted by Pratt. The words to Pratt's interpretation of Whitney's song were recorded by an unknown scribe. Whitney retained the original copy, and it was printed years later in the *Woman's Exponent*.[10] Whitney's song about Adam-ondi-Ahman, which is reproduced here, exemplifies a nineteenth-century form of charismatic discourse. The meter and topic of Whitney's song are very similar to those of William W. Phelps's hymn "Adam-ondi-Ahman."[11]

IN ANCIENT DAYS there lived a man,
Amidst a pleasant garden,
Where lovely flowers immortal bloom'd,
And shed around a rich perfume;
Behold, his name was Adam.

One of the nobles of the earth,
Had mighty power in blessing;
Received the priesthood, and went forth[12]
And blessed his seed, and gave the earth
Blessings for their possession.[13]

He sealed them for eternal life,
And all their generations,
Who should obey the gospel plan,
Down to the latest years of man—
A multitude of nations.

Isaac and Jacob, they in turn
Had power to bless their children:[14]
Hence, Jacob by his faith did learn,
And gave directions for his bones
To be conveyed to Canaan.[15]

By the same spirit, Joseph gave
A great and mighty blessing
To Ephraim, and Manasseh too,[16]

Whereby their seed were carried through
Long travels, though distressing.

By that same faith they built a ship,
And crossed the mighty ocean,[17]
Obtain'd the choicest land of earth,
Foretold the great Messiah's birth,
And all the great commotion.[18]

* * * * * * * *

The holy priesthood long remain'd
In all its power and glory,
Until the priests of God were slain,
Their records hid from wicked men
Within the hill Cumorah.

Their remnants sank in sorrow down,
Became a loathsome people.
To misery and sorrow doom'd,
Their pleasant fields o'erspread with gloom,
Ruled by a Gentile nation.

But now the priesthood is restored,[19]
And we partake its blessings;
Our parents and our children dear
With Joseph's remnants have a share
To latest generations.

As Adam blessed his family
In Adam-ondi-Ahman,[20]
So shall our aged father bless
His seed who dwell in righteousness
Upon the land of Zion.[21]

Elizabeth Ann Whitney, "A Leaf from an Autobiography," Woman's Exponent *7, no. 11 (Nov. 1, 1878): 83.*

WE ARE GOING TO DO SOMETHING EXTRAORDINARY

◇◇◇

EMMA HALE SMITH

Nauvoo Relief Society
Nauvoo, Illinois
1842–1844

Emma Hale Smith (1804–1879) met her husband, Joseph Smith, when he boarded at her parents' farm in Harmony, Pennsylvania, and they were married on January 18, 1827.[1] Her mother-in-law, Lucy Mack Smith, praised Emma: "I have never seen a woman in my life who would endure every species of fatigue and hardship, from month to month, and from year to year, with that unflinching courage, zeal, and patience, which she has always done."[2] Emma Smith briefly worked as a scribe for the translation of the Book of Mormon and assisted her husband in other ways.[3] For instance, she helped prepare early missionaries for their service and gathered with women to pray on behalf of Joseph Smith in New York.[4] Years later, she delivered a petition to the governor of Illinois, signed by nearly a thousand women in Nauvoo, Illinois, seeking protection for her husband.[5] She opened her home to the sick, the orphaned, and other visitors.[6] Smith was the mother of eleven children—nine biological and two adopted. Four of her children died at birth or shortly after, and two died as toddlers.[7]

In early July 1830, a short time after Emma Smith's baptism, Joseph Smith dictated a revelation directed to his wife, now known as section 25 of the Doctrine and Covenants. The revelation addressed Emma Smith as "an Elect Lady whom I have called" and told her that she would be "ordained . . . to expound scriptures and exhort the church according as it shall be given thee."[8] Her calling extended even further when she was elected president of the Female Relief Society of Nauvoo on March 17, 1842. At the first meeting of the organization, Joseph Smith read the 1830 revelation, explaining that at the time it had been given, "Presidentess" Smith had been "ordained . . . to expound the scriptures to all; and to teach the female part of the community." He went on to liken Emma Smith to the "Elect Lady" spoken of in the New Testament.[9] John Taylor called Emma a "mother in Israel," and instructed her to care for the needy and be a "pattern of virtue," to "preside and dignify her office" through teaching correct principles.[10] Though Emma Smith met with the society only twelve times in 1842 and four times in March 1844, her leadership was crucial in shaping the organization. Latter-day Saint women were not automatically enrolled in the Relief Society in the early days of the society—they were required to apply in order to prove their worthiness and commitment to the church. Emma directed membership recruitment efforts, encouraged unity, and instructed women on compassion and care for the poor. Emma Smith's public speaking established a pattern for Latter-day Saint women, who looked to the 1830 revelation—which declared that its exhortation to Emma was also the Lord's "voice unto all"—as justification for their own ministries.[11]

Emma Smith also maintained her charge to "walk in the paths of virtue" as instructed by the 1830 revelation.[12] National purity movements and moral reform groups formed by women all over the country at this time worked to instill virtue and uphold chastity and marital fidelity.[13] The Relief Society provided a public venue for Emma Smith to crusade in defense of virtue and promote moral reform. At the same time, Joseph Smith was privately introducing the principle of plural marriage to a small group of Latter-day Saints.[14]

While the Nauvoo Relief Society functioned in a discussion format rather than as a venue for traditional discourses, Emma Smith's words, which are excerpted here, show her leadership. Even at the final meeting of the Nauvoo Relief Society, Smith maintained her sense of spiritual authority, exhorting the women to repent as they strengthened each other and practiced charity.[15]

[March 17, 1842]

PRESIDENT EMMA SMITH remarked we are going to do something <u>extraordinary</u>. When a boat is stuck on the rapids with a multitude of Mormons on board we shall consider <u>that</u> a loud call for <u>relief</u>.[16] We expect extraordinary occasions and pressing calls. . . .

President E. Smith then arose and proceeded to make appropriate remarks on the object of the society, its duties to others, also its relative duties to each other, viz., to seek out and relieve the distressed, that each member should be ambitious to do good, that the members should deal frankly with each other, to watch over the morals and be very careful of the character and reputation of the members of the institution, etc. . . .

[March 24, 1842]

President E. Smith then rose and said that measures to promote union in this society must be carefully attended to. That every member should be held in full fellowship. As a society, hoped they would divest themselves of every jealousy and evil feeling toward each other, if any such existed. That we should bring our conduct into respectability, here and everywhere else. Said she rejoiced in the prospect before her. . . .

President E. Smith said, no one need feel delicate in reference to inquiries about this society. There is nothing private. Its objects are purely benevolent . . . , its objects are charitable: none can object to telling the good, the evil withhold. She hoped all would feel themselves bound to observe this rule. . . . She said it was the duty of every person to inquire into the condition of the poor and represent their true state. . . . We should assist each other in this way. . . .

[March 31, 1842]

President E. S. said we were going to learn new things. Our way was straight. Said we wanted none in this society but those who <u>could</u> and <u>would</u> walk straight and were determined to do good. . . .

[April 14, 1842]

President E. Smith arose and addressed the meeting. . . . Her desire was to do good. Wished all the members of this society to assist her. Said it was necessary to begin at home, to eradicate all evil from our own hearts, and warn those who wish to join with us to come calculating to divest themselves of everything wrong and unite to expose iniquity, to search it out and put it away. She said the society had other duties to attend to than seeing to the wants of the poor. Exhorted the members so to conduct as to have the honor of commencing a good work and of carrying it out. Enforced the necessity of walking in a manner that would be approbated of God. . . .

President Smith then called on those, if any present, who knew of cases of the poor to be represented.

[May 19, 1842]

Mrs. President continued by exhorting all who had erred to repent and forsake their sins. Said that Satan's forces were against this church. That every saint should be at the post. . . .

[May 27, 1842]

President E. Smith arose and addressed the congregation. She said all must have grace for themselves, etc. . . . She impressed the necessity of being united in doing good to the poor. . . .

[June 23, 1842]

Mrs. President said she was rejoiced to see the increasing union of the society. Hoped we should live right before God, among ourselves, and before the world. . . . Said we had nothing to do but to fear God and keep the commandments, and in so doing we shall prosper.

[August 4, 1842]

Mrs. President arose and addressed the society upon the necessity of being united among ourselves. Said we shall have sufficient difficulty from abroad without stirring up strife among ourselves and hardness and evil feelings one towards another, etc. . . .

We could govern this generation in one way if not another. If not by the mighty arm of power, we can do it by faith and prayer.[17] If we will try to live uprightly, said she believed we should not be driven.[18]

Mrs. President continued by saying God knows we have a work to do in this place. We have got to watch and pray and be careful not to excite feelings, not make enemies of one another, etc.

[March 16, 1844]

Mrs. President then arose and addressed the meeting upon the necessity of being united among ourselves and strengthening each other's hands in order that we may be able to do much good among the poor. . . . We must throw the mantle of charity around to shield those who will repent and do so no more. . . . She advised all to abide the Book of Mormon and Doctrine and Covenants. . . . Also exhorted them to look after the poor.

Nauvoo Relief Society Minute Book, Mar. 17, 1842–Mar. 16, 1844, 8–[126], in Jill Mulvay Derr, Carol Cornwall Madsen, Kate Holbrook, and Matthew J. Grow, eds., The First Fifty Years of Relief Society: Key Documents in Latter-day Saint Women's History *(Salt Lake City: Church Historian's Press, 2016), 32–130. Handwriting of Eliza R. Snow and Hannah M. Ells. Title supplied by the editors.*

AFTER THE ORDER OF HEAVEN

◇◇◇

SARAH CLEVELAND, ELIZABETH ANN WHITNEY, PRESENDIA BUELL, LUCY MACK SMITH, ELIZABETH DURFEE, ELIZA R. SNOW, AND PATTY SESSIONS

Nauvoo Relief Society
Lodge Room, Red Brick Store, Nauvoo, Illinois
April 19, 1842

Twenty women gathered for the first Relief Society meeting on March 17, 1842, and at the second meeting, President Emma Hale Smith taught the women "to promote union in this society" and encouraged all those who wished to join.[1] Counselors Sarah Marietta Kingsley Howe Cleveland (1788–1856) and Elizabeth Ann Smith Whitney (1800–1882) and secretary Eliza Roxcy Snow (1804–1887) contributed to the society's inclusive and welcoming spirit. By the fifth meeting, held on April 19, 1842, there were 158 members, including Lucy Mack Smith (1775–1856), Elizabeth Davis Goldsmith Brackenbury Durfee (1791–1876), Martha "Patty" Bartlett Sessions (1795–1892), Abigail Calkins Leonard (1795–1880), and others who participated in discussion, testimony, and service.[2]

Some women living outside of Nauvoo, Illinois, had heard about the organization and wanted to participate. Presendia Lathrop Huntington Buell (1810–1892), for example, lived in Lima, Ohio, about thirty miles south.[3] She traveled to Nauvoo, where her sister, Zina D. Huntington Jacobs [Young], lived, to attend the Relief Society, and the women welcomed her as a new member.[4] Other Relief Society groups met later in surrounding towns.[5] The Relief Society provided a central location to unite women across location, age, and socioeconomic status. Lucy Mack Smith "rejoiced in view of what was doing. As she came in and looked upon the sisters, it gave her feelings of deep interest. [She] wept . . . [and] hoped the Lord would bless and aid the society in feeding the hungry, clothing the naked . . . [and] felt to pray that the blessings of heaven might rest upon the society."[6]

Joseph Smith taught the Relief Society that their institution followed an ancient order that existed in the time of the Old and New Testaments.[7] As demonstrated in this April 19 meeting, women of the Relief Society participated in gifts of the Spirit with the belief that they were part of the restoration of the gospel of Jesus Christ.[8] They spoke in tongues, with others interpreting. They gave and received blessings of health and comfort, allowing them to participate in sacred rituals as well as build intimate social networks.[9] These experiences contributed to the "Spirit of the Lord which pervades this society" mentioned in this meeting. The Relief Society meeting was a participatory event—consisting more of discussion than a formal lesson or address. Many women spoke. Their public testimonies and personal blessings reveal the emotional relief they found in service and in communion.

A SPECIAL MEETING of the society being convened agreeably to previous appointment; President Emma Smith not being present, Counselor Cleveland presided.[10]

The meeting was opened with singing. Prayer by Counselor Cleveland. Singing by the choir. . . .

Counselor Cleveland then arose and addressed the meeting by saying that inasmuch as the meeting was specially called for the admission of Mrs. Buell, who resided at a distance, was deprived of the privileges enjoyed by the sisters in Nauvoo, and wished to become a member of this society; there was not much business to be attended to, therefore we might spend the time in religious exercises before the Lord. Spoke of the happiness she felt in the present association of females, and made very appropriate remarks respecting the duties and prospects of the society, that it was organized after the order of heaven, etc., etc.[11]

Counselor Whitney also made many interesting remarks and invited all present to speak their sentiments freely.

Mrs. Buell arose and said that she rejoiced in the opportunity, that she considered it a great privilege. She felt that the Spirit of the Lord was with the society and rejoiced to become a member, although residing at a distance and could not attend the meetings.

Joseph Smith's red brick store. Circa 1885–1886. The founding meeting of the Female Relief Society of Nauvoo took place on the second floor of this dry goods store on March 17, 1842. The red brick store became a location for women to gather and share needs, concerns, and spiritual ministry. Photograph taken or obtained by Brigham H. Roberts. (Church History Library, Salt Lake City.)

Mother Smith spoke very pathetically of her lonely situation, and the feelings she had as she reflected on the care which Father Smith always felt for the sisters when in life he presided over the meetings.[12]

Mrs. Durfee bore testimony to the great blessing she received when administered to, after the close of the last meeting, by President E. Smith and Counselors Cleveland and Whitney.[13] She said she never realized more benefit through any administration, that she was healed, and thought the sisters had more faith than the brethren.

Miss Snow, after making observations with regard to the society, the importance of acting in wisdom and walking humbly before God, etc., said she had a blessing for Mrs. Buell, that inasmuch as she had become a member of this society, as the spirit of a person pervades every member of the body, so shall the Spirit of the Lord which pervades this society be with her. She shall feel it and rejoice. She shall be blessed wherever she is, and the Lord shall open the way and she shall be instrumental in doing much. Through her own exertions and by the instrumentality of others, she shall be enabled to contribute much to the fund of the society. She shall warm up the hearts of those who are cold and dormant and shall be instrumental in doing much good.

Mrs. Leonard, Counselor W., and Counselor C. bore testimony to the truth of what Miss Snow had said to Mrs. Buell.

Counselor Cleveland stated that she many times felt in her heart what she could not express in our own language, and as the Prophet had given us liberty to improve the gifts of the gospel in our meetings, and feeling the power resting upon, desired to speak in the gift of tongues, which she did in a powerful manner.[14]

Mrs. Sessions arose and gave the interpretation of what Counselor C. had spoken in an unknown tongue, and said that God was well pleased with this society, that if we would be humble and faithful the Lord would pour out upon the members generally the gift of prophecy. That when the speaker laid her hand on the head of Sister Snow, she said that not only she should have the Spirit but that all should have it also. That the speaker then addressed herself to Mother Smith, saying that the prayers of Father Smith were now answered upon the members of the society. That the days of Mother S. should be prolonged and she should meet many times with the society, should enjoy much in the society of the sisters, and shall hereafter be crowned a mother of those that shall prove faithful, etc.[15]

The meeting was very interesting, nearly all present arose and spoke, and the Spirit of the Lord like a purifying stream refreshed every heart.

Mrs. Mary Smith recommended Elizabeth Eaton to the patronage of the society as a person skillful in needlework.

The meeting closed with prayer by Mother Smith and singing by the choir—after which Mrs. Leonard was administered to for the restoration of health, by Counselors Cleveland and Whitney.

Nauvoo Relief Society Minute Book, Apr. 19, 1842, [30–33], in Jill Mulvay Derr, Carol Cornwall Madsen, Kate Holbrook, and Matthew J. Grow, eds., The First Fifty Years of Relief Society: Key Documents in Latter-day Saint Women's History *(Salt Lake City: Church Historian's Press, 2016), 49–52. Handwriting of Eliza R. Snow. Title supplied by the editors.*

5

THIS GOSPEL OF GLAD TIDINGS TO ALL PEOPLE

◇◇◇

LUCY MACK SMITH

General Conference
Temple Grounds, Nauvoo, Illinois
October 8, 1845

Several months after the deaths of her sons Joseph, Hyrum, and Samuel Smith, Lucy Mack Smith (1775–1856) began writing her history.[1] At age sixty-nine, she was in poor health and felt "it a privilege as well as my duty . . . to give (as my last testimony to a world from whence I must soon take my departure) an account."[2] Impaired by fading memory and fueled by indignation and grief, at times she presented a "confused chronology and incomplete information"; nevertheless, Smith's account gives insight into her personality, attitude, emotions, beliefs, and understanding of Joseph Smith's role as prophet.[3] Smith devoted the summer of 1845 to final revisions, and her manuscript was completed by October, when she first publicly announced the project at general conference.[4] Her narrative informed the larger institutional history of the Latter-day Saints.[5]

Smith felt a pressing need to witness, and she spoke often in public, giving a firsthand account of many events in church history. "I have told over many things pertaining to these matters to different persons to gratify their curiosity—indeed, have almost destroyed my lungs giving these recitals to those who felt anxious to hear them," she wrote to her son William.[6] At a Relief Society meeting on March 31, 1842, she "wished to leave her testimony that the Book of Mormon is the book of God, that Joseph is a man of God, a prophet of the Lord set apart to lead the people. If we observe his words it will be well with us; if we live righteously on earth, it will be well with us in Eternity."[7] She spoke at another public meeting on February 23, 1845, describing the "trials and troubles she had passed through in establishing the Church of Christ and the persecutions and afflictions" she had experienced with the murders of her sons Joseph and Hyrum the previous year. Hosea Stout recorded that those who heard her speak "were deeply affected with the remarks of this 'Mother' of the 'mothers in Israel,' for she spoke with the most feeling and heartbroken manner of the troubles she had passed through."[8]

Smith's age and increasing physical ailments prevented her from the activity she had previously enjoyed. At the Relief Society's second meeting in March 1842, she wept and told the women "she was advanced in years and could not stay long." A few weeks later, she "spoke very pathetically of her lonely situation," but she also repeatedly shared her testimony, mingled with her history.[9] The Saints cared for the widow. Following the mob murders of Joseph and Hyrum Smith in June 1844, Relief Society member Sarah M. Kimball visited Mother Smith to offer comfort, allowing Smith to testify of the innocence of her sons.[10] Wilford Woodruff gave Lucy Mack Smith a blessing on August 23, 1844, calling her "the greatest Mother in Israel." He continued, "Thou hast lived and stood to see the fall of thy sons by the rage of gentile hands, and like an impenetrable rock in the midst of the mighty deep thou hast remained unmoved until God has given thee [the] desires of thy heart in seeing the keys of the kingdom of God held in the hands of thy posterity."[11] On July 9, 1845, Bishops Newel K. Whitney and George Miller provided a public dinner for members of the Smith family, including Lucy and Emma Hale Smith.[12] Brigham Young promised to care for Lucy Mack Smith as the Saints prepared to leave Nauvoo, Illinois, for the West, but she remained in Nauvoo with her three daughters and her daughter-in-law Emma.[13]

Mother Smith was seventy years old when she delivered this address at a general conference held at the Nauvoo temple.[14] The conference took place amid violence against Latter-day Saints in areas outside of Nauvoo during the previous month; Brigham Young had publicly agreed that the Saints would leave Nauvoo in the coming spring.[15] At the conference, Young and other leaders spoke of the upcoming exodus. On October 8, 1845, the last day of the three-day conference, Smith requested the podium to respond to the discussion about moving west. According to the church newspaper *Times and Seasons,* "She spoke at considerable length, and in an audible manner, so as to be heard by a large portion of the vast assembly."[16] Smith expressed her religious beliefs and shared her testimony while recounting events from the church's early history. This is the first account of a woman speaking in general conference.[17]

WELL, BROTHERS AND SISTERS, I have been looking around upon this congregation. I have long been waiting for the time when the Lord would give me strength to look upon you and my children.[18] I feel solemn. I want everyone to look into their hearts to see what they have come to this place for, whether they have come to follow Christ through evil and good report or for any other cause. I want to give you my advice. I want to have time to talk about my husband and Hyrum and Joseph. I want to give you all my advice. Brigham Young has done the errand, he has fixed it completely. For a long time I have been wanting to ask whether you would be willing to receive stolen goods or not.[19] I want to know if you believe in such things. There is one thing I want to speak of, there is maybe 2,000 people here that never were acquainted with Mr. Smith or my family. I raised up 11 children, 7 boys.[20] I raised them in the fear of God. When they were two or three years old I told them I wanted them to love God with all their hearts. I told them to do good.

I want all you to do the same. God gives us our children and we are accountable. In the fear of God I warn you. I want you to take your little children and teach them in the fear of God. I want you to teach them about Joseph in Egypt and such things, and when they are four years old they will love to read their Bible. I presume there never was a family more obedient than mine. I did not have to speak to them, only once. Set your children to work and try to bring them up to your comfort. Don't let them play out of doors.[21] If I can't talk to a few thousands here, how can I meet millions and talk in the celestial glory? I want the young men to remember that I love children, young folks, and everybody. I want them to be obedient to their parents. Be good and kind and do in secret as you would do in the presence of millions. I call you brothers and sisters and children. If you consider me a Mother in Israel I want you to say so. (President B. Young arose and said, "All who consider Mother Smith as a Mother in Israel signify it by saying yes." Loud shouts of "Yes!")[22]

My feelings have been hurt by hearing them say "Old Mother Smith"—"There goes Old Mother Smith." I have had my feelings hurt a great deal.

I want to speak about the dead. It was eighteen years ago last 22nd of September that Joseph took the plates out of the earth, and it was 18 years last Monday[23] since Joseph Smith the prophet of the Lord—

It was in a morning my son came to me and told me he had taken those plates out of the ground, and he said, "Go and tell all three of them (the Harrises) that I have taken the plates out of the ground,[24] and I want Martin should assist me. I want to take off some of the characters and send them to New York."[25]

I am now in my 70th year. It is 18 years since I began to receive this gospel of glad tidings to all people.[26] I have got it all in a history, and I want this people to be so good and so kind as to get it printed before you go west.[27] Martin Harris was the first person that helped Joseph about this work to get the Book of Mormon printed,[28] for the gospel could not be preached until this was done. Here was only my family and Martin Harris to do anything about it. Just as soon as they commenced, the Devil began to roar and attempt to destroy them. But a little while before we were turned out of house and home, Joseph went to Pennsylvania.[29] Hyrum and Samuel had to go and work in the woods all day and then at night had to go haul the wood and get means to help Joseph to publish the book. Two of them guarded the house.[30]

This was the way it commenced, and now see what a congregation is here who talk about going to the west, how easy this can be done. My family could go to work and get means to print the Book of Mormon. Do not be discouraged and say that you can't get wagons and things; as Brigham says you must be all honest or you will not get there.[31] If you feel cross you will have trouble.

My family made out to get the book printed. The angel of the Lord told them what to do. They began 18 years ago last Monday.

Thousands have come into the church since then and have not known Joseph, Hyrum, [Don] Carlos, or William, and they are all gone but poor William, and he is gone, I don't know where.[32]

I have 3 daughters at home; they have never had anything but have worked for the church.[33] After the book was printed, Samuel took some of them to sell and was turned out of doors three times.[34] He went into Brother Green's, a Methodist preacher.[35] Samuel said, "Don't you want to buy a book?" She asked, "What is it?" Samuel said, "It is a Book of Mormon that my Brother Joseph has translated from plates out of the ground." She asked her husband but he would not buy. Samuel left one till he returned. He had to sell them to buy us victuals. I want to speak of this that you may not complain of hard times. He went into a house and asked to have a breakfast and he would give a book for it.[36] He again went to Sister Green. She said he must take the book again. Samuel took the book and looked and looked.[37] She afterwards told me she never saw a man look so; she knew that he had the Spirit of God. He said, "The Spirit forbids me taking this book." She knelt and asked him to pray with her. She read the book and became a Mormon.[38] And thus the work began, and then it spread like a mustard seed.[39]

After the church began to grow we were driven from one place to another, to Kirtland then to Missouri.[40] William was taken sick, Samuel's wife and others;[41] and I had twenty or thirty sick to take care of during the mobbing.[42] I felt strong in health. I could take care of thirty sick then better than sit on my chair now.

While William lay sick he had a vision and saw the mob come in. He said he saw them come in thousands and thousands, and he said, "Mother, you will be driven," and, says he, "If I die I want you to take care of my wife. I want you to carry my corpse wherever you go." The first day William was able to walk as far as the door, the mob came. Ten of them came into my room after they had taken

Joseph and Hyrum into their camp.[43] There were thousands of them hallooing and screeching in my ears. How do you think I felt? Have you any feelings for me?

While they were in the camp I could not go to see them, and now my children are in the grave. Ten men came in and said, "We have come in to kill the heads of the family." Says I, "Do you want to kill me?" They said yes. I said, "I want you to do your work quick, for I would then be happy."[44] They then said, "God damn it, these Mormons had as lief die as live." They then tried Joseph and Hyrum and sentenced them to be shot in 15 minutes. A man came in and said, "Mother Smith, if you ever want to see Joseph again you must go now, for he is going to be shot in Jackson County."[45] He took me by the hand, and it was as much as we could do to get through the crowd to the wagon.

The men lifted up their swords and swore I should not see them. I finally got to the wagon and put up my hand. He took hold of my hand and kissed it. I said, "Joseph, let me hear your voice once more." Said he, "God bless you, my poor Mother." They were taken away. They were in bands and irons.[46] All this time my son William and his wife were sick.[47] Samuel's wife was sick and some others, and I had them all to take care of.[48] After that we had to move.

Joseph then went to the city of Washington.[49] It rained three days as hard as it could rain, but we had to travel and nothing to shelter us. I walked 6 miles in the bottom. My clothes were wet so high up I could scarcely walk, and when we got to the Quincy River it snowed, it rained, it hailed.[50] We lay our bed on the cold snow and a blanket over us and took off our wet stockings and did the best we could. In the morning the cover was frozen stiff. We could not make a fire for the snow.[51] Joseph then went to the city of Washington, as he had a revelation to importune at the governor's feet and the president's feet, and the Lord said if they would not heed him he would vex the nation.[52] When he got home he preached down between Mr. Durfee's and the Mansion House. He told the brethren and sisters that he had done all he could for them. Says he, "They are determined we shall not have justice while we stay in Nauvoo."[53] But, says he, "Keep good courage. You shall never suffer for bread as you have done before." Said he, "All these cases are recorded on earth, and what is recorded here is recorded in heaven.[54] Now," says he, "I am going to lay this case of their taking away our property, etc. I am going to take it up before the highest court in heaven." He repeated it 3 times. Little did I think he was going to leave us so soon to take this case to heaven. We never could get justice till he took it there.

The Lord has got even the marshal there.[55] They know all our sufferings and don't you think our case is being tried? I think they will do more for us there than they could if they were here. I feel that if every soul would stay at home they would be blessed. I feel as though God is vexing the nation a little here and there, and I feel that the Lord will let Brother Brigham take the people away. I don't know as I shall go, but if the rest of my family go I will go, and I pray that the Lord may bless the heads of the church, Brother Brigham and all of you, and when I go to another world I want to meet you all. Here lays my dead, my husband and children.[56] I want to lay my bones here so that in the resurrection I can raise with my husband and children, if so be that my children go. And I would to God that all my children would go. They will not go without me, and if I go I want to have my bones fetched back to be laid with my husband and children.[57]

Lucy Mack Smith, General Conference, Oct. 8, 1845, Nauvoo, Illinois, Historian's Office, General Church Minutes, 1839–1877, Oct. 6–8, 1845, 7–13, CHL. Handwriting of Curtis E. Bolton. Title supplied by the editors.

6

SEEK TO THE LORD FOR WISDOM

◇◇◇

PHOEBE M. ANGELL

Female Council of Health
Old Adobe Tabernacle, Temple Square, Salt Lake City, Utah Territory
August 14, 1852

Born to working-class parents in Guilford, Massachusetts, Phoebe Ann Morton (1786–1854) married James Angell in Providence, Rhode Island, at the age of sixteen. They had ten children, four of whom died while young.[1] Following the breakup of his mother's unhappy marriage, her son Truman O. Angell remembered how she had "seven children to support, and nothing but her hands for her fortune." He expressed sympathy for "my Mother's sufferings in consequence of the conduct of my Father toward her. . . . Her trials were truly great: she almost sank under them."[2]

Angell was baptized in January 1833 while living in New York.[3] The single mother moved with her family to Kirtland, Ohio, in 1834 or 1835, then moved again in 1838 to Far West, Missouri.[4] While there she served as midwife for Mary Fielding Smith in delivering Joseph F. Smith, then cared for the two while their husband and father, Hyrum Smith, was imprisoned in Liberty, Missouri.[5] She joined the Nauvoo Relief Society on April 14, 1842. Because she had little money and few items to donate, she volunteered her services to "repair old clothes if necessary when new material cannot be obtained."[6] After arriving in the Salt Lake Valley in 1848, she worked as a midwife and nurse and often visited and cared for women who were sick. At the end of her life in 1854, when her own health was failing, she received the same care in return.[7]

Many women in the eighteenth and nineteenth centuries, including Angell, practiced "social" medicine: they treated common ailments, sicknesses, and injuries with their own home-manufactured medicines, including salves, syrups, teas, ointments, poultices, and dressings.[8] At a time before modern medicine had attained high rates of success, many combined the then-popular Thomsonian use of natural remedies and herbs with faith and fervent prayer, often distrusting doctors and their unproven remedies.[9] Mormon women, like their American contemporaries, developed an informal health network within their communities in Nauvoo, Illinois, providing medical care for themselves, their families, and their neighbors. Church leaders asked individual women to act as midwives and nurses, even setting them apart for these appointments.[10] The Nauvoo Relief Society coordinated service for the sick and the poor. Even after the disbanding of the Nauvoo Relief Society in 1845, women gathered informally while crossing the plains to assist and care for each other.[11]

Willard Richards, an apostle and Thomsonian physician, organized the Council of Health in 1849 in Salt Lake City to address the health problems facing the Saints in their new, difficult living conditions.[12] Women participated and created a female branch for the training of midwives.[13] In 1852, Angell was president of the Female Council of Health; Patty Sessions and Susannah Liptrot Richards were her counselors. They met weekly and presented lectures or shared personal experiences and recipes for natural prescriptions. At times, they also spoke in tongues and performed blessings, a common practice among nineteenth-century Latter-day Saint women.[14]

At the August 14, 1852, meeting, Angell spoke about the importance of combining faith with practical knowledge and experience in treating the sick.

SISTER ANGELL SPOKE, exhorting the council not to trust in the knowledge which is obtained from books, or to trust in herbs altogether, but seek to the Lord for wisdom.[15] She referred to a circumstance in Nauvoo when much chill and fever was among the people. She cried to the Lord that he would show her something to do them good. In the night she received the following receipt as though a voice spoke to her:[16] "Take boneset, such a portion; lobelia, one handful; put it in one pint of vinegar, let it stand overnight, and administer it to the sick when the chill comes on, a tablespoonful once every hour."[17] She bore testimony of the great good this receipt did. She used one bushel of boneset that summer.[18]

Female Council of Health, Minutes, Salt Lake City, Utah Territory, Aug. 14, 1852, CHL. Handwriting of George D. Watt. Title supplied by the editors.

THIRTEENTH WARD RELIEF SOCIETY COVENANT

◇◇◇

MATILDA DUDLEY BUSBY

Salt Lake City Thirteenth Ward Relief Society
Private Residences, Salt Lake City, Utah Territory
June 14, 1854, and May 6, 1857

Matilda Matey Dudley Ferguson Paschall Busby (1819–1895) had a long history with American Indians. Her family history maintains that Indians attacked the Dudley family when she was a baby. Her father, Lawson, was scalped and killed, and she and her mother were kidnapped and later escaped, perhaps to Ohio, where Matilda later married her first husband, Stephen Ferguson.[1] Dudley was baptized in November 1849, then immigrated to the Salt Lake Valley in 1851 with her son, Henry Ferguson, where they lived in the Thirteenth Ward.[2]

When the Latter-day Saints arrived in the Salt Lake Valley in 1847, they began to cultivate relationships with local American Indians, negotiating conflicts over land, water, and other natural resources. Utes and other native peoples soon entered a devastating decade of disease, resulting from sickness spread by the Mormon settlers.[3] On January 24, 1854, several women from all over Salt Lake City met to consider "the importance of organizing a society of females, for the purpose of making clothing for the Indian women and children."[4] The next week they met at Matilda Dudley's home, elected her both president and treasurer of the new society, and resolved that all members should pay twenty-five cents in dues as well as donate work hours "for the benefit of those Indians that should seem to be most necessitous or most deserving of our sympathy and assistance."[5] This was one of several such organizations throughout the territory.[6]

A few months later, Brigham Young issued a formal call to the women in Salt Lake City to unite their efforts in sewing clothing for native peoples and instructed bishops to organize Relief Societies in each ward.[7] Dudley's Indian Relief Society disbanded, and she was a key participant in the organization of the Salt Lake City Thirteenth Ward Relief Society on June 7, 1854.[8] The next week, she presented a "covenant" for Relief Society members, which echoed counsel given by Emma Smith in the Nauvoo Relief Society for the sisters to be unified and not speak ill of each other or of church leaders.[9] The minutes of the Thirteenth Ward Relief Society meetings record the women making donations; sewing clothing, quilts, and carpet rags; and braiding straw hats, all of which was done "in the usual social, useful, and kindly manner." The organization took an annual winter hiatus when it was too cold to work together.[10]

Three years later, on May 6, 1857, Dudley, who had since married Joseph Busby and changed her surname, reissued the same covenant, nearly word for word. That covenant, which is reproduced here, may have been intended for new members who had joined after 1854 or as a reiteration of the purpose of the society.[11] In both its 1854 and 1857 versions, Dudley's brief speech illustrates her organizational vision for this local group and its connection to the broader Relief Society. The Thirteenth Ward Relief Society was discontinued in 1857 because of the pending arrival of the federal army, which had been sent by President James Buchanan in response to allegations of a Mormon rebellion in Utah.[12]

[June 14, 1854]

MOVED BY M. DUDLEY, seconded by A Cobb,[13] and carried unanimously, that the following covenant be made by all who become members of this society, viz., that we speak no evil of each other, nor of the authorities of the church, but endeavor by all means in our power to cultivate a spirit of union, humility, and love, and that this shall be the covenant into which all shall enter who become members of this society.

[May 6, 1857]

Sister M. Busby[14] proposed that the covenant entered into at the commencement of the first organization of the society should be renewed, which was as follows: That all who become members of this society shall speak no evil of each other while assembled, nor of the authorities of the church or any other person, but endeavor by all means in our power to cultivate a spirit of union, humility, and love, and that this shall be the covenant that all shall enter into who become members of this society.

Salt Lake City Thirteenth Ward, Salt Lake Stake, Relief Society Minutes, vol. 1, 1854–1857, June 14, 1854, May 6, 1857, [4], [14–15], CHL. Handwriting of Martha J. Coray and Elizabeth Goddard.[15] *Title supplied by the editors.*

WE HAVE EACH A MISSION TO PERFORM

◇◇◇

ELICIA A. GRIST

Address in *Latter-day Saints' Millennial Star*
Liverpool, England
May 4, 1861

British actress Elicia Allely Grist [Suhrke Garthwaite] (1827–1898) was baptized a member of the Church of Jesus Christ of Latter-day Saints in May 1853, about five months after her husband, John Grist.[1] As a result of Elicia's new church membership, her parents disinherited her.[2] Over the years, the Grist family moved around England and Ireland, between Birmingham, Dublin, and Liverpool, where this talk was published.[3]

In the eighteenth and nineteenth centuries, Britain experienced the profound economic, social, cultural, and political changes of the Industrial Revolution. The development of the steam printing press, for instance, made publications more accessible to the growing working class. The thriving print culture created a public space where people could more fully articulate their sense of personal identity, their values, and their church activity, as Grist demonstrated.[4] In addition, many individuals who experienced the dislocations of the Industrial Revolution were open to exploring new religious ideas and groups, and the church grew rapidly in Britain in the mid-nineteenth century. The church's semimonthly British periodical, the *Millennial Star,* which was first published in 1840, was "devoted to the spread of the fulness of the gospel" and communicated with Saints throughout the British Mission.[5]

The *Millennial Star* was particularly important because the Saints in Britain were spread out widely and lacked some of the formal organization of the church. For instance, the first British Relief Society was not formally organized until 1873.[6] The *Millennial Star* served in part as a forum for women—some of its articles, editorials, addresses, and messages spoke specifically to a female audience.[7]

In her address, Grist spoke of the distinct responsibilities of women. British women were experiencing new economic, cultural, and political opportunities as a result of the Industrial Revolution. Some mid-nineteenth-century Englishwomen who fought for women's rights and suffrage simultaneously defended the Victorian concepts of gendered spheres and woman's place in the home.[8] Grist used metaphors from her acting career in her discourse, encouraging women to recognize their performance in the various acts of life. She also spoke as a mother—the Grists had seven daughters, four of whom died in infancy.[9]

Grist personally completed the plan of emigration outlined in this address when her family moved to Utah in 1863 through the assistance of the Perpetual Emigrating Fund.[10] Upon arriving in Salt Lake City, she immediately began acting in the Salt Lake Theater, taking up again a pastime from her earlier life.[11] Whether she actually delivered this address orally or simply published it in the *Millennial Star* is unknown.

IN TAKING UPON MYSELF to address the sisters of the church, I do it with a view of stimulating and encouraging the best of feelings to exist among them; but by no means do I claim to be a dictator. I merely suggest what I consider would be a means of causing a more lively interest in each other's society, by becoming more united in our efforts and extending a goodly influence in the sphere in which we are called to move.

When we take into consideration the many opportunities and various ways of usefulness, and the amount of good that may be accomplished by us who are engaged in so great a cause, some of you may feel that it is not our prerogative to interfere in the least, or to take one step towards building up the kingdom of God. But I feel that it is a mistaken idea to suppose that we cannot perform acts that would ennoble our character and position, when we are so nearly allied to the brethren of the priesthood, and they are required to use strenuous efforts to advance the cause of God. Not that I would wish it to be understood as suggesting anything that would interfere with the rights and duties of their high and holy calling. But could we not cherish a loving, kindred spirit towards each other? If we cannot often meet together in a social capacity, we may individually retain a more saintly oneness, and imbibe in our thoughts and sentiments a greater desire to bless and build up—to strengthen and encourage, and thus be a means of diffusing abroad a more lively interest in the kingdom of our Father, whose adopted ones we claim to be. As we are all of one family, let us be united in doing all the good we can in our sphere; for we are able to accomplish much, if we feel like doing it. Also in our fellowship meetings much depends upon the part we take.[12]

We have each a mission to perform, if we were only to consider what responsibility there is devolving upon us in every act we perform, though we are the weaker vessels, and cannot be called to bear off the higher responsibilities which rest upon those holding the oracles of God.[13] But can we not, dear sisters, carry with us a pure sentiment of kindly feeling, and assist to create a lively spirit and devoted earnestness to the cause; and I need not name one great privilege we have, when there is ample opportunity afforded us for testifying and exercising the gifts of the Spirit. How many times have we been forcibly struck by the manifest power of God in our meetings![14] In many instances, when we have participated in these holy inspirations, our testimony may have caused some who have been present to reflect more deeply and closely upon what has been said.[15] The same also may be done on other occasions, while in company with our neighbor or friendly visitor, who may, perhaps, have called on us, desiring the loan of some book. Here we may have the chance of conversing upon the principles of the church, and disseminating the works of the church also; and who knows but that in this way we may be the means of convincing some honest lover of truth, and showing him or her the way of salvation! Many instances of this sort might be mentioned. But suffice it to say, I deem it unusual on my part to give such instructions to my sisters, who may fully understand their duties and the various ways of usefulness, and how they can be best engaged in spreading a knowledge of the truth, by inviting others to attend the assemblies and congregations of the Saints; for "a word in season, how good it is" to those who will take a hint![16]

We will now turn our attention to the domestic circle. Much depends upon us as to what kind of a spirit pervades our homes. As wives, we can create a little heaven there. When the head of a family returns from his daily toil, he necessarily looks for those comforts and attentions which it is unnecessary for me to mention, as all know best for themselves how to please and comfort those whom it is their privilege to look up to. There are also weighty responsibilities resting upon those of us that are mothers—namely, the proper training and instructing of our children. We cannot begin too early to instill into their young minds the principles of the church. I am frequently led into a train of serious reflections by questions asked by my little ones concerning the church. Their questions often arouse me to a sense of my duty. We are, dear sisters, held accountable to God for the manner in which we bring up our children. Do our little ones ever hear us pray for them? Do they ever see us kneeling by their little beds? For it is those children who hear their mothers pray who are most likely to pray for themselves.

I would also suggest another source of good to our children—namely, that of reading aloud to them, as often as we possibly can, the works of the church.[17] Their young minds are very susceptible, and impressions are soon made, and their interest easily excited to that which is good. Take, for instance, an idea lately suggested by some of the brethren of the priesthood—that of traveling to Zion at the rate of three miles a penny: so every penny saved will bring you three miles nearer to Zion![18] If we can only get our children to take an interest in this, it would check that natural desire so prevalent amongst them of running away to buy cakes and sweets that only do them an injury.

I will mention one incident that came under my notice, for the encouragement of the young who may read it, or hear it read. Two little ones belonging to a family in the church had twopence each given them, and they came running to their mother, with joy beaming in their faces—"Oh, mother, we are six miles nearer to Zion! Please to put it in the box." It would be well to encourage our children in this new movement. Although simple as it seems, our youngest children may in some instances be traveling three miles a day, and in a very easy way too, by putting their pence in a saving-box to their own credit.[19] This will cause them and us to have the interest of the gathering at heart.

I trust that these few scattered remarks, written in all humility, will be received in the same kindly feeling; and I hope some more talented sister will take up the subject, as by that course we may greatly benefit each other. I do not wish any to think that I profess to be perfect. Alas, no. I feel my own imperfections but am endeavoring to overcome those things which I know to be a hindrance to my progress in the kingdom of God.

Elicia Grist, "Address to the Sisters of the Church," Latter-day Saints' Millennial Star *23, no. 18 (May 4, 1861): 277–278. Title supplied by the editors.*

GOD WILL ENABLE US TO OVERCOME

◇◇◇

MARY ISABELLA HORNE

Salt Lake City Seventeenth Ward Relief Society
Union Hall, Salt Lake City, Utah Territory
July 30, 1868

On July 30, 1868, Mary Isabella Hales Horne (1818–1905) spoke to the Salt Lake City Seventeenth Ward Relief Society about faith in times of trial. The *Woman's Exponent* described Horne as a woman of "indomitable energy of character" who was "determined not to shrink from any responsibility placed upon her."[1] Born in England, she immigrated with her family to York [Toronto], Canada, in 1832, when she was thirteen years old. She met Joseph Horne at a Methodist camp meeting when she was fifteen and married him two years later. The couple became acquainted with Mormon missionaries Orson Pratt and Parley P. Pratt shortly after their marriage and were baptized in July 1836. The Hornes moved to Far West, Missouri, in 1838 and were driven out of Missouri to Illinois with other Mormons the following winter. She joined the Nauvoo Relief Society on June 9, 1842.[2]

Horne's Relief Society service continued in Salt Lake City. When the Salt Lake City Fourteenth Ward Relief Society was organized in 1856, she served as first counselor to President Phebe W. Woodruff. When the society was reorganized on December 12, 1867, she was made president.[3] She often traveled and spoke to different Relief Societies throughout Utah Territory, sharing her personal experience and conviction.[4]

In July 1868, Horne visited the neighboring Seventeenth Ward Relief Society.[5] Her friend Marinda N. Hyde, whose husband may have baptized Horne, presided over this Relief Society.[6] Prior to Horne's speech, Hyde spoke about the work of the Seventeenth Ward. She said they had produced "one quilt, a piece of carpet, and a piece of jeans, and I believe that we are blessed in our labors. I feel that our Heavenly Father will take care of us."[7] Hyde continued her message of hope when she referred to a recent invasion of crickets (local settlers called them grasshoppers or locusts) in the Salt Lake Valley.[8] The latest infestation likely prompted memories of a similar event two decades earlier in which crickets had attacked crops—a story that had become part of Mormon cultural memory.[9] Hyde remarked, "In relation to the grasshoppers which visited us last week, I never felt for a moment as though Father had forsaken us."[10] Horne echoed these sentiments of faith in her own talk.

I AM PLEASED to meet with you in the capacity of a Female Relief Society. I feel that these societies are stepping stones to much greater works, and that finally we shall reap the reward, but we must live faithful lives and successfully contend with evil and God will enable us to overcome. My faith never failed on account of the grasshoppers, for I knew that Father was willing and able to sustain us, and that sometimes he tries us to bring us nearer to him.[11] I know it is good for us to meet sometimes in this capacity; the interchange of thoughts and feelings in a good cause tends to our elevation. And if we are faithful, when our work is done on earth we shall reach the celestial kingdom of our God.

Salt Lake City Seventeenth Ward, Salt Lake Stake, Relief Society Minutes, vol. 2, 1868–1871, July 30, 1868, 97–98, CHL. Handwriting of Lydia Dunford Alder. Title supplied by the editors.

Mary Isabella Horne. Circa 1860s. Horne acted as president of the Ladies' Cooperative Retrenchment Association from 1870 to 1904, president of the Salt Lake Stake Relief Society from 1877 to 1903, and treasurer of the Relief Society general board from 1880 to 1901. She also served as chair of the executive committee of the Deseret Hospital from 1882 to 1894. Photograph by Edward Martin. (Church History Library, Salt Lake City.)

LET US CULTIVATE OURSELVES

◇◇◇

ELIZA R. SNOW

Salt Lake City Seventeenth Ward Relief Society
Union Hall, Salt Lake City, Utah Territory
February 18, 1869

As a young woman, Eliza Roxcy Snow (1804–1887) worked as a secretary for her father when he served as justice of the peace in Portage County, Ohio.[1] Early exposure to legal documents and parliamentary procedure prepared her to draft a constitution when Latter-day Saint women in Nauvoo, Illinois, proposed a women's sewing group in March 1842. When Snow submitted her constitution and bylaws for Joseph Smith's approval, he commended her efforts, then suggested that the women instead form an official church organization, which became the Relief Society.[2] She acted as secretary of the Relief Society and maintained the ledger containing the minutes and donation and membership records. In this capacity, Snow became acquainted with the intricate details and breadth of women's work, which she discussed in a talk twenty-five years later in the Salt Lake City Seventeenth Ward Relief Society.

Snow connected the foundation of the Nauvoo Relief Society with new official iterations of the society in Utah. She carried the Nauvoo Relief Society Minute Book from Nauvoo to Winter Quarters, Nebraska, and then to the Salt Lake Valley in 1847.[3] Several relief and benevolent societies emerged in Utah in the 1850s, although they did not survive through the Utah War and the Civil War. Snow participated minimally in these groups; at the same time, she was officiating in the Endowment House, which commanded much of her time and attention.[4] When Brigham Young called for the re-institution of the Relief Society, first in 1867 and then again in 1868, he appointed Snow to assist bishops in organizing Relief Societies in each ward.[5] She later remembered, "To me it was quite a mission, and I took much pleasure in its performance. I felt quite honored and much at home in my associations."[6] She took the Nauvoo Relief Society Minute Book with her as she traveled around Utah Territory and used it to show new Relief Society leaders how to keep minutes and hold proper proceedings.[7]

With Snow's influence, the Relief Society in Utah provided a forum for women to act, to understand their relationship with the priesthood and with male counterparts, and to develop a sense of female spiritual and secular authority.[8] In a two-part article in the *Deseret News* in April 1868, Snow explained: "This is an organization that cannot exist without the priesthood, from the fact that it derives all its authority and influence from that source." She explained that the Relief Society "was organized after the pattern of the Church of Jesus Christ of Latter-day Saints, with a presidentess, who chose two counselors."[9] She and others who attended the Nauvoo meetings later remembered Joseph Smith's explanation of women's responsibilities.[10]

As part of Snow's assignment to help organize ward Relief Societies and her effort to expound Joseph Smith's teachings to women, she visited the Seventeenth Ward, a ward society that had close ties to the Nauvoo Relief Society, on February 18, 1869.[11] In attendance were members of the Salt Lake stake presidency and several presidents and officers of other Salt Lake City Relief Societies.[12]

I HAVE OFTEN THOUGHT that unless we had more to do than what it seemed possible for us to accomplish, that we should not perform all that we might.[13]

It is a blessing to us that we, at times, are brought into circumstances which are calculated to bring into exercise every power and faculty which we possess. It is true, it may not seem very desirable for the time being, but it has a tendency to strengthen and develop our abilities and prepare us for greater usefulness.

We have been instructed that each one of us in our organizations is endowed with the germs of every faculty requisite to constitute a god or a goddess.[14] These little ones in their mothers' arms have the germs of all the capabilities which we exhibit, and what constitutes the difference between them and ourselves? Merely a lack of development in them, and this development requires cultivation, energy, and perseverance.

The organization of the Female Relief Society places the sisters in positions to bring into exercise and thus develop all of our faculties: thus in doing good to others, we benefit ourselves. "In blessing thou shalt be blessed."[15] And those who do thc most good shall be most blessed.

My sisters, let us cultivate ourselves, that we may be capable of doing much good. We are daughters of our Heavenly Father, and our position as Saints of the Most High is at the head of the world.

Let us try to realize our responsibilities and honor our position.

It is a delicate thing for us sisters to act in an organized capacity. Our brethren are accustomed to move in organized bodies—we are not, and we need a great deal of the Spirit and wisdom of God to direct us. Although we should meet with difficulties, let us never feel discouraged, but move forward in the path of duty, and through the blessing of God and the encouragement of our brethren, we shall surmount every obstacle.[16] When you see one step before you, take it, and do not wait to see where is the next—if we see one step, it is not for us to stand still until we can see the way clear in the distance, but move forward and the way will be opened before us, step by step. This is a principle. God requires us to make the effort and thus prove our faith and trust in him, and then he is sure to extend his aid. We have a gratifying illustration of this principle here before us. Sister Rich reports that Bro. Rich donates $50.00 worth of lumber to this society.[17] If the society had not made a move in preparing to build, this liberal donation would not have been made.[18]

This society has already done much. God has been with you, my sisters, or you could not accomplish what you have—you have also had the faith and prayers of the First Presidency and of your bishop.[19]

This organization is a portion of the holy priesthood, and stands in the same relation to the bishop that the society which was organized in Nauvoo by Joseph Smith stood to him; and the idea of the society acting in opposition to the bishop is not only preposterous, but an impossibility.[20] In all its movements it acts in accordance with his counsel, and the moment it takes a step aside from this, it ceases to exist in its proper order, and the spirit of the institution is withdrawn.

But I am not in the least anticipating such an event. You have a president and counselors who have learned by many years of experience to respect and be guided by the authorities placed over them.[21]

Yet, I feel to say to you be careful, move cautiously, yet with energy.

I feel to congratulate you on your success—you have done much. You have donated liberally, and you have disbursed as liberally.[22] I trust that in the ensuing year, the demands on your treasury will not be so heavy as in the past.[23]

And, by the way, I wish to caution my sisters a little with regard to sympathy: Our sympathies, as well as every other emotional feeling, require cultivation. This I have learned by practical experience. I could not believe that any person would solicit charity unless really needy, and I had been many times imposed upon before I dared to question my sympathies; but I "learned wisdom from the things I suffered."[24]

It is your duty and province as a society for the relief of the poor to make yourselves fully acquainted with the circumstances of those who solicit your aid.[25]

I have known instances of people being supported by charity when they had large boxes stored with good jewelry, etc.[26] Do not hesitate to inform yourselves—the really needy will not dissemble, neither will they shrink from investigation. You need the wisdom of God to direct you in these matters, that you may neither withhold from the destitute, nor unnecessarily drain your treasury.

Each member of the society should study to know her place, and honor herself by filling it honorably, and all move forward like machinery that is perfect in all its parts.[27] Let no one overstep her mark or in the least crowd against another. For instance, I would say to the teachers or visiting committee, it is for you to visit your respective blocks—to ascertain the circumstances of those you visit and report to the proper authorities whose province it is to deal out or administer as shall be requisite.[28] And if this principle shall be carried out in every department, the society will move on like clockwork.

We must learn to act from principle, not from feeling—we often have occasion to put the bit upon our feelings, and with a strong curb of restraint keep them under proper control, for through this channel the tempter will seek to stir up jealousies and envies—check every feeling of this nature. We may at times think we have not received due respect from this or that one, but let us ever remember "it is better to suffer wrong than to do wrong."[29] Let us act nobly, as becomes Saints of God and daughters of Abraham, and ever bear in mind the greatest and the noblest are the most condescending.

This is one branch—there are many branches but they all constitute one Female Relief Society, as it was organized by Joseph Smith. Let each member realize her responsibility, and seek to make the society honorable by being honorable herself. Let us be humble and cherish the Spirit of God, that we may increase in wisdom and knowledge, that we may attain to true and noble womanhood, that we may become what we were in the beginning created to be—helpmate to our brethren.

According to instructions by the Prophet Joseph at the time of its first organization, this society is designed to be a relief to the bishop and elders of Israel. In administering to the poor you have already aided your bishop and lessened his cares, and every labor that comes within the province of woman devolves upon the Female Relief Society.[30]

In a recent address by President Young before the F.R.S. [Female Relief Society] of the 15th Ward, he established a broad platform, and pointed out an extensive field, or fields of labor—almost too much, it might seem, to be accomplished in this generation.[31]

I desire fervently that we all may grow better day by day, that when the faithful shall be called out, as we have been instructed they will be, we may be one of the number.

My sisters, you have my blessing, and my prayer is that we may have grace to overcome evil with good—have power to withstand every temptation—attain to the faith of the ancients, and obtain victory over everything that opposes us on our way to the celestial kingdom.

Salt Lake City Seventeenth Ward, Salt Lake Stake, Relief Society Minutes, vol. 2, 1868–1871, Feb. 18, 1869, 148–152, CHL. Handwriting of Lydia Dunford Alder. Title supplied by the editors.

Zina D. H. Young. Circa 1867. Young served as the Relief Society general president from 1888 to 1901. She was also the first matron of the Salt Lake temple in 1893. Photograph by Edward Martin. (Church History Library, Salt Lake City.)

11

WE SERVE A JUST GOD

◇◇◇

ZINA D. H. YOUNG

Lehi Relief Society
Tabernacle, Lehi, Utah Territory
October 27, 1869

Zina Diantha Huntington Jacobs Young (1821–1901), who was known for having a "great mother-heart," spoke about motherhood at the Lehi Relief Society on October 27, 1869.[1] She maintained a close relationship with her mother, Zina Baker Huntington, and her sister, Presendia Huntington Buell Kimball.[2] She had two sons, Zebulon and Chariton, with husband Henry Jacobs, and a daughter, Zina Presendia Young [Card], with husband Brigham Young.[3] She also raised the three children of another of Brigham Young's wives, Clarissa Maria Ross Young, after Clarissa's untimely death in 1858.[4]

Susa Young Gates, the daughter of another of Brigham Young's wives, described Zina Young as the heart of women's work in the church.[5] Young expanded her female circle when she joined the Nauvoo Relief Society at its second meeting on March 24, 1842, at age twenty-one.[6] After Relief Society meetings ceased in 1845, Young continued to meet with the women in Nauvoo.[7] In Winter Quarters, she joined with friends to pray and exercise spiritual gifts.[8] She became an important influence in the development of the Relief Society in Utah in 1868, assisting Eliza R. Snow in organizing and training new presidencies. Public speaking was a new experience for Young, as it was for many of her contemporaries, but her wide life experience and knowledge of church teachings permeated her unpolished words. She later served as the third Relief Society general president from 1888 until her death in 1901. Gates remembered that "Sister Zina was all love and sympathy, and drew people after her by reason of that tenderness."[9]

The Relief Society in Lehi, Utah Territory, thirty miles south of Salt Lake City, was organized on October 27, 1868, under the direction of President Sarah Coleman.[10] A year later, on October 27, 1869, the Lehi Relief Society celebrated its first anniversary at the Lehi Tabernacle. Snow and Young attended both the morning and afternoon sessions, and President Brigham Young, apostles George A. Smith and Orson Pratt, and Joseph Young of the Quorum of the Seventy arrived in the middle of the afternoon session. The topic of motherhood was foremost at this meeting. Snow spoke of Eve and the responsibility to bear children.[11] That afternoon, Brigham Young taught about "the duties of mothers to their children. . . . The ladies were the mainspring of every nation, and if we wanted to know what a nation was we must see what their mothers were."[12] Such instruction likely resonated with the mothers in the congregation. Of the Relief Society presidency alone, Sarah Coleman had eight children, Barbara Evans had fifteen, Martha Thomas had ten, and Mary Ann Davis had eight.[13] Zina Young demonstrated sensitivity to those who had no children, including secretary Rebecca Standring, in her afternoon speech, which is presented here.[14]

I AM NOT ACCUSTOMED to public speaking[15] but pleased to look upon the faces of my sisters[16] and to know that we are engaged in this great work,[17] and I would exhort you to be faithful in the discharge of every duty; and to mothers I would say, fulfill your duties to your children, for they are blessings from God entrusted to your care; and to you my sisters who may not have children, be comforted. We serve a just God, and if you are faithful to his cause it will be no loss to you.[18] Let us seek after the Spirit of God and learn to bear all things and with each other, and if a sister should come to us with her griefs and sorrows, let us not encourage her in them but show her how the Lord will not put upon us more than we can bear,[19] and when we have endured all things and overcome we shall then inherit all things.[20] May God bless you and keep you faithful forever. Amen.

Lehi Ward, Utah Stake, Relief Society Minutes and Records, vol. 1, 1868–1879, Oct. 27, 1869, 30, CHL. Handwriting of Rebecca Standring. Title supplied by the editors.

BE FORBEARING AND FORGIVING

◇◇◇

JANE H. NEYMAN

Beaver Relief Society
Tabernacle, Beaver, Utah Territory
November 4, 1869

Jane Harper Neyman [Fisher] (1792–1880) addressed the Beaver Relief Society on November 4, 1869, speaking of human weakness and charity. Neyman was born and raised in western Pennsylvania. She was baptized in 1838, and she and her husband, William Neyman, moved in 1840 to Nauvoo, Illinois, where William died within a few months. Her second husband, Thomas G. Fisher, died soon after their March 1844 marriage. Neyman lost four other family members within the year.[1]

Neyman and her children suffered from poverty in Nauvoo. The Nauvoo Relief Society minutes record concern on April 28, 1842, for the "widow Neyman," who was "destitute."[2] Emma Hale Smith requested an inquiry into the Neyman home, evidently because Neyman's daughters Matilda and Margaret had been accused of sexual immorality with Chauncey Higbee.[3] The Neyman sisters testified before the Nauvoo high council in May 1842 that Higbee had seduced them by falsely invoking the authority of Joseph Smith.[4] The events must have caused a great deal of gossip; Jane Neyman's obituary recorded that "Joseph Smith was her unvarying friend; he rebuked those who falsely slandered her."[5] Her daughter Mary Ann Nickerson joined the Nauvoo Relief Society on May 12, 1842, but when Jane Neyman applied for membership on July 14, 1842, an objection was raised, most likely because of the events with her other daughters, and she was not admitted.[6]

Neyman later traveled to Utah with her daughters Rachel Neyman and Mary Ann Nickerson. She nursed the sick during a cholera epidemic on the plains, "believing that if she did all in her power to save others, the Lord would spare her, and thus it proved," according to her friend Louisa Barnes Pratt. Pratt explained, "In many instances, through her faith, was the power of God manifested in a marvelous manner."[7] The Neyman family settled in Beaver, Utah Territory, two hundred miles south of Salt Lake City, where Neyman served as the first president of the Relief Society when it was organized on January 11, 1868. When Neyman wrote a letter inviting "the honorable and benevolent ladies in Beaver" to form a Relief Society, she indicated that it would be "for the relief of the poor and afflicted among us; and for the mutual benefit of each other to encourage faithfulness in the cause of truth, and all the Christian graces; to visit the sick among our sex and administer to their wants both temporally and spiritually."[8] Her motto as president was "gather up the fragments, let nothing be lost." She resigned as president on March 4, 1869, at age seventy-eight, "thinking the burden too great for her, being far advanced in life."[9] At a meeting on November 4, 1869, "fifteen new members were admitted, all recommended by responsible persons," and Neyman spoke about charity and unity as necessary components of Relief Society membership, a common theme in nineteenth-century Mormon women's teachings.[10]

MOTHER NEYMAN ADDRESSED the meeting on the subject of charity, encouraging all to be forbearing and forgiving, refraining as much as possible from scrutinizing the conduct of our neighbors, remembering always that we are human and must therefore err. It seemed to be the unanimous agreement of the Spirit that presided over the meeting that tattling and slander should die a natural death; that charity, which covereth a multitude of sins,[11] which thinketh no evil, and suffereth long and is kind,[12] should dig the grave and help to bury all the malice and envy which at any time had intruded upon our peace and harmony;[13] and in their stead establish truth and integrity, twin sisters of charity, and then appoint the Mormon creed as a rear guard to repel the first attack of the enemy, that we might be timely warned to avoid an evil wherein our mutual confidence might be destroyed.[14] All this, though not expressed in so many syllables, was in substance the same, no doubt the sentiments of all present. We hope our new members will understand what will be expected of them in this honorable sisterhood: that they will live above reproach and by guarding the doors of their lips keep themselves from censure.[15]

Beaver First Ward, Beaver Stake, Relief Society Minutes, vol. 1, 1868–1878, Nov. 4, 1869, 25–26, CHL. Handwriting of Louisa B. Pratt. Title supplied by the editors.

THE PRAYER OF FAITH

◇◇◇

DRUSILLA D. HENDRICKS

Smithfield Relief Society
Private Residence, Smithfield, Utah Territory
August 7, 1871

When Drusilla Dorris Hendricks (1810–1881) spoke at the Smithfield Relief Society in August 1871, she talked about trusting the Lord when faced with significant challenges. She spoke from many years of experience, which she recorded in her life sketch. In that sketch, she remembered that when she was a very ill ten-year-old, the doctor, a Baptist minister, prayed that she "might become a mother in Israel and do much good in [her] days, all of which [she] never forgot."[1] As new converts to the Church of Jesus Christ of Latter-day Saints, she and her husband, James Hendricks, joined other members in Clay County, Missouri, in May 1836.[2] James was injured at the Battle of Crooked River, a skirmish between Latter-day Saint and Missouri militia forces on October 25, 1838.[3] He remained paralyzed for the rest of his life, and his wife both nursed him and provided for the family.[4]

At one particularly distressing time, when the family was out of food, she remembered that a voice told her, "Hold on, for the Lord will provide."[5] Hendricks found different ways to support her family, including growing, making, and selling food and beverages; taking in boarders and laundry; and producing and selling gloves and mittens.[6] In 1860, Hendricks and her husband followed their sons and daughters to settle in Richmond, Utah Territory, about one hundred miles north of Salt Lake City.[7]

Hendricks often visited her daughter Rebecca Roskelley in Smithfield, six miles south of Richmond. On August 7, 1871, they attended the Smithfield Relief Society, where her daughter was one of the founding members.[8] Roskelley spoke, as did Hendricks, sharing the story of her son William volunteering for the Mormon Battalion in Council Bluffs, Iowa, in 1846.[9] After lobbying by church leaders, the United States government had decided to enlist five hundred Latter-day Saint men for service in the Mexican-American War.[10] Because her husband was severely disabled and she faced the daunting task of caring for him as well as the rest of her family in crossing the plains, Hendricks hesitated to give approval for her sixteen-year-old son to go.[11] She later described how the Spirit reminded her to trust in God, who had provided for her in the past. Although the journey was difficult, the Hendricks family arrived safely in Salt Lake City, and William—after marching with the battalion from Iowa to California—reached the Salt Lake Valley ten days later. Hendricks added, "The hand of the Lord was in it; I have seen it since."[12]

SISTER DRUSILLA HENDRICKS, a visitor from Richmond, arose and addressed the meeting: Would rather sit and listen to her sisters but was always willing to bear her testimony to the truth and offer a cheering word; felt the necessity of living so as to have the prayer of faith continually in her heart; had realized the importance of it in past days; had worked day and night to support her family and pay her tithing when there was nothing else to sustain her but the prayer of faith and the consolation given in answer to it.[13]

After her husband was shot down in Missouri and then dragged about by the merciless mob when unable to help himself,[14] and they were driven from their home, when a call was made for volunteers to go in the Battalion she was so indignant at the way in which the Mormons had been treated she said her boy could not go, and kept him from making any preparations until the morning the company was to start.[15] Then, as she watched him go into the tall, wet grass which surrounded their encampment, to bring up the cow, the thought occurred to her, how easily he might be taken from her by death occasioned by the exposures and hardships he had to encounter remaining with her[16]—and then, how she should meditate, had he gone in the Battalion it might not have been! But again the feeling returned, "I cannot let him go!" Then came a peculiar sensation and it was as though a voice said to her, "Do you not want the highest glory?" She answered naturally, "Yes," and the voice continued, "How do you think to gain it save by making the greatest sacrifices?" She questioned—"Lord, what lack I yet?"[17] "Let the son go in the Battalion," was the answer received, but she argued, "It is too late now, they are starting—and besides, he is too young and not able to carry arms." Her heart was greatly disturbed.

Presently her boy came with the cow, and soon after came a man crying, "Turn out and volunteer to go in the Battalion—we lack a number of men yet,

James and Drusilla D. Hendricks with a grandchild. Circa 1852. Drusilla Hendricks was an early proponent of the Relief Society. She reminisced that before the Relief Society was organized in Nauvoo, she dreamed that women were holding meetings and keeping records of their work. Hendricks joined the Nauvoo Relief Society on April 14, 1842, and was appointed to a visiting committee in the Second Ward in Nauvoo. (Photograph in family possession.)

but we do not wish to press anyone."[18] She wanted her cow for a screen just then, and taking a bucket she knelt by the cow as if to milk, but in reality to pray. Her prayer was, "Lord, if you want my son, take him, only let him be restored to me again as was the son of Abraham," and the answer came in spirit—"So shall it be, even as thou hast said."[19] She arose and with the help of some of her neighbors quickly prepared her boy and sent him from her with the firm conviction that God would be as good as his word and restore her son to her again. During his absence it was her constant labor to pray for him, and he was restored to her as a recompense for her faithfulness.[20] So it will be with us all; we have to make sacrifices, but if done in meekness, with an eye single to the glory of God, we will never fail to reap a rich reward.[21]

Smithfield Branch, Cache Stake, Relief Society Minutes, vol. 1, 1868–1878, Aug. 7, 1871, 98–99, CHL. Handwriting of Louise L. Greene. Title supplied by the editors.

AN ELEVATION SO HIGH ABOVE THE ORDINARY

◇◇◇

ELIZA R. SNOW

Senior and Junior Cooperative Retrenchment Association
Fourteenth Ward Assembly Hall, Salt Lake City, Utah Territory
October 11, 1872

Eliza Roxcy Snow (1804–1887) encouraged women attending a meeting of the Senior and Junior Cooperative Retrenchment Association on October 11, 1872, to elevate their thoughts, beliefs, and actions through study and service. She was instrumental in the development of the retrenchment organization in 1870. The idea originated when Brigham Young visited various settlements in 1869. He noticed a pattern of women spending an inordinate amount of time preparing extravagant banquets and neglecting their spiritual and intellectual nourishment.[1] Young hoped that women would "retrench," or reduce energy and time spent preparing lavish meals and engaging in excessive fashion. He invited Mary Isabella Horne, president of the Salt Lake City Fourteenth Ward Relief Society, "to call the sisters of the Relief Society together, and ask them to begin a reform in eating and housekeeping."[2] Young, Horne, and Snow encouraged women to expand their priorities beyond domestic routines to also include broader issues of social reform, home manufacture, and intellectual and spiritual discussion.[3]

In her discourse, Snow referred to the role of women within the future organization of the "order of Enoch," a reference to a Latter-day Saint scriptural text that described Enoch's "City of Holiness, even Zion" in which the people were "of one heart and one mind, and dwelt in righteousness; and there was no poor among them."[4] Inspired in part by these scriptures, Brigham Young had encouraged economic cooperation through the establishment of cooperatives in Utah in the previous decade. The purposes, he taught, were self-sufficiency and the preservation of Latter-day Saint identity, especially in the face of the perceived threats of non-Mormon economic, social, and cultural intrusion into Utah Territory after the completion of the transcontinental railroad in 1869. Women were encouraged to participate in the cooperative movement.[5] They found ways to contribute their talents and resources, and they developed new skills. The Ladies' Cooperative Retrenchment Association provided a location for women to gather, educate themselves, and contribute to the cooperative movement.

Snow served as one of six counselors to Horne, president of the Ladies' Cooperative Retrenchment Association.[6] Separate from the Relief Societies, which oversaw benevolent work within each ward, the Retrenchment Association crossed ward boundaries and focused on cooperative assignments given to women, including silk production, cooperative stores, grain storage, home industry, and medical classes. The movement supported a "senior" group for the older women and a "junior" group for young ladies.[7] Unlike the junior groups, which met in individual wards, the Senior Retrenchment Association remained one large organization, meeting collectively in the Fourteenth Ward Assembly Hall in Salt Lake City.[8] These semimonthly meetings generally opened with a hymn, a prayer, and a second hymn. Minutes of the previous meeting were read and accepted or amended. The president or presiding officer began with introductory remarks, sometimes reading a published article or giving a travel report, discussing local current events, or introducing a thematic topic. Attendees then expressed feelings in a discussion format, speaking as moved upon.[9]

At the forty-second meeting of the Retrenchment Association on October 11, 1872, Snow announced the commencement of a new physiology class for women. Sarah M. Kimball would direct the class and follow Young's charge for women to be more engaged in education and medicine.[10] Snow then talked about spiritual and intellectual edification, as well as the proper development of domestic skills as part of the cooperative movement.

SAINTS OF GOD can be edified by nothing but the Spirit of God. We have attained to an elevation so high above the ordinary walks of life that nothing but the revelations of heaven would edify the Saints, their aspirations being so much higher. I was pleased with a remark in the minutes made by a sister saying it is uphill business.[11] It is uphill, and if you continue you will attain to something much higher than those who go downhill. How much more satisfying to you it will be if we can look back upon our preceding years, having done what God required of us to do. They who are opposed to the course the young ladies are pursuing may seem to enjoy themselves for a while, but they do not know what it is to taste true happiness. It is but the gratification of the lower faculties of the mind; the higher

Fourteenth Ward Assembly Hall. Circa 1886. Several different types of women's meetings were held in this hall in Salt Lake City, including retrenchment meetings and Mutual Improvement Association June conference sessions. Photograph by C. E. Johnson. (Courtesy Utah State Historical Society, Salt Lake City.)

emotions emanate from God. I am interested in my young sisters; they have taken a course that will elevate, prepare, and purify them for the presence of Goddesses in eternity.

This life is full of trouble. Then why should we concentrate our all in that which is fading and will pass away? My young sisters, do not grow cold, but be active in preparing yourselves to be of some use in the kingdom of God. Some seem to think they live for nothing but self-gratification. Our religion is not a fable; it is a reality. And if we live it so as to have the Spirit of God in our hearts, no matter what we are called to pass through, God is with us to comfort and strengthen us. I sometimes think we have all got to look upward, but it seems natural for women to lean sideways. That is not sufficient. My young sisters who meet together and have the Spirit of God in their hearts have a foretaste of eternal happiness.

Human knowledge can never impart the spirit and intelligence they possess.[12] We may talk with some for a generation and yet cannot by words enlighten their understanding. If we have influence with God to penetrate their hearts, it shows them the difference between the things of God and the things of the world. It is necessary for the young to meet together and exercise in religion; it is just as much use to them as to any. We should consider ourselves immortal beings and live for immortality. We should improve every opportunity of treasuring up knowledge and everything that will have a tendency to enlighten our understanding and make us useful, but not for aggrandizing ourselves. We should live for others; in doing so we benefit ourselves. The person that does the most good is the happiest. I was blessed when a child in realizing the advantage and superiority of doing good to being useless. I devoted my early life to studying. How it makes my heart ache over the waste of time and physical energies of some of the young by devoting themselves to amusement instead of study.[13] Not that I would discard amusement, but do not make a business of it. It then ceases to be a diversion.

I was very much pleased with the conference. In speaking of the people living so far beneath their privileges, President Young has said at three different times, "Yet out from this people the Lord will call a people that will do his will." I have wondered how, when, and to whom is this call to be made. In his remarks one day during conference, President Young spoke of establishing a colony composed of those who had sufficient confidence in each other to bind themselves in an indissoluble band.[14] Those that cannot see the order of Enoch will think it an excitement caused by the brethren. It rejoices my heart to see that God is working in our midst, and who are prepared to enter in? Those who have abided the whole law. When we all come to examine ourselves, we shall find the weaknesses of the flesh.

I am thankful to God that I am associated with good sisters. Know that many of them are thinking of something besides human grandeur and mortal wealth; know that you love and are seeking after things of God. Let us do it with our whole hearts. I suggest that we bring forward subjects that will improve and benefit us as daughters of the Most High. Let those things that are foreign to us be let alone. I would not have you think that spiritual exercises are going to perfect us. They alone will not do it. We come together to get our energies aroused to assist us in the duties of life. It is a difficult thing for mortals to take an even course, to devote to each duty that portion of time which belongs to it.

We want to study, reflect, pray, speak, sing, attend meetings, partake of the sacrament, seek out the poor and the needy and those who are losing the light of eternity from their bosoms. I do not believe in taking the course the sectarian world is pursuing, that is, looking after the heathen and neglecting their duties at home.[15] Do not leave those that are nearby to reach after those that are far from us. Our labors for the advancement of the kingdom of God will not be lost; they are sure to meet with their reward. We may labor for other things, and they will perish as the grass. I would exhort the aged to use their influence with the young in trying to get them interested in educational matters. We want to be good housewives. Our young ladies should learn trades and get all the book knowledge that they can. But the perfect knowledge of domestic duties lays the foundation of a thoroughly accomplished lady. This constitutes a foundation upon which you may heap a great many of the finer accomplishments, and she will not become top heavy. But the ornaments are of no use if we are deficient in the other acquirements. To become queens and priestesses we must be business women.[16] We are laying the foundation of the kingdom of God, and it is our duty to mold the character of this generation. We do not want to be ignorant in regard to the principles of the gospel or any department of education which elevates us for the field of action. We expect heaven to be of a higher and more perfect order and free from the weaknesses and impurity of the flesh.

Senior and Junior Cooperative Retrenchment Association, Minutes, Salt Lake City, Utah Territory, looseleaf, 1871–1874, Oct. 11, 1872, 42nd Meeting, [2–5], CHL. Handwriting of Maggie Mair. Title supplied by the editors.

Mary Ann Freeze. Circa 1880s. Freeze joined the Young Ladies' Mutual Improvement Association general board in 1898. She worked at the Salt Lake temple as well as the Bureau of Information on Temple Square. She also participated in the Utah Women's Press Club. Photograph by Fox and Symons. (Church History Library, Salt Lake City.)

15

OUR MISSION

◇◇◇

MARY ANN FREEZE

Salt Lake City Eleventh Ward Young Men's and Young Ladies' Mutual Improvement Associations
Salt Lake City, Utah Territory
January 1879

Mary Ann Burnham Freeze (1845–1912) spoke at a combined meeting of young women and young men of the Salt Lake City Eleventh Ward in January 1879 with a specific message: each individual has worth and purpose. Experience helped Freeze formulate her own life mission. Her father, James Burnham, died just four days before her birth in Nauvoo, Illinois. Her tenacious mother, Mary A. Huntly Burnham, worked for six years to finance the trip across the plains, then led her children to Bountiful, Utah Territory. Freeze wrote of her youth: "My girlhood days were not as happy as might have been, on account of our exceeding poverty, but I have many times since thought that it was for my greatest good that I was reared in want and loneliness; that it was a means of keeping me humble, the good spirit thereby finding a receptacle in my heart, giving me a desire to seek after truth and learn of the things of God."[1]

Throughout her life, Freeze worked with youth in family, professional, and ecclesiastical settings.[2] She taught school in Richmond, Utah Territory, and married the principal, James Freeze, in 1863 at the age of seventeen. The Eleventh Ward Young Ladies' Mutual Improvement Association (YLMIA) was organized under the direction of Zina D. H. Young on October 18, 1871, with the intent to encourage church activity among younger Latter-day Saints. At the age of twenty-six, Freeze was appointed president. At the first meeting, she confided, "This is a new business to me; still I wish to advance and answer to every call. By speaking, we gain confidence and improve in our language; also by speaking new ideas are elicited. Let us exert ourselves to bring more of the girls to our meetings. As Sister Eliza R. Snow says, let us retrench in our ignorance and assist each other to conquer our failings. By comforting others, we not only do them good, but we also comfort ourselves, and this principle will appear more plain and beautiful."[3] Susa Young Gates later described the Eleventh Ward YLMIA as "one of the strongest and best organizations in the city."[4]

In 1878, Freeze was named president of the first stake YLMIA.[5] She reported that she and her counselors "have visited the Associations as far as practicable, have enjoyed the spirit of our mission and feel assured we have been instrumental in the hands of God of doing much good."[6] By the time she gave the following talk in January 1879, she had grown confident in her role as a leader of the youth. Years later, Freeze served on the general board of the YLMIA. YLMIA general president Elmina S. Taylor said of Freeze, "When she visits [the young women] she takes with her the Spirit of God, and the spirit of humility, and the spirit of love. She tells the girls their duties, she inspires in them a desire to serve God, and as his handmaidens, to try to make themselves better day by day."[7]

MY YOUNG BROTHERS AND SISTERS, we were all sent here on the earth for a purpose, and we all have a mission to perform. It is the duty of each of us to understand that mission. We have been told by many of our great men that the noblest spirits were reserved to come forth in this our day because of the great and mighty work to be accomplished in preparing for the second coming of our Lord and Savior Jesus Christ.[8] I wonder how many of us realize that ours is one of those noble spirits, and do we ever ask ourselves the question, "Are we honoring and striving to bring our bodies into subjection to that pure and noble spirit that inhabits it, which ever invites to deeds of virtue and holiness, and would check us when prompted to do any evil or wrong?" How our hearts should swell with gratitude to God that for us was reserved this great privilege, which so many of our forefathers longed to enjoy but were denied.

How little we realized these great gospel truths until these organizations were instituted for the growth and development of the young.[9] Now we begin to know who we are, from where we came, and what will be our future destiny, if we are faithful to God and obey all his commands; and let us not think for a moment that we can do too much good the little time we stay, for it will be only through the utmost diligence on our part that we can earn a place in the celestial kingdom.[10] We must not only be able to say, "We have done harm to no one," but we must be able to say, "We have done all in our power for the furtherance and advancement of the Zion of God on the earth, being prompt in every good word and work." Let us attend faithfully to all our meetings and seek knowledge from every available source, for knowledge is power, and the more we possess the more capable we will be in assisting in the great latter-day work.

We all desire to be good and useful, so let us put our good desire into execution, for it is in our power so to do. It is probable that we covenanted with our Heavenly Father before we came here that we would be energetic in the cause of righteousness, if he would grant us the great and inestimable privilege of having a body on the earth; for we could then see how great the blessings to be thus obtained, which could be obtained in no other way. We cannot now see as we could then, but we have the holy gospel to lead and guide us into all truth and teach us our duty from time to time; we are also blessed with a living priesthood, through which we can receive the word of God, so we are not left to grope in the dark. These associations were organized through that living priesthood and consequently are from heaven; and any young man or woman who will faithfully attend these meetings, taking part as they may be called upon by those who preside, will advance with rapid strides, will know their mission, and will become great and mighty pillars in the church of God upon the earth; and finally be crowned in the presence of God and the Lamb, while those who take no part, or taking part shrink from duty, will also reap the reward of the deeds done in the body, and will receive only what they have justly earned. May we who are here this evening put on the whole armor of righteousness,[11] and battle bravely to overcome sin, and establish a reign of peace on the earth; and that we may receive all the glory we are capacitated to enjoy is the prayer of your sister.

Mary A. Freeze, "Our Mission: Read Before the Conjoint Meeting of the M. I. Associations of the 11th Ward, S. L. City, Jan. 1879," Woman's Exponent *7, no. 20 (Mar. 15, 1879): 209.*

ESSAY ON FAITH

◇◇◇

MARY B. FERGUSON

Spanish Fork Young Ladies' Association
Spanish Fork, Utah Territory
September 20, 1879

On September 20, 1879, Mary Tyndale Baxter Ferguson (1826–1909) addressed the young women of Spanish Fork, Utah Territory, about fifty miles south of Salt Lake City, on the topics of faith and work. Ferguson's experiences revealed her faith and commitment to God despite the challenges of life. She was born in Glasgow, Scotland, and orphaned at a young age.[1] Ferguson was raised by a hired nurse named Agnes Reid, for whom she developed a deep affinity; she did not learn she was adopted until years later. She attended school until age sixteen, then worked in a silk factory and a steam loom factory.[2] She grew up religious; Reid "taught her to read the Bible, fear God and lead a good, virtuous life," and Ferguson became active in different church groups.[3] After she was introduced to Mormon missionaries through her sister in the fall of 1845, Ferguson was apprehensive and determined to investigate the Bible to discover the authenticity of the Church of Jesus Christ of Latter-day Saints.[4] The more she studied, the more she was convinced. She was baptized in October 1846 and recorded that as a result, "all my companions left me and I had my good name cast out as evil, for the gospel's sake."[5]

At a church conference in Scotland, Ferguson met John Baxter, whom she married in 1849. They lived with his family, where Ferguson cared for his ailing siblings and mother. She nursed her husband through his poor health, the result of years of working in a coal mine. With hopes for a better situation in America, the family emigrated in 1851. They remained in St. Louis for two years while earning money to cross the plains to Utah. Not long after their arrival in the Salt Lake Valley in September 1853, her husband became discouraged with the unfamiliar climate and scarce resources in Utah and left for California, leaving Ferguson to support their two living children.[6] Baxter returned a year later, and the family moved to Utah County, living in Spanish Fork and Goshen, where five additional children were born. Baxter died in 1869 after years of sickness.[7]

According to Ferguson's obituary, "she had a very hard struggle to rear and care for so large a family of small children, but the Lord heard her cry and blessed her and fitted her back for its heavy burden."[8] In 1874, five years after the death of her first husband, she married Andrew Ferguson, a friend from Scotland who had both baptized her and officiated at her first marriage to Baxter in 1849.[9]

Ferguson served in the church at the same time she worked to support her family as a nurse and midwife.[10] The same year her first husband died, she was treasurer of the Goshen Relief Society. In 1873 she became a visiting teacher, a responsibility assigned to a small number of women in each ward during this period. The Goshen Relief Society minutes record her donations of potatoes, meat, and wool; her opening and closing prayers; and her remarks on several occasions. On July 6, 1871, she said, "It was good to be obedient in all things pertaining to Christ, for he was meek and humble and loved to bless the sick and poor. She hoped that her walk and conduct would be as a life of a Saint."[11] After she remarried and her family moved to Spanish Fork, Ferguson served for several years as president of the Relief Society there. Women during this time often attended meetings of several organizations. The Spanish Fork Relief Society and Young Ladies' Mutual Improvement Association (YLMIA) often reported to each other, so it was not unusual for Ferguson to visit and speak at a YLMIA meeting.[12]

AS FAITH IS THE FIRST PRINCIPLE of the gospel, it is necessary to inquire, What is faith? The scriptures tell us that "faith is the assurance of things hoped for, the evidence of things not seen";[13] for example, if I should tell you that by going to a certain place you could obtain a piece of gold or a pearl of great beauty, and consequently you go and find it, you manifest your faith by your works.[14] Thus it is when we obey the gospel, certain blessings follow; but if we say we believe and do not obey, then is our faith vain. It is like the body without the spirit, dead. It was this living faith, my young sisters, which caused your fathers and mothers to obey the gospel in their native lands and homes; in the midst of scorn and persecution, through faith they left homes and kindred and all they held dear and embarked on the mighty ocean, tossed upon the waves and billows for weeks and months, far from the sight of land, seasick and weary, but still trusting in the arm of Jehovah to bring them safely to a haven of rest; and many of them had never known the trials and hardships of life, leaving weeping friends distracted with grief, who had not faith, and did not understand the purposes of God.[15] Through faith they traveled across the plains with the slow wearisome travel of oxen—but still more wearisome traveled with handcarts. Think of it, my young sisters: your fathers and mothers traveling over a thousand miles drawing a handcart, with their rations and bedding, cooking utensils, clothing and etc., many of them with little children; fording rivers up to their waists and toiling through miles of heavy sand, and yet by the campfire at night their songs of praise resounded to God, for the principles of faith were planted in their bosoms;[16] they had an assurance of things not seen; by faith they arrived in these valleys; they were not then the rich fertile valleys you now see. By faith they subdued the sterile, barren soil and through the blessings of God succeeded in making the wilderness blossom as the rose.[17] It may yet be said of us in succeeding generations as it has been said of Moses: they struck the soil, and it brought forth abundantly; but it has taken years of arduous toil—toil that now tells on the constitution of those who have passed through it.

Time would fail me to tell you of the trials of our faith caused by crickets, grasshoppers, droughts, floods, and also by the persecution of our enemies; but in all we are an exceedingly blessed and happy people; and through faith we intend to grow and increase and spread abroad till, like Abraham of old, of our increase there shall be no end.[18]

Now, my dear young friends, you need not think that because we have done so much there is nothing for you to do; you have got to spread abroad. You need not think that the territory of Utah is going to hold the children of Zion. You will have to build up new colonies.

It is for our young people, as they are called upon, to leave fathers and mothers, for Zion's stakes must be strengthened and her "cords lengthened."[19] "Give us room that we may dwell, Zion's children cry aloud."[20] The scriptures are fulfilling right before our eyes; the wicked are afraid that we will take away their name and nation, but the prophecies must be fulfilled, though earth and hell should dare oppose.

Therefore, contend earnestly for the faith delivered in these last days to your fathers, that you may be enabled through faith to help bring to pass the purposes of Jehovah; and may the quickening influence of the Spirit of God rest upon the children of Zion, that it may be as a living fire within them, bringing forth much fruit unto righteousness. Then can you say with the poet:

> In danger, in trials and afflictions,
> We have shared with the worthies of yore,

That we at truth's banquet may join them,
When error's great conflict is o'er.[21]

Mary Ferguson, "Essay on Faith: Read at a Meeting of the Y.L.A.," Woman's Exponent *8, no. 9 (Oct. 1, 1879): 70–71.*[22]

17

THE FRUITS OF OUR LABOR

◇◇◇

LILLIE T. FREEZE

Salt Lake City Eleventh Ward
Young Ladies' Mutual Improvement Association
Salt Lake City, Utah Territory
October 18, 1880

Lelia "Lillie" Tuckett Freeze (1855–1937) addressed the transition from youth to adulthood in her talk to young women on October 18, 1880. A little more than twenty years earlier, Brigham Young called her mother, Mercy Westwood Tuckett, on a two-year mission to perform in the theater company at the Bowery and at the Social Hall in Salt Lake City. Freeze performed with her mother in plays at Camp Floyd, the federal army camp located forty-five miles southwest of Salt Lake City, at the age of four. When the theater company disbanded, Tuckett relocated to Nevada and California to pursue her theatrical career, essentially abandoning her children and husband. At the age of five or six, Freeze moved with her grandmother to southern Utah; she walked three hundred miles from Salt Lake City to St. George and then walked back a year later. In 1865, Freeze returned to live with her father and siblings in the Salt Lake City Eleventh Ward. She enjoyed participating in ward theater productions, and she wrote for the *Deseret News*, the *Woman's Exponent*, the *Improvement Era*, and the *Young Woman's Journal*.[1]

Freeze started her association with church youth programs at age sixteen when she joined the Young Ladies' Retrenchment Association of the Eleventh Ward in 1871, attending meetings in the home of Mary Ann Freeze, the first president. She served as a counselor from 1871 to 1881 and helped edit the *Improvement Star*, the manuscript newspaper of the Eleventh Ward Young Ladies' Mutual Improvement Association (YLMIA).[2] In 1875, Lillie married James Freeze as a plural wife, joining the family of her friend Mary Ann, Freeze's first wife.[3] Lillie Freeze was named the first secretary of the Primary general board in June 1880, a position she held for five years. In October 1888, she became the first counselor to Primary general president Louie B. Felt; at the same time, she served on the YLMIA general board under Elmina S. Taylor.[4] These leadership opportunities allowed her to share her experiences and encourage young people to embrace new, more progressive opportunities at the same time they held to core gospel principles.

As a counselor in the Eleventh Ward YLMIA, Freeze spoke often about the responsibilities of the youth and how they could fulfill them. On September 20, 1880, a month before she gave the discourse featured here, she urged the girls to improve their talents and to exert a positive influence on boys.[5] A week later, she encouraged them to "obtain spiritual food, that we may be better prepared to perform our duties."[6] She gave the following sermon at the ninth anniversary of the association on October 18, 1880.[7] Freeze's speech was published in the *Woman's Exponent* a month later.

IT IS NOW NINE YEARS since we began the task of remodeling ourselves,[8] since we commenced to realize the existence of our spiritual beings—that life was not given us that we might eat, sleep, make money, and die, but we began to learn the necessity of cultivating the mind, administering to the needs of an immortal soul, and training the heart in the ways of obedience to God and the light of inspiration. We caught a glimpse of a higher and more noble object of living.

Much has been done, but the field of labor seems to be but just opened. How many of the little girls who, years ago, flocked to the feast of their minds and souls, weekly prepared for them in our little meetings, are now happy wives (notwithstanding the fact that a large number entered the order of celestial marriage)[9] and are devoted mothers, all the better qualified to discharge the holy duties of motherhood and consequently are benefactors to society?[10]

From our ranks have gone to new fields of labor, and will still go, women whose names will be honored as far as the sound of the gospel can reach. The seeds of their success and honor were planted when they made their first feeble attempt to speak in an organized capacity,[11] and were cradled by a succession of untiring efforts, struggling hand to hand with the powers of darkness and the evil they were enabled to see in themselves. And they triumphed to a certain extent by fasting and mighty prayer, by singing and praising God, and count hours as only moments.

We scarcely stop to think seriously upon any subject but fashion.[12] Many of our aspirations reach no further than the feather that floats over our heads. Our eyes see little but the failings of each other, and our ears are open to scandal and prejudice, while our lips are but the servants of our idle, giddy brain. We are too easily satisfied with ourselves and our labors. While the great work of life rolls on constantly, calling for earnest, busy laborers in the cause of humanity, we, in our wild mania after pleasure, rush blindfolded past every avenue of doing good, and every wide open door of improvement, while our hungry, starved spiritual natures must stand aside and wait the time when they will be allowed to plead their just cause without being forever silenced by the harsh, unfeeling voice of our own selfish natures. Now let us stop in this soul- and body-destroying course, and listen to the reasoning that will keep us in the ways of peace, honor, and everlasting life.

Oh! that we the daughters of Zion would claim our privilege in leading out in all that is pure and refining. God requires this at our hands. Let us cultivate more true modesty and less prudery.[13] More sincere sisterly respect and charity for each other and indulge in less flattery, and let our daily intercourse at home and abroad be characteristic of pure nobility of soul. We can overcome our rough, uncouth ways, use only chaste and elegant language, and always manifest a respectful consideration for the feelings and opinions of others.[14] Thus fortified we can trust ourselves in the company of the cultured without a book of etiquette in our pockets.[15]

Let us seek for that guide which would preserve unsullied a spotless reputation and prevent us from associating with the rude and wicked. Let us take pride in maintaining the principles of truth that shall stand when nations now prosperous have gone to decay, fearing no ridicule, dreading naught but the punishment of our offended Creator. Let us not cut ourselves short of an inheritance with our Heavenly Father by folly and disobedience. God requires of us all that we are able to do, and in the end our hearts will swell with everlasting joy and gratitude, surpassing all mortal comprehension.

Lillie Freeze, "The Fruits of Our Labor: Read at the Annual Meeting of the Y.L.M.I.A., 11 Ward," Woman's Exponent *9, no. 12 (Nov. 15, 1880): 95.*

Eliza R. Snow. Circa 1875. Snow was a poet, a world traveler, and a renowned leader of Latter-day Saint women. She effectively linked the Nauvoo Relief Society to the resurgence of the organization in the Utah Territory by preserving the Nauvoo Relief Society Minute Book and traveling throughout Mormon settlements to help organize women and encourage them to speak. Photograph by Charles Carter. (Church History Library, Salt Lake City.)

18

EVERY SISTER SHOULD COME FORWARD

◇◇◇

ELIZA R. SNOW

Kanab Relief Society
Schoolhouse, Kanab, Utah Territory
February 13, 1881

On February 13, 1881, Eliza Roxcy Snow (1804–1887) spoke to women in Kanab, Utah Territory, three hundred miles south of Salt Lake City, about the individual quest for salvation.[1] Three months earlier, Snow left Salt Lake with travel companion Zina D. H. Young for an extensive tour of Latter-day Saint settlements in southern Utah.[2] They intended to participate in ordinances in the St. George temple, the only temple then functioning in the church.[3] They also visited and organized Relief Societies, Young Ladies' Mutual Improvement Associations (YLMIA), and Primaries throughout central and southern Utah.[4]

Snow and Young spent the second week of February in Kanab, about eighty miles east of St. George, just north of the Arizona border.[5] Due in part to its isolation, the settlement did not often receive guests. Kanab Stake president John Nuttall had previously noted, "We have not the privilege of visits from the leading sisters of the north; it takes all their time to travel and visit those that are surrounded by outside influences."[6] While in Kanab, Snow and Young attended a ward picnic, established the Kanab ward and stake Primary organizations, met with the Kanab Relief Society and YLMIA, and organized a silk association.[7] On Sunday, February 13, Snow, Young, and Minerva Snow, the stake Relief Society president in St. George, spoke to a combined meeting of the Relief Society and YLMIA.[8]

The women of Kanab welcomed their Salt Lake City visitors with a formal greeting, hailing them as "Lady Pioneers," "Mothers in Israel," and "Presidents of all the feminine portion of the human race."[9] In June 1880, Snow had been appointed general president of the Relief Society and had chosen Young as her first counselor.[10] In that role, Snow had authority to oversee the women's organizations of the church. Her personal relationships also contributed to her status in Latter-day Saint society. She had been a plural wife of Joseph Smith and, after his death, had married Brigham Young. Snow took Smith's last name in 1880, after the death of Brigham Young in 1877, the death of Emma Smith in 1879, and her appointment as Relief Society general president in 1880.[11] Snow believed and taught the women of Kanab that each woman is responsible for her own salvation.

SISTER SNOW SMITH said the time was when we thought that our husbands would save us, independent of our own exertions. Now we understand that instead of depending entirely on our husbands for salvation and position, we have to work them out ourselves.[12] The responsibility and labor that devolve upon women are becoming more important. If society is reformed, it is to a great extent because women are refined. And the well-being of her children depends much on her influence and example. These societies are to be helps to the bishops and take many cares from their hands. We are organized in ward and stake capacities, and it is necessary that every sister should come forward and take hold of this work for the benefit of their daughters. The Lord wants us to be a peculiar people. Felt that none of us draw as near to Father as we should. When we get the victory over ourselves, then we are saved. "I would say to my young sisters, never shrink from a duty.[13] God has put the means in your hands to become queens and priestesses in his kingdom, if you will only live for it."[14]

Eliza R. Snow, Discourse, Feb. 13, 1881, in "Kanab Relief Society," Woman's Exponent *9, no. 21 (Apr. 1, 1881): 165–166. Recorded by M. Elizabeth Little.[15] Title supplied by the editors.*

THE POWER OF PRAYER

◇◇◇

ELLENOR G. JONES

Salt Lake City Eleventh Ward
Young Ladies' Mutual Improvement Association
Salt Lake City, Utah Territory
February 1, 1882

Ellenor Georgina Reed Jones (1832–1922) taught the young women of the Salt Lake City Eleventh Ward about the power of prayer in 1882. Not much is known about her personal life. Born in Nashville, Tennessee, she was living in Cincinnati, Ohio, by 1850.[1] By 1860 she had married Berry Jones and moved to San Mateo, California, where they had three children.[2] After Berry's death in 1863, Ellenor Jones married Hugh Jones in San Francisco in 1865.[3] They separated after they had two children, and Hugh died in 1893.[4] She traveled back and forth between California and Utah from 1870 through the 1890s; a San Francisco city directory in 1873 listed her as a widow.[5] She died in Redding, California, in 1922.[6]

Born into a multiracial family and raised in the South at the height of slavery and hostility toward free blacks, Jones likely experienced racial prejudice. Census records indicate that her mother, Mary Jones, was born in Kentucky, and that Mary's spouse, Thomas Jones, from Virginia, was "black." Ellenor Jones, her mother, and her brothers and sisters—who were born in Mississippi, Ohio, and Tennessee—are listed on the census as "mulatto."[7] Later, in Utah and in California, Jones was registered as white in the census. No mention is made of Jones's multiracial heritage in Utah or Mormon records, which is especially significant at a time of the Civil War, racial unrest, and the church's ban on priesthood ordination for black men and temple admittance for black women and men.[8]

The traces Jones left in the historical record indicate that she was a devoted

Latter-day Saint. She and her family became acquainted with the church in Tennessee in the 1840s. Her older sister, Margaret, was baptized in 1842, and Jones followed in 1844. Jones was endowed in the Endowment House in Salt Lake City in 1869, and she lived in the Eleventh Ward.[9] She corresponded with Brigham Young in 1875, hoping to visit with him before she returned once more to California. She commented in a Young Ladies' Mutual Improvement Association (YLMIA) meeting about living among people of other faiths in California.[10] All four of her living children appeared in ward records. She and her children donated money for the construction of the Salt Lake temple in 1892.[11] Jones performed temple work for and with members of her family in the Logan temple in the 1880s and 1890s, when temple worship was denied to people of African descent.[12]

Jones wrote an article for her ward's YLMIA manuscript newspaper, the *Improvement Star*.[13] Several ward organizations produced manuscript newspapers, which were composed, edited, handwritten—often by different people for each issue—and then read aloud and discussed. At the Eleventh Ward YLMIA weekly meetings, the young women and their leaders would read lessons, talks, and editorials from the *Improvement Star* and the *Juvenile Instructor,* as well as chapters from the scriptures.[14] YLMIA president Mary Ann Freeze encouraged those in attendance to both write for and read the paper.[15] This article was read in a YLMIA meeting and then published by the *Woman's Exponent* on February 1, 1882. While Jones's discourse does not offer biographical information, her teaching on the principle of prayer suggests a trusting relationship with God and a profound connection to the divine in a tenuous world.

PRAYER IS THE KEY that will unlock the statehouse of knowledge.[16]

It is the foundation rock of every Christian's life; and we can safely say that there is no one that can attain to a position of usefulness in the kingdom of God without knowledge.

We learn that our Savior, whom we should all choose as our pattern, prayed often, and in the gospel according to St. Luke, chapter 22, verses 39 and 40, after he had administered the last supper to his apostles, we read: "And he came out and went, as was his wont, to the Mount of Olives, and his disciples also followed him; and when he was at the place he said unto them, 'Pray, that ye enter not into temptation.'"[17]

We learn from these few words spoken by our Savior that prayer is also a safeguard that will withhold us in the hour of temptation from doing evil.

Through prayer, our faith is strengthened and our powers of comprehension are quickened, and we receive power to discern good from evil.

Through prayer, we are led to search for truth, and learn to love and keep the laws of righteousness, laid down in his church and kingdom, through which we may be brought back into the holy and divine presence of our God.

Through prayer, the windows of heaven unclose, and blessings are showered down upon our heads and upon those we love and pray for.[18]

Through prayer, the darkness that had hovered over this earth for ages burst, and the light of everlasting truth shone forth; for it was while Joseph Smith, then but a boy, was praying to God to know which of all the different doctrines that he had heard preached was true, that truth was revealed, that those who lived in the days of Joseph, the Prophet, should know the truth, and for generations to come.

If you will read the Bible, the Book of Mormon, and other good books, you will learn that all good and great people were those who prayed to God, for it is the only way to become good and great. And, my young friends, it is well for you to remember, while traveling on this journey of life, that there is no prison so dark, no pit so deep, no expanse so broad, that the Spirit of God cannot enter; and when all other privileges are denied us, we can pray, and God will hear us.[19] No one can take this from us. But remember it is a most precious gift, it is something that must be cultivated; and when the still, small voice whispers, "Go and pray," you must obey; for if you do not, the Spirit will be grieved, and the voice in time becomes silent.

Should you at any time find yourself overwhelmed with disappointment and sorrow, remember that although your prayers may be like the wailings of the most feeble infant, God, being more loving than the most tender mother, will hear and answer you.[20] But we cannot say that he will always answer according to the desires of your mind; but in his great wisdom he sees and knows what is for your best good and will answer according to his wisdom.

To the young we will say, be prayerful; ask God to inspire your hearts with noble aspirations and to help you become good and great in his church and kingdom. And when you are done with this life, may you find that spirit of peace which was with our Lord when he appeared to his disciples, after the resurrection, when he spoke those sweet words, "Peace be unto you."[21]

May God give you his Spirit, that you may seek unto him, is my prayer, in the name of Jesus, amen.

E. G. Jones, "The Power of Prayer," in Improvement Star *1, no. 4, manuscript newspaper, 11th Ward Y.L.M.I.A.; reprinted in* Woman's Exponent *10, no. 17 (Feb. 1, 1882): 134–135.*

Elvira S. Barney. Circa 1880s. Barney practiced obstetrics and medicine in Utah. She was deeply committed to the work of women's rights and religious liberty. She spoke at a mass meeting on March 6, 1886, in Salt Lake City: "Oh, that my voice could reach the ears of those uninformed and misinformed of the United States. I would ask them to listen to the testimony of the ten thousand wives and mothers of Utah, with large, intelligent, loving families, of beautiful, pure children." (Church History Library, Salt Lake City.)

PRAYER

◇◇◇

ELVIRA S. BARNEY

Utah Woman Suffrage Association
Assembly Hall, Temple Square, Salt Lake City, Utah Territory
October 7, 1889

Elvira Stevens Woodbury Huntington Barney (1832–1909) gave the invocation at a meeting of the Utah Woman Suffrage Association, a prewritten prayer that was then printed in the *Woman's Exponent.* Her words demonstrate one way in which women engaged publicly in theological discourse and expanded the role of women in society.

Barney's sermon-like prayer exhibits a life of careful thought and involvement. She was born in Gerry, New York, the daughter of a merchant and a teacher. The family converted to the church in 1844 and moved to Nauvoo, Illinois. Shortly after their arrival, her father died from a brief illness in 1844, and her mother passed away three months later, purportedly of exhaustion.[1] Elvira traveled across the plains with her older sister Jane and Jane's family, arriving in Utah in 1848.[2] Two years later, she married John Woodbury, and together they served a mission to the Sandwich Islands (now known as Hawaii), along with a group including Barney's sister and a former brother-in-law, from 1851 to 1856.[3] After divorcing Woodbury, she married Oliver Huntington on December 28, 1856; they, too, divorced.[4] Barney then married Royal Barney Jr. as a plural wife on January 6, 1866, in Salt Lake City.[5]

Barney followed in the footsteps of her mother by teaching school, first in Winter Quarters and while crossing the plains, then in California before and after her mission, and later in Utah.[6] She attended the University of Deseret (now the University of Utah) in Salt Lake City and Wheaton College in Illinois from 1864 to 1866; she studied medicine in the eastern United States, then returned to Utah to teach medical courses for young women.[7] She demonstrated her father's knack for business in her work with the home manufacture movement, women's cooperative stores, and grain storage, all of which were closely associated with the Relief Society.[8]

Barney actively pursued political causes, including women's rights and suffrage. On February 12, 1870, the Utah territorial legislature granted suffrage to Utah women, following a precedent set in Wyoming the previous year. In response to the threat of federal legislation limiting Mormon women's voting rights because of polygamy, Barney spoke at a mass meeting on March 6, 1886. Notwithstanding these protests, the federal government rescinded the vote from Utah women the following year. In 1889, Utah women formed the Utah Woman Suffrage Association, an affiliate organization of the National Woman Suffrage Association that had been founded two decades earlier by Elizabeth Cady Stanton and Susan B. Anthony.[9] Nineteen local suffrage associations were organized throughout the counties of Utah Territory over the next few years, with representatives meeting often to coordinate efforts.[10] The territory organization convened in the Assembly Hall in Salt Lake City on October 7, 1889.[11] Delegates from each association in the territory were invited, and addresses were given by prominent speakers, including James E. Talmage, Charles W. Penrose, Zina D. H. Young, and Lula Greene Richards.[12]

The Utah Woman Suffrage Association was open to "all women, without regard to party, sect, or creed."[13] The territory association and various local associations had chaplains, allowing them to incorporate a religious component in a secular organization.[14] Sarah M. Kimball was the first listed chaplain for the territorial association on April 11, 1889, but at the July 19, 1889, meeting, Barney filled that role.[15] The prescribed responsibility of "minister" allowed her to engage in a pastoral role, leading both Mormon and non-Mormon women in prayer to God in a nondenominational manner, seeking his aid in the quest for woman suffrage.

O GOD, the Eternal, the Father of the heavens and the earth, in the name of thy Son, Jesus Christ, we, a small portion of the human family, have assembled ourselves together under this roof for an especial purpose, and we do pray thee, that thou wilt inspire both the speakers and the hearers with a portion of thy heavenly divine influence, that good shall be the result of our assembling together, that we may learn and prepare ourselves for storm or fair weather, for war or peace, for prosperity or adversity. Thou hast blest us in early youth, thou hast been with us all the journey of life thus far, and we pray thee that thou wilt forget us not in our declining years.

Thou didst cause that the earth should roll into existence, and from chaos it was formed. Thou didst cause that the earth should produce vegetation, and that the human and animal creation should subsist upon it, and dwell upon its face; and now we do implore thee that thou wilt bless the earth, that it may still bring forth vegetation, and that thou wilt cause the dews of heaven to descend, and the rains in due season.[16] Wilt thou temper the climate for the good of mankind and all animal creation, that we may feel to praise thy holy name that mankind does live. Wilt thou, the Great Eternal, command the lightning, the earthquakes, and the elements, that they may be manifested for the good of all vegetable and animal creation.[17]

We pray for the weak, we pray for the afflicted, and we pray for the strong, that they may be willing to help carry the burdens of the weak.[18] We pray that thou wilt, in thine own way and time, mellow the hearts of the wicked and immoral, that thy grace may spread and form a canopy over the whole earth, that sin and wickedness may not be known, and righteousness triumph. Wilt thou be with the rulers of the nation, that thy voice shall reach their ears in their council chambers, that they may fear to make unjust laws,[19] and that they may study to improve and make better those already formed, that the cries of the people may not reach thee because of oppression.[20] Wilt thou soften the hearts of the rigid, that the means that man has at his disposal may be used for the whole of humanity; may they not forget their benefactor but ever bend the knee in humble reverence to thee.[21]

Wilt thou be with woman as thou hast with man, to strengthen her where she is weak that she may aid in the defense of truth and right, and where her voice is heard throughout the broad face of the earth, may it have echo in the hearts of the honest, and may she serve to smooth the wrinkles of unjust laws, as she does and has, the pillows beneath the aching heads of thy soldiers and servants.[22] We pray thee that thou wilt bless thy handmaidens here in this little nook in the valleys of the mountains, that we may perform noble and grand acts that will compare with the grandeur of the mountains around.

Hear us, O Father, at this time, and accept of our humble offering, for we dedicate ourselves, our meeting, and our cause unto thee, asking a forgiveness of our sins, in the name of Jesus, amen.

Elvira S. Barney, "Prayer: By Dr. Elvira S. Barney, at the U.W.S.A. Convention Held in the S.L. Assembly Hall," Woman's Exponent *18, no. 12 (Nov. 15, 1889): 94.*

21

THE SCHOOL OF EXPERIENCE

◇◇◇

MATTIE HORNE TINGEY

World's Congress of Representative Women
Art Institute of Chicago, Chicago, Illinois
May 19, 1893

Martha "Mattie" Jane Horne Tingey (1857–1938) believed women had a responsibility to develop their intellects and their talents in order to influence their children and the world, as outlined in her 1893 speech before the World's Congress of Representative Women. The fourteenth of fifteen children of Joseph and Mary Isabella Horne, she grew up in Salt Lake City, where she participated actively in the Primary Association, the Sunday School, and the Young Ladies' Mutual Improvement Association (YLMIA).[1] As a child, she would often eavesdrop on the conversations of adults in her parents' parlor, many of whom were leaders in the church and the community.[2] As a teenager, Tingey edited the manuscript newspaper of her ward YLMIA and often read articles at joint meetings of the Young Ladies' and Young Men's Associations. She attended the University of Deseret,[3] and she was a member of the Wasatch Literary Association and a member and assistant secretary of the Tabernacle Choir.[4] While working as a typesetter, she met Joseph Tingey at the *Deseret News* office and married him on September 30, 1884. Together they had seven children.[5]

Like her mother, Tingey served actively in the church's women's organizations. She acted as a counselor in the Salt Lake City Fourteenth Ward Primary Association under Clara C. Cannon and as a counselor in the YLMIA for many years. In the summer of 1880, she was called as second counselor to Elmina S. Taylor, the first general president of the YLMIA, in which capacity she served for twenty-five years.[6] Tingey herself was sustained as general president of the YLMIA on April 4, 1905, and served until 1929.[7]

Even before the 1890 Manifesto ended the official sanction of plural marriage,

Mormon women worked to establish relationships with contemporary women's groups with similar beliefs and goals. But the 1890s became a period of unprecedented cooperation and coordination for Mormon women with national organizations.[8] As a delegate of the YLMIA, Tingey traveled to Chicago at her own expense in 1893 to attend the World Columbian Exposition.[9] The exposition, or world's fair, included a World's Congress of Representative Women, which had the purpose "of bringing together the representatives of all worthy organizations of women, whatever their nationality or their specific object."[10] The congress hoped to find solutions to the many problems associated with "the Woman Question."[11] Mormon women were requested to plan their visits to the fair in order to attend "this most important meeting."[12]

The YLMIA conducted an evening session of the congress on Utah Day, May 19, 1893, following the afternoon session sponsored by the Relief Society. Speakers included Elmina S. Taylor and other members of the YLMIA general board, addressing such topics as literature and art, the legal and political status of Utah women, and education.[13] Tingey was known for her impressive public speaking skills, "having a fine voice and clear articulation. She is modest, humble, and retiring in her disposition, yet firm, fearless, and unhesitating in expressing her convictions."[14] At this meeting she presented the address featured here on the role of women. She introduced significant Mormon beliefs—including the belief in a Heavenly Mother—to an audience of people from a variety of faith traditions.[15] The meeting was considered a success as several attendees—both men and women, both Mormon and those from other faiths—expressed "surprise and pleasure over the exalted, refined, and pure sentiments" presented at the session.[16]

Woman—Mother, Woman—Wife,
The sweetest words man ever knew.[17]

THE SCHOOL OF LIFE, in which we are all pupils, is a grand, a glorious institution. Of divine conception, it is perfect in organization, widespread and far-reaching in its operations, incomprehensible in its results. It extends back to man's pre-existence and reaches forward to the vast eternities to come.[18]

When we take up the study of nature and become somewhat acquainted with its beauties, its harmony, its grandeur and perfection, our minds expand, and we can but think of the Creator, the Organizer, the Power that controls so much life and intelligence; and almost unconsciously a feeling of reverence for that unseen Power, that great Intelligence, takes possession of our hearts, and the questions naturally arise in our minds: By what power were all these things brought into existence?[19] Who planned and controls such a perfect system, and what is the object of its creation? This spirit of inquiry as to the why and wherefore of our earthly existence is the first step in theology; for pure and undefiled religion is the true science of life.[20] According to the views of the so-called Mormon people, this earth is only one department of a great system of education which has been devised by our Heavenly Father for the cultivation and development of his children. The sacred scriptures—the Holy Bible—teach that all things were created first spiritual, then temporal, and man is no exception to the rule.[21] The primary department, or first grade, in this school of life was the spirit world, where the sons and daughters of God passed through a spiritual probation to enable them to gain the intelligence and experience necessary to prepare them for a future state of existence—in other words, to enable them to enter the preparatory department in the school of experience.[22] According to their diligence and faithfulness in the first department is their position or status in this the second or earthly probation. Time will not admit of our entering into the details of this organization; suffice it to say, that in the wisdom of God man has been placed in charge of this department; but to woman has been given the power, the honor to open the door through which all must pass ere they can enter that advanced stage of action and go forward in the work of progression which has been designed and marked out by our Heavenly Parents.[23] I say parents, because while we hear a great deal about our Heavenly Father, and very little, if anything, about our Heavenly Mother, reason and revelation both teach us that we must also have a Mother there.[24] This is true, pure motherhood—to give temporal bodies to heavenly spirits, that the spiritual and temporal may be united and continue on in the work of perfection.

I would ask this intelligent audience, is this a menial labor? Is there a greater or nobler work, or one that is more important and beneficial to the human family than that of motherhood? It is of equal importance to the high and the low, the rich and the poor. A man can never reach such a height of perfection, such a pinnacle of greatness that he can deny that he owes the possibility of his success to a woman—his mother. It is for this reason we impress upon our girls the necessity of preparing themselves to become pure, strong, intelligent wives and mothers, that their children may begin life upon this earth with fair prospects: strong, healthful bodies; bright, active minds; free from inherited disease and vice. And in order that this may be accomplished perfectly, it is woman's right—nay, more, it is her duty—to demand from the husband and father the same purity of life and character that she herself maintains and that he demands from her. For a man is under as great condemnation in the sight of God for unchastity and an unholy life as is woman. Else woman must be the superior power, the greater intelligence, if more is expected and required from her than from her brother man.[25]

Nor is this all of woman's work. For reasons best known to our Heavenly Father, the intelligence gained in our previous existence is for the time being taken from us, and we come upon the earth pure, innocent, helpless babes. Upon mothers has been placed the responsibility of nurturing and training these tender plants. It is during the period of childhood that the most lasting impressions are made upon the mind. Let us have educated, refined, common-sense mothers, and the home, society, the nation, and the world will reap the benefits. I once heard a prominent Utah man remark that if he could only educate a part of his family he would certainly educate his daughters rather than his sons. He realized woman's power and influence, especially when she becomes a mother, over present as well as future generations.[26]

Oh, if mothers would thoroughly understand, fully appreciate, and wisely use their God-given power, there would be no greater truism than the old adage, "The hand that rocks the cradle is the hand that rules the world."[27]

When women entertain the idea [of] a wife and mother [as was] advanced to me, that when she married she gave up her own individuality, she felt she had no mind nor will independent of her husband's, can we wonder that their children grow up with the idea that father and mother are one, and that one is the father? It has always roused an indignant feeling within me to hear a woman say in answer to her child's question, "Oh, I don't know anything about such things; go and ask your father." Every time she makes a remark of that nature the mother loses influence and the father gains it.

Let woman prepare herself to stand side by side, shoulder to shoulder with her husband in all the affairs of life, to be a wise counselor and helpmeet unto him, as her Creator designed she should be;[28] let mothers impress upon their children the principles of justice and equal rights, and the women of the next generation will not have to beg and plead for what rightfully belongs to them.

Why is it that today there is so much broader a view taken of woman's position than before? Because woman herself is beginning to feel that she is an intelligent, responsible being, with a mind capable of the highest intelligence, with talents that it is her duty to develop and use for the advancement and elevation of the human family. This feeling is gradually but steadily growing; it is being felt throughout the world, and it will continue to grow until it becomes a power in the earth.

All honor to the noble women of this Congress, who have stood firm in the face of severe opposition, bitter scorn ofttimes, and dared to maintain their convictions of truth and right. May their number increase, and their influence be felt until it reaches every nook and corner of the habitable globe.[29]

Mattie Horne Tingey, "Address of Mrs. Mattie Horne Tingey: Delivered in the Woman's Congress at Chicago, during the Services of the Y.L.M.I.A.," Young Woman's Journal *4, no. 12 (Sept. 1893): 547–549. Title supplied by the editors.*

Sarah M. Kimball. Circa 1890s. In her role as secretary for the Relief Society general board, Kimball coordinated a collection of autobiographical records of men and women in 1880. This time capsule effort celebrated the anniversary of the founding of the church and was retrieved in 1930. The artifacts were distributed to the oldest living female descendants of the original authors. (Church History Library, Salt Lake City.)

OUR SIXTH SENSE, OR THE SENSE OF SPIRITUAL UNDERSTANDING

◇◇◇

SARAH M. KIMBALL

National Council of Women
Metzerott's Music Hall, Washington DC
February 21, 1895

Sarah Melissa Granger Kimball (1818–1898) spent her life promoting women's public activity and private "spiritual understanding," as she explained in this 1895 speech delivered at the National Council of Women. Born in Phelps, New York, she and her family were baptized after her father read the Book of Mormon shortly following its publication.[1] As a young woman, Kimball attended both the School of the Prophets and the Hebrew School in Kirtland, Ohio, at least once.[2] After she and her husband migrated to Utah, Kimball supported her husband, Hiram, and their children by teaching school.[3] Her contemporary Emmeline B. Wells said Kimball "had a good faculty for teaching [and] could simplify lessons and adapt them to the understanding of those whom she instructed."[4] These educational endeavors from her youth and early adulthood laid the foundation for her intellectual inquiry later in life.

A natural organizer, Kimball became a noteworthy leader among Mormon women. She coordinated a ladies' sewing society in the spring of 1842 in Nauvoo, Illinois, which led to the formal organization of the Female Relief Society.[5] Fifteen years later, she became the president of the Salt Lake City Fifteenth Ward Relief Society when it was first organized.[6] As ward Relief Society president, she influenced Relief Societies throughout the church by helping define roles of leaders and supervising the construction of the first Relief Society hall.[7] Kimball also served as the secretary of the Relief Society general board from 1880 to her death, during which time she kept records and encouraged the creation of women's historical accounts.[8] Throughout her life, Kimball advocated for the equality and rights of women, including promoting women's suffrage in the 1870s and 1880s in Utah.[9]

Kimball participated in meetings of the National Council of Women, which coordinated efforts of various women's rights organizations.[10] The council's second triennial session was held in Washington DC from February 17 to March 2, 1895. Representatives of women's organizations from throughout the United States gathered to discuss topics such as religion, temperance, philanthropy, suffrage, industry, and education.[11] Elmina S. Taylor headed the Utah delegation, which also included Ellis R. Shipp, Emmeline B. Wells, Aurelia Spencer Rogers, Marilla Daniels, Minnie J. Snow, and Susa Young Gates. The Young Ladies' Mutual Improvement Association (YLMIA) and the Relief Society both conducted sessions, and representatives attended business meetings and lectures.[12]

A polished public speaker, Kimball was well known outside Utah for her representation of Mormon women.[13] Perhaps because of her age, Kimball did not attend the Washington DC conference. But she did prepare the address featured here, which was read by Marilla Daniels during an evening session of the conference; her speech explored philosophical ideas of spiritual enlightenment and eternal progress.[14] Susa Gates considered this paper "the best paper of our session . . . although so spiritual that it was not perhaps thoroughly appreciated by all." Although Gates described the warm welcome given to the women from Utah, she also noted that some in the audience expressed concern with distinct Mormon practices and beliefs.[15] Kimball's speech was printed in the *Woman's Exponent* and distributed widely among Latter-day Saint women.

Come Holy Spirit, heavenly dove,
With all thy quickening powers,
Kindle a flame of sacred love,
In these cold hearts of ours.[16]

IT IS PROPER on occasions like this to consider such topics as shall be of the highest benefit to womankind; and to my mind, it is fitting to discuss here that capacity of mind in which woman is preeminently fitted to excel. The contemplation of the sense of spiritual understanding first gives me a sense of my littleness and inability, then encourages me in the attempt to express a few thoughts on this absorbing theme.

This faculty, like our physical sense, is susceptible of cultivation. Its possibilities are limitless; it is the cause least understood; it is the divine of our nature; it brings to our understanding things not seen with the natural eye or discerned by mortal mind; it extends our correspondences. With the eyes and senses of our physical self, we are in correspondence with our physical surroundings; with our spiritual eyes and senses awakened and cultivated, we come into communion with infinitude.

The sixth sense links mortal with immortal existence; it testifies in unmistakable language of the immortality of the soul.[17] It educates, exalts, and refines those that heed its whisperings and follow its guiding influence. This sense leads to blissful heights of superior understanding; teaches the secrets of ever-existent life—our relationship to the past, present, and future—and brings us into harmony with the infinite fountain of life and intelligence.[18] It illumines the soul that cultivates it, purifies thoughts and actions, enlarges the sphere of comprehension, and exalts the aspirations. Its continued exercise brings its possessor nearer and nearer to the throne of the Almighty.

Those who answer the whisperings of this sense are sympathetically drawn toward each other, as exemplified in the Religious Congress held in Chicago in 1893, where religious pilgrims and would-be reformers from all lands, and of all creeds, met and harmonized in a bond of love. This was notably true of the woman's department of the memorable congress.[19]

The light of this sense has been foreshadowed in various ages of the world's history. In the nineteenth century, the searchlight of religion, philosophy, and science have united in exploring an untrodden pathway toward the haven of light which is unextinguishable.

The legitimate exercise of spiritual power obtained through the operations of this sense puts the individual in possession of keys of knowledge and clothes him with additional responsibility relating to the enlightenment and elevation of the human family.

They that seek, by faith and earnest prayer, find the light that leads to the golden gate.[20] They that knock with study and faith's assurance have the narrow way opened to them[21] and are received into communion with the Infinite Father and Mother,[22] are permitted to enter hallowed mansions, to attend the school of the prophets,[23] and by advancing steps, to reach the school of the gods, where they learn the processes by which worlds are organized by the combining of eternal, intelligent, obedient elements; the uses for which worlds are called into existence; the manner in which they are controlled; and the laws of progression by which all beings and animate things are perfected and glorified in their respective spheres.[24]

Students of this sense become, some more, some less, familiar with the state of that portion of the human family whose varied conditions are typified by the stars. They contemplate the intelligence, the glory, and the peace typified by the moon; and in progressive order this sense educates, disciplines, enlightens, and brings its possessor in harmony with the effulgence of celestial light and glory as typified by the sun.[25] All that enter this higher glory are heirs with Jesus Christ, our elder brother, in the preexistent state, to all the knowledge, power, exaltation, and glory possessed by the Father.[26]

When through our spiritual nature we are in communion with God, we are drawing nearer and nearer to each other, and our words and works will blend more and more harmoniously, until earth's dutiful children, recognizing universal spiritual kinship, hail the peaceful millennial dawn and participate in the triumphant reign of our God and his Christ.

Of the advanced thinkers and diligent workers who compose the Woman's Triennial Council much is expected.[27] Your labors of preparation have been arduous; the whisperings of this sense have disarmed opposition and brought you to a large measure of victory. The thought wave of many a prayer is wafted to you as inspiration; and in reciprocal order, the highest expression of your combined wisdom must radiate and inspire receptive souls in all the world, stimulating them to higher hopes and stronger activities in the cause of more enlightened civilization and a more perfect understanding of divine science, as revealed through our sixth sense, or the sense of spiritual understanding.

In closing, the writer, in loving sympathy, asks that increased spiritual light may illume the pathway of the various lines of good work represented in the Triennial Council.

Sarah M. Kimball, "Our Sixth Sense, or the Sense of Spiritual Understanding," Feb. 1895, typescript, CHL; see also Sarah M. Kimball, "Our Sixth Sense, or the Sense of Spiritual Understanding: Read at the Triennial Council of Women in Washington, February 21, 1895," Woman's Exponent *13, no. 18 (Apr. 15, 1895): 251.*

PRAYER

◇◇◇

ANN M. CANNON

Mutual Improvement Association June Conference
Fourteenth Ward Assembly Hall, Salt Lake City, Utah
June 4, 1901

Ann Mousley Cannon (1869–1948) was a woman of cultural and literary discernment, as well as business acumen. She was born in Salt Lake City, the daughter of Angus Munn and Sarah Maria Mousley Cannon. She and a brother joined the Salt Lake Choral Society and often attended musical productions.[1] When she was thirteen, she started working at another brother's office, learning business skills.[2] Beginning in 1883, at the age of fourteen, Cannon studied literature at the University of Deseret; she graduated in 1886 in a class that included two other young women.[3] After graduation, she worked at the Salt Lake County Recorder's office. Cannon never married; she devoted her life to her extended family, her church, and her community. She cared for her parents in their later years, and she helped raise the children of her sister. She always bought two tickets to cultural events and attended with a young person.[4]

Cannon served for decades in the Young Ladies' Mutual Improvement Association (YLMIA). She began her work in the Salt Lake City Fourteenth Ward YLMIA, being appointed assistant secretary in 1887, treasurer in 1888, second counselor in 1891, and first counselor later that same year.[5] Beginning in 1891, she served forty-six years on the YLMIA general board. During that time, she chaired the committee that explored joining the national program of Camp Fire Girls and eventually formed the Bee Hive program, a precursor to Personal Progress.[6] Twice she represented the board as a delegate to the National Council of Women, working directly with national women's rights leader Susan B. Anthony.[7] For nineteen years she was the general secretary of the

Young Ladies' Mutual Improvement Association general board. Circa 1905. The first YLMIA general board was organized in 1880 under Elmina S. Taylor. The board members traveled, coordinated the efforts of local associations, corresponded with local units, conducted training, developed curriculum and programs, and spoke at MIA June Conferences starting in 1896. Included in this photo are the following women who are mentioned in this volume: Maria Y. Dougall (seated row, first on right), Emma N. Goddard (seated row, second from right), Ann M. Cannon (seated row, third from right), Mattie Horne Tingey (seated row, fifth from right), Ruth May Fox (seated row, sixth from right); May Booth Talmage (first standing row, fifth from right); and Minnie J. Snow (second standing row, first on right). Tingey was YLMIA general president at the time this photo was taken. (Church History Library, Salt Lake City.)

YLMIA, and for ten of those years, including the time she gave this talk, she acted also as treasurer.[8] In her role as secretary, Cannon initiated the use of roll books with duplicate annual report blanks, a procedure that increased the efficiency of record-keeping.[9] Cannon chaired the literary committee of the *Young Woman's Journal* and edited the *Journal* for five years, from 1902 to 1907.[10] Years later, Cannon wrote, "The mutual [YLMIA] has been a great power for good in my life. . . . The richest experiences in my life have come through it, and what I am is largely the result of those experiences."[11]

Beyond administrative church assignments, religion was an important part of Cannon's everyday life.[12] She discussed prayer in a talk to officers at the annual conjoint conference of the YLMIA and the Young Men's Mutual Improvement Association in 1901.[13] Other speakers included members of the YLMIA general board: Maria Y. Dougall, Mattie Horne Tingey, Mary Ann Freeze, May Booth Talmage, and Emma N. Goddard. At the time, the two organizations oversaw fifty thousand young men and women. Cannon's speech was printed in the *Young Woman's Journal* two months later.[14]

THE SUBJECT OF PRAYER is one dear to me. I know that prayer can lift the greatest burdens and rest the weary.[15] Nothing else can give such perfect relief. Even the falling of a tear is prayer. There are times in the lives of all when we need extra strength and comfort.[16] Be not discouraged in praying again and again for the same thing.[17] God understands our needs, and he will bless us in his own way. The power in prayer seems to me much like that of electricity. As the wire is the conductor of the electric current, so, it seems to me, is prayer the channel through which inspiration comes to man.

Ann M. Cannon, "Prayer," June 4, 1901, in "General M.I.A. Conference," Young Woman's Journal *12, no. 8 (Aug. 1901): 366.*

Emmeline B. Wells and Bathsheba W. Smith. 1908. Smith (right) was the Relief Society general president from 1901 to 1910. She was the last Relief Society general president who was also a member of the Nauvoo Relief Society. Wells (left) succeeded Smith, serving as Relief Society general president from 1910 to 1921. Photograph by Olsen and Griffith. (Church History Library, Salt Lake City.)

WE HAVE STILL A GREATER MISSION

◇◇◇

BATHSHEBA W. SMITH

Address in *Woman's Exponent*
Salt Lake City, Utah
January 1906

As the fourth Relief Society general president, Bathsheba Wilson Bigler Smith (1822–1910) encouraged Relief Society members to rise up from the past and embrace the future with responsibility and action.[1] When she delivered this address in January 1906, she had been associated with Relief Society for sixty-four years, having joined the Nauvoo Relief Society at its first meeting.[2] Smith grew up on her parents' large farm in Virginia. She was remembered as a Southern girl who loved the outdoors and was particularly adept at horse riding. Her mother taught her typical housewifery skills, including carding, spinning, dyeing, and weaving wool, cotton, and flax, as well as fine stitchery and embroidery.[3] She also enjoyed music.[4]

As a young girl, Smith was drawn to religion; she considered herself "somewhat religiously inclined, loved honesty, truthfulness, and integrity. I attended to my secret prayers."[5] When she was fifteen, Latter-day Saint missionaries, including her future husband, George A. Smith, visited her neighborhood. She and her mother were baptized on August 21, 1837, and other family members were baptized around that same time. They joined the Latter-day Saints in Missouri, where they and others were accosted by mobs. She witnessed the death of apostle David W. Patten and the injury of other Mormons. She referred to these experiences in her 1906 address, perhaps seeking to link a younger generation with the rich history and heritage of the church.[6]

The temple played a central role in Smith's life. She was present at the laying of the cornerstone of the Nauvoo, Illinois, temple in 1841.[7] She participated in temple ordinances in Nauvoo, both in the home of Joseph and Emma Hale Smith and in the red brick store.[8] She worked in the temples in Nauvoo and St. George, Logan, and Salt Lake City, Utah, and in the Endowment House in Salt Lake City.[9] Soon after the Salt Lake temple was dedicated in 1893, Smith succeeded Zina D. H. Young as temple matron when Young became too ill to work. Smith "presided in the temple over the sisters there and gave four days in the week regularly to the temple work."[10] Smith continued this work until shortly before her death. Lula Greene Richards wrote that Smith "was ever anxious to be in her place in that holy edifice."[11]

Smith's Relief Society participation continued well past Nauvoo. When her husband became the church historian in Salt Lake City, she was the first counselor to Rachel Grant in the Salt Lake City Thirteenth Ward Relief Society. The Smith home doubled as the Church Historian's Office.[12] Eventually, after her husband's death, Smith moved to a different home and was appointed secretary, treasurer, and president of the Salt Lake City Seventeenth Ward Relief Society, serving in that capacity for eleven years.[13] She acted as the treasurer of the Salt Lake Stake Relief Society. Smith was also active in other organizations associated with the Relief Society. She was a counselor to Mary Isabella Horne in the Retrenchment Association and was on the board of directors of the Deseret Hospital.[14] In 1888, after the death of Eliza R. Snow, Zina D. H. Young was appointed general president of the Relief Society, and Young selected Smith to be her second counselor. When Young died in 1901, Smith became Relief Society general president, and she presided over a period of growth in the Relief Society.[15] She had been president for five years when she presented this address, which was printed in the *Woman's Exponent.*

List to the sound—that rolling chime,
Hark! 'tis the busy knell of Time;
The year has gone,
And borne along the hopes and fears,
The smiles and tears of multitudes unknown to song.
E. R. Snow[16]

THE CLOSING YEAR OF 1905, which is the hundredth birthday of the Prophet, stirs my mind with a multitude of thoughts.[17]

In fancy I go back to my childhood and youth in Virginia[18]—elders come crying, "Repent and be baptized for the kingdom of heaven is at hand,"[19] and, as of yore, I am stirred with the glad tidings of the restoration of the gospel of Christ;[20] once again I gather with the Saints in Missouri, and hear the horrid yells of the mobbers as Joseph and Hyrum are captured by them.[21] I see the wounded and dying; I am driven from Missouri but meet with joy at Quincy, in a conference of the church, Joseph and Hyrum, and the apostles, who are there called to labor in Europe.[22]

The Prophet I recall and his wondrous spiritual power, intelligence, loving kindness, and great goodness of heart![23] His sermons, sayings, the organization of our own Relief Society in 1842.[24] His revelations, persecutions, martyrdom, and the grief of the Saints thereat. There is little left save our homes and families in this world, but the gospel becomes even more to me. Now follows the burning of our homes and the forced exodus from Nauvoo in the dead of winter.[25] The elements rage upon and about us, but we are able to endure, to rest at last, though in the shadow of death, as it were, for here we part with a multitude of our loved ones.[26] But, rising from our weakness, in obedience to the servants of the Most High, we proceed, crossing trackless plains, fording swollen streams, scaling rugged mountain heights, and descending into "The Valley," to find rest from persecution and comfort in the desert.[27]

All the events of those trying years unite today, revealing to me, in the evening of life, the overshadowing importance of the plan of salvation. A comforting message from the Giver of all good seems to give me this sweet assurance that naught that was suffered and naught that was accomplished, no matter how dear the price, was without avail; yea, our wounds were seared over with wisdom, pain gave birth to patience, and our martyred Saints rose, peradventure, our best petitioners in the courts above.[28]

And I am convinced that it were better to be faithful and enduring to the end, showing worthiness in overmastering self and upholding the standard of truth, than to rest in apathy and ease, forgetful of God and unmindful of the weak, the weary, and desolate.

It is good to reflect on the past, but beyond and above its shades of sorrow and errors, our duty ever rises before us.

> Soothe the sad, succor the oppressed,
> Visit the widow and the fatherless.[29]

To go from house to house, seeking out the poor, the cast-down, minister to the sick, lay out the dead, gathering and distributing, as you have done, my sisters, for so many years, gifts and donations for relief.

And yet we have a larger mission—to teach the mother to rear her young in simplicity and in truth and virtue, that happy home circles may abound in our midst.[30]

And yet we have still a greater mission. We faint not in our efforts to teach others but display a great lack of true religion when our own faults remain unmended.

When will we learn that the beam is in our own eye and the mote only disturbs the vision of our neighbor?[31]

We are called upon by the still small voice, a whispering from our Father, to work out our own salvation.[32]

Briefly the constructive parts of the plan of salvation are these: What man is, God once was; what God is now, man may be;[33] the glory of God is intelligence.[34] Nothing can be annihilated and no act lost.[35] It is impossible to be saved in ignorance.[36] The Spirit of God, which is the Holy Ghost and the Comforter, surrounds us and pervades the universe, and is the medium by which we may receive the inspiration of God toward intelligence and through which it is our right to receive comfort; and finally that faith, hope, and charity are necessary for divine grace, but that the greatest of these is charity![37]

Therefore it is plainly necessary that women, as well as men, cease not while life lasts to study diligently for the knowledge which is of greatest worth. To me the best step towards this is for us to throw off the curse of drudgery by learning to do our work so well that we will love to do it and have cause for rejoicing over the achievements of our hands.

Let us learn of the handiwork of God by the study of nature, search out her flowers, her moods, her laws. Let us study to improve our thoughts, reaching up toward our Heavenly Father, praying for the inspiration of the Holy Ghost.

Let us improve our language in our homes and among our children, that our words be not idle, complaining, nor vain, but, as nothing can be lost, cheerful, hopeful, intelligent, reflecting a charitable spirit.

Let us open the books of life and salvation and study also the great authors, poets, and painters, that our minds may be clothed with intelligence and our hearts abound with human feeling.

And here I am inclined to offer a thought for the year's work before us. With our multifarious duties we may not be able to call upon some aged or invalid sister, to cheer her, but we may lend her a book to read at pleasure, and peradventure to the strengthening of her purpose, the cheering of her life, and the edification of her mind. Likewise after reading a good book, pass it to a sister, saying, "I commend this book to you. It has instructed me and may edify you, and when you have read, return, that I may lend again."

Another thought: Having done your part well, be satisfied to relinquish the load to some stronger woman when you become weary.

And now my sisters, God's choicest blessings be upon you, and peace be with you.

Bathsheba W. Smith, "Relief Society Annual Greeting: President Bathsheba W. Smith Addresses Associate Workers in All the World," Woman's Exponent *34, no. 7 (Jan. 1906): 41–42. Title supplied by the editors.*

Rachel H. Leatham. Circa 1906. Leatham worked as a guide at the Bureau of Information on Temple Square until 1911, when she married James Jensen. They lived in Bingham, Salt Lake City, and Sandy, Utah, where Leatham served in various auxiliary presidencies on the ward and stake level. (Photograph in family possession. Courtesy Mary Austin Ungerman.)

GOD HAS REVEALED IT UNTO ME

◇◇◇

RACHEL H. LEATHAM

Annual General Conference Outdoor Overflow Meeting
Temple Square, Salt Lake City, Utah
April 5, 1908

When returned missionary Rachel Hannah Leatham [Jensen] (1884–1979) spoke at an outdoor overflow meeting during the church's general conference on April 5, 1908, she became the second woman ever to be included in the church's official conference report.[1] Born and raised in Salt Lake City to a Scottish father and an English mother, Leatham was baptized on the eleventh anniversary of her mother's baptism, January 3, 1893, in the same location, on Temple Square.[2] Leatham attended Salt Lake City public schools, Salt Lake Business College, and the Latter-day Saint University (now LDS Business College). She worked at a business firm in Idaho Falls, Idaho, at the age of eighteen, then returned to Salt Lake City for additional employment opportunities.[3]

Leatham was among the first generation of unmarried women to serve proselytizing missions for the church.[4] In September 1906, at the age of twenty-two, she was assigned to serve in the Colorado Mission.[5] She worked mostly in and around Denver, splitting her time between duties in the mission office and proselytizing activities. In a letter to the mission president shortly after her arrival, she reported tracting and visiting: "I have had a number of good gospel conversations and have been fortunate in getting into the homes of the people."[6] She returned home to Salt Lake City on February 19, 1908.[7]

Upon her return, Leatham volunteered as a guide at the Temple Square Bureau of Information, along with over a hundred "suitable brethren and sisters."[8] The bureau had opened in 1902 under the direction of Leatham's former institute teacher Benjamin

Goddard, with the intent to provide accurate information and distribute church literature to visitors.[9]

At general conference during this era, those who could not be seated in the Tabernacle on Temple Square were directed to overflow meetings in the nearby Assembly Hall.[10] When the Assembly Hall was filled in April 1908, several hundred people congregated on the lawn near the Bureau of Information Building, where services were conducted at 2:00 p.m. under the direction of Goddard.[11] After Leatham's discourse, another returned missionary from the same mission, Martha M. Langenbucher, also spoke.[12] Their talks were included in the official conference report.

MY BROTHERS AND SISTERS: Some of you, I know, will appreciate my feelings as I stand before you. I think that I am one of the happiest girls in all the world, and it is the gospel that makes me feel this way, for I do know that the gospel is true. I do know that God our Father, and his Son, Jesus Christ, came down and brought the gospel and established it and spoke to the Prophet Joseph Smith. I know that Jesus is the Christ and that Joseph Smith is his prophet. I feel that if I could live forever, I could never thank my Heavenly Father enough for the blessings that have come into my life, for the privilege of going out into the world and bearing this testimony, telling them of the gospel being restored, of the authority Christ has given to his servants, and of the blessings that are in store for those who listen to and obey the words of truth, life, and salvation as they fall from the lips of the servants of God who are sent out to preach the gospel.

I sometimes think that we young folks at home do not fully realize the responsibilities that rest upon us. We do not always remember that those who stand at our head are aged, and that when our fathers and mothers are gone it will devolve upon us to assume their work; that we are the future responsible people of Zion. Are we doing our part, and are we preparing ourselves so that we will be able to do the work that our fathers have done? Are we ordering our lives so that the Spirit of God will dwell with us as it has dwelt with our parents? Do we realize the extent of the blessings that God has given us, and do we understand the words of life and salvation contained in the scriptures and in the Doctrine and Covenants? Are we able to tell what the promises are that God has made us, if we will keep his commandments?[13] Are we familiar with the ancient record of the inhabitants of this continent, the Book of Mormon? And are we familiar with the great truths that are taught therein and with those books that teach us the beauties of the work in which we are engaged today? I am afraid we are not sufficiently conversant with the principles of the gospel and that we are not as diligent as we should be.[14]

Where much is given, much is required; and you know, every one of you, how much has been given to us, and how much will be required at our hands.[15] Are we preparing ourselves so that we will not fall short? Let us live by every word that proceeds out of the mouth of God.[16] Let us live so that he will ever be willing to own us, and bless us, and love us.

I do not desire to speak longer, but I want once more to bear my testimony. I want to say again that I know the gospel is true. Not because my father knows it, not because my mother has always taught it to me, but I know that the gospel is true because God has revealed it unto me. His Spirit has borne witness unto my spirit, and that testimony is God's most precious gift to me.[17]

May God bless us all, I ask in the name of Jesus, amen.

Rachel H. Leatham, Discourse, Apr. 5, 1908, in "Outdoor Meeting," Seventy-Eighth Annual Conference of the Church of Jesus Christ of Latter-day Saints, *Apr. 4–6, 1908 (Salt Lake City: Deseret News, 1908), 81–82. Title supplied by the editors.*

Amelia Flygare. Circa 1910s. Flygare served as president of the Weber Stake Young Ladies' Mutual Improvement Association from 1911 to 1922. In addition to her YLMIA service, she also served as the first president of her ward Relief Society. She and her husband, Christian Flygare, were active in community organizations and city government. (Photograph in family possession. Courtesy Steve Coray.)

A GREAT LOCOMOTIVE

◇◇◇

AMELIA FLYGARE

Mutual Improvement Association June Conference
Assembly Hall, Temple Square, Salt Lake City, Utah
June 10, 1916

Amelia Margaret Hansen Flygare (1866–1948) believed that every person makes valuable contributions to the work of God, as she explained in her 1916 talk to Young Ladies' Mutual Improvement Association (YLMIA) officers. She was born in Brigham City, Utah, the daughter of Danish immigrants.[1] She married Christian Flygare in 1887, and they had six sons and three daughters.[2] Active in her community, she found ways to serve that were consistent with the circumstances of her family. When her children were in elementary school, for example, she was appointed first vice president of the Ogden kindergarten association.[3] When four of her sons served in World War I, she supported local patriotic causes, including the Ogden chapter of the American Red Cross and the Ogden Service Star Legion, an organization for relatives of people in war service.[4] She also founded the Weber County Daughters of Utah Pioneers, organized the Girl Scout program in Ogden, participated in the local Democratic Party, and chaired the Weber County women's chapter of the Democratic Party.[5]

Flygare was active in her church assignments, both in her Ogden ward and in the Weber Stake.[6] She served in the presidency of the Ogden Fifth Ward YLMIA for about seven years.[7] She was a counselor to two different presidents in the Weber Stake YLMIA and then became stake YLMIA president for eleven years.[8] The Weber Stake YLMIA was noted for its scholarly instruction. For instance, their stake curriculum in the summer of 1907 focused on famous musicians and authors and their works.[9]

Because of her local work and leadership, Flygare was also involved in YLMIA on a general level. Flygare and other stake leaders sometimes assisted in training local officers at the annual conjoint conference.[10] By 1916, the year of the talk featured here, the YLMIA had grown into a significant organization with over thirty-four thousand young women enrolled and over eight thousand officers.[11] The conference that year was held June 8–11. While some meetings were combined with Young Men leaders, separate training sessions were conducted on Saturday in the Assembly Hall by the YLMIA board members, with President Mattie Horne Tingey presiding. Flygare spoke to officers as part of a panel on the "Division of Responsibilities." Additional presentations that morning focused on the *Young Woman's Journal,* curriculum, and increasing enrollment. About seven hundred people were in attendance.[12] Flygare's five-minute talk was published with others from this meeting in the *Young Woman's Journal.*

THE SUBJECT ASSIGNED TO ME is "Responsibility of Officers"—musical directors, choristers, members of committees, and various other officers. Duty and responsibility go hand in hand.

I cannot help but refer this morning to the parable by our Savior that he has so beautifully given to us of the talents. He tells us in this parable that every member of this great organization has a talent. To some are given more than to another, but that does not signify that the one that has the least talent should not emphasize it and cultivate it and assume the responsibility of that talent. I won't go into detail about the talents, because they are in the 25th chapter of St. Matthew—they are there for us to read—there for our benefit—but I will say: When the men to whom God himself had given the talents were brought before him, the one to whom he had given five talents came and said, "I have doubled my talents that thou gavest me." Jesus said, "Blessed art thou; thou hast been faithful in few things, and I will make thee master over many." He said this also to the one to whom he had only given two talents.[13] That is such a stimulus to us, for whether we are called to the presidency, or to the counselor's office, or to any office, our place in this great work means just as much as the greatest place.[14] It can be compared, my brothers and sisters, with a great locomotive. Every little pin, every little wheel, every little mechanism, has its work to do in order to keep the whole machinery in harmony.[15] In our church we have an individual place, and no matter where we are called to work, no matter what our office may be, we should do our part and do it cheerfully, and as we do one part, our responsibilities and talents will be added to, and we will go onward and upward as it is destined that we shall go.

I want to call your attention to the chorister, for instance. In the first place, officers, we are expected to select our workers, as has been told us so beautifully this morning by our president, with wisdom and with a prayerful heart, so that we may select those fitted for special places, those whom God has blessed with particular talents, and then, when they are selected, we must place the responsibility with them.[16] Watch their progress or their failure, not saying, "Now we would like you to act in this capacity" and then turn around and say to someone else, "You see that she does it, will you?" Do you know that that weakens our strength and confidence and weakens the confidence of that particular member in us? If an officer can be made to feel that she is really a worker and that her position means something to that association, I believe she will assume her part.

I could not help, during this entire conference, thinking that it is almost useless for me to take five minutes. We have had example after example on this particular subject. We have had Sister Cooper lead us in singing.[17] We all know and feel that she is just inspired when she leads us, and it has helped to inspire our choristers that they will go home feeling that they, too, must assume the responsibilities of leadership in that particular calling. When we have placed even a small member on a small committee, that position too should be magnified, and once in a while it will not depreciate us in their opinion if we will occasionally go to these officers and say, "Well done; you certainly have done well, and we expect you to do many, many more things," and in that way, I feel that they feel that it would be a sin to betray the confidence that we have in them.[18]

I feel that perhaps it would not be amiss for me to tell you what I once heard President Woodruff say.[19] To me, President Wilford Woodruff was as perfect as any man I ever met. He was a little, unassuming man when I was a child, and he lived away off in the country with one of his families, and I was taught to reverence and respect him.[20] I do not know any other one man I was taught to respect quite so much. It was just in the time of my life when I yielded to that influence, and I heard him say in after years, when he stood at the head of this great organization, that he was blessed just as much as a humble elder in the church as he ever had been as president.[21] To me, that is a stimulus through life, and I very often tell it in our organization. Never mind what position you have; try to realize that unless that position shall be magnified, you would not have that position—in fact, there would be no position for you.

We must remember that in our organization, our strength and our power are measured by the support we give it—we, as Mutual Improvement members. Our power is only measured in this great Mutual organization by the individual responsibility that we assume in it; and so on in the whole church. By the responsibility which the members assume is the power and the progress of the church felt.[22]

Now, my dear sisters, I do not know whether I have strengthened your faith in regard to this, or whether I have left one thought with you, but remember with it all that we are God's children, and that we owe him everything that we can do in his service, and there should not be one position in it—not one—but what is worthy of our very best, and if we give our very best efforts to any calling that we are called to act in, the very best will come back to us.

May God bless this work and bless every earnest worker in it, that our influence may be felt throughout the length and breadth of this earth. I ask it in the name of Jesus, amen.

Amelia Flygare, Discourse, June 10, 1916, in "Division of Responsibility: Five Minute Talks by Stake Officers," Young Woman's Journal *27, no. 7 (July 1916): 445–446. Title supplied by the editors.*

27

KNOWLEDGE NOW WHICH IS DEFINITE

◇◇◇

ANNIE D. NOBLE

Mutual Improvement Association June Conference
Assembly Hall, Temple Square, Salt Lake City, Utah
June 11, 1916

Speaking at a Mutual Improvement Association conference in 1916, Annie Emma Dexter Noble (1861–1950) described her experience of gaining a personal witness of the gospel of Jesus Christ; she later wrote, "It is one thing to believe and another to have positive knowledge."[1] Noble was the tenth of thirteen children born to Abigail Tryphosa Dick and Walter Dexter in Friezland, England, where her father was an accomplished lace maker.[2] The family moved to Brooklyn, New York, for two years, then returned to England, leaving Noble in the care of a friend from their local Christian congregation. There she experienced a personal conversion to Jesus Christ. She returned to her family in England when she was seventeen.[3]

Noble married Abraham Noble, a Baptist, on May 26, 1885, in Nottingham, England, and they had seven children. In 1906, Abraham became ill with severe depression, which affected him physically for several years. The couple traveled around England and finally to the United States, seeking medical help. At one point, while visiting friends in Gainsborough, England, the Nobles met two young Mormon missionaries, an encounter that remained in Annie's memory. A short time later, in Brooklyn, she prayed fervently to know if her husband would ever be healed. She recalled that she heard a voice: "Your husband shall be completely restored—and he shall preach the gospel." The experience marked a transformative shift; not only did Abraham begin to improve, but Noble found herself seeking further contact with the divine. Two and a half years later, a Mormon missionary left a gospel tract at their home in Nottingham. After two years of study, Annie and one daughter were baptized on November 5, 1910. Her husband and other daughters were baptized fifteen months later.[4] The family immigrated to Utah in 1912.[5]

About a year after the family arrived in Utah, Noble's bishop asked her to preside over the ward Young Ladies' Mutual Improvement Association (YLMIA). She remembered, "It was a very great surprise and I felt my inability keenly, and also felt that others could fill the position far better than I." Notwithstanding her feelings of inadequacy, the bishop persisted, and she was appointed president of the Ogden Fifth Ward YLMIA on October 28, 1914, and served for seven years.[6]

In her role as a ward YLMIA president, Noble attended the 1916 annual conference for officers in the Young Men's and Young Ladies' Mutual Improvement Associations, held in Salt Lake City. The Sunday morning session consisted of a testimony meeting in the Assembly Hall on Temple Square.[7] The board minutes state that "the meeting was a most successful one," attended by President Joseph F. Smith and YLMIA general president Mattie Horne Tingey as well as Young Men's Mutual Improvement Association superintendent Heber J. Grant.[8] According to the minutes, "many bore strong testimonies concerning the work of the Lord, and the spirit of the gospel was greatly enjoyed by those present, the Holy Ghost being poured out in great measure upon those who spoke as well as upon those who listened."[9] Testimonies of twenty-one different leaders from a variety of stakes, both male and female, were printed in the *Young Woman's Journal,* including one by "Sister Noble, Weber Stake."[10]

MY BRETHREN AND SISTERS, I feel it a great honor to be in your midst this morning. I feel that I am among the aristocracy of the world, and I have been deeply impressed with the beauty of the countenances of the people of Zion.

I have been in this country only three and a half years, and not quite six years in the church. I am thankful to be here in Zion and for the great blessings which the Lord has poured out upon me.[11] In less than six years, my sons and daughters have been gathered into the fold of Christ, and each one by his or her own investigation. I realize that the foundation knowledge of the principles of the gospel makes us strong, and I rejoice today. And I can testify to the truth, and the knowledge and the strong testimony which my children have and my husband has. I bless the Lord that he has called us in this day to see the light of the gospel. It was a great thing to us. We had belonged for a great many years to the Baptist denomination, and I must say that for some years I had been very much exercised over what should be expected of me as a Christian.[12] And I thought to myself, how much ought I to do? I gave what I felt continuously to be right, and yet I had misgivings, and thought how lovely to know definitely how much was expected of us, both in service and in means. And I feel to rejoice that I have knowledge now which is definite, not only upon this point but on so many other points which have become quite clear to me and to all of us.

I wish to bear my testimony that I know this gospel is true, that I know Joseph Smith was a true prophet of the Lord. Not until nearly six months after I joined the church was I able to say that I knew that Joseph was a prophet of the Lord. I used to attend cottage meetings every week in Nottingham,[13] in the city that I came from, and when I heard the brethren and sisters bear testimony that the prophet was a true prophet of the Lord—I knew the gospel was true, I had a testimony of that, but oh, I used to feel I would like to say that I knew Joseph Smith was a prophet of the Lord. It seems a strange thing that I should have a testimony of the gospel and yet not have a testimony of the servants whom the Lord spoke through and delivered that gospel to; but so it was. One evening I was going as usual to the cottage meeting, when such a desire came to my heart as I went down the road that I could declare to my brothers and sisters that Joseph Smith was a true prophet of the Lord.[14] And in a moment it seemed like a voice said, You can say it now, and I said, Yes, I can say it; I know that he is a true prophet of the Lord. That is the answer that I received, and I went forward to the meeting and I declared it, and I have declared it ever since, the testimony that was given to me instantaneously.[15]

My dear sisters, I wish to tell you how much I love you all. I love my sisters in Weber Stake, and all my sisters. My heart is touched when I look at the sisters' faces, often whom I do not know at all personally, and my heart goes out in love for them, because I know that they are my sisters in the church, and I pray the Lord will bless you all and keep you in obedience. Obedience is the great thing. I pray the Lord will bless you all, in the name of Jesus, amen.

Annie D. Noble, Discourse, June 11, 1916, in "Fast Meeting," Young Woman's Journal *27, no. 10 (Oct. 1916): 626–627. Title supplied by the editors.*

THOU SHALT LOVE THY NEIGHBOR

◇◇◇

EMMA N. GODDARD

Mutual Improvement Association June Conference
Tabernacle, Temple Square, Salt Lake City, Utah
June 9, 1918

While World War I played out on the distant horizon, the 1918 general conference of the Young Ladies' and Young Men's Mutual Improvement Associations (YLMIA and YMMIA) in Salt Lake City addressed immediate needs of Latter-day Saint youth both on the battlefield and on the home front. A member of the YLMIA general board, Emma Jane Nield Goddard (1861–1940), taught youth leaders about raising a righteous generation in a time of chaos by focusing on loving neighbors.[1] Goddard was born in Lancashire, England, to parents who had joined the Church of Jesus Christ of Latter-day Saints before she was born.[2] Emma and her two older sisters, however, joined a local Baptist congregation. The three girls worked in a factory and remained in England when their parents and younger brother immigrated to Utah in the fall of 1875. About four years later, the Nield sisters became restless without their parents and decided to join the family. They traveled to America in 1879, where they were baptized members of the church.[3]

The Nield family settled in Meadow, Millard County, Utah Territory, about 160 miles south of Salt Lake City. Emma taught school for several years with her brother-in-law, Benjamin Goddard, in Kanosh, six miles south of Meadow, then married him as a plural wife in 1883.[4] In the winter of 1886, she took a break from teaching to attend the Brigham Young Academy in Provo with her brother.[5] In December 1886, she joined the Meadow Ward Relief Society; a few months later she became the assistant secretary.[6] In 1889, the Goddards moved to Salt Lake City, where, after three years, Emma became president of the Salt Lake City Twenty-First Ward YLMIA.[7] In May 1896, she was appointed to the YLMIA general board by President Elmina S. Taylor. In this office, she served on the Guide committee, where she helped with curriculum, and on the *Young Woman's Journal* committee.[8]

The twenty-third annual conference of the YLMIA and YMMIA was held in Salt Lake City on June 7–9, 1918, with a distinct focus on the pending crisis of world war. At the opening session of the conference, YLMIA president Mattie Horne Tingey presented the annual MIA slogan: "We stand for service to God and country." Speakers and musicians participating in the conference encouraged patriotism and war support.[9] The speakers at the conference also addressed the devastation wrought by World War I, acknowledging that youth and MIA officers alike were affected by having family and friends at war. Approximately twenty-one thousand individuals from Utah served in the United States armed forces, including over fifteen thousand Latter-day Saint men and young men.[10] On the home front, American Latter-day Saint youth contributed to Liberty Bonds, the American Red Cross, the United War Work Campaign, and the Soldiers' Welfare Fund; they also worked in local gardens to help with food production.[11]

Goddard addressed the YMMIA and YLMIA officers on Sunday morning, and her speech was later printed with others in the *Young Woman's Journal.* Goddard, who spoke on love of neighbor, was preceded by Levi E. Young, who spoke about the love of God, and followed by May Booth Talmage and Richard R. Lyman, who spoke about service to country.[12]

THOU SHALT LOVE THY NEIGHBOR—this was not a new law when given by the Lord in the meridian of time.[13] Under the Mosaic dispensation as recorded in Leviticus, the law was given unto Israel, "Thou shalt not avenge or bear any grudge against the children of thy people, but thou shalt love thy neighbor as thyself."[14] This injunction was beautifully emphasized by the Master in answer to the inquiry of a certain lawyer who stood saying,

> "Master, what shall I do to inherit eternal life?"
>
> He said unto him:
>
> "What is written in the law? How readest thou?"
>
> And he answering said: "Thou shalt love the Lord thy God with all thy heart, and with all thy soul, and with all thy strength, and with all thy mind; and thy neighbor as thyself."
>
> And he said unto him, "Thou hast answered right: this do, and thou shalt live."
>
> But he, willing to justify himself, said unto Jesus, "And who is my neighbor?"[15]

You will remember, and I need not repeat in detail, the beautiful yet plain, simple parable told by the Christ of the man who had fallen among thieves and was left bruised and bleeding by the wayside. How the priest and the Levite, each in turn, passed him by, and how finally the despised Samaritan came along and attended to him most kindly and lovingly, pouring oil and wine on his wounds, finally placing him upon his beast and taking him to the inn and even then leaving the message with the master of the inn that he should still be cared for and that when he came again that way he would remit all expenses. The Master then turned to the lawyer and said, "Which now of these three thinkest thou was the neighbor unto him that fell among thieves?" thus leaving the onus of the decision to his questioner. What else could he say than what he did say? "He that showed mercy on him." Then said Jesus unto him, "Go thou and do thou likewise."[16]

In answer to one of the scribes who asked which is the first commandment of all, Jesus answered, "The first of all the commandments is, Hear, O, Israel, the Lord our God is one Lord, and thou shalt love the Lord thy God with all thy heart, with all thy soul, and with all thy mind, and with all thy strength: this is the first commandment, and the second is like, namely this, thou shalt love thy neighbor as thyself. There is none other commandment greater than these."[17]

This injunction was evidently understood by the apostles and has come down to us through the ages. Paul, addressing the Romans who had not been trained in this law of ethics, stated:

"Owe no man anything, but to love one another, for he that loveth another hath fulfilled the law; for this, Thou shalt not commit adultery, Thou shalt not kill, Thou shalt not steal, Thou shalt not covet; and if there be any other commandment, it is briefly comprehended in this saying, namely, Thou shalt love thy neighbor as thyself."[18]

In like manner when addressing the Galatians, Paul repeated the injunction, saying, "For all the law is fulfilled in one word, even in this; Thou shalt love thy neighbor as thyself."[19]

If all Christian nations had been guided by this law, given by the Master as a rule of life for all of his followers, there would have been no war or contention, but peace on earth and good will to men would have prevailed.

As a consequence of the violation of this law, untold misery, sorrow, and death now exist in the world, and who can tell when the end will be?[20] Erelong our wounded boys may be brought home, and again there will be "lamentation and weeping and great mourning; Rachel weeping for her children and would not be comforted because they are not."[21] Under these conditions we shall have ample opportunity for demonstrating our faith in the Master's behest in striving to comfort and cheer the distressed, remembering that "pure religion and undefiled" is this, to visit the fatherless and widows in their affliction and keep ourselves unspotted from the world.[22] We are surrounded every day with opportunities to practice this divine injunction.[23]

But how does this beautiful commandment apply to us as officers of these great organizations? Because these boys and girls, these young men and women who are in our charge, are in very deed our neighbors. They need our help and assistance more at this critical time in our world's history than ever before. We need to throw every safeguard around them, for they are surrounded by temptations of the most subtle character. They are young and inexperienced and naturally love freedom and have their own ideas of obtaining pleasure. We must guide and counsel them in this adolescent period of their lives and help them to form strong and vigorous characters. We must enter the trenches of their temptations and help them to cope with and overcome them. We must study them and try to understand them, for often if we did, we would find a way to the heart of the apparently most careless and indifferent.

Edgar A. Guest has said:

When next you start in sneering,
And your phrases turn to blame,
Know more of him you censure,
Than his business and his name.

For it's likely that acquaintance,
Would your prejudice dispel,
And you'd really come to like him,
If you knew him very well.

When you get to know a fellow,
And you understand his ways,
Then his faults won't really matter,
For you'll find a lot to praise.[24]

Let us show our young people the glory of righteousness, rather than the hideousness of sin, that the living of gospel law brings lasting joy and peace rather than the anguish that follows the wasted life.

In order to reach their hearts we must live very near to the Lord ourselves. God is love, and the more of this attribute we possess the more successful we will be.[25] Our young people must feel this love, this all-absorbing desire of ours to help and bless them. But if after all our efforts, some few fall and become a prey to evil habits and are left bruised and bleeding by the wayside, what of them? Like the good Samaritan, we must reach out our hands and tenderly and lovingly, if possible, bring them back and plant their feet once more in the straight and narrow path.

Think gently of the erring one!
O, let us not forget
However darkly stained by sin,
He is our brother yet.

Speak gently to the erring ones!
We yet may hold them back
With holy words and tones of love,
From misery's thorny track.[26]

We must be earnest and sincere, ever showing by our own examples that we believe the gospel ourselves, that we love it with all our hearts and souls and are striving every day to live by its precepts. We must give ourselves with our gift, for as Lowell says:

Not what we give, but what we share,
For the gift without the giver is bare,
Who gives himself with his gift feeds three,
Himself, his hungry neighbor, and me.[27]

"God so loved the world that he gave his only begotten Son, that whosoever believed on him should not perish, but have everlasting life."[28]

J. S. Spalding says: "If justice is a universal law, love is a universal duty. Nothing but love can make us just to ourselves."[29] Our members must feel that we love each one of them and have real personal interest in them.

I know of no finer exemplar of this class of teacher than Doctor Karl G. Maeser.[30] He lived for his work. Each pupil felt his benign influence. A benediction appeared to follow in his wake. His students felt his presence. Whenever he entered the classroom, order reigned at once where had been the careless chatter of thoughtless boys and girls. A desire to be and do all that he taught took possession of his students. His smile of approval was sufficient reward for their most arduous efforts. Through his most sublime teachings they were led to consecrate their lives and their all to the profession for which they were qualifying themselves. He studied his individual pupils and understood them. He knew just when and how to administer a rebuke, or to offer a word of praise or encouragement and even to show further loving tender solicitude. We would do well to emulate this noble example. We must seek to lead, not coerce, remembering the Master's injunctions: "Follow me." "Feed my sheep."[31]

This coming season we must endeavor to enter into the social pleasures of our members and urge them to avoid even the appearance of evil. The natural escorts and protectors of our girls, viz., their brothers and sweethearts, have gone in the defense of their country's colors; hence, we must urge more than ever that in all of their excursions, especially when absent from home overnight, that they have a chaperone. We must teach them that the chaperone is not a spy, but a friend, a protector, a wise and loving counselor. In fact, that it is the proper thing for a party to be chaperoned and that good ethics demand it.

Youth is the time for sweet, innocent pleasures; hence, we should encourage such and, as much as possible, help provide them. But in addition to taking this interest in their social life, we must try to impress our young people with the seriousness of the conditions by which we are now surrounded, and the necessity of each one of them assuming some personal responsibility in helping to bring about victory to the cause of truth and liberty. We can all do our bit no matter how poor and humble, how rich or influential we may be. Our boys at the front are risking their all.[32] Should we not then be willing, gladly and cheerfully, to make some little sacrifice, some self-denial at home? A sacred obligation is resting upon each one of us, and the graveness of the situation demands that we curb our frivolities and offer our youthful strength and energy in supporting the call made upon us by our own great country and the allied nations in this world struggle for a reign of right, not might.

May God help us to sense the magnitude of the work devolving upon us and grant us strength and wisdom to perform our full duty in connection therewith. May we, during this conference, become thoroughly imbued with this spirit of giving and doing. Yea, consecrate our very lives, if necessary, for the establishment of peace and righteousness on the earth, thus fully demonstrating that we do indeed "Love our neighbors as ourselves."

By thus aiding in raising a righteous generation we shall surely do the best service to God and country.

Emma Goddard, "Thou Shalt Love Thy Neighbor," June 9, 1918, in "Addresses at the June Conference: 'We Stand for Service to God and Country,'" Young Woman's Journal *29, no. 8 (Aug. 1918): 434–437.*

FORGIVENESS IS LIKE MERCY

◇◇◇

JENNIE BRIMHALL KNIGHT

Relief Society General Conference
Assembly Hall, Temple Square, Salt Lake City, Utah
Thursday, April 3, 1924

Lucy Jane "Jennie" Brimhall Knight (1875–1957) served a mission to Great Britain from April to November 1898 as one of the first single sister missionaries in the church. Her mission companion and future sister-in-law, Inez Knight, served from April 1898 until June 1900.[1] As a missionary, Jennie spoke at meetings throughout the British Isles and spent several weeks on the European continent. According to an early history, her missionary work with Inez looked just like that of the elders with whom they served: "visiting, tracting, preaching, and exerting themselves to the utmost to spread a knowledge of the truth respecting their religion and their people."[2]

Jennie Knight married Jesse Knight on January 18, 1899, and received a pedagogy degree from the General Church Board of Education in May 1899. She served five years as president of the Young Ladies' Mutual Improvement Association in the Taylor Stake in Raymond, Alberta, Canada, and eight years in the same position for the Utah Stake when she returned to Provo, Utah.[3] She also engaged in public work supporting women and education, serving as matron of Brigham Young University from the fall of 1907 to the spring of 1911, with the assignment to see to the welfare of female students.[4] During World War I, Knight was vice president of the State Council of Defense, Woman's Division.[5]

Knight joined the Relief Society general presidency on April 1, 1921, as first counselor to President Clarissa S. Williams.[6] She continued to live in Provo after joining the general presidency, traveling to Salt Lake City each week for board meetings and throughout the church to attend stake Relief Society conventions.[7] Her journal

Jennie Brimhall Knight with sons Philip and Richard. Circa 1916. Some eighteen years before this photo was taken, Knight was one of the first single female church members to serve as a missionary. Photograph by Larson and Bygreen. (Photograph in family possession. Courtesy Jennifer Whatcott Hooton.)

chronicles her management of Relief Society and home responsibilities and notes her family members' contributions.[8] One day in 1922, for example, she recorded that she returned home from church duties after midnight, checked on her sleeping family members, and crept into bed. She woke the next morning to clean house and can peaches and then left again the next week to fulfill her church responsibilities in far-flung towns.[9]

Knight's service on the board involved not only speaking at local congregations but also participating in broader, national causes. In 1923, she traveled by train with Relief Society general secretary Amy Brown Lyman to attend a weeklong social welfare convention and a planning meeting for the National Council of Women in Washington DC.[10] She would return to Washington in 1925 to represent the Relief Society at a meeting of the International Council of Women.[11] Knight drew on her experience examining human nature and teaching church principles when she delivered the following contemplation of forgiveness at a 1924 Relief Society general conference.

MANY SPLENDID LESSONS have been given during this conference, and I am sure many resolutions have been renewed with the effect that we shall be better leaders, better pace-setters in our different communities, more sympathetic sisters, more devoted wives, and more understanding mothers.

The group assembled here today belongs to the class of women who have no time to be idle, no time to indulge in those things which we have been taught are a waste of time and not conducive to advancement. Our aim is to serve and in that service find joy in this life, and eternal life in the world to come.

Along the path of life that leads to happiness are many pitfalls which must be avoided if we reach our goal. One of these pitfalls I shall call unforgiveness. By it stands a little mound of forgiveness which, if mounted, will lift us above the petty things of life to see a bigger, broader plain and a well-defined path.

There are many actions of men and women of which we do not approve, take part in, or sanction, and while it is our mission to do all we can in the spirit of real charity and sisterly love to show the better way, the more perfect plan of peace, we need not hate our fellow beings because their ways are not ours. We must let our Father judge them.

The word of the Lord through the Prophet Joseph Smith, recorded in the Doctrine and Covenants, says, "I, the Lord, will forgive whom I will forgive, but of you it is required to forgive all men, and ye ought to say in your hearts, 'Let God judge between me and thee according to thy deeds.'"[12]

I heard the other day of a woman who lived on the same street as her father and yet she had not spoken to him for many years. I heard also a Relief Society president who, upon learning that one of the members of the society was offended because of some action on the part of the presidency of the Relief Society, went to the home of this sister and tried to talk matters over, to apologize, if necessary, and make things right, but this sister could find no place in her heart for forgiveness and so the president turned away sorrowing for that sister. Which of the two women would be happiest today? My father has often said: "Hate hurts the hater worse than the hated."[13]

Peter, on one occasion, said to Jesus, "How oft shall my brother sin against me, and I forgive him? till seven times?" And Jesus said unto him, "I say not unto thee until seven times, but until seventy times seven." Then he said, "Therefore is the kingdom of heaven likened unto a certain king, which would take account of his servants, and one was brought unto him which owed him ten thousand talents, but forasmuch as he had not to pay, his lord commanded him to be sold, and his wife, and children, and all that he had, and payment to be made. The servant, therefore, fell down and worshiped him, saying, Lord, have patience with me, and I will pay thee all. Then the Lord of that servant was moved with compassion, and loosed him and forgave him the debt.

"But the same servant went out, and found one of his fellow-servants which owed him an hundred pence; and he laid hands on him, and took him by the throat, saying, Pay me that thou owest. And his fellow-servant fell down at his feet and besought him, saying, Have patience with me, and I will pay thee all. And he would not; but went and cast him into prison.

"So when his fellow-servants saw what was done, they were very sorry and came and told unto their lord all that was done. Then the lord, after that he had called him, said unto him, O thou wicked servant, I forgave thee all that debt because thou desiredst me: Shouldst not thou also have had compassion on thy fellow-servant, even as I had pity on thee? And his lord was wroth, and delivered him unto the tormentors till he should pay all that was due unto him. So likewise shall my heavenly Father do also unto you, if ye from your hearts forgive not every one his brothers their trespasses."[14]

Is it not a truth that Jesus taught us to pray: Forgive us our trespasses as we forgive them that trespass against us?[15]

Martin Luther commenting on this said, "When thou sayest, 'I will not forgive,' and stand before God with your paternoster, and mumblest, 'Forgive us our debts,' it is the same as saying, 'I do not forgive him, so do not thou, God, forgive me.'"[16]

In our homes let us not hold grudges one toward another, but seek and pray daily to find a way to forgive one another, remembering that forgiveness is like mercy, "It is twice blessed, it blesses him that gives and him that receives."[17] If we could become as little children in this particular how much happier we would be, for whoever knew a little child who was not willing to forgive at the very first intimation of regret on the part of the offender; yes, and even before any repentance was shown on the part of the one who committed the offense. Did not God say, "Except ye become as little children ye can in no wise enter the kingdom of God"?[18]

To those who have been sorely tried and bitterly offended, remember it requires a prayerful, generous, and merciful heart coupled with a strong will to forgive, but remember also, an unforgiving heart places a barrier between itself and God's forgiveness, for is it not written, "He that forgiveth not his brother his trespasses, standeth condemned before the Lord, for there remaineth in him the greater sin."[19]

So let us each and all bury our grievances whether they pertain to our immediate family, our church, or our neighbor, and cover this pitfall that deprives us of happiness with a slab of forgetfulness and forgive as we hope to be forgiven.

Jennie B. Knight, Discourse, Apr. 3, 1924, Afternoon Session, in "General Meetings," Relief Society Magazine *11, no. 6 (June 1924): 307–309. Title supplied by the editors.*

Amy Brown Lyman at Social Service Training in Anaconda, Montana. Circa 1920. Lyman, bespectacled in the center of the front row, became a trained social worker after formative visits to Hull House in Chicago and was a leader in implementing social service work within the Relief Society. Lyman served on the Relief Society general board for thirty-six years, including her time as president. Photograph by Montgomery Studio. (Church History Library, Salt Lake City.)

THE VALUE OF FAITH

◇◇◇

AMY BROWN LYMAN

Relief Society General Conference
Assembly Hall, Temple Square, Salt Lake City, Utah
April 3, 1926

My first love had been Primary work," wrote Amy Brown Lyman (1872–1959), after nearly four decades of service on the Relief Society general board. In truth, she loved any program that concentrated on human development and flourishing. Before joining the board in October 1909, her major church work had been in the Young Ladies' Mutual Improvement Association. Lyman served on the Relief Society general board until 1945, the last five years as president. The first meetings she attended connected her to foundational Relief Society roots: Bathsheba W. Smith, who joined Relief Society as a nineteen-year-old in Nauvoo, was president. At that time the board met in the office of the *Woman's Exponent* in Salt Lake City's Templeton Building.[1]

When Lyman gave the following talk, she had been serving as Relief Society general secretary under Emmeline B. Wells since 1913 and was in the middle of a two-year term as secretary for the National Council of Women. As general secretary, Lyman fulfilled church president Joseph F. Smith's request that she modernize and supply the Relief Society offices, "that the business affairs of the organization, including those of stakes and wards, be conducted according to the best business practices."[2] Lyman obtained typewriters, filing cabinets, and adding and mimeograph machines; established professional bookkeeping procedures; and introduced uniform ward record books and visiting teacher report books. Lyman also worked in the business department of the *Relief Society Magazine* for more than thirty years, starting when it began publication in 1915. To finance the new magazine, she and Jeanette Hyde solicited advertisements. Their children helped them wrap and mail issues to subscribers each month.[3]

Social work was among the enduring pursuits of Lyman's life. When she accompanied her husband, Richard, to the University of Chicago in the summer of 1902, she took several courses. Her favorite was on the new discipline of sociology, and decades later she recalled, "It was at this time that I first became interested in social work and social problems."[4] She also did volunteer work with Chicago Charities and attended the lectures of Jane Addams, a prominent crusader against poverty, at Hull House, interviewing Addams several times for a class project. President Joseph F. Smith asked in 1913 that Lyman continue her previous study of social work with the hope of improving the church's current practices.[5] She joined a delegation of four women in 1917 for a special course in family welfare work taught by the University of Colorado and the Red Cross; she later credited that course as being crucial to her developing understanding of the field.[6]

A month before Lyman's husband joined the Quorum of the Twelve Apostles on April 6, 1918, Joseph F. Smith consulted with Amy Lyman about creating a new Relief Society social services department. By the beginning of the following year, Lyman had established a social welfare department at Relief Society headquarters, which she directed until 1934.[7] In 1920, she organized and taught a six-week course on family welfare work at Brigham Young University, the first of many courses that would train Relief Society members in the challenges and methods of social work.[8]

She served in the Utah House of Representatives in 1923 and was very pleased to introduce to the House the bill requesting state acceptance of the federal Sheppard-Towner Act, which provided funds for maternity and infant care. The bill passed, and Relief Society branches in the western states supported it by equipping and operating well-baby and health clinics.[9] These efforts contributed to 19 percent reductions in infant mortality and 8 percent reductions in maternal death rates by 1928.[10]

Lyman's understanding of faith, expressed in the following talk given in a general session of the Relief Society general conference in 1926, intimates why and how she pursued these many contributions.[11]

THE LACK OF FAITH in the world today, together with some recent personal experiences, has led me of late to appreciate more than ever before the value of faith and the great blessing it is to those who possess it.

I am sure that every woman in this audience has passed through trials and afflictions which would have been almost unbearable without faith in God and a testimony of the gospel, with all that it comprehends.

Faith in our Heavenly Father and in his Son Jesus Christ is an asset to any individual. It helps him to be a brave and courageous individual. It helps to make him a positive and forceful character as opposed to a negative and vacillating one. It helps him to have confidence in himself and confidence in others; to believe in himself and to believe in others; to be generous to those in need and charitable to those less fortunate; to be cheerful, hopeful, and optimistic.

Faith in the Father and the Son is a blessing—yes, one of the greatest blessings one can have. It is more far-reaching as a comforter than any other influence. It is a source of solace in times of sickness, sorrow, and despair. Faith helps an individual to be philosophical and to meet with comparative composure whatever comes, and to be resigned and reconciled to circumstances over which he has no control. It helps one to be meek and humble and to put his trust in God.

Faith in the Father and the Son presupposes a belief in their teachings which include a preexistent state and a life beyond the grave; and to a Latter-day Saint it comprehends the gospel plan of life and salvation as revealed to us through the Prophet Joseph Smith.[12] Such faith and such belief helps one to formulate a plan of life on the highest plane, and to set up worthy and worthwhile standards of living which conform to the standards of the gospel. It helps one to judge of values—to choose between those things which are really worthwhile, which are lasting and eternal—and those things which are temporary and passing. It makes one realize that life is a stepping stone to a higher life, and the better the life here the greater the happiness here and in the life to come. Faith fills the possessor with the desire to emulate the life of the Savior and to keep the commandments of God.

Sublime faith is one of the greatest of all gifts. Let us pledge our allegiance to our faith. Let us as individuals say, "No man may destroy my faith and hope and belief and leave me a stone." For I have observed that those who have no faith, and who tend to undermine and destroy faith in others, never, so far as I know, leave anything constructive in its place.

Let us not be influenced by doubters and cynics and atheists, nor by the wave of doubt and despair which is filling the earth today.[13] Let us cling to the belief that faith with good works is an asset,[14] a comforter, a blessing; it is the power of God unto salvation to everyone that believeth.[15] Let us cling to the belief that faith is our birthright, and let us sell it not for a mess of pottage.[16]

Amy Brown Lyman, Discourse, Apr. 3, 1926, in "Conference Addresses," Relief Society Magazine *13, no. 7 (July 1926): 381–382. Title supplied by the editors.*

SENSING RESPONSIBILITY OF OFFICE

◇◇◇

LALENE H. HART

Relief Society General Conference
Bishop's Building, Salt Lake City, Utah
April 4, 1933

Formal education, teaching, and life experience made Lalene Hendricks Hart (1885–1972) an expert in the field of home economics. She first studied household economics at Brigham Young College in Logan, Utah, and later at Simmons College in Boston, Massachusetts. Upon completing her training, she taught at the Night School in Nephi, Utah; at Cassia Stake Academy in Oakley, Idaho; and at Brigham Young College, where she became head of the Household Economics Department. She married Charles H. Hart, a widower with ten children, in 1915.[1] Beginning in 1923, she wrote numerous *Relief Society Magazine* articles full of housekeeping tips under the title "Of Interest to Women."[2]

Hart worked on the Relief Society general board under two presidents, Clarissa S. Williams from 1921 to 1928 and Louise Y. Robison from 1928 to 1939.[3] She maintained her position on the Relief Society general board when she accompanied Charles to Toronto, where he was president of the Canadian Mission from 1927 to 1930.[4] While presiding over the Relief Society in Canada, she traveled throughout the mission to attend conferences with female members, to give talks, and to proselytize.[5] She approached this mission as an extension of her service on the board. At a Relief Society conference on the eve of her departure in 1927, she said, "While I shall not for a time be permitted to meet with you in board meetings or in conference, perhaps I may feel your spirit by mothering the boys and the girls that will have the privilege of going into the Canadian mission. . . . I assure you with all my heart that I shall try to guide and protect as far as it is my duty to do, the boys and girls that come under my direction."[6]

As chair of the social service committee during the early 1930s, Hart reported on recent Relief Society Social Service Institutes, which prepared women to act as social workers in their own communities.[7] The Great Depression was in full swing, and Utah was not faring well. By 1930, only a third of the state's adult population was employed, the worst record of any state except for Mississippi. Social Service Institutes trained stake and ward Relief Society leaders in modern social-work techniques and lasted anywhere from several days to six weeks.[8] Relief Societies appointed at least one social service aide per stake and some at the ward level where necessary. This training helped the Relief Society to cooperate with government agencies and to address the overwhelming needs of their community members.

Relief Society efforts to cultivate a sense of social obligation also included monthly lessons dedicated to social service, which were published in the *Relief Society Magazine.* The Relief Society's social welfare programs included child placement, the Employment Bureau for Women and Girls, summer trips for malnourished children, and a storehouse for clothing and other supplies.[9] Hart gave the following talk on what it meant to be a leader in Relief Society at a Relief Society general conference meeting for officers in the Bishop's Building in 1933.[10]

THE LIFE OF EACH of us is largely governed by a threefold obligation: duty to ourselves, duty to our fellowmen, and duty to our God. The law of ethics prescribes certain rules whereby human relations and behavior are controlled.

The members of a Relief Society organization are in a school of training in ethics which is far superior to any other class or club. Besides gaining knowledge through outlined lessons, they learn other lessons in courage, tolerance, kindliness, and devotion. This school is also trying to create in its membership a sense of social obligation, to stimulate interest in the welfare of neighbors, and to develop interest in all classes and races of people.

Every woman who enters into the service of this organization as an officer[11] does so with some degree of ambition and determination to gain new ideas and experiences that will give her a broader view of life, will raise her own and others' standard of ideals, and efficiently serve those with whom she comes in contact. At no previous time has the preparation for better and more complete living been so intensive. Women are interested in more things and in more people than heretofore. They are eager to know more of human nature, their own personality and its development.

Those who have been given the responsibility for directing this preparation[12] must rise to their possibilities and offer opportunities and experiences to their respective groups, which will enable them to find a life freer from those things which discourage, worry, and annoy, and fuller of things that satisfy, stimulate, and inspire. This responsibility has not been solicited, but has been bestowed upon us as an honor. Any office, however, ceases to be an honor unless that office is honored. Ben Jonson says, "Great honors are great burdens, but on whom they are cast with envy he doth bear two loads. His cares must still be double to his joys in any dignity."[13]

To be worthy to preside over a well-organized society in dignity and poise is an officer's greatest achievement; it requires long, intensive labor to acquire.

The mission of officers is to create and develop in the lives of our members the spirit of the gospel and carry its message to all people, to encourage the distressed and disheartened.

As we approach the end of our season's outlined work, we may well ask ourselves, has this year's work been a success or failure as far as I am individually concerned? What is success, and how is it to be measured? Not by the length of the days or the accumulation of knowledge or influence, but by the continuous and unrelenting adaptation of the powers and capacities that we have to the opportunities and needs of our environment.

Such a result may be far short of the standard we have set for ourselves, or it may even exceed it, but nothing can excel in loftiness of purpose the desire to make the most effective use of our talents in the service of others.

That Relief Society officer has achieved success who has lived well, loved much, given generously, served willingly, and grown graciously through her responsibility. She has failed if she has ignored the truth, discarded her highest ideals, and lain aside the standards of her own organization and the church.

Let us sense seriously the responsibility that rests upon us to rise and shine and show the way to a doubting, waiting, skeptical world that there is a God in heaven, that Jesus Christ lives, and that he is interested in the welfare of his children.

Lalene H. Hart, "Sensing Responsibility of Office," Apr. 4, 1933, in "Officers' Meeting," Relief Society Magazine *20, no. 5 (May 1933): 271–272.*

Elsie Talmage Brandley. Circa 1930. The final editor of the *Young Woman's Journal,* Brandley was a popular writer and speaker as a member of the Young Ladies' Mutual Improvement Association general board, on which she served from 1924 until her untimely death in 1935. (Church History Library, Salt Lake City.)

THE RELIGIOUS CRISIS OF TODAY

◇◇◇

ELSIE TALMAGE BRANDLEY

Mutual Improvement Association June Conference
Assembly Hall, Temple Square, Salt Lake City, Utah
June 9, 1934

Elsie Talmage Brandley (1896–1935) had a facility for self-expression cultivated by her heritage. Her mother, May Booth Talmage, raised seven children, served on the Young Ladies' Mutual Improvement Association (YLMIA) general board for thirty-eight years, edited the *Young Woman's Journal* for nineteen months, and was a leader in Utah's suffrage movement.[1] James E. Talmage, her father, was a geologist, university president, prolific author of theological works, and member of the Quorum of the Twelve Apostles.[2] As a very young child, Brandley sneaked into her father's study after bedtime and overturned an ink bottle so that it spilled down her nightgown. When her mother saw her, she asked, "Don't you think you should be spanked?" Elsie replied, "I'd rather be loved."[3]

Brandley's relationship with ink proved enduring. As a student at Brigham Young University, she was student body vice president and associate editor of the *White and Blue,* a student periodical.[4] In 1923, six years after her graduation and marriage to Harold Brandley, she became associate editor of the *Young Woman's Journal.*[5] The mother of seven daughters, she darned stockings in between writing paragraphs or reading over proofs for the magazine.[6] She was general editor in 1929 when the magazine was combined with the *Improvement Era,* a periodical that aimed to serve both male and female readers. With the end of the *Young Woman's Journal,* Brandley immediately became associate editor of the *Improvement Era,* and she served in that position until her death in 1935.[7]

Brandley's service on the YLMIA general board spanned eleven years during the presidencies of Mattie Horne Tingey and Ruth May Fox.[8] She joined the board in 1924 and, in addition to working on the magazines, helped to write manuals, plays, songs, programs, and other material.[9] She was also a popular public speaker.[10] E. E. Ericksen, with whom she collaborated on MIA committees, said that her idea of saving souls was to help all of their abilities—cultural, moral, and spiritual. "The human personality was sacred to her, and its development the great spiritual objective," he said.[11] She also championed young people in asking and finding answers to their own questions. "You are the ones whose responsibility it is to insure the faith and unwavering trust in the gospel which is your heritage," she wrote.[12]

Many felt the world to be in moral, political, and economic crisis during the 1930s, in part because of post–World War I disillusionment and the Great Depression. Young people in particular were considered to be in crisis. With the onset of the Great Depression, high school dropout rates increased substantially, youth unemployment rose sharply, and by 1932, two hundred thousand young people had left their desperate home situations to wander the country.[13] Leaders of Latter-day Saint youth discussed such religious and moral crises at their general board meetings. For example, a few weeks before this conference, President Ruth May Fox exhorted the board members to pray constantly: "We are living in critical times and everything that can be shaken will be shaken."[14] Speakers at this conference were optimistic about ways the church fortified members to withstand such challenges.[15]

In the 1930s, the YLMIA and the Young Men's Mutual Improvement Association (YMMIA) worked closely through joint conferences, meetings, committees, and coordinated programs (including contests and dances).[16] Both organizations were in the midst of a shift from a focus on recreation and social service education for young people to an increased emphasis on Jesus Christ and gospel teachings.[17] The YLMIA also adopted a new name in 1934, becoming the Young Women's Mutual Improvement Association (YWMIA) because *women* was seen as a more dignified descriptor than *ladies*.[18] Brandley delivered the following discourse in the Assembly Hall on Temple Square after the MIA had conducted an "Attitudes of Youth" survey where two groups of young men and young women made presentations before MIA board members about their challenges.[19] Four board members—Brandley, Joseph Fielding Smith, Oscar A. Kirkham, and Melvin J. Ballard—responded to issues raised by these young people at the first general session of the June MIA conference.[20] The session was extremely popular, and the *Improvement Era* published the talks.[21] The talks by Brandley and Ballard were also reprinted in the *Millennial Star*.[22]

THIS IS A GATHERING of the leaders of youth—Latter-day Saint youth—and in the presence of you who give so generously of yourselves I stand in sincere tribute.[23] Yours is the gift of which the poet might have been speaking when he said, "Who gives himself with his gift feeds three—himself, his hungering neighbor, and me."[24]

I am glad and thankful to be living today and in my own particular generation—the middle generation of three now working in MIA—for we have an older, more experienced one to lead us with their wisdom and a younger one to fire us with enthusiasm and energy.[25] We have both of these to help in guiding us past our own individual problems into the almost frightening ones of a new day. To deny the fact that we are facing a new day is to close our eyes to the world about us; to prove ourselves blind and deaf to sights and sounds so significant that an intelligent mind not only must admit them but must integrate them into the shifting, colorful pattern which is life just ahead. With the passing of every generation emphases shift, certain problems give way to others, answers change with the changing times. In view of the amazing progress and drastic change of the past century it is easy to see something of the reasons why problems have become more acute and less easily soluble by old methods of discipline and pronouncement.

In the Church of Jesus Christ of Latter-day Saints, change has kept pace with that outside the church, and rightly so, for Mormonism is based on a foundation of modern revelation and therefore has greater right to change, under authoritative direction, than have many other existing organizations.[26] Changes have come and will continue to come in traditions, observances, methods. The Lord, we are told in the first section of the Doctrine and Covenants, spake to his servants after the manner of their language, that they might come to understanding.[27] Is it irreverent or sacrilegious to conclude that with deeper understanding language might become increasingly explicit or profound?

Of some things we are sure; to certain rooted principles we cling. As Latter-day Saints we accept the divinity of Jesus of Nazareth; we believe implicitly in the restored gospel as given through the Prophet Joseph Smith; we regard the General Authorities of the church as being divinely commissioned to speak in the name of God and bear testimony to the Godship of Christ; we accept the standard works of the church as authoritative utterances given for the spiritual guidance of man upon the earth.

A party of geologists, crossing a loose shale deposit on a steep incline, realized that the shale was slipping. Most of the party reached the opposite side of the hill in safety, but one, bringing up the rear, saw that the sliding rock was carrying him in its glacier-like grip toward a declivity which might mean death. Looking ahead, he saw in his path a trunk of an old tree and recognized there a chance of safety.

Reaching the stump, grasping it and clinging grimly, he was able to hold on while the entire deposit of loose shale passed. His knowledge of the stability of a tree to remain firmly rooted in spite of shifting surface rock gave him assurance; he could face apparent disaster clinging to that which was thus rooted. To the fundamental roots of church belief we cling; to them we anchor our faith; in them we believe. Differences which may arise between groups and individuals are not based upon these roots. Outside of this, which is basic, opinions may diverge. As leaders, let us examine possible evidences of differences and reasons for them, if they exist, and try to glimpse a possible solution.

Consider again the many new ways of life which are today presenting themselves for understanding and incorporation into a new system—politics, economics, technology, science, education, social welfare, recreation—innumerable others.[28] Any occasional misunderstanding between youth and maturity might be one chiefly of orientation—of finding orbits in the new system. Maturity goes hand in hand with youth in meeting most of the changes in fields of invention, of discovery, of scientific advancement, of recreation and vocational training, and of many new applications of accepted religious truth. If they part at a gate through which youth demands the right to pass and at which maturity hesitates, is it not, perhaps, because youth ever was curious and daring and inquiring, while age, having made its own ventures, longs for security?

Parents and leaders provide and administer education, and education teaches youth to explore, to experiment, to try new ways and find new paths. Is it consistent to resent what is found in these educational journeys? Do we strive to discover how far we leaders and parents might be lagging behind youth, instead of trying to measure how far they are getting away from us?

In the religious situation confronting us today the world finds old conditions inadequate. The Church of Jesus Christ of Latter-day Saints is having no more and perhaps much less difficulty in making religious adjustment than are others, but it is no longer possible for the church to remain apart from the world. In their reading, their studies, their observations, and their contacts, youth makes discoveries which to them seem new. When such discoveries appear to threaten time-honored religious traditions of their elders, concern inevitably is aroused.

The situation is not new in this age or in this church; people ever have held dear their religious beliefs and practices, major and minor, and have resented innovations which have endangered them. Five centuries ago Columbus was refused help in his attempt to prove the earth round because the Bible had spoken of the four corners of the earth and a sphere could not have four corners.[29] Five years ago a woman insisted upon her daughter refusing an anesthetic in childbirth on the grounds that the Bible had said that a woman should bring forth her children in sorrow and suffering.[30]

We must not, now and in the latter days and especially in the church of Jesus Christ, make the word of God grounds for unnecessary misunderstanding. Quoting from the statement of a late member of the Quorum of Twelve Apostles:

"Let us not try to wrest the scriptures in an attempt to explain away what we cannot explain. The opening chapters of Genesis and scriptures related thereto were never intended as a textbook of geology, archaeology, earth-science, or man-science; Holy Scripture will endure, while the conceptions of men change with new discoveries. We do not show reverence for the scriptures when we misapply them through faulty interpretation."[31]

According to my belief, to know the fundamental truths of the gospel is to leave one free to go far and wide, anchored by that knowledge, in search of all else that earth and sea and skies have to teach. Instead of making religious truths a bone of contention and source of differences, should we not, as leaders and individuals, try to make them a means of bringing order and harmony out of apparent confusion?

One of the influences bringing about a new day, an influence vital in its importance, is that of reading, but one of today's shale deposits is uncritical reading. Study of the printed page must be analytical, or it becomes either meaningless or too powerful—both dangerous conditions. I quote at random a line or two from various sources to remind you of what youth reads day by day—week by week—and ask: Could we have lived on such a diet of reading matter before our own ideas were defined clearly and established firmly, and remained uninfluenced? Must we not admit that forces surrounding youth today are more potent in encouraging them to question than were forces yesterday?

Robert Morse Lovett, in *Current History* for January 1934, describing the Fair at Chicago,[32] says:

> Evidences were abundant of the achievements of science—telephone, radio, television, airplane—but where was the evidence of the larger life of mankind, or promise of it? Disappointment was especially acute when people went to the halls of Social Science and Religion. The exhibits in the last two suggested a troubled doubt as to the meaning, reality, and future of progress toward a larger life. . . . Throughout the fair, comments on every hand were heard to the effect that modern improvements had mechanized life but had failed to enrich values of living.[33]

Albert Edward Bailey in the *Christian Century* for January 24, 1934, presents an imaginary dialogue between the architect of a new church and a dreamer who has ideas of what a church should be. The dreamer says:

> "See if you cannot find somewhere in the structure places for meditation—I see them as pathways to God. Take, for example, the pathways of service . . . with statuettes illustrating the parable of the Good Samaritan; wall frescoes showing Lincoln emancipating the slaves; the first use of anesthesia; Howard and prison reform; a Carnegie library; Jane Addams and Hull House. . . ." The architect replies, "This dream of yours means scrapping many of the old ideas and practices; I doubt you'll ever get the church as a whole to accept them," and the dreamer answers, "Well, aren't we in the midst of a social revolution of first magnitude? Why shouldn't the church do a little revolutionizing . . . if it would . . . bring the kingdom of God a little nearer?"[34]

Glenn Frank, in "The Will to Doubt," says:

> The will to believe has given us our great saints; the will to doubt has given us our great scientists. The goal of the intelligent man is a character in which the will to believe of the saint and the will to doubt of the scientist meet and mingle. Neither alone makes a whole man. A merely blind faith gives us a soft saint; a merely blind doubt gives us a hard scientist. Humanity owes much to the saint and much to the scientist, but humanity would fare badly if the world were peopled solely by saints with a blind faith or by scientists with a blind doubt. Modern science is modest. It suspends judgment when it does not know. In all other fields—religion, politics, and so on—we must learn to do likewise. We must act in the light of the best we know at any given moment, but we must be willing to hold our beliefs open to revision in the light of new facts. Thus can we combine saint and scientist.[35]

With thinkers such as these urging youth to question, why should they not? Mature leadership cannot afford to remain apart, aloof, waiting at a gate for youth to return from their explorations. We, the leadership of the MIA, must go with them and learn what they learn and see what they see. A young man of MIA prominence, asking his father a question, received answer: "I never want to hear you speak of such things again in my presence." This man refused to pass through the gate of inquiry with his son, and his power of leading the boy was lost. Leaders in MIA must not lose their contacts through such an attitude! Youth must ask in order to find answers; youth must analyze and harmonize. Their very eagerness to do so is indicative of their interest; indifferent passiveness would be death, but this intensity is life. Youth must be converted personally; only on the strength of a converted youth can this church realize its high and glorious destiny.[36]

On the other hand, youth must admit the fact that it accepts much without criticism and doubt: fruit is eaten without knowing botany; stars are loved in ignorance of astronomy; telegrams are sent with no knowledge of the Morse code; love and friendship, home and books and nature become dear and of great value with little attempt to explain technical reasons. Let us not encourage youth to segregate religion as the only phase of life upon which to concentrate doubtful inquiry; let us help them to see that they accept certain conditions with no stronger proof of their doing so than that they provide joy and hope and faith and courage; can they not accept religion, up to a certain point, with the same composure?

Quoting again from *The Earth and Man,* let us realize that:

> It is natural for the young and immature mind to think that what to it is new must of necessity be new to the world. Comparatively inexperienced students are discovering from time to time apparent discrepancies between the faith of their fathers and the development of modern thought, and these they are apt to magnify and exaggerate, when as a matter of fact their great-grandfathers met the same seeming difficulties and yet survived. Believe not those who assert that the gospel of Jesus Christ is in any way opposed to progress or inconsistent with advancement.[37]

Leaders of youth in the MIA—what can we do? Certain it is we cannot dismiss the individual problems of boys and girls simply because their great-grandfathers had similar problems; we must regard every young person who has a question as we would an investigator and give each the same prayerful consideration. The way of youth may not be our way; their language may seem frank and strange and irreverent to us; but to them we, perhaps, appear strange too. We might regard youth and maturity as travelers, bound for an oriental port. Youth may travel east, into the rising sun; age may go west, toward the evening shadows; but at their common destination they will meet and realize that both were headed straight in their course of travel; but there will always be between them the difference of experience along the way.[38] Has not the cumulative power of Mormonism in a century been sufficient to form a cement, joining all truths and desire for truth into a oneness—a unified search in which all members, regardless of age, can set forth together? Is there a place—a legitimate and reverent place—for inquiry in the building of a testimony? We answer—we *must* answer—yes, and say that the basis of doubt and inquiry has been the genius of the church, the power through which members have fought their way into it.

James E. Talmage, asked how he received his testimony, replied: "Though I seem to have been born with a testimony, yet in my early adolescence I was led to question whether that testimony was really my own or derived from my parents. I set about investigating the claims of the church, seeking a way out if its claims should prove to me unsound. After months of such inquiry . . . I was convinced of its truth once for all, and this knowledge is so fully an integral part of me that without it I would not be myself."[39]

Another conversion is described as follows:

> At first he was prejudiced against the doctrines, but as the elder continued to preach . . . it produced an extraordinary effect upon the mind of Daniel Spencer. For two weeks he closed his establishment and refused to do business with anyone; he shut himself up to study, and there alone with his God he weighed in the balance of his clear head and conscientious heart the message he had found. . . . One day . . . he exclaimed, bursting into a flood of tears: "The thing is true, and as an honest man I must embrace it, but it will cost me all I have on earth." He saw that in the eyes of his friends and townspeople he must fall from the social pinnacle on which he stood to that of a despised people, but he stepped off like a man.[40]

These, which have been the experiences of many born in the church and out, explain the marvel which is the power of the gospel. With a membership largely constituted of those who have joined the church after searching investigation—who have questioned the beliefs of their fathers—we cannot say, consistently, that youth has no right to question religion as any other human concern and evaluate it in terms of individual worth.

I wish I might be given inspiration to suggest to you leaders potent means of reaching and holding all the young people of the church; I shall leave what I hope might be one helpful thought, and it is this:

Listen to what they have to say; open your hearts and minds to their problems. Never bid them be silent, but inspire them to cry out to you the innermost questions of their souls. Forget your own convictions in listening to them; remember your convictions only when you come to make reply.

One woman has said: "The rapid social reorganization of the time has made flexibility necessary, and only those who are alert and vital, who are curious about life, elastic enough to assimilate new ways of thinking and living, can adjust themselves to altered circumstances and face the future without fear."[41]

Youth and age both can and will and do accept the rooted principles of the gospel—the fundamentals. As a church, I repeat, we accept the divinity of Christ, the restoration through Joseph Smith, and the authority of God held by those commissioned today to speak in his name. This is the anchor to which we must—and do—and will hold.[42] Securely anchored thus we may look into every new theory, every new belief, every new thought, and accept what is of value to us. As leaders, what can we do, I ask again; and again give answer: Listen to youth and learn from them; talk to youth and teach them! Lose no opportunity to light from your fire of belief the fuse which will ignite in them a spark of testimony—that electric force which will generate in them energy to work for the church; heat to warm them to the gospel; light to illumine their way toward a realization of that highest conception of intelligence as the glory of God. May God grant us the reward of seeing the crisis of religion today turned toward the great and glorious possibilities which are inseparably bound up in these latter days with our great and glorious church—the Church of Jesus Christ![43]

Elsie Talmage Brandley, "The Religious Crisis of Today," Improvement Era *37, no. 8 (Aug. 1934): 467–468, 496–497; see also Elsie Talmage Brandley, "The Religious Crisis of Today,"* Latter-day Saints' Millennial Star *96, no. 36 (Sept. 6, 1934): 561–566.*

PREPARE THY HEART

◇◇◇

LEONE O. JACOBS

Relief Society General Conference
Tabernacle, Temple Square, Salt Lake City, Utah
September 29, 1949

Before her Relief Society general board service, Maud Leone Openshaw Jacobs (1903–1990) and her husband, Joseph, served missions in Palestine and Syria.[1] Joseph left for his service as mission president in July 1937. Leone and their children, eleven-year-old Geraldine and seven-year-old Lamont, could not join him until December 1938, after Leone had undergone and recovered from major surgery.[2] Leone Jacobs's mission work included fellowshipping members, learning Turkish, hosting a Christmas party for church members, and preparing meals for mission guests and missionaries.[3] She also supported Relief Society and youth activities and played the organ for meetings.[4] After England declared war on Germany on September 3, 1939, the Jacobs family was called home, leaving behind seventy-nine members to maintain the church in Asia Minor.[5] Jacobs wrote a twelve-page report of her mission, describing Jewish efforts to settle Palestine, the roles of men and women in local culture, and a sad farewell with church members. The *Deseret News* published her report in two articles.[6]

Jacobs joined the Ensign Stake Relief Society presidency in 1941, the same year the United States entered World War II. She worked with other Relief Society members in sending soap, clothing, and bedding overseas; supporting the American Red Cross's Utah headquarters by sewing hospital gowns and bandages; and filling canning assignments at Welfare Square.[7] Materials were scarce, so the Relief Society had to be resourceful and act quickly to buy supplies to make blankets, clothing, and other items when such dry goods became available. Members of the stake Relief Society presidency pooled their gasoline ration stamps while Jacobs, the only presidency member with a car, drove them on their expeditions to look for fabric.[8]

At the war's end, new Relief Society general president Belle S. Spafford invited Jacobs to serve on the general board, which she did from 1945 to 1956, when heart disease forced her to resign.[9] Jacobs's assignments on the board included planning Relief Society conventions[10] and representing the board in community programs such as the Utah Safety Council and the Women's Legislative Council of Utah.[11] She gave the following talk on continually increasing in righteousness at a Relief Society general conference on September 29, 1949, in the Salt Lake Tabernacle.

PRESIDENT CLARK AND BROTHERS AND SISTERS, it is indeed an inspiration to look out into your faces and to contemplate the influence for good that you sisters are, and I am sure that if this influence could be measured in some way, it would exceed by far our most extravagant estimate.[12]

We do appreciate your loyalty to this organization and to the gospel, and appreciate the love and understanding that you exert in your communities.

I pray that the few moments that I stand before you I may have your faith and prayers and that our Heavenly Father will strengthen me.

One of the most glorious principles of life is that we can always rise above our present level. How discouraging life would be if once we found ourselves involved in unworthy conduct we could not lift ourselves up and out and on to better ways, but we do not have to remain as we are. Each day offers a fresh beginning.

An old man once was reviewing his life to a friend. "When I was thirty I was just no good," he said, "no good at all, not even to myself, and then one day I had the urge, the desire to right-about-face. I decided I was going to change my direction, and from that day to this I have led a life I was proud of."

A young college girl paused in her round of excitement one day and said: "I guess I am going with the wrong crowd. I do not think I want to go where they are going." She did not go that way.

A mother of three husky little boys had never deemed it necessary to give them any religious instruction. Oh, yes, she fed them well-balanced meals, kept them as clean as little boys can be kept, and saw that the bedtime was strictly observed. But one day she pondered thus: "I wonder if I am a really good mother. There seems to be much more to raising a family than merely feeding and clothing them. I seem to have time for my bridge club and our social engagements in the evening, but maybe I am neglecting some very important points."[13] She did something about it.

Lives can be changed, can they not? The course of our lives can be rerouted, but how? Let us call it preparing our hearts.

Well, what does preparing one's heart mean? It means checking up on oneself, scrutinizing one's daily life to see what is there, to see what is there of value and what should be thrown out. It means humbling oneself before the Lord. It means ridding oneself of bitterness and selfishness. It means complete forgiveness of all wrongs inflicted upon us, real or imagined. It means opening wide one's heart to righteousness, putting oneself in an attitude to receive good. It means clothing one's life differently.

Picture in your mind a field, plowed and harrowed from end to end, leveled near perfectly; weeds burned down along the fence line; everything possible done that is conducive to the growth of good seed. We can put our hearts in that very same condition, in an attitude of receptiveness to good. We can plow under the old useless habits and smooth down the rough places of error, but we hear someone say: "I wish I could enjoy working in the church like Mrs. So-and-so does. I wish I could enjoy living the gospel like she does."

They can. It is all in the set of the heart. It is all in preparing one's heart to want that sort of living. We hear other people say: "But I don't see how you ever get the time for it all."

In one of our recent Relief Society conventions a bishop said something that I think is very important for us to remember. It was this: "If you are too busy to serve the Lord, you are too busy."

Yes, if we are too busy to serve the Lord, we are too busy doing other things that are not worthwhile.

In the Old Testament we read this: "For Ezra had prepared his heart to seek the law of the Lord and to do it. . . . For Ezra had prepared his heart to seek the law of the Lord and to do it."[14]

What a lovely ideal for us to work to.

And in the Doctrine and Covenants the Lord said to the Prophet Joseph Smith: "Therefore, prepare thine heart to receive and obey the instructions which I am about to give unto you."[15]

I believe preparing one's heart is perhaps the most decisive point in progress toward any goal. True, the carrying out of our plans is important too, but once our hearts are fully and staunchly prepared, the action is comparatively easy. Like the poem says: "It is the set of the soul that determines the goal."[16]

And I fully believe that as far as living the gospel is concerned, we can do what we want to do, if we want to enough.

Now, in Relief Society we have much help in preparing our hearts for righteousness. We have much help in our wonderful lessons and in our work-day activity, and we not only have help in preparing our own hearts to live, but we have an opportunity to help prepare the hearts of others. Visiting teaching is a wonderful opportunity to help bring back those who are not as active as they should be, little by little, into greater activity in the gospel.

We know that living the gospel means sharing it with others, and visiting teaching is indeed a challenge in sharing the gospel. True, it takes great preparation, great thought and tact and wisdom, and I am quite sure that visiting teaching has not as yet reached its full possibility.

Recently I heard a bishop make a very urgent plea for the Relief Society members to put their arms around our sisters who have drifted away and estranged themselves from the church because they married outside the church. We certainly should endeavor to draw these sisters near to us and, through sheer love and personal interest, make them feel wanted, and that they belong and are needed in our organization.

Remember, if you are too busy to serve the Lord, you are too busy. Prepare your heart to seek the law of the Lord and to do it, and in every way possible help others to prepare their hearts for righteousness. I pray to our Heavenly Father that he will help us to plan the course of our lives in the straight and narrow path, and that we may diligently pursue that course, and I ask it, in the name of Jesus Christ, amen.

Leone O. Jacobs, "Prepare Thy Heart," Sept. 29, 1949, 246–251, in Relief Society Annual Conference Proceedings, 1945–1975, CHL; see also Leone O. Jacobs, "Prepare Thy Heart," Sept. 29, 1949, in "General Session," Relief Society Magazine *36, no. 12 (Dec. 1949): 819–820.*

CULTIVATING LIFE'S ETERNAL VALUES

◇◇◇

MARY J. WILSON

Relief Society General Conference
Tabernacle, Temple Square, Salt Lake City, Utah
September 29, 1949

Mary Jacobs Wilson (1896–1990) had substantial experience serving in the Relief Society when she was appointed to the general board in November 1946.[1] She had been president of two ward Relief Societies, a counselor in two stake Relief Societies, and stake Relief Society president, all in the Ogden, Utah, area.[2] Wilson and her husband, David, had five children.[3] When welcoming her to the Relief Society general board, fellow board member Maureen C. Neilsen described the home the Wilsons had created as possessing "welcome hospitality, music, laughter, humor, and the Spirit of the Lord."[4] Wilson had studied music and drama at Weber College and served as a student body vice president.[5]

Wilson served on the Relief Society board during the early years of Belle S. Spafford's presidency, along with sixteen other women (not including four presidency members).[6] In addition to serving on the music, literature, and poetry contest committees, she represented the Relief Society on the Women's Legislative Council, which studied state problems and legislative issues. In December 1946, the Relief Society was put in charge of developing the family home evening program with the assistance of its advisors in the Quorum of the Twelve, Joseph Fielding Smith and Mark E. Petersen.[7] Wilson chaired the Relief Society home evening committee. When Wilson began her service, board members were just completing fund-raising efforts to build a Relief Society building.[8]

During the years after World War II, many Americans, including Latter-day Saints in the Mountain West, enjoyed expanding professional and educational opportunities.

The postwar era also saw increased emphasis on a vision of the nuclear family that included distinct roles for women and men. Even though many Americans experienced rising prosperity, others—particularly racial and ethnic minorities—met barriers that hindered their economic movement. Neighborhoods and schools were segregated, and institutionalized racism prevented upward mobility.[9] These social and cultural changes after World War II form the context in which Wilson gave the following talk on prioritizing eternal salvation over wealth.

MY DEAR BRETHREN AND SISTERS, as a text for my message today I have taken verse seven from the 6th section of the Doctrine and Covenants: "Seek not for riches but for wisdom, and behold, the mysteries of God shall be unfolded unto you, and then shall you be made rich. Behold, he that hath eternal life is rich."

The most important responsibility resting upon any individual is to build a worthwhile and meaningful life. This objective is not achieved in a day, a week, or a month. In the words of J. G. Holland:

> Heaven is not gained at a single bound;
> But we build the ladder by which we rise
> From the lowly earth to the vaulted skies,
> And we mount to its summit round by round.[10]

With every person is born the God-given assignment to build a life. What then are the materials that we should use in building this worthwhile life?

America's great inspirational poet, Henry Wadsworth Longfellow, caught the vision:

> For the structure that we raise,
> Time is with materials filled;
> Our todays and yesterdays,
> Are the blocks with which we build.[11]

Nothing enduring can be built without a pattern or a plan. We must have purpose and direction in our building. What is the great plan by which we shape our lives? We, as Relief Society sisters, know the answer, for it is to know and to do the will of our Heavenly Father. "God," in the words of Tolstoy, "is he without whom we cannot live."[12]

Our time, our energy, and our means are limited, so we are of necessity confronted with the responsibility of making choices. How necessary it is, therefore, that we develop a pattern of life containing imperishable values and that we build them into the structure of our individual lives.

May I suggest some of the eternal qualities for which we must strive. They are sincere and abiding faith, prayer, interest in and love for our fellow men, and sincere devotion to our Heavenly Father's plan for the achievement of eternal life.

Faith is that which gives you vision to carry on and confidence in ultimate success, even in the face of personal discouragement. It is well to recall the story of Marie Curie.[13] How she worked or struggled, and went on and on, not letting any adversity defeat her in her plan, for she had faith; she knew that someday the goal for which she was working would be achieved.

In First Nephi, seventeenth chapter, we learn that Nephi was commanded to build a great ship. His brothers ridiculed him and laughed at him and called him fool, but he stood up before them and said: "If God had commanded me to do all things, I could do them. If he should command me that I should say unto this water, be thou earth, it should be earth; and if I should say it, it would be done."[14]

Such implicit faith.

Through faith we have the power to be selective, to know the wheat from the chaff. It was this kind of faith that made it possible for our pioneer forefathers to give up everything of a material nature and to turn to religion, and then to build this great western empire of ours.

In speaking of faith, I enjoy thinking back over the years to the faith possessed by my father and mother. One of our little brothers was taken suddenly ill. My father was not at home, but mother called her seven other children into that room where he was lying ill and we all knelt around his bed.[15] I do not now remember the words that mother spoke, but I do remember the feeling that was there, for she spoke to our Heavenly Father as if he were really present with us, and not one of us had a doubt but that mother's prayer would be answered, and it was, for that same evening our little brother was up again and playing with us.

Blessed indeed is the home, blessed are the children, who have parents with such implicit faith, the kind of faith that lifts us over the discouraging experiences of life, the kind of faith that enables us to project ourselves toward eternal goals and to see life's experiences in their eternal setting.

There is no more important element in building faith than prayer. It is the means of getting closer to God, and through this medium we learn his will. Do we always, though, say meaningful prayers, or are they a matter of habit and routine with us? The prayers that will enrich our souls and give us new vision and faith are the prayers through which we open our souls completely to God, with a faith and confidence that he will give us strength to face and overcome the things that are keeping us from achieving true spiritual growth, which is the destiny of all God's children, particularly each Latter-day Saint, who are entitled, if they live righteously, to the direction of the Holy Spirit.

An elder in the Uruguayan Mission recently told of a visit he had with an elderly Spanish couple. At their first meeting he told them of his being able to express his inner feelings and his ideas to God each time it was his turn to take part in family prayer. These people had only been able in their church to say a memorized prayer and one that they did not understand. They became very interested through this conversation and in a very short time were baptized members of our church.

Faith and prayer, however, cannot function in our lives in an effective way merely as abstract principles. In James we are told that faith without works is dead.[16] We must, therefore, reflect our faith in our service and love for our fellow men. The Savior himself said: "He that has served his fellow men has served his Heavenly Father."[17] One of the greatest statements in the Bible concerning the Savior is that he went around doing good.[18]

When service is mentioned, we are prone to cast about for an opportunity to serve in some big way in remote places. Our tendency is to forget the acres of diamonds lying around our own doors, in the same community or on the same block—or, perhaps, in our same households are those who are discouraged and impoverished for the want of words of love and words of hope.[19] There are those who are spiritually sick as well as those who are mentally and physically ill. On the whole, our fields of service lie within those acres about our own homes.

Two visiting teachers on one of their visits found a sister crushed with grief. She had passed through great sorrow, and she had lost faith in herself and faith in God. This afflicted sister had passed through a great deal, and these visiting teachers had a newly found interest in this unfortunate sister. They visited her often. They knew that they must in some way create an interest for living within that sister's heart. They must also rekindle within her a love for her God and faith in herself. This was accomplished, and this is only one example of true love and service that comes from our visiting teaching. There are thousands of such cases where people have been helped within our own Relief Society organization.

We must remember that no one ever finds life worth living. It has to be made worth living.

The true meaning of love is given to us in the 11th chapter of First Nephi, 21st to 23rd verses. The angel was speaking to Nephi and he said:

"Behold the Lamb of God, yea, even the Son of the Eternal Father! Knowest thou the meaning of the tree which thy father saw? And I answered him saying: Yea, it is the love of God, which sheddeth itself abroad in the hearts of the children of men; wherefore, it is the most desirable above all things. And he spake unto me, saying: Yea, and the most joyous to the soul."

Latter-day Saints have a marvelous concept of the meaning and necessity of growth through acquisition of knowledge. In the 18th and 19th verses of the 130th section of the Doctrine and Covenants we read: "Whatever principle of intelligence we attain unto in this life, it will rise with us in the resurrection."

How can we then cultivate knowledge and intelligence in our quest for eternal life? First, we must awaken within us the need for growth, and then we shall find the means and the opportunity for development.

When Michael Pupin, the great inventor, was leaving his home in Hungary for America, his mother said to him—she was blind because she could not read and write, and said she: "My boy, if you wish to go out into the world you must provide yourself with another pair of eyes, the eyes of reading and writing. There is so much wonderful knowledge and learning in the world which you cannot get unless you study." And then she concluded by saying: "Knowledge is the golden ladder over which we climb to heaven."[20]

We not only gain knowledge through the study of great books, but through prayer we also find ways and means of development. Let us not waste time.

Benjamin Franklin said: "Dost thou love life? Then do not squander time, for that is what life is made of."[21]

One often hears this expression: "If I just had time to do this or that," but we overlook what can be accomplished by small snatches of time. The late Charles W. Eliot of Harvard compiled the Harvard Classics as an answer to his claim that anyone could become well educated by spending fifteen minutes a day in intelligent study.[22]

Be ever alert to your opportunities. Study. Seek good companions. Insist upon filling your life with eternal riches. You have a great birthright. You live in a land choice above all others.[23] You have accepted as a pattern of life the gospel of Jesus Christ. Your opportunities are unbounded, but only you can fashion your individual lives into glorious eternal mansions.

May God bless all of us that we may get the vision necessary to see life at its best, and give us the strength to live according to an eternal pattern, is my humble prayer, in the name of Jesus, amen.

Mary J. Wilson, "Cultivating Life's Eternal Values," Sept. 29, 1949, in Relief Society Annual Conference Proceedings, 1945–1975, 238–246, CHL; see also Mary J. Wilson, "Cultivating Life's Eternal Values," Sept. 29, 1949, in "General Session," Relief Society Magazine *36, no. 12 (Dec. 1949): 817–819.*

GAINING KNOWLEDGE AND INTELLIGENCE

◇◇◇

MARIANNE C. SHARP

Relief Society General Conference
Assembly Hall, Temple Square, Salt Lake City, Utah
September 27, 1950

Growing up in Washington DC, Marianne Clark Sharp (1901–1990) had limited access to church gatherings—twice-monthly sacrament meetings were held at the home of apostle and United States senator Reed Smoot. Clark attended these meetings with her parents, Luacine and J. Reuben Clark Jr., and three siblings. Later she recalled, "We didn't have much formal study of the church, but it was just in the very air we breathed that we didn't do some things that other people did and that our roots were here in the West."[1] Yet she would heavily influence others' formal church experience. She began editing the *Relief Society Magazine* in 1943 and was editor in chief from 1945 to 1970.[2] She also helped to compile and edit *A Centenary of Relief Society,* which the Relief Society general board published in 1942.[3] And as first counselor in the Relief Society general presidency from 1945 to 1974, she oversaw curriculum, which changed substantially during her tenure.[4]

Sharp began amassing the editorial expertise needed for such projects early on: she edited the yearbook and the school paper before graduating as valedictorian from Western High School in Georgetown, Virginia.[5] In a 1977 interview, she noted the ways she felt God had guided her life and remarked, "If you do everything that you're asked to do eventually you keep building on to the next thing. That's why it's important to accept things."[6] She majored in ancient languages at the University of Utah, graduating with high honors in 1924 and receiving a teaching fellowship in Latin. After her marriage to Ivor Sharp in 1927, she lived in New York City for eleven years, where she chaired the Queens Branch genealogical committee and worked in the Relief Society.[7]

Marianne Sharp also represented the Relief Society on the National Woman's Radio Committee (NWRC).[8] The NWRC was organized in 1934 in response to radio soap operas, quiz shows, and an increasing dearth of educational programming. The women on the committee oversaw efforts to improve programming, including establishing the first radio programming awards. Committee members included representatives from the country's largest women's organizations and from diverse faith backgrounds: the National Council of Women, the National Women's Christian Temperance Union, the United Council of Church Women, Catholic Daughters of America, the National Council of Jewish Women, and others.[9] Relief Society representatives continued to attend meetings despite other members' prejudices against Latter-day Saints. For example, Sharp recalled a meeting when the committee called on every participating organization to give a report—except for the Relief Society.[10]

Sharp and her family returned to Salt Lake City in 1938, when she began work with Kate Barker on the Relief Society's Mormon Handicrafts Giftshop committee, and she was then appointed to serve on the Relief Society general board in 1940.[11] She accepted the position of first counselor to the new Relief Society general president, Belle S. Spafford, in 1945 and served until Spafford's release in 1974.[12] Sharp and Spafford learned from Sharp's research that the Relief Society had long sought to have its own building; a building then became one of the primary goals of the new presidency. Sharp wrote asking for five dollars from each Relief Society member in the church, except those from countries most devastated by the war.[13] She also encouraged ward Relief Societies to raise funds through bazaars and other means when individual members could not pay. In one year, ending October 1948, they raised $554,000, exceeding their goal of half a million dollars. Sharp also worked on the welfare committee and chaired the Relief Society general conference committee.[14] Sharp had been first counselor for five years when she shared the following insights on the relationship between intelligence and obedience during a Relief Society general conference meeting for stake and mission officers and board members in Temple Square's Assembly Hall.

MY BELOVED SISTERS, I pray that the Spirit of the Lord may be with me for the few minutes that I shall speak this morning and that I may have an interest in your faith and prayers.

We are now living in the midst of eternity, and we are enjoying those blessings to which we were entitled because of our faithfulness in the spirit world, and we are told that if we are true and faithful in this mortal existence, if we keep this, our second estate, that we will have glory added upon our heads forever and ever.[15]

Modern revelation tells us that the glory of God is intelligence,[16] and that as God is now, man may become.[17]

Wherefore every one of us should heed these words of the Lord found in section 131 of the Doctrine and Covenants, which say: "Whatever principle of intelligence we attain unto in this life, it will rise with us in the resurrection. And if a person gains more knowledge and intelligence in this life through his diligence and obedience than another, he will have so much the advantage in the world to come."[18]

Sisters, what do these words mean to us—mothers of Zion and officers in the Relief Society? Do they mean that those of us who may have had the opportunity of earning a college degree have thereby gained the advantage in the world to come, have earned sufficient knowledge and intelligence? Not as I read the scriptures. For if that were the case, then the Lord would have the learned men of the world as his chosen prophets.

There were many erudite scholars upon this land and in the world when the Lord gave that first glorious vision to that untutored lad of fourteen, Joseph Smith. You will remember that a few years later when the Prophet was translating the Book of Mormon, that Martin Harris was allowed to take a copy of part of the characters and the translation and show them to a learned man, Professor Anthon. You will recall the conclusion of that.[19] In foretelling this incident in the Book of Mormon it says, "Then shall the Lord God say unto him [meaning Joseph Smith]: The learned shall not read them, for they have rejected them, and I am able to do my own work; wherefore thou shalt read the words which I shall give unto thee."[20]

You will also recall that God hath taken the weak things of the earth to overcome those things which are mighty, wherefore I would conclude that a so-called higher education is not necessary for the gaining of knowledge and intelligence.

But if we are to travel the path of eternal progression we must be ever seeking and gaining knowledge and intelligence, for the Prophet Joseph said, "A man is saved no faster than he gets knowledge,"[21] and the Lord declares, "It is impossible for a man to be saved in ignorance."[22]

Since, then, knowledge and intelligence are the doorway into eternal life, how zealous we here today should be as Relief Society officers to see that we are ever gaining knowledge and intelligence. Probably a devotion of all our free time to such a pursuit would not give us the advantage in the world to come without diligent study. Then, how careful we should be that we do not fritter away our time in unfruitful pursuits, but that we take our time in giving it to a devotion of studying knowledge and intelligence, thereby to gain it.

And how difficult it is as mothers for us to study. Not for us the ivory tower nor the secluded cloister. We must study while our family affairs proceed normally, with one interruption to care for a child, and another one to stir the pot on the fire, and a third to answer the doorbell or telephone. Then how necessary it is that we should choose the right things when we study. And what should we study? In section 88 of the Doctrine and Covenants, the Lord gives us a list of some things which we should teach one another. It says, "And I give unto you a commandment that you shall teach one another the doctrine of the kingdom. Teach ye diligently and my grace shall attend you, that you may be instructed more perfectly in theory, in principle, in doctrine, in the law of the gospel, in all things that pertain unto the kingdom of God, that are expedient for you to understand; of things both in heaven and in the earth, and under the earth; things which have been, things which are, things which must shortly come to pass; things which are at home, things which are abroad; the wars and the perplexities of the nations, and the judgments which are on the land; and a knowledge also of countries and of kingdoms."[23]

Sisters, do you see how closely the subject matter which we are studying in Relief Society parallels in part the words of the Lord as to what we should study? How grateful we should be as Relief Society members to have the opportunity to study these lessons which are approved by the Brethren. And what a responsibility is ours, those of us who are here in this building this morning, to see that we are overseeing and encouraging and exhorting the sisters to teach them diligently one to another. But sisters, all the diligent study in the world is not sufficient for us to gain knowledge and intelligence, for we are told not only to gain it through diligence, but through obedience. Obedience to what? Obedience to the commandments of God, and we will gain knowledge and intelligence in this way which can be gained in no other way. All the studying of academic learning in the world, and even the studying of righteous principles, won't give us the advantage unless we are obedient to the commandments of God. We must be obedient. As Paul said, "And though . . . I understand . . . all knowledge . . . and have not charity, I am nothing."[24]

And what are the commandments of God? Nearly two thousand years ago this same question was put to the Savior, who answered, you all know the answer: "Thou shalt love the Lord thy God with all thy heart, and with all thy soul, and with all thy mind. This is the first and great commandment. And the second is like unto it, Thou shalt love thy neighbor as thyself."[25]

By obedience to these commandments, sisters, we will gain knowledge and intelligence.

Brigham Young said, "To live the gospel requires time, faith, the heart's affections, and a great deal of labor."[26] Sisters, are you not gaining knowledge and intelligence through your labors in clothing the naked, preparing food for the hungry, nursing the sick, comforting the sorrowing, and pouring balm on the disconsolate heart? Is that not your great work in this Relief Society? Does not Relief Society then give you the opportunity, both through diligence and obedience, to earn knowledge and intelligence? The Lord knew the kind of an organization which was needed upon this earth to perfect his daughters. And what a responsibility is ours to see that every Latter-day Saint woman will be given this opportunity of gaining knowledge and intelligence. And the Lord is never in our debt. As we labor mightily for the good of our sisters, as we labor for the good of ourselves, he pours forth saving knowledge and intelligence on our heads.

Sisters, I would like to bear my testimony to the work of Relief Society. There is nothing except the work which we do in our own homes which will bring us the blessings we may gain through our devotion and laboring mightily for Relief Society. And it is my prayer that each one of us here will realize the twofold objectives in Relief Society which will give us knowledge and intelligence, and that each one here will go home with a determination to see that the lessons in Relief Society are taught diligently, and to see that all sisters are given the opportunity to labor mightily for the Lord and for our own saving knowledge and intelligence. And this I pray in the name of Jesus Christ, amen.

Marianne C. Sharp, "Gaining Knowledge and Intelligence," Sept. 27, 1950, 4–8, in Relief Society Annual Conference Proceedings, 1945–1975, CHL; see also Marianne C. Sharp, "Gaining Knowledge and Intelligence," Sept. 27, 1950, Morning Session, in "Departmental Meeting," Relief Society Magazine *37, no. 12 (Dec. 1950): 812–814.*

UNTO THE LEAST OF THESE

◇◇◇

MARGARET C. PICKERING

Relief Society General Conference
Tabernacle, Temple Square, Salt Lake City, Utah
September 28, 1950

Margaret Aird Cummock Pickering (1891–1976) spent much of her life organizing and coordinating the work essential to institutions, serving as secretary or secretary-treasurer for several organizations. Born and raised in Salt Lake City, she attended Latter-day Saints University, the Utah Agricultural College, and the University of Utah.[1] She contributed to church programs long before serving on the Relief Society general board. First, she worked for the Young Men's Mutual Improvement Association, whose headquarters were in the Bishop's Building, down a long hall from the Relief Society offices. Then she worked for several years in the editorial department of the *Improvement Era,* an official church magazine, which was housed in the same building.[2] In 1917, she married Harold W. Pickering.[3] Before joining the Relief Society general board in October 1945, she also served as secretary-treasurer of both the Salt Lake City South Eighteenth Ward Relief Society and the Ensign Stake Relief Society.[4]

An avid participant in service work, Pickering volunteered for several local and state agencies in Salt Lake City both before and after joining the general board. She was the first executive secretary of the Woman's Civic Center, the first secretary of the Utah State Society for Mental Hygiene, a member of the executive committee of Community Chest, and for ten years, including during World War II, director of the Salt Lake County chapter of the American Red Cross.[5] During her tenure as Relief Society general secretary-treasurer from 1945 to 1956, Pickering managed a heavy load of correspondence and traveled throughout the church to attend stake Relief Society conventions.[6]

Pickering's Relief Society service work came during the early years of the Cold War, a time marked by fear and insecurity. Three months before Pickering gave this speech, the United States entered the Korean War. From a military standpoint, the country was not prepared to fight a war in Korea. Many veterans had resigned from military service at the end of World War II, leaving the armed forces understaffed. Seeking to save money, the Pentagon was slow to hire replacements, and the new personnel were inexperienced.[7] The government responded to this crisis with the unpopular announcement that it planned to draft eighty thousand men per month for the first three months of 1951.[8] The Korean War also increased American fears about communism and communist sympathizers.[9] This threatening atmosphere was the backdrop when Pickering gave the following speech about compassionate service in the Salt Lake Tabernacle during a Relief Society general conference.

MY DEAR BROTHERS AND SISTERS: The title of this talk that I am to give this afternoon is taken from Matthew, the 25th chapter, and refers to the last judgment when the Son of Man shall come in all his glory and all nations shall be gathered before him, and he shall separate them one from another as a shepherd divideth his sheep from the goats, and he shall say to those on his right hand,

> Come, ye blessed of my Father, inherit the kingdom prepared for you from the foundation of the world:
>
> For I was an hungred, and ye gave me meat: I was thirsty, and ye gave me drink: I was a stranger, and ye took me in:
>
> Naked, and ye clothed me: I was sick, and ye visited me: I was in prison, and ye came unto me.
>
> Then shall the righteous answer him, saying, Lord, when saw we thee an hungred and fed thee? or thirsty, and gave thee drink?
>
> When saw we thee a stranger, and took thee in? or naked, and clothed thee?
>
> Or when saw we thee sick, or in prison, and came unto thee?
>
> And the King shall answer and say unto them, Verily I say unto you, Inasmuch as ye have done it unto one of the least of these my brethren, ye have done it unto me.[10]

During the 108 years of Relief Society's existence, compassionate service—the tender, love-inspired ministrations which women, by their very natures, are peculiarly fitted to perform—has been an integral part of its program.[11] In fact, Relief Society had its inception in concern for the welfare of the immediate group in which the Saints lived and, from that time to the present, Relief Society has given the world a testament of faith that it sorely needs—a great, practical demonstration of brotherly love through its millions of friendly visits bearing cheerful and faith-promoting messages, through its care of the aged, needy, sick, and homebound, and through sympathetic service at the time of death. Emphasis has been placed on various aspects of this service over the years, according to the needs of the times. In the early years of Relief Society's existence, both in Nauvoo and later in the West, caring for the physical or temporal needs of the Saints was of paramount importance—making clothing and bedding, caring for the sick, and sharing scarce provisions—for limited crops and severe weather on the frontier made this necessary. But throughout these years, the spiritual needs were not forgotten, and as the wilderness was conquered and temporal needs became less acute, Relief Society continued to minister to the spiritual needs of the sisters. Up until the time the welfare plan was inaugurated, through which the temporal needs of the Saints are met, Relief Society continued to directly supply some of the temporal needs of the Saints, under the direction of the bishops.[12] During the last decade, however, Relief Society's efforts have been transferred from directly supplying such needs to assisting in producing welfare assignments and to more extensively ministering to the spiritual hungers of women.

All this is a testimony to me of the divine origin of this organization—that it is set up to serve how, when, and where it is most needed. Never in the history of civilization have more people of all ages and in all lands felt more restless, insecure, confused, afraid. Never has the world had greater need for a testament of faith through practical demonstrations of brotherly love. Relief Society has a great opportunity now. It does not do much good to talk about such big things as "humanity," "democracy," and the "brotherhood of man" unless we can bring them down and apply them to our next-door neighbor, as that is where international amity and the brotherhood of man begins. The Prophet Joseph said at one of the early meetings of the society: "Let your labors be confined mostly to those around you in your own circle."[13]

Relief Society, through precept and example for over a hundred years, has sought to help us develop the forces in our own natures through which we may enrich the lives of others and, in doing so, enrich our own lives. And to the extent that we as individuals have actively engaged in ministering "unto the least of these," to that extent has the organization through the individual been strengthened. While Relief Society officially records only those visits and services authorized by the president, it is aware of the fact that only the Master himself can note many of the heartwarming and soul-satisfying services rendered by our sisters, and it is about these services over and above the call of duty that I speak specifically.[14]

While visiting teachers through their monthly visits have unusual opportunities to discover persons in need of special attention and to discern ways to give help, there are in every neighborhood many aged, sick, lonely, or disturbed people who lack for no temporal needs—some members of the church, some not, but they need friendly interest, assurance, peace of mind. No one is better fitted to minister to their needs than friendly, faithful Latter-day Saint neighbors—Relief Society members backed by a tradition of a century of sympathetic service and understanding to inspire and guide them. President Spafford has referred to compassionate service as the "heartbeat of Relief Society—the kind word, the ray of hope, the warm handclasp."[15] It is the constant stimulation of this heartbeat through sincerity and frequency of application that increases the circulation of hope, cheer, brotherly love, and faith in God in the world today, and produces a warm, peaceful glow in the souls of men in exact proportion to the amount of stimulation applied.

What about the aged women in your neighborhood—some who don't see too well, who would appreciate a cheerful visit, an hour of reading or letter writing, or being escorted to church or to an entertainment? What about the homebound for whom you might run an errand or do some shopping? What about the mother in your neighborhood whose son is called to war and who is depressed, or the young wife whose husband has entered military service and she is confused and upset about the future; or the newcomer who feels strange and lonely, perhaps one of our own converts from a foreign land having difficulty with our language and customs, and needs them interpreted?

What about the chronically ill to whom a smiling face and fresh viewpoint would give new hope; a child confined to bed for a long period, such as in the case of rheumatic fever, to whom a cookie, or some simple dessert would bring happiness; what about staying occasionally some afternoon or evening with the children of a neighbor who seldom gets out because she cannot afford a babysitter. There are endless opportunities all around us to demonstrate sisterly love if we but open our eyes to them.

Recently I read a little paragraph on the magic of giving in connection with an article on overcoming loneliness. It read:

> To fight loneliness, you must give of yourself. Do you reach out to others in a friendly, helpful way? Do you make personal sacrifices? Do you visit the sick, do social service work, or otherwise give aid and comfort to those less fortunate than yourself? It is easy to make a money contribution or sign a check, but what does that give of your heart? If you go beyond routine gestures of

> helpfulness, thus establishing a bond of sympathy and affection for others, you cannot possibly be lonely.[16]

Yes, compassionate service benefits and blesses both the one who performs it and the one who receives it. In these times, when homes are being broken and plans being disrupted again by the call of our young men into military service and the specter of war hanging over us, there is great need for an acceleration of our compassionate services, not only as a means of encouraging and aiding our neighbors but to increase our own faith and quell our own fears, so that in following the example of our Savior, we shall be strengthened and can say with David of old, "What time I am afraid, I will trust in thee."[17]

That we may do this is my prayer and I ask it humbly, in the name of Jesus Christ, amen.

Margaret C. Pickering, "Unto the Least of These: Matt. 25:40," Sept. 28, 1950, 119–124, in Relief Society Annual Conference Proceedings, 1945–1975, CHL; see also Margaret C. Pickering, "Unto the Least of These," Sept. 28, 1950, in "General Session," Relief Society Magazine *37, no. 12 (Dec. 1950): 831–832.*

Relief Society General Conference. 1962. The first Relief Society general conference was held in 1889. This photograph of the Salt Lake Tabernacle shows a large crowd at one of the sessions of the October 1962 conference, at which Louise W. Madsen spoke. Photograph by Ross Welser. (Church History Library, Salt Lake City.)

UNION OF FEELING

◇◇◇

LOUISE W. MADSEN

Relief Society General Conference
Tabernacle, Temple Square, Salt Lake City, Utah
October 3, 1962

Life experience led Elen Louise Wallace Madsen (1909–1987) to develop the organizational, homemaking, and intellectual skills she would use during her service on the Relief Society general board. Beginning when she was thirteen years old, Madsen helped to raise her four younger siblings after her father died.[1] She graduated from LDS High School, then took courses in English, history, literature, and law at the University of Utah.[2] On June 1, 1928, she married Francis Madsen, and together the two established the Madsen Furniture Company, first in Ogden, Utah, and later expanding to Salt Lake City. Also while in Ogden, Louise Madsen hosted a radio program.[3] Her early church service included teaching seminary, leading the Gleaner Girls, and teaching literature and theology classes in the Relief Society.[4] She was also the Emigration Stake Relief Society president.[5] Madsen began her service on the Relief Society general board in December 1947, and by the time she became a second counselor to Belle S. Spafford in the Relief Society general presidency on August 11, 1958, she had served on many general board committees.[6]

Madsen's work in the presidency included directing homemaking activities (called work meetings until October 1966) and overseeing both the temple clothing department and the Mormon Handicraft Shop.[7] She oversaw a yearlong course of study inspired by the Red Cross home nursing program to educate Relief Society members in home nursing skills.[8] She also supervised the creation of a nursery program, which the Relief Society established to enable more young mothers to attend Relief Society meetings, to provide learning opportunities for young children, and to create service opportunities for Relief Society members who either supervised or volunteered in the nursery.[9] Madsen traveled around the world to instruct various Relief Societies and represented the Relief Society at the National Council of Women.[10] Many of Madsen's speeches and articles, for which she was celebrated, appeared in the *Relief Society Magazine* and the *Church News*.[11]

By the early 1960s, the United States was entangled in conflicts both internal and external. Awareness of racial violence in the United States had increased substantially during the late 1950s, following media coverage of a number of high-profile acts of violence against the African American community.[12] In 1962, the United States was also on the brink of war with the Soviet Union over the placement of ballistic missiles in Cuba.[13] During this period of heightened fears and disputes, Madsen spoke on how God rewards unity with power at a Relief Society conference in the Salt Lake Tabernacle in 1962.

MY DEAR BROTHERS AND SISTERS, just before he entered the Garden of Gethsemane on the night of his betrayal, the Lord "lifted up his eyes unto heaven"[14] and prayed to the Father. President McKay has spoken of this prayer as "the greatest, most impressive prayer ever uttered in this world."[15] His prayer was for those who had believed on him and for "them also which shall believe on" him. A sublime message contained therein is in this verse: "That they all may be one; as thou, Father, art in me, and I in thee, that they also may be one in us."[16]

This is a most beautiful expression of the principle of unity. It is this principle of unity, this spirit of being "one," with each other and with our God, which has been instrumental in enabling the church to progress and to accomplish the purposes for which it was established.

One of the statements of the Prophet Joseph Smith to Relief Society which has great and continuing significance is "By union of feeling we obtain power with God."[17] This is an expression of the principle of unity which shows how it works to fulfill purposes. He urged the sisters to obtain power from on high by being "one" in spirit and determination to do the work he would have them do. The fact that they have done so is attested by the growth and accomplishment of Relief Society throughout the world. Separation by vast expanses of land and oceans of water does not change or diminish the feeling for, or necessity of, "oneness." A quarter of a million women unified in feeling and purpose, seeking power from our Heavenly Father in righteousness, can exert a tremendous power for good wherever they may be.

What is this power we may obtain? Since it derives from our unity with God our Father and his son Jesus Christ, is it not in the words of Micah "to do what is good, to do what the Lord requires of us, to do justly and to walk humbly with our God"?[18] Is it not the privilege to serve we seek, the moving force of compassion to feel? Is it not the power of God-given strength and his blessing of knowledge we cherish? Is it not the power of unselfish thought and action, selflessness, the ability to rise above fault-finding and petty-mindedness we desire? The power to be instrumental in saving souls has been accorded to Relief Society. To build firm testimonies to the divinity of the Savior and of the gospel is our ultimate purpose. Charity, the true love of Christ, is our guiding principle.[19]

We are again reminded that these aspects of power are derived through "union of feeling," "union of feeling" among ourselves and with our Heavenly Father. This kind of unity cannot be successfully maintained with less than the best from each other. Dissatisfaction with mere mediocrity enhances the ability of the organization to use this heaven-given power to its fullest extent. Our vision and aim must be exalted and the integrity of purpose and dependability of each member must be heightened.

Those to whom power is given must assume the responsibilities that accompany it. One of these is wise leadership. To guide, persuade, and direct aright,[20] to fortify in righteousness, to educate and to give impetus to courageous action are facets of leadership for which Relief Society women are trained.[21] The strength of an organization dedicating itself to good, fitting itself for what needs to be done, and thoroughly believing that its work is basically and spiritually right, is the strength required of us by the Lord. Each Relief Society, no matter how small, no matter how isolated, must participate in this "union of feeling."

Paul, in his epistle to the Romans, speaks of the "mutual faith both of you and me,"[22] and beseeches his brethren to "strive together"[23] in all that must be done. He warns them to avoid "divisions and offences contrary to the doctrine."[24] A number of the sisters he singled out for special commendation:

> I commend unto you Phebe our sister, which is a servant of the Church at Cenchrea:
>
> That ye receive her in the Lord, as becometh saints, and that ye assist her in whatsoever business she hath need of you: for she hath been a succourer of many, and of myself also.
>
> Greet Priscilla and Aquila my helpers in Jesus Christ:
>
> Who have for my life laid down their own necks: unto whom not only I give thanks, but also all the churches of the Gentiles . . .
>
> Greet Mary, who bestowed much labour upon us . . .

> Salute Tryphena and Tryphosa, who labour in the Lord. Salute the beloved Persis, which laboured much in the Lord.[25]

That kind of commendation can also be given to many individual women in this dispensation. Great numbers of the sisters holding office in the society could be described in the words of Paul as having "laboured much in the Lord."[26] But it is the society as a whole, as an auxiliary of the church, receiving power from God by "union of feeling," which best serves to do the work he would have an organization of his daughters do.

Beautiful are the bonds of sisterhood! Uplifting are the ties of friendship. Glorious is the work of thousands of sisters unified in righteous purpose. Humbling is the realization that it is the Lord's work we are to do.

May he bless us with the desire to approach him in "union of feeling," and be one as Christ prayed his followers would be, I pray in the name of Jesus Christ, amen.

Louise W. Madsen, Discourse, Oct. 3, 1962, 44–46, in Relief Society Annual Conference Proceedings, 1945–1975, CHL; see also Louise W. Madsen, "Union of Feeling," Oct. 3, 1962, in "General Session," Relief Society Magazine *49, no. 11 (Nov. 1962): 804–805.*

MY YOKE IS EASY AND MY BURDEN IS LIGHT

◇◇◇

ALICE C. SMITH

Relief Society General Conference
Tabernacle, Temple Square, Salt Lake City, Utah
October 1, 1969

Alice Colton Smith (1913–2006) brought a cosmopolitan and scholarly perspective to the Relief Society general board. Smith moved from Vernal, Utah, to Washington DC after her father, Don B. Colton, was elected to the United States House of Representatives in 1921. Upon her graduation from Columbia University in 1934, she married bacteriologist-in-training Whitney Smith. Whitney completed his graduate education at the University of Wisconsin, and the Smiths then moved to southern California for his teaching job. They relocated in 1946 to Utah State University in Logan, Utah, where Alice earned a master's degree in sociology and subsequently joined the faculty.[1] She became an assistant professor and taught at Utah State until the mid-1970s, when she resigned so she could focus more on her general board work.[2]

Two major international experiences complemented the Smiths' academic careers. First, they lived in Israel from 1953 to 1954, where Alice Smith served as chair of the Embassy Committee on Israeli-American relations while her husband worked as research advisor in bacteriology to the Israeli government.[3] When they returned to Utah, Governor George D. Clyde appointed Smith to the Utah State Textbook and Curriculum Committee, where she served from 1958 to 1960.[4] From 1960 to 1963 they lived in Vienna, where they established the first Latter-day Saint mission headquartered in Austria, serving as mission president and Relief Society mission president.[5] When they returned, Governor Calvin L. Rampton appointed Smith to the Utah Committee for the White House Conference on the Family.[6] She joined the Relief

Society general board in 1964, serving for fourteen years under presidents Belle S. Spafford and Barbara B. Smith.[7]

Joseph Fielding Smith, then president of the Quorum of the Twelve Apostles, set Smith apart for her Relief Society board work. She recalled that he told her in the blessing, "You have been put upon this board not to be silent. You are to take an active role in everything that occurs." Spafford told Smith that such counsel had never been given to a board member during all the time she had been on the board, and Smith remembered Spafford repeating it at their next board meeting: "Now that really applies to all of you but I want you to know it applies to Alice."[8] Smith's board responsibilities included reviewing, editing, and critiquing Relief Society lessons, which assignment made good use of her candor and professional experience.[9] She also wrote the visiting teaching lessons.[10]

Smith believed that loving service was at the heart of following Christ: "I used to protest about 'Patty Perfect' all the time. I used to say that's not real, that's not the real world, nor is it the gospel. They would bring up this perfection and I'd say, yeah, but I think that the Lord meant be perfect in being loved. Be loving, kind, and merciful. He wasn't talking about getting up in the morning and combing your hair."[11] In 1979, Smith described herself as belonging "to the school that feels that Jesus was not a salesman but a teacher. . . . I believe that he was there to create behavioral changes that were permanent."[12]

Smith gave the following talk on visiting teaching at an officers' session of Relief Society general conference in the Salt Lake Tabernacle. The practice that came to be known as visiting teaching began when visiting committees in Nauvoo, Illinois, were formed in the spring of 1843. Committee members visited families both to identify and to supply their needs. They also visited church members to ask for donations. As part of the reestablishment of the Relief Society in Utah in 1868, Sarah M. Kimball and Eliza R. Snow drafted a document that further developed the responsibilities of teachers, adding that they should visit persons on their assigned blocks once per month.[13] The Relief Society general board began providing a uniform message for visiting teachers in 1921, and visiting teachers stopped collecting charity funds in 1944.[14] Smith composed visiting teaching messages for the year beginning in October 1969 under the theme "truths to live by" and focused them on messages from the Book of Mormon, "a shining light in our turbulently troubled times."[15]

> Come unto me, all ye that labour and are heavy laden, and I will give you rest.

> Take my yoke upon you, and learn of me; for I am meek and lowly in heart: and ye shall find rest unto your souls.
> For my yoke is easy, and my burden is light.[16]

ACROSS THE CENTURIES from the shores of the eastern Mediterranean comes this warm invitation from our Savior.

As Jesus climbed the dry hills of Galilee or trod the dusty roads of Judea, he met poverty, disease, afflictions of every kind. He found the sinner repentant and unrepentant. He met the suffering. And out of these experiences and his vast understanding came his compassionate solicitation, "Come unto me."

In 1830, the Prophet Joseph Smith declared that God is "the same unchangeable God."[17] So, it is no surprise that on July 28, 1843, sixteen women were appointed "to search out the poor and suffering . . . to relieve the wants of all."[18] Sixteen in a world of millions. But there had to be a beginning. In 1843, 16 visiting teachers; today, well over 100,000; tomorrow 200,000; the day after tomorrow two million.

A few weeks ago, I met a wonderful friend of mine. She has been active in Relief Society for many years. I love her. I was delighted to see her. I wanted to know all about her. I asked her what she was doing in the church now. There was a noticeable pause. Then, she answered, "Oh, I'm just a visiting teacher." Just a visiting teacher! After we parted, I thought, how would she feel if the Savior came to her next visiting teachers meeting and said to her, "I want you to be my emissary. I want you to tell the women in your district that I love them, that I am concerned about what happens to them and their families. I want you to be my helper, to watch over these sisters, to care for them so that all will be well in my kingdom."[19] If we met after such a meeting, wouldn't her reply be different? Hasn't he already called her through his priesthood as surely as if he stood in her presence?

How many of our visiting teachers think of themselves as "just visiting teachers"?

To the visiting teacher is given the great responsibility of searching out those in need. More, she tells all sisters by her visit that someone cares and that God cares.

The visiting teacher should be the best friend of everyone in her district. Oh, I don't mean the most intimate friend, but the best friend.

I hope everyone here has a best friend, for then you will know what I mean. What is a best friend? It is a friend in whom one can confide and know that her secrets will be safe. It is someone who listens and someone who wants to listen. It is someone who is interested in all that happens to her friend. It is someone who always helps when needed.

When I go to the door and find my best friend standing, waiting to come in, my heart glows. I can't open the door fast enough. I am delighted to see her. I know that she loves me as I love her.

The visiting teacher should evoke such a response in everyone over whom she watches. She should not be someone who rushes in the last day of the month and says, "I've just a few minutes—I know you've read the message and know it better than I do, and you don't need it anyway. How are you, and I'll see you at Relief Society next week." The visiting teacher should leave behind her a love that blesses both the visited sister and her home.

Years ago as I was leaving the chapel after a Relief Society meeting, my visiting teacher stopped me. "Alice," she said, "you have everything you need. I wish I could do something for you."

"You do something for me every month," I replied. "You bring me a message of love. I am comforted and strengthened by your concern for me and my family." But she did not seem entirely satisfied.

Less than two hours later she came to my door. In her hand was a loaf of freshly baked homemade bread. "After I left you today," she said, "I remembered that you told me once that your university duties keep you so busy that you never have time to bake bread. So there is something special I can do for you."

Five years ago we returned to our home after a three-year absence.[20] We were tired from a long overseas journey. We hadn't yet had time to go to the market. Twenty minutes after we walked in there was a knock at our door. There she stood, my visiting teacher (now long since released) with a loaf of freshly baked homemade bread and a jar of raspberry jam. I love the emblem of the Relief Society with its motto, "Charity Never Faileth," but my own private emblem of visiting teaching will always be a loaf of freshly baked homemade bread.[21]

We are "to relieve the wants of all."[22] In our confused and complex world, as in the world of Jesus, there is loneliness, despair, sin, and suffering. Who knows which day we will find them in the homes of our friends? We must be prepared.

Compassion is a way of life. Darlene, young, pretty, charming, the mother of a young baby, developed multiple sclerosis. Swiftly the disease progressed so that she could not take care of her baby. It was at this time that she was visited by two compassionate visiting teachers. "Pour oil and wine to the wounds of the distressed," counseled the Prophet Joseph Smith.[23] They continued to call and help.

Her other friends, at first attentive, began to visit less and less often as the years went on. Her husband deserted her. Darlene grew bitter. She met overtures of help with angry hostile words. Why should she lie helpless when others traveled, played, and worked as they wished? Why should she lie in bed and grow weaker and weaker? She railed against her fate. As she did, her friends ceased to come.

One of the visiting teachers moved away. The other was released, but her loving care did not stop. Through the years this dedicated ex-visiting teacher visited frequently, offering her continuing help. She saw through Darlene's angry, bitter words. Even when they were directed at her, she did not forsake the hurt and suffering one.

Recently Darlene's family moved to Utah. Darlene, now completely bedridden and still under forty, moved here also. Was that the end of her old visiting teacher's care? No. A long distance telephone call to a member of the visiting teacher's family in Utah: "Please visit Darlene. Let her know that I think of her and love her. Please go and see her whenever you can."

Compassion is a way of life. Years of care and distances do not matter when a visiting teacher is a concerned, loving best friend. The visiting teachers' messages are important. The rules that govern our visiting teaching are important, but beyond and above them all and far more important is the understanding, concerned, and loving heart.

Never were visiting teachers more needed. The visiting teacher may never meet a Darlene, but every month she finds those who need love and acceptance.

Each year as the church grows, the need for visiting teachers will grow greater. What is their future? They will help combat the loneliness which plagues our world and impersonality of the big cities. They will look after the stranger, the widow, the orphan, the wounded, and distressed, after all sisters with concerned, loving care. They will be needed as my grandmother was when she left her warm pioneer bed on stormy nights to drive miles with a horse and buggy in response to a cry of need.[24] As my mother during the depression found the hungry, so will they.[25] As my visiting teacher brought me a loaf of freshly baked homemade bread and love, so will they. They will help relieve physical, emotional, and mental suffering. They will aid the sinner and comfort the sorrowing. They will carry a message of gospel love to all our sisters throughout the world. As their warm, tender care spreads its web around the world, they will become a standard to the nations.[26]

> Come unto me, all ye that labour and are heavy laden, and I will give you rest.
>
> Take my yoke upon you, and learn of me; for I am meek and lowly in heart: and ye shall find rest unto your souls.
>
> For my yoke is easy, and my burden is light.[27]

God bless the visiting teachers. For when all work together the yoke is easy and the burden is light.

By this shall all men know that we are our Lord's disciples, if we have love one to another.[28] May it ever be so, I pray. Amen.

Alice C. Smith, Discourse, Oct. 1, 1969, 18–23, in Relief Society Annual Conference Proceedings, 1945–1975, CHL; see also Alice C. Smith, "'My Yoke Is Easy and My Burden Is Light,'" Oct. 1, 1969, in "Officers Meeting," Relief Society Magazine *57, no. 3 (March 1970): 174–177.*

RELIEF SOCIETY BRINGS HAPPINESS

◇◇◇

LUCRECIA SUÁREZ DE JUÁREZ

Mexico and Central America Area Conference
National Auditorium, Chapultepec Park, Mexico City
August 26, 1972

Lucrecia Suárez de Juárez (1896–1998) was stake Relief Society president when she gave the following talk during a Mexico and Central America area conference in 1972.[1] The child of Lucía Mejía and Paulino Suárez, Suárez de Juárez was born to a life of wealth. Family servants helped her ride horseback to school each day, and she had private teachers for lessons in music, painting, and French. But the Zapatista army raided the household several times after the Mexican Revolution began in 1910, and the family moved to Mexico City in reduced circumstances.[2] There Suárez de Juárez became a grade school teacher in 1918. She later met Aurelio Juárez at a dance; he was a professional musician who had fled to Mexico City after escaping Pancho Villa's army. The two married in 1924. When Aurelio died in 1947, two of their five children were under the age of seven. Suárez de Juárez would later help raise her grandson, Miguel Angel Romero.[3]

Suárez de Juárez joined the church in 1956, taught and baptized by missionary Rex E. Lee.[4] Beginning in 1961, she was the first director of Moctezuma Xocoyotzin, a church-run primary school on the east side of Mexico City, and she eventually became the Mexico City East Stake Relief Society president.[5]

By the time of the area conference in 1972 at which Suárez de Juárez delivered this address, Mexican women had been part of the Relief Society for nearly seventy years.[6] The church in Mexico continued to grow despite the political instability, war, and legislation that often limited the religious activities of non-Mexican church leaders and missionaries between 1913 and 1934.[7] Church membership grew rapidly after 1946: one mission had been divided into four by 1960, the first stake was organized in 1961, and a second stake was formed in 1967.[8]

Nearly seventeen thousand church members attended the first area conference in Mexico, many of whom traveled long distances and made great sacrifices to be there. Two-thirds of the members who attended struggled to obtain travel money. Members from Guatemala fasted and prayed so their employers would give them the requisite time off. In Tijuana, Mexico, members chartered a bus for the forty-eight-hour drive. After all seats were spoken for, ten members who earned enough money only at the last minute asked to join. Passengers took turns standing in the aisles to accommodate the latecomers. One woman from that area spent five months earning money by going door to door offering to wash laundry. Members from the agricultural north and central regions of Mexico sold tacos or tamales, washed cars, gardened, and sold their possessions to raise the necessary 200 pesos (roughly 16 U.S. dollars) for bus fare. Once they arrived, many people were out of money. They slept on hardwood gymnasium floors and fasted during the three-day conference. In some communities, members pooled their money and chose which of them might benefit most from attendance.[9]

This conference was the largest gathering of Spanish-speaking Saints to that time and the first time the Mormon Tabernacle Choir broadcast a performance from a non-English-speaking nation (on their 125th anniversary).[10] Over three thousand women gathered at the National Auditorium for the Saturday evening women's session, where Suárez de Juárez gave the following talk in Spanish on happiness, motherhood, and the collective power of Relief Society.[11]

DEAR SISTERS, what a beautiful and meaningful time this is for us, to think that in many areas of the world—in foreign lands, in towns, cities, and rural regions—there are sisters who are caring for their homes and families and dedicating themselves to the significant programs of the Relief Society.[12]

Welcome all of you, my sisters, and may our hearts be as one in love and humility before the Lord. There are no oceans, mountains, deserts, or land barriers that can separate the sisters of the Relief Society, because all of them are equal in faith and devotion, equal in their desires to follow the teachings of the gospel and be exemplary women before the world. The program and the spirit of Relief Society opens the door to an extensive field in which the most noble attributes of womanhood are cultivated, and these bring us happiness. Earning happiness and contributing to the happiness of others should be the most important goal in our lives.

Means to Happiness

The sisters who are able to develop these qualities should manifest them, first in their homes and then to their fellow men in general. Happiness comes to us by various means; if we give comfort to the ill and the needy, to the afflicted, to the dying, to the orphans and widows, our hearts are happy. When the Lord blesses us with a calling, we are frightened because we know we are incompetent; but if we put forth our will and efforts to fulfill it, then we are happy and we can say that blessed is the calling which made us go beyond our ability. We have many experiences in the work of the Relief Society, some satisfactory and others not. If an experience was a success, we are happy, and if we fail, we must be courageous and continue on with greater charity and love. Love towards our sisters must be proven with deeds in order to bring us happiness. Charity is a love so great that it makes us willing to give part of ourselves. We have the example of the visiting teachers who impart their messages of faith and comfort, and they are made happy. Useful and beautiful handiwork for our homes contributes to the happiness of our loved ones.[13] The sons that are raised in praise to God unite the sisters in spiritual communion, and this makes us feel joy.

Could one lone woman combat against the negative influences which harm our children? No, sisters, but we are gathered together as an army of righteous and determined women who can do something.

As sisters of the Relief Society and daughters of our Heavenly Father we must seek wisdom, peace, good fruits, and humility. What greater joy is there than to see our family living clean and righteously. On one occasion President McKay said that a woman must be intelligent and pure because she is the fountain of life, "the living fountain from which flows the stream of humanity."[14]

Role of a Mother

Let us now look at a woman in her role as a mother. The experience which I am going to relate shows us the preparation which Relief Society can give to a mother in order to train her children.

This young mother set her foot on the road of life. "Is the road long?" she asked. Her guide answered, "Yes, and the road is difficult, and you will be old before you get to the end, but the end will be better than the beginning." The mother was happy; she played with her children, gathered flowers for them by the side of the road, and bathed them in pure streams; the sun shone upon them and life was good. The young mother exclaimed, "Nothing could be better than this." Then night fell and the tempests came; the road was dark, and the children trembled from fear and cold. The mother went to them and covered them with her mantle, and the children said, "Mother, we are not afraid, because you are with us, and we know that no harm can come upon us." The mother said, "This is better than the light of day, because I have taught my children courage, and I am happy."

Taught about God

Dawn came and in front of them there was a hill; the children climbed and became tired, but she kept saying to them, "Be patient and in a little while we will reach the top." When the children arrived, they said, "We would never have made it here without you, Mother"; and while the mother rested happily that night, looking at the starry skies, she said, "This day has been better than yesterday, because my children have learned to have strength in the face of difficulties. Yesterday I gave them courage, and today strength." The next day there came strange clouds which darkened the earth—clouds of war, hate, and wickedness—and the children groped and stumbled, and the mother said, "Look up; raise your eyes to the light." The children raised their eyes, and saw above the clouds an everlasting glory which guided them and carried them beyond the darkness. That night the mother said, "I am happier than the other days, because I have taught my children about God."

The days passed, and the months and years, and the mother became old. She was small and frail, but her children were tall and strong, and she walked with courage. When the road was difficult and rough, they carried her because she was small and light. At last they came to a hill, and up over the hill they could see a brilliant road and a golden door which was open. The happy mother said, "I have come to the end of my journey, and now I know that the end is better than the beginning, because now my children can walk alone." And the children answered, "You will always be with us, Mother, even when you have gone through that door." They waited and saw her continue on alone, and the doors were closed behind her. Then the children, looking steadily into infinity, said, "We cannot see her, but she is with us yet."

And so it is, dear sisters. Our mother is not a sweet memory, it is as if she were with us. The happiness of mothers is found in the righteousness of their children, which is reached with the guidance of the Relief Society, the strong arm of the priesthood, and the courage of these mothers, as well as their faith in God.

Relief Society Brings Happiness

The thought that I have tried to leave with you is this: The Relief Society brings happiness into our lives, if we seek it diligently.

Our hearts tonight are filled with gratitude to our Heavenly Father for having blessed us with the presence of his chosen servants, whom we love deeply, because we know the word of God is with them.[15] My testimony is that God the Father and his Son Jesus Christ live, and that the soul of man can communicate with them through the Holy Ghost. My prayer tonight is that the coming work year in Relief Society will bring to each of us the strength to fulfill our duties, joy in serving, and success in accordance with our righteous efforts.

These humble thoughts I leave with you in the blessed name of our Savior, Jesus Christ, amen.

Lucrecia Suárez de Juárez, Discourse, Aug. 26, 1972, in "Sister Lucrecia Suarez de Juarez," Official Report of the First Mexico and Central America Area General Conference of the Church of Jesus Christ of Latter-day Saints, *Aug. 25–27, 1972 (Salt Lake City: Deseret Press, 1973), 82–84. Title supplied by the editors.*

Belle S. Spafford, Marianne C. Sharp, and Louise W. Madsen with the Relief Society general board. 1962. With members of the presidency at the head of the table (left to right: Madsen, Spafford, and Sharp), the Relief Society general board poses in the six-year-old Relief Society Building. Board members trained Relief Society units throughout the world, oversaw temple clothing production, published the *Relief Society Magazine,* and created Relief Society curriculum. Photograph by J. M. Heslop. (Church History Library, Salt Lake City.)

LATTER-DAY SAINT WOMEN IN TODAY'S CHANGING WORLD

◇◇◇

BELLE S. SPAFFORD

Brigham Young University Devotional
Marriott Center, Brigham Young University, Provo, Utah
February 11, 1975

Belle Smith Spafford (1895–1982) was her parents' seventh child, born eight months after the death of her father. Spafford's mother, Hester Sims Smith, had a number of favorite sayings that Spafford and her siblings would later remember and use, including, "Accept people as you find them, not as others represent them to be," and "No investment pays as high dividends as kindness." Spafford's mother influenced her to complete the teacher training program at the University of Utah, then to take courses at Brigham Young University (BYU) before teaching there in the Department of Education.[1]

When Spafford acquired a new responsibility, her typical response was to take courses—in social work when she wanted to better help her students, in composition and grammar when she became editor of the *Relief Society Magazine,* and in church history when she chaired a Relief Society committee on that topic.[2] Spafford first joined the Relief Society general board and edited the *Relief Society Magazine* in 1935.[3] Amy Brown Lyman asked Spafford and Marianne C. Sharp to compile a history of the first hundred years of the Relief Society to commemorate the upcoming centennial anniversary and then made Spafford her second counselor in 1942.[4] Spafford frequently referenced Relief Society history after her work on the centennial project, as she did in the talk reproduced here.

Spafford orchestrated landmark events during her own tenure as Relief Society general president from 1945 to 1974, including construction of the Relief Society Building in downtown Salt Lake City, translation of the *Relief Society Magazine* into Spanish, and tremendous growth in membership. Relief Society membership grew from one hundred thousand to nine hundred thousand while Spafford was president, with members in sixty-five countries.[5] The Relief Society also became responsible for single women in the church during that time.[6] Like her predecessor Amy Brown Lyman, Spafford devoted Relief Society attention to social work, which at the time included adoption services, care for single mothers, foster home care, and family casework.[7] She received honorary degrees from BYU and the University of Utah for this work.[8]

After declaring herself a Mormon the first time she attended a National Council of Women (NCW) meeting, Spafford felt unwelcome. Consequently, when she became Relief Society general president she wished to discontinue Relief Society participation in the council. But when she met with church president George Albert Smith regarding these plans, Smith's response redirected her intentions. He replied, "I think Mormon women have something to give to the women of the world and they may also learn from them. . . . Go back and make your influence felt."[9] Spafford took his advice seriously and was still involved with the council when she gave the speech featured here. She affiliated with the NCW for fifty-two years, eventually serving as chair of the International Council of Women, as second vice president of NCW, as a member of the executive committee, and as president.[10] Working with the council kept her apprised of current legislation and movements regarding women's welfare; this, in turn, led her to carefully weigh diverse visions of what would best promote female advancement. She said in 1975, "Right this very hour I've got to know what they [American women] think about birth control, what they think about abortions, what they think about the Equal Rights Amendment, what they think about voluntary service for women, what they think about women in politics."[11]

Spafford had recently completed thirty-nine years of Relief Society service at the general level when she delivered the following discourse about women and society to BYU students.[12] The proposed Equal Rights Amendment to the United States Constitution was being actively debated at this time, and both Spafford and her Relief Society successor Barbara B. Smith had made statements opposing the amendment.[13] Spafford reasoned that inequalities—such as unequal pay for equal work, discriminatory credit laws, and denial of property rights—would best be resolved through established legislative channels. At the same time she stated, "Women owe it to themselves to develop their full potential as women—to exercise their mental capacities, to enlarge upon their talents, and to increase their skills—in order that they may give to the world the best they have." She expressed worry over "new philosophies" that she felt threatened marriage and family life.[14]

IT IS ALWAYS A GREAT PLEASURE and a strengthening experience for me to speak to a group of Brigham Young University students. I enjoyed the chorus this morning, and I also appreciated being referred to as a young woman.[15] I was called the other day by the National Council of Women and asked if I would accept an appointment as a delegate to an international meeting in Paris. I thought, "Before I accept this, I should refer it to one of the members of the First Presidency." So I called President Tanner and said, "I have an invitation to serve as a delegate, and I don't think I should accept it because and because and because—."[16] I had a number of very good reasons, I thought.

He listened attentively, and then he said to me, "You know, I should think you'd take advantage of your opportunities while you're still young."

I'm particularly honored this morning to be invited by the chairman of the Women's Week program committee to speak at this devotional assembly. Since this is Women's Week, it seems appropriate that I address myself, in the main, to the role of the Latter-day Saint woman in today's changing world.[17] I'm sensitive to the fact that this group consists of men as well as women. In the governing structure of the church, men play an important role in relation to the women's activities as they relate to the work of the church. At early meetings of the Relief Society in Nauvoo, the Prophet Joseph Smith clearly defined this relationship. At the founding meeting, a presidency consisting of three women—a president, a first counselor, and a second counselor—was appointed to preside over the organization. Later in the meeting the Prophet Joseph said, "Let this presidency serve as a constitution—all their decisions be considered law, and acted upon as such. If any officers are wanted to carry out the design of the institution, let them be appointed and set apart. . . . The minutes of your meetings will be precedent for you to act upon—your constitution and law."[18] Nonetheless, at the third meeting of the society the Prophet gave this enduring directive: "You will receive instructions through the order of the Priesthood which God has established, through the medium of those appointed to lead, guide, and direct the affairs of the church in this last dispensation."[19]

Because of these mandates it seems imperative that not only the women but also the brethren of the priesthood should be knowledgeable regarding the role of women. The brethren will want to be familiar with the problems confronting women so that through an understanding of these and the duties and the responsibilities of the sisters they will be in a position to counsel and direct them in harmony with the design of the Lord. The advancement of the work of the church is a joint responsibility of the men and the women of the church, each working in his assigned sphere. The deeper understanding each has of the role of the other, the greater the total success of the work of the church is bound to be. Understanding is built primarily upon knowledge. Therefore, it does not seem inappropriate for me to speak about woman's role in today's changing world to this group, consisting as it does of men and women.

National Gains of Women

With the advent of this new year, 1975, our nation found itself and still finds itself struggling with many unusual and difficult circumstances. It was of interest to me to listen to a radio broadcast during which outstanding news broadcasters discussed what they considered to be the most significant news events of 1974 affecting the nation. Their conclusions, as I recall, were as follows: "inflation and the recession, the energy crisis, the resignation of the president of the United States, the Watergate trials, the pardon of the president, the growing wealth and power of the oil-producing nations, and the world food shortages."[20]

In my opinion the broadcasters bypassed one happening more significant, perhaps, in its long-range impact on home, community, and national life than any of those mentioned. I refer to the advancement made by women in their efforts toward emancipation from what they regarded as existing restraints that encumbered their full development and usefulness. Women have been active in working toward specific goals in relation to this for years, but 1974 was different. It was a year of intensified effort in a vast scope of diversified areas, and gains were pronounced. As an example of one gain, I cite those made in the field of political life. A record number of experienced, qualified, dedicated women ran for public office, and many won. The National Women's Political Caucus issued the following figures: 18 women representatives were elected to Congress, an unprecedented number; 599 women were elected to state legislatures; one woman was elected governor of one of our sovereign states; another woman was elected a lieutenant governor. "All across the country," declares the Women's Caucus, "it was a banner year for women."[21]

In some areas, however, gains were made which, in the opinion of some persons, raise questions as to the effect upon national life. While we rejoice in the correction of injustices, we must not lose sight of the need for sober evaluation of action that brings about change in the status of women—change which breaks with the traditional, time-tested patterns of life that have proved good and have contributed to the happiness and the well-being of families and of nations. We must not lose sight of the basic natures of women and their divinely ordained roles in life. James Kilpatrick, a prominent columnist, has pointed out that "we look to the Judeo-Christian ethic." He declares that we live by a body of rules or laws drawn from generations past; that they cannot be treated as if they do not exist. People care about these things because they have found them to be good and satisfying.[22]

Current Trends in Relation to Traditional Values

There are some present viewpoints and trends that give concern because they seem to run counter to traditional values. The Latter-day Saint woman finds herself in an ideal position to evaluate changes in the status of women and to intelligently and properly appraise trends and viewpoints because she has at her command unfailing measuring rods. These infallible calculators, if you will, are the divinely inspired guidelines in the revealed truths as set forth by the scriptures and in the words of our modern prophets. Yet some of us fail to use these unerring measuring rods because we are not sufficiently familiar with them. We do not know them. We may have failed to take advantage of the opportunities to learn them, to understand their full meaning, and to apply them in our individual and collective lives. Or we may be like Saul, the son of Kish, who loved the Lord and would do his will, but he lacked the courage to go against popular opinion.

In the Bible we are told, "Now there was a man of Benjamin, whose name was Kish. . . . And he had a son, whose name was Saul, a choice young man, and a goodly: and there was not among the children of Israel a goodlier person than he: from his shoulders and upward he was higher than any of the people. And the asses of Kish, Saul's father, were lost."[23] Saul was sent to find the animals, but he could not. He and his servant then went to inquire of God through God's servant Samuel, who was a prophet. (At that time he was called a seer, according to the scriptural account.) Samuel had been forewarned of Saul's coming and the Lord had revealed to Samuel that it was his will that Saul should reign over his people as their captain. Samuel showed unto Saul the works of God. Then he took a vial of oil and anointed Saul to be captain over his inheritance. He then counseled him as to the will of the Lord and how to proceed.[24]

The people, however, were not happy with this. They wanted a king, and Saul yielded to the will of the people. Then Samuel, learning of Saul's decision, went unto Saul, a Benjamite, and said:

> Thou hast done foolishly: thou hast not kept the commandments of the Lord thy God, which he commanded thee: for now would the Lord have established thy kingdom upon Israel for ever.
>
> But now thy kingdom shall not continue: the Lord hast sought him a man after his own heart, and the Lord hath commanded him to be captain over this people.[25]

> And Saul said unto Samuel, I have sinned: for I have transgressed the commandment of the Lord, and thy words: because I feared the people, and obeyed their voice.[26]

Too many of us today fear the voice of the people. Counseling on the desirability of representative government, King Mosiah made this significant statement: "It is common for the lesser part of the people to desire that which is not right."[27] Now, having this warning from a great Book of Mormon prophet, Latter-day Saints would do well to be particularly careful to weigh the voices of the people in the light of the teachings of our modern-day prophets. Even though the voices may be few, they are usually loud and convincing.

Possessing revealed truth and the words of the prophets as they relate to the responsibility of the Latter-day Saint woman and her role in life, we have an unwavering duty to uphold these teachings in our speech and actions, and to direct our lives in harmony with them. But I ask, "Do we have any further responsibility? Do we have a responsibility to share these teachings with those who may not have the light of truth?" In Matthew, our duty is made clear on this point. We read, "Ye are the light of the world. A city that is set on an hill cannot be hid. Neither do men light a candle and put it under a bushel, but on a candlestick; and it giveth light unto all that are in the house. Let your light so shine before men, that they may see your good works, and glorify your father which is in heaven."[28]

Relief Society Prophecy Fulfilled

I am reminded of an address given to Relief Society women by President George Albert Smith in the October 1945 general conference. This was the first conference he addressed as president of the church and the first conference I conducted as president of Relief Society.[29] For several years we had been denied conferences due to the restrictions of war.[30] The women gathered to that Relief Society conference with eager and receptive spirits to hear the message of their new prophet-president. The Spirit of the Lord rested mightily upon President Smith, and the spirit of prophecy prevailed as he spoke of the future of the women of the church. He made very clear the responsibilities we had to all womankind. An excerpt from his address is worthy of reading at this time. Said President Smith:

> I feel that I am standing on sacred ground, for in this pulpit have appeared some of the great men and women of the world, those who were anxious to do what the Lord would have them do. Here they bore testimony of the divine mission of our Lord and Savior Jesus Christ.

> You are more blessed than any other women in all the world. You were the first women to have the franchise;[31] the first women to have a voice in the work of a church. It was God who gave it to you, and it came as a result of revelation to a prophet of the Lord. Since that time think what benefits the women of this world have enjoyed. Not only you who belong to the church have enjoyed the blessings of equality, but when the Prophet Joseph Smith turned the key for the emancipation of womankind, it was turned for all the women of the world, and from generation to generation the number of women who can enjoy the blessings of religious liberty and civil liberty has been increasing.[32]
>
> Do you realize that you have opened this tabernacle to the first general conference we have had in years?[33] . . . Now the sky is the limit, and I am not so sure that by the time we have two or three more general conferences here we may have visitors from Australia, New Zealand, Africa, China, Japan, and elsewhere. They may leave their homes in airplanes and in about twenty-four hours be right here. It is marvelous what the Lord has given to us in this age.[34]

I was deeply moved by the remarks of that great president, and following the session I thanked him and poured forth the feelings of my heart. I inquired, "Would any of this take place during my administration?" Then I asked, "When and how will our message be carried to the women of the world?" While his reply is not recorded in the conference proceedings, it is recorded in my little notebook where I've kept notes of the various general conferences, and it is also recorded in my mind and in my heart.[35]

The prophet replied, "It could easily happen during your administration. The message of Mormon women will reach the women of the world when there is a special need for it. You don't need to worry about how," said he. "The Lord will see to that."

By way of showing prophecy fulfilled, a few years after President Smith's address my counselors and I noted a rather large number of women in attendance at our conference from overseas and foreign-language countries. We decided to hold a special meeting for them following the regular session of our two-day conference. We asked for a verbal roll call that morning. Each sister was to give her name, the country from which she came, and her method of transportation. Most of them had come by plane. Every country mentioned by President Smith in his 1945 address was represented except China. I noted that there was a woman there from Taiwan. I commented on this, adding that we did have a sister from Taiwan even though we did not have one from China. The sister from Taiwan then quietly arose and in perfect English said, "China is my homeland." Prophecy was fulfilled.[36]

Importance of Relief Society Today

Today the message of Mormon women is being carried to the world in a number of ways—through the great missionary program of the church, through Relief Society's affiliation with the National and International Councils of Women, through radio, television, the press, and other means of communication.[37] I assure you that the message of Mormon women is needed by women of the world today. Countless women are troubled as to the course they should pursue. Many are confused by new philosophies and new points of view. Relief Society holds a position of respect and influence among organized women of the world. While they may not always agree with our position on issues which to us are important, we are usually given ample opportunity to express ourselves, and our influence is felt. Often our position prevails.

The names of over 900,000 women are now on the Relief Society rolls. These include young women, many of them college women. Also, there are middle-aged women and those who are experienced and who have grown old in dedication to the work. It is our duty as Mormon women, regardless of our age or circumstances, to stand united and firm in support of church teachings. It was not a coincidence or a whim when Relief Societies were established on this campus and on other college campuses.[38] Nor was it a coincidence when President Harold B. Lee brought the young adult women and the special interest women under the auspices of Relief Society.[39] It was the will of the Lord. It was in fulfillment of prophecy by an earlier prophet-president, Joseph F. Smith. These are his prophetic words recorded in his book *Gospel Doctrine*:

> I will speak of the Relief Society as one great organization in the church, organized by the Prophet Joseph Smith, whose duty it is to look after the interests of all women of Zion and of all the women who may come under their supervision and care, irrespective of religion, color, or condition. I expect to see the day when this organization will be one of the most perfect, most efficient and effective organizations for good in the church, but that day will be when we shall have women who are not only imbued with the spirit of the gospel of Jesus Christ, and with the testimony of Christ in their hearts, but also with youth, vigor and intelligence to enable them to discharge the great duties and responsibilities

> that rest upon them. . . . We want the young women, the intelligent women, women of faith, of courage and of purity to be associated with the Relief Societies in the various stakes and wards of Zion. We want them to take hold of this work with vigor, with intelligence and unitedly, for the building up of Zion and the instruction of women in their duties—domestic duties, public duties, and every duty that may devolve upon them.[40]

Choice young Latter-day Saint women are augmenting the strength of Relief Society today because they are needed. The times demand their training, their leadership skills, their testimonies—coupled with the strength of the sisters long experienced in the work. Latter-day Saint women are concerned for the solidarity of the home and the eternal well-being of the family. They know good homes are the cornerstone of a good society and happy citizenry. Any change that adversely affects the home and the family is to be deplored. The Latter-day Saint doctrine of the eternity of the family unit was frequently referred to by the late Elder Stephen L Richards as "the most sublime of all theological doctrines."[41]

The gospel teaches women how to behave toward their husbands, and it teaches men to esteem womanhood and to honor and respect their wives. The church places no restrictions on a woman's going into the marketplace and into community service on a paid or a volunteer basis, if she so desires, when her home and family circumstances allow her to do so without impairment to them. Women are encouraged to develop their full potential as women, and the church affords abundant opportunity for them to do so. Well-directed compassionate service, which is according to the nature of women, is but the law of brotherhood in action. It is Latter-day Saint doctrine. These are a few of the measuring rods whereby you young women here today may evaluate change and determine your actions in life. The 900,000 women constituting the Relief Society membership can be a power for helping women the world over properly to evaluate change. Guided by church teachings, they can help themselves to move forward along proper lines in the development of their talents and skills and in their service to mankind. The church can enable women of the world to determine what should receive priorities in their lives. Latter-day Saint women have at their command the firm and infallible guidelines that lead toward the full development and total usefulness of womankind. The power for good inherent in our 900,000 women guided by the inspiration of priesthood leadership is incalculable. For Latter-day Saint women, the teachings of the church are eternal security. May we never lose sight of them I sincerely pray in the name of Jesus Christ, amen.

Belle S. Spafford, "Latter-day Saint Women in Today's Changing World," in Speeches of the Year: BYU Centennial Devotional and Fireside Addresses, 1975 *(Provo, UT: Brigham Young University Press, 1976), 41–50.*

DRIFTING, DREAMING, DIRECTING

◇◇◇

ARDETH G. KAPP

Brigham Young University Women's Conference
Ernest L. Wilkinson Center, Brigham Young University, Provo, Utah
February 2, 1980

Ardeth Greene Kapp (b. 1931) spent her formative years in the small town of Glenwood, Alberta, Canada, working in the country store owned by her mother, Julia "June" Greene, and helping her father, Edwin "Ted" Greene, on the farm.[1] June often gave food to clients who could not pay, and Ted raised turkeys and sometimes gave them to families in need (he also twice gave cows to Australian immigrants).[2] Ted was a bishop when he brought a couple of missionaries to join the family for dinner, including a young man named Heber Kapp. Ardeth and Heber corresponded after that evening until he returned from his mission in Canada to his home in Utah.[3]

Ardeth moved to Provo, Utah, to attend Brigham Young High School for her senior year, and she and Heber began to date.[4] They married in 1950.[5] Ardeth Kapp worked for telephone companies in Utah and California until, by 1960, she was the employment and personnel representative at the Mountain States Telephone Company, the highest phone company position available to a woman at that time.[6]

The Kapps were unable to have children, so they sought to learn the lessons they felt having children would teach them, including patience, tolerance, charity, and serving at inconvenient times.[7] This goal influenced Kapp's decision to become an educator. While attending her aunt's funeral in Glenwood, Kapp felt an impression to go to college.[8] She earned a bachelor's degree from the University of Utah in elementary education in 1964 and a master's degree in curriculum development from Brigham Young University (BYU) in 1971, after which she taught grade school in Davis County, Utah, and then supervised student teachers at BYU.[9] She also wrote a series of instructional television programs and, by the time of the talk featured here, had published four books.[10] From 1966 to 1972, she was a faculty member in teacher education at BYU.[11]

Kapp worked on church curriculum from 1967 to 1972, initially through the youth correlation committee. In that capacity, she and her fellow committee members reviewed every proposed church publication related to church members aged twelve to twenty-eight, including magazines and curriculum.[12] In 1971, she moved to the new curriculum development committee, formed to plan and coordinate—but not to write—all church curriculum.[13] Throughout this period, she sought to ensure that curriculum materials focused on gospel values.[14] Kapp became a counselor in the Young Women general presidency in 1972, serving with President Ruth Hardy Funk.[15] As a member of the general presidency, she continued to teach and train church members while overseeing curriculum development.[16]

Kapp gave the following talk at a BYU Women's Conference two years after completing her assignment as counselor in the Young Women general presidency and two years before becoming president of that organization. Kapp spent these intervening years working on a committee to update the church's teacher development program, caring for her ailing mother, lecturing to church groups, writing for the *New Era* magazine, writing a fifth book, supporting her husband as stake president, conducting time-management seminars, and running two miles at 5:30 every morning. In 1979, she said, "Sometimes when you're released you wonder if you've passed the peak of your service. But in my patriarchal blessing there's a statement that says, 'You'll be surprised in the days to come the blessings the Lord has in store for you.' And I suppose that could be said of every one of us."[17]

The text presented here is an excerpt of Kapp's original speech; roughly the first quarter of the talk has been omitted.

IT HAS BEEN MY OBSERVATION, and it is my confession as a former participant, that many people drift along with the crowd in the church. Many good people drift to sacrament meeting and Sunday School, even family home evening, and they drift through a casual study of the scriptures. The drifters fall into at least one of two groups: In the first are those who step into the mainstream, getting deeply involved with church activity and floating with the current, comfortable with a sense of false security that they are in the right place. Others, who form the second group, accepting a few selected principles, resist being part of the flow, the mainstream, and choose to get out into the eddies at the edge, freed from the demands of full participation. It is difficult to decide of these two groups which is better, or worse. Those of us who are, on the basis of activity alone, very much in the church may not necessarily have the church very much in us; and if we left, the church might hardly recognize the difference. Following the practices, doing the right thing but without coming to know, understand, accept, and apply the saving principles and doctrines, we may be compared to one who spends his entire life stringing the instrument—never once hearing the music for which the instrument was created or incapable of recognizing it if he did.

In matters of principle, let us stand as solid as a rock. In matters of practice, may all that we do be based upon these saving principles, and may we understand the intrinsic relationship of principles and practices. It is in making the decision to follow the admonition of the prophet and to become scholars of the scriptures that we gradually learn the doctrine that prepares us to stand on the rock of revelation and to experience less and less the restless sense of drifting, wandering, questioning, and searching.

There are many good people who are very faithful (and may I emphasize *faithful*) in following the traditions and practices. I'm reminded of a song we used to sing in Sunday School:

"Never be late for the Sunday School class, come with your bright smiling faces."

The chorus ended with:

"Try to be there, always be there, promptly at ten in the morning."[18]

Ten in the morning became a practice, a tradition, for a long time. It was not a principle. Yet there were those among the faithful who felt uncomfortable about change, not unlike the feelings expressed by some today as practices and traditions are modified. When changes come, and they always will, for some it may be a test to survive because their foundation is based on practices alone, without an understanding of the eternal, unchanging principles.

Being faithful does not necessarily develop faith. The first principle of the gospel is faith in the Lord, Jesus Christ.[19] To have faith in him is to know him, to know his doctrine, and to know that the course of our life is in harmony with and acceptable to him. It is relatively easy to be faithful, but faith is born out of study, fasting, prayer, meditation, sacrifice, service, and, finally, personal revelation. Glimpses of understanding come line upon line, precept upon precept. Our Father is anxious to feed us just as fast as we can handle it, but we regulate the richness and the volume of our spiritual diet. And we do this by the same method used by the sons of Mosiah:

> They had waxed strong in the knowledge of the truth; . . . they had searched the scriptures diligently, that they might know the word of God. But this is not all; they had given themselves to

> much prayer, and fasting; therefore they had the spirit of prophecy, and the spirit of revelation, and when they taught, they taught with power and authority of God.[20]

Faithfulness without faith, practices without principles, will leave us and our families seriously wanting as we move closer to that time spoken of by Heber C. Kimball when he said, "The time is coming when no man or woman will be able to endure on borrowed light. Each will have to be guided by the light within himself. If ye do not have it, you will not stand."[21]

May we find ourselves doing less and less drifting as we make right choices based on personal revelation that give direction to us and our families each day of our lives. And with that direction, let us develop "a program for personal improvement" that will cause us to "reach for new levels of achievement," as the prophet has admonished us.[22]

He has also promised us that the Lord "will help us from day to day on the allocation of our time and talent. We will move faster if we hurry less. We will make more real progress if we focus on the fundamentals."[23] Certain principles are essential in our struggle to avoid the wasteful experience of drifting.

Now what of dreamers? Many of us are dreamers at times, wanting in some way to escape ourselves, to be free of our own limitations. I often ponder the words: "With voluntary dreams they cheat their minds."[24] It has been said that if fate would destroy a man, it would first separate his forces and drive him to think one way and act another. It would rob him of the contentment that comes only from unity within. Choices must be decisive so that dreams and actions can be in harmony with each other. When we do something different than we know we should, it is like going into a final examination and putting down the wrong answer, even though we know the right one.

Dreaming, however, can also serve a very positive function when it fits Webster's definition of having "a goal or purpose ardently desired."

In the popular musical *South Pacific* is the delightful little song that goes, "If you don't have a dream, / How ya gonna make a dream come true?"[25] I am concerned for some of our sisters who have a magnificent dream but who will never fully realize its fulfillment because they feel that their righteous husband will take care of it, and they fail to prepare for their part in this eternal partnership.

There are some sisters who ponder the administrative structure of the church and trouble themselves with what they think they don't have without ever coming to a full understanding of their own special and unique mission and the great blessings reserved specifically for them. We hear it expressed in terms that suggest that because women don't have the priesthood they are shortchanged.

There are still others of our sisters who have the misunderstanding that priesthood is synonymous with men, and so they excuse themselves and have no concern for studying its importance in their own lives. The term *priesthood* is used without qualification, whether it is referring to a bearer of the priesthood, priesthood blessings, or priesthood ordinances. Our hearts should cry out in either case, and we should raise our voices and shout warnings to sisters whose dreams are built on such faulty foundations.

Our greatest dreams will be fulfilled only as we come to understand fully and experience the blessings of the priesthood, the power of the priesthood, and the ordinances of the priesthood in our own lives. If we were to begin with the time a child is given a name and a blessing and then continue on through baptism, confirmation, the sacrament, callings and being set apart, patriarchal blessings, administrations, the endowment, and finally celestial marriage, we would quickly realize that all the saving blessings of the priesthood are for boys and girls, men and women. And while that divine mission of motherhood is paramount, it is not all-inclusive. To help another gain eternal life is a companion privilege. This privilege, indeed this sacred responsibility, this noblest of callings, is denied to no worthy person. To assist in bringing to pass the eternal life of man, and to do it in dignity and honor, is the very pinnacle of my own personal dream. And for us to close our eyes to these eternal truths and not recognize them as priesthood blessings and ordinances is to keep us on the fringe area of the very saving principles—the only principles—that can make our eternal dreams come true.

It is true that as sisters we do not experience a priesthood ordination that carries an administrative function, nor do we have the tremendous, weighty burden of having that sacred responsibility heaped upon us in addition to the mission of creating and nurturing in partnership with God, first in giving birth to the Lord's spirit children and then in raising those children to serve the Lord and keep his commandments.

I have come to know that we can all, both men and women, rejoice in the sacred calling of motherhood. To give birth is but one part of this sacred calling.

After drifting and dreaming, now may we consider the directing of one's life. At my high school graduation, Oscar A. Kirkham stood at the pulpit, looking into the eyes of idealistic, enthusiastic graduates, and in his husky voice he offered this challenge: "Build a seaworthy ship. Be a loyal shipmate, and sail a true course."[26] I don't remember anything else that he said, or what anyone else said, for that matter. But I've pondered that challenge many times over the years. In directing our lives we want to be sure of the true course and its ultimate destination. We cannot risk being caught in the disillusionment of the fellow who was committed to going north and was in fact traveling north—but on an iceberg that was floating south.

"True points," like stars in the heavens to guide us, are readily available for anyone earnestly seeking direction. These true points of doctrine are found in the true church.[27] Conversion to the truth comes by accepting true doctrine, and the truth of doctrine can be known only by revelation gained as a result of obedience. The Savior taught: "My doctrine is not mine, but his that sent me. If any man will do his will, he shall know of the doctrine, whether it be of God, or whether I speak of myself."[28]

The skeptic of two thousand years ago might have said, "Look, if I knew for sure that the star (the sign of the Savior's birth) would appear in the heavens tonight, I would be obedient." That's like standing in front of a stove and saying, "Give me some heat, and then I'll put in the wood." We must put in the wood first, and then we feel the warmth and the heat; then we can bear testimony of its reality. In the twelfth chapter of Ether we read: "Dispute not because ye see not, for ye receive no witness until after the trial of your faith."[29] And as our faith is tried and we are found standing firm even in times of storm, we will rejoice with increased confidence as we discover within ourselves the loyal shipmate that we really have as we sail a true course.

Apostles and prophets have been provided in the church for the purposes of identifying and teaching true doctrine, lest men be "tossed to and fro and carried about with every wind of doctrine."[30] Now, we can follow the Brethren blindly, as one of my non-Mormon friends claims that we do—and I might add that it is far safer and better to follow them blindly than not at all—but that could be an abdication of our responsibility to direct our own lives and become spiritually independent. Again, following the practices alone is not enough. We must come to know the reason, indeed the doctrinal bases, for that practice; otherwise, when the practice or tradition is questioned or changed, those who do not understand the principle are prone to waver. They may even abandon or reject the very practice intended as a schoolmaster to carry them to an understanding of a saving and eternal principle.

There were those in King Benjamin's time who were caught up in exacting the law of Moses. With blinders they followed the practices—an eye for an eye and a tooth for a tooth—until King Benjamin taught them that their practices availed them nothing unless they accepted the mission of the Savior and his atonement.[31] Without that commitment their practices were for naught.

While Adam was offering the firstlings of the flock, an angel appeared and asked him why he was doing it, why this practice. You will remember Adam's response. He said, "I know not, save the Lord commanded me."[32] The practice was offering a sacrifice, but the principle, in this instance, was obedience. And then

Adam received a witness, after the trial of his faith. The angel explained: "This thing is a similitude of the sacrifice of the Only Begotten of the Father."[33]

As we direct our lives, it is important to understand practices and principles, their relationship as well as the differences between them. In my mind's eye, I visualize the practices as a horizontal line, a foundation, a schooling, a testing, a preparation; and the saving and exalting eternal principles or doctrine as a vertical line that links our souls to heaven and builds the relationship with God and faith in the Lord, Jesus Christ, and his mission.

There will continue to be much opposition to true doctrine; but by and by the storm subsides, the clouds disperse, the sun breaks forth, and the rock of truth is seen again, firm and lasting. There never was a true principle that was not met by storm after storm of opposition and abuse, until that principle had obtained such influence that it no longer paid to oppose it. But until that time, the opposition and the abuse have ebbed and flowed like the tide. It was a strong doctrine that rid Jesus of his weak disciples, and the same testing process continues today in determining those worthy of his kingdom. The Prophet Joseph Smith stated:

> God has in reserve a time . . . when he will bring all his subjects, who have obeyed his voice and kept his commandments, into his celestial rest. This rest is of such perfection and glory, that man has need of a preparation before he can, according to the laws of that kingdom, enter it and enjoy its blessings. This being the fact, God has given certain laws to the human family, which, if observed, are sufficient to prepare them to inherit this rest. This, then, we conclude was the purpose of God in giving his laws to us.[34]

In our goal to apply principles and proceed with direction, it isn't intended that we arrive before we experience that witness of the Spirit. The witness sustains us in our journey. In a few lines of prose, given so eloquently, President Kimball tells how the gospel came into the life of an unlearned, Bolivian woman.[35] In hearing of the mission of the Savior and the doctrine of the atonement, the Spirit bore witness to her soul. With her golden-brown face turned upward, her dark eyes wide and trusting, with tears rising to overflowing, she whispered her emotions, "You mean, he did that for me?" With the confirmation of her question received, she again whispered, this time not in question but in reverent awe, "You mean, he did that for me!"

And to this eternal and saving principle, I bear my fervent testimony that he did that for you and for me. With that conviction, I think with soberness of the penetrating observation by Truman Madsen, "The greatest tragedy of our life is that our Savior paid the awful price of suffering so that he could help us, but is forbidden to because we won't let him. We look down instead of up."[36] We choose to remain enclosed in marble. But if we would free ourselves and come to know this truth through personal revelation, the time might come when even our routine practices could become life-giving and done in the Lord's name with his Spirit so that the whole of our lives becomes a sacred experience as we labor for him continuously.

It was not long ago that I witnessed what until then had been something of a routine for me, the blessing on the food. Picture with me my aged father, his body deteriorated by the devastation of stomach cancer, while his spirit was magnified and refined through suffering. He sat at the kitchen table; he then weighed less than a hundred pounds. Bowing his head, resting it in his frail, trembling hands over a spoonful of baby food—all that he could eat—he pronounced a blessing on the food—as though it were a sacred sacrament—and gave thanks with acceptance and submission, with truth and faith, because he knew to whom he was speaking.

It is in coming to know our Savior and the saving principles that he taught through the gospel of Jesus Christ that we become different. And we need to be recognized as being different. The majority of the world doesn't see the options. It is our responsibility to be obviously good and obviously right—and able to articulate our values and be an advocate for truth. We may have a temple recommend and attend our meetings and practice the principles, but how we look and act, what we say and do, may be the only message some people will receive. Our acts should show that there is a power and an influence with us that the inhabitants of the world do not understand. What is it that distinguishes us from others? The distinction is that we profess to be guided by revelation. And it is because of this principle that we are peculiar, since all of our actions can be under divine guidance. Having made the choice, we must stand and be visibly different. Until we make that choice, we remain anonymous, subject to the current of the meandering multitudes.

President Kimball has said:

> Much of the major growth that is coming to the church in the last days will come because many of the good women of the world (in whom there is often such an inner sense of spirituality) will be drawn to the church in large numbers. This will happen to the degree that the women of the church reflect righteousness and articulateness in their lives and to the degree that they are seen as distinct and different—in happy ways—from the women of the world.[37]

That is our direction. That is our challenge. All individuals are what they are and where they are by a composite of choices that direct their life each day. The responsibility of directing is not only for our own lives, but also for others who may be looking for the light. As we build a seaworthy ship and then sail a true course, many sails will navigate safely through troubled waters into the peaceful harbor because of the unflickering light radiating from the bow of our craft. As I consider our responsibility to others I am inspired by the words of the song:

> Brightly beams our Father's mercy from his lighthouse evermore,
> But to us he gives the keeping of the lights along the shore.
>
> *Chorus*
> Let the lower lights be burning; send a gleam across the wave;
> Some poor fainting, struggling seaman you may rescue; you may save.
>
> Dark the night of sin has settled; loud the angry billows roar.
> Eager eyes are watching, longing, for the lights along the shore.
>
> *Chorus*
>
> Trim your feeble lamp, my brother; some poor sailor, tempest tossed,
> Trying now to make the harbor, in the darkness may be lost.
>
> *Chorus*[38]

Elder Neal A. Maxwell recently wrote, "As other lights flicker and fade, the light of the gospel will burn ever more brightly in a darkening world, guiding the humble but irritating the guilty and those who prefer the dusk of decadence."[39]

Now my dear sisters, may our lights be bright without a flicker, as we tend the lights along the shore. Let us each one reach out and touch another. Let us help carry one another's burdens. In cooperation we can overcome great odds. Let us rejoice with one another. It may be just a smile, a note, a call, an encouraging word that says, "I care; I understand; I will stand by you and help you." These are life-saving measures in times of storm.

Recently I was privileged to read part of a blessing received by one of our sisters that stated that her life would continue over a period when she would see great devastation and that she would be called to go into homes of the sorrowing, the suffering, the sick and afflicted, to minister unto them, to bind up their wounds, and to cheer them.

I believe that we have all been called to minister unto those in need, to bind up not just their physical wounds but also their spiritual wounds, social wounds, and wounds that are kept hidden, sometimes festering until someone cares enough to tend the lights along the shore.

These are matters of eternal consequence, and we can, if we desire, reach far enough to experience an awakening of things we have known before. Remember, President Kimball said:

> In the world before we came here, faithful women were given certain assignments while faithful men were foreordained to certain priesthood tasks. While we do not remember the particulars, this does not alter the glorious reality of what we once agreed to. We are accountable for those things which long ago were expected of us just as are those whom we sustain as prophets and apostles.[40]

It is my fervent and humble testimony that the heavens are very much open to women today. They are not closed unless we, ourselves, by our choices, close them. And this reality can be just as evident as in any time past. As I read of the great spirituality of women of the past and realize how the Lord communicated with them, I thrill with the spiritual manifestations that have accompanied their missions in life, literally a power evidencing the will of God made known through their instrumentality. I think of Eliza R. Snow, of whom Joseph F. Smith said, "She walked not in the borrowed light of others, but faced the morning unafraid and invincible."[41]

The Spirit whispers to me that there are Eliza R. Snows among us even today, and there can be many, many more. We can pull down the blessings of heaven through obedience to law. These divine and sacred blessings are not reserved for others alone. Visions and revelations come by the power of the Holy Ghost, and the Lord has said, "And on my servants and on my handmaidens I will pour out in those days of my Spirit; and they shall prophesy."[42]

Now let us go forth with the faith, the vision, the direction, and the decision to abide the laws that ensure these blessings not only for ourselves and our families but for all of God's children everywhere.

As we leave this conference, let us each feel deeply the power and strength and influence for good of our collective and united resolves. With renewed determination and confidence and commitment to the covenants we have made, let us become truly and in every way "Women of God." Let us go forth in faith and confidence and prepare for the noble calling spoken of by the prophet—to be a righteous woman during the winding-up scenes on this earth before the second coming of our Savior.

Ardeth G. Kapp, "Drifting, Dreaming, Directing," in Blueprints for Living: Perspectives for Latter-day Saint Women, *ed. Maren M. Mouritsen (Provo, UT: Brigham Young University, 1980), 77–88.*

Elaine A. Cannon speaking at general women's meeting. 1983. A writer, editor, and television and radio personality, Cannon actively endorsed the creation of a magazine for young people in the church and served as an associate editor when the *New Era* began publication in 1971. She also petitioned for Young Women to have Sunday religious instruction in addition to their weekday meetings. The church adopted this policy in 1980 while she was Young Women general president. Photograph by Marty Mayo. (Church History Library, Salt Lake City.)

SEASON OF AWAKENING

◇◇◇

ELAINE A. CANNON

Young Women Fireside
Tabernacle, Temple Square, Salt Lake City, Utah
March 28, 1981

As a young person, Elaine Anderson Cannon (1922–2003) was independent and active. Her parents had high expectations and invested in a variety of lessons and activities for their oldest daughter: piano, elocution, drama, singing, debate, and different kinds of contests.[1] She started writing when she was young, first a few stories, then a daily journal starting in sixth grade.[2] When she was eleven years old she wrote in that journal: "I'm writing this down so that when I'm a grown-up working with youth I will remember what it felt like to be young."[3]

Even before her service on the board of the Young Women's Mutual Improvement Association (YWMIA), Cannon devoted much of her life to church service, in addition to working as a writer, editor, television and radio personality, and popular speaker. Many of her service opportunities focused on young people and education, including the youth correlation committee, the curriculum planning and writing committee, and lecturing for the Church Educational System.[4] Cannon also raised six children with her husband, James.[5]

Cannon was not always able to achieve an objective on the first try. She reflected, "I am willing to go to the Lord and say, 'Okay, I really care about this. If it's something you're interested in, then help me. Together we can go and do whatever we need to do.'"[6] When leading the Young Women, she would tell the general board members, "If we can't get to it this way, then we'll just go like this to get there, around whomever or whatever obstacles."[7] She insisted the key to knowing when to persevere was to be alert to God's will.[8] For instance, she felt strongly that it was God's will that young people should have their own periodical, instead of the "Era of Youth" insert in the *Improvement Era* that she and Marion D. Hanks coedited from 1959 through 1970.[9] Cannon's and Hanks's initial efforts to start a youth magazine were stymied. So Cannon asked Hanks, an assistant to the Quorum of the Twelve Apostles, to get them an appointment with Spencer W. Kimball, then president of the Quorum of the Twelve. She fasted and prayed, and at the meeting they made their pitch. Kimball swirled his chair around, pounded his fist on the desk, and said, "Let's do it, and I will be the first subscriber."[10]

While serving on the YWMIA general board from 1961 to 1963, Cannon tried without success to implement Sunday religious instruction for young women.[11] At the time, young women studied the gospel briefly during their weeknight meetings, but not on Sundays. Young men had weeknight activities, but they also attended priesthood meetings on Sundays. Cannon felt that young women should have more structured opportunities to study the gospel. When she became general president of the Young Women in 1978, she returned to this cause.[12] This time, Cannon's efforts coincided with church development of a consolidated Sunday meeting schedule.[13] She fasted, prayed, and expressed her feelings to the First Presidency. On September 1, 1979, she wrote in her journal that Sunday instruction for young women had been approved as part of the new consolidated meeting schedule.[14] Around the time of the talk reproduced here, she was working to instigate a general women's meeting, where members of the Young Women and the Relief Society would meet together annually instead of in separate meetings.[15]

Cannon believed a crucial part of her mission was, as her daughter put it, "to give an identity and a place to the young women of the church that reflected the equal value the Lord places on both his young men and young women."[16] She gave the following talk advising young women to develop a relationship with God while serving as general president of the Young Women organization, which she led until 1984.[17] Young women attended this second annual fireside with general board members and local leaders; it was broadcast throughout the world.[18] The theme was "For God hath not given us the spirit of fear; but of power, and of love, and of a sound mind (2 Tim. 1:7)."[19] Camilla E. Kimball spoke first, followed by her husband, church president Spencer W. Kimball, then Cannon.[20] Four young women spoke after Cannon: Julie Fullmer, Becky Goates, Becky Smith, and Kirsten Brady. Marvin J. Ashton of the Quorum of the Twelve gave remarks that concluded the evening.[21]

AS A YOUNG WOMEN PRESIDENCY we want you to know that we are committed to sustaining President Kimball and the Brethren and to helping the Lord Jesus Christ in his great mission "to bring to pass the immortality and eternal life of man."[22] And our special concern is with the young women between the ages of twelve and eighteen. It is a privilege to be serving this very royal generation of young women.[23]

Now, in Utah where this program is originating, we are coming into the greening time. It is the season of the awakening. Buds are thickening on the branches. Brave early bloomers are brightening Temple Square. It is spring! While over there in Australia and New Zealand—that part of the world where so many of you are listening right now—the seasons are completely reversed. It is almost the time of the harvest.

So it is with us in this congregation. There are over a quarter of a million young women—girls who are in the spring of their lives. There are also over 35,000 adult presidencies—guardians of the girls who are, some of us, pushing the summer of our lives to the very limit.

Somewhere in between our seasons of spring and harvest time, the nurturing, pruning, and enriching in our lives must happen before the miracle of the harvest can occur. We pray for us all that one day the yield of our lives will be acceptable before God.

For you who are in the season of the awakening, in the spring of your life, that special song that the choir sang to open this meeting was dedicated to you. It was as if each one of you might be saying:

> Who am I?
> What special purpose is mine?
> I follow winged sparrow . . . and I yearn to soar.
> I hear the ocean's thunder. There is pow'r!
> But what am I?
> I see lilies blooming where the winter storms have swept the field.
> I feel the sun; by its radiance I see all that God created.
> I, too, am God's creation, and he knows me as his own.
> Tenderly, I know him in my heart.
> Who am I? [What special purpose is mine?]
> I am a daughter of God.[24]

So you are—a daughter of God, a member of his family. Being a member of a family usually means you do what the family does; you keep the family's standards; you live as the family lives; you speak as the family speaks. You love after the manner of the family. Your kindnesses are done in the name of the family. Now, while all of your dreams haven't come true yet and the growing pains are often grim, I think it really helps to remember that the head of this heavenly family is a Patriarch who, with his great caring, his great quality, his infinite wisdom and superb capacity, loves you—loves you anyway. While you are away from Heavenly Father, wandering here on earth, experiencing and learning, he's watching. He's waiting. He wants you to come home again. He wants you to make it.

No doubt you have had some moments when you've felt a kind of inner longing, a loneliness even while surrounded by people. You've felt a kind of eternal homesickness, as some people have spoken of it. You have a vague remembrance that you do have a special link with Heavenly Father. I think that knowing this ought to make a difference in how *you* feel about *yourself.* It ought to make a difference in how you *are* and in the things you do and the choices you make. We believe that each of you should develop a sweet and saving relationship with the Lord, because when you have that, everything else will begin to fall into place—things like personal purity, temple endowment, honoring your parents, and learning all you can about the plan of life and the principles to live it. See, it really doesn't matter, really it doesn't matter, whether you are skinny or wide or tall or small. It's what you are inside that counts; that's all. You develop yourself with a new confidence, a new purpose, and you begin to contribute to others of our Heavenly Father's children.

Remember, he's standing by to help.

In the Bible we are told, "The Spirit itself beareth witness with our spirit, that we are the children of God."[25] Spiritually, then, you are rooted in God. This is the most important knowledge to obtain. The second most important knowledge, perhaps, is the purpose of your physical bodies.

Physically you are descendants of father Abraham and are entitled to all the blessings God promised Abraham's posterity.[26] I think it is well to remember that you are also indebted to all of your recent ancestors who have gone before you and laid foundations for you to build upon.

The poet Walt Whitman says something I'd like you to think about in terms of your own parents, family, and the place you call home. He says:

> There was a child went forth every day;
> And the first object he look'd upon, that object he became;
> And that object became part of him for the day, or a certain part
> of the day, or for many years, or stretching cycles of years.
>
> The early lilacs became part of this child. . . .
> The streets themselves, and the facades of houses, and goods in
> the windows. . . .
> The horizon's edge, the flying sea-crow, the fragrance of salt marsh
> and shore mud,
> These became part of [him].

[*lines out of sequence*]

His own parents,
He that had father'd him, and she that had conceiv'd him in her
womb, and birth'd him,
They gave this child more of themselves than that;
They gave him afterward every day—they became part of him. . . .
The family usages, the language, the company, the furniture—
the yearning and swelling heart,
Affection that will not be gainsay'd—the sense of what is real. . . .
These became part of that child who went forth every day, and
who now goes, and will always go forth every day.[27]

Sisters, with apologies for editing Mr. Whitman somewhat, in the interest of time, let me suggest that what has been written so beautifully in poetry by him is true in life. All that you learn and see and choose to do, all that home and friends and church and school are to you, you are! You are rapidly becoming what you are going to be.

But you have a remarkable advantage over other people in the world—you can have a patriarchal blessing.[28] Only a fraction of the earth's population is so privileged. A member in good standing of the Church of Jesus Christ of Latter-day Saints is entitled to have hands placed upon her head by an ordained patriarch and through the power of the priesthood of God receive a very personal blessing from her Heavenly Father. This is one way to learn more about yourself and what you might do with your life. I think it is God's special gift to us.

Studying your patriarchal blessing frequently, especially in times of decision or trial or depression, will quickly remind you and give you the vision of who you really are and what your relationship with God is, and especially what his will for you is. It can comfort you when you feel unloved and unworthy and inadequate or forgotten. It can point you toward your own special purpose in life.

I am going to be personal for a moment and tell you that when I was about the age of many of you young women, I had my patriarchal blessing. It was late spring. The season was at its best, and I wanted to be, too; so I had prepared myself to receive what Heavenly Father would have to say to me personally. There had been some repenting, some fasting and praying, and deep discussions about the meaning of it all with my parents and a very special boyfriend. I remember well the night before my appointment with Patriarch Jones, up there on Capitol Hill behind the Tabernacle.[29] I felt a strong need to gather myself together with Heavenly Father, and I went outside through the screen door and stood there for a time listening to the years of my childhood sift by on the night song of the crickets. I felt very grown-up that moment. Then suddenly I felt once again the pull of the stars. Kind of self-consciously at first, I stretched down on my back on prickly grass, as I had done so often as a child. (You know what I mean.) Then once again I took a deep breath and turned my face skyward. I studied the heavens; I found the familiar constellations and got placement with the North Star. And then there came to me the mind-stretching, soul-searing experience of feeling lifted up into the universe—almost into the presence of God, it seemed to me. It set my heart pounding. I knew my prayers had reached home in heaven. The witness of the Spirit to me that God lives and was mindful of little me warmed me to tears. The next day when I went for my blessing, I knew that the blessings and instructions that were given to me by that wonderful patriarch were personal.

That was a green spring for me. It was the season of awakening for me as I tried thereafter to make decisions according to God's will for me and to commit myself to a way of life that would ensure fulfillment of all his sacred promises.

Now, in the time of the harvest in my life, I can say it is so. God lives. He loves us.

Most of you are in the green springtime of your life—the time of awakening—and you have so much going for you. You can do anything you want to with your one chance at life, if you want to badly enough.

We have talked about your spiritual endowment—your spiritual roots—heredity, environment—they all have their important places in you.[30] Your patriarchal blessing is a unique and sacred and strengthening gift to you. But there is yet another factor. It is that particular quality or essence that has always and forever been you, and it determines how you'll respond to the challenges of life.

When I was visiting in Russia, I bought a hand-carved and hand-painted peasant doll. Actually it is many dolls of graduating sizes that nest one inside the other. You'd never suspect what is inside that big doll by looking at the outside of it. I love that doll. It stands as a reminder to me that there is more to a person than meets the eye. I think we need to think about this in terms of ourselves. And it would be well if we remembered it about others as well.

You have a lot to you, too, girls, more than meets the eye. Beautiful as you are, there is more to you than meets the eye. Now, what are you going to do about it?

One of the basic teachings of the gospel is that everyone is responsible for his or her own salvation. That is the prime purpose of life on earth. You can be taught; you can be prayed over; you can be preached to; you can be endowed; but you cannot be forced into the presence of your Heavenly Father. You earn that privilege by learning and by doing with the givens of your life.

Heavenly Father loves you, but true love doesn't force. He will not force you to do his will. He will not force you even to accept his blessings. He will not deny you your choice. Since you are personally accountable for your own actions and choices, how soon will you start shouldering the powerful and precious responsibility for yourself? When, little sister, you who are a daughter of God? When?

Deep in your heart, as I talk to you now, I'm certain you sense all of this. You know you are his. You know Heavenly Father loves you. Those deep feelings that you are having right this minute are from him. Like the song says, "Tenderly [you] know him in [your] heart," and "he knows [you] as his own."[31]

Then turn to him. Want him in your life. Love him enough to keep his commandments, and all will be well with you.

I hope you'll write about your feelings in your journal. I hope you'll record what you are learning through this meeting.

And now a final scripture to consider:

"Blessed is the [one] that trusteth in the Lord, and whose hope the Lord is.

"For [she] shall be as a tree planted by the waters, and that spreadeth out her roots by the river, and shall not see when heat cometh, but her leaf shall be green; and shall not be careful in the year of drought, neither shall cease from yielding fruit."[32]

My sisters, whether we are in Utah or Australia or somewhere in between, whether we are in the season of youth and spring or the time of the harvest in our lives, if we put our trust in the Lord and our roots in his gospel, all will be well with us. When the heat of temptation or pressure comes into our lives, we will not wilt, neither shall we become unproductive.

As the Young Women presidency, we love you. And we love the Lord. We love the opportunity President Kimball and the Brethren have given us to serve you. We pray for you on our knees. We leave these thoughts and our love with you in the name of Jesus Christ, amen.

Elaine A. Cannon, "Season of Awakening," New Era *11, no. 6 (July 1981): 9–12.*

Francine R. Bennion. 1995. Bennion served on the general boards of the Young Women and Relief Society in the 1970s and 1980s. Photograph by Busath Photography. (Courtesy Francine Bennion.)

A LATTER-DAY SAINT THEOLOGY OF SUFFERING

◇◇◇

FRANCINE R. BENNION

Brigham Young University Women's Conference
Harris Fine Arts Center, Brigham Young University, Provo, Utah
March 28, 1986

What I'm passionate about," said Francine Russell Bennion (b. 1935), "is human existence, and the relationships between people and God, and what works and what doesn't."[1] In an interview, Bennion explained that when she taught a Relief Society or Gospel Doctrine lesson she never wanted to brush off reality and speak only of ideals. Instead, she tried to present fresh, useful, and reality-affirming perspectives that would lift and enhance human relationships.[2]

Born to Latter-day Saint parents in Lethbridge, Alberta, Canada, Bennion is a classically trained pianist who studied at the Banff School of Fine Arts and has degrees from the Royal Schools of Music in London, England, and the Western Board of Music. She earned a bachelor's degree in French from Brigham Young University (BYU) and a master's degree in English from Ohio State University, where her husband, Robert C. Bennion, earned a doctorate in clinical psychology at the same time.[3] Together they raised three children. Bennion taught reading, writing, and logic courses part time at Ohio State between 1957 and 1961. Between 1961 and 1997, she taught courses in English, piano, Book of Mormon, and history of civilization at BYU.[4] Throughout her career and church service, she expressed her devotion to logic, words, and ideas.

During the 1970s, Bennion served on ad hoc committees both at the general level of the church and at BYU. One of these committees was foundational to forming the Women's Research Institute at BYU.[5] Bennion also worked on the church's instructional development committee, writing curriculum for both the Relief Society and the Young Women programs.[6] She served on the Young Women general board under President Ruth Hardy Funk from 1976 to 1978.[7] When Barbara B. Smith was general president of the Relief Society, Bennion and Aileen H. Clyde were asked to develop a workshop about depression, since many church members were reporting a struggle with depression to their bishops. From 1980 to 1982 Bennion and Clyde tested and conducted the workshop in various settings, including a twelve-week Sunday School course in two wards, selected Relief Society groups, and some all-day Saturday meetings.[8] In 1983, Smith asked Bennion to join the Relief Society general board, where she served until Smith's release in 1984.[9]

Bennion had long thought about the assumptions undergirding human opinions and behavior. "Human experience is an endless revealer of underlying assumptions. . . . Being real means trying to make sense of what truly is good and real—and what is consistent with a God who is love and joy," she expressed.[10] In response to a request from the BYU Women's Conference committee that she focus on the topic of suffering, Bennion gave the following talk designed to address "vital issues in the lives of all thoughtful Latter-day Saints."[11]

IT IS NOT MY PURPOSE here to give careful definition of the term *suffering* or to distinguish between various kinds of suffering. For purposes of this discussion, *suffering* is anything that hurts badly, in any way.

Nor is it my purpose to answer all questions about suffering, or even to suggest that we all have the same questions. We have our own quests, and the search for peace must be our own. My intent is to discuss the reservoir to which many of us go for understanding and comfort in time of anguish.

My friend Sheila Brown came out of brain surgery with one side of her body paralyzed and with her speech and sight badly impaired. As we worked one day at stretching and relaxing her muscles, Sheila asked me what I was going to talk about at the BYU Women's Conference.

"A Latter-day Saint theology of suffering."

"Oh," she said, searching for words and trying to form them, "I think—you should talk about theology of—courage—hope—like looking out a window."

"I think it's the same thing," I replied.

We are accustomed to talking of fragments of theology—a topic here, an assumption or tradition there, often out of context with the whole. We are a people accustomed also to fragments of scripture out of context—a phrase here, a verse there, words that say something appropriate to the matter at hand, and ring with clarity and conviction. We have to do it; we haven't time or ability to say everything at once. Sometimes, however, the clarity becomes blurred and the conviction open to question when a person puts some fragments with others. For example, what do you make of the following?

2 Nephi 2:25	"Men are, that they might have joy."
Job 5:7	"Man is born unto trouble, as the sparks fly upward."
Deuteronomy 4:29–31	"But if from thence thou shalt seek the Lord thy God, thou shalt find him, if thou seek him with all thy heart and with all thy soul. When thou art in tribulation, and all these things are come upon thee, even in the latter days, if thou turn to the Lord thy God, and shalt be obedient unto his voice; . . . he will not forsake thee."
Psalm 22:1–2	"My God, my God, why hast thou forsaken me? why art thou so far from helping me, and from the words of my roaring? O my God, I cry in the daytime, but thou hearest not; and in the night season, and am not silent."
Matthew 27:46	"My God, my God, why hast thou forsaken me?"
Abraham 3:18	"Spirits . . . have no beginning; they existed before, they shall have no end, they shall exist after, for they are gnolaum, or eternal."
2 Nephi 2:14	"God . . . hath created all things, both the heavens and the earth, and all things that in them are, both things to act and things to be acted upon."
Proverbs 3:13	"Happy is the man that findeth wisdom, and the man that getteth understanding."
Ecclesiastes 1:18	"In much wisdom is much grief: and he that increaseth knowledge increaseth sorrow."

One function of theology is to provide a comprehensive framework that gives meaning to the fragments and the seeming contradictions or paradoxes which they suggest. Theology provides a framework that binds diversity and complexity into a more simple net with which we can make some sense even of things we don't fully understand.

If we live long enough, we find diverse views and contrasting fragments not only in scripture but also in life. For example, Dorothy Bramhall went to Hawaii in February for the birth of a grandchild.[12] She went also for a visit with a longtime friend, not LDS, who had lost two sons in a traffic accident and then struggled with her own cancer and amputations for many years. Dorothy wrote:

> It's been a week of varied emotions. My friend, Jean Kerr, died the morning after I arrived.[13] It seems I'm destined to spend part of my beach time in Hawaii contemplating the death of a good friend. The beach, at least for me, like the mountains, is a good place for such contemplation. Again, my thoughts have been drawn to the "why" of it all. For those of us in the church, there are at least a few answers to that question. But as I look at my friend and wonder what her purpose in life was—it seems that suffering has been the *only* purpose. . . . Suffering without a sense of purpose seems bitter indeed. Her mother said her husband prayed all night for her to die. Does one who doesn't believe pray to anyone or anything? Or is it merely another way of saying—he yearned for or hoped that she would die? Do you think such a prayer will be heard when all those given for her healing have not been?
>
> Enough! My grandson was born at 5 a.m. Sat. Eight lbs., 8 ozs.! I don't know where she put him—from the back you would never know she was pregnant. He has lots of black hair, and I'm hoping maybe this one will be brown eyed. This is a miracle baby. When he was born the doctor showed them that the cord was knotted. The reason the baby survived is that his cord was unusually long, and the knot was never pulled tight. They are feeling very blessed. It's always such a humbling feeling to look at a newborn—such utter perfection! I can hardly wait to hold him.[14]

The same week, the daughter of another of my friends gave birth to a premature Down's syndrome child who has already had two of the six operations needed for survival. On March 2, a report released by the World Bank estimated that 730 million people in poor countries, not including China, lacked the income in 1980 to buy enough food to give them the energy for an active working life.[15]

One function of any religion is to explain such a world as this, to provide a theology that makes sense of love and joy and miracles but also of suffering and struggle and lack of miracles. Good theology makes sense of what is possible but also of what is presently real and probable. In this twentieth century, it is not enough that a theology of suffering explain *my* experience; it must also explain the child lying in a gutter in India, the woman crawling across the Ethiopian desert to find a weed to eat, and the fighting and misery of many humans because of pride, greed, or fear in a powerful few.[16] Satisfying theology must explain the child sexually abused or scarred for life, or the astronaut who is blown up and leaves a family motherless or fatherless.[17] Good theology of suffering explains *all* human suffering, not just the suffering of those who feel they know God's word and are his chosen people.

It is not enough that theology be *either* rational *or* faith promoting. It must be both. It is not enough that satisfying theology be mastered by a few expert scholars, teachers, and leaders. It must be comfortably carried by ordinary people. It is not enough that theology help me to understand God. It must also help me to understand myself and my world.

Theology does not prevent all hurt and anguish. No knowledge of theology can remove all pain, weakness, or nausea from all terminal cancer. Nor can it fill an empty stomach. What sound theology *can* do is to help those who believe it to make some sense of the suffering, of themselves, and of God, such sense that they can proceed with a measure of hope, courage, compassion, and understanding of themselves even in anguish.

There is no single theology of suffering in our church, one framework uniform in all respects in the minds of all leaders and all other members. Though we may share the same scripture, the same revelation, prophets, and belief that God and Christ are real, we have various frameworks for putting them together and for seeing suffering, either our own or someone else's. One person thinks God sends suffering to teach us or to test us. Another thinks God or Satan can affect only our response to the suffering, and some think it is Satan who is causing the suffering. Others think there should be no suffering at all if we are righteous and certainly no misunderstanding at all about why it is happening. These are only a few of the varieties of LDS belief about the origins of suffering, and however contradictory they be, each can be supported by fragments of scripture.[18]

We do not use identical principles or patterns to bind together fragments of scripture and life. In this twentieth century, with the history of the world before us, each of us has taken ideas and patterns from various sources to form our personal theologies of suffering. The complexity and power of those sources are evident in the story of Jephthah.

According to the book of Judges, chapter 11, Jephthah was asked to lead Israel against invading Ammonites.

> And Jephthah said unto the elders of Gilead, If . . . the Lord deliver them before me, shall I be your head?
>
> And the elders of Gilead said unto Jephthah, The Lord be witness between us, if we do not so according to thy words.

> Then Jephthah went with the elders of Gilead, and the people made him head and captain over them. . . .
>
> Then the Spirit of the Lord came upon Jephthah. . . .
>
> And Jephthah vowed a vow unto the Lord, and said, If thou shalt without fail deliver the children of Ammon into mine hands,
>
> Then it shall be, that whatsoever cometh forth of the doors of my house to meet me, when I return in peace from the children of Ammon, shall surely be the Lord's, and I will offer it up for a burnt offering.
>
> So Jephthah passed over unto the children of Ammon to fight against them; and the Lord delivered them into his hands.
>
> And he smote them . . . with a very great slaughter. Thus the children of Ammon were subdued before the children of Israel.
>
> And Jephthah came to Mizpeh unto his house, and, behold, his daughter came out to meet him with timbrels and with dances: and she was his only child; beside her he had neither son nor daughter.
>
> And it came to pass, when he saw her, that he rent his clothes, and said, Alas, my daughter! thou hast brought me very low, and thou art one of them that trouble me: for I have opened my mouth unto the Lord, and I cannot go back.
>
> And she said unto him, My father, if thou hast opened thy mouth unto the Lord, do to me according to that which hath proceeded out of thy mouth; forasmuch as the Lord hath taken vengeance for thee of thine enemies, even of the children of Ammon.
>
> And she said unto her father; Let this thing be done for me: let me alone two months, that I may go up and down upon the mountains, and bewail my virginity, I and my fellows.
>
> And he said, Go. And he sent her away for two months: and she went with her companions, and bewailed her virginity upon the mountains.
>
> And it came to pass at the end of two months, that she returned unto her father, who did with her according to his vow which he had vowed.[19]

As the story is told, Jephthah makes the sacrifice because he believes it to be right. At the core of his and his daughter's theology are these principles: God controls human events and determines either victory or defeat in battle. God can be bargained with. God gives Israel victory *because* of Jephthah's all-encompassing vow, his willingness to give God anything he has. God's law requires that the vow be kept. According to our record in the book of Numbers, "If a man vow a vow unto the Lord, or swear an oath to bind his soul with a bond; he shall not break his word, he shall do according to all that proceedeth out of his mouth."[20]

A human being's function is to obey the law. If God had wanted the obedient daughter saved, he could have prevented her from dancing out at so inopportune a moment.

We do not all read the same things into Jephthah's story, or into sacrifice.[21] Even in so short a story, the context for suffering is complex and today provokes questions such as these: Who is really responsible for the suffering in this story? Jephthah? God? The religious leaders who taught the theology that contributed to the making and keeping of the vow? Persons who developed a social system in which a daughter is her father's property? What of Jephthah's wife, who isn't even mentioned? What about Jephthah's father and harlot mother, and the half-brothers who threw Jephthah out of the house earlier in his life and perhaps contributed to his great desire for the power that victory would bring?[22] What about Jacob, who set a precedent by bargaining with God?[23] Or Moses, who, without regard to circumstances, seemed to teach that keeping a vow was more important than "selfish" compassion?

This list does not, of course, exhaust the questions, which go beyond reasons for Jephthah's vow; for example, is obedience always a virtue? Is the major difference between God and Satan just a matter of who's in charge, demanding obedience?

Custom can make the whole matter of Jephthah's vow seem simple, and we tend to like simplicity and clarity, even if it means ignoring some things. There is power in simplicity. Some thousand and more years after the time of the judges, Paul the apostle praised Jephthah for his faith without condemning him for ambition or rashness.[24]

Today, many who do think Jephthah rash nevertheless have "simply" made his version of God their own: a God who controls all human events; a God who can and must be bargained with; a God who considers unquestioning obedience to be the highest good—not just the *means* to goodness, but goodness itself; a God who causes suffering in the innocent and also authorizes theology that fosters it. Many who believe in such a God either ignore or are confused by inconsistency with other scriptures that seem to speak of God's valuing agency above obedience,[25] love above tradition,[26] and the human heart above ritual sacrifice.[27]

What do *you* think about Jephthah, his vow, and his God? Your answer will depend in part upon your own version of theology.

Does it really matter what we think? Can't we just be kind and patient, without worrying about various points of theology?

It matters. For one thing, our assumptions affect how kind and patient we are likely to become. What Jephthah *believed* was central to what he did about suffering, and what we *believe* is central to what we do about it. For example, if we believe that inflicting suffering will further God's work or glory, we may inflict it, as Irish and Lebanese and Iranians are currently doing, or as a father did by punishing his young son by putting his hands under scalding water, which nearly destroyed them, or as a husband is doing by telling his wife she can do nothing unless he tells her she can.[28]

If we believe God wants suffering, we may not take responsible action to relieve or prevent it. Thirty-five years ago, one of my schoolteachers would not take medical help for a lump in her thigh because "God had given it to her." In Relief Society one Sunday last year, a class member told us we shouldn't concern ourselves with events in the newspaper because God is planning destruction before the Millennium anyway, and all we should concern ourselves with is our own righteousness and that of our children, and then we'll be all right. A few years ago, one young woman's confusion about God and suffering was central to her anguish and paralysis in the face of repeated violence: "I don't know what it is God's trying to teach me with my husband's temper."

Many who believe God is causing the suffering will not, or feel they cannot, ask him for help or comfort at the very time they need it most.

Another of the reasons our theology of suffering matters is that we may live comfortably with a framework which has inherent holes and contradictions as long as the suffering is someone else's or as long as our own suffering isn't very great. But holes and contradictions have a way of becoming very important when anguish is our own or when we feel the pain of persons we care about. Job's friends said to him:

> Behold, thou hast instructed many, and thou hast strengthened the weak hands.
>
> Thy words have upholden him that was falling, and thou hast strengthened the feeble knees.
>
> But now it is come upon thee, and thou faintest; it toucheth thee, and thou art troubled.[29]

If, like Job, we find that the comforts we've offered others aren't sufficient for our own experience, then the suffering itself, however great, is not the only problem. The problem is also that the universe and our ability to make sense of it have fallen apart, and we are without hope or trust in ourselves or in God.

Theology can become an even heavier problem than the anguish of suffering itself. If we believe suffering shouldn't exist, but it does; or suffering is God's way of testing and teaching, but what can a wailing infant be proving or learning; or prayer should cure the problem, but it hasn't—then it is not only the suffering that troubles us but also the great cracks in a universe that should make sense but doesn't. I have seen the pain of persons in this place, the pain of persons fumbling with their long-held assumptions when the ancient questions rise afresh, though they had thought them already answered: Why is this happening? Can I stand it? What can I do? What am I? Is God real, or powerful, or good? What is life for? What does he want us to do with it?

Important to one's struggles with such questions are the implications of elements at the core of one's theology—for example, Latter-day Saint belief that we can become more like God, our Eternal Father, not just obey him or imitate him or follow his Son, though these things are part of the process, but become gods ourselves with his help.

For many Christians, such doctrine is scandalous, radical, heretical. On February 17, 1600, the Dominican priest Bruno of Nola was burned at the stake as a heretic. Among other things, he had taught that there is an infinity of worlds, the universe is eternal, and "from a more vile creature I become a God."[30] Today there is widespread agreement that there is indeed an infinity of worlds, and that so-called matter or energy is eternal, though fluctuating in form and state. But the idea of humans becoming gods is still considered by traditional Christians to be a vain, presumptuous, heretical notion.[31]

Even among those who believe it, the idea of our possible state as gods sometimes remains as nebulous as traditional views of pink clouds and golden harps. A group of BYU Honors students was discussing Voltaire and "the best of all possible worlds."[32]

"Tell me," I said, "what you consider to be the best of all possible worlds."

"It would be like the celestial kingdom."

"What is that like?"

"Well, there won't be problems like we have here."

"What kind of problems?"

"Well, for one thing, everyone will be—happy. There won't be any unkindness. No one there will be rejected or abused, or laughed at, or ignored."

"Oh," I said. "Are you suggesting that God experiences none of these things now?"

And then there was silence, for a moment.

In wanting to get to the celestial kingdom, these students had more awareness of traditional struggle-free utopias than of our own God and our own world. The celestial kingdom was a place to get away from suffering, not a place to understand it and address it in ways consistent with joy and love and agency.

It is not only professed points of doctrine such as potential godhood or the celestial kingdom that matter but also the meaning and larger framework that a person gives to them. The larger framework gives meaning to the fragments. I haven't heard anyone in or out of our church ask why God caused seven persons to fall in bits to the bottom of the sea when the space shuttle *Challenger* exploded. We are accustomed to a methodical framework for space travel, and we looked within that framework for explanations of the disaster. A commission began to examine video reruns, O-rings, materials, workmanship, memos, organization, and decision making, among other things, to identify and address problems before proceeding with the next manned space project. The process was complex, but even minor steps had been recorded, and a meticulous report was possible.

We can make such a report to trace the steps in many kinds of suffering, but usually we have neither time nor ability to reduce all causes and all effects to a satisfying xeroxed page.[33] Even when we can do it quite accurately, we are most likely reporting *how* the suffering came about, not *why*. Some twenty years ago, a man watched his mother die miserably of cancer and then, closing up the house, said, "I cannot pray to a God who would let my little mother suffer like that." He did not want a step-by-step report on how cancer causes pain, or how she got the cancer. He wanted to know why cancer exists at all, why there is pain, why God doesn't prevent it, why the innocent suffer, why a small frail human would have such undeserved hurt. What purpose could justify such anguish? What comprehensive model of existence could make sense of it?

We have not the mind of God. We see through a glass darkly now and will till we meet him and ourselves face to face and "know as we are known."[34] There are times we must say, "I don't know." If we think we know everything, it is a sure sign we do not. But we are capable of learning much about this world and of considering what difference LDS doctrines can make to how we put together our experience, our diverse scriptures, our traditions, and well-supported but contradictory theological explanations. The better we understand what *is* at the core of LDS doctrine, the better we can distinguish what is *not*. We need not shroud ourselves helplessly in a crazy quilt stitched haphazardly from Old Testament theology, such as that of Jephthah, with a few patches of utopian thought and LDS doctrine embroidered on top. We can extend our understanding of LDS principles and use them as the core for a framework with which to make some sense of contradictory fragments.

Of course it may seem simpler to stay on well-worn traditional ground, but God—and this is one of the most important things we believe about him—has invited us to go further, to make suffering worth the trouble and to meet it as well as we can. We can be in the process of learning to do that whatever our current limitations or circumstances. Though our search for understanding be long or incomplete, it can lead us to courage, peace, and an increasingly truer sense of ourselves and God.

The traditional views are that we are alive because God put us here, or because Eve and Adam fell from innocence and trouble-free paradise through disobedience. These views are expressed in scripture. The Latter-day Saints believe, however, that these traditional views are fragmentary because they leave out several important things—for example, that we have existed without beginning and that we are here because we chose to come.[35] We are here not just because God decided it would be a good idea and made it happen, not just because Adam and Eve fell and we automatically followed, but because *we chose to come.* However essential what God or Eve or Adam did to make it possible, we believe the decision to be born was our own. Our very brief accounts of life before this earth suggest that we chose as Eve chose, and we defended that choice in whatever kind of war can take place among spirits.[36] Our birth is evidence of courage and faith, not helplessness, shame, and disobedience, and yet we must make sense of conflicting reports about it, seemingly contradictory fragments about it. If we are to make sense of them, we had better understand well the implications of those brief fragments we have about our existence before human life began.

We don't know if there were several possibilities of which we have no record, but I doubt there was a never-never land where we could have been happy children without responsibility forever.[37] Apparently there was a point at which we had to grow up or choose not to. Our scriptures suggest that there were unavoidable decisions to be made consciously and responsibly by all inhabitants in the premortal council, as in Eden. We could not be mere observers, only thinking about the decision, only imagining what might happen if we made it, only talking about the meaning of it all. At any rate, God's directive to Alma when he watched good women and children being burned alive in Ammonihah suggests that it was not enough to imagine what might have happened if they were burned to death, or what might have become of the persons who were doing it.[38] God didn't want to know just what *could* happen and neither, apparently, did they in the beginning.

At any rate, we are told that there were two alternatives. Lucifer proposed a way so different from God's that it would have destroyed this universe in which God speaks of *I* and *thou, they* and *we,* this universe in which Elohim and Jehovah speak of their own names and also address *by name* Eve, Joseph, Moses, Mary, Abraham, Helaman, Peter, and Emma.[39] Lucifer would have for all of us only one name, one will, one identity: his own. It was not obedience and "success" (by his definition) he would prevent; rather it was disobedience and failure he would not allow. In his universe, no one would be hurt or afraid. He would allow only whatever experience and identity he chose for us, and if we met pleasure, pain, or success, it would be wholly because of himself, not because of ourselves. The wonder is that Lucifer's intended universe is exactly the universe many now attribute to God, or want from him.

God offered a profoundly different possibility, that with his help we meet and create reality as individuals in a universe of law and personal agency, and ultimately choose who we want to be, choosing to become more like himself if that is what we want, choosing to become gods if that is what we truly want for all eternity.[40] Law in God's universe is a matter of processes or relationships that are knowable and predictable, not whimsical or inconsistent. Such law is inherent in all matters. Agency in such a universe is not only the capacity for moral choice, but more largely, the capacity for real thought, action, and invention, with inherent consequences for oneself and others. An agent is one whose self cannot be permanently determined by other persons, or by events and circumstances. The implications of this doctrine are important to our suffering whether we live in England or Africa, with or without current understanding of God's ways.

We wanted life, however high the cost. We suffer because we were willing to pay the cost of *being* and of being here with others in their ignorance and inexperience as well as our own. We suffer because we are willing to pay the costs of living with laws of nature, which operate quite consistently whether or not we understand them or can manage them. We suffer because, like Christ in the desert, we apparently did not say we would come only if God would change all our stones to bread in time of hunger. We were willing to *know* hunger. Like Christ in the desert, we did not ask God to let us try falling or being bruised only on condition that he catch us before we touch ground and save us from real hurt.[41] We were willing to *know* hurt. Like Christ, we did not agree to come only if God would make everyone bow to us and respect us, or admire us and understand us. Like Christ, we came to be ourselves, addressing and creating reality. We are finding out who we are and who we can become regardless of immediate environment or circumstances.

What is the point of that? What is the point of knowing reality and being ourselves, of suffering as Dorothy's friend Jean Kerr suffered and as many other people suffer daily? Why did this matter so much?

One reason we were willing to pay the high costs of continuing to address reality and become ourselves is that God told us we can become more like himself. We can become more abundantly alive, with ultimate fulness of truth, joy, and love—fulness impossible for souls unable to take real part in creating it, souls ignorant of good or evil, pleasure or pain, souls afraid of the unknown.

According to my understanding of scripture, we are not preparing now to begin in the next life to become more like God. We are not simply waiting to get started with the process. We are in it here and now. The implications of this are many, and there is time here to suggest only a few relevant to suffering.

If we are to become more like God, we must experience and understand the reality of physical law. Nobody in our world or in God's universe is manipulating mass, energy, motion, gravity, or quantum leaps so that they have no more reality than a TV movie or some imaginary adventure. For God, these matters of quantum leaps and mass and motion are real, and for us they are real. God functions according to laws that we are experiencing and trying to learn here. We have many scriptures indicating that our God is a God of law, and we are coming in contact with the same kind of laws he understands.[42] Laws are real for him, and the same laws are real for us. If they were not, we would have either incomprehensible chaos or the kind of existence which Lucifer offered.

Important to our experience is the reality of operations we can learn to depend upon and predict. Where would we be if gravity were inconsistent and we tried to sit down? Where would we be if gravity were working for some of us and not for others? Yet, when a child falls out of a high window, some wish gravity were not in effect at the moment, or suppose that God is using it to cause suffering, or look to him to stop it. The same thing occurs with other laws of mass and motion. We want to drive to the grocery store or across the country, but the same laws of motion and mass that take us on these trips can result in accidents that disfigure people for life or leave them helpless in bed for thirteen years unable to move. We live with natural law.

Nobody is manipulating every human decision that would affect every human experience. If God did, we would have the kind of existence now that Lucifer offered permanently. For God, the agency and real existence of other souls is of prime value, value that exceeds any reason for his arbitrarily controlling all they experience and become. God does not make himself the only reality, or the only source of reality.

"All truth is independent in that sphere in which God has placed it, to act for itself, as all intelligence also; otherwise there is no existence."[43] We cannot exist without agency and its results. Neither can we become like God if we think others must be deprived of their agency so that we can be ourselves. We are not coddled toddlers in playschool or Disneyland; we are not preparing to meet reality someday. We are in it here and now.

Soon after I learned to read, I discovered folk tales and myths on a bottom shelf in the public library and devoured all that were there. Heroes and heroines were kind and brave, sharing bread with persons much uglier and very different from themselves; they were able to ride the wind east of the sun and west of the moon, and they met mountains and forests and giants and persons who could turn them to stone, and they would emerge always triumphant and happy. I was one of them and walked to school disguised as an ordinary Canadian girl in the early 1940s and thought myself kind and brave. I could meet those things and would, as the people in the stories did. I didn't know then what it was really like to be turning into stone, so to speak, or what it was like trying to swim beyond my strength, but I know now. Though I would certainly share my bread with ugly old hags or anyone else who was starving, I didn't understand compassion for someone hurting me in their own ignorance. I thought only evil persons could hurt me. The folktales were imaginary; life is real.

There is a fragment of Isaiah which illuminates the matter for me. It is better in context with surrounding chapters and best in context with all scripture but is useful even alone:

> Whom shall he teach knowledge? and whom shall he make to understand doctrine? them that are weaned from the milk, and drawn from the breasts.
>
> For precept must be upon precept, precept upon precept; line upon line, line upon line; here a little, and there a little:
>
> For with stammering lips and another tongue will he speak to this people.
>
> To whom he said, This is the rest wherewith ye may cause the weary to rest; and this is the refreshing: yet they would not hear.
>
> But the word of the Lord was unto them precept upon precept, precept upon precept; line upon line, line upon line; here a little, and there a little; that they might go, and fall backward, and be broken, and snared, and taken.[44]

Why would he speak to us in a way that would let us "fall backward, and be broken, and snared, and taken"? For many years the passage puzzled me. I couldn't understand it. And yet, I think, if we are to understand God we must understand that passage.

I learned much about it one day in sacrament meeting, not from anything I heard but from watching a little boy playing in the row ahead of me. He had a quiet book open to a page with colored shapes—a purple square, an orange circle, red rectangle, green triangle, and on top of these, attached with Velcro, matching shapes and colors. The boy was clearly inexperienced. He pulled off all the shapes, then stuck a purple square on a green triangle, pulled his father's knee, and beamed up at him in utter delight because he had put a purple square on a green triangle and it stayed there. The father looked down, saw the mistake, shook his head, and turned his attention back to the speaker. The boy pulled the purple square off the green triangle, stuck it on an orange circle, pulled his father's knee, and beamed up at him with utter joy and delight. The father looked down, saw the mistake, shook his head, and turned back to the speaker. The boy pulled off the purple square and put it on a purple square, *discovered* the match, pulled his father's knee, and beamed up at him in utter delight. The father nodded and turned back to the speaker, and the boy began to experiment with the removable green triangle.

Of course, this is not a perfect metaphor for our experience with suffering or with God, but it suggests much to me in conjunction with the Isaiah passage. The boy was learning about shapes and colors, not just about being a good boy and pleasing his father by matching the right shapes and colors. Shapes and colors, useful though they be, were part of more comprehensive matters he was learning: he *can* learn, ignorance or mistakes need not be indelible, he is becoming himself, he is not the circumference of everyone else's universe, there is delight in discovery and invention, some "utter" joys are better than others, and so forth. The learning was his own, and he was taking part in creating as well as discovering that which he learned.[45]

Beyond the specifics of suffering, we too are being "weaned from the milk and drawn from the breasts" and are agents learning comprehensive matters, however brief, painful, or severely restricted earth experience might be. Even an infant born yesterday and dead of starvation or abuse within a week will experience physical reality, the quantum leaps, elements, motions, or processes which constitute physical existence. Even such an infant experiences something of how agents can affect each other and be affected by each other. Even such an ignorant child discovers that with God's help one can survive pain, imbecility, anguish, or death, and transcend them. What we meet in the way of suffering is far more important than purple squares, but we too are discovering that we can learn, and that we can take help from our Father in order that we might survive.

The history of the earth, the history of religion, is the history of human problems with understanding our Father in Heaven. We have the verse from Deuteronomy which says that if we seek the Lord with all our hearts, he will not forsake us.[46] We have also, in the Twenty-second Psalm and in the words of Christ on the cross, "Why hast thou forsaken me?"[47] Can we trust God? Is he a reliable help in times of trouble?

In response to such questions, some vigorously nod their heads, some look doubtful, some vigorously shake their heads, and some go to sleep. Our perceptions are not identical. God is not making them identical. He is not the only source of our understanding of him or our relationship with him. *We* take part in creating the understanding and the relationship. He invites us to come to *know* him, not just to know about him. The way to know him better is to become more like him.

If we are to find help from scriptures in this process, we must read them all in context with the writers' own language and understanding, and choose what is most important and most meaningful.[48] If we take some writings, we may look to God only for vengeance, fury, and infliction of suffering when we make any mistake or are in need of help. But I believe other writings are more expressive of LDS belief in the love of Elohim and Jehovah, their love, their relationship with us, and their preservation and enhancement of our agency. For example:

> For I am persuaded, that neither death, nor life, nor angels, nor principalities, nor powers, nor things present, nor things to come,
>
> Nor height, nor depth, nor any other creature, shall be able to separate us from the love of God, which is in Christ Jesus our Lord.[49]

> For we have not an high priest which cannot be touched with the feeling of our infirmities; but was in all points tempted like as we are, yet without sin.
>
> Let us therefore come boldly unto the throne of grace, that we may obtain mercy, and find grace to help in time of need.[50]

> Ye were also in the beginning with the Father; that which is Spirit, even the Spirit of truth;
>
> And truth is knowledge of things as they are, and as they were, and as they are to come;
>
> And whatsoever is more *or less* than this is the spirit of that wicked one who was a liar from the beginning.[51]

> He doeth not anything save it be for the benefit of the world; for he loveth the world.
>
> . . . he inviteth them all to come unto him and partake of his goodness; and he denieth none that come unto him, black and white, bond and free, male and female; and he remembereth the heathen; and all are alike unto God, both Jew and Gentile.[52]

I know the love of God. It is one of the very few things I do know with absolute certainty. I think suffering on this earth is an indication of God's trust, God's love. I think it is an indication that God does not want us to be simply obedient children playing forever under his hand, but wants us able to become more like himself. In order to do that we have to know reality. We have to be real ourselves and not dependent on externals. If we are to be like God, we cannot live forever in fear that we may meet something that will scare us or that will hurt us. We have to be able, as he is able, to meet what comes of others' agency, and of living in a lawful universe that allows creation of a habitable planet only when it allows also the difficulties that come in natural operations of such a planet.

We exist now as adolescents between ignorance and full truth, with real interactions among ourselves and the universe more numerous and complex than we yet observe or comprehend. It is within this context that I trust God and his commandments. I do not believe I could do it within the traditional framework where his love and power are supposed to keep us from pain or struggle if we are good. Neither could I find it easy to trust him if I believed him to make a habit of manipulating natural law and other persons to give me just what I need to test or teach me—in other words, to make me the center of the world without regard to other persons' agency or experience, and without regard to consistent, knowable law. In LDS theology, I believe, it is the *large* context for *all* humans that gives meaning to suffering. Within the context of LDS theology, I find hope for understanding and changing what I can, but also hope for transcending what I cannot: "Here is my dragon now, here is my magician who might turn me to stone, but I am able with God's help to be myself. I'm able to hurt and survive."

Some of the most difficult questions about suffering are why does God seem to intervene at some times but not others, and why should we pray for his protection. There are times we just have to say, "I don't know," and then trust God. I find this more satisfying within the context I've suggested than within traditional theologies; however, it is within the *traditional* framework that many LDS persons ask questions about suffering and God's part in it. Whatever they may say they believe about law or human agency, when the anguish comes, many LDS believers look to Jephthah's version of God and his power. In LDS theology, the power, goodness, and love of God as defined in traditional theologies are not the issues at question. Our being alive and meeting the suffering are evidence of his power, goodness, and love.

The real question is what is God's present relationship with us? I believe he loves us for ourselves, not only for himself. I believe he is our help, our guide, the means of our present existence, our comforter, but I believe these things must be understood in a larger context than may be immediately apparent. When Elijah calls for rain to end local drought, the writer of his story does not discuss relevant necessary changes in large weather systems circling the earth, or the results of them for India or Japan.[53]

God's power is real. The power of faith is real—it is not that God arbitrarily awards help to a person good enough to have sufficient faith, but that the faith itself is power.[54] Physical laws inherent in the universe are also real. God has repeatedly urged that we ask his help, with faith that he will do what is good. In every case, his definition of what is good is a matter of truth and law, not arbitrary whim. We may not comprehend all the specifics, or all the interactions involved, but we can understand the theological context within which the fragments occur.

Knowing that we can stumble or fall, knowing that some do not have the gospel, or lack freedom or capacities—in other words, knowing our various limitations here—I find sense in LDS doctrine that our learning goes on after this life, and that when we fall, it need not be permanent. Many causes and effects of suffering are evident in our sense of who we are and what we can do about it. Because of our ignorance and inexperience, we are hampered by things we don't understand and also by things we assume we do understand. What other persons have taught us, whatever their intentions, may hamper as much as help us. One of my prayers to my Father is that my children will be healed of my ignorance and will not bear forever the difficulties caused by things I have mistakenly done or not done as a parent. As I think of the atonement of Christ, it seems to me that if our sins are to be forgiven, the results of them must be erased. If my mistakes are to be forgiven, other persons must be healed from any effects of them. In the same way, if other persons are to be released by the atonement, then we must be healed from their mistakes. I think that is an essential part of understanding God's gift: He did not make a plan whereby we simply prove ourselves already right or wrong. Rather, we must make sense of the fact that who we are and who we become is not wholly dependent on where we are now, and on never having made a mistake. Christ's atonement makes it possible for us to go through the meeting of reality, the falling, the hungering, the screaming, the crawling on the floor, the being disfigured and scarred for life psychologically or physically, and still survive and transcend it. If that were not true, then our whole universe would have no meaning, and we had just as well be what Lucifer suggested, simply obedient robots.

I know the goodness of God, and I also know the hurts of this life. Of the very few things I truly know, the most certain, drawn from the most vivid and inexpressible experience of my life, is this: God is love, and our becoming so is what matters. I pray we may gain courage and faith to affirm the choice we made, to remember that we are active and alive and meeting suffering here because God knew we could and because we believed we could.

Let us choose well the theology with which we frame our experience. Let us trust ourselves and God, asking continually for the help which is good. Let us love each other, mourn with each other, and sacrifice fear for courage. Let us seek reality and truth, forgiving ourselves and each other, learning to help ourselves and each other as we can. Let us become more like our God, who is good.

Francine R. Bennion, "A Latter-day Saint Theology of Suffering," in A Heritage of Faith: Talks Selected from the BYU Women's Conferences, *ed. Mary E. Stovall and Carol Cornwall Madsen (Salt Lake City: Deseret Book, 1988), 53–76.*

THE UNKNOWN TREASURE

◇◇◇

JUTTA B. BUSCHE

Brigham Young University Women's Conference
Marriott Center, Brigham Young University, Provo, Utah
April 6, 1990

Jutta Baum Busche (b. 1935) grew up in Dortmund, Germany, with three older brothers who, she reported, "kept me from being spoiled."[1] Since schools were closed during and immediately after World War II, her education was driven primarily by her own voracious appetite for reading and music. Eventually she attended a math high school for boys.[2] Her uncle was the first solo cellist for the Berlin Philharmonic and frequently practiced in her home. She often listened to classical programming on the radio as well, and when she heard something unfamiliar, she looked for background information in the family's encyclopedia.[3] She married Enzio Busche in 1955, and the two were baptized on January 19, 1958, in a Dortmund public swimming pool.[4]

In October 1977, Jutta and Enzio attended a conference in Berlin so that Enzio, a church regional representative, could translate for church president Spencer W. Kimball.[5] During a reception at the end of the conference, Kimball spoke privately with Enzio and asked him to join the First Quorum of the Seventy—a full-time position that would require the Busches to move from their home. Then Kimball met with Jutta Busche and asked her what she thought of the invitation. "I want to die," she exclaimed. The Busches spent the night walking around the city.[6] They had recently finished remodeling their house, which Jutta had designed exactly the way they wanted. They also kept an apartment for vacationing on the Baltic Sea. Jutta later explained that she had spent too much time focusing on material things like wallpaper. "Of course they are nice," she said, "but not as high" in importance as eternal things.[7]

Their first assignment was in Munich, Germany, where Enzio led the mission for two years; then they moved to Utah in 1980.[8] They traveled a great deal, visiting church members all over the world, and Jutta spoke at regional conferences with her husband.[9] Shortly before the dedication of the Frankfurt temple in 1987, they became its president and matron.[10] Busche had never been a temple worker, and Gordon B. Hinckley advised her at a training seminar, "The most important thing is to have love and love and love."[11] She took his counsel to heart. She taught the temple workers to smile when people came in and showed their recommends, reassuring patrons instead of frowning if there was a problem with the recommend. She asked temple workers to make it their top priority to help patrons feel God's Spirit.[12]

After her return to Utah in September of 1989, Busche was invited to speak on a panel at Brigham Young University's Women's Conference, which she had done several times before. Then one day, while she was doing the laundry, she received a call saying the conference organizers had changed their minds. Instead of speaking on a panel, they wanted her to give the conference's closing address at the Marriott Center. Once she heard the conference theme, "the power within," she knew she could give the speech.[13] "You feel by yourself what is wrong or what is not wrong," she has said.[14] "This is why we are here on the earth to learn. . . . We have to learn here to have the Spirit with us. God loves us and God loves everybody. We cannot judge."[15] Busche believes that individuals will figure out for themselves what they need to change when they have enough experience with feeling unconditional love.[16] She wrote the following talk in English with language editing assistance from Enzio Busche's assistant, Joy Baker.[17]

ONE EVENING IN LATE SUMMER of 1940, the Baum family—the mother, two sons, one adopted son, two daughters, and a little baby—gathered in their dining room in the absence of the father, who was a soldier in the war.[18] The mother had been busy all afternoon improvising a supper from such limited supplies as dandelion greens, turnips, and potatoes. As she placed the food on the table and looked around at the children, she asked, "Where is Jutta?" Startled, the three boys looked at one another, and then one by one guiltily dropped their eyes. The mother repeated her question more urgently: "Where is Jutta?" Finally, one of the boys said in a subdued voice, "She is still tied to a tree in the forest. We forgot to loosen her. We were playing a war game."

This incident was typical of my childhood. At the time I was only five and already a tomboy. I grew up mainly among boys and enjoyed participating in their war games. I served principally as their "weapons carrier," though occasionally I stood in as "the enemy." I am grateful to my Heavenly Father that I was born at that time in Germany. Wartime was full of sacrifices, fear, panic, pain, and hardships, but it was also a time of vivid memories, learning, and growth, because real learning often happens only in times of hardship.[19]

During the war years, I remember, each evening as darkness came, I would take a small backpack containing some extra underclothing, a pair of stockings, and a pair of shoes, and walk about three kilometers (just under two miles) from home to a tunnel to spend the night alone in a compartment of a stationary train kept there to furnish shelter for civilians who were afraid of the almost nightly air raids. I also remember the first banana I ever had and how good it tasted. The war had just ended, and a merciful soldier from the occupying forces gave it to me. I remember very vividly our meager diet of water soups, nettle spinach, dandelion greens, turnips, and the molasses that people in our town were fortunate to obtain from a damaged railroad car. I remember very well the smell of sheep wool, which we sheared ourselves and spun into yarn, making sweaters and dresses for ourselves. I saw, as a consequence of our lack of food and medical assistance during those years, my sixteen-year-old sister and my nineteen-year-old brother become ill and finally die. The death of my brother, to whom I was very close, hurt me terribly and filled me with a deep awareness of how fragile life is.

In our home there was little religious education, although my parents were Protestant.

My family simply did not talk about religion. But my father's brother was a Protestant minister. I remember a time when this uncle's wife came to visit. Before my aunt arrived, my father instructed us, "When she is here, we must have a prayer before we eat." I will never forget how comical and strange it was to hear my father offer a blessing on the food in words and tone of voice so unfamiliar to us that it struck me as hypocritical. Yet, as I grew up, frequently in the evening I knelt at my bedside on my own initiative to pray to my Heavenly Father because, even without religious instruction, I felt in my heart that there must be someone whom I could trust and love—someone who knew me and cared about me. What a privilege it would have been to be reared in a family that was well grounded in the restored gospel!

When the missionaries first came to our door in Dortmund, Germany, my husband and I had not been married long. Our first son was only three months old. I was and always will be grateful each minute of my life for the message that came to us through these young missionaries. I was impressed with many things about these young men. One was the loving way they talked about their families. Another was their attitude about their message. There was no facade. I sensed such humble honesty in their expressions of testimony that I was compelled to listen. What they told me about angels and golden plates intrigued me enough that I wanted to learn why such nice young men could believe in such strange things.

I learned from them that we are all children of a loving Heavenly Father and that we are here on this earth to learn, to grow, and to love. I learned that we lived with God as his spirit children, his sons and daughters. We walked and talked with him. We knew him and he still knows us. We raised our hands in support of the plan to come to this earth.[20] Achieving our full potential in our journey here depends on our free choices. That message needs to penetrate every act of our daily lives.

I have since discovered that one great stumbling block to our progress in faith is rule-keeping that does not spring from an honest heart. Too many people imply in their attitude toward others that our Heavenly Father expects a perfect conformity to established rules. But Jesus Christ never condemned the honest in heart. His wrath was kindled against the hypocritically empty rule-keeping of the Pharisees.[21] Jesus preached that through repentance we become free from sin; *however, only as we become honest do we feel the necessity of repentance.*

When at age thirteen I was confirmed a member of a Protestant faith, the minister quoted John 8:32: "Ye shall know the truth and the truth shall make you free." This scripture had no meaning for me until I found the true gospel and learned the value of free agency—the right to make one's own decisions in one's own way. For me the truth that makes one free is twofold: the truths of the restored gospel, which provide a map of eternal realities, and the skill of being truthful with oneself and others, which leads to genuine repentance and integrity.

Self-honesty is the foundation for developing other spiritual strengths. Self-honesty will determine whether obstacles and problems we face in life are stepping stones leading to blessings or stumbling stones leading to spiritual graveyards. Marcus Aurelius, an ancient Roman philosopher, observed the connection between honesty and spiritual growth nearly two thousand years ago: "A man's true greatness lies in the consciousness of an honest purpose in life founded on a just estimate of himself and everything else, on frequent self-examinations, and a steady obedience to the rule which he knows to be right, without troubling himself about what others may think or say, or whether they do or do not do that which he thinks and says and does."[22] According to Marcus Aurelius, then, self-honesty is both a prerequisite to greatness and the core quality of integrity.[23]

A time of great insight into the principle of self-honesty came for me when my husband accepted a full-time call in the Lord's service, making it necessary for us to say good-bye to all those whom we had grown to love in our home ward in

Dortmund and everyone with whom we had been associated. The transition was not easy for us.[24]

I remember well the adjustments we had to make when we went to live in Utah. My first call in our ward was to serve as a Relief Society teacher. I watched the other teachers very closely and was deeply impressed with their striving for perfection in their teaching. Even their hairdos and immaculate dress showed their striving for perfection. I admired how fluent and articulate they were in the English language. How could I, with my poor English, compete with them and be their teacher? I was eager to learn and was so glad to hear that there was a stake preparation class for Relief Society teachers.

When I attended the training meeting for the first time, I was full of high hopes. I was not prepared for the question I was asked about what kind of centerpiece I would use when I gave my lesson. How incompetent I felt! I had no idea what a centerpiece was or what its purpose in the presentation of a lesson could be. Negative feelings about myself began to undermine my confidence.

Other efforts to fit in were equally discouraging. I felt very intimidated by my many wonderful neighbors with their seven, eight, or nine children.[25] I became very shy when I had to reply that we had only four, and I could not even mention to these people the deep hurt I had experienced when I found that for health reasons my family would have to be limited to four children.

I continued to feel inferior as I watched the sisters in my ward and saw them planting gardens and canning the produce.[26] They exercised daily by jogging. They sewed and bargain-shopped. They went on heart fund drives and served as PTA officers.[27] They took dinners to new mothers and the sick in their neighborhoods. They took care of an aged parent, sometimes two. They climbed Mount Timpanogos.[28] They drove their children to and from music or dancing lessons. They were faithful in doing temple work, and they worried about catching up on their journals.[29]

Intimidated by examples of perfection all around me, I increased my efforts to be like my sisters, and I felt disappointed in myself and even guilty when I didn't run every morning, bake all my own bread, sew my own clothes, or go to the university. I felt that I needed to be like the women among whom I was living, and I felt that I was a failure because I was not able to adapt myself easily to their lifestyles.

I could have benefited at this time from the story of a six-year-old who, when asked by a relative, "What do you want to be?" replied, "I think I'll just be myself. I have tried to be like someone else. I have failed each time!" Like this child, after repeated failure to be someone else, I finally learned that I should be myself. That is often not easy, however, because our desires to fit in, to compete and impress, or even simply to be approved of lead us to imitate others and devalue our own backgrounds, our own talents, and our own burdens and challenges. I had to learn not to worry about the behavior of others and their *code* of rules. I had to learn to overcome my anxious feeling that if I didn't conform, I simply did not measure up.

Two challenging passages in the Bible remind me that I must overcome self-doubts. One is Proverbs 23:7. "For as he thinketh in his heart, so is he." The other is Romans 12:2: "Be not conformed to this world: but be ye transformed by the renewing of your mind, that ye may prove what is that good, and acceptable, and perfect, will of God." When I tried to *conform,* it blocked my being *transformed* by the Spirit's renewing of my mind. When I tried to copy my wonderful sisters as I taught my class with a special centerpiece and other teaching techniques that were unfamiliar to me, I failed because the Spirit still talks to me in German, not in English. But when I got on my knees to ask for help, I learned to depend on the Spirit to guide me, secure in the knowledge that I am a daughter of God. I had to learn and *believe* that I did not need to compete with others to be loved and accepted by my Heavenly Father.

Another insight from Marcus Aurelius is, "Look within. Within is the fountain of good, and it will ever bubble up, if thou wilt ever dig."[30] Sometimes our great potential for good is veiled from us by the negative judgments of others. For instance, one day in Germany I had a meeting with our eleven-year-old son's school teacher. I was very saddened to hear that she judged our son to be lacking in sufficient intelligence to follow the course of mathematics of that school. I knew my son better than the teacher did; I knew that, on the contrary, mathematics was his real interest and within the scope of his capabilities. I left feeling very depressed. When I got home, I saw in the eyes of my son his high expectations as he enthusiastically inquired about what his teacher had said. I knew how devastated he would be if I were to tell him his teacher's exact words. It was the Spirit that gave me the wisdom to rephrase his teacher's concerns. I told him that the teacher recognized his great talent for mathematics and that only his lack of diligence would separate him from great achievements, for his teacher held high hopes for his future. My son took this to heart, and it did not take long before he became the best student of mathematics in his class. I do not even dare to think what would have become of him had I reported exactly the teacher's negative remarks.

God works through the positive power of his love. When we truly learn to love God, we learn to love all things—others, ourselves, all creation, because God is in all, with all, and through all. We need not be afraid, and we need not hide behind a facade of performance. When we come to understand this *unknown treasure*—the knowledge of who we really are—we will know that we are entitled to the power that comes from God. It will come when we ask for it and when we trust his leadership in our lives. Our efforts should not be to *perform* nor to *conform* but to be *transformed* by the Spirit. Again, "Be not conformed to this world: but be ye transformed by the renewing of your mind, that ye may prove what is that good, and acceptable, and perfect, will of God."[31]

Many pressures bind us to the world. Being honest in heart frees us to discover God's will for our lives. I am always touched in our monthly ward testimony meetings where my faith is strengthened by my neighbors who tell how they have been *buoyed up* to meet the challenges and trials that have come their way. So often their testimonies reveal serious challenges they have had to face—challenges that are not evident unless one opens up one's heart to another. I know that as I walk down our street and pass all the beautifully tended homes of my neighbors, I am inclined to think that all is well with them, that they do not struggle as I do. It is through the honest testimonies they bear that I learn to see their hearts, and we become united in feelings of love.

We, the children of the covenant whose eyes have been opened, have a great responsibility to be always aware of who we are.[32] Although we might be absorbed in meeting our daily challenges and opportunities for growth, we cannot afford to live one day or one minute without being aware of the power within us. What a privilege I had to serve as the first matron in the Frankfurt temple![33] I had to depend constantly on the Spirit; otherwise, it would have been impossible to succeed. The challenge to establish a fully functioning temple seemed overwhelming, but the more overwhelming our tasks are, the more we understand that there is only One who can help, our Heavenly Father. Only when we draw unto him can we learn how real he is, how much he understands, and how much he is willing to help. He knows that we are not perfect and that we are struggling; and when we accept ourselves with our weaknesses in humility, sincerity, and complete honesty, then he is with us. As Paul told the Corinthians, "Eye hath not seen, nor ear heard, neither have entered into the heart of man, the things which God hath prepared for them that love him."[34]

Jutta Baum Busche, "The Unknown Treasure," in Women and the Power Within: To See Life Steadily and See It Whole, *ed. Dawn Hall Anderson and Marie Cornwall (Salt Lake City: Deseret Book, 1991), 21–28.*

Jayne B. Malan, Ardeth G. Kapp, and Elaine L. Jack, Young Women general presidency. 1989. Kapp served as Young Women general president from 1984 to 1992. This presidency oversaw the creation of the Young Women theme and Young Women values, and they updated the Personal Progress program. Jack was Relief Society general president from 1990 to 1997. Pictured here, left to right, are Malan, Kapp, and Jack. (Church History Library, Salt Lake City.)

GET A LIFE

◇◇◇

ELAINE L. JACK

Church Educational System Fireside
Marriott Center, Brigham Young University, Provo, Utah
January 3, 1993

Elaine Low Jack (b. 1928) believed she brought a degree of independence to her church work because her parents had allowed her to be independent. While growing up in Cardston, Alberta, Canada, her mother's ill health left her with additional responsibilities at home, and she also earned extra money working in a beauty shop and a retail store. She played the organ in Sunday School and, during high school, transcribed patriarchal blessings for her grandfather John Anderson, who was a stake patriarch.[1] Jack devised her own version of shorthand for recording these blessings, which Anderson often gave in a room off the lobby in the Cardston temple.[2] In 1948 she would marry her husband, Joseph Jack, in that temple.[3]

President Belle S. Spafford invited Jack to join the Relief Society general board in 1972, where she worked on the curriculum and general conference committees, among others, from 1972 to 1974. She continued to work on the board until the end of Barbara B. Smith's presidency in 1984, chairing the curriculum committee and working on recreation and community outreach committees.[4] In 1987, she became second counselor to Ardeth G. Kapp in the Young Women and oversaw the development of leadership materials.[5] When assuming this position she remarked, "What brings me joy is to look back on my life and see growth."[6]

Jack's Young Women responsibilities ended when she became Relief Society general president and chose Chieko N. Okazaki and Aileen H. Clyde as her counselors.[7] The new Relief Society presidency, hoping to motivate members, revised the organization's purpose statement to read: "Build personal testimony, bless the individual woman, develop and exercise charity, strengthen families, enjoy a unified sisterhood, be full participants in the blessings of the priesthood."[8] They wanted women to have an increased feeling of self-worth and ability to progress. Said Jack, "We felt like we were on the threshold of something and that it was time for women to really be acknowledged and invested, and feel part of a very viable organization."[9] Jack wanted to acknowledge the diversity of Relief Society members while also building unity among them, and she felt the resulting focus on the individual woman was historically significant as it shifted the direction of Relief Society without changing the basic purpose.[10]

Jack trusted local Relief Society leaders to uphold and also to adapt basic principles as they sought to strengthen those in their stewardship. "You have the inspiration of your calling," she taught them. The basement of the Relief Society Building had a large resource room where visiting Relief Society members could find information to help them in their duties. Etched at the bottom of a large mirror in that room were the words, "You Are Your Best Resource." She felt that local leaders were "called of the Lord" and that she should strengthen and encourage them to have confidence in themselves.[11]

The Relief Society sesquicentennial celebrations in 1992 provided another occasion where Jack encouraged personal initiative, making service and literacy the hallmarks of her administration. As part of the celebrations, each individual church unit devised its own service project, which was to include as many Relief Society members as possible, both as planners and as participants.[12] The Cergy-Pontoise Relief Society in France, for example, made patchwork quilts for hospitals and retirement centers, and donated clothing and sweets to needy children.[13] The Magrath Stake in Alberta, Canada, made and froze fifty-six meals for the Lethbridge Soup Kitchen, sewed seventy nightshirts and thirty toiletry bags for Harbour House Women's Shelter, and wrote twenty-five letters to government officials "regarding moral issues," among other activities.[14] Members of the Aba Nigeria Stake improved the path to a water hole in Nigeria.[15] Jack felt the projects succeeded when they not only improved communities but also showed Relief Society members what they could accomplish.[16] Jack's presidency also launched a churchwide gospel literacy effort in December 1992; its purpose was to teach basic literacy skills to church members who could not read or write and to encourage all members to study the gospel throughout their lives.[17]

Early in her presidency, Jack attended a Priesthood Executive Council meeting at which she, Okazaki, and Clyde made a thirty-minute presentation about the work they were doing.[18] After their presentation, they were excused. They realized that changing their approach to that biannual meeting could make it more worthwhile, so the next time they attended they asked council members to respond to the Relief Society report with their own findings and suggestions and asked, "How can we be of better help to you?" The ensuing conversation was very useful, and thereafter they were invited to attend monthly meetings and stay for the entire meeting.[19] Jack also encouraged initiative and action in the following talk, which she gave at a fireside meeting for young adults in the Marriott Center on January 3, 1993.

JUST BEFORE THE CHILDREN OF ISRAEL crossed into the promised land, Moses, their leader, gave them a great final lecture. Their leader for forty years, Moses delivered this sermon about the essential knowledge of life, knowing full well he would not accompany his people into their new homeland. What would he have said this last time? Moses told his people the most important things to know if they were to live happily and return to their Heavenly Father.

Near the end of his message he laid out their choices very clearly. He said these significant words:

"I call heaven and earth to record this day against you, that I have set before you life and death, blessing and cursing: therefore choose life, that both thou and thy seed may live:

"That thou mayest love the Lord thy God, and that thou mayest obey his voice, and that thou mayest cleave unto him: for he is thy life, and the length of thy days."[20]

My dear brothers and sisters, like Moses, I stand watching you, the young adults of the church, prepare to cross into many lands of promise. Tonight I repeat Moses's words and ask you to choose life, to understand with your heart and your head that the Lord is indeed your "life, and the length of thy days."

To "choose life" is only possible when we understand that we have the power to do it. In the book of Moses we read about Enoch's discussion with the Lord. At one point Enoch recorded,

> The God of heaven looked upon the residue of the people, and he wept. . . .
>
> And Enoch said unto the Lord: How is it that thou canst weep, seeing thou art holy, and from all eternity to all eternity?
>
> And were it possible that man could number the particles of the earth, yea, millions of earths like this, it would not be a beginning to the number of thy creations; and thy curtains are stretched out still; and yet thou art there, and thy bosom is there; and also thou art just; thou art merciful and kind forever; . . . how is it thou canst weep?
>
> The Lord said unto Enoch: Behold these thy brethren; they are the workmanship of mine own hands, and I gave unto them

> their knowledge, in the day I created them; and in the Garden of Eden, gave I unto man his agency;
>
> And unto thy brethren have I said, and also given commandment, that they should love one another, and that they should choose me, their Father; but behold, they are without affection, and they hate their own blood.[21]

The power of agency is enormous. From the beginning of men and women's journey through mortality on this earth, agency has been a critical factor. The Lord gave us agency so we might choose for ourselves. When Moses told us to "choose life," he wasn't speaking lightly. He was suggesting that when it comes right to the bottom line, each of us makes a decision to obey the commandments or not to obey them.

There are many and varied circumstances that exist in each individual's life that govern our views of the world. But agency is still there, given to all. Your ability to choose can be one of your greatest blessings, if you learn to use it well.

A young man newly out of graduate school got a new job, bought a home, and made all kinds of plans to remodel it into his dream home, complete with a gym and study. Within seven months he got engaged to a woman with three young daughters. Six months after they were married his wife was expecting a baby. Things weren't easy for this family. The young man's job was promising but not lucrative. To meet expenses he took a second job as a newspaper delivery man.

One Saturday morning, cold and early, he pulled out of his driveway listening to a blues song on the radio. He resonated to the song about love and life and the pain of trying to get ahead in a grueling world, and he sank right into the blues himself. As he drove from site to site making his deliveries, the blues deepened into what you might call the *blue funk.* Now, to be in the blue funk is to feel like two cents looking for change. It is to think hope has gone south for the winter and has forgotten to come back.

As the sun crept into a new day, he thought about his life. He mentally looked at the faces of each one in his family and walked through the halls of his home. He considered his profession, his extended family, his neighborhood, and his church responsibilities. He weighed the complexities and challenges, the satisfactions and pleasures. And into his mind came one sentence: "Life doesn't get any better than this."

He said, "It was a realization that arrived unbidden. It didn't mean life couldn't get any easier or that I wanted to have the blues. It simply meant I had everything I needed. And it hadn't been that way when I lived alone and roamed my house, planning the interior."[22]

Some years later he invited his aging parents to come live with him and his family. As he rose at 3 a.m. daily to help his mother with her needs, he often thought, "Life doesn't get any better than this." He never got his library or gym, but in the midst of his very full house, he thanked the Lord often for what was also a very full life.

In the midst of finals, a romantic crisis, or a conflict with a spouse or roommates, it's a sign of spiritual and emotional maturity to remember "life doesn't get any better than this." That's because it's your life right now, and nothing is more invigorating than living your life, which is truly the process of making your choices based on the gospel of Jesus Christ. To do so is to really live.

A woman came into my office a few months ago. She was in tears as she described the challenges of living in these days. Her husband was in school and working, but he wasn't as satisfied with his job as he thought he could be. Her children were healthy and prospering, but they didn't have all the things she wanted to give them. Her house was comfortable, but it wasn't as large as she had dreamed it would be at this point in her life. Her friends were supportive, but they didn't give her as much time and attention as she wished they would. Her in-laws loved her, but her mother-in-law couldn't help her with the children as often as this young mother thought she should.

Another woman wrote me that she had lost hope of ever finding a man she could marry. She described in detail her failed relationships and efforts to find a husband. She talked about her diminished feelings of self-worth and her questions about whether or not the Lord really loved her as she'd been taught in church all her life. She has a good job, good health, good friends, good family. Yet she spoke of life in dismal terms and referred to herself as a second-class citizen in the church.[23] Fully realizing that I don't walk in either woman's shoes and that each has justified concerns, I still want to give this bit of counsel: Get a life. We are sons and daughters of God. We have the fulness of the gospel of Jesus Christ. We are called to rise, not wallow. Brothers and sisters, let's get a life.

At this time of year I find myself reading the story of Lehi and his family. Few stories in scripture tell more about the process of getting a life. After years in the wilderness and a lot of what he could justifiably complain about, Nephi wrote, "We did pitch our tents by the seashore; and notwithstanding we had suffered many afflictions and much difficulty, yea, even so much that we cannot write them all, we were exceedingly rejoiced when we came to the seashore."[24]

Difficulty is an essential element in the bedrock underlying mortality and does not preclude rejoicing. Everything doesn't have to be marvelous for us to rejoice. Earlier in the same chapter of 1 Nephi, Nephi says this about their journey: "And so great were the blessings of the Lord upon us, that while we did live upon raw meat in the wilderness, our women did give plenty of suck for their children, and were strong, yea, even like unto the men; and they began to bear their journeyings without murmurings."[25]

Nephi then adds what is almost a postscript about this experience: "And thus we see that the commandments of God must be fulfilled. And if it so be that the children of men keep the commandments of God he doth nourish them, and strengthen them, and provide means whereby they can accomplish the thing which he has commanded them."[26]

To get a life is to build on the good bedrock of your own experiences and testimony. Nephi made his choice young. He chose life, and despite the remarkable series of trials that came into his own life, he did not waver. He knew where he was going spiritually, so he could hold on even while he was lost in a desert wilderness.

To get a life is to be strong. The two women I just referred to are leading good lives, but they've lost heart for the tasks that are theirs. President Hinckley's stirring message at the October 1992 priesthood meeting is instructive to all of us. He said, "Be strong," and he talked about how we can do that through self-discipline, standing for the right, showing mercy, simple honesty, and having personal faith.[27] Personal faith requires strength and is a source of strength at the same time. As Nephi explained about his family's experiences in the wilderness, the Lord will nourish and strengthen us and give us the means to accomplish the thing he commands us.

Personal faith is a reality you need in your life. It's a source of strength and comfort and resolution under the happiest and most trying moments of your life. If you want to get a life, get a testimony. Yours may be a life of little or lots of money, considerable or conservative success, a married life or a single life. In every circumstance choose to be strong so, like Nephi, you can weather the thousands of circumstances that will be part of mortality.

To get a life is to rejoice in the dailiness of living. Leo Tolstoy wrote in *Anna Karenina* about Levin, a Russian landowner. One day he chose to mow hay with the peasants who worked his fields. At first all he could think of were the developing blisters on his hands and the constant aching of his bent back. The rows seemed longer and longer as he worked through them. He feared he wouldn't be able to keep up with the others. But then Tolstoy describes this, just as Levin was about to give in:

> Another row, and yet another row, followed—long rows and short rows, with good grass and with poor grass. Levin lost all sense of time, and could not have told whether it was late or early now. A change began to come over his work, which gave him immense

> satisfaction. In the midst of his toil there were moments during which he forgot what he was doing, and it came all easy to him.[28]

There's a kind of magic in getting into a task so thoroughly that you relish the process itself. Maybe that's why some of us get so much satisfaction from full jars of fruit in a storage room. Others may find it in a completed term paper or in an overhauled motorcycle or in cleaning the neighbor's garage. The tasks give us the opportunity to literally throw ourselves into work that brings us joy.

Looking at a freshly mowed lawn, a completed family group sheet, a photocopied dissertation, loaves of perfect homemade bread, a washed and polished car, a poem just written with an elegant turn of phrase, or an exam well taken and then reflecting that it is good—these are some of the most satisfying experiences of life. Life at its best is in these moments. We're rejoicing in the harvest and reaffirming that we are indeed made in our Creator's likeness, for he, too, paused after his six days of labor, looked on everything that he had made, and saw that it was good. Rejoicing in the harvest goes hand in hand with acknowledging our Creator. One who looks at a full granary and remembers the plowing time, the planting time, the weeding time, and the gathering time must also remember the miracle beyond his own power that brought that seed to fruition.

To get a life is to be grateful. When we see most clearly, we see the Lord's hand in everything. The truly grateful, like Nephi, dwell on the goodness of life even while acknowledging that there may be more adversity than there are even words to describe it. Perhaps the biggest difference between Nephi and his elder brothers was Nephi's unwavering ability to graduate through all kinds of spiritual levels as he increased in gratitude and faith while Laman and Lemuel never progressed past murmuring, withholding, and rebellion—low-level pursuits, indeed.[29]

Each of us only has so much energy and time in a day. Nephi put his energy into activities reflecting his faith and thanksgiving. Laman and Lemuel sowed their energies in the barren fields of discontent, disaffection, and disbelief. Their lack of gratitude led to endless mortal trouble for Nephi and endless eternal trouble for themselves.

In my experience I've learned that the people who are spiritually mature are people who are truly grateful. I've felt humbled to meet people whose very lives as well as their words express their gratitude for the blessings of life and for the blessings of truth. In the Philippines a young mother was thankful for a small, old-fashioned sewing machine that had allowed her to earn the extra money she needed for their family with eight children to travel to the Manila temple to be sealed together.[30] Thousands of Saints are leading a rich life, whether they are living in a mansion in Jakarta or in a home with a leaking roof. In a home with a leaking roof, a sister expressed gratitude that two of her daughters had done extremely well in final tests that qualified them to be midwives, and then explained to me that sometimes she has to "wear an umbrella" in the kitchen when it rains.

Sometimes I fear we have expectations that the good life is the life being led by someone else. The truth is that the good life is the life you have, for it's the only one you can lead. I believe Nephi understood that—with a full heart he could thank the Lord in the midst of trials that often were life threatening. To thank the Lord for his blessings to us is to understand how good life is, even when it seems unpleasant, unsuccessful, or just plain hard.

To get a life is to think about and to do for others. During 1992, Relief Society women throughout the world have joined together in service projects in their own communities. I know many of you were involved. A sister from Peru wrote that the women of her Relief Society had helped a family whose mother had died. The sister said, "We felt fellowshipped and strengthened spiritually, and we were happy to have been able to imitate our Lord, Jesus Christ, by serving our needy brothers and sisters."

Women in the Apia Samoa East Stake told us,

> We . . . decided to approach the government if it was all right for the stake Relief Society sisters to plant some flowers around the town clock. We chose the town clock because it is right in the middle of the town, and we felt it would be just the right place to have a beautiful garden. Its flowers would bear the theme of the Relief Society, "Charity Never Faileth." The government was thrilled. . . . They thanked us wholeheartedly, and then they asked us if there was any way we could paint the 20-foot clock tower as well. We told them . . . we would see what we could do. . . . The stake did not have money, which did not worry us a bit. We only wanted them to approve it, as we had a strong feeling and belief if it was the will of the Lord, things will work out. . . . Paints and equipment were donated, professional painters offered themselves and their time, and the priesthood of our . . . stake also helped out with the work. The sisters of the eight units of our stake worked in scraping the old paint off, scrubbing and cleaning the clock tower, and, of course, in planting the flowers. We will be taking turns in maintaining the gardens there for the whole year. Again, the sisters were generous and willing.

I love these stories and the many others that sisters have sent to Relief Society. Can you imagine the good that has been done in over a hundred nations by thousands of Relief Society sisters? Can you imagine the blessings that have come into the lives of those women? If you do not learn to do for others, yours will be a dull life.

I think the best experiences I've had in my life have all involved helping others. Maybe it was setting up a game at a family reunion or merit badge counseling. Such good times have come from working in church callings, in directing a road show or teaching Laurels or in neighborhood projects, maybe organizing a worthy fund drive.[31] In every case I've enjoyed situations in which I could work with others on some good cause.

The motto of Relief Society is "Charity Never Faileth."[32] What a great thing to base an organization on the most important values of our faith.

To get a life is to remain open to new ideas. Not long ago I heard the story of a man who was leaving a long career in one industry. Still a relatively young man, he had to get another job to support his family. The transition would be rough since he had never worked anywhere other than at his first job. At the meeting of a community group of which he was a member, a subject relating to this longtime job came up. He leaned back in his chair and immediately began to tell the group how things were in that industry, all the problems currently in the marketplace, and why he was right. After a rather lengthy oration, he critiqued the ideas being proposed and basically left the group without hope that anything could be done.

When the meeting adjourned one committee member said to another, "I think our friend will have a hard time getting another job. The ability to pontificate is not very marketable these days." How true that is! It's easy to use old knowledge and experiences to shoot down current or future possibilities. It's easy to say, "Well, in my mission field it was done like this," or, "In my last job we did it like that."

It's a lot harder and a lot wiser to use what you know as the basis of creating something new and better. The Lord commanded Nephi, "Thou shalt construct a ship, after the manner which I shall show thee, that I may carry thy people across these waters."[33] Nephi responded, "Lord, whither shall I go that I may find ore to molten, that I may make tools to construct the ship after the manner which thou hast shown unto me?"[34]

Probably Nephi had some knowledge of toolmaking and possibly of building. I doubt he knew much about ships. But he was willing to apply what he knew to a new situation. His brothers, on the other hand, had no desire to enter into this new domain—an unknown domain. Instead, they did what people often do when they're afraid, unsure, unskilled, or lazy—they criticized and demeaned Nephi. Nephi noted:

> And when my brethren saw that I was about to build a ship, they

> began to murmur against me, saying: Our brother is a fool, for he thinketh that he can build a ship; yea, and he also thinketh that he can cross these great waters.
>
> And thus my brethren did complain against me, and were desirous that they might not labor, for they did not believe that I could build a ship.[35]

You recall that it took divine intervention before Laman and Lemuel would get to work.[36]

Lack of belief is a convenient excuse for not undertaking new projects. New tasks can be very frightening, but they are good for us, too. They force us out of our current comfort zones. Sometimes we need to leave our spiritual comfort zone. The hard work we do spiritually will benefit us in many, many ways, just as the hard work you are currently doing intellectually and professionally will have lifelong value.

To get a life is to respect others. There are many times in our working relationships when we would do well to check our egos at the door along with our coats. Church callings are one of those times. We all serve along with others. We work in presidencies and bishoprics or as members of the corps of teachers in Sunday School or in the auxiliaries or quorums. We serve two by two as home or visiting teachers or as missionary companions. Presidents serve with counselors or advisors. All of this togetherness is for a good purpose. These working relationships teach us to work together. We have the benefit of others' ideas and spiritual insights. We join as brothers and sisters in synergistic relationships that benefit those who serve and those we serve. These working relationships may not always be easy.

In the church we are not building a kingdom, we are building *the* kingdom. We only do this when we are unified and truly working together. An early church leader, George Q. Cannon, remarked, "We are not the people of God when we are not united. Union is one of the fruits of the Spirit."[37] When we fail to work in unity in our church positions, we prevent the Lord from blessing us as he could. When was the last time you asked those with whom you serve, "How can I help?" "What do you need?"

You will realize great growth in sincerely asking those questions often and then acting on the responses you get. These questions suggest humility, the ability to listen, to learn, to collect feedback from others. They help us realize that we know we are not the center of the universe but rather one important worker in the Lord's kingdom, a kingdom that is eternal in scope and significance. We are valuable, each of us; and because we are, we should treat each other with respect.

To get a life is to be kind. Few things are as healing as simple kindnesses—a gentle touch, a pat on the arm, an encouraging word, patient silence, a probing question when something is obviously wrong, a withholding of judgment until all the facts are known. If we are sincere about being followers of Christ, if we really mean it when we partake of the sacrament on Sunday or attend a temple session, we will be kind.

We are called to kindness by the scriptural definitions of charity and godlike working relationships. Paul wrote, "Charity suffereth long, and is kind."[38] Mormon said, "Charity suffereth long, and is kind."[39] Joseph Smith penned, "No power or influence can or ought to be maintained by virtue of the priesthood, only by persuasion, by long-suffering, by gentleness and meekness, and by love unfeigned; by kindness."[40]

We owe each other kindness. Kindness can be shown in so many small ways. The scriptures don't say that we should go on a date with someone we don't choose to be with. They only say we must be kind in saying no to the offer. The scriptures don't say we have to loan money to a brother or sister, or to a roommate. They don't tell us we have to write a paper for a boyfriend, girlfriend, or spouse. They do say clearly that we must be kind about our dealings with one another. Kindness does require that we measure our own responses against a righteous standard. Sometimes kindness means we should keep quiet or leave a situation. Sometimes kindness requires us to remain and try to make things right. Ask yourself before you act or speak, "Is what I am about to do or say kind?" If it is, proceed confidently. If it isn't, frame another response.

To get a life is to love life. In Edgar Lee Masters' *Spoon River Anthology* is a wonderful poem entitled "Lucinda Matlock." In this poem, which reads almost as an epitaph, Lucinda tells of her hard life, her challenges, and joys. She concludes:

> What is this I hear of sorrow and weariness,
> Anger, discontent and drooping hopes?
> Degenerate sons and daughters,
> Life is too strong for you—
> It takes life to love Life.[41]

Two friends were talking. The one was outlining her concerns about graduate school and her upcoming finals. She was also worried about her boyfriend and getting married before she graduated. She wondered if she could find work after she did get her degree. Her father wasn't very well, and she was worried about getting together enough money to go visit him. She was feeling some stress in her roommate situation, too, and wondered about trying to find another place to live.

The friend listened carefully and then asked, "Which of these problems can you really do anything about right now and which are just recreational anxiety?"

The next time you consider spending some time in recreational anxiety, consider Nephi's words about our Savior: "And the world, because of their iniquity, shall judge him to be a thing of naught; wherefore they scourge him, and he suffereth it; and they smite him, and he suffereth it. Yea, they spit upon him, and he suffereth it, because of his loving kindness and his long-suffering towards the children of men."[42]

Nephi reminds us that our Savior suffered willingly because of his love for us. There is nothing we experience that our Lord does not understand.

I know this to be true. At times when I feel overwhelmed or alone, unsure or defeated, I remember that I have a Savior who understands and loves me. His atonement was personal; it was for me. He knows. He understands.

When Moses gave the last lecture I referred to at the beginning of these remarks, he knew what he was sending his people into. He told them, "Be strong and of a good courage, fear not, nor be afraid . . . for the Lord thy God, he it is that doth go with thee; he will not fail thee, nor forsake thee."[43] He knew they were not going into a new land alone. Unfailing help was with them, for the Lord was with them. Moses could, therefore, with confidence counsel that they be strong and of a good courage, for he knew there was a sure base for their strength and courage.

We go through mortality with the same promise. The Lord is with us and will not forsake us. A friend of mine tells her older children, "Pray at night, plan in the morning." What she means is that night is the time for rest for body, mind, and soul. Day is the time for action. I like the sign one of my neighbors has over her kitchen sink: "Every night I turn my worries over to God. He's going to be up all night anyway."

When the urge for recreational anxiety hits, remember courage, for the Lord knows and understands, and he loves you. Six years ago Elder Bruce R. McConkie, a member of the Council of the Twelve Apostles for twelve years, lay on his deathbed.[44] His wife, Amelia, leaned down to him and said, "Bruce, do you have a message for me?" Though weak and dying, he responded in a firm voice with his last words, "Carry on."[45]

To carry on—what a grand message. What a way to live and love life.

The choices Moses laid out are *the* choices. You are wonderful. Get a life by choosing the Lord, "for he is thy life." I say this in the name of Jesus Christ, amen.

Elaine L. Jack, "Get a Life," in Brigham Young University 1992–1993 Devotional and Fireside Speeches *(Provo, UT: Brigham Young University, 1993), 47–55.*

BASKETS AND BOTTLES

◇◇◇

CHIEKO N. OKAZAKI

Annual General Conference
Tabernacle, Temple Square, Salt Lake City, Utah
April 6, 1996

Through both her words and her leadership, Chieko Nishimura Okazaki (1926–2011) brought increased attention to the church's global membership. When she joined the Young Women general board in 1961, Okazaki became the first person of color to hold a church calling on the general board level. She was also the first woman to serve on all three of the women's auxiliary boards: Young Women from 1961 to 1966, Primary from 1988 to 1990, and Relief Society from 1990 to 1997.[1] When her husband, Edward Okazaki, established the new Japan Okinawa mission in 1968, Chieko was president of the mission Relief Society, Young Women, and Primary auxiliaries.[2]

Chieko Okazaki grew up in a Buddhist family of Japanese ancestry that was employed on Hawaiian plantations. The family sacrificed for her education, and education became her life's work. Hatsuko Nishimura, Okazaki's mother, was forced to quit school in sixth grade after the death of her own mother. To help finance her daughter's education, she and other family members—her husband, Kanenori, and their two sons—supplemented their income from plantation labor by making *zori* shoes of *lauhala* leaves at the rate of fifty cents per pair.[3]

First attending Latter-day Saint church meetings when she was eleven, Okazaki chose to join when she was fifteen, leaving home shortly thereafter to work as a maid to pay for high school.[4] She sold jewelry for Sears-Roebuck and worked as a clerk at the Swedish consulate to pay for her degree in education at the University of Hawaii in Honolulu.[5] She also earned a master's degree in education from the University of

Northern Colorado in 1977 and a degree in educational administration from Colorado State University in 1978.[6] She taught elementary school in Maui, Hawaii; Salt Lake City, Utah; and Littleton, Colorado, and for ten years was the first principal of Sunrise Elementary School in Littleton.[7]

By the time she was fifteen, Okazaki had come to acknowledge the complexity of her ethnic and cultural status. Worried about how others would perceive them after the Japanese military bombed Pearl Harbor, Hawaii, Okazaki and her mother gathered and burned every Japanese memento they owned. But then she looked in the mirror and contemplated her Japanese face. She thought, "I have never set foot in Japan. I am not Japanese in my heart. If a Japanese submarine landed on our beach and Japanese soldiers came ashore, I would run away from them. But I cannot run away from myself. My eyes, my skin, and my hair are Japanese."[8] Not long after her marriage to Edward Okazaki on June 18, 1949,[9] the couple moved to Utah for Ed to study social work at the University of Utah.[10] Okazaki described herself and her husband as "Japanese in our ancestry, Hawaiian by place of birth, and mainland American by place of residence. . . . We had claims on three cultures but did not totally belong in any one of the three."[11] She confronted racism throughout her life. Okazaki began teaching at Uintah Elementary in Salt Lake City in September 1951, soon after World War II when anti-Japanese sentiment still ran high in the United States. Three mothers refused to allow their children to be in her second-grade class. But Okazaki, radiant on the first day in a fuchsia dress and with a flower tucked behind her ear, soon won them over. The three mothers asked if their children could be in Okazaki's class after all.[12]

Okazaki repeatedly worked to foster unity despite language and cultural barriers. For example, after joining the Relief Society general presidency in 1990, she felt a strong desire to communicate with church members in their own languages. Before she traveled to other lands, the church's translation department translated the talks she wrote into Spanish, Tongan, and Korean; then she practiced and practiced her delivery. Korean posed a particular challenge for her. Sunae Mackelprang, whose husband, Gary, translated the talk, spoke it into a recorder for Okazaki, so she could play it over and over to guide her pronunciation.[13] Still, she struggled to pronounce the words in a comprehensible way and wondered whether she should give up and rely on a translator. She felt prompted to write the talk down in Hiragana characters—Chinese characters that Japanese speakers also use—and after that painstaking work, the pronunciation, grammatical structure, and intonation finally made sense to her. Her audience was able to understand the talk and was astonished and gratified that she could deliver it without a translator.[14]

In 1996, Okazaki oversaw Relief Society curriculum, Relief Society history, leadership, and visiting teaching, among other programs.[15] She delivered the following talk on unity and diversity during the Saturday morning session of general conference.

Chieko N. Okazaki delivering a general conference address. 1996. Okazaki was a prolific writer and popular speaker. A former elementary school teacher and principal, she frequently employed visual aids when she spoke. Photograph by Welden C. Anderson. (Church History Library, Salt Lake City.)

MY DEAR BROTHERS AND SISTERS, aloha! In February, I rejoiced with you when the number of members outside the United States edged ever so slightly past the number of members inside the United States.[16] That slight shift is an important symbol of the international nature of the church. I thought of Paul's statement to the Galatians: "There is neither Jew nor Greek, there is neither bond nor free, there is neither male nor female: for ye are all one in Christ Jesus."[17] This week I celebrate the 54th anniversary of my baptism. People like me who are converts know the promise of Paul: "For by one Spirit are we all baptized into one body."[18]

Brothers and sisters, today I want to talk about the beautiful oneness that we share in the gospel. I just returned from the Philippines, Australia, New Zealand, Tonga, and Fiji three weeks ago, where Sister Susan Warner and I participated in leadership training.[19] Earlier assignments have taken me to Mexico, Honduras, Guatemala, Samoa, Korea, and Japan.

In all these places we worked hard and long. People have said, "Oh, you must have been so tired." On the contrary, there was a feeling of being borne up "as on eagles' wings,"[20] because we have seen the daughters of Zion "awake, and arise . . . and put on [their] beautiful garments"[21] in response to the good news of the gospel. We taught, but—and this is the point I want to stress—we also learned.

The most important lesson was that we are truly all one in Christ Jesus.[22] We are one in our love of the Savior. We are one in our testimonies of the gospel. We are one in faith, hope, and charity. We are one in our conviction that the Book of Mormon is the inspired word of God. We are one in supporting President Hinckley and the other General Authorities.[23] We are one in loving each other.

Are we perfect in any of these things? No. We all have much to learn. Are we exactly the same in any of these things? No. We are all at different points on our journey back to our Father in Heaven. Did the Jews and Greeks whom Paul addressed in his epistle to the Galatians stop being Jews and Greeks when they were baptized? Did the men stop being men and the women stop being women? No. But they had all "been baptized into Christ" and had "put on Christ."[24]

Nephi explains the same principle in these terms: The Savior "inviteth . . . all to come unto him and partake of his goodness; and he denieth none that come unto him, black and white, bond and free, male and female . . . and all are alike unto God."[25]

God has given us many gifts, much diversity, and many differences, but the essential thing is what we know about each other—that we are all his children.

Our challenge as members of the church is for all of us to learn from each other, that we may all love each other and grow together.

The doctrines of the gospel are indispensable. They are essential, but the packaging is optional. Let me share a simple example to show the difference between the doctrines of the church and the cultural packaging. Here is a bottle of Utah peaches, prepared by a Utah homemaker to feed her family during a snowy season. Hawaiian homemakers don't bottle fruit. They pick enough fruit for a few days and store it in baskets like this for their families. This basket contains a mango, bananas, a pineapple, and a papaya. I bought these fruits in a supermarket in Salt Lake City, but they might have been picked by a Polynesian homemaker to feed her family in a climate where fruit ripens all year round.

The basket and the bottle are different containers, but the content is the same: fruit for a family. Is the bottle right and the basket wrong? No, they are both right. They are containers appropriate to the culture and the needs of the people. And they are both appropriate for the content they carry, which is the fruit.

Now, what is the fruit? Paul tells us: "The fruit of the Spirit is love, joy, peace, longsuffering, gentleness, goodness, faith, meekness, [and] temperance."[26] In the sisterhood of Relief Society, in the brotherhood of priesthood quorums, in the reverent coming together to partake of the sacrament, the fruit of the Spirit unites us in love, joy, and peace whether the Relief Society is in Taipei or Tonga, whether the priesthood quorum is in Montana or Mexico, and whether the sacrament meeting is in Fiji or the Philippines.

All over the world, as brothers and sisters in the gospel, we can learn from each other, grow closer together, and increase in love for each other. Our unity grows from what we have in common all around the world. They are the doctrines and ordinances of the gospel, our faith in the Savior, our testimonies of the scriptures, our gratitude for guidance from living prophets, and our sense of ourselves as a people striving to be Saints. These are the principles of the gospel.

Let us be sensitive to the unchanging and powerful core principles of the gospel. Let us understand that they matter most. Let us build firm foundations on these principles. Then when the rains fall and the floods come, our house will be "founded upon a rock" and it will not fall.[27]

Then, building on that firm foundation, let us rejoice with each other, listen to each other, learn from each other, and help each other apply those principles as we deal with our different circumstances, different cultures, different generations, and different geographies.

For six years now, I have been listening to the Relief Society women of the church. I have learned from all of them. I have learned from divorced mothers who are struggling to raise their children alone. I have learned from women who long to be married but are not, from women who yearn for children but cannot bear them, from women who are at risk from emotional and physical abuse in their homes. I have learned from women who work in their homes and women who work outside their homes. I have learned from women who endure chemical dependencies, experiences of childhood sexual abuse, and chronic illness.

Not many of these women thought they were giving me a gift. Most of them thought they were asking for help. But all of them blessed me as I listened and learned from them.

When I was called to the Relief Society general presidency six years ago this month, President Hinckley counseled me: "You bring a peculiar quality to this presidency. You will be recognized as one who represents those beyond the borders of the United States and Canada and, as it were, an outreach across the world to members of the church in many, many lands. They will see in you a representation of their oneness with the church." He gave me a blessing that my tongue might be loosed as I spoke to the people.[28]

President Hinckley, I want to bear witness to the Lord before you and this congregation that your counsel and your blessing have been literally fulfilled.

I do not speak Korean or Spanish or Tongan. But when I received my assignment to go among the Relief Society sisters and their priesthood leaders in lands where those languages were spoken, I was filled with a great desire to speak to them in their own language. I drew strength from President Hinckley's words of comfort and blessing. With the help of the church Translation Department and good coaches who spent hours working with me, I was blessed to deliver my addresses in Spanish, Korean, and Tongan as I went among those people.[29] I could feel the Spirit carrying my words to their hearts, and I could feel "the fruit of the Spirit"[30] bringing back to me their love, their joy, and their faith. I could feel the Spirit making us one.

Brothers and sisters, whether your fruits are peaches or papaya, and whether you bring them in bottles or in baskets, we thank you for offering them in love. Father in Heaven, may we be one and may we be thine,[31] I pray in the sacred name of our Savior, Jesus Christ, amen.

Chieko N. Okazaki, "Baskets and Bottles," Ensign *26, no. 5 (May 1996): 12–13.*

47

DECISIONS AND MIRACLES: AND NOW I SEE

◇◇◇

IRINA KRATZER

Brigham Young University Women's Conference
N. Eldon Tanner Building, Brigham Young University, Provo, Utah
April 27, 2000

Irina Valentinovna Kratzer (b. 1965) spent her first seven years in Kazan, Russia, with her physician parents, Minareta Kotova and Valentin Kotov.[1] The family then moved to Barnaul, Siberia, where Kratzer went to medical school and became a cardiologist.[2] Kratzer married a surgeon and had one daughter, Anastasia Davydova.[3] Medicine was not a lucrative field; months would go by when the hospital did not distribute paychecks.[4] After divorcing her abusive husband in 1996, Kratzer reported feeling exhausted and hopeless as she worked extra night shifts trying to support her mother and daughter on low wages. Sometimes Kratzer's patients brought her thank-you gifts of milk or foodstuffs.[5] She and her mother also grew food at her parents' dacha, a small country house three hours away by bus and tram.[6] Kratzer had been raised in a robustly atheist environment and did not believe in God. Nevertheless, one night she ventured a request: "All right, God, if you're there, just let me know, because you probably don't even care about me. Who am I to you, a little thing here trying to survive?"[7]

A few weeks later, in August 1996, Kratzer met a man who would introduce her to the church and help her travel to the United States to study English. In the United States, Kratzer not only had to learn medical terminology in a second language, but she had to learn new technologies and different approaches to medicine. She took an exam preparation course and studied twelve hours a day for three months for the first of her four board exams; she was the only member of her class to pass the first exam. Eight months after her arrival in Utah, in April 1998, Irina married Tay Kratzer. Tay had three young children at the time of their marriage. Anastasia, Kratzer's daughter, had stayed with her grandmother in Siberia, and the day after their wedding, the Kratzers filed the paperwork to bring Anastasia to Utah.[8]

Following her marriage, Kratzer decided to discontinue the practice of medicine. She was a teacher in an Orem, Utah, Relief Society when she was invited to speak at the Brigham Young University Women's Conference. Her husband helped her to edit the language in the following talk, which she wrote in English.[9]

THERE WAS A TIME in my life when I was touched by love and the light of Christ. My life has since changed forever.

I know how it is to live without the gospel. I lived that way for thirty years. I was born in Russia of goodly parents. They gave me tender love and care and an opportunity to have a good education. They did their best for me to be happy. For most of my life, I lived in Siberia. When I grew up, I got married and gave birth to a lovely baby girl. Soon I successfully graduated from the university and got a job I really liked. And yet, regardless of everything, I was far from being happy.

From the beginning, my marriage did not seem to work and gradually fell apart. Economic situations in Russia were getting worse every day. I was hardly able to provide simple food for my daughter and me. I sinned. I made one wrong choice after another. Hunger, depression, and poor decisions made my life miserable. I was blaming bad fortune, not realizing that in many ways I was suffering the natural consequences of my sins. But how could I know that? Sin did not exist according to what I had been taught. Let me explain.

Religion in Russia was prohibited after the Communist Revolution in 1917.[10] I was taught from kindergarten that there is no such thing as God and that only the Communist Party and Grandpa Lenin could bring happiness to the Russian people.[11] Religious people were badly persecuted in our society. Believers lost their jobs, were not allowed to go to school, and were labeled "crazy."[12] Everybody was required to take atheism classes at the university, where we proved that God does not exist. Although over time socialism in our country collapsed, and communist ideology proved to be not viable, atheism still lived in people's minds. It had deep roots in my mind also. I just did not think of God. Yet I felt pain in my heart about my poor choices. Later I would learn that the pain I felt was the Light of Christ giving me a sense of conscience to tell right from wrong.[13] But society opposed my feelings of pain. In other people's eyes, I was not doing anything particularly bad.

Elder M. Russell Ballard said: "The standards of the world have shifted like the sands of a wind-blown desert. That which was once unheard of or unacceptable is now commonplace."[14] That's how I lived. If there is no God, there is no sin; if there is no sin, it is absolutely up to you what you do with your life. Enjoy it. Take advantage of it. Because when you are gone, everything else will be gone also.

In the Book of Mormon, I have read about this same philosophy taught by the anti-Christ, Korihor: there is "no atonement made for the sins of men, but every man fare[s] in this life according to the management of the creature; therefore every man prosper[s] according to his genius, and . . . every man conquer[s] according to his strength; and whatsoever a man [does is] no crime."[15]

This philosophy appealed to me at first, but after a while, life seemed to me like a dark tunnel with only the grave at the end. I felt I was slowly dying. It is written in the scriptures that men are to have joy.[16] We came to this earth with the instinct to seek happiness, no matter where we live—in Russia, Africa, or blessed America. I did not know how to pray, so I dreamed. I am a big dreamer. I dreamed that one day I would run away from everything miserable in my life and would start again from the beginning—happy and bright. I wanted so much for my daughter to have a better life than I did. I dreamed about America. Somehow Russian people, and probably many other people in the world, associate America with a good life, success, and happiness.

Even when we do not know God's ways, he knows our hearts and listens to our dreams. One day a retired American doctor came to visit my city in Siberia.[17] His name was Dr. Woodmansee, and he was a Mormon from Utah.[18] All I'd heard about Mormons was that they did not drink tea and coffee, and that seemed strange. I was assigned to show Dr. Woodmansee around the hospital where I worked. At the end of our fifteen-minute visit he asked me, "Would you come to America to continue your education if I helped you?" Later he told me that in coming to Russia he never planned to make such an offer, but he followed a sudden prompting of the Spirit.

After that, for ten long months I corresponded with Dr. Woodmansee as we arranged for my coming to America. His acquaintance, Brother Ray Beckett, helped us communicate through the Internet and proved to be the best LDS missionary I've ever known.[19] Very often he shared his testimony with me. In one of his letters he promised me that my coming to America would change my life forever. He saw God's hand in what was going on in my life. He also arranged to send my documents through the church mail system, so that I could pick them up at the Novosibirsk mission office in Siberia.[20] That's how I met the LDS missionaries, who gave me a Book of Mormon. I was not interested in reading this book and put it somewhere on the shelf. During my next visit to the Novosibirsk mission home, I was given an *Ensign*.[21] I was trying to learn English at that time, so

I was very glad to receive such a present. It would help me in my English studies. The first article I read was about how the Book of Mormon had changed the lives of so many people, bringing them happiness and peace. These stories intrigued me and I decided to look closer into this book.

That is how the Book of Mormon came into my life. I read one chapter every morning before I went to work. Reading this book, I learned that God lives, that Jesus is his Son, and that he came to this earth to help sinners like me. The more I read this book, the more I saw the gap between the teachings of Christ and the way I lived. I learned that was why my life was so miserable. I felt pain and I had a great desire to change.

In 1997, President Thomas S. Monson said: "The decision to change one's life and come unto Christ is, perhaps, the most important decision of mortality. Such a dramatic change is taking place daily throughout the world."[22] At this time in my life, I received a new vision and understanding of life and could no longer live the way I had before. I was ready for a dramatic change. I will always remember the night in Russia when I cried the whole night through, realizing that my life was not good, that my poor decisions had hurt people I loved the most. It was the most painful experience of my life. I sobbed and pled the whole night, "Lord, please, help me!" By the end of the night I was exhausted and had no more tears. When the first morning light broke through, peace and relief came to me. I heard the words: "Here is my hand. I will lead you and guide you. But you have to promise me that you will change." And I did; I promised. I wanted this guidance and help more than anything else.

Alma the Younger related a similar experience to his son Helaman:

> But I was racked with eternal torment, for my soul was harrowed up to the greatest degree and racked with all my sins.
>
> Yea, I did remember all my sins and iniquities, . . . and that I had not kept his holy commandments. . . .
>
> And . . . while I was harrowed up by the memory of my many sins, behold, I remembered also to have heard my father prophesy unto the people concerning the coming of one Jesus Christ, a Son of God, to atone for the sins of the world.
>
> Now, as my mind caught hold upon this thought, I cried within my heart: O Jesus, thou Son of God, have mercy on me, who am in the gall of bitterness, and am encircled about by the everlasting chains of death.
>
> And now, behold, when I thought this, I could remember my pains no more; yea, I was harrowed up by the memory of my sins no more.

> And oh, what joy, and what marvelous light I did behold; yea, my soul was filled with joy as exceeding as was my pain!
>
> Yea, I say unto you, my son, that there could be nothing so exquisite and so bitter as were my pains. Yea, and again I say unto you, my son, that on the other hand, there can be nothing so exquisite and sweet as was my joy.[23]

I did not know, on that painful and joyous night in Russia, how great Christ's promises are. I did not know then that in just a little while I would travel to America where I would learn more about the gospel, and I would soon be baptized. I did not know that in less than a year from that eventful night, I would marry a wonderful man with three beautiful little children, a man who is so precious to my heart now, and with whom I want to live forever. I did not know that my daughter would come to America to join us in happiness with our newly formed family. Oh, I did not know then how great his promises are.

Now I know how much every soul is important to God. For me to get baptized, he took me out of cold Siberia and put me in sunny Utah to warm up my heart with friendly and kind people. He gave me so many miracles that I did not have even a little chance to doubt his divine hand in my life. I agree with President Monson. The decision to get baptized was the most important decision in my life, and my conversion was the biggest miracle for me.

But what about after my baptism? Do miracles still happen? Yes, they do! The fact that I no longer live with pain but with joy is the miracle that I have now daily. Like everybody else, I have my up and down days, but I have found true happiness on this earth. I was looking for it for thirty years, but I searched in all the wrong places, following the directions of the world and not knowing the Spirit.

Many other miracles, small and great, have come about in my life. And what matters most is what I have learned from them. First, I have learned that almost every miracle I have experienced since my baptism has come as a result of prayer and effort. God requires effort and faith on our part. Second, I have learned that the faith and testimony we gain require constant nourishment. Daily scripture study helps us to do that. Without effort on our part, our testimonies will fade, and the feelings of joy will fade also. If we don't go forward, we will go back. The third lesson I learned was that to receive daily miracles, we need to ask for them and then recognize them when they come. We recognize them not only to thank God, but to bring to our own awareness the ways in which God has blessed us. This process builds further faith.

Now in my dreams and in my letters, I return to Russia, to my friends, to people I love, and ask them: "Do you know who you are? Do you know where you come from? Please, listen. Listen to what I've learned." The fire burns in my soul day and night. The fire of joy, the fire of love, the fire of gratitude. And I cannot be still. I need to tell the whole world what I know now. Once I was blind, and now I see. Once I lived in darkness, and now I live in the brightest light.

Walk with Christ! Hold onto his hand! Feast upon his word. Drink in his light with your every pore, with all your soul. In times of hardships, you won't be left in a dark tunnel but in the light of his love with brighter light always ahead of you.

Irina Kratzer, "Decisions and Miracles: And Now I See," in Arise and Shine Forth: Talks from the 2000 Women's Conference *(Salt Lake City: Bookcraft, 2001), 102–107.*

48

KNOWING WHO YOU ARE—AND WHO YOU HAVE ALWAYS BEEN

◇◇◇

SHERI L. DEW

Brigham Young University Women's Conference
Marriott Center, Brigham Young University, Provo, Utah
May 4, 2001

Sheri Linn Dew (b. 1953) was born in Ulysses, Kansas, where Main Street had a total of four stoplights. She was the oldest of five children, and by the time she finished fifth grade, she was driving a large John Deere tractor, working from sunup to sundown on the family grain farm. On Sundays, her grandmother Maudie Dew would pick her up early for church, which was held in the Odd Fellows Hall. They would sweep up cigarette butts, beer cans, and wine bottles to prepare the room for sacrament meeting. Dew was "exquisitely shy," but participating in a small church branch meant she did a lot of speaking and teaching from a very young age.[1] She became the branch pianist when she was in seventh grade (replacing her grandmother, who died not long before Dew turned twelve) and served in her branch Primary presidency when she was sixteen.[2]

After earning a history degree at Brigham Young University (BYU) in 1978, she took a job with Bookcraft, a publishing company, where she became an editor. After four years at Bookcraft, she worked as editor and associate publisher of *This People* magazine, until she joined Deseret Book in 1988. She became an executive vice president at Deseret Book in 2000.[3]

Both Maudie Dew and Sheri's mother, JoAnn Petersen Dew, told her repeatedly that she was from a chosen generation and that there was something special about her. She believes their words helped her to push through her painful shyness and to accept increasingly high-level responsibilities.[4] She was thirty-five years old when she joined the Relief Society general board during the presidency of Barbara W. Winder and subsequently served as the president of the Sandy East Stake Relief Society from 1991 to 1996. When she became Mary Ellen W. Smoot's second counselor in the Relief Society general presidency in 1997, she was only forty-three.[5]

In her writing and speaking, Dew has frequently taught her audiences that they should learn to rely on the Holy Spirit and that the Spirit would teach them on an individual basis. "The reality is that when I'm allowed to do something that blesses someone else, that's the Spirit. It's the work of the Spirit," she said. "You go on assignment from the Lord to do different things; and if the Spirit is present, it works. And if the Spirit is not present, it doesn't work."[6] In her own life, she remembers that as her father confirmed her a member of the church, she felt the Holy Ghost so strongly that she began to weep deeply.[7] She could not stop and continued to weep after she returned to her seat. She reported that this experience taught her early that "the Holy Ghost was real and that it really could make a difference in my life."[8] Years later, when she felt unable to understand spiritual direction on a particular question, a friend suggested she could ask in prayer what it felt like for her when the Spirit spoke to her. She has continued the practice of praying for help to understand the "language of revelation" and has acquired firm confidence in her ability to do so, which she feels is vital.[9]

During her tenure in the general Relief Society presidency, Dew expressed her belief that Relief Society members needed to be better at reaching out and bringing in those who feel peripheral, including women making the transition at age eighteen from the Young Women program to the Relief Society. She believed one important way to make people feel included was to trust them with work to do: "My belief is that most of our young women who have a hard time making a transition wouldn't have a hard time making a transition if we put them to work, and got them involved, and valued them."[10] On the other hand, she had little sympathy for members who waited passively for the church to make their lives better. She said it is not the Relief Society president's job to make her happy. The Relief Society president's job is "to allow me to participate fully, and to have a full church experience."[11] Dew exhorted audience members to understand their worth and to participate fully during her discourse at the 2001 BYU Women's Conference.

SISTERS, YOU ARE JUST SPECTACULAR! You're not perfect, but you are spectacular! From Siberia to Seattle, you have won my heart and my deepest respect. I believe there is more righteous courage and determination inherent within the sisters of this church today than there has ever been among any group of women who have ever lived. And today I want to tell you why.

Recently, my sixteen-year-old niece Megan and two of her friends came for a sleepover. As we talked that evening, one of them asked me what it had been like growing up on a farm in the olden days. (This is not as bad, however, as what happened a few days ago when a handsome young returned missionary said to me, "Sister Dew, if I were just forty years older . . ." You know, if I ever do get married, I hope my husband does better math than that.) Anyway, I told Megan and her friends that in the "olden days," I had been painfully shy and had absolutely no self-confidence.

"How did you get over feeling that way?" Megan asked. A pat answer was on the tip of my tongue when I stopped, sensing that these terrific young women were receptive to more. So I told them that the reason was a spiritual one: It wasn't until I began to understand how the Lord felt about me that my feelings about myself and my life slowly began to change. Their questions then came in a flurry: How did I *know* how the Lord felt? And how could they find out how he felt about them?

For several hours, scriptures in hand, we talked about how to hear the voice of the Spirit, about how eager the Lord is to unveil the knowledge stored safely inside our spirits concerning who we are and what our mission is, and about the life-changing difference it makes when we know.

My message to you today, my dear sisters, whom I love, is the same: There is nothing more vital to our success and our happiness here than learning to hear the voice of the Spirit. It is the Spirit who reveals to us our identity—which isn't just who we are but who we have always been. And that when we know, our lives take on a sense of purpose so stunning that we can never be the same again.

As a people, we talk and sing constantly about who we are. Three-year-olds know the words to "I Am a Child of God."[12] The Proclamation on the Family declares that we each have a divine destiny.[13] The second Young Women's value is divine nature.[14] And the very first words in the Relief Society Declaration are, "We are beloved spirit daughters of God, and our lives have meaning, purpose, and direction."[15] And yet, with all our talking, do we really believe? Do we really understand? Has this transcendent doctrine about who we are—meaning who we have always been and, therefore, who we may become—permeated our hearts?

Our spirits long for us to remember the truth about who we are, because the way we see ourselves, our sense of identity, affects everything we do. It affects the way we behave, the way we respond to uncertainty, the way we see others, the way we feel about ourselves, and the way we make choices. It affects the very way we live our lives. So, today, I invite you to ponder in a new way not just who you are but who you have always been.

President Lorenzo Snow taught that "Jesus was a god before he came into the world and yet his knowledge was taken from him. He did not know his former greatness, neither do we know what greatness we had attained to before we came here."[16] But President Snow also taught that during the Savior's life "it was revealed unto him who he was, and for what purpose he was in the world. The glory and power he possessed *before* he came into the world was made known unto him."[17] Sisters, just as the Savior came to remember and to know exactly who he was, so may we.

Unveiling this knowledge would be easier if we could remember what happened in our premortal life. But we can't. We can't remember the glory of our former home. We have forgotten the language we spoke there and our dear companions with whom we associated. We cannot recall the "first lessons [we learned] in the world of spirits" or the identities of our heavenly tutors.[18] We cannot remember what promises we made to ourselves and to others and to the Lord. Nor can we remember our place in the Lord's heavenly kingdom or the spiritual maturity we achieved there.

There are, however, some remarkable things that we do know. We know that *we were there,* in the heavenly councils before the foundations of this earth were laid. *We were there* when our Father presented his plan, and we saw the Savior chosen and appointed, and we sanctioned it.[19] We were there among the heavenly host who sang and shouted for joy.[20] And when Satan unleashed his fury against the Father and the Son and was cast out of heaven, we were there, fighting on the side of truth. In fact, President George Q. Cannon said that "we stood loyally by God and by Jesus, and . . . *did not flinch.*"[21] We believed. We followed. And when we fought for truth in the most bitter of all confrontations, we did not flinch.

Because of our premortal valor, we were chosen to be born into the house of Israel, which lineage President Harold B. Lee called the "most illustrious lineage" of all who would come to earth, and which Elder Bruce R. McConkie said was reserved for those who sought the greatest of all premortal talents, the talent of spirituality.[22]

Now we are here, separated from the safety of our heavenly home, serving a mission in this lone and dreary world—a mission to prove whether or not we want to be part of the kingdom of God more than we want anything else. The Lord is testing our faith and our integrity to see if we will persevere in a realm where Satan reigns. Happily, despite taking this test in the stormy twilight of the dispensation of the fulness of times, we have once again chosen to follow Jesus Christ.[23] We have chosen to follow him because we remember him and we recognize him.

We are among the elect whom the Lord has called during this "eleventh hour" to labor in his vineyard, a vineyard that "has become corrupted every whit" and in which only a few "doeth good."[24] We are those few. God, who saw the "end from the beginning," foresaw perfectly what these times would demand.[25] Thus, said President George Q. Cannon, "God . . . reserved spirits for this dispensation who [would] have the courage and determination to face the world, and all the powers of the evil one," and who would "build up the Zion of our God, fearless of all consequences."[26]

Can you imagine that God, who knew us perfectly, reserved us to come now, when the stakes would be higher and the opposition more intense than ever? When he would need women who would help raise and lead a chosen generation in the most lethal spiritual environment? Can you imagine that he chose us because he knew we would be fearless in building Zion?

I can, because of what the Spirit has repeatedly whispered about you as I have sought the Lord in your behalf during this calling. Though we are sometimes far too casual about our spiritual lives; though we sometimes get distracted by the world and live beneath ourselves—the fact remains that we have always been women of God. We have repeatedly made righteous choices, on both sides of the veil, that demonstrate our faithfulness. We have bound ourselves to the Lord with the most binding covenants of mortality. We have been and are so much more valiant than we think. We have so much more divine potential than we yet comprehend.

The Lord told Abraham that he was among the "noble and great ones" chosen for his earthly mission before he was born.[27] And President Joseph F. Smith saw in vision that many—many—choice spirits reserved to come forth in this dispensation were also "among the noble and great."[28] Said Elder Bruce R. McConkie: "A *host* of mighty men and *equally glorious women* comprised that group of the 'noble and great ones.' . . . Can we do other than conclude that Mary and Eve and Sarah and myriads of our faithful sisters were numbered among them? Certainly these sisters . . . fought as valiantly in the War in Heaven as did the brethren, even as they in like manner stand firm . . . in mortality, in the cause of truth and righteousness."[29]

So, sisters, what about us? What about you and me? Is it possible that we were among the noble and great?

I have to tell you, I believe it is more than possible. The Prophet Joseph taught that "every man who has a calling to minister to the inhabitants of the world was ordained to that very purpose . . . before this world was."[30] President Spencer W. Kimball added that "in the world before we came here, faithful women were given certain assignments."[31] I simply cannot imagine that we who have been called to bear and rear and lead and love a chosen generation of children and youth this late in the final dispensation were not among those deemed noble and great.

Noble and great. Courageous and determined. Faithful and fearless. That is who you are, and that is who you have always been. Understanding that truth can change your life, because this knowledge carries a confidence that cannot be duplicated any other way. I doubt many of us feel noble or great. But then neither did Enoch, who was stunned when the Lord called him into service: "Why is it that I have found favor in thy sight, and am but a lad, and all the people hate me; for I am slow of speech?"[32] The Lord responded to Enoch by promising to walk with him and give power to his words. This encounter with the Lord gave Enoch a new vision of himself, and the result was magnificent, for so powerful was his word that his people were "taken up into heaven."[33] But that happened *after* Enoch understood who he was and that he had a mission to perform.

Saul, who made sport of persecuting Christians, was instantly converted after seeing the Savior and learning that he was a chosen vessel.[34] There surely wasn't a Christian breathing who would have described Saul of Tarsus as "chosen"—at least not based on his earthly conduct. He must have been chosen before. And when Saul understood that, he changed his life and his name. The Apostle Paul's conversion was at least partly about coming to understand who he had always been.

As we come to understand the same thing, we will feel a greater sense of mission and more confidence living as a woman of God in a world that doesn't necessarily celebrate women of God. We will cheer each other on rather than compete with each other, because we'll feel secure in our standing before the Lord. And we'll be eager to stand for truth, even when we must stand alone—for every consecrated woman will have times when she must stand alone.

Satan, of course, knows how spiritually potent the knowledge of our divine identity is. He hates women of the noble birthright.[35] He hates us because he is almost out of time, while we are en route to everlasting glory. He hates us because of the influence we have on husbands and children, family and friends, the church and even the world. It is no secret to him that we are the Lord's secret weapon.

Thus it should not surprise us that the master of deceit is going all out to keep us from comprehending the majesty of who we are. He offers an array of seductive but sorry substitutes—everything from labels and logos to titles and status—hoping to preoccupy us with the world's artificial identifiers. Not long ago a book listing *The 100 Most Influential Women of All Time* caught my attention.[36] I was interested to find out who the 100 most influential women of all time had been. Here's what you'll find interesting. Eve, the mother of all living—now catch the irony here, the woman without whom we wouldn't even be here—didn't make the list.[37] Come on! This pitiful list demonstrates how absurd the world's view and valuation of women is.

In a prominent magazine, a recent cover story entitled "The Quest for Perfection" promoted a definition of perfection that was disgusting and, frankly, evil. It listed every available lift, tuck, and augmentation, while not so much as mentioning virtue or values, marriage or motherhood—or anything, for that matter, that matters to the Lord.

Clearly, Satan wants us to see ourselves as the world sees us, not as the Lord sees us, because the world's mirror, like a circus mirror in which a 5'10" woman (that's me) appears two feet tall, distorts and minimizes us. Satan tells us we're not good enough. Not smart enough. Not thin enough. Not cute enough. Not clever enough. Not *anything* enough. And that is a big, fat, devilish lie. He wants us to believe that there is no status in being a mother. That is a lie, an evil lie. He wants us to believe that the influence of women is inherently inferior. And that is a lie.

Yet we often buy into Satan's superficialities. After speaking in a general women's meeting on satellite, I received a letter that said this: "Sister Dew, I can relate to you because I can see that you know what it means to have a bad-hair day." Sisters, this was no news flash; I've had years of bad-hair days. But though we don't always see beyond our hair and our clothing, the Lord does. For he "seeth not as man seeth, for man looketh on the outward appearance, but the Lord looketh on the heart."[38]

Thus Satan's all-out attempt to prevent us from understanding how the Lord sees us, because the more clearly we understand our divine destiny, the more immune we become to Satan. When Satan tried to confuse Moses about his identity, saying, "Moses, son of man, worship me," Moses refused, responding: "I am a son of God."[39] He knew who he was because the Lord had told him, "Thou art my son; . . . and I have a work for thee."[40]

Surely one reason Moses prevailed while the great deceiver ranted and railed was that Moses knew clearly who he was. So it is with us. We will never be happy or feel peace; we will never deal well with life's ambiguities; we will never live up to who we are as women of God until we overcome our mortal identity crisis by understanding who we are, who we have always been, and who we may become.

The Spirit is the key, for as President Joseph F. Smith taught, it is through the power of the Spirit that we may "catch a spark from the awakened memories of the immortal soul, which lights up our whole being as with the glory of our former home."[41] It is the Spirit that allows us to pierce the veil and catch glimpses of who we are and who we have always been. Thus our need to be able to hear what the Lord through the Spirit has to say. Asking in faith, fasting and praying, repenting regularly, forgiving and seeking forgiveness, worshiping in the temple where we may "receive a fulness of the Holy Ghost,"[42] and being obedient—all help us better hear the voice of the Lord in our minds and hearts.[43] Conversely, there are things we cannot do—movies we cannot watch, clothes we cannot wear, gossip we cannot spread, Internet sites we cannot visit, thoughts we cannot entertain, books we cannot read, and dishonesty we cannot tolerate—if we want the Spirit to be with us.

I can think of nothing more deserving of our energy than learning to better hear the voice of the Spirit. When the Nephite Twelve pleaded with the Father for "that which they most desired," it was the gift of the Holy Ghost.[44] Why? Because the Holy Ghost "will show unto [us] all things," including who we are.[45] I know this is true. One day while rocking a niece who was then three months old, I was overwhelmed with an impression about the valor of her spirit. My tears flowed as I rocked and wondered just whom I was rocking. Now that my niece is older, I have told her about that experience, hoping to encourage her onward.

Similarly, when I was that shy farm girl, both my mother and my grandma often told me that there was something chosen about me and my generation.[46] I couldn't quite imagine it, but my spirit wanted me to believe. So I quietly hung on their words and hoped they were true. Is there anything more meaningful a mother or a grandmother or any of us can do for the youth we love than help them begin to see who they *really* are?

As vital as this knowledge is, however, it alone doesn't make mortality fail-safe. President Lee warned that there are many who may "have been among the noble and great" but who "may fail of that calling here in mortality."[47] In other words, "many are called, but few are chosen."[48] And, frankly, we do the choosing, because the sobering reality is that whether or not we live up to our premortal promises is entirely up to us.

But the effort required is well worth it, for if we could comprehend how glorious a righteous woman made perfect in the celestial kingdom will be, we would rise up and never be the same again. We would gladly take upon us the name of Jesus Christ—which means following him, becoming like him, and dedicating ourselves to him and his work.[49] Women of God who honor their covenants look differently, dress differently, and act and speak differently from women who have not made the same covenants. Thus women of God who know who they are have unusual and sometimes unexpected influence.

There is a shop in New York City I visit when I am there. Frankly, I don't care for the shop's atmosphere, but because they carry skirts long enough for a tall woman, I endure the experience. On a recent visit, I made plans to meet a friend at this shop, and when I walked through the door, a saleswoman was already waiting for me. "Mizz Dew?" she said with a charming accent. "Yeah?" I responded. "Follow me. Your friend is waiting for you downstairs."

I had never had such a warm reception, but then, for the next hour, my friend and I became acquainted with this delightful European woman. After a while she said, "There is something different about you two. What is it?"

"Do you really want to know?" we asked her. When she nodded yes, I said, "Sit down." For an hour, my friend and I told her what made us different. Since then we've sent materials explaining more. And we've just sent her something else—missionaries who will call on her using our names.

What does knowing who we are and who we have always been have to do with bearing record and testifying of Jesus Christ? It has everything to do with our mandate to take the gospel to every nation, kindred, tongue, and people. Once we understand who we really are, we are not only beholden to the Lord to help others discover the same truths but we simply cannot be restrained from doing so. If a missionary moment can unfold in a stuffy New York dress shop, it can happen anywhere. And it will happen as the joy of the gospel and the reality of our mission lights our faces and energizes our lives.

I know a woman who responded to a nonmember friend wanting to sell her cosmetics by saying, "You can give me a facial if I can talk about the gospel." Both agreed, and both are here today. There is no more persuasive missionary messenger than a woman of God who knows who she is and who is thrilled with what she knows. I hasten to add that the most important missionary work we will ever do will be within our families, as their conversion is our highest priority.

Our objective through all of this isn't to build a bigger church. It is to bless the lives of people—mothers and fathers, sons and daughter—who deserve to know who they are, who they have always been, and who they may become.

Let's not make this harder than it needs to be. We can begin by simply praying for opportunities to serve, for we will do more missionary work through our examples than we ever will pounding a pulpit. Last year the sisters in an Arizona ward provided service, no strings attached, to a nonmember family whose infant son was undergoing open-heart surgery.[50] Those simple acts of kindness launched a remarkable sequence of events, and two weeks ago that family was baptized. I am happy to tell you that the mother of that family is here with us this morning, and she and her husband and their three darling little boys are beginning to find out who they are.

Repeatedly, President Gordon B. Hinckley has pleaded with us to "become a vast army with enthusiasm for this work."[51] In the last general Relief Society meeting, I invited every sister to look for missionary opportunities. And last month at the general Young Women meeting, Sister Margaret Nadauld asked every young woman to reach out to one girl and bring her into full activity this year.[52] Within a week, several of my teenage nieces had already made contacts with nonmember friends. They enlisted immediately in the army.

Can we do any less? If the women and young women of this church would join together in this glorious work, we would become a vast, enthusiastic part of the Lord's army. None of us can reach everyone, but we can all reach someone—and over time, many someones. The gospel kingdom will not move forward as it must until we as mothers and sisters and favorite aunts become full and eager participants.

Sisters, I am asking you today to respond to our prophet's call to enlist in the Lord's army. And in doing so I make this promise: As soon as we, the sisters of this church, commit fully to this work, it will explode in an unprecedented way because of our unique, nurturing influence and because of the spirit that attends righteous women. It will flourish because youth who see their mothers and leaders fearlessly sharing the gospel will do likewise.

More than twenty years ago President Kimball prophesied: "The female exemplars of the church will be a significant force in both the numerical and the spiritual growth of the church in the last days."[53] He was talking about us. Imagine the impact if this year every woman with a testimony helped one other woman gain a testimony and begin to find out who she is and was and may become.

I'll take the challenge. Will you join me? Ask the Lord to help you, and he will. Begin by reading Doctrine and Covenants 138 and Abraham 3 about the noble and great ones, and see what the Spirit reveals to you about *you.* When you understand that *you* were chosen and reserved for now, and when you live in harmony with that mission, you'll be happier than you have ever been before.

Listen to these words from President Gordon B. Hinckley:

"Woman is God's supreme creation. . . .

"Of all the creations of the Almighty, there is none more . . . inspiring than a . . . daughter of God who walks in virtue with an understanding of why she should do so."[54]

"Rise above the dust of the world. Know that you are daughters of God . . . and that there is for you a great work to be done which cannot be left to others."[55]

My dear sisters, will you seek to remember with the help of the Holy Ghost who you are and who you have always been? Will you remember that you stood by our Savior without flinching? Remember that you were reserved for now because you would have the courage and determination to face the world at its worst and to help rear and lead a chosen generation. Remember the covenants you have made and the power they carry. Remember that you are noble and great and a potential heir of all our Father has. Remember that you are the daughter of a King.

God is our Father, and his Only Begotten Son is the Christ. May we rejoice in once again standing tall for the Savior and serving with valor and vigor in his vineyard. And may we be fearless in building up the Zion of our God—because we know who we are and who we have always been. In the name of Jesus Christ, amen.

Sheri Dew, "Knowing Who You Are—and Who You Have Always Been," BYU Women's Conference address, May 4, 2001, Brigham Young University, Provo, UT, accessed Apr. 19, 2016, womensconference.ce.byu.edu.

Virginia H. Pearce, Janette Hales Beckham, and Bonnie D. Parkin, Young Women general presidency. 1994. The goal of Beckham's presidency, which served from 1992 to 1997, was to help "every young woman to become a righteous, problem-solving woman of faith." Parkin later served as the Relief Society general president from 2002 to 2007. Pictured here, left to right, are Pearce, Beckham, and Parkin. Photograph by Busath Photography. (Church History Library, Salt Lake City.)

WITH HOLINESS OF HEART

◇◇◇

BONNIE D. PARKIN

General Relief Society Meeting
Conference Center, Salt Lake City, Utah
September 28, 2002

While growing up in Herriman, Utah, Bonnie Dansie Parkin (b. 1940) learned independence and devotion to the Relief Society from her grandmother Agnes Kunz Dansie. Dansie was active in the Relief Society and proud that she had donated to the Relief Society Building fund. An ardent proponent of education in general, and education for women in particular, Dansie occasionally sent Parkin dollar bills to support her while she studied elementary education at Utah State University, where she earned her degree in 1962. Dansie earned these dollars by writing a column for the *Midvale (Utah) Sentinel* and by selling eggs from her chickens.[1]

Throughout her life, Parkin found strength in covenant-keeping. In Seattle, Washington, she was a new mother with very little money and a husband, James L. Parkin, who was often absent to fulfill responsibilities both as a medical resident at the University of Washington and as a member of the bishopric.[2] During this busy time, Parkin made her church commitments a priority, serving as the Primary president and studying the Book of Mormon and Bible with a friend.[3] The Parkins also continued to pay their tithing, even when their income was so low that the bishop asked whether they were paying what they ought, wondering how they could live on so little.[4] One way the Parkins emphasized covenants with their four sons was by enthusiastically celebrating baptisms. They prepared by having lessons and discussions in family home evening, buying new clothes, inviting grandparents and friends to attend, and sharing a meal afterward at their home.[5]

Parkin was on the Relief Society general board from 1990 until 1994, when she joined the Young Women general presidency.[6] Just six months after accepting this new position, she spoke in general conference.[7] She had written her talk and was entertaining houseguests just before conference when she realized she had prepared "the wrong talk."[8] So she started over, this time writing a talk about covenants, highlighting the covenants in Mosiah 18:8–9 to "bear one another's burdens, . . . mourn with those that mourn; . . . comfort those that stand in need of comfort, and . . . stand as witnesses of God at all times." She also described covenants in terms of temple promises to "be obedient, to sacrifice, to keep ourselves worthily pure, to contribute to the spreading of truth, to be chaste, to pray, to live the gospel."[9]

On the morning of February 25, 2002, the Parkins received a phone call asking them to meet with church president Gordon B. Hinckley. After speaking with them, Hinckley looked at Bonnie and said, "I'm calling you to be the Relief Society general president."[10] Parkin had specific priorities as president. For example, she felt an urgency to help young women learn to love Relief Society.[11] During her earlier general board service, she was on the committee assigned to help young women transition comfortably to Relief Society from the Young Women organization.[12] Parkin's priorities as general president were also influenced by her visits to Relief Societies in England, while she and her husband presided over the London South mission.[13] She admired how Relief Society members had openly shared at their meetings both the difficult and the good things in their lives. Even outside of meetings, they diligently supported each other through visiting teaching and compassionate service, despite the logistical inconvenience of sprawling ward boundaries. Many of the members were new converts who frequently described how their covenants blessed them.[14]

Parkin and her new counselors made covenants a part of their mission statement. They wanted to help women "feel the Lord's love in their lives daily, keep their covenants, exercise charity, and strengthen families."[15] Parkin gave the following talk, also about covenants, at a general Relief Society meeting six months after becoming president.[16]

ALTHOUGH OUR NUMBERS are much greater than those Relief Society sisters in Nauvoo, the spirit of our gathering is the same.[17] Like us, they lifted, nurtured, and inspired each other; they prayed for each other; they consecrated all that they had to the kingdom. President Hinckley has described us as "a vast reservoir of faith and good works, . . . an anchor of devotion and loyalty and accomplishment."[18] How remarkable that whether we are in the Conference Center or in a chapel in Mexico or in a branch in Lithuania, we are sisters in Zion with a great work to do. And together, led by a prophet of God, we will do it! I hope you feel the love I have for you—love that is shared by my counselors, who are a rich blessing to me.

To say I was overwhelmed when President Gordon B. Hinckley called me to serve as Relief Society general president is a huge understatement! Can't you relate? But, voice trembling, I responded, "Here am I; send me."[19] After a Jewish friend learned what my calling entailed, she looked at me like I was crazy and asked, "Bonnie, why would you do that?" (At times like these, I often ask myself the same thing!) But there is only one reason I did it: I have made covenants with the Lord, and I know what that requires. Plus, I knew that you and I would serve together and that my willingness was on behalf of all of us.

For centuries, righteous women have been stepping forward to join the cause of Christ. Many of you have only recently been baptized; your covenants are fresh in your hearts, your sacrifices still tender. As I think about you, I am reminded of Priscilla Staines from Wiltshire, England.[20] Nineteen-year-old Priscilla joined the church in 1843.[21] Alone. She had to steal away in the night to be baptized, because of the persecutions of her neighbors and the displeasure of her family. She wrote: "We waited until midnight . . . and then repaired to a stream of water a quarter of a mile away. Here we found the water . . . frozen over, and the elder had to chop a hole in the ice large enough for the purpose of baptism. . . . None but God and his angels, and the few witnesses who stood on the bank with us, heard my covenant; but in the solemnity of that midnight hour it seemed as though all nature were listening, and the recording angel writing our words in the book of the Lord."[22]

Her words "None but God and his angels . . . heard my covenant" touch my soul, for like Priscilla—no matter our age, our gospel knowledge, our time in the church—we are all women of covenant. That is a phrase we often hear in the church, but what does it mean? How do covenants define who we are and how we live?

Covenants—or binding promises between us and Heavenly Father—are essential for our eternal progression. Step by step, he tutors us to become like him by enlisting us in his work. At baptism we covenant to love him with all our hearts and love our sisters and brothers as ourselves.[23] In the temple we further covenant to be obedient, selfless, faithful, honorable, charitable.[24] We covenant to make sacrifices and consecrate all that we have. Forged through priesthood authority, our kept covenants bring blessings to fill our cups to overflowing. How often do you reflect that your covenants reach beyond mortality and connect you to the Divine? Making covenants is the expression of a willing heart; keeping covenants, the expression of a faithful heart.

Sounds so simple on paper, doesn't it? Of course, the doing is where we prove who we really are. Thus, every time we reach out with love, patience, kindness, generosity, we honor our covenants by saying, "Here am I; send me." Usually we speak these words softly, unaccompanied by brass bands.

When have someone else's covenants with the Lord blessed *your* life, brought you peace, nurtured your soul? When my husband and I were missionaries in England, we saw many elders and sisters whose lives were directly influenced by the covenants of worthy women.[25] I was so thankful for mothers, sisters, aunts, teachers—like so many of you—whose honored covenants extended blessings to others by the way they taught those future missionaries.

Covenants not only coax us out of comfort zones and into new growth but lead others to do the same. Jesus said, "The works which ye have seen me do that shall ye also do."[26] His covenant keeping encourages ours.

Covenants save us from needless suffering. For example, when we obey the prophet's guidance, we are keeping a covenant. He has counseled us to avoid debt, maintain a food supply, and become self-reliant.[27] Living within our means blesses us beyond that obedience. It teaches us gratitude, restraint, unselfishness; it brings peace from financial pressures and protection from materialism's greed. Keeping our lamps filled means that unforeseen circumstances do not hinder opportunities to declare with devotion, "Here am I; send me."

Covenants renewed invigorate and refresh a weary soul. Each Sunday when we partake of the sacrament, what happens in our hearts when we hear those words to "always remember him"?[28] Do we improve the following week by refocusing on what matters most? Yes, we face hard things; yes, making changes is strenuous. But have you ever wondered how our sisters survived being driven from Nauvoo, many walking the entire trek?[29] When their feet were tired, they were carried by their covenants! What else could grant such spiritual and physical fortitude?

Covenants also protect us from being "tossed to and fro, and carried about with every wind of doctrine, by the sleight of men, and cunning craftiness."[30] Women of covenant stand firm when evil is called good and good is called evil.[31] Whether it be in the college classroom, around the water cooler, or watching TV's latest "experts," remembering our covenants keeps us from being led astray.

Covenants can keep us and those we love spiritually safe and spiritually prepared by putting first things first. For instance, when it comes to families, we cannot afford indifference and distraction. Childhood is a vanishing wonder; so few have had the sunny days I knew growing up on a farm. President Hinckley has said: "Our problems, almost every one, arise out of the homes of the people. . . . If there is to be a change, . . . it must begin in the home. It is here that truth is learned, that integrity is cultivated, that self-discipline is instilled, and that love is nurtured."[32]

Sisters, the Lord needs women who will teach children to work and learn and serve and believe. Whether they are our own or another's, we must stand up and state, "Here am I; send me to watch over your little ones, to put them first, to guide and protect them from evil, to love them."

Sometimes we are faced with keeping our covenants when there seems to be no logical reason to do so. I listened to a single sister tell of her experience of "coming to trust the Lord completely." Her life had not worked out as she had expected. Sound familiar? This period of soul-searching was marked by changing jobs, new financial pressures, tugs from worldly philosophies. Now listen to what she did. She sat down with other sisters in her ward and found that they too were searching to find the peace the gospel brings. She asked for a priesthood blessing. She valiantly carried forward in her calling. She studied and tried to more fully commit her love, appreciation, and conviction to Jesus. She prayed. "I cried to the Lord," she said, "and told him I would do whatever he would ask of me." She did all this despite those difficulties. And do you know what happened? No, her eternal companion did not appear on her doorstep. But peace made its way into her heart, and life got better.

Sisters, we keep our covenants when we share our life's wisdom to encourage another, when we visit teach with genuine compassion, when we help a younger sister know that her fresh perspective will bless us in Relief Society. We can do that!

When young Priscilla, our British convert of 1843, crossed the Atlantic, she was befriended by a woman the age of her mother.[33] This older sister also felt the fire of covenants she had made. When they docked at the wharf in Nauvoo, she was by Priscilla's side. Together, bold and believing, they joined with the Saints of God.[34]

The spiritual integrity to keep our covenants comes from consistency in scripture study, prayer, service, and sacrifice. Such simple steps nurture our souls so we can say, "Send me to help a sister and her newborn; send me to tutor a struggling student; send me to love an outsider. Send me where you need me, when you need me."

The Lord has called us to do all that we do with "holiness of heart."[35] And holiness is a product of covenant living. I love the words of this hymn and the way they make me feel:

> More holiness give me,
> More strivings within,
> More patience in suff'ring,

More sorrow for sin,
More faith in my Savior,
More sense of his care,
More joy in his service,
More purpose in prayer.[36]

Holiness prompts the words "Here am I; send me." When Priscilla Staines made her midnight covenant in those icy waters, she stepped forward into a new life, clothes nearly frozen yet heart warmed with joy. "There was no turning back," she said. "I . . . set out for the reward of everlasting life, trusting in God."[37]

President Hinckley, with the Relief Society sisters around the world, I commit to you that we stand united as women of covenant and hearken to your voice.[38] In a host of different languages, hear the words of each Relief Society sister as we say, "Here am I; send me."

May our individual covenants that bind us to our loving Heavenly Father guide us, protect us, sanctify us, and allow us to do likewise for all his children, I so pray in the name of Jesus Christ, amen.

Bonnie D. Parkin, "With Holiness of Heart," Ensign *32, no. 11 (Nov. 2002): 103–105.*

PRAYER: A SMALL AND SIMPLE THING

◇◇◇

VIRGINIA H. PEARCE

Brigham Young University Women's Conference
Marriott Center, Brigham Young University, Provo, Utah
April 28, 2011

From childhood, Virginia Hinckley Pearce (b. 1945) found that her parents wove prayer and church service into the fabric of their everyday lives. She remembers that when she or one of her siblings was particularly worried over a situation, her father, Gordon B. Hinckley, would say, "Just say your prayers and go to bed. Get up in the morning; it'll be clearer."[1] Pearce has applied that good advice; her own restatement of it is, "Just say your prayers, go to bed, and when you get up in the morning, go back to work."[2] Gathering for family prayer, going to church, and working on church assignments felt like a natural part of her family life, not something on a list she had to complete. She saw that church work for her mother, Marjorie Pay Hinckley, was "part of who she was," and that she always seemed energized by doing that work, not pressured or annoyed.[3]

Pearce majored in history and minored in English at the University of Utah, completing her final year in 1967 at the University of Nebraska while her husband, Jim, attended Creighton University School of Medicine.[4] Her first children came in close succession: when her oldest daughter was two, Pearce had twin daughters, and eighteen months later she had another daughter. She waited several years before having another daughter and son.[5] As time drew near for her youngest son to begin first grade, she contemplated going to graduate school and realized that what she liked about both history and literature was watching people grow and learning how to facilitate that process.[6] She decided to study social work, completing a master's degree at the University of Utah in 1988. Then she worked briefly for the Salt Lake County mental health department before joining the Primary general board later that year.[7] After finishing her degree, Pearce also saw clients in a private practice, stopping in 1992 when she became first counselor in the Young Women general presidency.[8]

Although her time practicing social work was short, Pearce reports having felt compelled to complete that training and believes that experience has informed all of her church service work since then. In her responsibilities with the Primary and Young Women, she worked to train local leaders and to support international church members. She brought an informed understanding of the nature of adolescence to her Young Women work, including what a young person's search for identity means and how to best support a teenager's growth.[9] With the other members of the Young Women presidency, she "wanted every young woman to become a righteous, problem-solving woman of faith."[10]

Pearce's own identity has been closely linked to stories about her heritage. Family stories mean a lot to her, as did her relationship with her paternal grandfather, who lived in a house behind hers until he died when she was in her early teens.[11] She edited an innovative biography of her mother, which included Pearce's own prose alongside reminiscences from a broad range of sources.[12] Pearce lives in the house in which her husband was raised, and she wrote an unpublished history of the people who have lived in that house.[13]

Pearce also loves to teach and is a popular public speaker. She learned from her father both to try new approaches and to keep moving forward when a lesson or talk does not work. She says that everyone has times when what they try does not work, although sometimes we later learn our efforts were helpful to a person on the back row.[14] She sees prayer as central to the process of doing good work and feeling good about one's work: "There's a scripture in Words of Mormon," she says. "He's talking about writing on the plates, and he says he doesn't know why he's doing it. Then there's a sentence about how he believes that God works in him to do his will.[15] I think that's what happens when you pray all the time. You don't need to panic too much—am I making the right choice or the wrong choice? You can trust that he works in you and you do what he wants you to do."[16] Pearce gave the following talk on prayer as the keynote speaker for the 2011 Brigham Young University Women's Conference.

I AM DELIGHTED to be with you, my dear Relief Society sisters. I believe I know something of the preparations you have made to leave family, jobs, and other duties behind. I happen to have five daughters here this morning, and so I have seen up close and personal what it takes to arrange to leave their lives, and among them twenty-two children, and figure out how this day was—how today and tomorrow those people were going to get along without them. And when I multiply that times all of you, I am stunned. I think the invasion on Normandy Beach was nothing, child's play in terms of coordination and planning, to this.

I think I also know something of your expectations and desires for this time together. I love you and I have full confidence that there will be a generous outpouring of the Spirit of the Lord today and tomorrow.

Our theme comes from the thirty-seventh chapter of Alma—a verse we all know so well, memorable in its alliteration and paradoxical in its promise. Alma, speaking to his son Helaman about the importance of keeping the scriptural record, said, "Now ye may suppose that this is foolishness in me; but behold I say unto you, that by small and simple things are great things brought to pass."[17]

Isn't that comforting in our world, where extravagant, larger-than-life, huge events and expectations are before our eyes continually? I have a little tiny sign on my computer at home— it's not embroidered, cross-stitched, or framed. It's just a little sticky note and it says:

> KEEP IT SMALL.
> KEEP IT SIMPLE.
> GIVE IT TIME.

Reading these words—sometimes out loud—never fails to settle me down.

One of our great Relief Society forebears, Emmeline B. Wells, said it much more poetically:

> Faith urges on the weak, and gives them grace.
> And thus we often see the fragile ones outdo
> Those who were strong when starting in the race.[18]

Given time, our very smallness—our fragileness—actually allows God's grace to work in us and to triumph over those who might have seemed stronger and larger in the beginning.

My mother wore this simple gold band on her finger. As she grew older, with arthritic hands, she often wore the ring on a chain around her neck—this chain, in fact. She and I went to lunch one afternoon a couple of years before her death.[19] We were talking about nothing in particular when she stopped and asked me if I knew the story about the gold band. "It's 18K gold, you know, more than one hundred years old, and I want to be sure you know its story." And then she proceeded to tell me again about my great-grandmother's ring.

Martha Elizabeth Evans was seventeen years old when she first met George Paxman. He was new in town—lean, with a fine bone structure and deep-set blue eyes. She was a petite, five-foot-two young woman with smooth skin and an abundance of fine hair, unbelievably soft to the touch.

They fell in love and two years later, in the fall of 1885, as they made eternal promises to one another, he put this gold band on the fourth finger of her left hand.

The hopeful young couple moved into a two-room adobe house with a dirt roof while George's carpenter skills played their part in building a majestic white limestone temple, towering on a hill above the little adobe village of Manti, Utah. The young husband worked eight hours a day and received scrip for a weekly $4.00 worth of goods in the local store and produce from the tithing office. It was a sweet way to begin married life.

On a June evening in 1887, a month before their first little girl turned one year old, George came home from working on the temple, where he had helped hang the large east doors. He was in terrible pain. Alarmed, Martha loaded him in a wagon and made the strenuous trip through the mountains to a hospital, where he died three days later of a strangulated hernia. Eight months later, Martha gave birth to a second little girl—my grandmother—whom she named Georgetta after her beloved George.

A twenty-two-year-old widow with two little girls, her faith in God, and a gold band on her finger, Martha faced the future.

But now comes the story my mother wanted to be sure I knew. One day, several years after George's death, Martha was invited by a neighbor to replenish her mattress tick with new straw. In Martha's words: "Just as I finished filling the tick, I looked at my hand and my ring was gone. I could have cried. When I got home I spread sheets out on the floor and went through the straw piece by piece, but no ring was there. I decided to go back [to the neighbor's] anyway and looked around the straw again. I prayed that I might find it."[20] Well, the neighbor helped her look, but it seemed to be of no use. And just as she had given up, she kicked the straw with the toe of her shoe and the ring appeared.

Martha told and retold this story to her daughters and their children. Her grandmother's story convinced my mother that prayers are heard and that prayers are answered. This ring is a loving link honoring marriage and eternal loyalty, but to me it is a reminder about the power of prayer.

I believe in prayer, and have felt impressed to speak today about this small and simple practice by which great things are brought to pass.

Prayer is certainly the most basic religious ritual—of all faiths. All those who believe in God seek him in some form of prayer. It is the earliest religious behavior we teach to our tiny children. And yet, the process of prayer cannot be fathomed by the human mind. None of us understands how it works, even though we may have had a lifetime of experience with it.

But we do know some things.

The first thing we know is that *prayer rests on the principle of faith.* We have faith in the doctrine that we are children of a Heavenly Father, that we are separated from him during this time of mortality, and that our goal is to become like him so that we can once again return to his presence. Think about that. When we understand that God is our Father and we are his children, then prayer becomes natural and instinctive.[21]

We also know that *prayer is an expression of agency.* Earnest, sincere, heartfelt prayer is a deeply personal choice. No one can force us to reach out with all of our hearts. No one can compel us to feel after our Maker. I love the way Isaiah expresses this heartfelt desire to pray: "With my soul have I desired thee in the night; yea, with my spirit within me will I seek thee early. . . ."[22]

And so, our small and simple choice to pray allows God to unlock the powers of heaven in our behalf. The Holy Ghost is free to fill our minds and hearts, leading us towards him and our eternal destiny. I can think of no greater thing.

We know also that *prayer grows out of humility*: When we pray it signals a recognition that we cannot live this life alone, that we are dependent upon the Father and his Son for our very breath. Now, I know some very smart people. And I know some gifted and highly skilled people. I know some very, very rich people. But I have never met any person who has sufficient resources to meet all the demands of this life on his or her own. We need God. And if our troubles can take us to God, we can be thankful for them.

This painting, by Carl Bloch, is called *Christus Consolator.* It, along with other magnificent pieces, is on display this week in the BYU Museum of Art.[23] I hope, if you haven't seen this exhibit yet, you'll take an opportunity to visit it during the next two days.

I love to look at each individual who seeks consolation from Christ. You can see the troubles of mortality on their faces. These are they who know they cannot do it alone. Bloch described the joy we can take in adversity when we know it brings us to Christ. He said: "When things are at their worst they then become their absolute best. I think then that I have so much to thank God for, and it would be foolish to demand that one should be happy in this life. By that I mean always sparkling, always seeing the ideal under the light sky.[24]

"No, grey skies and rain splashing are part of it—one must be washed off thoroughly before one goes in to God."[25]

I like that artist's image—being washed off thoroughly by the grey skies and rains of life as we kneel in humility, in our fragileness, asking for God's help. "Be thou humble; and the Lord thy God shall lead thee by the hand, and give thee answer to thy prayers."[26]

I have a good friend whom I will call "Jane." Jane is a covenant-keeping member of the Church of Jesus Christ of Latter-day Saints. Her life has many facets: church service, full-time work, devotion to family, neighborliness, church callings. She is smart and funny and faithful. And, like all of us in mortality, she confronts heart-rending challenges—the greatest of which has to do with her family. As her children matured, some of them began to choose different paths. She witnessed them making choices that she knew would lead to unhappiness, and she was heartbroken—even frantic. She went over and over her parenting decisions of the past and was filled with guilt. Maybe this was all her fault. She found herself anxious and fearful—wondering what she could say and how and when she could say it so that the errant child would see the light and return. She worried about every interaction with the child—her own, as well as her husband's, the ward members', the neighbors'—everyone's! To say she felt tormented and out of control would be accurate.

And she prayed. My, did she pray! Her heart was "drawn out in prayer unto him continually for [her own] welfare, and also for the welfare of [the children]."[27]

One afternoon in fast meeting, she listened to a friend she admired describe how she had been troubled with a particular problem with one of her children and had determined to go to the temple once a week. The friend then testified in gratitude that after many months her prayers had been answered, and the problem had been miraculously solved.

Jane was touched, she came home, kept praying, and felt inclined to make a personally ambitious yearly goal of temple attendance. She felt sure that the Lord would honor such a significant personal sacrifice.

Now I am going to interrupt our story here to point out some of the things we have talked about. Jane had faith. She understood her relationship to her Father in Heaven. She exhibited humility, an understanding that she needed divine help. And she made an individual personal choice to pray. As she continued her very personal conversation with the Lord, kept her covenants, and went to church, the Holy Ghost sent the words of her friend's testimony deeply into her heart.

Continuing to pray, Jane acted on the promptings she received to attend the temple more often.

Now let me continue with her story. Quoting Jane, "After ten years of increased temple attendance and constant prayer, I am sorry to say that my children's choices have not changed."

And then there was a pause. . . .

"But I have. I am a different woman."

"How?" I asked her.

"I have a softer heart. I am filled with compassion. I can actually do more and am free of my fear, anxiety, guilt, blame, and dread. I have given up my time limits and am able to wait on the Lord. And I experience frequent manifestations of the Lord's power. He sends tender mercies, small messages that acknowledge his love for me and my children. My expectations have changed. Instead of expecting my children to change, I expect these frequent tender mercies and am full of gratitude for them." She continues, "I have a new openness and sensitivity to the Spirit, and I no longer worry myself to death over what I will say and how I will say it. If I feel inclined to speak, I don't hesitate, and the words feel as if they are given to me.

"All of my relationships are better, especially with my children and husband. I can do and say things that I could never do or say before. My children are respectful of my temple devotion. They are sweet and supportive of me, as is my husband. He and I are cemented together by these difficulties rather than blaming and pulling apart. Our marriage has never been more joyful. My ability to appreciate and enjoy the good things of my life is heightened. I am simply more present.

"My prayers are changed. I express more love and am more thankful. I pray to be equal to the tasks before me. I pray for an increase of charity and patience and faith. I am grateful for the trials that led me here. I wouldn't change a thing that has happened. The Lord works in marvelous ways, and I truly am filled with the peace that passeth all understanding."[28]

Prayer and temple attendance are not dramatic, sensational, or one-time activities. But repeated over and over, year after year, they are small and simple things by which great things come to pass. In fact, this gradual process of change seems to be the way the Lord often works with us. Yes, we have scriptural stories of seemingly sudden and complete change, but more often we become "new creatures"[29]—like those in the city of Enoch—"in process of time."[30]

I find the word *consecration* intriguing. It means "to make holy and sacred . . . to sanctify." Consecration means that we dedicate our thoughts, our actions—our very lives to God. And in turn, he can consecrate our experiences—sanctify them, make them holy—no matter how difficult, foolish, or destructive.

It is written: "In everything give thanks; waiting patiently on the Lord, for your prayers have entered into the ears of the Lord. . . . He giveth this promise unto you, with an immutable covenant that they shall be fulfilled; and *all things wherewith you have been afflicted shall work together for your good,* and my name's glory, saith the Lord."[31]

All things shall be for our good? How does that work?! I don't know, but I believe the words of Nephi: "Ye must pray always, and not faint; that ye must not perform any thing unto the Lord save in the first place ye shall pray unto the Father in the name of Christ, that he will consecrate thy performance unto thee, that thy performance may be for the welfare of thy soul."[32]

When I listened to Jane, I felt how the Lord had consecrated her difficulties with her children to the eternal welfare of her soul. Wasn't it something to hear her describe the changes? I thought I could see before my very eyes someone who had prayed with all the energy of her heart and who had been filled with pure charity—a gift bestowed freely on all true followers of Christ.[33]

How could this not also be helpful to her children?

Nephi talks about his prayers for his people. Think of Jane and her prayers for her children. Think of yourself and your prayers for those you love. "[For] behold, there are many that harden their hearts against the Holy Spirit, that it hath no place in them; . . . I pray continually for them by day, and mine eyes water my pillow by night, because of them; and I cry unto my God in faith, and I know that he will hear my cry. And I know that the Lord will consecrate my prayers for the gain of my people."[34]

I don't know how he will do this—agency must be exercised—but my faith tells me that someday when those loved ones make a choice to come to Christ and his atonement begins to operate in their lives, our prayers will be part of a miracle that can not only change their future but can consecrate their past experience to the welfare of their souls.[35] Perhaps rather than creating torment and bitterness and despair, their past sins will become experiences that deepen their compassion toward others and their gratitude for their Savior. Isn't that an amazing transformation, possible only through the Savior's infinite power?

Like Jane, we often add fasting, temple worship, and priesthood blessings to our prayers as we importune the Lord in times of exceptional need. I don't know how that works either, but as I have added these things, I have personally experienced the power of increased consecration and felt my heart open wider to receive the will of the Lord. And one of the great outcomes of effective prayer is that through it my will and the will of the Father become one and the same.

I also know that as others have joined their prayers, fasting, and temple worship on behalf of me and mine, I have indeed felt an increase in the Lord's presence. And why would that not be so? Faith coupled with pure charity—the love we extend when we pray, fast, and add names to temple rolls—makes a difference. It unifies us with one another. It unifies us with the Lord.

Sister Julie Beck encourages us as Relief Society sisters to pray.[36] She said, "Think of our combined strength if every sister had sincere prayer every morning and night or, better yet, prayed unceasingly as the Lord has commanded."[37]

Praying for one another brings strength. It knits our hearts together in unity and love.[38] And this pure love—charity—opens our hearts to receive the blessings that the Lord desires to give us, but that are made conditional on our asking for them.[39]

Sometimes answers to prayer are quite clear—simple and direct. But often prayer becomes a long and personal conversation. We continue to pray and work, and we find that in inexplicable ways the problems are gradually resolved or changed. Sometimes even our righteous and heartfelt desires are modified. Gradually, our desires become his desires. Our pleading becomes part of the experience.

Elder Neal A. Maxwell taught that the Lord works on us through the very process of prayer: "Some have difficulty with the reality that prayers are petitions even though God knows all and loves all anyway. True, we are not informing God, but we are informing ourselves by reverently working through our real concerns and our real priorities and by listening to the Spirit. For us merely to say, ritualistically, 'Thy will be done' would not be real petitionary prayer. This would involve no genuine working through of our feelings. There would be no experience in agonizing, in choosing, and also in submitting."[40]

And so, the power of praying is more than saying at the end of the prayer, "Thy will be done." It is actually finding that his will has become our will. Often the change in our part of the conversation is almost imperceptible. It is small and simple and occurs over time. It is difficult to talk about because by its very nature it is personal and unique—something that is happening between the Father and the individual. And it is unpredictable. He may answer me so immediately and distinctly at one time and so gradually at another that I think nothing is happening. But if I make the choice to keep believing, and I demonstrate that choice by continuing to pray, I am quite sure his will *will* be made manifest, and it will, in the end, seem to me to be just right.

Sometimes we may feel we are simply left on our own to do the best we can. I believe that if we were to wait to act every time we prayed until we recognized a clear answer, most of us would be waiting and wasting a good part of our lives.

Elder Richard G. Scott asks the question, "What do you do when you have prepared carefully, have prayed fervently, waited a reasonable time for a response, and still do not feel an answer?" He continues: "You may want to express thanks when that occurs, for it is an evidence of his trust. When you are living worthily and your choice is consistent with the Savior's teachings and you need to act, proceed with trust. . . . God will not let you proceed too far without a warning impression if you have made a wrong choice."[41]

President Gordon B. Hinckley had a personal motto that is quite practical. He taught it in many settings: "Things will work out. If you keep trying and praying and working, things will work out. They always do."[42]

And so we have to pray and then keep moving forward, trusting that if it is a direction that will *not* be for our good, the Lord will help us know. Otherwise, we trust that the Lord is bound to own and honor the decisions we have made using our own best judgment.[43]

Back to my great-grandmother Martha Elizabeth. She prayed for the ring. She looked down and she found it. She acknowledged the answer. I think of other prayers Martha Elizabeth must have offered—many more critical to her future than the one about the ring. I think of the desperate prayers she must have offered as she drove her husband in the carriage in search of a doctor. That prayer was not answered as Martha would have hoped. Somehow it was not part of his plan for Martha and George that they should have a full lifetime together.

But on the day that Martha lost her ring, God granted her prayerful desire. However, I believe that finding the ring was a minor miracle when compared to the real message. I think the real message to Martha was that God was aware of her sadness and love for her long-gone sweetheart whom the ring represented. He was telling her that he knew and loved her and that he was there for her. And stunningly, this reassurance of his presence and love is much greater than any other possible outcome.

My friend Jane talked about receiving those kinds of messages from Heavenly Father, those frequent manifestations of the Lord's power, the tender mercies, the small messages that acknowledged his love for her and her children. And she began to expect those tender mercies—frequently—and to be full of gratitude for them.

In Martha's life, in Jane's life, surely in yours, and most certainly in mine, God has not always granted those things that we have wanted—even asked for desperately. But he frequently puts his divine signature[44] on small events of the day. And his presence—the indescribably settling quality of his great love—more than recompenses for all tragedies and disappointments. He says, with these tender mercies: "I am here. I care about you. You are living your life with my approval. Everything will work together for your good. Trust me."

And so the miracle of prayer doesn't reside in the ability to manipulate situations and events, but in the miracle of creating a relationship with God.[45]

Think about that carefully, would you? What does it do for you to have an assurance that the Lord is with you? Everything.

In October of 2008 my husband and I were busily preparing to respond to a mission call. It had been a year of perpetual motion for us. My father had died in January, necessitating the business of dividing and distributing all of his "stuff." Oh, we do leave lots of things behind when we cross to the other side, don't we? Just as we were finishing that, my husband retired from his medical practice, and we were loading and unloading more boxes of "stuff" into an ever-crowded basement. There were lots of family events, some travel, and the preparation of our mission papers. And now, here we were with a mission call, making arrangements to rent out our home—yes, moving more stuff—when everything stopped.

Responding to some symptoms that were becoming increasingly problematic, my husband went in for tests and was diagnosed with a fatal and untreatable disease. He lived just short of one year from the day of diagnosis.[46]

It was a unique year for us—one of quiet and slow living—of unbusyness. President Dieter F. Uchtdorf explained, "When growing conditions are not ideal, trees slow down their growth and devote their energy to the basic elements necessary for survival." He continued, "It is good advice to slow down a little, steady the course, and focus on the essentials when experiencing adverse conditions."[47]

We did just that.

We talked, we cried, we read and reread verses of scripture, we pored over talks from the Brethren, we spent sweet time with family and friends. We went to bed every night and got up every morning. Most of all, though, we prayed. We prayed together, we prayed separately, we prayed vocally, we prayed silently. We prayed with loved ones. We fasted and prayed. We went to the temple and prayed. We prayed constantly. We pled with our Father in Heaven in the name of his Son, Jesus Christ.

I tell you this by way of personal testimony. Prayer works. It does indeed call down the powers of heaven. It reconciles our will with the will of the Father. It consecrates even our most adverse experiences to the welfare of our souls. Through combined prayer we experience love, unity, and power that are impossible to describe. We may not be granted that which we desire, but we end up grateful with all of our hearts for that which the Lord gives us.

And along the way we experience tender mercies over and over—those unmistakable messages from him: "I am here. I love you. You are living your life with my approval. Everything will work together for your good. Trust me."

Even though we may not see, minute to minute, that we are moving forward and making progress, I believe we will be able to one day look back at our lives and see that we were, in fact, doing just what we needed to be doing at just the right time in just the right place. We can trust that the Lord will work in and through us. Mormon expressed it beautifully: "And now, I do not know all things;

but the Lord knoweth all things which are to come; wherefore, he worketh in me to do according to his will."[48]

Like Mormon, I do not know all things, but I do know that the Lord works in faithful, prayerful people to do according to his will. I know that by small and simple means are great things brought to pass.[49]

Of that I bear testimony, in the name of Jesus Christ, amen.

Virginia H. Pearce, "Prayer: A Small and Simple Thing," BYU Women's Conference address, Apr. 28, 2011, Brigham Young University, Provo, UT, accessed Jan. 8, 2016, womensconference.ce.byu.edu; see also Virginia H. Pearce, "Prayer: A Small and Simple Thing," in By Small and Simple Things: Talks from the 2011 BYU Women's Conference *(Salt Lake City: Deseret Book, 2012), 227–239.*

WHY WE ARE ORGANIZED INTO QUORUMS AND RELIEF SOCIETIES

◇◇◇

JULIE B. BECK

Brigham Young University Devotional Address
Marriott Center, Brigham Young University, Provo, Utah
January 17, 2012

Julie Bangerter Beck (b. 1954) lived in Sao Paulo, Brazil, from ages four to nine while her parents supervised the Brazilian Mission. Missionary work pervaded Beck's childhood and those of her siblings: instead of playing house or soccer, they played "missionary," acting out missionary work while wearing the old clothing of former missionaries.[1] The baptisms in the Brazilian Mission took place in the same backyard where the Bangerter children played.[2] Beck said she never knew her parents outside of a setting of "complete devotion and dedication to church service and the story of faith that drove them both."[3]

In 1974, not long after Beck had married Ramon P. Beck and moved to their hometown of Alpine, Utah, her parents left to open the Portugal Lisbon Mission.[4] She says that at that time, "Relief Society became my mother. Those women stepped in and became my role models."[5] Because at the time different church organizations met during the week instead of in one three-hour period on Sundays, Beck could teach in the Relief Society as well as in Primary and also be a visiting teacher. "All the Relief Society sisters helped teach Primary, and we all knew we were Relief Society sisters who took other assignments to build the kingdom," she recalled.[6] In Alpine, Beck was in the stake Relief Society presidency for seven years.[7] She served on the Young Women general board under Margaret D. Nadauld, where she oversaw the committee for revising the Personal Progress program.[8] When Susan W. Tanner became Young Women general president in 2002, she chose Beck as her first counselor. As a member of the general presidency, Beck spoke in Portuguese for a broadcast to Spain and Portugal in 2006.[9] The first time she served as a Relief Society president was as general president, beginning in 2007.[10]

A major legacy of Beck's presidency was the book *Daughters in My Kingdom,* which was translated into twenty-three languages and distributed to adult female members of the church.[11] Beck visualized Eliza R. Snow carrying the Nauvoo Relief Society Minute Book across the country to the Salt Lake Valley, then taking it from ward to ward as she worked to reestablish the organization of the Relief Society. She felt that God put that image in her head to guide her to produce *Daughters in My Kingdom,* so every home could have a book that, like the Nauvoo Relief Society minute book, gives a clear sense of the history and purpose of the Relief Society.[12]

A study of Relief Society history also led Beck to redefine and emphasize the purpose of the Relief Society. The original purposes of the Relief Society in Nauvoo were to care for the poor and needy and to save souls.[13] Beck's presidency built on these ideas in an effort to make them applicable to a worldwide church and to align with the mission of the church, which was "to bring to pass the salvation and exaltation of [God's] children."[14] She summed up the essential focal points of the new purpose statement as "faith, family, and relief."[15] Beck also emphasized visiting teaching as a way church members could fill the purpose of the Relief Society.[16] When Beck visited branches around the world as Relief Society general president, she saw that members were sometimes apologetic about the small size of their groups. She would remember her small childhood branch in Brazil and think, "Oh, that's not a worry. This is where the church is good and strong, where we have a small branch and everybody helping."[17] She gave the following discourse at a Brigham Young University devotional toward the end of her presidential tenure.

THANK YOU FOR YOUR WELCOME today at Brigham Young University. I love this university, and I feel blessed by every opportunity to feel the spirit that is unique to this campus. Because of my service on the Church Board of Education, I can testify of the Lord's interest in this marvelous institution, and, in your honor, I wore my best BYU blue today.[18]

As I have pondered this opportunity to speak to you, a number of different subjects came to my mind. The Spirit has persisted in giving me ideas about why we are organized into quorums and Relief Societies.

Although this is probably an unusual topic for most of you to consider, I hope the Spirit will use me to teach you some things that will bless your lives as you continue to strengthen your faith in the Lord Jesus Christ and contribute to building his kingdom.

When I was a young girl my father was called to preside over the Brazilian Mission.[19] At that time there was only one mission in Brazil. There were no stakes or wards; there wasn't an elders quorum in the country. That means there were no home teachers. There were over forty branches, which were generally presided over by missionaries who conducted a weekly sacrament meeting and sometimes held Sunday School and branch activities. My father had served as a stake president and a bishop prior to his call as a mission president, and he had an understanding of how to establish the Lord's church. He began to organize branches and districts in the pattern we are familiar with today in anticipation of future stakes and wards.

To begin the organization, some priorities were followed. First, a branch president and then an elders quorum president and a Relief Society president were called. It was understood that there could be no functioning branch without a quorum president and a Relief Society president.

As the Prophet Joseph Smith began establishing the church in this dispensation, the Lord directed him to follow similar inspired patterns. When he set the course for the Relief Society, he told the sisters they were organized "under the priesthood after the pattern of the priesthood."[20] This gave the sisters official responsibilities in the restored church and the authority to function in those responsibilities. This was a pattern similar to that given to a president of a quorum of elders, who was to counsel with his presidency.[21]

Before we can understand why we are thus organized, it may be helpful to review the definition of a priesthood quorum and a Relief Society. Many people have the mistaken idea that a quorum or a Relief Society is merely a class or a place to sit during the third hour of church on Sunday. Perhaps some of this misunderstanding started to develop when the church combined its major meetings into a three-hour block on Sunday.[22] Before that time, quorum and Relief Society meetings were not connected with sacrament meeting or Sunday School.

A priesthood quorum is a group of men with the same office of priesthood who are to perform a special labor. Membership in a quorum has been called "a steady, sustaining citizenship."[23] President Boyd K. Packer has said that quorums are "selected assemblies of brethren given authority that [the Lord's] business might be transacted and his work proceed."[24] He also said that "in ancient days when a man was appointed to a select body, his commission, always written in Latin, outlined the responsibility of the organization, defined who should be members, and then invariably contained the words *quorum vos unum,* meaning, 'of whom we will that you be one.'"[25]

President Spencer W. Kimball taught that "the Relief Society is the Lord's organization for women. It complements the priesthood training given to the brethren."[26] The word *society* has a meaning nearly identical to that of *quorum.* It connotes "an enduring and cooperating . . . group" distinguished by its common aims and beliefs.[27] When Joseph Smith organized the sisters, he told them that "there should be a select society, separate from all the evils of the world, choice, virtuous, and holy."[28] President Joseph F. Smith taught that Relief Society has its own unique identity and that it was "divinely made, divinely authorized, divinely instituted, divinely ordained of God to minister for the salvation of the souls of women and men."[29]

The purposes of Relief Society are to increase faith and personal righteousness, strengthen families and homes, and seek out and provide relief for those who are in need.[30] The quorum is to serve others, build unity and brotherhood, instruct quorum members in the doctrines and principles of the gospel, and watch over the church.[31]

Being part of a Relief Society or quorum is a designation for a way of life. We are to serve in the association of a Melchizedek Priesthood quorum or a Relief Society for a lifetime. From the quorum or Relief Society, we are called to serve in other church assignments and organizations, such as missionary work, temple service, Sunday School, seminary or institute, Young Men, Primary, Young Women, and so forth. No matter where we serve, we always retain our "citizenship" in and our responsibility to the quorum or Relief Society. President Packer has taught that all service in the church strengthens the higher priesthood and Relief Society and is a demonstration of our devotion to Relief Society and quorum membership.[32]

It is true that each of us is responsible for becoming a faithful, covenant-keeping disciple of the Lord Jesus Christ. Some may argue that we can accomplish this as individuals without the benefit of a supporting group. But President David O. McKay said that if priesthood men only needed "personal distinction or individual elevation, there would be no need of groups or quorums. The very existence of such groups, established by divine authorization, proclaims our dependence upon one another, the indispensable need of mutual help and assistance."[33]

Inasmuch as the Lord chose to organize us in this way, it is important for us to seek for a greater understanding as to why we are thus organized and then to seek to fulfill the vision he has for us. To help facilitate that understanding I have drawn heavily from the scriptures and words of prophets to illustrate, only briefly, five important reasons why we are organized into quorums and Relief Societies.

One of the reasons we have quorums and Relief Societies is to organize us under the priesthood and after the pattern of the priesthood.[34] Our God is a God of order, and all that he does to build his kingdom is done through his priesthood patterns.

One of those patterns is the organization of wards and stakes, each with a geographic boundary. Each ward is guided by a bishop who holds the keys, or the Lord's authority, for his ward. He is the shepherd of the Lord's flock within his ward and has the charge to see to the temporal and spiritual needs of that flock. Only he can authorize the ordinances that are essential for the salvation of the members of that flock. His responsibility is monumental and is the more difficult because he is only one man who cannot possibly watch over all of the sheep at once. The quorum and Relief Society leaders are seen by the bishop as under-shepherds who magnify, enhance, and distribute his watchcare.

The formation of a presidency is also a priesthood pattern. Every ward elders quorum president and Relief Society president presides over and directs the activities of the elders quorum or Relief Society in the ward.[35] Quorum and Relief Society leaders have a measure of divine authority given to them regarding the government and instruction of those they are called to lead.[36] They are men and women who are "called of God, by prophecy, and by the laying on of hands."[37] To preside means to stand guard, to superintend, and to lead.[38] This means that Relief Society and quorum leaders in a ward carry the responsibility to supervise, oversee, and regulate the work of the Relief Society and the quorums on behalf of the bishop.

Sustaining those who are called to lead is also a priesthood pattern. We do not select our leaders by popular vote as is common in organizations outside the church. It is an act of our faith in the Lord and those who are called to lead in his church to sustain their actions and support them in their responsibilities to lead us. When Joseph Smith organized the Relief Society, he "exhorted the sisters always to concentrate their faith and prayers for, and place confidence in, those whom God has appointed to honor, whom God has placed at the head to lead."[39]

One of the priesthood patterns we enjoy is the ability to receive revelation. When Joseph Smith organized the Relief Society, he said the sisters were "to get instruction through the order which God has established—through the medium of those appointed to lead."[40] This ability and promise regarding personal revelation is one of the remarkable blessings that come to every quorum and Relief Society presidency. When the Lord said that each of us was to learn our duty and act in the office to which we are appointed, he provided a way for us to do just that.[41] I have seen humble Relief Society and quorum presidencies in many parts of the world leading with great and inspiring ability because they are organized under the priesthood and after the order of the priesthood. They follow patterns that allow them to get revelation for the work they have been set apart to do.

At the time of the Relief Society centennial the First Presidency wrote:

> We ask our Sisters of the Relief Society never to forget that they are a unique organization in the whole world, for they were organized under the inspiration of the Lord. . . . No other woman's organization in all the earth has had such a birth.[42]

A second reason we are organized into quorums and Relief Societies is to focus Heavenly Father's sons and daughters on the work of salvation and to engage them in it. Quorums and Relief Societies are an organized discipleship with the responsibility to assist in our Father's work to bring about eternal life for his children. We are not in the entertainment business; we are in the salvation business. Entrance into an elders quorum or a Relief Society usually follows a significant investment from the Lord and his leaders in the teaching and preparation of younger members of the church for such a work. The work of salvation includes missionary work and retaining in activity those who are converted. We are to do all we can to bring back into activity those of our group who have weakened in their faith. The work of a quorum and a Relief Society also focuses on temple and family history work. We carry the responsibility to teach the gospel and exemplify righteous living to one another.

The work of salvation also includes improving our temporal and spiritual self-reliance. And as a group we ensure that the needy and the poor are cared for. Elder John A. Widtsoe defined the saving work of the Relief Society as the "relief of poverty, relief of illness, relief of doubt, relief of ignorance—relief of all that hinders the joy and progress of woman."[43] These same kinds of responsibilities are given to a quorum. They are honorable and heavy responsibilities. They connote a sacred trust and imply a significant contribution to the Lord's work of salvation—a work that is both a burden and a blessing. When quorums and Relief Societies are unified in this work, they each essentially take an oar in the boat—each helping move us toward salvation.

When we are organized into Relief Societies and quorums, our personal discipleship is extended and we become engaged with others in the saving work that was modeled by the Savior. It is never modest or inconsequential. It forces us to a higher path of discipleship and a greater spiritual maturity. It is often a long-suffering and patient work and can seem thankless because there is usually a noticeable absence of public recognition for the good we do. Elder Widtsoe taught that "to save souls opens the whole field of human activity and development."[44] The work of salvation is guided by the Spirit, who confirms our actions, assures us of the Lord's approval, and supplies the true joy that comes with an affirmation of our success.

A third reason we are organized into quorums and Relief Societies is to help bishops wisely manage the Lord's storehouse. The Lord's storehouse includes the "time, talents, compassion, materials, and financial means" of the members of the church.[45] The talents of the Saints are to be used to help care for the poor and the needy and to build the Lord's kingdom. The Lord envisions "every man seeking the interest of his neighbor, and doing all things with an eye single to the glory of God."[46]

Bishops have charge of the Lord's storehouse, and they depend on the quorums and Relief Societies to help them seek out and care for all in their wards. Every ward is unique and can be said to have its own DNA. This makes it essential that the leaders of the quorums and Relief Societies work in councils to help bishops manage and apportion the Lord's assets. Together they evaluate the strengths and abilities of individuals and ensure that the Lord's sheep are cared for.

Our Savior taught this principle in many ways during his mortal ministry, and the scriptures contain many examples of how he looked after those who were in need. In every ward there are always a few dedicated souls who would do all of the work while others would neglect their duty and fail to offer their gifts. Quorum and Relief Society leaders have the responsibility to organize and carry out an inspired ministry to help all brothers and sisters keep their covenants to remember the Savior and consecrate their lives to his work.

If we were left to ourselves, we might prefer to care only for the popular, charming, and grateful people in our wards. It is much more challenging to care for those who are difficult to love, who have grave and complicated challenges, or who do not seem to appreciate our help. The Savior said:

> Love your enemies, bless them that curse you, do good to them that hate you, and pray for them which despitefully use you, and persecute you;
>
> That ye may be the children of your Father which is in heaven: for he maketh his sun to rise on the evil and on the good, and sendeth rain on the just and on the unjust.
>
> For if ye love them which love you, what reward have ye? do not even the publicans the same?
>
> And if ye salute your brethren only, what do ye more than others? do not even the publicans so?
>
> Ye are therefore commanded to be perfect, even as your Father who is in heaven is perfect.[47]

One of the most significant ways this kind of watchcare is apportioned is through home teaching and visiting teaching. President Henry B. Eyring said,

"The only system [that can] provide succor and comfort across a church so large in a world so varied would be through individual servants near the people in need."[48] Elder Bruce R. McConkie, who served faithfully as an Apostle of the Lord Jesus Christ, called an elder "a shepherd serving in the sheepfold of the Good Shepherd." He taught that home teachers "have status" and that "their calls are official." They are "sent by their quorum president, by the bishop, and by the Lord." It was his feeling that "the greatest defect of the home teaching system in the church is that it remains almost unused."[49]

President Thomas S. Monson said:

> The home teaching program is a response to modern revelation commissioning those ordained to the priesthood to "teach, expound, exhort, baptize, and watch over the church . . . and visit the house of each member, and exhort them to pray vocally and in secret and attend to all family duties, . . . to watch over the church always, and be with and strengthen them; and see that there is no iniquity in the church, neither hardness with each other, neither lying, backbiting, nor evil speaking" (D&C 20:42, 47, 53–54). . . .
>
> From the Book of Mormon, Alma "consecrated all their priests and all their teachers; and none were consecrated except they were just men. Therefore they did watch over their people, and did nourish them with things pertaining to righteousness" (Mosiah 23:17–18).
>
> In performing our home teaching responsibilities, we are wise if we learn and understand the challenges of the members of each family.[50]

A visiting teacher should also consider her assignment "as a call from the Lord."[51] President Kimball said to the sisters, "Your duties in many ways must be much like those of the [home] teachers, which briefly are 'to watch over the church always'—not twenty minutes a month but always."[52]

Visiting teaching and home teaching become the Lord's work when our focus is centered on people rather than on percentages. The perfection of our statistics is often not a good measure of our watchcare.[53] We can never say, "My home teaching or visiting teaching is done!" When we represent the Lord we are always on his errand. President Thomas S. Monson taught, "Home teaching is more than a mechanical visit once per month, that the statistical report of the ward will be pleasing. Ours is the responsibility to teach, to inspire, to motivate, to bring to activity and to eventual exaltation the sons and daughters of God."[54] When we give an account of our stewardship each month, we are to report the spiritual and temporal well-being of those we are assigned to care for. We can also report any service we render. Special or urgent needs should always be reported immediately.[55] The only true measures of our success in this effort are the confirmations of the Spirit for our efforts and when those we are assigned to watch over can say three important things: (1) "My home teacher or visiting teacher helps me grow spiritually"; (2) "I know my home teacher or visiting teacher cares deeply about me and my family"; and (3) "If I have problems, I know my home teacher or visiting teacher will take action without waiting to be invited."

The Lord said, "And if any man among you be strong in the Spirit, let him take with him him that is weak, that he may be edified in all meekness, that he may become strong also."[56] When these measures are our aim, then we organize and function in an inspired rather than a programmatic way.

A fourth reason for why we are organized into quorums and Relief Societies is to provide a defense and a refuge for Heavenly Father's children and their families in the latter days. President Thomas S. Monson has said: "Today, we are encamped against the greatest array of sin, vice, and evil ever assembled before our eyes. . . . The battle plan whereby we fight to save the souls of men is not our own."[57]

We are all in the midst of a mortal experience. We all chose this experience, and the Lord will ensure that we all have one. An age-old anti-Christ deception implies that people who are smart enough or rich enough can avoid challenges.[58] This is not so! In our lives and the world today we are experiencing in full measure the "perilous times" of the last days the Apostle Paul described to Timothy.[59] As our times become ever more difficult, the faithful brothers and sisters in quorums and Relief Societies are to protect the homes of Zion from the shrill voices of the world and the provocative influence of the adversary.

We have been taught by Elder Dallin H. Oaks that "one of the great functions of Relief Society is to provide sisterhood for women, just as priesthood quorums provide brotherhood for men."[60] It is our blessing to be part of a sisterhood or a brotherhood that provides "a place of healing, love, kindness, care, and belonging."[61] President Packer said: "This great circle of sisters will be a protection for each of you and for your families. The Relief Society might be likened to a refuge. . . . You will be safe within it. It encircles each sister like a protecting wall."[62] He said: "How consoling it is to know that no matter where [a family may] go, a church family awaits them. From the day they arrive, he will belong to a quorum of the priesthood and she will belong to Relief Society."[63]

Elder D. Todd Christofferson recounted the story of Brother George Goates, who in six days lost his son Charles and three of Charles's small children during the flu epidemic of 1918.[64] That week Brother Goates made the caskets, dug the graves, and helped prepare the burial clothing. His child and grandchildren died during the week he was to harvest his sugar beet crop, which was left freezing in the ground. After the burials, he and another son went to their fields to see if they could salvage any of their crop. When they arrived, they saw the members of his quorum leaving the empty field. His quorum had harvested every sugar beet. It was then that this man who had shown tremendous strength in the previous week sat down and sobbed like a child. He looked up to the sky and said, "Thanks, Father, for the elders of our ward."[65]

Whatever our mortal experience, we can have this feeling of fellowship and have the support and strength of many around us. The Lord said, "Also the body hath need of every member, that all may be edified together, that the system may be kept perfect."[66] It is in the sisterhood of Relief Society and the brotherhood of the quorums that we should find refuge and protection from the storms of life and the calamities of the latter days.

A fifth purpose for being organized into quorums and Relief Societies is to strengthen and support us in our family roles and responsibilities as sons and daughters of God. Though many of our responsibilities in the church are parallel, Heavenly Father's sons and daughters each have unique and distinct responsibilities in the family and in the church. Quorums and Relief Societies are to teach our Heavenly Father's sons and daughters and inspire them to prepare for the blessings of eternal life. Our Father sees the potential of his sons and his daughters to be family leaders. Therefore, everything we do in quorums and Relief Societies is to help the Lord with his mission of preparing his children for the blessings of the eternal life he envisions for us. In these settings we are meant to learn how to become part of our Heavenly Father's eternal family.

The quorum and the Relief Society assist family leaders and future family leaders and help them establish patterns and practices of righteous behavior and covenant keeping in their lives. Brothers and sisters encourage one another to pray always, pay tithes and offerings, and renew covenants on the Lord's holy day. They are to help one another be sufficiently mature to make and keep sacred temple covenants.

The quorum and the Relief Society should help us become who our Heavenly Father needs us to become. Joseph Smith taught the sisters from 1 Corinthians about the importance of developing godlike qualities. He said the sisters were organized "according to [their] natures" and were "placed in a situation in which [they could] act according to those sympathies which God has planted in [them]."[67] It is for this reason that the motto of Relief Society, "Charity never faileth," was chosen.[68]

Sister Eliza R. Snow, second Relief Society general president, said to the sisters:

> We want to be ladies in very deed, not according to the term of the word as the world judges, but fit companions of the Gods and Holy Ones. In an organized capacity we can assist each other in not only doing good but in refining ourselves, and whether few or many come forward and help to prosecute this great work, they will be those that will fill honorable positions in the Kingdom of God. . . . Women should be women and not babies that need petting and correction all the time. I know we like to be appreciated, but if we do not get all the appreciation which we think is our due, what matters?[69]

It is in the quorum that brothers are taught to "rise up" as "men of God" and "have done with lesser things. Give heart and soul and mind and strength to serve the King of Kings."[70] The work of the quorum and the Relief Society clarifies the unique identities and responsibilities of sons and daughters of God and unifies them in defense of his plan. President Harold B. Lee stated:

> It seems clear to me that the church has *no choice*—and never has had—but to do more to assist the *family* in carrying out *its* divine mission, not only because that is the order of heaven, but also because that is the most *practical* contribution we can make to our youth—to help improve the quality of life in the Latter-day Saint homes. As important as our many programs and organizational efforts are, these *should not* supplant the home; they should *support* the home.[71]

As the Lord said to Emma Smith, we are to "lay aside the things of this world, and seek for the things of a better. . . . Cleave unto the covenants which thou hast made. . . . Keep my commandments continually, and a crown of righteousness thou shalt receive."[72] Each of us is a beloved daughter or son of God with sacred personal responsibilities. In our quorums and Relief Societies we are to be taught and inspired to become who our Father in Heaven created us to become.

There is much work a quorum must do as a quorum and much a Relief Society is to do as a circle of sisters, and there is much that is to be coordinated between them. Because "the Lord's church is governed through councils,"[73] it is important for the Relief Society president to be included in priesthood executive meetings in which confidential welfare matters are discussed and in which bishops can facilitate the coordination of home teachers and visiting teachers.[74]

President Gordon B. Hinckley said:

> It will be a marvelous day, my brethren . . . when our priesthood quorums become an anchor of strength to every man belonging thereto, when each such man may appropriately be able to say, "I am a member of a priesthood quorum of the Church of Jesus Christ of Latter-day Saints. I stand ready to assist my brethren in all of their needs, as I am confident they stand ready to assist me in mine. Working together, we shall grow spiritually as covenant sons of God. Working together, we can stand, without embarrassment and without fear, against every wind of adversity that might blow, be it economic, social, or spiritual."[75]

President Packer recently declared to the brethren of the church: "We need everyone. The tired or worn out or lazy and even those who are bound down with guilt. . . . Too many of our priesthood brethren are living below their privileges and the Lord's expectations."[76] "In one of the first meetings of the Female Relief Society of Nauvoo, Joseph Smith admonished the sisters to 'live up to [their] privilege.'"[77] In a similar vein, President Packer said to the sisters of Relief Society:

> Rally to the cause of Relief Society! Strengthen it! Attend it! Devote yourselves to it! Enlist the inactive in it and bring nonmember sisters under the influence of it. It is time now to unite in this worldwide circle of sisters. A strong, well-organized Relief Society is crucial to the future, to the safety of this church.[78]

Much of what has been taught today can be found in *Daughters in My Kingdom: The History and Work of Relief Society.* This new resource from the First Presidency can help brothers and sisters learn how to fulfill their responsibilities. Through this and other instructions, we "know how to act and direct [the] church, how to act upon the points of [the Lord's] law and commandments, which [he has] given." We are now to "bind [ourselves] to act in all holiness before [him]."[79]

What the Lord envisioned regarding quorums and Relief Societies has not yet been fully utilized. Many quorums and Relief Societies are at present much like sleeping giants waiting for you to breathe new life into them.

I bear you my testimony that the true restored gospel of Jesus Christ is upon the earth. My testimony of that restoration has been strengthened by knowing that quorums and Relief Societies were established so the Lord could organize his sons and daughters under the priesthood and after the pattern of the priesthood. By this means he engages his children in his work of salvation and in wisely managing his storehouse. Quorums and Relief Societies are meant to be a safety and a refuge in these difficult days and to support and strengthen the identity, roles, and responsibilities of Heavenly Father's sons and daughters. We are "called by the voice of the Prophet of God to do it,"[80] and, as we do so, "the angels cannot be restrained from being [our] associates."[81] Of this I testify in the name of Jesus Christ, amen.

Julie B. Beck, "Why We Are Organized into Quorums and Relief Societies," BYU Devotional address, Jan. 17, 2012, Brigham Young University, Provo, UT, accessed Apr. 27, 2016, speeches.byu.edu.

Judy Brummer as a missionary in Queenstown, South Africa. Circa 1980. A native of South Africa, Brummer (pictured here, second from the right) was the first Latter-day Saint missionary fluent in the Xhosa language. (Photograph in family possession. Courtesy Judy Brummer.)

OUR FATHER IN HEAVEN HAS A MISSION FOR US

◇◇◇

JUDY BRUMMER

Fireside
Salt Lake City, Utah
April 28, 2012

Judy Bester Brummer (b. 1956) grew up on a farm in South Africa, where her father, Johan Bester, raised Merino sheep for wool, Angora goats for mohair, and cattle to compete in agricultural shows.[1] Her mother, Gwenna Rundell Stocks Bester, managed their home and homeschooled the children until they turned ten, when by law they had to attend school. The family had long-term relationships with their servants, who were members of the Xhosa tribe.[2] When Gwenna arrived at the family ranch as a new bride, Maggie (Notholi Dikane) was the cook; when the elderly Gwenna moved into a care center many years later, Maggie was still the cook. Jane (Nowinsi Xhashimba) was the housekeeper, and Lizzie (Nowinele Skeyi) did the laundry.[3] Lizzie's daughter Sindie (Sintombi Skeyi) and Jane's daughter Tombe (Ntombisi Xhashimba) were Brummer's best friends. Of the girls, only Brummer spoke English, so the friends always communicated in Xhosa.[4]

The first Latter-day Saint missionaries assigned to serve in Africa arrived in South Africa in 1853, but work proceeded sporadically until missionaries returned permanently in 1944.[5] The first South African stake, in Johannesburg, was organized in 1970, followed by one in Durban in 1981 and another in Cape Town in 1984, both close to the time Brummer served a mission in Queenstown.[6] Membership growth was slow in part because many nineteenth-century converts immigrated to areas with larger concentrations of church members.[7] There were also long periods when war disrupted missionary work in the country. Further, before 1978, the church restricted men of black African descent from priesthood ordination and black men and women from temple worship;

as a result, church membership in South Africa was primarily white, and the church was mainly established in the English- and Afrikaans-speaking areas. Serving from 1980 to 1982—a few years after the restriction on priesthood ordination and temple worship ended—Brummer was among the first wave of missionaries to proselytize primarily in the townships and tribal homelands of black South Africans. Her fluency in Xhosa proved crucial to her missionary work. After her mission, she also helped translate large portions of the Book of Mormon into Xhosa.[8]

After her mission, Brummer married South African André Brummer, who had been leader of her missionary district during the last months of her mission.[9] Raising young children, they tired of the high crime rate in their country, where they had to unlock four or five security gates for their child to go outside and ride a bicycle. They moved to Utah in 1993 for André to study international relations at Brigham Young University, and they stayed as he found employment with an online genealogy company.[10]

Brummer estimates she has given versions of the following talk hundreds of times since 2001, speaking two or three times per month.[11] Most often she speaks in Utah, although she has also traveled to speak in California, Texas, Arizona, and Oklahoma.[12] She says that she makes this effort because she believes, based on what listeners have told her, that "people's testimonies have been strengthened."[13] The text presented here is an excerpt of a version of Brummer's talk, given at a ward meetinghouse in Salt Lake City; it was recorded by Dan and Edith Baker, missionaries serving in the Family and Church History Mission at church headquarters.

I AM VERY HONORED and happy to be here this morning and thank you all for coming. I am so grateful.

As I tell you the story about how I grew up in South Africa, I want you to think and ask yourself this question: Does our Father in Heaven prepare a way ahead of time, or is this all one big coincidence?

I grew up on a ranch in the Karoo in South Africa.[14] I was born to a Methodist family. I love my Methodist family; they are very hardworking, good, honest, decent, farm, country-bumpkin people. I am truly grateful for the heritage that I have and to be born into that family.

My mother attended the most expensive private school on the African continent; she went to Rhodes University, and she had two university degrees.[15] She passed away two summers ago at the age of eighty-five.[16] In those days it was extremely unusual even for white women in South Africa to have had that type of education; because she had no brothers, the education was afforded to her. My mother had a bachelor of science degree in mathematics. She was a very intelligent woman, and personally I don't believe that you have to have a bachelor of science in mathematics to read the Bible and to figure out that one and one and one are three separate individuals.

I had a Methodist mom who taught me Mormon doctrine. Another thing that I'm eternally grateful for is my mother, and I hope that every mother here today tries to do this for her children or her future children. My mom taught us about the power of God. She taught us that Almighty God is not called "Almighty" for nothing. He can do anything, anywhere, anytime. How grateful I am to have grown up in a home where you believe that Heavenly Father can reach out to you and intervene in your life or answer your prayers. How much more likely is it you will ask for his help if you truly believe he can do anything, anywhere, anytime?

The longer I live, the more I believe that my mother had quite a lot in common with Moroni, who in the very last chapter of the Book of Mormon uses the word "power" not once, not twice, but nine times.[17] And let us remember that Moroni was not typing on a laptop; he was carving on golden plates when he wrote in Moroni 10: "Deny not the power of God." Then he repeated: "If ye deny not the power of God . . ." I think Moroni wanted us, in these last days, to acknowledge, remember, and believe in the power of the Almighty.[18] I am extremely grateful to my mother for teaching me those two things.

If you grew up in the Karoo where I grew up, at the age of six you were shipped off to an all-white boarding school in the city because of apartheid.[19] Parents were not allowed to homeschool their children if they lived in the outback, unless the teaching parent was qualified as a teacher. Think of the movie *Australia*—we lived in the outback in this white homestead.[20] If you stood in the front yard and you did a 360-degree twirl, there was no sign of any other human habitation. My father owned a 10,000-acre ranch, and so I thought he owned the whole world when I was growing up.

In South Africa there are eleven official languages, and if you were white, you grew up speaking English, if you were of British heritage like me; or you grew up speaking Afrikaans, like my husband did. It's mostly Dutch with a bit of German and French mixed in it. The Black African people are from nine different tribes, and they each have their own language. For instance, the Zulus speak isiZulu, the Sotho speak isiSotho, the Tswana speak isiTswana, and the Xhosa speak isiXhosa. The families that we had living on our ranch spoke isiXhosa. They were of the Xhosa tribe. I am sure you've heard of Nelson Mandela or Thabo Mbeki; these are Xhosa men belonging to the Xhosa tribe, and they speak isiXhosa.[21]

Our servants all belonged to the Xhosa tribe, so as a baby, I learned to speak two languages at once. I have no recollection of learning to speak Xhosa. I just grew up and thought, "Well, when you look at a black person you click your tongue, and when you look at a white person you speak English." As a baby I had no idea that I was even learning two languages at once, but they were both my "mother tongue" because I had one white mother and three black moms that raised me.

I'm going to fast-forward now to when I was at boarding school. Because my mother had those two degrees, she was permitted by the strict government guidelines to homeschool us for four years. Instead of being shipped off to a white boarding school at the age of six, I only got shipped off to a white boarding school at the age of ten. By the time you are ten years old, if you have been speaking a language for ten years, it is pretty much bolted into the back of your brain and you don't forget it. Some of the white kids that grew up in the area forgot the African languages when they got sent off to the white schools. But think about my mother—because she had this education, which was extremely unusual, I was permitted to stay on the ranch until I was ten.

When I was at boarding school during high school, I read a book by a minister called *The Cross and the Switchblade,* and I remember thinking, "What a noble thing to do."[22] David Wilkerson, that minister, wrote about how he used the gospel to lift people who were downtrodden after World War II. I thought perhaps I would do the same thing. So when I left boarding school and graduated from high school, I went to Rhodes University and signed up to study some social science classes. I thought perhaps I could do some social welfare or social work.

I had a friend from boarding school, and she looked at me one day and said, "Judy, you speak Xhosa fluently. Why don't you sign up to study Xhosa?" because I needed one more subject. When you are eighteen you are always looking for the easy way out. She said, "That will be an easy thing for you to study." So purely by accident, I signed up for a Xhosa class. I could speak it fluently and I had spoken it my whole life, but I had never learned to read and write it. I found myself in a Xhosa class with a white professor, who had spent many hours trying to learn this clicking language. Xhosa is the most difficult language on the face of the earth, because when you speak Xhosa sometimes you are making sounds by inhaling and other times by exhaling. When you speak English, you are exhaling, and all the sounds are made by blowing air out of your lungs, but when you speak Xhosa it is different.

In the middle of 1978, around about the same time that our beloved prophet, Spencer W. Kimball, received the revelation that every worthy male member can receive the priesthood—I am sure some of you in this room can remember exactly where you were and what you were doing that day[23]—at that time, I was still Methodist and I was living in Cape Town, the most beautiful city. In fact, if you ask any international pilot, they will tell you that Rio de Janeiro and Cape Town are the two most beautiful cities. They have the mountains and the ocean. I was living in Cape Town in 1978 with a very good friend of mine from boarding school, Vivienne. At the time, I landed a job that was nothing as noble as social work. It was the most glamorous overpaid, underworked job in all of Cape Town. A friend of mine that was studying advertising saw there was a full-page advertisement in the Sunday paper, and she looked at me and she said, "Judy, they're describing you here. You should apply for this job, and it's so overpaid." I said to her, "I already have a job, and I'm really not going to bother." So she wrote a letter on my behalf, and I landed this overpaid, underworked job, which was for Christian Dior cosmetics. I had a brand new car each year, and I had to travel around the southwestern tip of South Africa and represent Christian Dior and go to five to eight stores a day. You could do that in an hour or two and then go to the beach for the rest of the day.

My roommate, Vivienne, said, "Judy, you are the luckiest person on the earth. You have the perfect family, the perfect boyfriend, and now the perfect job." She made me feel guilty. You do have a certain amount of guilt when you grow up in a country where there are a lot of underprivileged people and you are so blessed. So we decided to go to church to say thank you for our blessings. There were four of us girls: my roommate, Vivienne, and me; and two friends from upstairs. We decided we would go to church to say thank you for Judy Bester's job. My friends had perks too. They got all the half-empty testers that I had to take back when I gave a full tester to a department store, so my friends always smelled of Christian Dior.

As we went to different churches in the middle of 1978, we started to go to church to say thank you for my job. We would go, and every Sunday we would look at each other and say, "We are never going back there again." Then the next week we would try a different church and say the same thing, "We are never going back there again." Eventually we gave up. The four of us sat down together and we made a pact that we would not attend any of those churches again. That was the most boring thing you could possibly do on a Sunday. So we decided that we would read our Bibles and be "good people," which we were not, and we would go to Clifton Beach every Sunday. We gave up our search altogether.

You can guess who came knocking on our door. I always said that Heavenly Father knew better than to send elders to that door where those four crazy girls lived. There were two South African sister missionaries. Anyone here who has raised a missionary or supported a missionary or been on a mission, I thank you from the bottom of my heart, because I can remember this day as clearly as if it happened yesterday. Vivienne, my roommate, and I were playing field hockey outside. We had a coach and he really tried to whip us into shape. We were sweaty and had just walked in the door of our apartment in Rondebosch, Cape Town.

It was January of 1979. Now January is watermelon season; it is midsummer in the Southern Hemisphere, and we were in the kitchen quenching our thirst with watermelon when there was this big, loud knock on the door. I went to the door and I saw these two sisters. I was twenty-two years old at the time and Sister Dicks was twenty-two years old, Ronell Dicks—she's now Ronell Wrench—and Sister Louise Bell. She was an older lady in her forties and a widow. Sister Dicks was a brand-new green missionary and was quite nervous, and in one breath she said, "Good afternoon, we are missionaries from the Church of Jesus Christ of Latter-day Saints—more commonly known as the Mormons—would you like to know more?" I looked at her name tag and I saw the Savior's name, and that was before they'd even enlarged it. I remember thinking, "How did we miss that church?" Then I suddenly thought I had better ask my roommate, Vivienne, if she would like to hear as well, because a few weeks prior I had allowed a homeless man into our flat—when I say flat, I mean apartment—and we could not get rid of him. My roommate Vivienne was quite cross with me and said, "Don't you let any more weirdos into this flat." I said to the sisters, "Just wait a minute and I will ask Viv." I took a few steps to the right, and I said to my roommate, "Vivienne, would you like to hear about the 'Morbid church'?" She had a mouthful of watermelon which she spat all over the kitchen table, and she was holding her stomach and was hysterical. You will understand that we laughed at things that are not really funny. I started to laugh and the two of us just stood there and we were just guffawing, just hysterical.

All of a sudden this thought came into my head: "Don't you dare laugh at those girls; you would never have the courage to do what they are doing. Allow them in." So I went to the door and said to them, "Please come in." They sat us down, and we had two friends that came from upstairs, and they taught us the very first discussion. I remember clearly how they taught about the First Vision, about this young farm boy—and I love farm people.[24] We are really simple people and I related. There's something special about farm people; I just love farm people.

When they said he was a farm boy from upstate New York and fourteen years old, and he didn't know which church to join, that sounded vaguely familiar. Then he went into a grove of trees; and then he asked God, the Eternal Father, which church he should join. And the heavens were opened and Almighty God, our Father and Jesus the Son, two separate beings, appeared to the boy prophet Joseph Smith; and they personally restored his church back to the earth in these latter days. I remember thinking, "*Wow.*"

The First Vision took place in the year 1820. I remember my very first thought was, "This is the most significant event in all Christianity since that very first Easter of the resurrection of our Lord and Savior, Jesus Christ. And how come it takes 160 years for that news to travel across the Atlantic?" I could not believe that I had never heard of the First Vision before. We considered ourselves educated and enlightened, and yet we had never heard of the most significant event, the most important event.

My first thought was, "What's the matter with BBC and CNN?" My father was a news junkie and he subscribed to all the news magazines. We had all the newspapers, he listened to the news on the radio at least five times a day, and yet we never heard—I felt a little peeved and cheated. So I thought, "I better start telling my family about the Restoration." I was on the phone telling them, I was so excited. I told everybody about what the missionaries taught me. I called all my family and friends afterwards, after each lesson.

I was very startled at the reaction. I received an avalanche of anti-Mormon literature. Even three ministers were sent to our flat to tell me not to join this evil cult from America that had a false prophet. I was quite cheeky, fortunately. When the ministers came in their black robes and white collars to tell me not to join the Mormon church, I asked them, "Why?" And one minister said, "Oh, because they're not Christian." I defended the Mormons; I said, "I beg your pardon, reverend, how can you possibly say that Mormons are not Christian? They have name tags with the Savior's name, and I've been to their church a few times and it's written in brass letters and stuck on the bricks outside." I said, "How can you possibly say they're not Christian?" And he said, "Because they don't belong to the WCC." I said, "What's the WCC?" He said, "The World Council of Churches."[25]

Fortunately I had some ammunition. I said, "Excuse me, I have just read my Bible from cover to cover. Can you please show me the chapter and the verse where Jesus says you have to belong to the WCC? I was just reading in James chapter one, and it tells us how to recognize pure religion.[26] And I believe the Mormons are the best Christians I have ever met. I have been to their Relief Society; they run around and take casseroles to the sick, and they look after people's children when they are having babies, and they take care of the widows, and they take care of the poor. They do this awful thing: they fast once a month and give their money to the poor." I said, "In James 1:22 it says, 'But be ye doers of the word, and not hearers only, deceiving your own selves,' and in verse twenty-six it says, 'If any man among you seem to be religious, and bridleth not his tongue, but deceiveth his own heart, this man's religion is vain.' Verse twenty-seven: 'Pure religion and undefiled before God and the Father is this, to visit the fatherless and the widows in their affliction, and to keep himself unspotted from the world.'"

I remember telling the minister that these Mormons were the most unspotted people I had ever met, that they lived their religion.

I was baptized in April of 1979. The reason I was baptized was because I prayed with a sincere heart, with real intent of changing my worldly ways. I asked God to please tell me if the Book of Mormon was the word of God, and the Holy Ghost witnessed to me, in my heart, with such power that I could not dismiss it as an emotion. I knew from that very prayer that the Book of Mormon was the word of God. I can still remember that feeling. I have a very bad memory generally, but I remember kneeling with a missionary on either side of me and asking God, knowing that he was quite capable of telling me if the Book of Mormon was the word of God.

I remember that feeling in my heart. It burned a hole in my heart. It wasn't just a slight feeling—it was a very powerful feeling—and from that prayer onwards, I knew that the Book of Mormon was the word of God, and no minister could tell me that this was not the church that Jesus himself restored to the earth through the Prophet Joseph Smith. But even earlier, I recognized the truth when the missionaries knocked on my door. I felt the Spirit. I am so grateful that they were worthy to have the Holy Ghost with them as they taught me and my friends, though none of my friends were baptized.

A year later I decided to go and serve a mission. That was when my family thought I had crossed the sanity line. My mother called me. (They were still living in the country, and the Methodist minister was telling them that the Mormons were not Christians.) I told my parents, "I believe with all my heart that this is the church that Jesus has brought back to the earth in preparation for his second coming. I believe that with all my heart." They said, "Don't resign that overpaid job; you will never find a job like that again, and we're not going to support you during your mission or after your mission." Once again I was very cheeky and said, "I know this is the Lord's church. Don't worry about me; he'll take care of me in eighteen months if I just have the faith to walk that plank. He will catch me when I get to the other end."

In 1980 I told my branch president that I would like to go on a mission, and two weeks later I was in the mission field.[27] It was an urgent call from Salt Lake City because somebody heard that I could speak this clicking language. There was an African man who called himself Bishop Kowa who had some church literature given to him, and he decided he was not going to wait 160 years for the missionaries to come and teach him, so he got a piece of corrugated iron, painted on it "The Church of Jesus Christ of Latter-day Saints," and put it outside his mud hut in Steynsburg and went around preaching the gospel.[28] He had congregations all around the Ciskei and Transkei, East London, Cemazili, Sada, Illinge, and more. All these places he had preached the gospel.[29]

I heard this from an AP [assistant to the president] missionary that was on a mission at the time. He said that Bishop Kowa decided to register the Church of Jesus Christ of Latter-day Saints in South Africa, only to discover it had already been registered by the headquarters of the church in Salt Lake City. So he wrote a letter to the prophet, President Kimball, and asked if he would like to merge with his church. The letter was written in Afrikaans; I think he thought maybe President Kimball would understand Afrikaans. The letter was translated and sent back and forth.

In about 1979 they sent two missionaries, both South Africans; one was Peter Boyton.[30] They sent him to visit this Bishop Kowa, who now had a large number of people in his church, and he was living off the tithes of the people. Bishop Kowa could not understand English, and these two elders could not speak the clicking language. Since there was no communication, they were eventually pulled out. Then the mission president had heard that I could speak this language. Two weeks later I was in the mission field, and we were speaking to Bishop Kowa. That was 1980.

The Lord had prepared people of the Xhosa tribe, through Bishop Kowa, and by the time we got there, there were congregations of people to teach. I interpreted for the American and the South African missionaries on my mission. I spent eighteen months in Queenstown, which is about two hours away from where I grew up. We traveled the Transkei and the Ciskei, teaching these people.[31] Bishop Kowa would come with us and he would say, "You must listen to these people." We had an enormous amount of success because the people were prepared by the Lord.

We baptized thirty, forty, fifty people at a time. I remember once we had fifty-four people ready for baptism, and we only had a couple missionary and my companion and myself, so there was one priesthood holder.[32] We had to phone East London and say, "Send us some elders, because it is not easy to baptize fifty-four people with an elderly gentleman."[33] My mission president, Lowell D. Wood, told me on the phone, "I'm awfully sorry, but we're not transferring you, because you're the only one who can speak Xhosa." So I spent my entire eighteen-month mission in Queenstown. Eventually they brought in more missionaries until we had twelve missionaries in that area, and what an experience. I *loved* my mission. I was on such a high learning curve since I had only been in the church for one year, but I learned the basics over and over again. I am so grateful that I was able to sell everything I had and go on a mission.

The church does everything in order. When I was on my mission I was asked to translate a number of things, and I think the very first thing I was asked to translate was the name of the church, and that is: *Ibandla lika Yesu Krestu Yaba Ngcwele beMihla yokuGqibela.* Have any of you seen the movie *The Gods Must Be Crazy*? Well, that is a similar language.[34] When we were teaching people and baptizing people, we had the Bible in Xhosa, which was a very poor translation, but nevertheless we had a Bible. But there was no Book of Mormon in Xhosa. So when we were teaching and the missionaries read out of the Book of Mormon to teach the gospel, I would just translate it verbally. Things like the sacrament prayer and the baptismal prayer, I wrote that on paper so that they could be said the exact same way each time.

What an honor and privilege it was for me to see these people who I love come to the gospel. I had grown up with the Xhosa people, and I absolutely love them. They are very spiritual people, very humble people. I remember that every time one of them got the priesthood, I would look at this little twelve-year-old boy and I would say to him, "Do you know that you have more authority than most ministers that are famous and recognized on the earth?" It would just blow me away to think that those little twelve-year-old barefoot boys had the priesthood. I cannot describe to you the joy and the thrill to see these people as they were baptized and see how the gospel lifted them out of some of the dire situations that they were in.

One of my favorite scriptures is found in John 8:32. It says, "And ye shall know the truth, and the truth shall make you free." The truth, as taught by the missionaries of the Church of Jesus Christ of Latter-day Saints, is the best truth you can possibly have. That is the best freedom you can possibly have. I remember telling these African people, "You might be oppressed under apartheid, but you now have the priesthood. You now have the greatest freedom on earth."

If any of you know about Africa, there are a lot of problems, not just in South Africa, with things like witchcraft, ancestor worship, AIDS, and things that have brought the African continent to its knees. The gospel helps people; it lifts people out of that state. It is such a thrill for me now to receive letters from people that we baptized thirty years ago. Their children are serving missions and going to the temple. I cannot tell you the joy. I just heard a few weeks ago that South African missions had the highest retention rate as far as people staying in the church.[35]

As I was on my mission, I was often asked to interpret when people confessed their sins because the church leaders were all white. People would have to tell me their sins, and then I would have to tell the stake president or the bishop. I would just think to myself, "Some of these sins are so bad and scary!" I said to my mission president one day, "I often think, 'How can I make it sound a little bit better?'" because these American leaders were not familiar with witchcraft. A person would say, "This one is putting a curse on that one," and I thought, "Oh, my goodness, how can I translate this?" Some people had actually committed murder. My mission president said, "If you do not say it exactly like it is, if you misinterpret it, their sins are going to be on your head." And I said, "Thank you, I have plenty of my own sins. I am going to say exactly as they say from now on."

After my mission, Elder Brummer—now I have to confess my own sins, because I was Judy Bester when I started, and toward the end of my mission, Elder Brummer was my district leader. Okay, I married my district leader after my mission. Elder Brummer came to me and said, "The church needs to buy your air ticket or train ticket. Where are you going?" I had sold everything I had to go on a mission, and when I started my mission I had a suitcase of fabulous clothing, but after eighteen months I had a suitcase of worn-out clothing and not two pennies to rub together. I had no idea where I was going, and remember how cheeky I was to my mother? There was no way I could go home like a prodigal daughter. So I kept saying to Elder Brummer, "I'll tell you next week," and he would come up to me and say, "We need to buy you a plane ticket. Where are you going?" I said, "I'll tell you next week. I'll tell you next week," because I had no clue where I was going to go with no money and worn-out clothing.

Then about three weeks before my mission ended, I got a telegram, not from my boss in Cape Town but his boss at the head office in Johannesburg—a telegram is like a text message on paper, for you young ones. I still have that telegram. It said, "Contact me urgently, Alec." So I ran and I called my boss's boss and he said to me, "When are you finished being a nun?"[36] I think nonmembers do not quite understand the vocabulary in the church. I am sure you know that Mormons speak differently. We have a different vocabulary. I said to him, "I have three weeks left on my mission. I am not a nun." And I said, "I finish on that Friday." He said, "Monday morning, eight o'clock, I want you in the Durban office." I got the exact same job, only on the east coast. They gave me a 50 percent increase in salary. Guess who I called? My mom. And guess how cheeky I was then? I said, "Guess whose church this is? Didn't I tell you that if I did this eighteen-month mission, the Lord would take care of me afterwards? And he did."

I know, my sisters, that the power of God should never be denied. We need to have the faith to walk that plank, and do what our Heavenly Father wants us to do, when he wants us to do it, and know that he will take care of us when we get to the end.

After my mission I was asked to translate a few things for the church, and one of them was this pamphlet *Ubungqina Bukamprofethi UJoseph Smith,* the testimony of the Prophet Joseph Smith.[37] Elder Brummer and I traveled to the Salt Lake temple and we were married there because there was no temple in South Africa in 1983. We moved right back to South Africa, lived in Johannesburg for about ten years. We have four children now, but at the time we only had three children. The church's translating department came to my door in North Johannesburg and said, "We have enough members of the Xhosa tribe, good, honest, tithe-paying members, to now translate scriptures into their language." I remember my very first reaction—yours most likely would have been the same: the most correct book on earth, as Joseph said,[38] into the most difficult language on earth—my first reaction was to run and hide. I made all the excuses. I said, "Well, my husband is the bishop right now, I have three little kids at my ankles right now—there's no way I can do it." I said, "There is a university with a black Xhosa professor. I am sure he can do it." They gave the black professor *Selections of the Book of Mormon,* and he did not understand the English, the thees and thous, and so he just wrote a different story. They gave him a few chapters, and they brought it to me to proofread. My friend said she can still remember how furious I was because he just made stuff up and he thought, "Oh, they will never know."

So then I spoke to Bob Eppel, who was over church translating in South Africa. I said, "You know this is just not good enough. I am not volunteering to do it, but I just want you to know it is not good enough."[39] One day the translating people came to my home in Johannesburg. It was a couple from Salt Lake and a couple from South Africa, and they had Elder Gene R. Cook with them of the Seventy.[40] They said, "You pick three sisters in the ward to come and babysit your kids, to take turns every day while you do the translation, and we will pay them. We really feel strongly that you need to do this work." Elder Cook laid his hands on my head, and he gave me a blessing. Everybody in that room knew that that was why I was born to a Methodist mother who taught me Mormon doctrine. That was why I was allowed to stay on that ranch for ten instead of six years, and that was why I signed up, accidentally, for a Xhosa class.

Had I known back then I was going to join the church and be asked to translate scripture, I would have stayed in that class a lot longer and paid more attention.

In closing, I would like to tell you three things that happened to me which did not take place when I was translating pamphlets or other things. I translated the *Gospel Principles* manual,[41] some materials for the Relief Society and Young Women, and some songs. But these last three things took place only when I had the Book of Mormon, the *Selections of the Book of Mormon* in English, and I was translating it into Xhosa by hand.

The first was opposition. We were hit with enormous opposition. My kids got sick; one child almost died. Opposition did not just affect André and me; it also affected my three babysitting friends who were going to make the work possible.

One day we sat down and we said, "What's going on?" There were broken legs and smashed cars, sick children, and almost dying children. Then suddenly we realized that the adversary did not want the Book of Mormon to be translated into the mother tongue of about eight million people, because when you read the Book of Mormon in your own mother tongue it touches an extra heartstring, and that I know. We refused to be depressed, and we rolled up our sleeves and said, "We're going to fight back, and we're not going to let Satan win," and then the opposition dissipated.

The second thing that happened to me: I was reading the English Book of Mormon and I understood it with a clarity that I cannot even explain to you. It was so clear. It was almost like I was there. I knew exactly what every word meant in English. So it was easy to translate into Xhosa, which does not happen to me now. I understood it with a clarity that I cannot explain, even the portions from Isaiah. I kept saying to myself, "I feel like there is a lightbulb that lit up in my brain. I am not usually this smart," and I know now that it was a gift from God. I did not do it alone; I had help.

I know this very, very certainly because one day I got out of bed on the wrong side, and I snapped at everybody in my family. I was in a bad mood and I went to translate and I could not do it. I was stuck on one word. I had the Xhosa Bible and I was trying. I was cross-referencing dictionaries, and I remember saying to myself, "I am not enjoying this at all. This is suddenly not easy," and it was because I was in a bad mood and the Spirit left me. The gift of translation was removed hastily when I behaved badly. So I thought, "It is much easier to humble yourself and to repent," and the next day I was fine again.

The third and the final thing is the characters of the Book of Mormon. I know that the Book of Mormon was written by ancient prophets who lived on this continent, and that they cared about us enough to write for us so that we can have the truth in the last days about God, the truth that makes us free. I felt the different personalities. I felt the different characters. Sometimes when you are translating, there is not the perfect word; there are two words, or three words. I would pray and I would ask Heavenly Father, "Please help me to know which word Alma would use." And instantly I would know. Some of the prophets felt more strict, and some more lenient. Just like when you have a different stake president or a different bishop, the church is still true but they have their different personalities. I felt the personalities of the prophets who wrote in the Book of Mormon. I know that they were helping me, and the veil was very thin. I did not do it alone, and I know that they were very close to me. I know that the Book of Mormon is the most powerful book; it changed my life from night to day, and I have watched it change many more souls' lives from night to day.

I would like to close with bearing you my testimony. I am going to try to translate it into Xhosa, since I can still speak Xhosa. I have very many Xhosa friends who call me regularly on the telephone, so I still speak it all the time, but I can't remember what I said two seconds ago, so that is the reason why it is not going to be perfect.

I would like to leave you my testimony that I know that God can do anything, anywhere, anytime; that he is Almighty; that he loves us with an infinite love. [*Speaking Xhosa*] I know that Jesus is the Christ, that he atoned for my large sins and your little sins equally. [*Speaking Xhosa*] I know that the Holy Ghost witnesses truth to the hearts of human beings. [*Speaking Xhosa*] I know that this is the Lord's work. I felt the passion that Moroni had when he said we are going to be triumphant in these last days and that we need to take the gospel to every nation, kindred, tongue, and people.[42] We need to prepare this earth for our Savior's return.

I am so happy, and I know there is a fine line between being unashamed and being proud and I am right up against that line. I am so unashamed that I am almost proud of being a Mormon because I truly believe that you are the best Christians on the face of this earth. And I leave this with you and I thank you for your dedication, for your efforts to build this kingdom. I am so grateful for all of you and for the opportunity to be here today to share my testimony. I leave this with you in the name of Jesus Christ, amen.

Judy Brummer, "Our Father in Heaven Has a Mission for Us," Fireside, Apr. 28, 2012, Salt Lake City, Utah, edited transcript of audio recording, CHL.

OUR SABBATH DAY GIFTS

◇◇◇

LINDA K. BURTON

Utah South Area Conference
Marriott Center, Brigham Young University, Provo, Utah
September 13, 2015

Linda Kjar Burton (b. 1952) moved with her family to Wellington, New Zealand, in 1966, when her parents, Morris and Marjorie Castleton Kjar, served a three-year term overseeing the New Zealand South Mission. Burton and her sisters attended Church College of New Zealand, a boarding school north of Wellington that was sponsored by the church.[1] After returning to Utah, Burton met her future husband, Craig P. Burton, while studying elementary education at the University of Utah. They married August 7, 1973, and together had six children.[2] In 2005, Linda Burton joined the Primary general board, where she worked on the Spanish, music, and training committees, planning instructional programs for Primary leaders and choristers.[3]

The Burtons moved to Seoul, South Korea, in 2007, where Craig was mission president.[4] At zone conferences, Linda Burton taught gospel messages, trained missionaries on how to teach, and instructed them on health issues. She spent much of her time caring for missionaries, fielding medical questions, and when necessary, coordinating care with a medical doctor or psychiatrist in Japan. She also prepared many meals for missionaries, as well as visitors and local church leaders. Every Sunday, the Burtons spoke at a branch, ward, or stake conference. And nearly every week on preparation day, they attended the temple with missionaries.[5]

Soon after their return from South Korea in 2010, Burton was appointed to the Relief Society general board.[6] The board and presidency were preparing for the worldwide distribution of *Daughters in My Kingdom,* a history of the Relief Society written for adult female church members. Burton was responsible for preparing the Relief

Society web pages for President Julie B. Beck's successor, unaware that she would be the one to fill that role until she was called to it in January 2012.[7] Since becoming Relief Society general president in March 2012, her major goal has been to encourage members to fulfill the Relief Society's purpose as it appeared in the church's *Handbook 2* at the time of her call: "Relief Society prepares women for the blessings of eternal life by helping them increase their faith and personal righteousness, strengthen families and homes, and help those in need."[8] To help women increase their faith, Burton's presidency has expounded on the object of that faith: Jesus Christ and his atonement. The presidency has emphasized ordinances and covenants as a way to help women strengthen home and family and has taught the importance of unity—with God, with Jesus Christ, with priesthood holders, and among sister organizations—when planning how to help those in need. In 2015 Burton became the first woman to serve on the church's Priesthood and Family Executive Council.[9] Burton also announced the "I Was a Stranger" program, which called on church members to aid refugees in an effort to increase unity and give meaningful service.[10]

In June 2015, church leaders announced new measures to help members improve the quality of their Sabbath observance. These measures included encouragement for all wards to hold sacrament meeting at the beginning of the three-hour block, for ward councils (instead of only bishopric members) to plan sacrament meeting programs together, and for families and congregations to focus more clearly on Sundays as a time to worship God.[11] Three months after the increased emphasis on the holiness of the Sabbath day, Burton addressed the topic of Sabbath observance at a multistake conference that was broadcast to 365 stakes.[12] In preparing her talk, she pondered Russell M. Nelson's general conference talk from earlier that year, particularly his depiction of the Sabbath as a delight, as a way to keep oneself unspotted, as a sign of love for God, and as a "two-way gift," from God to us and from us to God.[13]

MY BELOVED BROTHERS AND SISTERS, I count it a sacred privilege to speak to you today from this magnificent Marriott Center in Provo, Utah, as you are gathered together in your buildings. Among you are some of our own precious family members and cherished friends. I consider it a sacred privilege to accompany Elder Ballard, Elder Hallstrom, and Bishop Davies this morning.[14] I testify that they are chosen servants and dedicated disciples of the Lord Jesus Christ and plead with you to listen, learn, and live what the Spirit whispers to you through them this morning.

In our most recent general conference President Russell M. Nelson asked, "What did the Savior mean when he said that 'the Sabbath was made for man, and not man for the Sabbath?'" President Nelson then answered his own question, "I believe he wanted us to understand that the Sabbath was his gift to us."[15]

What did YOU do the last time someone gave a gift to you? Did you express gratitude in words, either written or spoken? Did you use the gift to show that you value, cherish, and appreciate it? For example, did you hang a piece of artwork one of your children or grandchildren or a member of your Primary class made especially for you? Did you take time to read a book, letter, email, or card offered in love for you?

I am sorry to admit that as a newlywed on our first Christmas together as husband and wife, I failed to show appreciation for a gift my husband gave to me. We had agreed that since we had very little money that we would not give each other gifts for Christmas that first year. However, my sweet husband noticed that I needed a new pair of shoes. He surprised me with a brand new pair of brown shoes for Christmas at great sacrifice to himself. But guess what? They weren't the kind of shoes I would have chosen for myself. As a very young and immature bride, I thought they looked like "brown grandma shoes." And instead of wearing them to show how much I appreciated my husband's thoughtfulness, I asked if he had kept the receipt and promptly returned them to the shoe store the next day.

Did my husband give me a bad gift? Certainly not! It was a good gift given with great love. Did I turn the good gift into a bad gift by not accepting it in the spirit in which it was given? If I am to be perfectly honest, I must admit that I did. I wish I had known then what I know now about good gifts. In the New Testament we read what Jesus Christ has to say about the gifts God gives us. In Matthew 7:9–11 we read, "What man is there of you whom if his son ask bread, will he give him a stone? Or if he ask a fish, will he give him a serpent? If ye then, being evil, know how to give good gifts unto your children, how much more shall your Father which is in heaven give good things to them that ask him?"

This brings us back, then, to President Nelson's observation about the Sabbath day being a gift from our Heavenly Father. Is the Sabbath day a bad gift? Of course not! The Lord is perfect and gives only good gifts to his children—to us! He loves us and knows what is best for us and wants to bless us with the best gifts. We need to remember, however, that the Sabbath day really belongs to him.

In Isaiah 58:13–14 we read, "If thou turn away . . . from doing thy pleasure on my holy day; and call the sabbath a delight, the holy of the Lord, honourable; and shalt honour him, not doing thine own ways, nor thine own pleasure, nor speaking thine own words: Then shalt thou delight thyself in the Lord; and I will cause thee to ride upon the high places of the earth."

President Nelson reminded us that one way we can "delight in the Lord" is to freely give him a sign that we love and remember the Sabbath is his day. We do this as we remember the perfect life and perfect sacrifice of his beloved Son, our Savior and Redeemer.

What signs do we give to those we love to demonstrate we love, respect, and cherish our relationship with them? We might remember them on a birthday or other special day by eating foods they choose, allowing them to choose what activities they most enjoy, or listening to music they prefer, among other things. These demonstrate we remember and honor them. Let me share a couple of personal examples to illustrate.

While we were serving our mission in Korea a few years ago, my husband was deeply touched and felt greatly honored to learn how our family had chosen to remember and honor him on his birthday, although we were thousands of miles away from each other. All of our children and grandchildren gathered together and went to my husband's favorite restaurant, ate his favorite kind of food, and all ordered his favorite dessert. This was a sign between our family and my husband that they remembered him on his special day.

Last year my father passed away.[16] We dearly love and miss him. To keep his memory alive in the hearts and minds of his posterity, we gathered together at his grave on the anniversary of his death and celebrated his wonderful life by sharing memories, food, and music that he loved. Similarly, we can give a sign of love to our Heavenly Father and the Savior by choosing to do things on the Sabbath day that demonstrate our love.

At my own home stake conference a couple of weeks ago, my heart was overflowing with love as I was blessed to hear about the efforts of several who are trying harder to keep the Sabbath day holy as a sign of their love for our Heavenly Father. The first was a darling young single adult sister who shared her feelings. She said, "When I live the gospel, I tend to make it more complicated than it needs to be." She continued, "As I was thinking about how I can best keep the Sabbath day holy, I decided the best way is to simply love the Lord. If I view my behavior as an expression of my love for God," she said, "I will know how to keep his day holy." As she pondered this in her heart, the Holy Ghost had whispered to her and magnified her thoughts.

Another family reported on their efforts to prayerfully consider how to better observe the Sabbath day and felt the need to improve in another way. This family mentioned that their tendency was to focus only on the needs of their own family on the Sabbath day. But as they prayed with the real intent to change, they felt some gentle urgings from the Holy Ghost. The feelings they received have resulted in using the Sabbath to reach beyond their own comfort zone of family, opening up their home to include the lonely, the less active, and others. It is their sign to the Lord that they love him by loving his children.

At that same stake conference, I learned from another young family how they are striving to improve their observance of the Sabbath day and keep it in a way to show their love for the Lord. As they counseled together as husband and wife, then as a family that includes three children, ages eight, five, and three, they came up with a plan. The inspiring thing about counseling together is that as we talk with and listen to each other with the intent to do better, the Holy Ghost brings thoughts to our minds and feelings to our hearts that magnify our efforts. This was the case with this striving young family. As they counseled together, they felt they could do better by making the sacrament more meaningful for their young, active family. They hoped to improve their sacrament experience in three ways: in their preparation before attending church together, trying to better feel the Spirit during the ordinance of the sacrament, and then following up afterwards at home.

Their family plan included being more consistent in their individual and family prayers and scripture study and trying harder during the week to repent more and forgive more. They also decided, as part of their preparation, they would select a Savior-centered scripture, hymn, Primary song, or picture in the gospel art kit to help them focus their thoughts during the sacrament. Now before leaving for church, they stop and review what they have decided to focus on together during the ordinance of the sacrament. During the sacrament they each think of that one thing and report how they felt and what they learned when they return home later that day.

Partaking of the sacrament is more than just renewing our baptismal covenant, for we are cleansed again each time we worthily partake and remember him. Doing so helps us repel the stains of the world and keep "unspotted" from it. Recall with me the commandment the Lord gives in the 59th section of the Doctrine and Covenants. "Thou shalt offer a sacrifice unto the Lord thy God in righteousness, even that of a broken heart and a contrite spirit. And that thou mayest more fully keep thyself unspotted from the world, thou shalt go to the house of prayer and offer up thy sacraments upon my holy day."[17]

As I share the following story with you, consider what the sister in the story learned from her service in the temple that we could apply to keeping ourselves "unspotted from the world" on the Sabbath day. These are the words of Sister Julie Thompson:

> A few years ago, I arrived at the Bountiful Utah Temple to fulfill a late-night cleaning assignment. The turnout for the assignment was impressive, and I wondered for a moment if some would be sent home. I was more than ready to volunteer to leave early. Then I cynically thought to myself, "Of course they won't let us go early. They will find menial jobs for all of us, thinking it is

their duty to keep us here the entire two hours." I remembered a previous assignment during which I had dusted for more than an hour, only to return a cloth that looked as clean as it had been when it was given to me. I prepared myself to spend two hours cleaning things that didn't appear to need cleaning. Obviously, I had come to the temple that night out of a sense of duty more than from a desire to serve.

Our group was led to a small chapel for a devotional. The custodian who conducted the devotional said something that will forever change the way I look at temple cleaning assignments. After welcoming us, he proceeded to explain that we were not there to clean things that didn't need cleaning but to keep the Lord's house from ever becoming dirty. As stewards of one of the most sacred places on earth, we had a responsibility to keep it spotless.

His message penetrated my heart, and I proceeded to my assigned area with a new enthusiasm to protect the Lord's house. I spent time with a soft-bristled paintbrush, dusting the tiny grooves in door frames, baseboards, and the legs of tables and chairs. Had I been given this assignment on an earlier visit, I might have thought it ridiculous and carelessly brushed over the areas in an effort to appear busy. But this time, I made sure the bristles reached into the tiniest of crevices.

Because this job was neither physically nor mentally taxing, I was blessed with time to ponder while I worked. I first realized that I never paid attention to such minute details in my own home but cleaned those areas that others would see first, neglecting those known only to members of my family and me.

I next realized that there were times when I had lived the gospel in a similar fashion—living those principles and fulfilling those assignments that were most obvious to those around me while ignoring things that seemed known only to my immediate family or me. I attended church, held callings, fulfilled assignments, went visiting teaching—all in full view of members of our ward—but neglected to attend the temple regularly, have personal and family scripture study and prayer, and hold family home evening. I taught lessons and spoke in church but sometimes lacked true charity in my heart when it came to interactions with others.

> That night in the temple, I studied the paintbrush in my hand and asked myself, "What are the little crevices in my life that need more attention?" I resolved that rather than plan to repeatedly clean the areas of my life that needed attention, I would try harder never to let them become dirty.[18]

Let's pause for a brief moment and ponder what the Spirit is teaching us right now. Let's ask ourselves, "How does this story apply to me?" "What are the places in my life that I need to be sure to keep clean so they will never become dirty?" "Are there areas I may be neglecting that need some special attention?" Because the Sabbath day is the Lord's day, I know he would be pleased to have us each consider how we might better keep ourselves and our homes "unspotted from the world."

> In January of 1982, [Elder Robert D. Hales] spoke in a devotional [here in the Marriott Center].[19] [He] invited the students to imagine that the church was on one side of the podium . . . and the world was just a foot or two away on the other side. This represented the "very short distance between where the world was and where the church standards were" when [he] was in college. Then, standing before the students 30 years later, [he] held up [his] hands in the same manner and explained, "The world has gone far afield; [it has traveled; it is nowhere to be seen;] it has proceeded way, way out, all the way out of this [building and around the world]."[20]

This sobering reminder from Elder Hales is surely applicable to how the world observes or, more accurately, ignores the observance of the Sabbath day today. It is vastly different from how the Lord intended it to be.

It is interesting to note that one of the charges frequently brought against our Savior was that of Sabbath breaking, but this was because he failed to conform to the traditions and man-made regulations concerning the Sabbath.[21] Satan doesn't really care whether we break the Sabbath by over-regulating it the way the Pharisees did—with unending rules and regulations—or whether we throw out all the rules and use it as a lazy day to do nothing or simply make it just another day of the week. He loves to deal in the extremes. We will know in our hearts if we are keeping the Sabbath day holy and remembering to honor the Lord if what we are doing are things he would do if he were here—especially and most importantly in our homes.

In Matthew 12:12 we read the Savior's own words, "Wherefore it is lawful to do well on the Sabbath days." And President Spencer W. Kimball taught, "The

Sabbath is a holy day in which to do worthy and holy things. Abstinence from work and recreation is important, but insufficient. The Sabbath calls for constructive thoughts and acts."[22] I think President Kimball was inviting more intentional or thoughtful behavior in how we observe the Sabbath day.

My dear friend and counselor in the Relief Society general presidency, Sister Linda S. Reeves, recently shared how and why she lives this counsel. As a mother of thirteen children, she recalled that when her children were all living at home, she found it was absolutely necessary to prepare for the Sabbath day well in advance in order to make it a holy day. She then admitted that she had slipped out of that habit for a time since only she and her husband were then at home. She said that recently she recommitted to preparing more diligently for the Sabbath on Saturday. She said something like, "I saw it as sort of a sign or a love letter to my Heavenly Father that I would more intentionally remember him on his special day." Then she testified that in her efforts to remember him by preparing ahead to worship him and have temporal things in order, that in return, he has blessed her with a special reassurance of his love. She said, "It is as if he is sending me a love letter in return."[23]

Twenty years ago, Elder Neal A. Maxwell said something in general conference that sank deep into my heart. As I felt my heart burn within me, I knew the Holy Ghost was confirming to me that what Elder Maxwell was teaching was not only true, but meant especially for me. It feels applicable to how we observe the Sabbath day. He said, "The submission of one's will is really the only uniquely personal thing we have to place on God's altar. . . . It is the only possession which is truly ours to give!"[24]

May we decide today to do one small thing to submit our will to his to improve our observance of the Sabbath day as a sign of our love for our Heavenly Father and our Savior Jesus Christ. Wonderful Elder Ballard, who is with us today, lovingly taught, "Great things are wrought through simple and small things. . . . Our small and simple acts of kindness and service will accumulate into a life filled with love for Heavenly Father."[25]

I testify that the gift of the Sabbath day is from our loving Heavenly Father as a sign of his love for us. He has given it to us to help us remember his greatest gift—the gift of his Beloved Son. That we will "always remember him" as our gift in return is my prayer, in the name of Jesus Christ, amen.[26]

Linda K. Burton, "Our Sabbath Day Gifts," Utah South Area Conference, Sept. 13, 2015, Brigham Young University, Provo, UT, typescript, CHL.

RESOLVING CONFLICTS USING GOSPEL PRINCIPLES

◇◇◇

GLADYS N. SITATI

Brigham Young University Women's Conference
Gordon B. Hinckley Alumni and Visitors Center,
Brigham Young University, Provo, Utah
April 27, 2016

Gladys Nang'oni Nassiuma Sitati (b. 1952) was raised to be a teacher.[1] The oldest of ten children, she attended Toloso primary school in her village of Chwele, Bungoma, Kenya. Her father taught English and math at a school farther away, and when he saw that his daughter learned readily, he took her with him to work so that he could personally prepare her to attend good boarding schools. By the age of eight, both of her parents had also taught her to cook so she could help care for the family when she was home.[2] Sitati met Joseph W. Sitati during her first year at the University of Nairobi, and she married him upon completion of her bachelor's degree in education in 1976.[3]

Joseph Sitati was also from Chwele; in fact, the two attended the same primary school but did not know each another because boys and girls studied separately. The Sitatis lived in Mombasa and later in Nairobi, having five children between 1977 and 1983 and at the same time supporting their younger brothers and sisters in their education. At the beginning of her teaching career, Gladys Sitati taught the school classes of three of her younger siblings. In 1983, she accepted a job in the overseas department at the Ministry of Education, working to facilitate the college education of Kenyan students outside of the country in places like India, Great Britain, and the United States.[4]

In 1985, an American Latter-day Saint couple living in Nairobi met the Sitatis at a friend's house and invited them to church. They were baptized in 1986.[5] Four years later, as Sitati was recovering from a surgery, she and her husband were thinking seriously

Gladys N. Sitati. 2016. Sitati is a former teacher and employee of Kenya's Ministry of Education. With her husband, Joseph Sitati, the first black African general authority, Sitati has addressed church congregations around the world. Photograph by James Findlay. (Courtesy Gladys Sitati.)

about church president Ezra Taft Benson's counsel that mothers should reject "the marketplace" and stay home full time with their children.[6] Deciding whether to keep her job was difficult. The Sitati children and Gladys's siblings worried whether the family would have enough money without her income. Further, it was common in Nairobi at the time for men to abandon their wives and children to start new families with other women, leaving their first families destitute. Confident her husband would continue to be faithful and that God would help to provide for their needs, Sitati resigned from her job.[7]

In Johannesburg, South Africa, in 1991, Joseph and Gladys Sitati and their children became the first Kenyan family to be sealed in the temple. Joseph received many church assignments, including as the first Kenyan district president, president of Kenya's first stake, area authority, president of the Nigeria Calabar Mission, and the first black African general authority. During these years, Sitati taught Sunday School, Primary, Young Women, Relief Society, and seminary. She wrote a brief history of the church in Kenya and served alongside her husband in the Nigeria Calabar Mission.[8]

During her mission in Nigeria, Sitati prayed to learn what to do for the missionaries in her care. Although most missionaries spoke some English, the majority needed help to improve both their spoken and written English. Sitati decided to teach thirty-minute English lessons every six weeks at zone conferences, and the mission eventually provided both a dictionary and the book *Common Mistakes in English* to every missionary. At zone conferences she assigned homework, and when missionaries sent their completed work to her, she would review and comment on it and then return it at the next zone conference.

Sitati also looked after missionaries' health concerns. They were entirely reliant on local doctors, who often felt insulted if patients wanted to know what they were being treated for. Sitati changed this practice, stipulating that doctors must communicate both with the missionaries and with her to continue working as physicians for the mission. She kept a health file on each of their eighty-six missionaries, and when health issues were routine, she treated them herself, reading up on diseases prevalent in the area. Common health problems led her to encourage missionaries to take their malaria pills, to eat healthy meals, and to exercise. She and Joseph prayed for the missionaries every day. "[We took] care of them the way [we] would [our own] children," she said. "I [couldn't] do it alone. . . . Whatever treatment I [prescribed] for them, [God would] add the healing." In addition to mentoring missionaries, Joseph arranged for them to have refrigerators and generators so they could keep their food fresh and have electric light for early morning and evening study.[9]

When Joseph's sister died in 2004, the Sitatis adopted her two children and two additional children of a deceased cousin. Although the youngest Sitati child was nineteen, all the children still lived at home, and almost doubling their family size was an adjustment. The Sitatis had held family councils as needed since they learned of them when first investigating the church, and family councils helped through this adjustment as well. The Sitati children continued to hold family councils on their own while their parents served a mission. Sitati often spoke about cultivating peace in companionships when she addressed missionaries—she had seen how cultural differences and disobedience could interfere with their working relationships. She gave the following discourse on the topic of contention at a Brigham Young University Women's Conference.[10]

THE SCRIPTURES WARN that "he that hath the spirit of contention is not of me."[11] However, we live in a world with differences of opinion and conflict. In our families, church classes, councils in the church, and interactions with our neighbors, we must avoid contention. What doctrines and principles teach us how to resolve conflict? In what ways can being "peaceable followers of Christ" help us deal with conflict as we also "stand as witnesses of God"?[12]

Sisters and brothers, I would like to share some personal thoughts and experiences about resolving conflicts and avoiding contention as we strive to live as peaceable followers of Jesus Christ and as we stand as his witnesses, according to the covenants we have made.

As I considered the topic of our discussion, I wondered if there is anyone I know who has lived a life without conflict and contention. Contention comes easily, even with those we truly love and desire the best for. It is difficult to always be on guard and to always remember who we are when those we love and are close to do things that we sincerely disagree with or things that provoke us.

Let me mention a few areas from which contention between people can arise:

1. Lack of communication, which leads to misunderstanding, wrong expectations, and undesirable conclusions, distrust, and suspicion.
2. Making rush judgments and assumptions about others, which leads to misrepresentation of other people's intentions and to hurting other people's feelings.
3. A competitive spirit driven by pride, which fuels dislike, feelings of anger, and isolation.
4. Differing cultural values, which often lead to distrust, suspicion, prejudice, and profiling of others.

Conflict and contention are not inevitable. What we do to prevent or escalate it is a choice we make. In the Book of Mormon, we read of a people who lived a peaceful and happy life together for many generations—after they were visited and taught by the resurrected Christ.

> And it came to pass that there was no contention in the land, because of the love of God which did dwell in the hearts of the people.
>
> And there were no envyings, nor strifes, nor tumults, nor whoredoms, nor lyings, nor murders, nor any manner of lasciviousness; and surely there could not be a happier people among all the people who had been created by the hand of God.
>
> There were no robbers, nor murderers, neither were there Lamanites, nor any manner of -ites; but they were in one, the children of Christ, and heirs to the kingdom of God.
>
> And how blessed were they! For the Lord did bless them in all their doings; yea, even they were blessed and prospered until an hundred and ten years had passed away; and the first generation from Christ had passed away, and there was no contention in all the land.[13]

How did these people manage to live such a peaceful life for many generations? The people embraced the teachings of the Savior, which became the standard by which they governed all their relationships, with God and with each other.

As a convert to the Church of Jesus Christ of Latter-day Saints, I have come to understand that if we, who are followers of Jesus Christ, adopt and emulate his life and teachings as our standard of personal living and the norm by which we relate to other people, we would eradicate conflict in our families and communities and also bring happiness and peace in all the land, as these Nephites did in their time.

May I share with you five of the principles we have been taught that can help us to avoid conflict and contention.

The first principle is having faith in the Lord Jesus Christ.

The Apostle Paul taught that "faith is the substance of things hoped for, the evidence of things not seen."[14]

And Christ has said, "If ye will have faith in me ye shall have power to do whatsoever thing is expedient in me."[15]

Faith is a principle of action and power, and whenever we work toward a worthy goal, we are exercising our faith.[16] When we believe in Christ, we have hope in what we do; we exemplify his attributes in our lives; and for these things, he blesses us.

In the course of our labors, as we exercise patience, meekness, and humility, with purity of heart, our spirituality will grow and flourish. Our actions can then transcend all human barriers, including cultural, economic, and political associations.

I have seen this type of faith in a branch in Salt Lake City, known as the Swahili Branch, where most of the members are refugees from Swahili-speaking countries of East Africa.[17] These members have been joined by volunteer citizens of this country, who have given of themselves, their resources, and their time to teach these brothers and sisters and their families a variety of skills—such as how to live and travel in the USA, where to find schools and jobs, how to prioritize the family, and the importance of teaching the gospel in the home. When these volunteers initially meet these refugee families, they communicate through an interpreter, as many of these brothers and sisters are not yet fluent in the English language. The helpers soon learn a few words of the tribal dialects spoken by the refugees, which increases trust between them and enhances the learning and the understanding. Eventually, their relationship becomes cordial. These devoted helpers teach and work with these brothers and sisters, with much faith and diligence, to first, enable them to become rooted in Christ, and second, to settle down so they no longer see themselves as strangers in this land. At ward gatherings, for example, they enjoy eating each other's food. Recently, I was delighted to see a photo of some of these sisters on the cover page of the general conference issue of the *Ensign* and *Liahona,* as they sang in the stake choir at the women's session of conference.[18] You can imagine how far they have come, through much love and much diligence made possible by the infinite power of God.

Elder Richard G. Scott counsels us: "Reach out to those living in adverse circumstances. Be a true friend. This kind of enduring friendship is like asphalt that fills the potholes of life and makes the journey smoother and more pleasant. . . . Welcome into your home others who need to be strengthened by such an experience. . . . Recognize the good in others, not their stains. At times a stain needs appropriate attention to be cleansed, but always build on his or her virtues."[19]

The Savior teaches us, "And if any man among you be strong in the Spirit, let him take with him him that is weak, that he may be edified in all meekness, that he may become strong also."[20]

If we do this, any prejudices and fears we may have had will melt away, as our knowledge and our love for those we live among increases.

The second principle that can help us avoid conflict is being worthy to have the companionship of the Holy Ghost in our lives.

One of the main influences of the Holy Ghost is to help us find peace in this life and fill our hearts with love for ourselves and for others, through his guidance.

"By the power of the Holy Ghost ye may know the truth of all things."[21]

In a situation of developing conflict, the Holy Ghost may help us best when we deliberately think about the problem in advance. This counsel given to Oliver Cowdery may also apply to us:

"Behold, you have not understood; you have supposed that I would give it unto you, when you took no thought save it was to ask me.

"But, behold, I say unto you, that you must study it out in your mind; then you must ask me if it be right."[22]

We could therefore write down several possible actions to take that could help us avoid the contention. After pondering and deciding on the best action to take, we could humbly go to Heavenly Father in prayer to ask for his approval. He will send the Holy Ghost to provide a confirming witness and to guide us on actual things to do. To have the full benefit of that witness and guidance, we need to trust the Lord and his timing and be ready to do all that we can.

The third principle that can help us is prayer.

Prayer often goes together with fasting, especially when we are petitioning the Lord for a special blessing.

Prayer affirms our faith in our Heavenly Father and in the Lord Jesus Christ. It affirms our humility and our trust in the Savior's atoning power to intervene on our behalf. In a letter to the Romans, Paul explained it this way: "The Spirit also helpeth our infirmities: for we know not what we should pray for as we ought: but the Spirit itself maketh intercession for us with groanings which cannot be uttered. . . . And we know that all things work together for good to them that love God. . . . If God be for us, who can be against us?"[23]

The Lord also teaches us that when we are sincere and persistent in our prayers, we shall be answered.[24]

Who should we pray for?

Christ taught: "Ye have heard that it hath been said, Thou shalt love thy neighbour, and hate thine enemy. But I say unto you, Love your enemies, bless them that curse you, do good to them that hate you, and pray for them which despitefully use you, and persecute you."[25]

A story told by President Howard W. Hunter when he was a bishop illustrates the workings of this principle. A member of his ward came to him to tell him there was a man in the congregation he did not like. President Hunter told the brother to go home and pray for this man morning and evening and then report back after two weeks. When the brother came back, he said that he had learned that the man had problems and needed help. He was going to help the man.[26] Such experiences give us the hope to pray for those we have bad feelings against or those who have done wrong against us. Who knows? They probably need our help.

I wish to add here that most things that we fret about—what someone has said about us or done to us—do not contribute to their salvation or to ours. They are things of no consequence compared to what God has for all of us in his glorious realm. Our human exteriors may be different, but inside of us, we are the same. We feel bad when we are treated unfairly by others or when we are dismissed, not respected, or discriminated against. If thinking well of other people does not come easily to us, let us pray for this valuable gift. "Let virtue garnish thy thoughts unceasingly; then shall thy confidence wax strong in the presence of God."[27]

If our thoughts are pure, the Spirit will confirm this reality to those we associate with. I have come to know that the Spirit of God does not lie.

Recently, I read an article in the *Deseret News* on prayer, by Kelsey Dallas, which I will summarize thus: She refers to prayer as a conflict resolution tool that couples can use to strengthen and establish peace in their marriages. Individual and joint prayer practices can lay the groundwork for relatively conflict-free companionships, especially when couples view God as a Deity who loves them and who can bless their relationship to be happy and successful. Such couples, as they pray daily, will call upon God to bless them to mind each other's well-being.[28]

The fourth principle I wish to talk about is forgiveness.

Suppose we have done our very best to live peacefully with our neighbors, but somehow conflicts arise. What shall we do?

Peter was interested in the answer to that question and asked: "Lord, how oft shall my brother sin against me, and I forgive him? till seven times? Jesus saith unto him, I say not unto thee, Until seven times: but, Until seventy times seven."[29]

Following this pattern will enable us to resolve all disputes, find peace, and make many friends.

On this subject of forgiveness, President Gordon B. Hinckley taught: "We see the need for [forgiveness] in the homes of the people, where tiny molehills of misunderstanding are fanned into mountains of argument. We see it among neighbors, where insignificant differences lead to undying bitterness. We see it in business associates who quarrel and refuse to compromise and forgive when, in most instances, if there were a willingness to sit down together and speak quietly one to another, the matter could be resolved to the blessing of all. Rather, they spend their days nurturing grudges and planning retribution."[30]

Many of us find it difficult to forgive those who have wronged us. We need to pray that we may be able to do so with the help of the Savior's atoning power.

Those who have forgiven know the joy and freedom that attends forgiving. We are happier, less complaining, and pleasant to be around.

The fifth principle is love.

Speaking during the Sunday morning session of general conference two years ago, President Thomas S. Monson taught:

> Love is the very essence of the gospel, and Jesus Christ is our Exemplar. His life was a legacy of love. . . .
>
> May we begin now, this very day, to express love to all of God's children, whether they be our family members, our friends, mere acquaintances, or total strangers. As we arise each morning, let us determine to respond with love and kindness to whatever might come our way.

President Monson also said,

> We cannot truly love God if we do not love our fellow travelers on this mortal journey. Likewise, we cannot . . . love our fellowmen if we do not love God, the Father of us all. . . . We are all spirit children of our Heavenly Father and, as such, are brothers and sisters. As we keep this truth in mind, loving all of God's children will become easier.[31]

This truth, as taught by President Monson, is the perfect way to be at peace with other people, starting with our families. We start by acknowledging each other. Asking family members how they slept when they wake up in the morning brings a good spirit in the home.

Among people of the islands of the Pacific and in Africa (except in the cities), when you meet someone, you stop and greet them. You inquire after their families. In this way, you get to connect with the person and to establish a friendly rapport.

The Savior commands us to love all men:

> For if ye love them which love you, what reward have ye? do not even the publicans the same?

> And if ye salute your brethren only, what do ye more than others? do not even the publicans so?
>
> Be ye therefore perfect, even as your Father which is in heaven is perfect.[32]

I have found that love is a powerful tool in our hands. We are created to love and to be loved. But the spirit of love has been overtaken by worldly aspirations, such as the desire to be seen as being better than others, greed, lust, selfishness, pride, and other ungodly habits.

Our Savior Jesus Christ is the embodiment of love. When he had been nailed on the cross, was experiencing extreme pain, and the soldiers were abusive to him, he prayed to the Father to forgive them, saying that they knew not what they were doing. What love! We need to have this kind of love in our hearts to live peacefully with other people.

As I grew up in a family of ten children, we sometimes disagreed with each other, but there were no prolonged hurtful feelings because our parents took care to instill a peaceful, loving environment in the home. When we grew up and each of us left home to settle down on our own, we continued working together cooperatively as we united in efforts to support our aging parents. This arrangement worked well until a few years ago when my father passed away.

The bond that held us together started to weaken. True to the patterns we read about in the Book of Mormon, groups started to form and faultfinding became a favorite pastime for some.

Being the oldest child of my parents, I listened to each one's complaints and counseled with them individually over a number of years. But the situation continued to get worse. So, while preparing to go for our home leave last December, we decided we would try to bring peace between the various groups that had formed and called a family meeting.

To resolve the contention, everyone was given time to speak out their feelings without interruption. As each spoke, we realized that some of them had been hurting for a long time. They spoke earnestly as they addressed my husband, as if pleading with him to help. Next, my husband addressed each speaker, paraphrasing their complaints and asking if they agreed with the summary. Then he asked each one again, from the first speaker to the last one, what they were personally willing to do to bring peace, irrespective of what anyone else did.

Next, we discussed the responses using the wonderful scripture found in Philippians, which reads:

> Fulfil ye my joy, that ye be likeminded, having the same love, being of one accord, of one mind.

> Let nothing be done through strife or vainglory; but in lowliness of mind let each esteem other better than themselves.
>
> Look not every man on his own things, but every man also on the things of others.[33]

Concluding that family meeting, my husband thanked everyone for their openness and expressed hope that we would find peace in our lives by frequently referring to the wise counsel of the Apostle Paul. There was a spirit of great relief and peace at the end of the meeting. We observe that in the last four months since that meeting, we have not heard about any more contention, for which I am deeply grateful to the Lord.

Elder Dallin H. Oaks, in his address during the October 2014 general conference, counseled us, among other things, to follow after the things that make for peace as we live among other people; to practice civility when others have different opinions, to forgo contention and practice respect, and to be kind to those who choose not to keep the commandments of God. He emphasized that kindness is powerful.[34]

As much as we can, we should keep in touch with those we disagree with, especially family members. We let them know we love them by inviting them to family activities and finding good things to say about them. Given time, the Lord may soften their hearts. I believe that an important ingredient in the success of our family meeting is that we gave a special family gift to each of my siblings so that as they came to the meeting, no one was in any doubt about our feelings toward them.

When we have a troubled relationship, we need to ask ourselves these questions: What do I honestly desire for this relationship? What would I do if I were in their shoes? What am I willing to give up to establish peace?

This counsel from King Benjamin is helpful as it reminds us of the covenants we have made with God:

> And again I say unto you as I have said before, that as ye have come to the knowledge of the glory of God, or if ye have known of his goodness and have tasted of his love, and have received a remission of your sins, which causeth such exceedingly great joy in your souls, even so I would that ye should remember . . . his goodness . . . and humble yourselves even in the depths of humility, calling on the name of the Lord daily, and standing steadfastly in the faith. . . .
>
> And behold, I say unto you that if ye do this ye shall always rejoice, and be filled with the love of God. . . .

> And ye will not have a mind to injure one another, but to live peaceably, and to render to every man according to that which is his due.[35]

Let me summarize again the five principles we can apply to resolve conflict and contention in our associations:

First, faith in the Savior Jesus Christ is the beginning of a desire to trust the Lord in our circumstances, knowing that he will share our burdens and bring comfort to our souls.

Second, faith in the Lord Jesus Christ leads us to do those things that invite the companionship of the Holy Ghost, which can fill us with "hope and perfect love" toward all people and all things.[36]

Third, "diligence unto prayer" helps us to continue to enjoy the companionship of the Holy Ghost, to be filled with love, and to overcome the temptations of the adversary that may come through provocation to conflict.[37]

Fourth, filled with the love of God, we can not only forgive others but help to give them a vision and a better hope of what they can become.

Finally, filled with the love of God, we can transcend all barriers to peace, harmony, and unity with all people.

As I conclude my thoughts, I would urge each one of us to "press forward with a steadfastness in Christ . . . and a love of God and of all men" and to heed the Savior's counsel that contention is of the devil and should be done away with.[38]

May each one of us find love and peace wherever we are in the world that we may stand as true witnesses of our Lord and Savior Jesus Christ and through his atoning power be able to do all things.

This I leave with you, in the name of Jesus Christ, amen.

Gladys N. Sitati, "Resolving Conflicts Using Gospel Principles," BYU Women's Conference address, Apr. 27, 2016, Brigham Young University, Provo, UT, typescript, CHL.

REFERENCE MATERIAL

APPENDIX

◇◇◇

LATTER-DAY SAINT WOMEN SPEAKERS IN GENERAL CONFERENCE

THIS TABLE CONTAINS the names of all the women who have spoken in the semiannual general conference of the Church of Jesus Christ of Latter-day Saints, or in special meetings that occurred in conjunction with general conference. For example, Aaronic Priesthood meetings, also called bishop's conferences, were held from 1921 through 1963 and attended by male ward and stake leaders who oversaw the daily workings of their congregations, including the Aaronic Priesthood and Young Women. Welfare sessions, sometimes called agricultural meetings, began in 1937 and trained male and female stake and ward welfare workers on resources and procedures. Welfare sessions were discontinued in 1982. Other special sessions or meetings discussed missionary work, the Indian Placement Program, and genealogical work. On occasion, women spoke at these meetings.

The table does not include women's speeches from Relief Society general conferences or women's meetings, MIA June conferences, Young Women meetings and firesides, Primary conferences, or Sunday School conferences. Women spoke regularly at these auxiliary conferences and meetings, and their words were recorded in the *Woman's Exponent, Relief Society Magazine, Young Woman's Journal, Improvement Era, Children's Friend, Ensign, New Era, Liahona, Deseret News,* and elsewhere. Auxiliary conferences ended in 1975, replaced by various iterations of a general women's meeting and by training conducted on a regional and stake level. Beginning in the fall of 2014, the general women's meeting was recognized as a session of general conference; it is included on this table from that date.

Sources for information in this table include official Conference Reports, the *Deseret News,* and audiovisual collections of welfare sessions at the Church History Library in Salt Lake City.

Date	Speaker	Session
Oct. 8, 1845	Lucy Mack Smith	general session
Oct. 7, 1879	Zina D. H. Young	priesthood and MIA meeting
Apr. 5, 1908	Rachel H. Leatham	outdoor overflow meeting
Apr. 5, 1908	Martha Mary Langenbucher	outdoor overflow meeting
Apr. 4, 1909	Lillian V. Jones	outdoor overflow meeting
Oct. 5, 1929	Louise Y. Robison	general session
Oct. 5, 1929	Ruth May Fox	general session
Oct. 5, 1929	May Anderson	general session
Apr. 9, 1930	Louise Y. Robison	general session
Apr. 9, 1930	Ruth May Fox	general session
Apr. 9, 1930	May Anderson	general session
Oct. 5, 1930	Louise Y. Robison	general session
Oct. 5, 1930	Ruth May Fox	general session
Oct. 5, 1930	May Anderson	general session
Oct. 2, 1937	May Anderson	Aaronic Priesthood meeting
Oct. 5, 1940	Amy Brown Lyman	welfare meeting
Apr. 5, 1941	Marguerite Burton	welfare meeting
Apr. 5, 1941	Zephyr Doyle	welfare meeting
Apr. 5, 1941	Donna D. Sorensen	welfare meeting
Oct. 4, 1941	Alice M. Graves	welfare meeting
Oct. 4, 1941	Amy Brown Lyman	welfare meeting
Oct. 5, 1945	Verna W. Goddard	Aaronic Priesthood meeting
Apr. 4, 1947	Belle S. Spafford	Aaronic Priesthood meeting
Apr. 6, 1948	Mildred Thompson	Aaronic Priesthood meeting
Apr. 5, 1949	Belle S. Spafford	welfare meeting
Apr. 3, 1959	Theda Farnsworth	missionary meeting
Apr. 7, 1967	Belle S. Spafford	welfare session
Sept. 30, 1967	Carolyn Dunn	welfare session
Sept. 30, 1967	Belle S. Spafford	welfare session
Apr. 6, 1968	Belle S. Spafford	welfare session
Oct. 4, 1968	Virginia Casuse	Indian Placement meeting
Oct. 5, 1968	Belle S. Spafford	welfare session

Date	Speaker	Session
Apr. 5, 1969	Belle S. Spafford	welfare session
Oct. 4, 1969	Belle S. Spafford	welfare session
Apr. 4, 1970	Belle S. Spafford	welfare session
Oct. 3, 1970	Belle S. Spafford	welfare session
Apr. 3, 1971	Belle S. Spafford	welfare session
Oct. 2, 1971	Belle S. Spafford	welfare session
Apr. 8, 1972	Belle S. Spafford	welfare session
Oct. 7, 1972	Belle S. Spafford	welfare session
Apr. 7, 1973	Belle S. Spafford	welfare session
Oct. 6, 1973	Belle S. Spafford	welfare session
Apr. 6, 1974	Belle S. Spafford	welfare session
Oct. 5, 1974	Belle S. Spafford	welfare session
Apr. 5, 1975	Barbara B. Smith	welfare session
Oct. 4, 1975	Barbara B. Smith	welfare session
Apr. 3, 1976	Barbara B. Smith	welfare session
Oct. 2, 1976	Barbara B. Smith	welfare session
Apr. 2, 1977	Barbara B. Smith	welfare session
Oct. 1, 1977	Barbara B. Smith	welfare session
Apr. 1, 1978	Barbara B. Smith	welfare session
Sept. 30, 1978	Barbara B. Smith	welfare session
Oct. 6, 1979	Barbara B. Smith	welfare session
Apr. 5, 1980	Shirley W. Thomas	welfare session
Oct. 4, 1980	Barbara B. Smith	welfare session
Apr. 4, 1981	Barbara B. Smith	welfare session
Oct. 3, 1981	Barbara B. Smith	welfare session
Oct. 3, 1981	JoAnn Randall	welfare session
Apr. 3, 1982	Barbara B. Smith	welfare session
Oct. 2, 1982	Barbara B. Smith	welfare session
Apr. 7, 1984	Elaine A. Cannon	general session
Apr. 7, 1984	Barbara B. Smith	general session
Apr. 8, 1984	Barbara Ann Winder	general session
Apr. 8, 1984	Ardeth G. Kapp	general session
Apr. 3, 1988	Dwan J. Young	general session
Oct. 2, 1988	Michaelene P. Grassli	general session
Apr. 2, 1989	Joy F. Evans	general session
Oct. 1, 1989	Jayne B. Malan	general session

Date	Speaker	Session
Apr. 1, 1990	Barbara W. Winder	general session
Apr. 1, 1990	Elaine L. Jack	general session
Oct. 7, 1990	Ruth B. Wright	general session
Apr. 7, 1991	Janette C. Hales	general session
Oct. 6, 1991	Aileen H. Clyde	general session
Apr. 5, 1992	Ardeth G. Kapp	general session
Apr. 5, 1992	Janette C. Hales	general session
Oct. 4, 1992	Betty Jo N. Jepsen	general session
Apr. 4, 1993	Chieko N. Okazaki	general session
Oct. 3, 1993	Virginia H. Pearce	general session
Apr. 2, 1994	Elaine L. Jack	general session
Apr. 3, 1994	Ruth B. Wright	general session
Oct. 1, 1994	Michaelene P. Grassli	general session
Oct. 2, 1994	Patricia P. Pinegar	general session
Apr. 1, 1995	Aileen H. Clyde	general session
Apr. 2, 1995	Bonnie D. Parkin	general session
Sept. 30, 1995	Janette Hales Beckham	general session
Oct. 1, 1995	Anne G. Wirthlin	general session
Apr. 6, 1996	Chieko N. Okazaki	general session
Apr. 7, 1996	Susan L. Warner	general session
Oct. 5, 1996	Virginia H. Pearce	general session
Oct. 6, 1996	Elaine L. Jack	general session
Apr. 5, 1997	Patricia P. Pinegar	general session
Apr. 6, 1997	Elaine L. Jack	general session
Oct. 4, 1997	Mary Ellen Smoot	general session
Oct. 5, 1997	Janette Hales Beckham	general session
Apr. 4, 1998	Anne G. Wirthlin	general session
Apr. 5, 1998	Margaret D. Nadauld	general session
Oct. 3, 1998	Virginia U. Jensen	general session
Oct. 4, 1998	Susan L. Warner	general session
Apr. 3, 1999	Carol B. Thomas	general session
Apr. 4, 1999	Sheri L. Dew	general session
Oct. 2, 1999	Sharon G. Larsen	general session
Oct. 3, 1999	Patricia P. Pinegar	general session
Apr. 1, 2000	Coleen K. Menlove	general session
Apr. 2, 2000	Mary Ellen W. Smoot	general session

Date	Speaker	Session
Oct. 7, 2000	Margaret D. Nadauld	general session
Oct. 8, 2000	Virginia U. Jensen	general session
Mar. 31, 2001	Sydney S. Reynolds	general session
Apr. 1, 2001	Carol B. Thomas	general session
Oct. 6, 2001	Sheri L. Dew	general session
Oct. 7, 2001	Sharon G. Larsen	general session
Apr. 6, 2002	Mary Ellen W. Smoot	general session
Apr. 7, 2002	Gayle M. Clegg	general session
Apr. 7, 2002	Bonnie D. Parkin	general session
Oct. 5, 2002	Coleen K. Menlove	general session
Oct. 6, 2002	Margaret D. Nadauld	general session
Apr. 5, 2003	Kathleen H. Hughes	general session
Apr. 6, 2003	Susan W. Tanner	general session
Oct. 4, 2003	Anne C. Pingree	general session
Oct. 5, 2003	Sydney S. Reynolds	general session
Apr. 3, 2004	Gayle M. Clegg	general session
Apr. 4, 2004	Julic B. Beck	general session
Oct. 2, 2004	Bonnie D. Parkin	general session
Oct. 3, 2004	Elaine S. Dalton	general session
Apr. 2, 2005	Coleen K. Menlove	general session
Apr. 3, 2005	Kathleen H. Hughes	general session
Oct. 1, 2005	Susan W. Tanner	general session
Oct. 2, 2005	Cheryl C. Lant	general session
Apr. 1, 2006	Julie B. Beck	general session
Apr. 2, 2006	Anne C. Pingree	general session
Sept. 30, 2006	Elaine S. Dalton	general session
Oct. 1, 2006	Margaret S. Lifferth	general session
Mar. 31, 2007	Bonnie D. Parkin	general session
Apr. 1, 2007	Vicki F. Matsumori	general session
Oct. 6, 2007	Mary N. Cook	general session
Oct. 7, 2007	Julie B. Beck	general session
Apr. 5, 2008	Cheryl C. Lant	general session
Apr. 6, 2008	Susan W. Tanner	general session
Oct. 4, 2008	Silvia H. Allred	general session
Oct. 5, 2008	Elaine S. Dalton	general session
Apr. 4, 2009	Margaret S. Lifferth	general session

Date	Speaker	Session
Apr. 5, 2009	Barbara Thompson	general session
Oct. 3, 2009	Vicki F. Matsumori	general session
Oct. 4, 2009	Ann M. Dibb	general session
Apr. 3, 2010	Julie B. Beck	general session
Apr. 4, 2010	Cheryl C. Lant	general session
Oct. 2, 2010	Rosemary M. Wixom	general session
Oct. 3, 2010	Mary N. Cook	general session
Apr. 2, 2011	Jean A. Stevens	general session
Apr. 3, 2011	Silvia H. Allred	general session
Oct. 1, 2011	Barbara Thompson	general session
Oct. 2, 2011	Elaine S. Dalton	general session
Mar. 31, 2012	Cheryl A. Esplin	general session
Apr. 1, 2012	Julie B. Beck	general session
Oct. 6, 2012	Ann M. Dibb	general session
Oct. 7, 2012	Linda K. Burton	general session
Apr. 6, 2013	Elaine S. Dalton	general session
Apr. 7, 2013	Rosemary M. Wixom	general session
Oct. 5, 2013	Carole M. Stephens	general session
Oct. 6, 2013	Bonnie L. Oscarson	general session
Apr. 5, 2014	Linda S. Reeves	general session
Apr. 6, 2014	Jean A. Stevens	general session
Sept. 27, 2014	Linda K. Burton	general women's session
Sept. 27, 2014	Jean A. Stevens	general women's session
Sept. 27, 2014	Neill F. Marriott	general women's session
Oct. 4, 2014	Cheryl A. Esplin	general session
Oct. 5, 2014	Carol F. McConkie	general session
Mar. 28, 2015	Cheryl A. Esplin	general women's session
Mar. 28, 2015	Carole M. Stephens	general women's session
Mar. 28, 2015	Bonnie L. Oscarson	general women's session
Apr. 4, 2015	Linda K. Burton	general session
Apr. 5, 2015	Rosemary M. Wixom	general session
Sept. 26, 2015	Rosemary M. Wixom	general women's session
Sept. 26, 2015	Linda S. Reeves	general women's session
Sept. 26, 2015	Carol F. McConkie	general women's session
Oct. 3, 2015	Neill F. Marriott	general session
Oct. 4, 2015	Carole M. Stephens	general session

Date	Speaker	Session
Mar. 26, 2016	Cheryl A. Esplin	general women's session
Mar. 26, 2016	Neill F. Marriott	general women's session
Mar. 26, 2016	Linda K. Burton	general women's session
Apr. 2, 2016	Mary R. Durham	general session
Apr. 3, 2016	Bonnie L. Oscarson	general session
Sept. 24, 2016	Jean B. Bingham	general women's session
Sept. 24, 2016	Carole M. Stephens	general women's session
Sept. 24, 2016	Bonnie L. Oscarson	general women's session
Oct. 1, 2016	Carol F. McConkie	general session
Oct. 2, 2016	Linda S. Reeves	general session

ACKNOWLEDGMENTS

◇◇◇

MANY INDIVIDUALS AND INSTITUTIONS have made this volume possible. We give special thanks to administrators and officials of the Church of Jesus Christ of Latter-day Saints, Salt Lake City, for sponsoring the project, and to the management and staff of the Church History Library, Salt Lake City, where the majority of the documents reproduced in this volume are located.

We acknowledge with appreciation the contributions of many other individuals from the Church History Department. Richard E. Turley Jr. provided helpful direction throughout the process. Lisa Olsen Tait reviewed the entire manuscript and offered crucial feedback. Jeff Crossley and Matthew Geilman translated Spanish correspondence. Leslie Sherman helped establish styles for the endnotes. Stephanie Steed and Adam McLain provided editorial assistance. Jeffrey G. Cannon and Kay Darowski assisted with illustrations and permissions. Ben Ellis Godfrey organized the accompanying website, churchhistorianspress.org; Ben Godfrey, John Heath, and Debra Xavier helped with marketing. Kiersten Olson provided administrative support.

A number of other people, many of them missionaries, student interns, and volunteers at the Church History Library, contributed their research skills to the volume: Craig Dee Anderson, Megan Beth Armknecht, Marlene Breti, Lilly Christensen, Rebekah Clark, Steven James Fluckiger, Cathy Gilmore, Elise Marchant Godfrey, Joan Harding, Janelle Higbee, Tara Jes Huish, Cathryn Jane Hulse, Shalyn Schmelter, Amy Amelia Anne Wallace, and Kristine Lee Wright.

Thanks to the management and staff of Deseret Book Company, Salt Lake City, for their expertise in designing, printing, distributing, and marketing the volume. We particularly acknowledge Sheri L. Dew, Laurel Christensen Day, Lisa Roper, Richard Erickson, and David Kimball. We are also grateful to Margaret A. Hogan for careful proofreading and to Rachel Lyon for creating the index in this volume.

We extend special thanks to Jill Mulvay Derr, formerly of the Church History Department; Colleen McDannell of the University of Utah; Susanna Morrill of Lewis and Clark University; and Jana Reiss of the Religion News Service, each of whom reviewed a draft of the volume and offered valuable comments and feedback.

In addition to the Church History Library, several other libraries and repositories have provided critical materials and assistance: L. Tom Perry Special Collections, Harold B. Lee Library, Brigham Young University; Special Collections, J. Willard Marriott Library, University of Utah; Utah State Historical Society; and International Society Daughters of Utah Pioneers.

NOTES

◇◇◇

Sources presented in the notes include the full reference for the first mention in each chapter, after which a short citation form is generally used within the notes for that chapter. Citations to the Book of Mormon and other Latter-day Saint scriptures usually reference to modern editions. Sources come from a variety of repositories and publications. The names of the following frequently cited repositories are abbreviated in citations: Church History Library, the Church of Jesus Christ of Latter-day Saints, Salt Lake City (CHL); Family History Library, the Church of Jesus Christ of Latter-day Saints, Salt Lake City (FHL); L. Tom Perry Special Collections, Harold B. Lee Library, Brigham Young University, Provo (BYU); and Special Collections and Archives, J. Willard Marriott Library, University of Utah, Salt Lake City (UU). Chapter numbers, rather than chapter titles or page numbers, are used in internal cross-references.

INTRODUCTION

1. Sarah S. Leavitt, Autobiography, 1875, 10, 15, Juanita Leone Leavitt Pulsipher Brooks Papers, 1928–1981, Utah State Historical Society, Salt Lake City; see also Sarah Sturtevant Leavitt, "History of Sarah Studevant Leavitt," ed. Juanita Leavitt Pulsipher [Brooks], typescript, 1919, 8, 12, CHL; Jeremiah 20:9; and 1 Corinthians 14:15.
2. "Exhort," and "expound," in *An American Dictionary of the English Language,* ed. Noah Webster (New York: S. Converse, 1828).
3. Revelation, July 1830 (Doctrine and Covenants 25), in Jill Mulvay Derr, Carol Cornwall Madsen, Kate Holbrook, and Matthew J. Grow, eds., *The First Fifty Years of Relief Society: Key Documents in Latter-day Saint Women's History* (Salt Lake City: Church Historian's Press, 2016), 17–21.
4. Along with other women, Emma Smith organized prayer groups and feasts for the poor in the 1830s. She opened her home to the sick, the orphaned, and other visitors. (Carol Cornwall Madsen, "The 'Elect Lady' Revelation [D&C 25]: Its Historical and Doctrinal Context," in *Sperry Symposium Classics: The Doctrine and Covenants,* ed. Craig K. Manscill [Provo, UT: Religious Studies Center, Brigham Young University, 2004], 124, 126; Mark Lyman Staker, *Hearken, O Ye People: The Historical Setting of Joseph Smith's Ohio Revelations* [Salt Lake City: Greg Kofford Books, 2009], 244–245; Lucy Mack Smith, History, 1844–1845, 18 books, bk. 14, [5]; bk. 15, [12], CHL; Linda King Newell and Valeen Tippetts Avery, *Mormon Enigma: Emma Hale Smith,* 2nd ed. [Urbana: University of Illinois Press, 1994], 84–90, 132).
5. See chapter 3 herein.
6. Nauvoo Relief Society Minute Book, Mar. 17, 1842, 8, in Derr et al., *First Fifty Years,* 32. For much of the nineteenth century, the terms *ordain* and *set apart* were used interchangeably (and sometimes together) in connection with women's appointment to offices. (See Derr et al., *First Fifty Years,* xxxiii.)
7. Nauvoo Relief Society Minute Book, June 9, 1842, [63], in Derr et al., *First Fifty Years,* 79.
8. See 1 Timothy 2:11–12; and Ann Braude, "Women's History *Is* American Religious History," in

Retelling U.S. Religious History, ed. Thomas A. Tweed (Berkeley: University of California Press, 1997), 87–107.

9. See Ann Braude, *Sisters and Saints: Women and American Religion* (New York: Oxford University Press, 2008), 31–35.
10. See Titus 2:1–5; and Thomas Hutchinson, *The History of the Province of Massachusetts-Bay, from the Charter of King William and Queen Mary, in 1691, until the Year 1750* (Boston: Thomas and John Fleet, 1767), 485.
11. Jon Butler, *Awash in a Sea of Faith: Christianizing the American People* (Cambridge, MA: Harvard University Press, 1990), 164–166, 170, 178; Catherine A. Brekus, *Sarah Osborn's World: The Rise of Evangelical Christianity in Early America* (New Haven, CT: Yale University Press, 2013), 183–187; Rebecca Larson, *Daughters of Light: Quaker Women Preaching and Prophesying in the Colonies and Abroad, 1700–1775* (New York: Alfred A. Knopf, 1999), 10, 303–304; Stephen J. Stein, *The Shaker Experience in America: A History of the United Society of Believers* (New Haven, CT: Yale University Press, 1992), 133, 241, 256–272; Catherine A. Brekus, *Strangers and Pilgrims: Female Preaching in America, 1740–1845* (Chapel Hill: University of North Carolina Press, 1998), 8.
12. See Nathan O. Hatch, *The Democratization of American Christianity* (New Haven, CT: Yale University Press, 1989), 5; see also Doctrine and Covenants 43:8.
13. See chapters 1 and 2 herein.
14. Brekus, *Strangers and Pilgrims,* 280–281.
15. John H. Wigger, *Taking Heaven by Storm: Methodism and the Rise of Popular Christianity in America* (New York: Oxford University Press, 1998), 152–157; Brekus, *Strangers and Pilgrims,* 133.
16. See, for example, Maureen Ursenbach Beecher, "Women in Winter Quarters," in *Eliza and Her Sisters* (Salt Lake City: Aspen Books, 1991), 75–97; and Patty Bartlett Sessions, *Mormon Midwife: The 1846–1888 Diaries of Patty Bartlett Sessions,* ed. Donna Toland Smart (Logan: Utah State University Press, 1997), 32–124.
17. During the nineteenth century, Latter-day Saint women frequently administered blessings; at that time, Latter-day Saints generally understood the gift of healing as a gift of the Spirit available to all believers through their faith. On the administration of blessings, see "Joseph Smith's Teachings about Priesthood, Temple, and Women," Gospel Topics, accessed May 2, 2016, lds.org; Derr et al., *First Fifty Years,* xxi–xxv; Jonathan A. Stapley and Kristine Wright, "The Forms and the Power: The Development of Mormon Ritual Healing to 1847," *Journal of Mormon History* 35, no. 3 (Summer 2009): 42–87; and Jonathan A. Stapley and Kristine Wright, "Female Ritual Healing in Mormonism," *Journal of Mormon History* 37, no. 1 (Winter 2011): 1–85.
18. Derr et al., *First Fifty Years,* 179–182, 188–197, 221–226, 248; see also chapter 7 herein.
19. See chapters 9, 10, 11, 14, and 18 herein.
20. Derr et al., *First Fifty Years,* 561–564.
21. Lori D. Ginzberg, *Women and the Work of Benevolence: Morality, Politics, and Class in the Nineteenth-Century United States* (New Haven, CT: Yale University Press, 1990), 13–14.
22. Robert H. Abzug, *Cosmos Crumbling: American Reform and the Religious Imagination* (New York: Oxford University Press, 1994), 190–193, 204–220; Gerda Lerner, *The Grimké Sisters from South Carolina: Pioneers for Women's Rights and Abolition* (Chapel Hill: University of North Carolina Press, 2004).
23. Abzug, *Cosmos Crumbling,* 183–187; Elizabeth Cady Stanton, Susan B. Anthony, and Matilda Joslyn Page, eds., *History of Woman Suffrage,* 6 vols. (Rochester, NY: Susan B. Anthony, 1887), 1:70–71; Ginzberg, *Women and the Work of Benevolence,* 90, 101–103.
24. See Minutes of "Ladies Mass Meeting," Jan. 6, 1870, in Derr et al., *First Fifty Years,* 305–306.
25. See chapters 20, 21, and 22 herein.
26. For more on sacrament meetings and other church meetings in the nineteenth century, see Ronald W. Walker, "'Going to Meeting' in Salt Lake City's Thirteenth Ward, 1849–1881: A Microanalysis," in *New Views of Mormon History: A Collection of Essays in Honor of Leonard J. Arrington,* ed. Davis Bitton and Maureen Ursenbach Beecher (Salt Lake City: University of Utah

Press, 1987), 138–161; and William G. Hartley, *My Fellow Servants: Essays on the History of the Priesthood* (Provo, UT: BYU Studies, 2010), 343–349, 415–422.

27. See Madsen, "The 'Elect Lady' Revelation," 124; and Hartley, *My Fellow Servants,* 422–423.
28. These annual meetings—often called conjoint conferences or June conferences—were held around the first of June each year in honor of Brigham Young's birthday. (Susa Young Gates, *History of the Young Ladies' Mutual Improvement Association of the Church of Jesus Christ of Latter-day Saints* [Salt Lake City: Deseret News, 1911], 140–142, 221–222.)
29. Latter-day Saint women began participating in missionary work soon after the church was organized, often informally. Some married women served missions with their husbands before 1898. (See "Women with a Mission: Series Introduction," accessed May 24, 2016, history.lds.org; see also Carol Cornwall Madsen, "Mormon Missionary Wives in Nineteenth-Century Polynesia," in *Proclamation to the People: Nineteenth-Century Mormonism and the Pacific Basin Frontier,* ed. Laurie F. Maffly-Kipp and Reid L. Neilson [Salt Lake City: University of Utah Press, 2008], 142–169.)
30. Catherine A. Brekus, "Protestant Female Preaching in the United States," in *Encyclopedia of Women and Religion in North America,* ed. Rosemary Skinner Keller and Rosemary Radford Ruether, 3 vols. (Bloomington: Indiana University Press, 2006), 2:970–972; see also Pamela S. Nadell, *Women Who Would Be Rabbis* (Boston: Beacon Press, 1999).
31. See, for example, Debra Renee Kaufman, *Rachel's Daughters: Newly Orthodox Jewish Women* (New Brunswick, NJ: Rutgers University Press, 1991); Kathleen Sprows Cummings, *New Women of the Old Faith: Gender and American Catholicism in the Progressive Era* (Chapel Hill: University of North Carolina Press, 2009); and R. Marie Griffith, *God's Daughters: Evangelical Women and the Power of Submission* (Berkeley: University of California Press, 1997).
32. Women taught Sunday School courses to children and youth very early on in Utah. (Hartley, *My Fellow Servants,* 429–430; Walker, "'Going to Meeting' in Salt Lake City's Thirteenth Ward," 149–151.)
33. See, for example, Tremonton Ward, Bear River Stake, General Minutes, vol. 4, 1918–1923, Feb. 3, 1918, Aug. 28, 1921–Sept. 25, 1921, 3, 58–59; vol. 6, 1928–1930, Oct. 12–21, 1930, 158–160; vol. 7, 1931–1936, Mar. 17, 1935, 199, CHL; and Eleventh Ward, Ensign Stake, General Minutes, vol. 7, 1921–1922, Feb. 13, 1921, 101; vol. 8, 1923–1925, Jan. 28, 1923, Apr. 15, 1923, 2–3, 7; vol. 9, 1925–1934, Jan. 29, 1933, Sept. 24, 1933, 156, 169; vol. 10, 1934–1951, Aug. 8, 1937, May 30, 1943, 81, 211, CHL. While women spoke in meetings, only men who held the Aaronic or Melchizedek priesthood were permitted to pray in sacrament meeting from 1968 to 1978. (*General Handbook of Instructions,* no. 20 [Salt Lake City: The Church of Jesus Christ of Latter-day Saints, 1968], 44; Marvin K. Gardner, "Report of the Seminar for Regional Representatives," *Ensign* 8, no. 11 [Nov. 1978]: 100.)
34. *Handbook of Instructions,* no. 17 (Salt Lake City: The Church of Jesus Christ of Latter-day Saints, 1944), 48–49.
35. The first general Relief Society conference was held in 1889, and the organization continued to hold semiannual conferences until 1945. From 1945 to 1975, the Relief Society held only one conference per year, in September or October. That annual meeting was eventually replaced by today's general women's session. (Derr et al., *First Fifty Years,* 561–564; Jill Mulvay Derr, Janath Russell Cannon, and Maureen Ursenbach Beecher, *Women of Covenant: The Story of Relief Society* [Salt Lake City: Deseret Book, 1992], 378–379, 473n85; see also Appendix herein.)
36. "Verbatim Report of the Relief Society Annual General Conference of the Church of Jesus Christ of Latter-day Saints in Salt Lake City, Utah," Sept. 30–Oct. 2, 1975, 113, in Relief Society Annual Conference Proceedings, 1945–1975, CHL. In 1933, United States president Franklin D. Roosevelt popularized the notion of fireside chats with the first in a series of radio broadcasts by that name. The Latter-day Saint tradition of firesides began with Salt Lake Institute of Religion founder Lowell L. Bennion in 1935. Bennion invited students to join him for evening gospel discussions in a University Ward room that had a fireplace. (Douglas B. Craig, *Fireside Politics: Radio and Political Culture in the United States, 1920–1940* [Baltimore: Johns Hopkins University Press, 2000], 83–89; Sheridan R. Sheffield, R. Scott Lloyd, and Mike Cannon, "Some Things Uniquely LDS," *Church News,* Jan. 25, 1992.)

37. "Women's Fireside Addresses," *Ensign* 8, no. 11 (Nov. 1978): 102; "Young Women Fireside 1980," *New Era* 10, no. 6 (July 1980): 7.
38. Ernest L. Wilkinson and W. Cleon Skousen, *Brigham Young University: A School of Destiny* (Provo, UT: Brigham Young University Press, 1976), 67, 177, 608–610; Rose Marie Reid, "How the Gospel Influenced My Life," July 1, 1953, Brigham Young University Devotional Speeches, CHL.
39. Carol Lee Hawkins, "Brigham Young University Women's Conference: A History," June 1992, 1–4, in editors' possession. Oversight for the conference moved to the university president's office in 1984, and the conference has been cosponsored with the Relief Society since 1990.
40. The first general conference of the church was held in 1830, and general conference became a regular, semiannual event around 1840. (Paul H. Peterson, "Accommodating the Saints at General Conference," *BYU Studies* 41, no. 2 [2002]: 5–7; Kenneth W. Godfrey, "150 Years of General Conference," *Ensign* 11, no. 2 [Feb. 1981]: 66–74; M. Dallas Burnett, "General Conference," in *Encyclopedia of Mormonism*, ed. Daniel H. Ludlow, 5 vols. [New York: Macmillan, 1992], 1:307; see also Appendix herein.)
41. "General Relief Society Meeting," *Ensign* 10, no. 11 (Nov. 1980): 102. There was also a general women's meeting held in 1978. (Derr, Cannon, and Beecher, *Women of Covenant,* 378.)
42. "General Women's Meeting," *Ensign* 12, no. 5 (May 1982): 93.
43. "General Women's Meeting," *Ensign* 13, no. 11 (Nov. 1983): 81; Julie A. Dockstader, "Gift of Eternal Life Is Available to All," *Church News,* Oct. 2, 1993; *Ensign* 23, no. 11 (Nov. 1993): 3; *Ensign* 24, no. 5 (May 1994): 3.
44. "New Women's Meeting," *Church News,* Nov. 10, 2013.
45. Tad Walch, "LDS Church Confirms Women's Meeting Now Part of General Conference," *Deseret News,* Oct. 30, 2014; *Ensign* 44, no. 11 (Nov. 2014): 1.
46. See chapter 11 herein.
47. Morgan Utah Stake Relief Society Minutes and Records, vol. 1, 1878–1912, Oct. 24, 1879, 24, CHL.
48. Derr et al., *First Fifty Years,* 546–547.
49. Emily S. Richards, in "General Conference Relief Society," *Woman's Exponent* 30, no. 7 (Dec. 1901): 54.
50. Orson F. Whitney, *History of Utah,* 4 vols. (Salt Lake City: George Q. Cannon and Sons, 1904), 4:605.
51. Joseph Fielding Smith, "Relief Society—An Aid to the Priesthood," *Relief Society Magazine* 46, no. 1 (Jan. 1959): 4.
52. See chapter 1 herein.
53. As apostle Dallin H. Oaks taught in 2014, "When a woman—young or old—is set apart to preach the gospel as a full-time missionary, she is given priesthood authority to perform a priesthood function. The same is true when a woman is set apart to function as an officer or teacher in a church organization under the direction of one who holds the keys of the priesthood." (Dallin H. Oaks, "The Keys and Authority of the Priesthood," *Ensign* 44, no. 5 [May 2014]: 51.)
54. See chapter 45 herein.
55. See chapter 12 herein.
56. See chapter 47 herein.
57. Russell M. Nelson, "A Plea to My Sisters," *Ensign* 45, no. 11 (Nov. 2015): 97. As an apostle in 1940, Joseph Fielding Smith taught that while a major revelation for the church would come only through the church president, "the word of the Lord, as spoken by other servants at the general conferences and stake conferences, or wherever they may be when they speak that which the Lord has put into their mouths, is just as much the word of the Lord as the writings and the words of other prophets in other dispensations." (Joseph Fielding Smith, "What a Prophet Means to Latter-day Saints," *Relief Society Magazine* 28, no. 1 [Jan. 1941]: 6–7.)
58. Carol F. McConkie, email to Kate Holbrook, Dec. 4, 2015; Carol F. McConkie, "Live according to the Words of the Prophets," *Ensign* 44, no. 11 (Nov. 2014): 77–79.

59. Leavitt, Autobiography, 10; Revelation, July 1830 (Doctrine and Covenants 25), in Derr et al., *First Fifty Years,* 20.
60. Nelson, "A Plea to My Sisters," 96–97.
61. Julie B. Beck, "Fulfilling the Purpose of Relief Society," *Ensign* 38, no. 11 (Nov. 2008): 108.

FINDING, SELECTING, AND PRESENTING THE DISCOURSES

1. Jill Mulvay Derr, Carol Cornwall Madsen, Kate Holbrook, and Matthew J. Grow, eds., *The First Fifty Years of Relief Society: Key Documents in Latter-day Saint Women's History* (Salt Lake City: Church Historian's Press, 2016), xxi–xxv.
2. *Handbook of Instructions of the Relief Society of the Church of Jesus Christ of Latter-day Saints* (Salt Lake City: General Board of Relief Society, 1931), 75.
3. Maren M. Mouritsen, ed., *Blueprints for Living: Perspectives for Latter-day Saint Women* (Provo, UT: Brigham Young University Press, 1980).
4. Carol Lee Hawkins, Mary Stovall Richards, and Maren Mouritsen, interview by Kate Holbrook, Oct. 27, 2015, 30, CHL.

CHAPTER 1: LUCY MACK SMITH, "WHERE IS YOUR CONFIDENCE IN GOD?"

1. William Smith, *William Smith on Mormonism* (Lamoni, IA: Herald Steam Press, 1883), 6–7.
2. Irene M. Bates, "Lucy Mack Smith—First Mormon Mother," in *Lucy's Book: A Critical Edition of Lucy Mack Smith's Family Memoir,* ed. Lavina Fielding Anderson (Salt Lake City: Signature Books, 2001), 6–7.
3. Karen Lynn Davidson, David J. Whittaker, Mark Ashurst-McGee, and Richard L. Jensen, eds., *Histories, Volume 1: Joseph Smith Histories, 1832–1844,* vol. 1 of the Histories series of *The Joseph Smith Papers,* ed. Dean C. Jessee, Ronald K. Esplin, and Richard Lyman Bushman (Salt Lake City: Church Historian's Press, 2012), 366.
4. Larry C. Porter, "'Ye Shall Go to the Ohio': Exodus of the New York Saints to Ohio, 1831," in *Regional Studies in Latter-day Saint Church History: Ohio,* ed. Milton V. Backman Jr. (Provo, UT: Department of Church History and Doctrine, Brigham Young University, 1990), 14–15, 23.
5. Lucy Mack Smith, History, 1844–1845, 18 books, bk. 11, [2–3], [8–10], CHL; Anderson, *Lucy's Book,* 511n3. Smith's history is generally considered reliable, but it also reflects her perceptions from many years later.
6. Smith, History, bk. 11, [6].
7. Smith, History, bk. 11, [6–7]; bk. 12, [1–2].
8. Porter, "Ye Shall Go to the Ohio," 18.
9. At one point on the journey, Smith reprimanded mothers in the company who neglected their children. She remembered that the women later complained to her: "It does seem to me that we would have done better to have remained at home, for there we might set in our rocking chairs and take as much comfort as we were a mind to, and here we are tired out and no place to rest ourselves." (Smith, History, bk. 11, [5].)
10. At the beginning of the journey, as the company was organizing their leadership and resources, Smith discovered that there were about twenty people with fewer than two meals on hand. Smith recalled that she supported those without money as well as the thirty children on board. (Smith, History, bk. 11, [2–3].)
11. Luke 8:25.
12. See 2 Corinthians 2:16; and Doctrine and Covenants 20:15.
13. See John 5:25.

CHAPTER 2: ELIZABETH ANN WHITNEY, "ADAM-ONDI-AHMAN"

1. Elizabeth Ann Whitney, "A Leaf from an Autobiography," *Woman's Exponent* 7, no. 6 (Aug. 15,

1878): 41; Emmeline B. Wells, "Elizabeth Ann Whitney," *Woman's Exponent* 10, no. 20 (Mar. 15, 1882): 153–154; Edward W. Tullidge, *The Women of Mormondom* (New York: Tullidge and Crandall, 1877), 32–34.

2. Whitney, "A Leaf from an Autobiography," *Woman's Exponent* 7, no. 7 (Sept. 1, 1878): 51; Wells, "Elizabeth Ann Whitney," 153–154; Tullidge, *Women of Mormondom,* 41.
3. Tullidge, *Women of Mormondom,* 41–42.
4. Whitney, "A Leaf from an Autobiography," *Woman's Exponent* 7, no. 7 (Sept. 1, 1878): 51; Wells, "Elizabeth Ann Whitney," 153.
5. See Mark 16:17–18; 1 Corinthians 12:1–11; Doctrine and Covenants 46; and Richard Lyman Bushman, *Joseph Smith: Rough Stone Rolling* (New York: Alfred A. Knopf, 2005), 147–152; see also Nathan O. Hatch, *The Democratization of American Christianity* (New Haven, CT: Yale University Press, 1989), 50–55; and Michael Hicks, *Mormonism and Music: A History* (Urbana: University of Illinois Press, 1989), 35.
6. Tullidge, *Women of Mormondom,* 208–209; Hicks, *Mormonism and Music,* 35–39; Linda King Newell, "Gifts of the Spirit: Women's Share," in *Sisters in Spirit: Mormon Women in Historical and Cultural Perspective* (Urbana: University of Illinois Press, 1987), 111–150.
7. "Elizabeth Ann Whitney," Patriarchal Blessings, 1833–2011, CHL; Whitney, "A Leaf from an Autobiography," *Woman's Exponent* 7, no. 11 (Nov. 1, 1878): 83; Parley P. Pratt, *The Autobiography of Parley Parker Pratt,* ed. Parley P. Pratt Jr. (New York: Russell Brothers, 1874), 140. Often people gathered in groups to receive patriarchal blessings. In Kirtland, these meetings occurred in private homes or in the temple. (Irene M. Bates and E. Gary Smith, *Lost Legacy: The Mormon Office of Presiding Patriarch* [Urbana: University of Illinois Press, 1996], 38–39.)
8. Pratt, *Autobiography of Parley Parker Pratt,* 141.
9. Whitney, "A Leaf from an Autobiography," *Woman's Exponent* 7, no. 11 (Nov. 1, 1878): 83; Wells, "Elizabeth Ann Whitney," 153–154. Whitney sang "inspirationally," sometimes in tongues, throughout her life. In 1854, Wilford Woodruff recorded such an instance: "Sister Whitney sung in tongues in the pure language which Adam and Eve made use of in the garden of Eden. This gift was obtained while in Kirtland through the promise of Joseph. He told her if she would rise upon her feet (while in a meeting) she should have the pure language. She did so and immediately commenced singing in the language. It was as near heavenly music as anything I ever heard." (Wilford Woodruff, Journal, Feb. 3, 1854, CHL; see also, for example, Wells, "Elizabeth Ann Whitney," 153–154; and Eliza R. Snow, *The Personal Writings of Eliza Roxcy Snow,* ed. Maureen Ursenbach Beecher [Logan: Utah State University Press, 2000], June 3, 1846, 135.)
10. Whitney, "A Leaf from an Autobiography," *Woman's Exponent* 7, no. 11 (Nov. 1, 1878): 83. The concept of the pure language of Adam stemmed from the Tower of Babel and the preservation of language for the Brother of Jared as outlined in Ether 1:33–37; see also Genesis 11:1–9. (Samuel Brown, "Joseph [Smith] in Egypt: Babel, Hieroglyphs, and the Pure Language of Eden," *Church History* 78, no. 1 [Mar. 2009]: 26–65.)
11. The Kirtland high council, including William W. Phelps, met the same day Whitney uttered these words and discussed the hymnbook compilation by Emma Smith (created with the help of Phelps as editor). Phelps's hymn, "Adam-ondi-Ahman," was printed in Smith's 1835 hymnal and sung at the dedication of the Kirtland temple. (Minutes, Sept. 14, 1835, in Matthew C. Godfrey, Brenden W. Rensink, Alex D. Smith, Max H Parkin, and Alexander L. Baugh, eds., *Documents, Volume 4: April 1834–September 1835,* vol. 4 of the Documents series of *The Joseph Smith Papers,* ed. Ronald K. Esplin, Matthew J. Grow, and Matthew C. Godfrey [Salt Lake City: Church Historian's Press, 2016], 412–415; Emma Smith, ed., *A Collection of Sacred Hymns, for the Church of the Latter Day Saints* [Kirtland, OH: F. G. Williams, 1835], no. 23, 29–30.)
12. Joseph Smith taught that "the Priesthood was first given to Adam." (Joseph Smith, Report of Instructions, July 1839, in Willard Richards Pocket Companion, 63, CHL, accessed Sept. 6, 2016, josephsmithpapers.org; see also Doctrine and Covenants 78:15–16.)
13. See Doctrine and Covenants 107:40–42, 53.
14. See Genesis 27:23–29; 28:1–4; 48:9–15.

15. See Genesis 47:29–30; 50:5, 13.
16. See Genesis 48:5, 13–20.
17. The Book of Mormon recounts that Lehi, a descendant of Joseph of Egypt, traveled by ship to the Americas with his family. (See 1 Nephi 17–18.)
18. See Helaman 14:2–6, 14, 20–28; and 3 Nephi 1:15–20; 8:1–25.
19. Oliver Cowdery to W. W. Phelps, *Latter Day Saints' Messenger and Advocate* 1, no. 1 (Oct. 1834): 15–16; Joseph Smith—History 1:71–72.
20. In spring 1835, Joseph Smith described the valley of Adam-ondi-Ahman as a place where Adam gave a "last blessing" to his children. In 1838, Smith specified that Adam-ondi-Ahman was located in modern-day Missouri. ("Adam-ondi-Ahman," accessed Oct. 4, 2016, josephsmithpapers.org.)
21. Doctrine and Covenants 116:1.

CHAPTER 3: EMMA HALE SMITH, "WE ARE GOING TO DO SOMETHING EXTRAORDINARY"

1. Richard Lyman Bushman, *Joseph Smith: Rough Stone Rolling* (New York: Alfred A. Knopf, 2005), 53.
2. Lucy Mack Smith, History, 1845, 190, CHL.
3. Mark L. Staker, "'A Comfort unto My Servant, Joseph': Emma Hale Smith (1804–1879)," in *Women of Faith in the Latter Days, Volume One, 1775–1820,* ed. Richard E. Turley Jr. and Brittany A. Chapman (Salt Lake City: Deseret Book, 2011), 353–356.
4. Smith, History, 1845, 189–190; John S. Reed, "Some of the Remarks of John S. Reed, Esq., as Delivered before the State Convention," *Times and Seasons* 5, no. 11 (June 1, 1844): 551.
5. Nauvoo Female Relief Society, Petition to Governor Thomas Carlin, ca. July 22, 1842, CHL, in Jill Mulvay Derr, Carol Cornwall Madsen, Kate Holbrook, and Matthew J. Grow, eds., *The First Fifty Years of Relief Society: Key Documents in Latter-day Saint Women's History* (Salt Lake City: Church Historian's Press, 2016), 136–141.
6. Lucy Mack Smith, History, 1844–1845, 18 books, bk. 14, [5]; bk. 15, [12], CHL; Linda King Newell and Valeen Tippetts Avery, *Mormon Enigma: Emma Hale Smith,* 2nd ed. (Urbana: University of Illinois Press, 1994), 84–90, 132.
7. Staker, "A Comfort unto My Servant, Joseph," 345.
8. Doctrine and Covenants 25:3, 7.
9. See 2 John 1:1.
10. Nauvoo Relief Society Minute Book, Mar. 17, 1842, 8–9, in Derr et al., *First Fifty Years,* 32–33. "Presidentess" was a nineteenth-century term for female president. For an explanation of the word *ordain,* see Derr et al., *First Fifty Years,* xxxi–xxxiv.
11. Doctrine and Covenants 25:16.
12. Doctrine and Covenants 25:2.
13. Mary P. Ryan, "The Power of Women's Networks: A Case Study of Female Moral Reform in Antebellum America," *Feminist Studies* 5, no. 1 (Spring 1979): 66–85; Lori D. Ginzberg, *Women and the Work of Benevolence: Morality, Politics, and Class in the Nineteenth-Century United States* (New Haven, CT: Yale University Press, 1990), 113–114.
14. See Derr et al., *First Fifty Years,* 97–99, 142–144; Glen M. Leonard, *Nauvoo: A Place of Peace, A People of Promise* (Salt Lake City: Deseret Book, 2002), 226; Bushman, *Rough Stone Rolling,* 460, 494–499; and Newell and Avery, *Mormon Enigma,* 96, 142–147, 151–156.
15. In that meeting, Emma Smith "exhorted them to cleanse their hearts and ears. . . . [She] also exhorted to look after the poor . . . and said if there ever was any authority on the earth, she had it, and had it yet." (Nauvoo Relief Society Minute Book, Mar. 16, 1844, [125–126], in Derr et al., *First Fifty Years,* 130–131.)
16. The "rapids" refers to the Des Moines or Lower Rapids, an eleven-mile stretch of the Mississippi River just north of Keokuk, Iowa, where the river dropped about twenty-two feet. These rapids were impassable for steamboats during months of low water and were potentially treacherous during many other months. (Louis C. Hunter, *Steamboats on the Western Rivers: An Economic and Technological History* [New York: Dover, 1993], 188.)

17. See Deuteronomy 9:29; and Doctrine and Covenants 123:6.
18. This may be a reference to the Saints being driven from Missouri in 1839 and the hope that the Saints would not also be driven from their present location in Nauvoo.

CHAPTER 4: SARAH CLEVELAND, ELIZABETH ANN WHITNEY, PRESENDIA BUELL, LUCY MACK SMITH, ELIZABETH DURFEE, ELIZA R. SNOW, AND PATTY SESSIONS, "AFTER THE ORDER OF HEAVEN"

1. Nauvoo Relief Society Minute Book, Mar. 17, 1842, 6; Mar. 24, 1842, 15, in Jill Mulvay Derr, Carol Cornwall Madsen, Kate Holbrook, and Matthew J. Grow, eds., *The First Fifty Years of Relief Society: Key Documents in Latter-day Saint Women's History* (Salt Lake City: Church Historian's Press, 2016), 30, 37.
2. Nauvoo Relief Society Minute Book, Mar. 17–Apr. 19, 1842, 6–26, in Derr et al., *First Fifty Years,* 30–47.
3. Presendia Lathrop Huntington Kimball, "A Brief Sketch of the Life of Presendia Lathrop Huntington Kimball," Apr. 16, 1881, [2], CHL.
4. Nauvoo Relief Society Minute Book, Apr. 19, 1842, [31–32], in Derr et al., *First Fifty Years,* 50–51.
5. Relief Society branches may have existed in Macedonia, La Harpe, and Lima, Illinois. (Jill Mulvay Derr, Janath Russell Cannon, and Maureen Ursenbach Beecher, *Women of Covenant: The Story of Relief Society* [Salt Lake City: Deseret Book, 1992], 35.)
6. Nauvoo Relief Society Minute Book, Mar. 24, 1842, 17, in Derr et al., *First Fifty Years,* 38.
7. Nauvoo Relief Society Minute Book, Mar. 31, 1842, 22, in Derr et al., *First Fifty Years,* 43; see also Exodus 19:6; and Revelation 1:6.
8. For more information about spiritual gifts and the Relief Society, see Derr et al., *First Fifty Years,* xxi–xxv.
9. Jonathan A. Stapley and Kristine Wright, "Female Ritual Healing in Mormonism," *Journal of Mormon History* 37, no. 1 (Winter 2011): 1–85.
10. This meeting was held in the upper room of Joseph Smith's red brick store, sometimes known as the "lodge room" because it also hosted some meetings of the Nauvoo Masonic Lodge. It is not known why Emma Smith did not attend this particular meeting. In Emma Smith's absence, following parliamentary procedure, her counselors presided and conducted. (Andrew H. Hedges, Alex D. Smith, and Richard Lloyd Anderson, eds., *Journals, Volume 2: December 1841–April 1843,* vol. 2 of the Journals series of *The Joseph Smith Papers,* ed. Dean C. Jessee, Ronald K. Esplin, and Richard Lyman Bushman [Salt Lake City: Church Historian's Press, 2011], Mar. 17, 1842, 45.)
11. Sarah M. Kimball later recalled that the society was organized "after the pattern, or order, of the priesthood." (Sarah M. Kimball, "First Organisation," ca. June 1880, in "Relief Society Record, 1880–1892," 5, CHL.)
12. Joseph Smith Sr. was ordained a patriarch in December 1834 in Kirtland, Ohio, and often presided at blessing meetings, where individuals would gather to receive their patriarchal blessings. Joseph Smith Sr. died on September 14, 1840, in Nauvoo. (See Dean C. Jessee, Mark Ashurst-McGee, and Richard L. Jensen, eds., *Journals, Volume 1: 1832–1839,* vol. 1 of the Journals series of *The Joseph Smith Papers,* ed. Dean C. Jessee, Ronald K. Esplin, and Richard Lyman Bushman [Salt Lake City: Church Historian's Press, 2008], 139, 440.)
13. For additional information on the nineteenth-century practice of female healing, see Derr et al., *First Fifty Years,* xxi–xxv; and "Joseph Smith's Teachings about Priesthood, Temple, and Women," Gospel Topics, accessed May 2, 2016, lds.org.
14. In March 1831, Joseph Smith dictated a revelation explaining the diverse gifts of the Spirit, and that revelation discussed the gifts of speaking in tongues and interpreting tongues. Joseph Smith attended the next Relief Society meeting on April 28, 1842, and provided additional explanation on the use of the gift of tongues. (Revelation, Kirtland, Ohio, ca. Mar. 8, 1831, in Michael Hubbard MacKay, Gerrit J. Dirkmaat, Grant Underwood, Robert J. Woodford, and William G. Hartley,

eds., *Documents, Volume 1: July 1828–June 1831,* vol. 1 of the Documents series of *The Joseph Smith Papers,* ed. Dean C. Jessee, Ronald K. Esplin, and Richard Lyman Bushman [Salt Lake City: Church Historian's Press, 2013], 280–283; Doctrine and Covenants 46; Nauvoo Relief Society Minute Book, Apr. 28, 1842, [40–41], in Derr et al., *First Fifty Years,* 59.)

15. Before his death, Joseph Smith Sr. blessed his wife with a prolonged life: "You must stay to comfort the children when I am gone, so do not mourn but try to be comforted. Your last days shall be your best days." She passed away fourteen years later on May 14, 1856. (Lucy Mack Smith, History, 1844–1845, 18 books, bk. 18, [9], CHL.)

CHAPTER 5: LUCY MACK SMITH, "THIS GOSPEL OF GLAD TIDINGS TO ALL PEOPLE"

1. Smith was assisted by Martha Knowlton Coray, a Nauvoo schoolteacher, and her husband, Howard Coray, who had acted as a scribe and a historian for Joseph Smith. Smith was encouraged by the Quorum of the Twelve Apostles to write the history. (Howard Coray, "Journal of Howard Coray," typescript, 16, CHL; Lucy Mack Smith to William Smith, Jan. 23, 1845, 2, CHL.)
2. Lucy Mack Smith, History, 1844–1845, 18 books, bk. 1, CHL; see also Coray, "Journal of Howard Coray," 16.
3. Jan Shipps, *Mormonism: The Story of a New Religious Tradition* (Urbana: University of Illinois Press, 1987), 95–96; Richard Lyman Bushman, *Joseph Smith: Rough Stone Rolling* (New York: Alfred A. Knopf, 2005), 8–9.
4. Lavina Fielding Anderson, ed., *Lucy's Book: A Critical Edition of Lucy Mack Smith's Family Memoir* (Salt Lake City: Signature Books, 2001), 90.
5. Shipps, *Mormonism,* 92.
6. Lucy Mack Smith to William Smith, Jan. 23, 1845, 4.
7. Nauvoo Relief Society Minute Book, Mar. 31, 1842, 24, in Jill Mulvay Derr, Carol Cornwall Madsen, Kate Holbrook, and Matthew J. Grow, eds., *The First Fifty Years of Relief Society: Key Documents in Latter-day Saint Women's History* (Salt Lake City: Church Historian's Press, 2016), 45.
8. Lucy Mack Smith spoke at a meeting at the home of Bishop Jonathan Hale, at which she encouraged parents to raise their children in obedience. (Hosea Stout, Journal, Feb. 23, 1845, CHL; also available in Juanita Brooks, ed., *On the Mormon Frontier: The Diary of Hosea Stout, 1844–1861* [Salt Lake City: University of Utah Press, 1964].)
9. Nauvoo Relief Society Minute Book, Mar. 24, 1842, 17; Apr. 19, 1842, [31], in Derr et al., *First Fifty Years,* 38, 50.
10. Sarah M. Kimball to [Serepta] Heywood, ca. 1844, Joseph L. Heywood Letters, CHL.
11. Wilford Woodruff, Journal, Aug. 23, 1844, CHL.
12. "Dinner to the Smith Family," *Nauvoo Neighbor,* July 16, 1845.
13. William Clayton and Thomas Bullock, "Conference Minutes," *Times and Seasons* 6, no. 16 (Nov. 1, 1845): 1014. Emma Smith remained estranged from Brigham Young and the Church of Jesus Christ of Latter-day Saints. (Bushman, *Rough Stone Rolling,* 554–555.)
14. The church's newspaper recorded of this conference that "about five thousand Saints had the inexpressible joy and great gratification to meet for the first time in the House of the Lord in the city of Joseph." ("First Meeting in the Temple," *Times and Seasons* 6, no. 16 [Nov. 1, 1845]: 1017.)
15. Brigham Young, "To the Brethren of the Church of Jesus Christ of Latter Day Saints, Scattered Abroad throughout the United States of America," *Times and Seasons* 6, no. 16 (Nov. 1, 1845): 1018.
16. Clayton and Bullock, "Conference Minutes," 1013. The *Times and Seasons* reported this conference and included a brief synopsis of Smith's talk. The talk has previously been published with annotation in Ronald W. Walker, "Lucy Mack Smith Speaks to the Nauvoo Saints," *BYU Studies* 32, nos. 1–2 (1991): 276–284.
17. The next woman to speak in a general conference session was Zina D. H. Young, who spoke briefly at a combined priesthood and Mutual Improvement meeting on October 7, 1879. ("General Conference. Second Day," *Deseret News,* Oct. 15, 1879; see also Appendix herein.)
18. Two months prior to the conference, Lucy's son William Smith noted that "Mother Smith is rather

unwell this summer." (William Smith to J. Grant Jr., Aug. 12, 1845, in *Nauvoo Neighbor,* Aug. 20, 1845.)

19. Smith is referring to comments made by Brigham Young about Mormons stealing in response to perceived threats from people opposed to the Latter-day Saints. Since the 1838 conflict in Missouri, anti-Mormon factions frequently had alleged that Mormons were stealing goods. (Historian's Office, General Church Minutes, 1839–1877, Oct. 8, 1845, CHL; see also "Affidavits," *Quincy [IL] Whig* 8, no. 26 [Oct. 16, 1845]: 1–2; and John E. Hallwas and Roger D. Launius, eds., *Cultures in Conflict: A Documentary History of the Mormon War in Illinois* [Logan: Utah State University Press, 1995], 243–245.)
20. Nine of Smith's children lived to adulthood: Alvin, Hyrum, Sophronia, Joseph, Samuel, Katharine, Don Carlos, and Lucy. One child was stillborn and another died in infancy. ("Joseph Smith Pedigree Chart," accessed Sept. 3, 2015, josephsmithpapers.org.)
21. General advice for raising children at the time in Nauvoo included admonitions to keep boys at home instead of allowing them to wander the streets, causing problems. ("Boys," *Nauvoo Neighbor,* Apr. 30, 1845; Brigham Young, sermon, May 4, 1845, General Church Minutes.)
22. On the historical use of the phrase "Mother in Israel," see Carol Cornwall Madsen, "Mothers in Israel: Sarah's Legacy," in *Women of Wisdom and Knowledge: Talks Selected from the BYU Women's Conferences,* ed. Marie Cornwall and Susan Howe (Salt Lake City: Deseret Book, 1990), 179–201.
23. When Lucy Mack Smith said "it was 18 years last Monday," she was off by a week. Joseph Smith recorded that he obtained the plates on September 22, 1827, eighteen years and two weeks earlier than the October general conference at which Lucy Mack Smith spoke. (Karen Lynn Davidson, David J. Whittaker, Mark Ashurst-McGee, and Richard L. Jensen, eds., *Histories, Volume 1: Joseph Smith Histories, 1832–1844,* vol. 1 of the Histories series of *The Joseph Smith Papers,* ed. Dean C. Jessee, Ronald K. Esplin, and Richard Lyman Bushman [Salt Lake City: Church Historian's Press, 2012], 14–15.)
24. Lucy Mack Smith, History, 1844–1845, bk. 6, [3–4]. At the time, Martin and Lucy Harris had Lucy's widowed sister, Polly Harris Cobb, living with them. (Madge Harris Tuckett and Belle Harris Wilson, *The Martin Harris Story: Special Witness to the Book of Mormon* [Provo, UT: Maasai, 1983], 17–18.)
25. According to his account, Joseph Smith copied characters from a portion of the gold plates. Martin Harris, an early church member who gave financial support to Joseph Smith, then took the document to New York City and showed it to scholars including Charles Anthon, a professor of classical studies and literature. (Michael Hubbard MacKay, Gerrit J. Dirkmaat, Grant Underwood, Robert J. Woodford, and William G. Hartley, eds., *Documents, Volume 1: July 1828–June 1831,* vol. 1 of the Documents series of *The Joseph Smith Papers,* ed. Dean C. Jessee, Ronald K. Esplin, and Richard Lyman Bushman [Salt Lake City: Church Historian's Press, 2013], 355–357.)
26. See Luke 2:10.
27. Lucy Mack Smith, *Biographical Sketches of Joseph Smith the Prophet, and His Progenitors for Many Generations* (Liverpool: Orson Pratt, 1853), was not published until 1853. The book is better known today as *History of the Prophet Joseph Smith by His Mother.* While he initially supported Lucy Mack Smith writing the history, Brigham Young later disapproved of the book because he believed it contained inaccuracies.
28. Harris mortgaged his land to provide the $3,000 payment necessary to publish five thousand copies of the Book of Mormon. (MacKay et al., *JSP,* D1:86–88.)
29. The Smiths lost their newly constructed home in foreclosure of a mortgage on April 1, 1829. Joseph Smith moved to Susquehanna County, Pennsylvania, to escape mounting opposition against him in Palmyra, New York, in the spring of 1828. (Walker, "Lucy Mack Smith Speaks to the Nauvoo Saints," 282n15; Davidson et al., *JSP,* H1:238–239.)
30. Joseph Smith procured a copyright for the Book of Mormon, then returned to Pennsylvania with the plan to have guards protect the manuscript at all times. (Lucy Mack Smith, History, 1845, 158–159, CHL.)
31. Brigham Young spoke just before Lucy Mack Smith, encouraging members in Nauvoo to be honest

in their dealings with their neighbors and not return violence for violence. (General Church Minutes, Oct. 8, 1845; see also "Journal of Thomas Bullock," *BYU Studies* 31, no. 1 [Winter 1991]: 24–25.)

32. William Smith, a member of the Quorum of the Twelve Apostles, had returned from a mission to the eastern states in May 1845. Disputes quickly arose between Smith and the other apostles regarding Smith's behavior while in the East, his authority as church patriarch, the authority of Brigham Young as president of the Twelve Apostles, and Smith's public teaching of plural marriage. Smith left Nauvoo in the middle of the night on September 12, 1845. Two days prior to his mother's address, on the first day of the general conference, Smith was not sustained as a member of the Quorum of the Twelve Apostles as a result of objections. He was excommunicated on October 19, 1845. (Kyle R. Walker, *William B. Smith: In the Shadow of a Prophet* [Salt Lake City: Greg Kofford Books, 2015], 229–245, 257–258, 298–300; Clayton and Bullock, "Conference Minutes," 1008; Willard Richards, "Notice," *Times and Seasons* 6, no. 16 [Nov. 1, 1845]: 1019; Hosea Stout, Journal, Oct. 19, 1845.)
33. Joseph Smith Sr. and Lucy Mack Smith had three daughters: Sophronia Smith [Stoddard], Katharine Smith [Salisbury], and Lucy Smith [Millikin]. The three sisters and their families remained in Illinois following the Saints' move west. (See Kyle R. Walker, ed., *United by Faith: The Joseph Sr. and Lucy Mack Smith Family* [American Fork, UT: Covenant Communications, 2005], 187–195, 326–332, 416–418.)
34. Shortly after the publication of the Book of Mormon, in late June 1830, Samuel Smith went on a mission and took a number of books to sell. On his first day, he traveled twenty-five miles and was rejected by several potential buyers. (Smith, History, 1845, 169–170.)
35. John Portineus Greene was a member of the Methodist Episcopal Church and the Methodist Reformed Church in Mendon, New York. His wife, Rhoda Young Greene, was a sister to Brigham Young. (Walker, "Lucy Mack Smith Speaks to the Nauvoo Saints," 283n19.)
36. Samuel Smith slept under an apple tree, then had breakfast with a widow. In gratitude, he gave her a copy of the Book of Mormon. (Smith, *Biographical Sketches of Joseph Smith the Prophet,* 152.)
37. According to Lucy Mack Smith's history, Rhoda Greene took the book and then burst into tears. (Smith, History, 1845, 187.)
38. The Greenes were baptized in April 1831. (John P. Greene to Brother D. C. Smith, Jan. 29, 1841, in *Times and Seasons* 2, no. 3 [Feb. 15, 1841]: 325–326.)
39. See Luke 13:19. On a subsequent mission to Mendon, New York, Samuel Smith presented a Book of Mormon to Phineas Young, brother of Rhoda Young Greene and Brigham Young, which eventually led to the conversion and baptism of Heber C. Kimball and others. (Dean L. Jarman and Kyle L. Walker, "Samuel Harrison Smith," in Walker, *United by Faith,* 210–211.)
40. The Smith family moved from New York to Ohio in 1831 and then from Ohio to Missouri in 1838. They stayed in Missouri for only seven months. (Lavina Fielding Anderson, "Lucy Mack Smith," in Walker, *United by Faith,* 62–66.)
41. In the summer of 1838, William Smith and his wife, Caroline Grant Smith, became sick and were unable to care for themselves or their children. William's brother Samuel took them to their parents' home in Far West, Missouri. Samuel Smith's wife, Mary Bailey Smith, gave birth to a third child on August 1, 1838. (Walker, *William B. Smith,* 263; Smith, History, 1845, 247; Jarman and Walker, "Samuel Harrison Smith," 225.)
42. In 1838, opposition to the Latter-day Saints' expanding settlements in Missouri resulted in violent clashes between the Saints and non-Mormon Missourians. Lucy Mack Smith refers here to Latter-day Saints who had been displaced from their homes during the conflict. The acre of ground in front of the Smith tavern was "completely covered with beds, lying in the open sun, where families were compelled to sleep exposed to all kinds of weather. . . . It was enough to make the heart ache to see the children, sick with colds and crying around their mothers for food, whilst their parents were destitute of the means of making them comfortable." (Alexander L. Baugh, *A Call to Arms: The 1838 Mormon Defense of Northern Missouri,* Dissertations in Latter-day Saint History [Provo, UT: Joseph Fielding Smith Institute for Latter-day Saint History; BYU Studies, 2000]; Smith, History, 1845, 282.)

43. On October 31, 1838, Major General Samuel D. Lucas of the Missouri militia presented several conditions to the Latter-day Saints to ensure peace. Believing that Lucas was open to additional negotiations, Joseph Smith and four other church leaders submitted to arrest and entered the militia camp outside of Far West. On November 1, Hyrum Smith was arrested and placed with the other prisoners. (Samuel D. Lucas to Lilburn W. Boggs, Nov. 2, 1838, Mormon War Papers, Missouri State Archives, Jefferson City; Hyrum Smith, "To the Saints Scattered Abroad," *Times and Seasons* 1, no. 2 [Dec. 1839]: 21; Baugh, *A Call to Arms,* 141.)
44. Smith is likely referring to the militia's chaotic occupation of Far West, Missouri, in November 1838, when anti-Mormons were permitted to harass the Saints in the city. (See Michael Arthur to Clay County Representatives, Nov. 29, 1838, Mormon War Papers; see also Smith, History, 1845, 247–249, 253.)
45. On November 1, 1838, Joseph Smith and six other prisoners were tried by a court-martial in the militia camp and sentenced to be executed the following morning on the town square in Far West. Brigadier General Alexander Doniphan, however, opposed the ruling and halted the executions. Major General Samuel D. Lucas then decided to transport the prisoners to his headquarters in Independence, Jackson County, Missouri, leading to rumors that the executions would occur there. Lucy Mack Smith most likely added the detail of "15 minutes" to the story as dramatic flair. Joseph Smith spoke with his mother and sister from his prison wagon on November 2, 1838, and was later imprisoned in the jail in Liberty, Missouri, until April 1839. He eventually escaped from prison. (Heman C. Smith et al., *History of the Reorganized Church of Jesus Christ of Latter Day Saints,* 8 vols. [Independence, MO: Reorganized Church of Jesus Christ of Latter Day Saints, 1896–1903 (vols. 1–4), 1969–1976 (vols. 5–8)], 2:260–262; Eliza R. Snow to Isaac Streator, Feb. 22, 1839, in "Eliza R. Snow Letter from Missouri," *BYU Studies* 13, no. 4 [Summer 1973]: 547; Hyrum Smith, Testimony, Nauvoo, IL, July 1, 1843, Nauvoo [Illinois] Records, 13–16, CHL; Joseph Smith, Bill of Damages, June 4, 1839, Joseph Smith Collection, CHL; Bushman, *Rough Stone Rolling,* 356–382; Smith, History, 1845, 281.)
46. Lucy Mack Smith and her daughter Lucy were led to the wagon through crowds. As they were not allowed to see the prisoners, they shook hands with both Hyrum and Joseph under the strongly secured canvas covering the wagon. (Smith, History, 1845, 280–281.)
47. Lucy Mack Smith remembered that Samuel Smith brought to her home his brother and sister-in-law, William and Caroline Grant Smith, both of whom were ill. (Smith, History, 1845, 250.)
48. While Mary Bailey Smith, wife of Samuel, was living in Daviess County, Missouri, a mob dragged her and her children (including a newborn baby) out of their home into inclement weather and burned the house to the ground. Samuel Smith was absent at the time. With continuing exposure and lack of nutrition, Mary Smith never fully recovered. (Jarman and Walker, "Samuel Harrison Smith," 225.)
49. Joseph Smith left for Washington DC on October 29, 1839. He and Elias Higbee met with President Martin Van Buren, Senator John C. Calhoun, and members of the Illinois congressional delegation, reporting losses of $2 million and presenting a litany of abuses against Mormons in Missouri. They did not, however, receive federal support, either financially or in the form of federal intervention into state affairs. (Bushman, *Rough Stone Rolling,* 392–393, 396–397; Spencer W. McBride, "When Joseph Smith Met Martin Van Buren: Mormonism and the Politics of Religious Liberty in Nineteenth-Century America," *Church History* 85, no. 1 [Mar. 2016]: 19–27.)
50. Perhaps the Mississippi River near Quincy, Illinois.
51. In forced compliance with Governor Lilburn W. Boggs's order, about eight thousand church members began the arduous migration out of Missouri in early 1839, with many finding refuge in Quincy, Illinois, on the eastern side of the Mississippi River. In February 1839, Lucy and her husband joined the exodus to Illinois, walking in mud and camping in snow. (William G. Hartley, "'Almost Too Intolerable a Burthen': The Winter Exodus from Missouri, 1838–39," *Journal of Mormon History* 18, no. 2 [Fall 1992]: 6–40; Smith, History, 1845, 286; Jarman and Walker, "Samuel Harrison Smith," 228.)
52. Doctrine and Covenants 101:86–89; see also Doctrine and Covenants 123:6.

53. Joseph Smith reported on his visit to Washington DC at a conference held on April 8, 1840. Mr. Durfee may have been Jabez Durfee, whose wife, Elizabeth Durfee, was a member of the Nauvoo Relief Society. (Robert B. Thompson, "Conference Minutes," *Times and Seasons* 1, no. 6 [Apr. 1840]: 93.)
54. Doctrine and Covenants 127:7.
55. Smith may be referring to the September 10, 1845, death of Miner R. Deming, the Hancock County sheriff who was sympathetic to the Mormons during the May 1845 trials of the five men accused of murdering Joseph and Hyrum Smith. Deming's death terminated an uneasy peace between Mormons and non-Mormons over local concerns and led to increased mob violence. (Dallin H. Oaks and Marvin S. Hill, *Carthage Conspiracy: The Trial of the Accused Assassins of Joseph Smith* [Urbana: University of Illinois Press, 1975], 193–194.)
56. Five members of Lucy Mack Smith's family were buried in Nauvoo: Joseph Smith Sr., who died September 14, 1840; Don Carlos Smith, who died August 7, 1841; Joseph Smith Jr. and Hyrum Smith, who died June 27, 1844; and Samuel Smith, who died July 30, 1844. ("Joseph Smith Pedigree Chart.")
57. By the end of Lucy Smith's discourse, her voice grew weak and much of the congregation could not hear her words. Brigham Young then stood to relate the following: "Mother Smith proposes a thing which rejoices my heart: she will go with us. I can answer for the authorities of the church; we want her and her children to go with us; and I pledge myself in behalf of the authorities of the church, that while we have anything, they shall share with us. We have extended the helping hand to Mother Smith." (Clayton and Bullock, "Conference Minutes," 1014.)

CHAPTER 6: PHOEBE M. ANGELL, "SEEK TO THE LORD FOR WISDOM"

1. Laura P. Angell King, "Mother and Midwife and Nurse," Laura P. Angell King Papers, 1, CHL.
2. Truman O. Angell, "Autobiography," 1884, 3, 6, CHL. This first breakup was temporary, lasting three to four years. They reunited for more than a decade, then separated permanently.
3. Angell, "Autobiography," 7; King, "Mother and Midwife and Nurse," 2; see also Paul L. Anderson, "Truman O. Angell: Architect and Saint," in *Supporting Saints: Life Stories of Nineteenth-Century Mormons,* ed. Donald Q. Cannon and David J. Whittaker (Provo, UT: Religious Studies Center, Brigham Young University, 1985), 134.
4. "Obituary Notice," *Deseret News,* Feb. 1, 1855; Angell, "Autobiography," 6–7.
5. King, "Mother and Midwife and Nurse," 2–3.
6. Nauvoo Relief Society Minute Book, Apr. 14, 1842, 26; June 16, 1843, [91], in Jill Mulvay Derr, Carol Cornwall Madsen, Kate Holbrook, and Matthew J. Grow, eds., *The First Fifty Years of Relief Society: Key Documents in Latter-day Saint Women's History* (Salt Lake City: Church Historian's Press, 2016), 46, 101.
7. King, "Mother and Midwife and Nurse," 4; Patty Bartlett Sessions, *Mormon Midwife: The 1846–1888 Diaries of Patty Bartlett Sessions,* ed. Donna Toland Smart (Logan: Utah State University Press, 1997), 181, 194, 203, 209, 210.
8. For more information on the practice of social medicine among women in the eighteenth and nineteenth centuries, see Laurel Thatcher Ulrich, *A Midwife's Tale: The Life of Martha Ballard, Based on Her Diary, 1785–1812* (New York: Vintage Books, 1991), 11–12, 47, 61–66.
9. Samuel Thomson, *New Guide to Health; or, Botanic Family Physician, Containing a Complete System of Practice,* 3rd ed. (Boston: J. Howe, 1831), 38–48, 70–71; Z[ebedee] Snow, "Speeches Delivered at the Assembly of the Council of Health, on Ensign Peak," *Deseret News,* July 24, 1852; Christine Croft Waters, "Pioneering Physicians in Utah, 1847–1900" (master's thesis, University of Utah, 1976), 14, 16.
10. Elizabeth Ann Whitney remembered that Joseph Smith ordained her and set her apart to "administer to the sick" in Nauvoo. Also in Nauvoo, Brigham Young and Heber C. Kimball appointed Patty Sessions as a "doctor for women." (Elizabeth Ann Whitney, "A Leaf from an Autobiography,"

Woman's Exponent 7, no. 12 [Nov. 15, 1878]: 91; Phoebe C. Sessions, "Biographical Sketch," *Woman's Exponent* 27, nos. 1–2 [June 1 and 15, 1898]: 294.)

11. Maureen Ursenbach Beecher, *Eliza and Her Sisters* (Salt Lake City: Aspen Books, 1991), 75–97; Derr et al., *First Fifty Years,* 178.
12. Historian's Office, Journal History, vol. 73, Feb. 21, 1849, CHL. By 1852, these meetings were held in Representatives Hall, on Ensign Peak, in various ward halls, or in the old adobe tabernacle, and were attended by anywhere from forty to three hundred people. ("Council of Health," *Deseret News,* Mar. 20, 1852; "[Untitled]," *Deseret News,* May 15, 1852; "[Untitled]," *Deseret News,* June 26, 1852; "Extracts from J. W. Cummings' Address before the 'Council of Health' and Their Friends, on Ensign Hill, June 16th," *Deseret News,* July 10, 1852; "Speeches Delivered at the Assembly of the Council of Health on Ensign Peak," *Deseret News,* July 24, 1852; "[Untitled]," *Deseret News,* Aug. 21, 1852; Jessie Del Macdonald Clawson, "Pioneer Physicians," in *Museum Memories* [Salt Lake City: International Daughters of Utah Pioneers, 2010], 2:83.)
13. The Female Council of Health was organized by July 1851. For more information and an image of the August 14, 1852, meeting reproduced here, see Derr et al., *First Fifty Years,* 179–180. Willard Richards, his wife Hannah, and his brother Phineas taught courses in nursing, midwifery, and childcare at Angell's house. ("[Untitled]," *Deseret News,* May 15, 1852; Claire Wilcox Noall, "Utah's Pioneer Women Doctors," *Improvement Era* 42, no. 1 [Jan. 1939]: 16; Richards Family Collection, "Phineas Richards Journal," May 6–Dec. 20, 1851, CHL.)
14. Sessions, *Mormon Midwife,* 169, 181, 194, 203; Richards Family Collection, "Phineas Richards Journal," May 6–Dec. 20, 1851; "Council of Health," *Deseret News,* Mar. 20, 1852; "[Untitled]," *Deseret News,* Apr. 3, 1852; "[Untitled]," *Deseret News,* Aug. 21, 1852; Thomas Carter, *Building Zion: The Material World of Mormon Settlement* (Minneapolis: University of Minnesota Press, 2015), 210–212. For more information on the nineteenth-century practice of female healing, see Derr et al., *First Fifty Years,* xxi–xxv; and "Joseph Smith's Teachings about Priesthood, Temple, and Women," Gospel Topics, accessed May 2, 2016, lds.org.
15. Brigham Young expressed these same sentiments: "It appears consistent to me to apply every remedy that comes within the range of my knowledge, and to ask my Father in Heaven, in the name of Jesus Christ, to sanctify that application to the healing of my body; to another this may appear inconsistent. . . . But it is my duty to do, when I have it in my power. Many people are unwilling to do one thing for themselves, in case of sickness, but ask God to do it all." (Brigham Young, "Discourse," *Deseret News,* Sept. 10, 1856.)
16. According to Noah Webster's *American Dictionary of the English Language* (1828), *receipt* was a commonly used word for *recipe.*
17. Boneset, or thoroughwort, an herb and a common home remedy in the nineteenth century, was used as a diuretic, particularly during flu epidemics. Lobelia was a common wild plant sometimes known as "Indian tobacco," and its leaves were used for respiratory ailments, asthma, coughs, and lung afflictions; it was also used to cleanse the stomach and to induce vomiting. (Thomson, *New Guide to Health,* 38–48, 70–71; W. A. Newman Dorland, *The American Illustrated Medical Dictionary* [Philadelphia: W. B. Saunders, 1900], 244, 364; S. Henry Dessau, "The Treatment of Epidemic Influenza," *New York Medical Times* 22, no. 4 [Apr. 1894]: 97.)
18. Following Angell's speech, "Sister Gibbs," Dr. Samuel Sprague, and Patty Sessions gave recipes for various ailments. This could be Sarah Waterous Gibbs [Eldredge], who later operated a "hospital home" and provided care for sick children. (*Pioneer Women of Faith and Fortitude,* 4 vols. [Salt Lake City: International Society of Daughters of Utah Pioneers, 1998], 1:884.)

CHAPTER 7: MATILDA DUDLEY BUSBY, "THIRTEENTH WARD RELIEF SOCIETY COVENANT"

1. See Elsie Helm, Reminiscence, typescript, accessed Sept. 1, 2015, ancestry.com. For details on Indian attacks, scalping, and kidnapping in Pennsylvania and Ohio, see *The History of Wyandot County, Ohio* (Chicago: Leggett, Conaway, 1884).
2. Endowment House, Sealings and Endowments of the Living, vol. A, 1851–1854, Matilda Paschall,

July 14, 1852, 43, microfilm 183,393, FHL; "Matilda M. Dudley Ferguson Paschall," Mormon Pioneer Overland Travel, 1847–1868, accessed Sept. 1, 2015, history.lds.org. Little is known about Busby's first and second husbands—only that her son had the last name of Ferguson and that she then took the name Paschall before she married Joseph Busby in 1856. Because she crossed the plains under the surname of Paschall, it appears she may have divorced Ferguson and married Paschall before making the trek to Utah. Mr. Paschall, however, does not appear to have traveled to Utah with her. She apparently started going by Dudley again sometime after her arrival in the Salt Lake Valley—she is called "M. Dudley" in the June 14, 1854, minutes of the Salt Lake City Thirteenth Ward Relief Society, which are presented here. The Thirteenth Ward was located between Main Street and 300 East, and South Temple and 300 South. (Andrew Jenson, *Encyclopedic History of the Church of Jesus Christ of Latter-day Saints* [Salt Lake City: Deseret News, 1941], 748–749.)

3. Jared Farmer, *On Zion's Mount: Mormons, Indians, and the American Landscape* (Cambridge, MA: Harvard University Press, 2008), 50–58, 80–88. In the fall of 1853, Brigham Young outlined various proselytizing missions to the Indians, which were set to depart in the spring of 1854. (Richard L. Jensen, "Forgotten Relief Societies, 1844–67," *Dialogue: A Journal of Mormon Thought* 16, no. 1 [Spring 1983]: 107–109.)
4. Amanda Barnes Smith, Journal, Jan. 24, 1854, CHL; Jill Mulvay Derr, Carol Cornwall Madsen, Kate Holbrook, and Matthew J. Grow, eds., *The First Fifty Years of Relief Society: Key Documents in Latter-day Saint Women's History* (Salt Lake City: Church Historian's Press, 2016), 188–190.
5. Amanda Barnes Smith, Journal, Feb. 9, 1854; Thirteenth Ward, Salt Lake Stake, Relief Society Records, 1854–1857, June 7, 1854, CHL; Derr et al., *First Fifty Years,* 190–191.
6. The first organized relief efforts in Utah occurred in the early 1850s, beginning with the Salt Lake City Second Ward's sewing meetings. Lydia Goldthwaite Knight coordinated a Relief Society specifically for the Salt Lake City First Ward in 1854, and Bishop Shadrach Roundy appointed Patty Sessions as president of the Salt Lake City Sixteenth Ward Relief Society in June of that year. Other societies started between 1854 and 1857. Ward societies organized in Salt Lake City included the Third, Sixth, Seventh, Eleventh, Fourteenth, and Fifteenth Wards. (Second Ward, Salt Lake Stake, manuscript history and historical reports, typescript, 7, CHL; Susa Young Gates, "Relief Society Beginnings in Utah," *Relief Society Magazine* 9, no. 4 [Apr. 1922]: 185–190; see also Jensen, "Forgotten Relief Societies.")
7. Historian's Office, General Church Minutes, 1839–1877, June 4, 1854, CHL.
8. Thirteenth Ward Relief Society Records, June 7, 1854; Louisa R. Taylor, "Records of the Female Relief Society Organized on the 9th of Feb,y in the City of Great Salt Lake 1854 Utah Territory," June 13, 1854, 30, BYU; Derr et al., *First Fifty Years,* 197.
9. Thirteenth Ward Relief Society Records, June 14, 1854; Nauvoo Relief Society Minute Book, Mar. 24, 1842, 15; Apr. 14, 1842, [27]; May 26, 1842, [53]; Aug. 4, 1842, [77], in Derr et al., *First Fifty Years,* 37, 47, 70–71, 91.
10. Thirteenth Ward Relief Society Records, July 19, 1854; "Historical Sketch of the 13th Ward Relief Society," Thirteenth Ward, Salt Lake Stake, Relief Society Minutes and Records, Minute Book "A," 1868–1898, Mar. 17, 1892, 646, CHL; Leonard J. Arrington, *From Quaker to Latter-day Saint: Bishop Edwin D. Woolley* (Salt Lake City: Deseret Book, 1976), 337–338.
11. Thirteenth Ward Relief Society Records, May 6, 1857. She married her third husband, Joseph Busby, who became a foreman for the territorial legislative assembly, on March 13, 1856. (Kate B. Carter, comp., "The Year of 1864," in *Our Pioneer Heritage,* 20 vols. [Salt Lake City: Daughters of Utah Pioneers, 1965], 8:4; Endowment Index, 1846–1969, Matilda Dudley, microfilm 1,262,865, FHL; Thirteenth Ward Relief Society Minutes and Records, 646.)
12. Thirteenth Ward Relief Society Minutes and Records, 646; Jill Mulvay Derr, Janath Russell Cannon, and Maureen Ursenbach Beecher, *Women of Covenant: The Story of Relief Society* (Salt Lake City: Deseret Book, 1992), 80.
13. Augusta Adams Cobb was from the Boston area. She married Brigham Young as his second plural wife and moved to Utah in 1848. She served as first counselor to Matilda Dudley. (Jeffery Ogden Johnson, "Determining and Defining 'Wife': The Brigham Young Households," *Dialogue: A Journal*

of Mormon Thought 20, no. 3 [Fall 1987]: 60; "Augusta Adams Cobb," Mormon Pioneer Overland Travel, 1847–1868, accessed June 13, 2016, history.lds.org; Thirteenth Ward Relief Society Records, June 7, 1854.)

14. Dudley had married Joseph Busby and taken his surname in the time since the June 1854 meeting.
15. George Busby donated the Relief Society minute book belonging to his mother, Matilda Dudley Busby, to the Church Historian's Office about twenty-three years after her death. (Clarissa Smith Williams and Amy Brown Lyman, "The Official Round Table," *Relief Society Magazine* 6, no. 1 [Jan. 1919]: 43.)

CHAPTER 8: ELICIA A. GRIST, "WE HAVE EACH A MISSION TO PERFORM"

1. "Death of Mrs. Garthwaite," *Salt Lake Tribune,* Sept. 25, 1898.
2. John Knapp Grist, *Journal of John Knapp Grist* (Spanish Fork, UT: Liberty Press, n.d.), [2]. At the time of the Grists' baptisms, some thirty thousand Latter-day Saints lived in the British Mission, where the church had been established for about sixteen years. ("Statistical Report of the Church of Jesus Christ of Latter Day Saints in the British Islands, for the Half-Year Ending June 30th, 1853," *Latter-day Saints' Millennial Star* 15, no. 31 [July 30, 1853]: 510.)
3. Grist, *Journal of John Knapp Grist,* [63, 65, 79, 83].
4. Jennifer L. Goloboy, "Introduction," in *Industrial Revolution: People and Perspectives,* ed. Jennifer L. Goloboy (Santa Barbara, CA: ABC-CLIO, 2008), xx; Paul J. Erickson, "Readers and Writers," in Goloboy, *Industrial Revolution,* 85, 94–95.
5. Peter Crawley, *A Descriptive Bibliography of the Mormon Church, Volume One, 1830–1847* (Provo, UT: Religious Studies Center, Brigham Young University, 1997), 108–113.
6. Rebecca Bartholomew, *Audacious Women: Early British Mormon Immigrants* (Salt Lake City: Signature Books, 1995), 89, 109–118; Leonard J. Arrington, "Mormon Women in Nineteenth-Century Britain," in *Coming to Zion,* ed. James B. Allen and John W. Welch (Provo, UT: BYU Studies, 1997), 285.
7. See Hannah Selina Pegg, "Friendly Suggestions to My Young Sisters," *Latter-day Saints' Millennial Star* 23, no. 16 (Apr. 20, 1861): 252–254; see also Elizabeth Tullidge, "Life," *Latter-day Saints' Millennial Star* 21, no. 2 (Jan. 8, 1859): 21–22; Emily G. Teasdale, "Woman—Her Sphere and Duties," *Latter-day Saints' Millennial Star* 21, no. 13 (Mar. 26, 1859): 206–208; and Mary [Fielding] Smith and M. R. [Mercy Fielding] Thompson, "To the Sisters of the Church of Jesus Christ in England: Greeting," *Latter-day Saints' Millennial Star* 5, no. 1 (June 1844): 15.
8. Bartholomew, *Audacious Women,* 103–106.
9. At the time Grist wrote this address, her daughters Evangeline and Alice were eight and nine years old. (See Grist, *Journal of John Knapp Grist,* [3].)
10. The Perpetual Emigrating Fund, launched in 1849, provided financial assistance for and coordinated organization among Latter-day Saints moving to Utah. (*Names of Persons and Sureties Indebted to the Perpetual Emigrating Fund Company from 1850 to 1877 Inclusive* [Salt Lake City: Star Book and Job Printing Office, 1877], 59; see also Richard L. Jensen and Maurine Carr Ward, "Names of Persons and Sureties Indebted to the Perpetual Emigrating Fund Company, 1850 to 1877," *Mormon Historical Studies* 1, no. 2 [Fall 2000]: 141–142.)
11. "Death of Mrs. Garthwaite"; A. A. [Annie Adams] Kiskadden, "Greenroom Memories at the Salt Lake Theatre," *Deseret Evening News,* Dec. 15, 1906. Grist was one of a large number of British Saints immigrating to Utah who brought with them theatrical experience. In a letter to Brigham Young about British Saints, George Sims described the Salt Lake Theatre as "a loud preacher" because its existence encouraged cultured British Saints to immigrate to Utah, where they could find cultural activities. (George E. Sims to Brigham Young, Mar. 5, 1863, 3, Brigham Young Office Files, 1832–1878, CHL; see also Lynne Watkins Jorgensen, "The Mechanics' Dramatic Association: London and Salt Lake City," *Journal of Mormon History* 23, no. 2 [Fall 1997]: 155–184.)
12. "Fellowship meeting" may have been a British term for testimony meeting. (See "The Visitor: The Fellowship Meeting," *Latter-day Saints' Millennial Star* 21, no. 4 [Jan. 22, 1859]: 57–58.)

13. See 1 Peter 3:7. Perceptions of the fall of Adam and Eve in the nineteenth century often focused on Eve being deceived by Satan; interpreters of the Bible commonly placed emphasis on women as physically and emotionally weaker than—and therefore submissive to—men. (Amanda W. Benckhuysen, "The Prophetic Voice of Christina Rossetti," in *Recovering Nineteenth-Century Women Interpreters of the Bible,* ed. Christiana de Groot and Marion Ann Taylor [Atlanta: Society of Biblical Literature, 2007], 170.)
14. A London-based poet described these British fellowship meetings as having "burning words of inspiration" given in "tongues unknown, and prophecy." The Saints were greatly blessed through those meetings: "Faithful Saints refresh'd and strengthen'd / Drooping ones reviv'd and cheer'd; / Thus their happy days are lengthen'd, / Thus Jehovah's name's rever'd." (T. J. D., "Fellowship Meeting," *Deseret News,* Dec. 14, 1854.)
15. See Doctrine and Covenants 46:14.
16. See Proverbs 15:23. Many British women invited neighbors and friends to learn more about the Church of Jesus Christ of Latter-day Saints. For three examples, see Arrington, "Mormon Women in Nineteenth-Century Britain," 282, 292, 297.
17. Grist's advocacy for children's education ran counter to the prevailing ideas in British society at the time, when most children faced many barriers to formal learning, including poverty and class distinction. Orson Pratt engaged a press in Liverpool under the auspices of the British Mission to publish scriptures, hymnals, poetry books, histories, theological pamphlets, catechisms, periodicals, and various works in French, German, Italian, Danish, and Welsh, as well as portraits of significant male church leaders in Utah. (Arrington, "Mormon Women in Nineteenth-Century Britain," 284; *Catalogue of Works Published by the Church of Jesus Christ of Latter-day Saints, and for Sale by Orson Pratt at Their General Repository, and "Millennial Star" Office* [Liverpool: ca. 1856].)
18. As part of the Perpetual Emigrating Fund, people were encouraged to save their own money and deposit it with approved agents to pay for their travel to Utah. The *Millennial Star* often printed information detailing the specific costs of ship passage, rail passage, and overland transportation, as well as suggested supply lists. (See, for example, "Individual or Penny Emigration Fund," *Latter-day Saints' Millennial Star* 19, no. 36 [Sept. 5, 1857]: 570–571; and "Emigration," *Latter-day Saints' Millennial Star* 23, no. 1 [Jan. 5, 1861]: 9–10.)
19. The obituary of Alice Grist Allen, a daughter of Elicia Grist, stated that Alice walked most of the way across the plains. ("Alice Alalee Allen," *Salt Lake Tribune,* Jan. 29, 1933.)

CHAPTER 9: MARY ISABELLA HORNE, "GOD WILL ENABLE US TO OVERCOME"

1. [Emmeline B. Wells], "A Representative Woman: Mary Isabella Horne," *Woman's Exponent* 11, no. 4 (July 15, 1882): 25; no. 8 (Sept. 15, 1882): 59.
2. Mrs. Joseph Horne [Mary Isabella Horne], "Migration and Settlement of the Latter Day Saints," 1884, 1–2, 4–6, 10, Bancroft Library, University of California, Berkeley; [Wells], "A Representative Woman," *Woman's Exponent* 10, no. 24 (May 15, 1882): 185; [Wells], "A Representative Woman," *Woman's Exponent* 11, no. 1 (June 1, 1882): 1; Nauvoo Relief Society Minute Book, June 9, 1842, [64], in Jill Mulvay Derr, Carol Cornwall Madsen, Kate Holbrook, and Matthew J. Grow, eds., *The First Fifty Years of Relief Society: Key Documents in Latter-day Saint Women's History* (Salt Lake City: Church Historian's Press, 2016), 80.
3. Derr et al., *First Fifty Years,* 209–210; "Address of Mrs. M. Isabella Horne," *Woman's Exponent* 20, no. 18 (Apr. 1, 1892): 138; [Wells], "A Representative Woman," *Woman's Exponent* 11, no. 8 (Sept. 15, 1882): 59.
4. Emmeline B. Wells and others remembered how Horne had earlier struggled with public speaking. She was "so very timid that she could not vote in the members of the society, without being supported by leaning on other sisters. To see her now stand up in the congregations of the Saints, and hear the words of instruction which flow from her lips, one could scarcely credit that she was ever so afraid of her own voice." ([Wells], "A Representative Woman," *Woman's Exponent* 11, no. 8 [Sept. 15, 1882]: 59.)

5. Seventeenth Ward, Salt Lake Stake, Relief Society Minutes and Records, vol. 2, 1868–1871, July 30, 1868, 97–98, CHL.
6. Seventeenth Ward, Salt Lake Stake, Manuscript History and Historical Reports, typescript, CHL. Like Horne, Hyde had joined the Nauvoo Relief Society. (Nauvoo Relief Society Minute Book, Mar. 17, 1842, 7, in Derr et al., *First Fifty Years,* 30.)
7. Jeans were work pants made of durable twilled cotton cloth. (Seventeenth Ward Relief Society Minutes, July 30, 1868, 97.)
8. The *Deseret News* reported several problems with grasshoppers throughout Utah Territory. The day before this meeting, the paper reported millions of grasshoppers eating gardens and lots in Salt Lake City. ("Items," *Deseret News,* July 29, 1868.)
9. Orson Hyde referred to the 1848 incident in a talk on September 24, 1853, saying that "the hand of Providence prepared agents, and sent them to destroy the destroyer." (Orson Hyde, "Common Salvation," in *Journal of Discourses,* 26 vols. [Liverpool: Various publishers, 1855–1886], 2:114; see also William G. Hartley, "Mormons, Crickets, and Gulls: A New Look at an Old Story," *Utah Historical Quarterly* 38, no. 3 [Summer 1970]: 233.)
10. Seventeenth Ward Relief Society Minutes, July 30, 1868, 97.
11. Writing of the 1848 incident when the Saints had tried to fight off the insects, Horne remembered her faith that God "would send deliverance never wavered. In their extremity the Saints united in calling upon the Lord in mighty faith, and he came to the rescue by sending large flocks of seagulls to devour the crickets and save us from starvation. It was one of the greatest miracles of this dispensation." (Mary Isabella Horne, "Pioneer Reminiscences," *Young Woman's Journal* 13, no. 7 [July 1902]: 294; see also Horne, "Migration and Settlement," 28.)

CHAPTER 10: ELIZA R. SNOW, "LET US CULTIVATE OURSELVES"

1. Eliza R. Snow, "Sketch of My Life," in *The Personal Writings of Eliza Roxcy Snow,* ed. Maureen Ursenbach Beecher (Logan: Utah State University Press, 2000), 6; Maureen Ursenbach Beecher, "Eliza of Ohio: The Early Years," in *Eliza and Her Sisters,* ed. Maureen Ursenbach Beecher (Salt Lake City: Aspen Books, 1991), 33.
2. Sarah M. Kimball, "Auto-Biography," *Woman's Exponent* 12, no. 7 (Sept. 1, 1883): 51. Kimball, who visited the second meeting of the reorganized Salt Lake City Seventeenth Ward Relief Society on February 13, 1868, recounted the story of Eliza R. Snow's initial constitution for the Nauvoo Relief Society. (Seventeenth Ward Relief Society Minutes and Records, vol. 2, 1868–1877, Feb. 13, 1868, 58, CHL.)
3. "Jedediah M. Grant—Joseph B. Noble Company (1847)," Mormon Pioneer Overland Travel, 1847–1868, accessed Dec. 21, 2015, history.lds.org; Jill Mulvay Derr and Carol Cornwall Madsen, "Preserving the Record and Memory of the Female Relief Society of Nauvoo, 1842–92," *Journal of Mormon History* 35, no. 3 (Summer 2009): 90.
4. Richard L. Jensen, "Forgotten Relief Societies, 1844–67," *Dialogue: A Journal of Mormon Thought* 16, no. 1 (Spring 1983): 105–125; see also Eighteenth Ward, Salt Lake Stake, General Minutes, vol. 5, 1854–1857, Sept. 6, 1855, 9, CHL; Snow, "Sketch of My Life," 32, 265n49.
5. Brigham Young, "Remarks," *Deseret News,* Dec. 18, 1867; Brigham Young, "Remarks," *Deseret News,* May 13, 1868; Snow, "Sketch of My Life," 35. Portions of Eliza R. Snow's sketch are also published in Jill Mulvay Derr, Carol Cornwall Madsen, Kate Holbrook, and Matthew J. Grow, eds., *The First Fifty Years of Relief Society: Key Documents in Latter-day Saint Women's History* (Salt Lake City: Church Historian's Press, 2016), 268–269.
6. Snow, "Sketch of My Life," 35; Derr et al., *First Fifty Years,* 268.
7. Derr and Madsen, "Preserving the Record and Memory," 88–117.
8. See Derr et al., *First Fifty Years,* xvii–xxxix.
9. Eliza R. Snow, "Female Relief Society," *Deseret Evening News,* Apr. 18, 1868. For a transcript of the two-part article, see Derr et al., *First Fifty Years,* 270–275.
10. Sarah M. Kimball later remembered that Joseph Smith organized the women "under the priesthood, after the pattern of the priesthood." John Taylor, who was present at the first meeting, stated that the

women were now "organized according to the law of Heaven." (Kimball, "Auto-Biography," 51; Nauvoo Relief Society Minute Book, Mar. 17, 1842, 14, in Derr et al., *First Fifty Years,* 36; see also, for example, Bathsheba W. Smith's speech to the Pioneer Stake, in Clara L. Clawson, "Pioneer Stake," *Woman's Exponent* 34, nos. 2–3 [July–Aug. 1905]: 14; Mercy R. Thompson, "Recollections of the Prophet Joseph Smith," *Juvenile Instructor* 27, no. 13 [July 1, 1892]: 398–400; and Eliza R. Snow, in Spring City Ward, Sanpete Stake, Relief Society Minutes and Records, vol. 2, 1878–1901, June 23, 1878, 16, CHL.)

11. At its first meeting, on August 16, 1856, Bishop Thomas Callister taught the women that this new organization was "a continuation of that which was organized in Nauvoo." At the following meeting, Callister reiterated his hope that "this society . . . be organized according to the pattern that was set up in Nauvoo. He wanted it set up on a permanent foundation." He read aloud a sermon from Joseph Smith to the Nauvoo Relief Society and invited women to share their personal memories. The Seventeenth Ward was located on nine blocks between 200 North and South Temple, and Main Street and 200 West. (Seventeenth Ward, Salt Lake Stake, Relief Society Minutes and Records, vol. 1, 1856–1870, Aug. 16 and 21, 1856, CHL; Andrew Jenson, *Encyclopedic History of the Church of Jesus Christ of Latter-day Saints* [Salt Lake City: Deseret News, 1941], 751.)
12. Sarah M. Kimball, Zina D. H. Young, Marinda N. Hyde, Margaret T. Smoot, and Bathsheba W. Smith also spoke. Each woman had been a member of the Nauvoo Relief Society. This meeting celebrated the one-year anniversary of the Seventeenth Ward Relief Society. (Seventeenth Ward Relief Society Minutes and Records, Feb. 18, 1869, 145.)
13. Snow described her perception of Brigham Young's views regarding women: "If any of the daughters and mothers in Israel are feeling in the least circumscribed in their present spheres, they will now find ample scope for every power and capability for doing good with which they are most liberally endowed. . . . President Young has turned the key to a wide and extensive sphere of action and usefulness." (Snow, "Female Relief Society.")
14. See Doctrine and Covenants 76:58; 132:20. In an address at the Salt Lake Tabernacle on August 8, 1852, Brigham Young stated that "the Lord created you and me for the purpose of becoming gods like himself; when we have been proved in our present capacity, and been faithful with all things he puts into our possession. We are created, we are born for the express purpose of growing up from the low estate of manhood, to become gods like unto our Father in Heaven." (*Journal of Discourses,* 26 vols. [Liverpool: Various publishers, 1855–1886], 3:93; see also "Becoming like God," Gospel Topics, accessed May 4, 2016, lds.org.)
15. See Genesis 22:17.
16. At the beginning of the meeting, Albert Merrill "said he was glad to see the spirit manifested by the sisters in striving to do good and in assisting to build up the church of God. He said there is work for all, both male and female. . . . We all have an interest in building up this kingdom, if we are citizens of it we shall inherit it forever and ever." (Seventeenth Ward Relief Society Minutes and Records, Feb. 18, 1869, 146.)
17. According to its annual report, the Seventeenth Ward Relief Society had acquired $150 worth of lumber for their building. This lumber may have been donated by Joseph C. Rich, who had attended and spoken at a society party earlier. (Seventeenth Ward Relief Society Minutes and Records, "Annual Report for 1868," 144; Feb. 18, 1869, 152.)
18. At a meeting of the visiting committee, Rhoda Marie Carrington proposed that the committee seek money to fund the building of a meeting hall for the Relief Society. Discussion of the building was featured in a subsequent meeting of the visiting committee a month later. (Seventeenth Ward Relief Society Minutes and Records, Dec. 10, 1868, 136; Jan. 14, 1869, 153.)
19. In February 1869, the First Presidency included Brigham Young, first counselor George A. Smith, and second counselor Daniel H. Wells. While Seventeenth Ward bishop Nathan Davis was abroad on business in February 1869, George Morris served as "acting bishop." Brigham Young had specifically counseled the bishops: "Now, bishops, you have smart women for wives, many of you; let them organize Female Relief Societies in the various wards. We have many talented women among us. . . . You will find that the sisters will be the mainspring of the movement." (Andrew Jenson, *Latter-day*

Saint Biographical Encyclopedia: A Compilation of Biographical Sketches of Prominent Men and Women in the Church of Jesus Christ of Latter-day Saints, 4 vols. [Salt Lake City: Andrew Jenson History Co., 1901–1936], 1:37, 62; Seventeenth Ward Relief Society Minutes and Records, Feb. 18, 1869, 147; Brigham Young, "Remarks," *Deseret News,* Dec. 18, 1867.)

20. See Derr et al., *First Fifty Years,* xxvi–xxxiv; see also Dallin H. Oaks, "The Keys and Authority of the Priesthood," *Ensign* 44, no. 5 (May 2014): 49–52.
21. Seventeenth Ward Relief Society president Marinda N. Hyde was a member of the Nauvoo Relief Society, having joined at its first meeting on March 17, 1842. She had served as the treasurer of the Seventeenth Ward Relief Society, replacing Bathsheba W. Smith, on August 21, 1856. A president, two counselors, and other officers were "to carry out the designs of the institution," as recommended by Joseph Smith in the Nauvoo Relief Society. (Seventeenth Ward Relief Society Minutes and Records, vol. 1, 1856–1870, Aug. 21, 1856; Nauvoo Relief Society Minute Book, Mar. 17, 1842, 8, in Derr et al., *First Fifty Years,* 31.)
22. For example, during this time period, donations listed in the Seventeenth Ward Relief Society minutes included fabric, peaches, sugar, carpet rags, paper, yarn, flour, coffee, apples, cash, pork, soap, clothes, shoes, and candles. (Seventeenth Ward Relief Society Minutes and Records, Feb. 13–Apr. 23, 1868, 62–76.)
23. The treasurer was Elizabeth A. Felt. According to the annual report given at this meeting, the Seventeenth Ward Relief Society had collected a total of $1,238.32 for the past year, including cash and donations. They had disbursed $854.85 in cash, $12.50 in store orders, and $188.12 in merchandise and retained $182.85 in cash. (Seventeenth Ward Relief Society Minutes and Records, "Annual Report for 1868," 144.)
24. See Hebrews 5:8.
25. Acting bishop George Morris had given particular details "of individual cases of persons in the ward who were wholly dependent on charity for support. He expressed his entire satisfaction of the course pursued by the F.R.S. [Female Relief Society]." (Seventeenth Ward Relief Society Minutes and Records, Feb. 18, 1869, 148.)
26. At a meeting three months later, the visiting committee reported an encounter with a Mrs. Frazier. Heeding this instruction from Snow to investigate the circumstances of the needy, the visitors asked to look in her trunks to ascertain her financial situation. Frazier at first refused, then partially lifted the lid of one trunk, but shut it down to prevent the women from seeing what was inside. The bishop instructed that no aid be given to Frazier and indicated he would work with her directly. (Seventeenth Ward Relief Society Minutes and Records, May 27, 1869, 177.)
27. George B. Wallace, acting president of the Salt Lake Stake, had said earlier in the meeting, "Every calling is honorable: the honor consists in doing honor to the calling unto which we are called, and in honoring ourselves in that calling." (Seventeenth Ward Relief Society Minutes and Records, Feb. 18, 1869, 146.)
28. Seventeenth Ward Relief Society president Marinda N. Hyde had earlier instructed the visiting teachers that they "must consult with their president upon any subject that claims the attention of the society, and all will work well together." (Seventeenth Ward Relief Society Minutes and Records, July 9, 1868, 94.)
29. Plato, *Gorgias,* 473a–475e.
30. Earlier in the meeting, George Morris said, "The object of this society is to labor in connection with the priesthood, to aid the bishop by looking after and administering to the wants of the poor—in comforting the sick and afflicted, etc." (Seventeenth Ward Relief Society Minutes and Records, Feb. 18, 1869, 147.)
31. On February 4, 1869, Brigham Young addressed the Relief Societies of the church from the Fifteenth Ward meetinghouse, praising women's efforts and activities. He encouraged girls to get a formal education, counseled women to seek meaningful employment to contribute to the community, and spoke about the responsibility of mothers to discipline children and educate them formally in school. He also encouraged women to learn bookkeeping and work in mercantile businesses and telegraph offices, relieving men for more physical work. At the next meeting of the Seventeenth

Ward Relief Society, Serepta M. Heywood asked that Young's speech be read aloud. "It was motioned and passed unanimously that the address be recorded in the Record Book of the Society." (Brigham Young, "An Address to the Female Relief Society," *Deseret News,* Feb. 24, 1869; Seventeenth Ward Relief Society Minutes and Records, Mar. 4, 1869, 153, 154–161.)

CHAPTER 11: ZINA D. H. YOUNG, "WE SERVE A JUST GOD"

1. E. B. [Emmeline B.] Wells, "Zina D. H. Young," *Young Woman's Journal* 12, no. 6 (June 1901): 254.
2. See, for example, Zina D. H. Young, "How I Gained My Testimony of the Truth," *Young Woman's Journal* 4, no. 7 (Apr. 1893): 317–319; Oliver B. Huntington, Diaries, vol. 9, 1843–1907, May 16, 1848, 88, BYU; Jill Mulvay Derr, Carol Cornwall Madsen, Kate Holbrook, and Matthew J. Grow, eds., *The First Fifty Years of Relief Society: Key Documents in Latter-day Saint Women's History* (Salt Lake City: Church Historian's Press, 2016), 655; "In Memoriam," *Woman's Exponent* 20, no. 15 (Feb. 15, 1892): 117.
3. Young was sealed to Joseph Smith in Nauvoo, Illinois. After Smith's death, she married Brigham Young. (Richard Lyman Bushman, *Joseph Smith: Rough Stone Rolling* [New York: Alfred A. Knopf, 2005], 439–440; Derr et al., *First Fifty Years,* 689. For more information on plural marriage in the 1840s, see "Plural Marriage in Kirtland and Nauvoo," Gospel Topics, accessed Feb. 8, 2016, lds.org.)
4. Clarissa Young's children were Maria, Willard, and Phebe. Zina Presendia Young remembered how her father asked her mother to take care "of his little ones whose mother was dead. She consented, and this event entirely changed my after-life; from being the pet and only child I now had to share with these motherless children. It was a trial in many ways, but my precious mother taught me to be unselfish and thank God for all his blessings and not complain, and I am thankful to say, following her advice without once alluding to the fact that my mother was not their own. Thus it proved to be the best lesson of my life, and a great blessing." ([Emmeline B. Wells], "A Distinguished Woman: Zina D. H. Young," *Woman's Exponent* 10, no. 14 [Dec. 15, 1881]: 107; Martha Sonntag Bradley and Mary Brown Firmage Woodward, *Four Zinas: A Story of Mothers and Daughters on the Mormon Frontier* [Salt Lake City: Signature Books, 2000], 207; Augusta Joyce Crocheron, *Representative Women of Deseret, a Book of Biographical Sketches to Accompany the Picture Bearing the Same Title* [Salt Lake City: J. C. Graham, 1884], 122–123.)
5. Susa Young Gates, *History of the Young Ladies' Mutual Improvement Association of the Church of Jesus Christ of Latter-day Saints* (Salt Lake City: Deseret News, 1911), 21.
6. Nauvoo Relief Society Minute Book, Mar. 24, 1842, 16, in Derr et al., *First Fifty Years,* 38.
7. Derr et al., *First Fifty Years,* xxi; Zina D. H. Young, Diary, 1844–1845, June 18, 1844; July 4, 1844, CHL.
8. Eliza R. Snow, *The Personal Writings of Eliza Roxcy Snow,* ed. Maureen Ursenbach Beecher (Logan: Utah State University Press, 2000), Jan. 1, 1847, 151; see also [Wells], "A Distinguished Woman," 107.
9. Gates, *History of the Young Ladies' Mutual Improvement Association,* 21.
10. Lehi Ward, Utah Stake, Relief Society Minutes and Records, vol. 1, 1868–1879, Oct. 27, 1868, 1, CHL.
11. Lehi Ward Relief Society Minutes, Oct. 27, 1869, 26–30. Eliza R. Snow did not bear children, but she was referred to as a "Mother in Israel" and spoke often about the divinity of motherhood. (See [Susa Young Gates], "The Mother of Mothers in Israel," *Relief Society Magazine* 3, no. 4 [Apr. 1916]: 189–190.)
12. Lehi Ward Relief Society Minutes, Oct. 27, 1869, 30–31.
13. Mrs. E. J. T., "Sarah Thornton Coleman," *Woman's Exponent* 20, no. 21 (May 15, 1892): 168; Hamilton Gardner and Lehi Centennial Committee, *Lehi Centennial History, 1850–1950* (Lehi, UT: Free Press, 1950), 371, 301, 242.
14. Lehi Ward Relief Society Minutes, Oct. 27, 1869, 30; Gardner, *Lehi Centennial History,* 297.
15. Both Young and Snow struggled initially with public speaking. When Eliza R. Snow first addressed the Lehi Relief Society earlier that morning, she said, "Your presidentess has desired me to address you. I do not of myself feel competent to do so, but with your faith and prayers and the Spirit of the

Lord I may be able to say something that will comfort and bless you." Thirteen years later, after Young had gained much experience, Emmeline B. Wells praised her public speaking ability: "Had she been educated for the platform, and spoken upon other subjects, she would doubtless have received many encomiums of praise and won distinction in the lecture field; but being only a 'Mormon,' she is content with the love of her own people, and ambition to do good to others inspires her to move forward wherever duty calls her for the benefit of womankind and the interests of Zion. And in pursuing this course she finds her highest happiness." (Lehi Ward Relief Society Minutes, Oct. 27, 1869, 26; [Wells], "A Distinguished Woman," *Woman's Exponent* 10, no. 16 [Jan. 15, 1882]: 123.)

16. Snow said in the morning session, "While sitting here I have been looking upon the faces of my sisters and can see the form of Deity there." (Lehi Ward Relief Society Minutes, Oct. 27, 1869, 26.)
17. Snow also said, "I have been reflecting on the great work we have to perform, even in helping in the salvation of the living and the dead." (Lehi Ward Relief Society Minutes, Oct. 27, 1869, 26.)
18. Snow taught, "We know the Lord has laid high responsibilities upon us, and there is not a wish or desire that the Lord has implanted in our hearts in righteousness but will be realized." (Lehi Ward Relief Society Minutes, Oct. 27, 1869, 27.)
19. See 1 Corinthians 10:13; and Alma 13:28.
20. See Revelation 21:7.

CHAPTER 12: JANE H. NEYMAN, "BE FORBEARING AND FORGIVING"

1. Louisa Barnes Pratt, "Obituaries," *Woman's Exponent* 9, no. 1 (June 1, 1880): 4; "Jane Harper Neyman Fisher," *The First Fifty Years of Relief Society*, accessed June 17, 2016, churchhistorianspress.org; "Neyman, William," Old Nauvoo Burial Ground Inventory of Markers and Graves, Nauvoo Death Records, Neibaur to Nye, 1837–1851, Nauvoo Restoration, Inc., Early Residents Files, CHL; Lyndon W. Cook, *Nauvoo Deaths and Marriages, 1839–1845* (Orem, UT: Grandin Book, 1994), 112; Fred E. Woods, "The Cemetery Record of William D. Huntington, Nauvoo Sexton," *Mormon Historical Studies* 3, no. 1 (Spring 2002): 150.
2. Nauvoo Relief Society Minute Book, Apr. 28, 1842, [42], in Jill Mulvay Derr, Carol Cornwall Madsen, Kate Holbrook, and Matthew J. Grow, eds., *The First Fifty Years of Relief Society: Key Documents in Latter-day Saint Women's History* (Salt Lake City: Church Historian's Press, 2016), 61.
3. Nauvoo Relief Society Minute Book, Apr. 28, 1842, [42], in Derr et al., *First Fifty Years,* 61.
4. Andrew H. Hedges, Alex D. Smith, and Richard Lloyd Anderson, eds., *Journals, Volume 2: December 1841–April 1843,* vol. 2 of the Journals series of *The Joseph Smith Papers,* ed. Dean C. Jessee, Ronald K. Esplin, and Richard Lyman Bushman (Salt Lake City: Church Historian's Press, 2011), 63. Neyman's older daughter, Mary Ann Neyman Nickerson, remembered that "there was John C. Bennett and Law and the Higbees and others all trying to lead the youth away, and we found it so. They were holding secret meetings in all parts of the city, saying it was the prophet's teachings." (Mary Ann Nickerson, "A Woman's Testimony," *Woman's Exponent* 36, no. 7 [Feb. 1908]: 51.)
5. Pratt, "Obituaries," 4; Louisa Barnes Pratt, *The History of Louisa Barnes Pratt: Being the Autobiography of a Mormon Missionary Widow and Pioneer,* ed. S. George Ellsworth (Logan: Utah State University Press, 1998), 377.
6. Nauvoo Relief Society Minute Book, July 14, 1842, [76], in Derr et al., *First Fifty Years,* 89–90. On March 31, 1842, Joseph Smith said "that none should be received into the society but those who were worthy—proposed that the society go into a close examination of every candidate." During that same meeting, Emma Smith said, "We wanted none in this society but those who could and would walk straight and were determined to do good and not evil." (Nauvoo Relief Society Minute Book, Mar. 31, 1842, 22–23, in Derr et al., *First Fifty Years,* 42–44.)
7. Pratt, "Obituaries," 4.
8. Neyman's counselors were Louisa Barnes Pratt and Caroline Barnes Crosby, who were sisters. (Beaver First Ward, Beaver Stake, Relief Society Minutes, 1868–1878, Jan. 11, 1868, [1], CHL.)
9. Beaver First Ward Relief Society Minutes, Feb. 1868, 4, 13.

10. Beaver First Ward Relief Society Minutes, Nov. 4, 1869, 25.
11. 1 Peter 4:8.
12. 1 Corinthians 13:4–5.
13. See Colossians 3:8.
14. The Mormon creed: "Mind your own business." (Michael Hicks, "Minding Business: A Note on 'The Mormon Creed,'" *BYU Studies* 26, no. 4 [Fall 1986]: 125–132.)
15. See Psalm 141:3.

CHAPTER 13: DRUSILLA D. HENDRICKS, "THE PRAYER OF FAITH"

1. Her illness continued for at least two years and perhaps longer. (Drusilla Dorris Hendricks, "Historical Sketch of James Hendricks and Drusilla Dorris Hendricks," typescript, 1877, 2, CHL.)
2. Hendricks, "Historical Sketch," 9; "Died," *Deseret News,* July 20, 1870.
3. Alexander L. Baugh, *A Call to Arms: The 1838 Mormon Defense of Northern Missouri,* Dissertations in Latter-day Saint History (Provo, UT: Joseph Fielding Smith Institute for Latter-day Saint History; BYU Studies, 2000), 99–113.
4. James Hendricks progressed to where he could hold things in one of his hands and walk short distances with the assistance of others or with a cane. He passed away on July 8, 1870, after a long sickness. (Hendricks, "Historical Sketch," 11–21; "Died.")
5. Neighbors and friends often helped the Hendricks family. Hendricks remembered, "I have just found out how the widow's crust and barrel held out through the famine. . . . Just as it was out, someone was sent to fill it." (Hendricks, "Historical Sketch," 14–16.)
6. Hendricks, "Historical Sketch," 15.
7. Of their five children, four settled in Cache Valley, Utah Territory, and one passed away before the family moved to Cache Valley. (Richmond Branch, Cache Stake, manuscript history, typescript, 1860, CHL; Hendricks, "Historical Sketch," 21.)
8. Smithfield Branch, Cache Stake, Relief Society Minutes, vol. 1, 1868–1878, May 13, 1868, 2, CHL.
9. Smithfield Branch Relief Society Minutes, Aug. 7, 1871, 98–99.
10. The Mormon Battalion served from July 1846 to July 1847 but never saw battle. (See Larry C. Porter, Clark V. Johnson, and Susan Easton Black, "Mormon Battalion," in *Encyclopedia of Latter-day Saint History,* ed. Arnold K. Garr, Donald Q. Cannon, and Richard O. Cowan [Salt Lake City: Deseret Book, 2000], 783–785; and Larry C. Porter, "The Church and the Mexican-American War," in *Nineteenth-Century Saints at War,* ed. Robert C. Freeman [Provo, UT: Religious Studies Center, Brigham Young University, 2006], 41–76.)
11. William Hendricks was one of the youngest members of the Mormon Battalion. (Martha Hendricks Aylworth, "A Sketch of the Life of William Dorris Hendricks," typescript, n.d., 1, CHL; Tim Vitale, "William Dorris Hendricks," *Portraits in Time: Notes from Cache Valley's Pioneer Past* [Logan, UT: Logan Herald Journal, 1997], 58.)
12. Hendricks, "Historical Sketch," 17–19.
13. Hendricks recounted paying tithing by making gloves and mittens. With the family's yoke of cattle, her son William also "hauled rock for the temple to pay our tithing." (Hendricks, "Historical Sketch," 15.)
14. In a later reminiscence, Hendricks wrote of her husband, "He was a martyr for the cause of truth. . . . He often wanted the brethren to lay hands on him to ease him from pain." (Hendricks, "Historical Sketch," 11–12, 21.)
15. Brigham Young supported the raising of the Mormon Battalion in hopes of receiving financial assistance needed to cross the plains and to demonstrate loyalty to the United States. However, many rank-and-file Latter-day Saints viewed the battalion with considerable suspicion and believed it was a conspiracy to further persecute them. (Porter, "The Church and the Mexican-American War," 43–44, 51–52; Matthew J. Grow, *"Liberty to the Downtrodden": Thomas L. Kane, Romantic Reformer* [New Haven, CT: Yale University Press, 2009], 58.)
16. In her reminiscence, Hendricks wrote of this experience, "My eyes followed as he started through

the tall heavy grass wet with dew. I thought how easy something might happen, for that was a sickly climate." (Hendricks, "Historical Sketch," 18.)

17. See Matthew 19:20.
18. Hendricks remembered, "William raised his eyes and looked me in the face. I knew then that he would go as well as I know now that he has been. I could not swallow one bite of breakfast but I waited on the rest thinking I might never have my family all together again. I had no photograph of him, but I took one in my mind and said to myself, If I never see you again until the morning of the Resurrection, I shall know you are my child." (Hendricks, "Historical Sketch," 18.)
19. Hendricks wrote, "I thought the cows would be shelter for me, and I knelt down and told the Lord if he wanted my child to take him, only spare his life and let him be restored to me and to the bosom of the church. I felt it was all I could do. Then the voice that talked with me in the morning answered me, saying, 'It shall be done unto you as it was unto Abraham when he offered Isaac on the altar.' I don't know whether I milked or not, for I felt the Lord had spoken to me. . . . I don't think that Abraham felt any worse than we did; I cannot tell the hardships we endured by his going. . . . We bore it with the patience of Job." (Hendricks, "Historical Sketch," 18–19; see also Genesis 22:1–13.)
20. Martha Hendricks Aylworth, William Hendricks's daughter, wrote about how while on duty, her father "thought of his mother's parting words, 'Son, if you are ever in trouble, kneel down and ask the Lord for help.' He knelt down and prayed earnestly for deliverance." (Aylworth, "Sketch of the Life of William Dorris Hendricks," 1.)
21. See Doctrine and Covenants 4:5; 82:19.

CHAPTER 14: ELIZA R. SNOW, "AN ELEVATION SO HIGH ABOVE THE ORDINARY"

1. While visiting Washington, Utah Territory, Young reportedly retired to bed while the women stayed up all night cooking. (Robert Glass Cleland and Juanita Brooks, eds., *A Mormon Chronicle: The Diaries of John D. Lee, 1848–1876,* 2 vols. [Salt Lake City: University of Utah Press, 1983], 2:114.)
2. Brigham Young, "Remarks," *Deseret News Weekly,* Nov. 24, 1869.
3. Although the formal assignment was given to Horne, Snow played an important supporting role. Horne expressed concern about her ability to bear the responsibility of the new movement: "It was some time before I could gain sufficient courage to perform this labor, but Sister Snow urged me to do my duty, so with fear and trembling I endeavored to do so." (Mary Isabella Horne, "Address of Mrs. M. Isabella Horne," *Woman's Exponent* 20, no. 18 [Apr. 1, 1892]: 138.)
4. Moses 7:18–19.
5. Leonard J. Arrington, *Great Basin Kingdom: An Economic History of the Latter-day Saints, 1830–1900* (1958; repr., Salt Lake City: University of Utah Press, 1993), 195, 235, 251–254. Snow's brother Lorenzo Snow organized a successful cooperative community in Brigham City, Utah Territory, starting in 1864. This initial experiment laid the groundwork for later attempts in the 1870s. (Arrington, *Great Basin Kingdom,* 324–325.)
6. The other counselors were Zina D. H. Young, Margaret T. Smoot, Sarah M. Kimball, Phebe Woodruff, and Bathsheba W. Smith. (Susa Young Gates, *History of the Young Ladies' Mutual Improvement Association of the Church of Jesus Christ of Latter-day Saints* [Salt Lake City: Deseret News, 1911], 34, 37.)
7. The junior group first became known as the Young Ladies' Retrenchment Association; that name was later changed to Young Ladies' Mutual Improvement Association and eventually Young Women. (Eleventh Ward, Salt Lake Stake, Young Women's Mutual Improvement Association Minutes and Records, vol. 1, 1871–1877, Oct. 18, 1871, 1, CHL; Gates, *History of the Young Ladies' Mutual Improvement Association,* 150–151; "Death Closes Rich Career of Church Worker, Mother," *Deseret News,* Mar. 24, 1937.)
8. Gates, *History of the Young Ladies' Mutual Improvement Association,* 36; see also Jill Mulvay Derr, Janath Russell Cannon, and Maureen Ursenbach Beecher, *Women of Covenant: The Story of Relief Society* (Salt Lake City: Deseret Book, 1992), 114–115. The development of different levels of the

Relief Society and retrenchment organizations followed specific needs. Wards organized Relief Societies first, starting in 1867, while senior retrenchment meetings were held on a more central level, rather than in local wards. Stake Relief Society organizations commenced in 1877 to coordinate ward societies, and the semimonthly retrenchment meeting later morphed into the Relief Society general board. For more information on these organizations and for minutes of some of the first meetings, see Jill Mulvay Derr, Carol Cornwall Madsen, Kate Holbrook, and Matthew J. Grow, eds., *The First Fifty Years of Relief Society: Key Documents in Latter-day Saint Women's History* (Salt Lake City: Church Historian's Press, 2016), 338–349, 353–357.

9. Derr, Cannon, and Beecher, *Women of Covenant,* 114.
10. Kimball explained that the class was actually an "educational society," with implicit instruction for women to "make this grow into something that will benefit us." (Senior and Junior Cooperative Retrenchment Association, Minutes, Salt Lake City, Utah Territory, looseleaf, 1871–1874, Oct. 11, 1872, 42nd Meeting, [1–2], CHL.)
11. At the beginning of the meeting, minutes were read from meetings of the Cooperative Retrenchment Association, the Salt Lake City Seventh Ward Relief Society, the Salt Lake City Ninth Ward Relief Society, and the Salt Lake City Eleventh Ward Relief Society.
12. When she was baptized in 1835 at the age of thirty-three, Snow recalled an experience in which she saw a candle with a long flame directly over her feet. "I sought to know the interpretation, and received the following, 'The lamp of intelligence shall be lighted over your path.' I was satisfied." (Eliza R. Snow, "Sketch of My Life," in *The Personal Writings of Eliza Roxcy Snow,* ed. Maureen Ursenbach Beecher [Logan: Utah State University Press, 2000], 10.)
13. As a young woman, Snow learned secretarial skills by assisting her father in his public business. Her mother considered housekeeping an important foundation for all female accomplishments and felt that "useful knowledge was the most reliable basis of independence." Snow's parents taught her and her siblings the value of both labor and education; Snow remembered, "Book studies and schooling were ever present—intermingling with every other industry, not omitting music and singing." In Kirtland in 1836, she taught at a girls' school. (Snow, "Sketch of My Life," 6–7, 10.)
14. Snow may be paraphrasing one of at least two talks that Brigham Young gave in general conference about building the kingdom of God through sacrifice and the future organization of select Saints in the order of Enoch. (Brigham Young, Oct. 9, 1872, in *Journal of Discourses,* 26 vols. [Liverpool: Various Publishers, 1855–1886], 15:158–167, 220–229.)
15. In the nineteenth century, the term *heathen* referred to peoples without a Judeo-Christian background, and many Christian sects were proselytizing in nations that lacked a substantial Christian presence. Some Mormon missionaries went to places such as South Africa, China, India, and islands of the Pacific during the second half of the century. (See William R. Hutchison, *Errand to the World: American Protestant Thought and Foreign Missions* [Chicago: University of Chicago Press, 1987]; Rex Thomas Price Jr., "The Mormon Missionary of the Nineteenth Century" [PhD diss., University of Wisconsin–Madison, 1991], 83; and *Oxford English Dictionary,* s.v. "heathen.")
16. Latter-day Saints believed that through participation in temple ceremonies and faithfulness in their lives, they could become "kings and priests" and "queens and priestesses" in eternity. (Carol Cornwall Madsen, "Mormon Women and the Temple: Toward a New Understanding," in *Sisters in Spirit: Mormon Women in Historical and Cultural Perspective,* ed. Maureen Ursenbach Beecher and Lavina Fielding Anderson [Urbana: University of Illinois Press, 1987], 90–91, 102–103.)

CHAPTER 15: MARY ANN FREEZE, "OUR MISSION"

1. James Burnham quarried stone for the Nauvoo temple and died as a result of bleeding in the lungs. The family remained in Nauvoo until the fall of 1846, long after the majority of the Saints had left. From Winter Quarters, Mary Burnham sent her two sons to the Salt Lake Valley with another family because she was unable to provide for them. The rest of the family arrived in October 1852. (Augusta Joyce Crocheron, *Representative Women of Deseret, a Book of Biographical Sketches to Accompany the Picture Bearing the Same Title* [Salt Lake City: J. C. Graham, 1884], 51–53.)
2. At Freeze's funeral in 1912, Joseph F. Smith called her "a minister of love among the young women

of the Church of Jesus Christ of Latter-day Saints." He went on to say, "She has labored diligently and earnestly in trying to persuade the daughters of Zion to come to a knowledge of the truth as she possessed it. She seemed to be thoroughly established in it." ("Address of President Joseph F. Smith Delivered at the Funeral Services of Sister Mary A. Freeze," *Young Woman's Journal* 23, no. 3 [Mar. 1912]: 129.)

3. Susa Young Gates, *History of the Young Ladies' Mutual Improvement Association of the Church of Jesus Christ of Latter-day Saints* (Salt Lake City: Deseret News, 1911), 66.
4. Gates, *History of the Young Ladies' Mutual Improvement Association,* 65.
5. The first stake to have a stake YLMIA organization was the Salt Lake Stake. (Mary E. Connelly, "Mary A. Freeze," *Young Woman's Journal* 23, no. 3 [Mar. 1912]: 125.)
6. Crocheron, *Representative Women of Deseret,* 55.
7. Connelly, "Mary A. Freeze," 126.
8. See Abraham 3:22–23.
9. Freeze attended several meetings of the Senior Retrenchment Society and recorded that on January 8, 1875, the group discussed the importance of "encouraging the young in the great work they had begun." (Mary Ann B. Freeze, "Diaries" [1875–1899], Jan. 8, 1875, BYU.)
10. Freeze wrote often about the importance of diligence: "I am striving to purify myself, and keep all of the commandments of God, to be diligent in the performance of every duty assisting to roll forth the great work our Father has established in the last days, that I may be worthy to receive the blessings which have been pronounced upon my head; for they are great and many, and I know I shall receive them if found worthy." (Crocheron, *Representative Women of Deseret,* 55.)
11. See 2 Corinthians 6:7; and 2 Nephi 1:23.

CHAPTER 16: MARY B. FERGUSON, "ESSAY ON FAITH"

1. Ferguson's obituary states that she was "stolen from her mother," but in her autobiography she wrote that her mother was very ill and placed her in the care of a hired nurse. (Amelia Gourley, Julia M. Okelberry, and Lucy P. Taylor, "Tribute of Love," *Woman's Exponent* 38, no. 6 [Jan. 1910]: 46; Mary Tyndale Ferguson, "Biography of Mary Tyndale Ferguson (Pioneer)," typescript, Daughters of Utah Pioneers, Goshen, UT, [1–2].)
2. Ferguson's uncle, Andrew Welsh, the brother-in-law of her birth mother, Magdalene Heathen Tyndale, supported her financially during her childhood, including paying for her education. Shortly after leaving school and finding a job at the age of sixteen, Ferguson supported herself. (Ferguson, "Biography of Mary Tyndale Ferguson," [1–2].)
3. Ferguson attended Sunday School and a minister's class, and she was president of a missionary society. (Gourley, Okelberry, and Taylor, "Tribute of Love"; Ferguson, "Biography of Mary Tyndale Ferguson," [2].)
4. Ferguson recalled that "in the fall of 1845, my sister Catherine and her husband joined the Mormons." Catherine Heathen, the daughter of Ferguson's birth mother and her first husband, has no record of baptism. Her foster sister, Catherine Douglas, who also lived with Agnes Reid and who worked at the loom factory, was baptized with her husband, Andrew Ferguson, in 1845. (Ferguson, "Biography of Mary Tyndale Ferguson," [1–2]; Andrew Ferguson, autobiography, 1852, 2–3, BYU.)
5. Ferguson, "Biography of Mary Tyndale Ferguson," [2].
6. The Baxters' oldest son, Henry, died of scarlet fever in January 1854. (Ferguson, "Biography of Mary Tyndale Ferguson," [3–4].)
7. Ferguson, "Biography of Mary Tyndale Ferguson," [4].
8. Gourley, Okelberry, and Taylor, "Tribute of Love."
9. Andrew Ferguson's first wife, Catherine Douglas, at one point lived with Agnes Reid, Mary Ferguson's adoptive mother. (Ferguson, "Biography of Mary Tyndale Ferguson," [2], [4]; Ferguson, autobiography, 2, 244.)
10. Ferguson, "Biography of Mary Tyndale Ferguson," [4].
11. Goshen Ward, Utah Stake, Relief Society Minutes and Records, vol. 1, 1870–1872, Nov. 3, 1870, 1; Dec. 1, 1870, 2; Jan. 5, 1871, 3; June 1, 1871, 11; July 6, 1871, 11–12, CHL.

12. Spanish Fork Ward, Utah Stake, Relief Society Minutes and Records, vol. 2s, 1875–1884, Oct. 18, 1879, 168; Oct. 22, 1880, 202.
13. Hebrews 11:1, Joseph Smith Translation.
14. See Matthew 13:46; and James 2:18.
15. Ferguson remembered, "My mother and brothers felt very bad about our decision to leave, and my brother William offered me every inducement if I would leave the Mormons." (Ferguson, "Biography of Mary Tyndale Ferguson," [3].)
16. Of her own experience crossing the plains in 1853, Ferguson wrote: "I was very sick all of the way, but I had faith in God and had laid up prayers against an evil day and my Father in Heaven heard my supplication and answered them. It was a year of high waters, which made our journey more difficult, but with all we were blessed and our lives preserved under dangerous circumstances." She added that she was pregnant for most of the trip: "My son John was born on this journey at Black Fork, forty-five miles from Salt Lake, September 6, 1853." (Ferguson, "Biography of Mary Tyndale Ferguson," [3].)
17. See Isaiah 35:1.
18. See Genesis 13:16; and Abraham 3:14; see also Isaiah 9:7.
19. Isaiah 54:2.
20. Ferguson is quoting a Protestant hymn by Irishman Thomas Kelly, published in several different hymnals starting in 1820, including Emma Smith, ed., *A Collection of Sacred Hymns, for the Church of Jesus Christ of Latter Day Saints* (Nauvoo, IL: E. Robinson, 1841), 169–170; and *Sacred Hymns and Spiritual Songs, for the Church of Jesus Christ of Latter-day Saints in Europe,* 9th ed. (Liverpool: F. D. Richards, 1851), 57–58.
21. Alexander Ross, "God's Kingdom or Nothing at All," *Latter-day Saints' Millennial Star* 27, no. 31 (Aug. 5, 1865): 496.
22. No minutes exist for the Spanish Fork Young Ladies' Association from this time period.

CHAPTER 17: LILLIE T. FREEZE, "THE FRUITS OF OUR LABOR"

1. "Death Closes Rich Career of Church Worker, Mother," *Deseret News,* Mar. 24, 1937; Andrew Jenson, *Latter-day Saint Biographical Encyclopedia: A Compilation of Biographical Sketches of Prominent Men and Women in the Church of Jesus Christ of Latter-day Saints,* 4 vols. (Salt Lake City: Andrew Jenson History Co., 1901–1936), 4:284; Susa Young Gates, *History of the Young Ladies' Mutual Improvement Association of the Church of Jesus Christ of Latter-day Saints* (Salt Lake City: Deseret News, 1911), 149–150.
2. Eleventh Ward YWMIA Minutes and Records, vol. 1, 1871–1877, Oct. 18, 1871, 1, CHL; Jenson, *LDS Biographical Encyclopedia,* 4:284; Eleventh Ward YWMIA Minutes and Records, vol. 2, 1878–1889, Feb. 21, 1881, 195; Oct. 24, 1881, 227. For more on the manuscript newspaper, see chapter 19 herein.
3. Gates, *History of the Young Ladies' Mutual Improvement Association,* 151. Mary Ann Freeze recorded in her diary on their wedding day: "This has been a most eventful day to us all, as we have had an addition made to our family in the shape of a new wife. We have all been at the Endowment House to witness the ceremony, and I had the pleasure of giving the bride away." James Freeze eventually had four plural wives. (Mary Ann Burnham Freeze, Diary, June 14, 1875, BYU; Jenson, *LDS Biographical Encyclopedia,* 4:260.)
4. Elmina S. Taylor, general president of the YLMIA, thought it would be an advantage to both associations to have Freeze act as an officer on both the Primary and YLMIA general boards and represent both while traveling. (Gates, *History of the Young Ladies' Mutual Improvement Association,* 151; "Death Closes Rich Career"; Jenson, *LDS Biographical Encyclopedia,* 4:284.)
5. Freeze was concerned about the use of tobacco among local boys. (Eleventh Ward YWMIA Minutes and Records, Sept. 20, 1880, 171–172.)
6. Eleventh Ward YWMIA Minutes and Records, Sept. 27, 1880, 174.
7. Also present and speaking were Elmina S. Taylor, first YLMIA general president; Mary Isabella Horne, first Salt Lake Stake Relief Society president and president of the Retrenchment Association;

Sarah M. Kimball, president of the Salt Lake City Fifteenth Ward Relief Society and secretary of the first general Relief Society presidency; Serepta M. Heywood, counselor in the Salt Lake City Seventeenth Ward Relief Society presidency; Hannah Tapfield King, president of the Seventeenth Ward Relief Society; Clara Cannon, second counselor in the Primary general presidency; and Elizabeth Howard, president of the Big Cottonwood Ward Relief Society and counselor to Horne in the Retrenchment Association. (Eleventh Ward YWMIA Minutes and Records, Oct. 18, 1880, 174–175.)

8. The Salt Lake City Eleventh Ward Junior Retrenchment Association was organized in 1870. Freeze joined almost immediately. (Gates, *History of the Young Ladies' Mutual Improvement Association,* 150–151.)
9. Nineteenth-century Latter-day Saints generally used the term "celestial marriage" to refer to plural marriage.
10. Articles and editorials in church-sponsored magazines often highlighted girls' responsibility to prepare for marriage and motherhood. (See, for example, L. W. E., "Young Ladies' Associations," *Contributor* 1, no. 7 [Apr. 1880]: 167.)
11. A fear of public speaking persisted among the young women, even ten years after their first gathering. A month before this October meeting in 1880, Eleventh Ward YLMIA counselor Louie White "spoke about the timidity which we were possessed of when we tried to arise and speak. Said we should try to conquer that feeling, for it was our duty to speak of the goodness of God. Said none were too young to do this." (Eleventh Ward YWMIA Minutes and Records, Sept. 20, 1880, 172.)
12. In July 1877, the Eleventh Ward YLMIA adopted resolutions, including one "that we will not follow after the foolish and disgusting fashions of the world, but will dress in a plain, neat, and becoming manner, strictly avoiding all extravagance, and devote the means saved thereby to the upbuilding of the kingdom of God." (Eleventh Ward YWMIA Minutes and Records, July 1877, 497.)
13. An 1899 dictionary defined *modesty* as "a sense of propriety; freedom from arrogance, boldness, or presumption; unobtrusiveness, bashfulness, diffidence; bashful reserve. . . . Moderation; freedom from excess, extravagance, or exaggeration. Chastity; purity of manners; decency; freedom from lewdness or unchastity." *Prudery,* by contrast, meant "affected or excessive niceness or preciseness; coyness." (Robert Hunter and Charles Morris, eds., *Universal Dictionary of the English Language* [New York: Peter Fenelon Collier, 1899], 3168, 3794.)
14. The Eleventh Ward YLMIA also decreed "that we will cease to speak evil of each other or of any of the Lord's anointed." (Eleventh Ward YWMIA Minutes and Records, July 1877, 497.)
15. Freeze later wrote articles for the *Young Woman's Journal* on etiquette. (See Lillie T. Freeze, "Chapter on Etiquette," *Young Woman's Journal* 3, nos. 6 and 8 [Mar. and May 1892]: 280–282, 382–383.)

CHAPTER 18: ELIZA R. SNOW, "EVERY SISTER SHOULD COME FORWARD"

1. Brigham Young dedicated Kanab, located in the arid southern Utah desert, in 1870, a few years after settlers had first grazed cattle there and built a fort. (Martha Sonntag Bradley, *A History of Kane County,* Utah Centennial County History Series [Salt Lake City: Utah State Historical Society, 1999], 60–62, 74.)
2. Snow recorded that she and Young had "traveled one thousand miles by team over jolting rocks and through bedded sand, occasionally camping out at night on long drives." They returned to Salt Lake City in March 1881. (Eliza R. Snow, "Sketch of My Life," in *The Personal Writings of Eliza Roxcy Snow,* ed. Maureen Ursenbach Beecher [Logan: Utah State University Press, 2000], 37; see also Jill Mulvay Derr, "Mrs. Smith Goes to Washington: Eliza R. Snow Smith's Visit to Southern Utah, 1880–81," in *Honoring Juanita Brooks: A Compilation of 30 Annual Presentations from the Juanita Brooks Lecture Series, Dixie State University,* ed. Douglas D. Alder [St. George, UT: Dixie State University, 2014], 475–510.)
3. Derr, "Mrs. Smith Goes to Washington," 495–498.
4. Snow formed organizations throughout the Mormon settlements in the West. She remembered, "I have traveled from one end of Utah Territory to the other—into Nevada and Idaho in the interests

of these organizations—have organized hundreds of the Young Ladies' and Primary Associations since their introduction." (Snow, "Sketch of My Life," 37.)

5. The group camped for three nights on the way from St. George to Kanab, an eighty-mile trip. They also visited Long Valley, Orderville, Glendale, and Johnson—all in southern Utah—before returning to St. George. (Eliza R. Snow Smith, "Trip to Kanab," *Woman's Exponent* 9, no. 20 [Mar. 15, 1881]: 157.)
6. Kanab Utah Stake Relief Society Minutes and Records, vol. 1, 1878–1921, Dec. 6, 1878, 3, CHL. Elizabeth Little noted at the official welcome to Snow and Young, "A long cherished hope is realized in the happy event. Here, on the frontier of Utah, in comparative isolation, it is the first time that any of our representative ladies have visited us." (M. Elizabeth Little, "A Welcome," *Woman's Exponent* 9, no. 21 [Apr. 1, 1881]: 165.)
7. Snow Smith, "Trip to Kanab," 157; M. Elizabeth Little, "Kanab Relief Society," *Woman's Exponent* 9, no. 21 (Apr. 1, 1881): 165–166. The Kanab Relief Society was established on November 12, 1873, and the Kanab Stake Relief Society held its first quarterly conference on December 6, 1878. (Kanab Ward, Kanab Stake, Relief Society Minutes and Records, Minute Book A, 1873–1883, Nov. 12, 1873, 3–4, CHL; Kanab Utah Stake Relief Society Minutes and Records, Dec. 6, 1878, 1–4.)
8. Snow and Young stayed with Minerva Snow during their time in St. George, and she accompanied them on their trip to Kane County. (Derr, "Mrs. Smith Goes to Washington," 483, 491.)
9. Little, "A Welcome," 165.
10. Emmeline B. Wells, "Salt Lake Stake Relief Society Conference," *Woman's Exponent* 9, no. 3 (July 1, 1880): 21–22.
11. Derr, "Mrs. Smith Goes to Washington," 479–482.
12. Young spoke after Snow, encouraging women to accept and honor the principle of plural marriage and never to speak disrespectfully of their husbands. "My sisters," Young said, "we have had a feast of correct principles." (Little, "Kanab Relief Society," 166.)
13. Minerva Snow spoke after Young and encouraged the women: "We should overcome our failings. What are the little trials of this life to the great blessings that are before us if we are faithful?" (Little, "Kanab Relief Society," 166.)
14. The bulk of this discourse was paraphrased by Elizabeth Little, who took the minutes, but in these last two sentences, Little is apparently quoting Snow directly. Snow told the Santa Clara Relief Society on November 27, 1880, that "the young ladies of Zion are greater than the queens of the earth. We can become what we desire." (Santa Clara Ward, Saint George Stake, Relief Society Minutes and Records, vol. 3, 1873–1893, Nov. 27, 1880, 47, CHL.)
15. Little's report of the meeting was sent to Emmeline B. Wells in Salt Lake City and printed in the *Woman's Exponent.* There is no report of the February 13, 1881, meeting in the Kanab Ward Relief Society minutes or the Kanab Stake Relief Society minutes, but the minutes of the next meeting make reference to the visit and to Snow's speech. (Kanab Ward Relief Society Minutes, Mar. 3, 1881, 165.)

CHAPTER 19: ELLENOR G. JONES, "THE POWER OF PRAYER"

1. Ellen Jones, 1850 U.S. Census, Cincinnati Ward 4, Hamilton Co., OH. The members of the family are listed as "free inhabitants." (Eleventh Ward, Salt Lake Stake, Record of Members, "Temple Donations Paid from April 1st 1892 to the Dedication of the Temple," CHL; Death Certificate, Redding, Shasta Co., CA, Mar. 21, 1922.)
2. Ellen Jones, 1860 U.S. Census, Township 1, San Mateo Co., CA; Deeds, San Mateo, CA, Aug. 3, 1869, 10:358–365. Their third son, Joseph M. Jones, died in 1869 at the age of four in San Francisco. (California, San Francisco Area Funeral Home Records, N. Gray and Co., Register, 1863–1878, 286, San Francisco History Center, San Francisco Public Library.)
3. "Married," *Sacramento Daily Union,* Nov. 20, 1865. It is unknown whether there was any relation between Berry Jones and Hugh Stevenson Jones. Ellenor Jones was a woman of some financial means. She acted as the administrator of her first husband's estate, which was worth between six and ten thousand dollars. ("[Untitled]," *Daily Alta California,* Aug. 9, 1866; Deeds, San Mateo Co., CA,

Aug. 3, 1869, 10:358–365; Nov. 27, 1872, 18:334–336; Apr. 5, 1875, 24:400–401; Oct. 10, 1882, 34:589–591.)

4. "H. S. Jones 1832–1893," Gravestone, Gavilan Hills Memorial Park, Gilroy, CA; Ellinor Jones, 1870 U.S. Census, Salt Lake City Ward 13, Salt Lake Co., Utah Territory; Elenor Jones, 1880 U.S. Census, Salt Lake City Ward 11, Salt Lake Co., Utah Territory; Hugh S. Jones, 1880 U.S. Census, Gilroy, Santa Clara Co., CA.
5. Ellinor Jones, 1870 U.S. Census, Salt Lake City Ward 13, Salt Lake Co., Utah Territory; Elenor Jones, 1880 U.S. Census, Salt Lake City Ward 11, Salt Lake Co., Utah Territory. Eleanor G. Jones is listed as a widow in the *San Francisco Directory, 1873* (San Francisco: Henry G. Langley, 1873), 333.
6. California, Death Index, 1905–1939, Surnames E–L, 5503; Death Certificate.
7. Thomas Jones, 1880 U.S. Census, New Jasper, Greene Co., OH. The 1850 U.S. Census lists Ellenor and her siblings, as well as their mother, listed as Maria Jones, as "mulatto." One of Ellenor's sisters married a "free colored" man. (Ellen Jones, 1850 U.S. Census, Cincinnati Ward 4, Hamilton Co., OH; Jesse Beckley, 1840 U.S. Census, Alexandria, Alexandria Co., District of Columbia; Jesse Beckley, 1850 U.S. Census, Cincinnati Ward 4, Hamilton Co., OH.)
8. W. Paul Reeve, *Religion of a Different Color: Race and the Mormon Struggle for Whiteness* (New York: Oxford University Press, 2015), 140–170.
9. Endowment House, Endowments of the Living, vol. G, 1868–1872, Eleanor Georgina Jones, Sept. 6, 1869, 109, microfilm 1,239,501, FHL; Endowment House, Endowments of the Living, vol. H, 1872–1878, Margaret Elizabeth Reed Beckley, Nov. 29, 1877, 385, microfilm 183,407, FHL.
10. Ellenor G. Jones to Brigham Young, Nov. 1, 1875, Brigham Young Incoming Correspondence, 1839–1877, CHL; Eleventh Ward, Salt Lake Stake, Young Women's Mutual Improvement Association Minutes and Records, vol. 2, 1878–1889, Aug. 1, 1881, 219, CHL.
11. Eleventh Ward Record of Members.
12. In 1896 Jones was proxy in the sealing of her second husband, Hugh Stevenson Jones, to his first wife. In 1898, Jones's daughter was proxy in the sealing of Jones's first husband, Berry Jones, to his first wife. In 1885 Jones was proxy for her mother's temple work. Jones was sealed in the Endowment House on September 15, 1869, to Bishop Alexander McRae of the Salt Lake City Eleventh Ward, becoming his third wife, but she never took his name nor did they live together or have children. (Logan Temple, Sealings for the Dead, vol. E, 1896–1903, Hugh Stevenson Jones and Mary Francis Blain, Oct. 2, 1896, 21, and Berry Jones and Mary Stevenson Jones, Jan. 19, 1898, 101, microfilm 178,064, FHL; Logan Temple, Endowments for the Dead, vol. A, 1884–1885, Maria Maxwell, Mar. 4, 1885, 367, microfilm 177,955, FHL; Endowment House, Sealings of the Living, vol. F, 1869–1870, Alexander McRae and Eleanor Georgena Jones, Sept. 15, 1869, 19, microfilm 1,149,515, FHL.)
13. This issue was edited by Gertie Sampson. On February 2, 1882, Sampson and other sisters read from the *Improvement Star,* and YLMIA president Mary Ann Freeze "said the last article read was very significant, and it contained a good moral. Said, 'I do not think the Lord will hear and answer our prayers unless our lives accord with them.'" (Eleventh Ward YWMIA Minutes and Records, Feb. 2, 1882, 243.)
14. See Eleventh Ward YWMIA Minutes and Records, Jan. 22, 1882, 242.
15. Freeze said "she was pleased with the paper, for it contained many good maxims. We should sustain our paper and write for it. We are hearing good things day after day, and if we do not improve it is not for the want of knowing better." (Eleventh Ward YWMIA Minutes and Records, Jan. 16, 1882, 241; see also Dec. 19, 1881, 238.)
16. A state house is "a building in which the governing body or legislative assembly of a nation meets." (*Oxford English Dictionary,* s.v. "state house.")
17. See also Mark 14:38.
18. See Malachi 3:10.
19. See Doctrine and Covenants 122:6–9.
20. See Isaiah 49:15; 66:13.
21. Luke 24:36.

CHAPTER 20: ELVIRA S. BARNEY, "PRAYER"

1. After the death of their mother, the family's farm and household goods were sold, and each son or daughter received ten dollars to fit them for the western journey. Barney never saw her twin brother again; he died six years later. (Augusta Joyce Crocheron, *Representative Women of Deseret, a Book of Biographical Sketches to Accompany the Picture Bearing the Same Title* [Salt Lake City: J. C. Graham, 1884], 76–77.)
2. Jane Stevens Lewis; her husband, Philip Lewis; and their children were a part of the Brigham Young Company. While traveling, Barney provided medical care to her ill sister and set her brother-in-law's broken arm. ("Stevens, Elvira," and "Brigham Young Company, 1848," Mormon Pioneer Overland Travel, 1847–1868, accessed Dec. 7, 2015, history.lds.org; Laron A. Wilson, "Biographical Sketch of Dr. Elvira Stevens Barney," in Elvira Stevens Barney, *The Stevens Genealogy, Embracing Branches of the Family Descended from Puritan Ancestry, New England Families Not Traceable to Puritan Ancestry and Miscellaneous Branches Wherever Found* [Salt Lake City: Skelton Publishing, 1907], 261.)
3. Nauvoo Sealings and Adoptions, vol. A, 1846–1857, John Stillman Woodbury and Elvira Stevens, Dec. 23, 1850, 781, microfilm 183,374, FHL; R. Lanier Britsch, *Unto the Islands of the Sea: A History of the Latter-day Saints in the Pacific* (Salt Lake City: Deseret Book, 1986), 103, 105. Also on the mission to Hawaii were Barney's sister Jane Stevens Lewis and her husband, Philip Lewis, and Jonathan and Caroline Crosby. Barney's sister Amelia Althea Stevens had been married to Jonathan Crosby as a plural wife in Nauvoo. She separated from Crosby and remained in the Midwest. (Caroline Barnes Crosby, *No Place to Call Home: The 1807–1857 Life Writings of Caroline Barnes Crosby, Chronicler of Outlying Mormon Communities,* ed. Edward Leo Lyman, Susan Ward Payne, and S. George Ellsworth [Logan: Utah State University Press, 2005], 515; Barney, *Stevens Genealogy,* 239.)
4. Crosby, *No Place to Call Home,* 398–399, 412, 541n36; Oliver B. Huntington, Diary, 1847–1900, part 2, pp. 108, 119, BYU. Nineteenth-century territorial Utah had relatively liberal divorce laws to protect women in unfavorable plural marriages. (See Kathryn M. Daynes, *More Wives Than One: Transformation of the Mormon Marriage System, 1840–1910* [Urbana: University of Illinois Press, 2001], 147–148, 193, 203–204.)
5. Endowment House, Sealings of the Living, vol. D, 1861–1866, Royal Barney and Elvira Stevens, Jan. 6, 1866, 575, microfilm 1,149,514, FHL.
6. Crocheron, *Representative Women of Deseret,* 77, 80; Laron A. Wilson, "Biographical Sketch of Dr. Elvira Stevens Barney," in Barney, *Stevens Genealogy,* 258, 262, 266; Huntington, Diary, 108, 110, 118.
7. Wilson, "Biographical Sketch of Dr. Elvira Stevens Barney," 266, 270; Crocheron, *Representative Women of Deseret,* 80–81; Emmeline B. Wells, "Woman's Tribute to Dr. Elvira S. Barney," *Deseret Evening News,* Jan. 16, 1909; Miriam B. Murphy, "The Working Women of Salt Lake City: A Review of the *Utah Gazetteer,* 1892–1893," *Utah Historical Quarterly* 46, no. 2 (Spring 1978): 124–125.
8. "Notice," *Woman's Exponent* 3, no. 21 (Apr. 1, 1875): 161; "Home Industry," *Woman's Exponent* 38, no. 8 (Mar. 1910): 60; "R. S. Reports," *Woman's Exponent* 4, no. 3 (July 1, 1875): 18; "General Meeting of Central and Ward Committees: On the Grain Movement," *Woman's Exponent* 5, no. 13 (Dec. 1, 1876): 99.
9. Emmeline B. Wells, "Utah," in *The History of Woman Suffrage,* ed. Susan B. Anthony and Ida Husted Harper, 6 vols. (Rochester, NY: Susan B. Anthony, 1902), 4:939–941; "Woman Suffrage Meeting: An Association for Utah," *Woman's Exponent* 17, no. 16 (Jan. 15, 1889): 121–122. For a more detailed timeline, see Kathryn L. MacKay, comp., "Chronology of Woman Suffrage in Utah," in *Battle for the Ballot: Essays on Woman Suffrage in Utah, 1870–1896,* ed. Carol Cornwall Madsen (Logan: Utah State University Press, 1997), 311–318.
10. Wells, "Utah," 941; Emmeline B. Wells, "Woman Suffrage Column: Utah W.S.A.," *Woman's Exponent* 23, nos. 15–16 (Feb. 1 and 15, 1895): 233.
11. See "U.W.S.A.," *Woman's Exponent* 18, no. 11 (Nov. 1, 1889): 85.
12. "Editorial Notes," *Woman's Exponent* 18, no. 9 (Oct. 1, 1889): 68; "U.W.S.A.," 85. James E. Talmage

was president of the Latter-day Saints College, a budding theologian, and a future apostle. Charles W. Penrose was a newspaper editor, author, territorial legislator, and future apostle. Lula Greene Richards was the first editor of the *Woman's Exponent* and a member of the YLMIA general board.

13. "Woman Suffrage Meeting," 122.
14. See "Woman Suffrage Meeting," *Woman's Exponent* 17, no. 23 (May 1, 1889): 182; "Woman Suffrage in Ogden," *Woman's Exponent* 17, no. 24 (May 15, 1889): 189; "Suffrage Meeting," *Woman's Exponent* 18, no. 2 (June 15, 1889): 13; "Meetings at Fillmore," *Woman's Exponent* 18, no. 2 (June 15, 1889): 15; "Morgan County W.S.A.," *Woman's Exponent* 18, no. 3 (July 1, 1889): 21; and "Woman's Suffrage at Ogden," *Woman's Exponent* 18, no. 6 (Aug. 15, 1889): 46.
15. "Woman Suffrage Meeting," 182; "W.S.A. Meeting," *Woman's Exponent* 18, no. 6 (Aug. 15, 1889): 46.
16. See Deuteronomy 11:4; 32:2.
17. See Psalm 107:25.
18. See Galatians 6:2; and Mosiah 18:8.
19. Congress passed the Edmunds Act in 1882, disenfranchising all men and women in polygamous marriages, and the Edmunds-Tucker Act in 1887, disenfranchising all women in Utah Territory. (Joan Iversen, "The Mormon-Suffrage Relationship: Personal and Political Quandaries," in Madsen, *Battle for the Ballot,* 156–159; Wells, "Utah," 939–940.)
20. Following this prayer, James E. Talmage spoke about the role of women. He concluded, "In this age may God assist to remove error, and grant his divine favor upon the efforts being made to elevate woman." ("U.W.S.A," 85.)
21. See Doctrine and Covenants 76:110; and Mosiah 27:31.
22. Charles W. Penrose spoke later in the meeting. He claimed that "some argue that women can't vote because they can't go to war and fight." He encouraged women to claim responsibility and to "become conversant with these subjects and with the laws of municipalities and counties, states, etc." ("U.W.S.A," 85.)

CHAPTER 21: MATTIE HORNE TINGEY, "THE SCHOOL OF EXPERIENCE"

1. "Pioneer Woman Goes to Her Rest," *Deseret Evening News,* Aug. 26, 1905; Emmeline B. Wells, "Our Picture Gallery: Martha Jane Horne Tingey," *Young Woman's Journal* 2, no. 4 (Jan. 1891): 147, 149–150; "Martha Horne Tingey," *Young Woman's Journal* 16, no. 6 (June 1905): 260.
2. Tingey's mother, Mary Isabella Horne, served as president of the Salt Lake City Fourteenth Ward Relief Society, president of the Salt Lake Stake Relief Society, executive chair of the Deseret Hospital board, and leader of the Retrenchment Association. (Augusta Joyce Crocheron, *Representative Women of Deseret, a Book of Biographical Sketches to Accompany the Picture Bearing the Same Title* [Salt Lake City: J. C. Graham, 1884], 20–21.)
3. Susa Young Gates, *History of the Young Ladies' Mutual Improvement Association of the Church of Jesus Christ of Latter-day Saints* (Salt Lake City: Deseret News, 1911), 287; see also chapter 9 herein.
4. Wells, "Our Picture Gallery," 150. The Wasatch Literary Association was a reading society for young adults that was organized in 1874 to promote appreciation of culture. Members of the group performed dramatic readings and small-scale theatrical productions and presented lectures, debates, and poetry. (Ronald W. Walker, "Growing Up in Early Utah: The Wasatch Literary Association, 1874–1878," *BYU Studies* 43, no. 1 [2004]: 61–63.)
5. She also worked as a typesetter for the *Woman's Exponent.* (Crocheron, *Representative Women of Deseret,* 23; Wells, "Our Picture Gallery," 149; "The New Class of Young Ladies," *Woman's Exponent* 2, no. 6 [Aug. 15, 1873]: 45; "Martha Horne Tingey," 260–261.)
6. "Martha Horne Tingey," 260; Gates, *History of the Young Ladies' Mutual Improvement Association,* 287–288.
7. Clarissa A. Beesley, "President Martha H. Tingey," *Young Woman's Journal* 40, no. 5 (May 1929): 310–311.

8. Carol Cornwall Madsen, "Decade of Detente: The Mormon-Gentile Female Relationship in Nineteenth-Century Utah," *Utah Historical Quarterly* 63, no. 4 (Fall 1995): 298–300.
9. "Martha Horne Tingey," 261.
10. Hubert Howe Bancroft, *The Book of the Fair* (Chicago: Bancroft, 1893), 921–922; May Wright Sewall, ed., *The World's Congress of Representative Women: A Historical Résumé for Popular Circulation,* 2 vols. (Chicago: Rand McNally, 1894), 1:46–48. The decision to hold the congress separate from the Chicago World's Fair meant that attendees would not have to pay entrance fees. ("World's Congress of Representative Women," *Young Woman's Journal* 4, no. 8 [May 1893]: 380.)
11. May Wright Sewall and Rachel Foster Avery, "The World's Congress Auxiliary of the World's Columbian Exposition: Woman's Branch of the Auxiliary," *Young Woman's Journal* 4, no. 1 (Oct. 1892): 43–45.
12. "Editor's Department," *Young Woman's Journal* 4, no. 4 (Jan. 1893): 183.
13. Tingey's mother, Mary Isabella Horne, spoke in the afternoon at the Relief Society session. (Gates, *History of the Young Ladies' Mutual Improvement Association,* 202–204.)
14. "Martha Horne Tingey," 261. Susa Young Gates described Tingey as "always a convincing speaker, and at times [she] pours forth her soul in the true language of eloquence. She has a dignified manner and is quiet in speech, though aggressive in her opinions. She has the prudence to restrain speech when silence is golden. If asked to name the most marked trait in Mrs. Tingey's character, the answer would be sincerity, genuineness." (Gates, *History of the Young Ladies' Mutual Improvement Association,* 288.)
15. Reid L. Neilson, *Exhibiting Mormonism: The Latter-day Saints and the 1893 Chicago World's Fair* (New York: Oxford University Press, 2011), 98–99.
16. "Miscellaneous," *Young Woman's Journal* 4, no. 9 (June 1893): 429; Neilson, *Exhibiting Mormonism,* 100–101.
17. The origin of this verse is unknown. A similar idea is found in a poem by Eliza R. Snow, "A Dialogue, between Jenny and Carry," which was published in the *Juvenile Instructor* in 1866. (Jill Mulvay Derr and Karen Lynn Davidson, eds., *Eliza R. Snow: The Complete Poetry* [Provo, UT: Brigham Young University Press; Salt Lake City: University of Utah Press, 2009], 728.)
18. *Pre-existence* refers to a period of life prior to mortal birth. (See Gayle Oblad Brown, "Premortal Life," in *Encyclopedia of Mormonism,* ed. Daniel H. Ludlow, 5 vols. [New York: Macmillan, 1992], 3:1123–1125.)
19. See Doctrine and Covenants 93:36.
20. See James 1:27.
21. Genesis 2:4–5; see also Moses 3:4–5; and Doctrine and Covenants 29:30–32.
22. See Alma 13:3; and Doctrine and Covenants 138:56.
23. Nineteenth-century Latter-day Saints and contemporary Americans often viewed women as gatekeepers to both birth and death. (See Susanna Morrill, "Relief Society Birth and Death Rituals: Women at the Gates of Mortality," *Journal of Mormon History* 36, no. 2 [Spring 2010]: 128–159.)
24. Her statement here echoes a line from a popular hymn, "O My Father," written by Eliza R. Snow in 1845, based on a teaching from Joseph Smith. This hymn was originally published under the name "My Father in Heaven." (Derr and Davidson, *Eliza R. Snow: The Complete Poetry,* 312–314; see also Jill Mulvay Derr, "The Significance of 'O My Father' in the Personal Journey of Eliza R. Snow," *BYU Studies* 36, no. 1 [1997–1996]: 85–126; Jill Mulvay Derr, Carol Cornwall Madsen, Kate Holbrook, and Matthew J. Grow, eds., *The First Fifty Years of Relief Society: Key Documents in Latter-day Saint Women's History* [Salt Lake City: Church Historian's Press, 2016], 173–175; and "Mother in Heaven," Gospel Topics, accessed May 9, 2016, lds.org.)
25. In the same meeting, Julia Farnsworth compared the purity and capability of men and women. She said of women in history, "We find that in accordance with the influence and power she has been allowed to wield in society, there also is purity, morality, and refinement of a high order." The conflicting ideas of separate gendered spheres and equal rights permeated the late nineteenth-century woman's movement. (Julia Farnsworth, "Woman in All Ages: Address Delivered in the World's Fair Congress at Chicago, during the Services of the Y. L. M. I. A.," *Young Woman's Journal* 4, no. 11

[Aug. 1893]: 513–514; Nancy F. Cott, *The Grounding of Modern Feminism* [New Haven, CT: Yale University Press, 1987], 16–20.)

26. This particular example of female education is often attributed to Brigham Young, but no reliable source can be found linking it to him. Rather, Tingey was probably referring to Joseph F. Smith, who had recently stated, "Whatever was good and noble was necessary for women to learn. He went still farther. He stated that so necessary did he consider the improvement of woman that if there must be an inequality of chances, let the first and best be given to women." ("The Intelligent Advancement of Woman," *Young Woman's Journal* 3, no. 12 [Sept. 1892]: 566.)
27. "The Hand That Rocks the Cradle" is a poem by William Ross Wallace praising motherhood as the preeminent force for change in the world, first published in 1865. The verse was repeated often in the *Woman's Exponent,* and an anonymous person wrote a Mormon version of the poem with similar ideas. (See Martin H. Manser, *The Facts on File Dictionary of Proverbs,* 2nd ed. [New York: Facts on File, 2007], 114; "R.S. Reports," *Woman's Exponent* 6, no. 15 [Jan. 1, 1878]: 114; and Hope, "The Hand That Rocks the Cradle," *Woman's Exponent* 7, no. 8 [Sept. 15, 1878]: 57.)
28. See Genesis 2:18. In her speech at this same meeting, Farnsworth spoke about Adam and Eve being true partners, "placing her by his side as companion and wife." (Farnsworth, "Woman in All Ages," 513.)
29. Speeches, discussion, and planning at the World's Congress of Representative Women involved 837 women from about 15 countries. (Sewall, *World's Congress of Representative Women,* 5–6.)

CHAPTER 22: SARAH M. KIMBALL, "OUR SIXTH SENSE, OR THE SENSE OF SPIRITUAL UNDERSTANDING"

1. Sarah M. Kimball, "Auto-Biography," *Woman's Exponent* 12, no. 7 (Sept. 1, 1883): 51.
2. Fifteenth Ward, Salt Lake Stake, Relief Society Minutes and Records, vol. 5, 1874–1894, Apr. 11, 1894, and vol. 8, 1893–1899, Nov. 25, 1896, 140, CHL; "President Sarah M. Kimball," *Woman's Exponent* 27, no. 14 (Dec. 15, 1898): 77. The School of the Prophets in Kirtland was initially organized to train missionaries. Meetings occasionally included women. The Hebrew School was an educational program instituted by Joseph Smith in Kirtland in January 1836 for the study of the Hebrew language. (Matthew C. Godfrey, Mark Ashurst-McGee, Grant Underwood, Robert J. Woodford, and William G. Hartley, eds., *Documents, Volume 2: July 1831–January 1833,* vol. 2 of the Documents series of *The Joseph Smith Papers,* ed. Dean C. Jessee, Ronald K. Esplin, and Richard Lyman Bushman [Salt Lake City: Church Historian's Press, 2013], 378–380; "Hebrew School," accessed Feb. 9, 2016, josephsmithpapers.org.)
3. Kimball, "Auto-Biography," 51.
4. Emmeline B. Wells, "L.D.S. Women of the Past: Personal Impressions," *Woman's Exponent* 37, no. 1 (June 1908): 1.
5. Kimball, "Auto-Biography," 51; Jill Mulvay Derr, Carol Cornwall Madsen, Kate Holbrook, and Matthew J. Grow, eds., *The First Fifty Years of Relief Society: Key Documents in Latter-day Saint Women's History* (Salt Lake City: Church Historian's Press, 2016), 24.
6. Salt Lake Stake Relief Society Record, 1880–1892, 69, CHL. Kimball served as ward Relief Society president from 1857 until her death. ("President Sarah M. Kimball," 77.)
7. Sarah M. Kimball, "Duty of Officers of FR Society," ca. May 1868, in Derr et al., *First Fifty Years,* 285–289; see also Jennifer Reeder, "'To Do Something Extraordinary': Mormon Women and the Creation of a Usable Past," PhD dissertation, George Mason University, 2013.)
8. Salt Lake Stake Relief Society Record, 1880–1892, 7, 52–54. When the Relief Society was legally incorporated in October 1892, Kimball was elected one of the vice presidents, a position she also held until her death. ("President Sarah M. Kimball," 77.)
9. In January 1870, Kimball was elected president of a ladies' mass meeting held in protest of federal antipolygamy legislation. She also worked with Susan B. Anthony and others as president of the Utah Suffrage Association. (Fifteenth Ward, Salt Lake Stake, Relief Society Minutes and Records, vol. 1, 1868–1873, Jan. 6, 1870, 139; see also Derr et al., *First Fifty Years,* 305, 310; "President Sarah M. Kimball," 77; and Wells, "L.D.S. Women of the Past," 1.)

10. Louise Barnum Robbins, ed., *History and Minutes of the National Council of Women of the United States, Organized in Washington, D.C., March 31, 1888* (Boston: E. B. Stillings, 1898), 1–6.
11. "Woman's Council: Topics to Be Discussed at the Coming Gathering," *Evening Star* (Washington DC), Feb. 9, 1895.
12. Susa Young Gates, "Utah Women at the National Council of Women," *Young Woman's Journal* 6, no. 9 (June 1895): 391, 397, 417. Elmina S. Taylor was the first general president of the YLMIA, from 1880–1904. Ellis R. Shipp, one of the first female doctors in Utah, was involved in the Relief Society and YLMIA. Emmeline B. Wells was the editor of the *Woman's Exponent* from 1877 to 1914 and was appointed the general secretary of the Relief Society in 1892. Aurelia Spencer Rogers founded the Primary organization in 1878. Marilla Daniels was the first counselor in the Utah County Stake Relief Society. Minnie J. Snow was president of the Box Elder Stake YLMIA from 1879 to 1894 and also served on the general board starting in 1892. Susa Young Gates founded the *Young Woman's Journal* and was appointed to the YLMIA general board in 1888.
13. "President Sarah M. Kimball," 77. According to Wells, Kimball "was a very good public speaker, concise in language and expression, used as few words as possible to convey her meaning, and invariably handled her subjects well." In 1891, Kimball represented the Utah Woman Suffrage Association in Washington DC, at the National Woman Suffrage Association meetings. (Wells, "L.D.S. Women of the Past," 2; Jill Mulvay Derr, *Sarah M. Kimball* [Salt Lake City: Signature Books, 1976], 2.)
14. Emmeline B. Wells presided over the evening session, and she presented a paper after Kimball's entitled "Forty Years in the Valley of the Great Salt Lake." She was followed by Alleseba Bliss, president of the Girls' Industrial School in Adrian, Michigan. Marilla Daniels had been a delegate of the Utah Woman Suffrage Association a few weeks earlier at the National Woman Suffrage Association meetings in Atlanta. ("Women and the Flag: Patriotism Made the Subject of Today's Addresses," *Evening Star* [Washington DC], Feb. 22, 1895; "Notable Utah Women: Mrs. Marilla Daniels," *Deseret Evening News,* Nov. 24, 1900.)
15. Gates, "Utah Women at the National Council of Women," 416–417.
16. This hymn was written by Isaac Watts in 1707 and published in several hymnals of the Church of Jesus Christ of Latter-day Saints, including the 1840 Manchester hymnal, the 1841 Nauvoo hymnal, and various editions of the Liverpool hymnal. (John Julian, ed., *A Dictionary of Hymnology: Setting Forth the Origin and History of Christian Hymns of All Ages and Nations,* 2 vols. [New York: Dover Publications, 1907], 1:247; Emma Smith, ed., *A Collection of Sacred Hymns for the Church of Jesus Christ of Latter Day Saints* [Nauvoo, IL: E. Robinson, 1841], 47–48; Shane J. Chism, comp., *A Selection of Early Mormon Hymnbooks, 1832–1872: Hymnbooks and Broadsides from the First 40 Years of the Church of Jesus Christ of Latter-day Saints* [Tucson, AZ: printed by the author, 2011], 310–311.)
17. Kimball was not the first person to consider the idea of a sixth sense. Eighteenth-century theologian Jonathan Edwards spoke of a sense of the heart, in addition to the five regular senses, whereby one could sense the holiness of God. Additionally, Eliza R. Snow discussed the concept of a "sixth sense" in a poem presented at the Polysophical Society on February 27, 1855: "The sixth, the spirit-sense will lead / If to its dictates we give constant heed; / And its refining process will prepare / Us for a full and free reception there." The concept of a sixth spiritual sense was also discussed by Emmeline B. Wells, Lucy Clark, and Lula Greene Richards at a Utah Women's Press Club meeting in 1893. (See William Dean, *American Religious Empiricism* [Albany: State University of New York Press, 1986], 22, 83; Eliza R. Snow, "Nationality," in *Eliza R. Snow: The Complete Poetry,* ed. Jill Mulvay Derr and Karen Lynn Davidson [Provo, UT: Brigham Young University Press; Salt Lake City: University of Utah Press, 2009], 486–490; and Ella W. Hyde, "U.W.P. Club," *Woman's Exponent* 21, no. 19 [Apr. 1, 1893]: 150.)
18. See Doctrine and Covenants 93:29, 36.
19. The 1893 World Columbian Exposition in Chicago included a World's Congress of Representative Women that focused in part on religion. Delegates came from several countries and represented 126 organizations engaged in civil, political, and moral reform; religion; charity and philanthropy; and education. The National Council of Women helped coordinate this conference. Kimball offered the invocation at the Relief Society session. (May Wright Sewall, ed., *The World's Congress of*

Representative Women: A Historical Résumé for Popular Circulation [Chicago: Rand McNally, 1894], 5; Reid L. Neilson, *Exhibiting Mormonism: The Latter-day Saints and the 1893 Chicago World's Fair* [New York: Oxford University Press, 2011], 92–102; see also chapter 21 herein.)

20. See Doctrine and Covenants 109:7; 103:36.
21. See Matthew 7:7.
22. For more on the Latter-day Saint doctrine of a Mother in Heaven, see "Mother in Heaven," Gospel Topics, accessed May 9, 2016, lds.org; and David L. Paulsen and Martin Pulido, "'A Mother There': A Survey of Historical Teachings about Mother in Heaven," *BYU Studies* 50, no. 1 (2011): 70–97.
23. Historically, early American Congregationalist and Presbyterian churches employed "schools of the prophets" to prepare clergy for ministerial service. Kimball is probably using the term more generally in the sense of divine training and preparation. (Joseph F. Darowski, "Schools of the Prophets: An Early American Tradition," *Mormon Historical Studies* 9, no. 1 [Spring 2008]: 1–13.)
24. See Doctrine and Covenants 101:32–34.
25. See 1 Corinthians 15:40–41.
26. Romans 8:17.
27. The National Council of Women was founded in 1888, and its first triennial session was held in Washington DC in 1891. The World's Congress of Representative Women held in conjunction with the World Columbian Exposition in Chicago in 1893 was held in lieu of the National Council of Women triennial session; therefore, the second triennial was this meeting held in Washington DC in 1895, two years later. (Robbins, *History and Minutes of the National Council of Women,* 161.)

CHAPTER 23: ANN M. CANNON, "PRAYER"

1. Leonard J. Arrington, *Madelyn Cannon Stewart Silver: Poet, Teacher, Homemaker* (Salt Lake City: Publishers Press, 1998), 3–6. Cannon's half brother Charles Mousley Cannon was the son of Angus Munn Cannon and plural wife Ann Amanda Mousley Cannon. (Ruth Stewart Barth, "Needs: The Biography of Ann Mousley Cannon," n.d., 44, UU.)
2. Cannon worked in the office of her brother George Mousley Cannon. (Susa Young Gates, *History of the Young Ladies' Mutual Improvement Association of the Church of Jesus Christ of Latter-day Saints* [Salt Lake City: Deseret News, 1911], 174–175.)
3. T. D. Lewis, "Remarks," in Funeral Services for Ann Mousley Cannon, Salt Lake City, UT, Nov. 9, 1948, 10, in family possession; Barth, "Needs," 7.
4. Barth, "Needs," 14, 44. Cannon's attentions had a powerful influence on her niece, the poet Madelyn Cannon Stewart Silver. (Arrington, *Madelyn Cannon Stewart Silver,* 17–18; Madelyn Stewart Silver, "A Story of Vision and Accomplishment . . . Ann Mousley Cannon," *Improvement Era* 53, no. 2 [Feb. 1950]: 135.)
5. Fourteenth Ward, Salt Lake Stake, Young Ladies' Mutual Improvement Association Minute Book, vol. 3, 1887–1896, Oct. 25, 1887, 3; Sept. 30, 1888, 32; Jan. 13, 1891, 118; Oct. 13, 1891, 136–137, CHL; Gates, *History of the Young Ladies' Mutual Improvement Association,* 175.
6. Marba C. Josephson, *History of the YWMIA* (Salt Lake City: Young Women's Mutual Improvement Association, 1955), 12, 44–45, 53; Barth, "Needs," ii, 21–27; Silver, "A Story of Vision and Accomplishment," 107, 134–135.
7. Cannon served as secretary of the resolutions committee of the National Council of Women in 1902. She presented speeches before the triennial sessions in 1899 and 1902. (Barth, "Needs," 32–40; Silver, "A Story of Vision and Accomplishment," 135.)
8. Barth, "Needs," ii; Gates, *History of the Young Ladies' Mutual Improvement Association,* 175.
9. Barth, "Needs," 20.
10. Ann M. Cannon, "Recollections," *Young Woman's Journal* 25, no. 10 (Oct. 1914): 621–623, 637; Josephson, *History of the YWMIA,* 115–118; Barth, "Needs," 49–50. Susa Young Gates said of Cannon, "Her editorial work gives proof of a logical mind endowed with superior power of analysis. The literary style developed in this connection is one of sweetness and simplicity." (Gates, *History of the Young Ladies' Mutual Improvement Association,* 175.)
11. Ann M. Cannon to Madelyn Stewart Silver, 1945, in Barth, "Needs," 16.

12. Cannon was known for her "deeply religious character," as one speaker at her funeral noted. (Lewis, "Remarks," in Funeral Services for Ann Mousley Cannon, 13.)
13. Young Women General Board Minutes, vol. 4, 1899–1901, June 2, 1901, 214; June 3, 1901, 253–254, CHL; Sixth General Conference of the Young Men's and Young Ladies' Mutual Improvement Associations, Salt Lake City, UT, Meeting Program, June 1901, CHL. In 1896, the general leaders of the YLMIA began holding annual meetings on Temple Square, known as conjoint conferences, with their counterparts in the Young Men's MIA to train local officers. These annual general conferences were held around the first of June each year in honor of Brigham Young's birthday. (Gates, *History of the Young Ladies' Mutual Improvement Association,* 140–142, 221–222.)
14. "Annual June Conference," *Young Woman's Journal* 12, no. 7 (July 1901): 292; "General M.I.A. Conference," *Young Woman's Journal* 12, no. 8 (Aug. 1901): 362–368.
15. See "Did You Think to Pray?" *Hymns of the Church of Jesus Christ of Latter-day Saints* (Salt Lake City: The Church of Jesus Christ of Latter-day Saints, 1985), no. 140. This hymn entered Latter-day Saint hymnody in 1884 in the second edition of the *Deseret Sunday School Union Music Book.* Cannon shared a room with her niece, Judith Silver Poulsen, as leukemia brought Cannon's life to a close. Recalling overhearing Cannon's nightly prayers, Poulsen said, "I never felt she was just 'saying her prayers.' Instead, I knew she was talking to a trusted friend." (Karen Lynn Davidson, *Our Latter-day Hymns: The Stories and the Messages* [Salt Lake City: Deseret Book, 1988], 166; Judy Silver Poulsen, email to Kate Holbrook, Oct. 15, 2015.)
16. See Alma 31:31.
17. In a draft of a letter to a suitor, Cannon wrote, "For near seven years I have been striving to make my will subservient to the Father's and have prayed every day for guidance. I cannot think my prayer unavailing; I know I will have the light when the right time comes." (Draft Letter, Oct. 26, 1903, Ann Mousley Cannon Papers, UU; Barth, "Needs," 11.)

CHAPTER 24: BATHSHEBA W. SMITH, "WE HAVE STILL A GREATER MISSION"

1. Smith's 1906 "annual greeting" was addressed to the "associate workers in all the world." The Industrial Workers of the World organization was formed the previous year, encouraging the solidarity of workers from various industries.
2. Nauvoo Relief Society Minute Book, Mar. 17, 1842, 6, in Jill Mulvay Derr, Carol Cornwall Madsen, Kate Holbrook, and Matthew J. Grow, eds., *The First Fifty Years of Relief Society: Key Documents in Latter-day Saint Women's History* (Salt Lake City: Church Historian's Press, 2016), 30.
3. Andrew Jenson, *Latter-day Saint Biographical Encyclopedia: A Compilation of Biographical Sketches of Prominent Men and Women in the Church of Jesus Christ of Latter-day Saints,* 4 vols. (Salt Lake City: Andrew Jenson History Co., 1901–1936), 1:699; Emmeline B. Wells, "A Loving Tribute," *Woman's Exponent* 39, no. 3 (Sept. 1910): 18; Wells, "Bathsheba W. Smith," *Woman's Exponent* 35, no. 4 (Oct. 1906): 25; Wells, "Bathsheba W. Smith," *Woman's Exponent* 35, no. 9 (May 1907): 65.
4. Smith sang in a temple choir in Nauvoo. Her children played instruments, sang, and danced. (Bathsheba W. Smith, "Autobiography," n.d., 84, CHL; Horace G. Whitney, "Music in Early Utah Days," *Young Woman's Journal* 24, no. 7 [July 1913]: 416; Augusta Joyce Crocheron, *Representative Women of Deseret, a Book of Biographical Sketches to Accompany the Picture Bearing the Same Title* [Salt Lake City: J. C. Graham, 1884], 44.)
5. Smith, "Autobiography," 1.
6. George A. Smith later became a member of the Quorum of the Twelve Apostles. (Smith, "Autobiography," 2–6; Wells, "A Loving Tribute," 18.)
7. Smith, "Autobiography," 6. The Nauvoo temple cornerstones were laid on April 6, 1841. ("Celebration of the Anniversary of the Church," *Times and Seasons* 2, no. 12 [Apr. 15, 1841]: 375–377.)
8. Bathsheba Smith, "Affidavit," in Affidavits about Celestial Marriage, 1869–1915, CHL; "Latter-day Temples," *Relief Society Magazine* 4, no. 4 (Apr. 1917): 185–186.
9. Smith, "Autobiography," 11, 38; Jenson, *LDS Biographical Encyclopedia,* 1:702; L. L. Greene Richards, "Sister Bathsheba in the House of the Lord," *Woman's Exponent* 39, no. 3 (Sept. 1910): 17.

10. "In Memoriam: President Bathsheba W. Smith," *Woman's Exponent* 39, no. 3 (Sept. 1910): 20.
11. Richards, "Sister Bathsheba in the House of the Lord," 17; Smith, "Autobiography," 78; Jenson, *LDS Biographical Encyclopedia,* 1:702. Emmeline B. Wells stated, "There is no woman living that has such a record in this line of work. . . . She has ministered to thousands and tens of thousands of the daughters of Zion, who rise up and call her blessed." (Wells, "Bathsheba W. Smith," *Woman's Exponent* 35, no. 9 [May 1907]: 66.)
12. "In Memoriam," 20; Smith, "Autobiography," 38, 83; Jenson, *LDS Biographical Encyclopedia,* 1:702.
13. "In Memoriam," 20; Crocheron, *Representative Women of Deseret,* 45; Jenson, *LDS Biographical Encyclopedia,* 1:702. Smith served as Seventeenth Ward Relief Society president from 1886 to 1897, when she asked to be released so she could devote more time to her temple duties and other Relief Society assignments. (Seventeenth Ward, Salt Lake Stake, Relief Society Minutes, vol. 5, 1871–1886, May 19, 1886, 585; vol. 9, 1886–1907, Feb. 6, 1897, 219, CHL.)
14. Jenson, *LDS Biographical Encyclopedia,* 1:702.
15. Smith was appointed president on October 31, 1901, and was sustained at a special conference on November 10, 1901. The Relief Society general board reported in 1899 a total of 26,943 members in 566 branches. According to a 1906 article, the Relief Society numbered over 35,000 members. ("In Memoriam," 20; Relief Society General Board Minutes, vol. 2, 1892–1910, 49, CHL; Wells, "Bathsheba W. Smith," *Woman's Exponent* 35, no. 4 [Oct. 1906]: 25.)
16. Eliza R. Snow wrote "The Year Has Gone" in 1840, commenting on the persecutions suffered by Latter-day Saints in Missouri. (Jill Mulvay Derr and Karen Lynn Davidson, eds., *Eliza R. Snow: The Complete Poetry* [Provo, UT: Brigham Young University Press; Salt Lake City: University of Utah Press, 2009], 105–107.)
17. Joseph Smith was born on December 23, 1805, in Sharon, Vermont. As part of the centennial anniversary of his birth, the church dedicated a monument to him at his birthplace. ("A Hundred Years of Progress: The Boy Prophet," *Woman's Exponent* 34, no. 7 [Jan. 1906]: 45–46.)
18. Shinnston, Harrison County, Virginia (now West Virginia). ("In Memoriam," 20.)
19. Doctrine and Covenants 42:7; see also Matthew 3:2; 4:17.
20. Smith recounted her conversion by remembering that after her baptism and confirmation, "the Spirit of the Lord rested upon me, and I knew that he accepted of me as a member in his kingdom." (Smith, "Autobiography," 2.)
21. Smith here refers to the arrest of Joseph and Hyrum Smith at Far West, Missouri, in late fall 1838. She also remembered seeing "thousands of mobbers arrayed against the Saints, and I heard their shouts and savage yells when our Prophet Joseph and his brethren were taken into their camp. I saw much, very much of the suffering that were brought upon our people by those lawless men. . . . In these distressing times, the Spirit of the Lord was with us to comfort and sustain us, and we had a sure testimony that we were being persecuted for the gospel's sake." (Smith, "Autobiography," 4–5.)
22. On July 8, 1838, Joseph Smith dictated a revelation calling the Twelve Apostles to go on a mission "over the great waters" and to depart from "the city Far West, on the twenty-sixth day of April next [1839]." On April 26, 1839, a majority of the Twelve Apostles returned to Far West from Illinois to comply with this revelation. George A. Smith was an apostle at the time; he left for England on September 21, 1839, returned to Nauvoo in 1841, and then married Bathsheba Smith. (Joseph Smith, Journal, July 8, 1838–A [D&C 118], in Dean C. Jessee, Mark Ashurst-McGee, and Richard L. Jensen, eds., *Journals, Volume 1: 1832–1839,* vol. 1 of the Journals series of *The Joseph Smith Papers,* ed. Dean C. Jessee, Ronald K. Esplin, and Richard Lyman Bushman [Salt Lake City: Church Historian's Press, 2008], 54; Smith, "Autobiography," 8–9, 42.)
23. In Nauvoo, Smith had ample opportunity to become acquainted with Joseph Smith. She remembered, "Here I continued my punctuality in attending meetings, had many opportunities of hearing Joseph Smith preach, and tried to profit by his instructions, and received many testimonies to the truth of the doctrines he taught." According to Emmeline B. Wells, when George A. Smith died in 1875, he encouraged his wife to "live and bear testimony of the Prophet Joseph Smith and the work of the Lord established through his divine mission." (Smith, "Autobiography," 6; Wells, "A Loving Tribute," 18.)

24. See Nauvoo Relief Society Minute Book, Mar. 17, 1842, 6–15, in Derr et al., *First Fifty Years,* 28–37; Jill Mulvay Derr and Carol Cornwall Madsen, "'Something Better' for the Sisters: Joseph Smith and the Female Relief Society of Nauvoo," in *Joseph Smith and the Doctrinal Restoration: The 34th Annual Sidney B. Sperry Symposium* (Provo, UT: Religious Studies Center, Brigham Young University, 2005), 123–143.
25. In her autobiography, Smith reported that mobbers burned 175 Nauvoo homes. Her husband, George A. Smith, released men from working on the temple to form a posse to disperse the mobs, but the posse was shut down by the state militia. This act, according to Smith, prompted the exodus from Nauvoo. Bathsheba and George A. Smith left Nauvoo with their family in February 1846. (Smith, "Autobiography," 10–12.)
26. The Smith family lost multiple family members in Winter Quarters. Bathsheba gave birth to a son, who lived only a few hours, and she remained sick for some months after. Her mother died, as did one of George A. Smith's plural wives and her child. (Smith, "Autobiography," 15.)
27. The Smith family arrived in the Salt Lake Valley in the fall of 1849. (Smith, "Autobiography," 19, 25.)
28. Lucy Mack Smith expressed a similar sentiment in her 1845 conference address, "This Gospel of Glad Tidings to All People," chapter 5 herein.
29. See James 1:27.
30. See Jill Mulvay Derr, Janath Russell Cannon, and Maureen Ursenbach Beecher, *Women of Covenant: The Story of Relief Society* (Salt Lake City: Deseret Book, 1992), 157–160.
31. See Matthew 7:3–5; and Luke 6:42.
32. See Philippians 2:12; and Mormon 9:27.
33. Smith is paraphrasing a popular teaching from former church president Lorenzo Snow. Building on teachings from Joseph Smith, Snow taught: "As man is now, God once was; as God is now man may be." In a sermon given at the funeral of church member King Follett on April 7, 1844, Joseph Smith taught, "God himself, who sits enthroned in yonder heavens, is a man like unto one of yourselves. . . . If you were to see him to-day, you would see him in all the person, image, and very form as a man; for Adam was created in the very fashion and image of God; Adam received instruction, walked, talked, and conversed with him, as one man talks and communes with another." ("President Snow's Response," *Deseret Evening News,* June 15, 1901; "Conference Minutes," *Times and Seasons* 5, no. 15 [Aug. 15, 1844]: 613–614.)
34. Doctrine and Covenants 93:36.
35. Brigham Young said, "There is no such thing as annihilation, for you cannot destroy the elements of which things are made." A hymn written by William W. Phelps in 1856 also illustrated this point. This hymn is included in the current Latter-day Saint hymnal as "If You Could Hie to Kolob," *Hymns of the Church of Jesus Christ of Latter-day Saints* (Salt Lake City: The Church of Jesus Christ of Latter-day Saints, 1985), no. 284. (Brigham Young, "Consecration," in *Journal of Discourses,* 26 vols. [Liverpool: Various publishers, 1855–1886], 2:302; William W. Phelps, "There Is No End," *Deseret News,* Nov. 19, 1856; *The Latter-day Saints' Psalmody: A Collection of Original Tunes* [Salt Lake City: Deseret News, 1896], no. 252.)
36. Doctrine and Covenants 131:6.
37. Doctrine and Covenants 130:22; 88:6–13; John 14:26; 1 Corinthians 13:13.

CHAPTER 25: RACHEL H. LEATHAM, "GOD HAS REVEALED IT UNTO ME"

1. See Appendix herein.
2. Rachel Hannah Hill was baptized on January 3, 1882, in the Endowment House on Temple Square, after emigrating from England to Utah to join her family. She subsequently married James Leatham. Their daughter Rachel Hannah Leatham was baptized in the Salt Lake Tabernacle. (Rachel Hannah Leatham Jensen, "Rachel Hannah Leatham Jensen," personal history, in family possession; Louis S. Leatham, *The Letham or Leatham Family Book of Remembrance: The Story of Robert Letham and His Wife Janet Urquhart with Historical-Genealogical and Biographical Data on Their Ancestry and Descendants* [Ann Arbor: Edwards Brothers, 1955], 343–362.)

3. Leatham worked as a stenographer and bookkeeper at the Merchants' Protective Association and the National Tea Importing Company in Salt Lake City. (Jensen, "Rachel Hannah Leatham Jensen"; Leatham, *Leatham Family Book of Remembrance,* 363.)
4. For additional context on the history of women serving missions, see "Women with a Mission," accessed May 11, 2016, history.lds.org; Tally S. Payne, "'Our Wise and Prudent Women': Twentieth-Century Trends in Female Missionary Service," in *New Scholarship on Latter-day Saint Women in the Twentieth Century,* ed. Carol Cornwall Madsen and Cherry B. Silver (Provo, UT: Joseph Fielding Smith Institute for Latter-day Saint History, 2005), 125–140; Calvin S. Kunz, "A History of Female Missionary Activity in the Church of Jesus Christ of Latter-day Saints, 1830–1898" (master's thesis, Brigham Young University, 1976); and chapter 29 herein.
5. Leatham was set apart on October 9, 1906, and arrived in Denver on October 12. The mission's name was changed during Leatham's service to the Western States Mission. (Leatham, *Leatham Family Book of Remembrance,* 363; Colorado Denver South Mission Manuscript History and Historical Reports, 1896–1977, vol. 1, Apr. 1, 1907, CHL; "Returned Missionaries," *Deseret Evening News,* Feb. 22, 1908; Colorado Denver South Mission General Minutes, vol. 4, 1906–1909, Oct. 12, 1908, 257, CHL.)
6. Colorado Denver South Mission General Minutes, Oct. 31, 1906, 95.
7. "Returned Missionaries"; Colorado Denver South Mission Manuscript History, Feb. 13, 1908.
8. "Bureau of Information and Church Literature," *Improvement Era* 5, no. 11 (Sept. 1902): 900. Leatham worked on Sunday mornings and holidays. Two of her daughters followed her example and served missions. (Leatham, *Leatham Family Book of Remembrance,* 363, 365.)
9. Benjamin Goddard, "Bureau of Information and Church Literature," *Young Woman's Journal* 13, no. 11 (Nov. 1902): 483–488; Leatham, *Leatham Family Book of Remembrance,* 363. Almost twenty years after its inception, it was said that "the Bureau has grown to be one of the best missionary institutions in the Church." (Edward H. Anderson, "The Bureau of Information," *Improvement Era* 25, no. 2 [Dec. 1921]: 139.)
10. For more information on overflow meetings during general conference, see Paul H. Peterson, "Accommodating the Saints at General Conference," *BYU Studies* 41, no. 2 (2002): 17–22.
11. *Seventy-Eighth Annual Conference of the Church of Jesus Christ of Latter-day Saints,* April 4–6, 1908 (Salt Lake City: Deseret News, 1908), 73.
12. Sister M. M. Langenbucher, in *Seventy-Eighth Annual Conference,* 82. Leatham and Martha Maria Langenbucher departed to and returned from their missions on the same days and sent letters to the mission president together. ("Returned Missionaries"; Colorado Denver South Mission General Minutes, Dec. 29, 1907, 365.)
13. Records from Leatham's mission show her belief in the promises of God that she describes here: "During the past month my faith in the gospel has been greatly strengthened. I have seen two wonderful manifestations of God's goodness to his children." (Colorado Denver South Mission General Minutes, Jan. 28, 1907, 149.)
14. Leatham's monthly letters to her mission president reveal her diligence as a common theme. On February 25, 1907, she wrote, "I have endeavored to do my duty and found great satisfaction in my labors." (Colorado Denver South Mission General Minutes, Feb. 25, 1907, 166.)
15. See Luke 12:48; and Doctrine and Covenants 82:3.
16. See Deuteronomy 8:3; Matthew 4:4; and Doctrine and Covenants 84:44.
17. See Romans 8:16.

CHAPTER 26: AMELIA FLYGARE, "A GREAT LOCOMOTIVE"

1. Amelia Hansen, 1880 U.S. Census, Brigham City District 4, Box Elder Co., UT.
2. "Amelia H. Flygare Dies at Afton, Buried in Ogden," *Star Valley (WY) Independent,* Aug. 26, 1948.
3. "Personal Mention," *Kindergarten Review* 8, no. 7 (Mar. 1898): 483; see also Amelia Flygare, 1900 U.S. Census, Ogden Ward 4, Weber Co., UT.
4. "Amelia H. Flygare Dies at Afton"; "The Larger Outside Cities: Ogden," *Deseret Evening News,*

Mar. 10, 1917; Lilliebell Falck, *"Lest We Forget": Our World War Heroes* (Ogden, UT: privately printed, 1927), 43.

5. "Funeral Rites Set for Mrs. Flygare," *Deseret News,* Aug. 24, 1948.
6. Flygare became the first Relief Society president of the Ogden Eighteenth Ward in 1924. (Ogden Eighteenth Ward, Mount Ogden Stake, Relief Society Minutes and Records, vol. 1, 1924–1925, Sept. 2, 1924, 11, 77, CHL.)
7. Flygare was appointed first counselor to Bertha M. Eccles on September 8, 1901. She was named president on October 1, 1905. She concluded that service in January 1909, after she was asked to serve as a counselor in the Weber Stake YLMIA presidency in December 1908. (Ogden Fifth Ward, Weber Stake, Young Women's Mutual Improvement Association Minute Book, vol. 2, 1896–1904, Sept. 8, 1901, 299; Oct. 1, 1905, 41, CHL; "Officers' Notes," *Young Woman's Journal* 20, no. 4 [Apr. 1909]: 196; Ogden Fifth Ward YWMIA Minute Book, vol. 3, 1904–1909, Jan. 12, 1909, 160.)
8. Flygare was appointed second counselor to Aggie H. Stevens on December 23, 1908. When Stevens was replaced as stake YLMIA president by Martha B. Cooley on May 5, 1909, Flygare became first counselor. Flygare was named president on April 23, 1911, ending her service in 1922. ("Officers' Notes," 196; "Officers' Notes," *Young Woman's Journal* 20, no. 11 [Nov. 1909]: 571; Weber Stake Young Women's Mutual Improvement Association Conference Minute Book, vol. 5, 1904–1918, Apr. 23, 1911, 39, CHL; "M.I.A. Notes," *Young Woman's Journal* 33, no. 7 [July 1922]: 406.)
9. Susa Young Gates, *History of the Young Ladies' Mutual Improvement Association of the Church of Jesus Christ of Latter-day Saints* (Salt Lake City: Deseret News, 1911), 482.
10. Lucy F. Stringham, president of the South Davis Stake YLMIA, spoke after Flygare at this training meeting, focusing on the value of reliability. ("Officers' Notes: The June Conference," *Young Woman's Journal* 27, no. 7 [July 1916]: 446; see also chapter 23 herein.)
11. Laura P. Nicholson, "Division of Responsibility," *Young Woman's Journal* 27, no. 7 (July 1916): 444.
12. Young Women General Board Minutes, vol. 8, 1914–1917, June 10, 1916, 55, 57, CHL; "Officers' Notes: The June Conference," 440–449.
13. See Matthew 25:14–30.
14. Just before Flygare spoke, Laura P. Nicholson, president of the Ensign Stake YLMIA, talked about the division of work: "Division of responsibility in Mutual Improvement work is one of vital importance and one upon which depends the success of any association. The work is so great that no president or presidency can carry it alone and make it a success. . . . Each member has a certain line of work to look after, and thus the responsibility is divided and the efficiency increased." (Nicholson, "Division of Responsibility," 444.)
15. A counselor in the YLMIA general presidency, Ruth May Fox, spoke after Flygare and used another metaphor to teach the same principle: "It is the spirit of the hive that accomplishes things. There is no seen force in the hive to direct, and yet every bee and every little community of bees knows just exactly what to do because of the spirit of the hive; and so, in our church, and in our organizations, it is the spirit that is the great moving power. It is necessary for us to understand and to put into practice all this detailed work, but we must rely upon the spirit of the work to do it successfully." (Ruth May Fox, "Enlistment Work," *Young Woman's Journal* 27, no. 7 [July 1916]: 446.)
16. An earlier article in a church periodical also extolled the importance of choristers: "There is probably no reason why choristers should not feel as if they had a mission; why they should not be set apart to this end; or why, when so acting, that they also are the veritable servants and handmaidens of God, and of Zion and its prophets." (H. W. Naisbitt, "Music and Her Sister, Song," *Contributor* 12, no. 6 [Apr. 1891]: 237.)
17. Mabel M. Cooper, a member of the YLMIA general board and assistant music director, spoke earlier in the meeting about the new YLMIA songbook published by the general board. ("Officers' Notes: The June Conference," 441; *YLMIA Song Book, Volume 1: Quartettes, Trios, Solos and Duet for Ladies' Voices* [Salt Lake City: Young Ladies' Mutual Improvement Association, 1916].)
18. Fox responded to Flygare: "As Sister Flygare indicated about the girl who had done her work dutifully, and to whom we should say, 'You have been a good girl, you have done your work well, and I am going to give you lots of work,' so we say to you, the more you do and the better you do it, the

more you will be asked to do. And this will be so even in the kingdom—the greatest reward that the Latter-day Saint expects in the kingdom of God is that the Lord will say, 'You have been faithful over a few things, and I will make you a steward over many things.' . . . The more you do and the better you do it, the more you will be asked to do here and hereafter." (Fox, "Enlistment Work," 447.)

19. Wilford Woodruff was the fourth president of the church from 1889 to 1898.
20. Flygare may be referring to the time Woodruff spent with his plural wife Sarah Elinore Brown Woodruff at their farm in Randolph, Rich County, Utah. (Thomas G. Alexander, *Things in Heaven and Earth: The Life and Times of Wilford Woodruff, a Mormon Prophet* [Salt Lake City: Signature Books, 1991], 135, 222–227.)
21. Wilford Woodruff, "Discourse Delivered at the Weber Stake Conference, Ogden, Monday, October 19th, 1896," *Deseret Weekly,* Nov. 7, 1896, 641. Before becoming church president, Woodruff was named general superintendent of the Young Men's Mutual Improvement Association at the general church conference held on April 6, 1880. ("Association Intelligence," *Contributor* 1, no. 8 [May 1880]: 190–192.)
22. YLMIA president Mattie Horne Tingey opened this meeting with a discussion about the responsibility of officers: "There is no one thing in which you need to be more careful and more particular and in which you need to seek the Lord for wisdom and guidance more than in the selection of your class leaders. . . . Their influence over the girls is great, and you want to be sure that they are women of good, strong character and have the love of God in their hearts, the love of Mutual Improvement work in their hearts, and a thorough love for the girls and a desire to help them." (Martha H. Tingey, "Greeting," *Young Woman's Journal* 27, no. 7 [July 1916]: 441.)

CHAPTER 27: ANNIE D. NOBLE, "KNOWLEDGE NOW WHICH IS DEFINITE"

1. Annie Emma Dexter Noble, "Some Sacred Experiences in the Life of Annie Emma Dexter Noble, 1931–1940," 14, CHL.
2. Noble, "Some Sacred Experiences," 1.
3. The Dexter family were active members of the Church of Christ in England, but when they lived in Brooklyn, they attended a neighborhood Christian church with similar worship practices. Noble recorded that at the age of fourteen, she heard Dwight L. Moody, a famous evangelist, speak to the local Brooklyn congregation. In her effort to obtain a personal witness of Jesus Christ, she prayed to trust God, "and immediately it was as though a heavy stone was lifted out of my heart and the room was as a bright light, and I was filled with joy and happiness indescribable." (Noble, "Some Sacred Experiences," 3–5, 38, 60–67.)
4. Annie Noble joined the Baptist church when she married her husband. After meeting Latter-day Saint missionaries, she was baptized in the Nottingham baths in 1910; her husband was baptized in the Leicester baths. (Noble, "Some Sacred Experiences," 8–13, 69, 71, 73, 80.)
5. The Nobles departed from Liverpool and arrived in Montreal. Noble recalled receiving a spiritual impression that she would serve a mission, and indeed, the Nobles later returned to their hometown of Nottingham, England, from 1920 to 1922 to preach the gospel. (Manifests of Passengers Arriving at St. Albans, VT, District through Canadian Pacific and Atlantic Ports, 1895–1954, Records of the Immigration and Naturalization Service, National Archives Microfilm Publication M1464, Oct. 27, 1912; Noble, "Some Sacred Experiences," 26–28, 33–37.)
6. Noble, "Some Sacred Experiences," 33; Ogden Fifth Ward, Weber Stake, Young Women's Mutual Improvement Association Minutes and Records, vol. 4, 1909–1915, Oct. 28, 1914, 161, CHL.
7. Attendees were instructed to share their feelings "regarding the divinity of this work. . . . We desire to hear brief testimonies of the goodness of the Lord to us as his children, as members of his church and of these Improvement Associations." ("Officers' Notes," *Young Woman's Journal* 27, no. 10 [Oct. 1916]: 618.)
8. Young Women General Board Minutes, typescript, vol. 8, 1914–1917, "Twenty-First General Annual Conference of the Y.M. and Y.L.M.I.A.," June 8–11, 1916, 58, CHL.

9. Young Men Minutes, typescript, vol. 16, 1916, "The Twenty-First General Annual Conference of the Y.M. and Y.L.M.I.A.," 100.
10. "Officers' Notes," 618–629.
11. Years later, Noble wrote about the events leading to her conversion. She described the fear and confusion she felt before she decided to be baptized and recalled a voice of inspiration that spoke peace to her soul. She also described receiving blessings for paying her tithing, as well as an ability to find lost property, which she considered a gift from the Lord. (Noble, "Some Sacred Experiences," 75–78, 15–16, 20–22.)
12. Noble had been very active in her Baptist church. "I sang a great deal at concerts and church affairs and was the chief soprano in the choir of the Baptist church," she remembered. When she contemplated joining the Church of Jesus Christ of Latter-day Saints, she worried about offending her husband, family, and friends who remained faithful Baptists. (Noble, "Some Sacred Experiences," 29, 76–77.)
13. After her baptism, Noble typically attended morning service at the Baptist church with her husband, then went to Latter-day Saint meetings in the evening. (Noble, "Some Sacred Experiences," 78–79.)
14. Noble later recorded: "Some might think it strange for a person to join the Mormon church without a testimony that Joseph Smith was a true prophet. However, in my case I believed with all sincerity that Joseph Smith was authorized to establish this church; otherwise, I could not have joined it." (Noble, "Some Sacred Experiences," 14.)
15. She also recounted this experience in her autobiography: "In the spring after joining the church in the November previous, I was walking along Muster's Road on my way to cottage meeting about 7:30 in the evening. I was alone. The air was very mild, and the trees which grew all along the road for a mile were in the fresh, green leaf. A soft yearning came into my heart to know something more than I already had, and an earnest desire and prayer went to God that I, like the rest of the Saints, might be able to say at cottage meeting that I too knew without doubt that Joseph Smith was a prophet of God. In a moment the Spirit whispered, 'You do know,' and I have known it ever since! As I continued to walk, I understood, as I had never understood before, the meaning of Christ's words to Nicodemus: 'The wind bloweth where it listeth and thou heareth the sound thereof, but canst not tell whence it cometh and whither it goeth; so is it with everyone that is born of the Spirit.' I had hands placed upon me for the reception of the Holy Ghost, thereby being born of the Spirit and thus entitled to receive (I know not just how) a positive knowledge!" (Noble, "Some Sacred Experiences," 14.)

CHAPTER 28: EMMA N. GODDARD, "THOU SHALT LOVE THY NEIGHBOR"

1. "Addresses at the June Conference: 'We Stand for Service to God and Country,'" *Young Woman's Journal* 29, no. 8 (Aug. 1918): 429–439; "Editorial Department," *Young Woman's Journal* 29, no. 8 (Aug. 1918): 484.
2. Jane Standring Nield was baptized on April 26, 1851, and Joseph Merrick Nield was baptized on November 18, 1844. (Endowment House, Endowments of the Living, vol. I, 1878–1884, Jane Standring Nield and Joseph M. Nield, Apr. 9, 1883, 320–321, microfilm 183,408, FHL.)
3. Martha Alice Nield, Emma Nield, and Hannah Nield were baptized in the summer of 1879. Benjamin Goddard was baptized on April 3, 1879. (Emma Jane Nield Goddard, "My Life Story," typescript, 1–3, in family possession.)
4. Benjamin Goddard was married to Martha Nield and had emigrated with the Nield sisters in 1879. Emma Goddard worked with her husband throughout her life. He directed the Bureau of Information center on Temple Square, starting in 1902, and she worked in the office. While Benjamin directed the bureau, he and Emma went on many business trips to various cities to gather material for their brochures and to promote the church. He served on the YMMIA board from 1903 to 1929, and Emma served on the YLMIA board from 1896 to 1935. (Goddard, "My Life Story," 3–5, 8–11; Andrew Jenson, *Latter-day Saint Biographical Encyclopedia: A Compilation of Biographical*

Sketches of Prominent Men and Women in the Church of Jesus Christ of Latter-day Saints, 4 vols. [Salt Lake City: Andrew Jenson History Co., 1901–1936], 4:239, 260; Susa Young Gates, *History of the Young Ladies' Mutual Improvement Association of the Church of Jesus Christ of Latter-day Saints* [Salt Lake City: Deseret News, 1911], 210–211.)

5. Goddard, "My Life Story," 3–5; St. George Temple, Sealings for the Living, vol. A, 1877–1886, Ben Goddard, Martha Alice Nield, and Emma Jane Nield, Oct. 3, 1883, 101, microfilm 170,579, FHL.
6. Meadow Ward, Millard Stake, Relief Society Minute Book, vol. 1s, 1870–1895, Dec. 2, 1886, 82; Apr. 7, 1887, 88, CHL.
7. Goddard, "My Life Story," 5, 9; Gates, *History of the Young Ladies' Mutual Improvement Association,* 209–210. Goddard was released as president of the YLMIA in her ward in October 1896. (Twenty-First Ward, Emigration Stake, Young Ladies' Mutual Improvement Association Minute Book, vol. 1, 1894–1898, Oct. 27, 1896, 83, CHL.)
8. Goddard, "My Life Story," 9–11; Gates, *History of the Young Ladies' Mutual Improvement Association,* 210; see also *Guide to the First Year's Course of Study in the Young Ladies' Mutual Improvement Association* (Salt Lake City: George Q. Cannon and Sons, n.d.).
9. Young Men's Mutual Improvement Association General Board Minutes, vol. 18, 1918, June 6–9, 1918, 106–111, CHL. The *Young Woman's Journal* reported the following about the conference: "A feeling of deep patriotism, a willingness to make any sacrifice necessary, unswerving faith in the over-ruling providence of God, confidence in the final outcome of the present great struggle pervaded the meetings." ("The June Conference," *Young Woman's Journal* 29, no. 7 [July 1918]: 422.)
10. Joseph F. Boone, "The Roles of the Church of Jesus Christ of Latter-day Saints in Relation to the United States Military" (PhD diss., Brigham Young University, 1975), 219–220; "Editors' Table," *Improvement Era* 22, no. 1 (Nov. 1918): 80. Some sources put the total Utah enlistment as high as twenty-four thousand. (Boone, "The Roles of the Church," 218–219.)
11. YMMIA General Board Minutes, 106–111.
12. "M.I.A. Notes," *Young Woman's Journal* 29, no. 6 (June 1918): 355. Levi Edgar Young served as a church general authority from 1909 to 1963 and on the general board of the YMMIA from 1913 to 1929. May Booth Talmage served on the general YLMIA board from 1892 to 1930. Richard R. Lyman was newly appointed as an apostle on April 6, 1918. (Jenson, *LDS Biographical Encyclopedia,* 3:760; 4:251, 266–267.)
13. See Matthew 22:39.
14. Leviticus 19:18.
15. See Luke 10:25–29.
16. Luke 10:30–37.
17. Mark 12:29–31.
18. Romans 13:8–9.
19. Galatians 5:14.
20. World War I ended on November 11, 1918, five months after this talk was given.
21. Matthew 2:18; see also Jeremiah 31:15.
22. James 1:27.
23. The *Deseret Evening News* summarized Goddard's speech as follows: "As officers of a great organization like the Y.L.M.I.A., Mrs. Goddard said all members should visit the widows and orphans doing everything possible to alleviate their sufferings." ("Slogan Read at Joint Session of M.I.A. Officers," *Deseret Evening News,* June 10, 1918.)
24. Edgar A. Guest, "When You Know a Fellow," in *A Heap o' Livin'* (Chicago: Reilly and Lee, 1916), 12.
25. See 1 John 4:16.
26. *The Latter-day Saints' Psalmody: A Collection of Original and Selected Tunes,* 5th ed. (Salt Lake City: Deseret News, 1912), no. 138. In *Psalmody,* the second line of the last stanza reads, "We yet may lead them back."
27. James Russell Lowell, *The Vision of Sir Launfal* (Cambridge, UK: John Bartlett, 1849), 26. The published text of the poem says "alms" rather than "gift" in the third line.
28. John 3:16.

29. "If justice is a universal law, love is a universal duty; for nothing but love can make us just to our fellow men." (John Lancaster Spalding, *Aphorisms and Reflections: Conduct, Culture and Religion* [Chicago: A. C. McClurg, 1901], 264.)
30. Karl G. Maeser was a well-known educator in Utah who served as principal of Brigham Young Academy when Goddard attended in the 1880s. Maeser believed in following the example of Christ in his teaching, inviting students to follow and choose to learn. (A. LeGrand Richards, *Called to Teach: The Legacy of Karl G. Maeser* [Provo, UT: Religious Studies Center, Brigham Young University, 2014], xxviii–xxix, 397–399, 431–433.)
31. See Matthew 4:19; John 1:43; 21:16–17; and Doctrine and Covenants 112:14.
32. See Boone, "The Roles of the Church," 215–222.

CHAPTER 29: JENNIE BRIMHALL KNIGHT, "FORGIVENESS IS LIKE MERCY"

1. Calvin S. Kunz, "A History of Female Missionary Activity in the Church of Jesus Christ of Latter-day Saints, 1830–1898" (master's thesis, Brigham Young University, 1976), 34–37, 54; Andrew Jenson, *Latter-day Saint Biographical Encyclopedia: A Compilation of Biographical Sketches of Prominent Men and Women in the Church of Jesus Christ of Latter-day Saints,* 4 vols. (Salt Lake City: Andrew Jenson History Co., 1901–1936), 4:177–179. Brimhall's family insisted that she return for fear that damp winter weather in England would cause recurrence of the pneumonia she had previously suffered. (Orson F. Whitney, *History of Utah,* 4 vols. [Salt Lake City: George Q. Cannon and Sons, 1904], 4:615.)
2. Whitney, *History of Utah,* 4:614.
3. "Mrs. Jennie Brimhall Knight," *Relief Society Magazine* 8, no. 7 (July 1921): 380–381; Whitney, *History of Utah,* 4:615.
4. Lillian C. Booth, "Research Made during the Summer of 1956 on Matron, Dean of Women, and Counselor for Women," 1, 7–8, CHL. The first Matron of Women on record at Brigham Young University was Zina Presendia Young Card, who held the post from 1879 to 1884. The university, initially named Brigham Young Academy, was founded in November 1875. (Booth, "Research Made during the Summer of 1956," 1–2; Ernest L. Wilkinson, ed., *Brigham Young University: The First One Hundred Years,* 4 vols. [Provo, UT: Brigham Young University Press, 1975], 1:66.)
5. Inez Knight Allen, "Jennie Brimhall Knight," *Relief Society Magazine* 15, no. 12 (Dec. 1928): 647. After its formation in August 1916, the Council of National Defense requested that each state form its own Council of Defense to help coordinate activities "for the general good of the nation and the successful prosecution of the war." In response, Utah formed a state council on April 26, 1917. Governor Simon Bamberger formed the Committee on Women's Work on August 3, 1917, to direct women's war efforts; Knight served on this committee. (Noble Warrum, *Utah in the World War: The Men behind the Guns and the Men and Women behind the Men behind the Guns* [Salt Lake City: Arrow Press, 1924], 86–87, 121.)
6. Knight served as a counselor to Williams until Williams's release in October 1928 and then continued on the board until 1939. (Mary Jane Groberg Fritzen, *Lucy Jane [Jennie] Brimhall Knight: An Expression of Love and Gratitude for Her Exemplary Life* [Idaho Falls, ID: Delbert V. and Jennie H. Groberg, 1997], 4, 42.)
7. Allen, "Jennie Brimhall Knight," 647; Fritzen, *Lucy Jane (Jennie) Brimhall Knight,* 42, 106.
8. Fritzen, *Lucy Jane (Jennie) Brimhall Knight,* 4, 105. Knight's grandniece wrote in her biography that Knight also hired babysitting and household help. (Fritzen, *Lucy Jane [Jennie] Brimhall Knight,* 4.)
9. This entry was likely written in September. (Fritzen, *Lucy Jane [Jennie] Brimhall Knight,* 48, 49.)
10. Fritzen, *Lucy Jane (Jennie) Brimhall Knight,* 49.
11. Fritzen, *Lucy Jane (Jennie) Brimhall Knight,* 49; Allen, "Jennie Brimhall Knight," 647.
12. Doctrine and Covenants 64:10–11.
13. Knight's father, George Brimhall, was president of Brigham Young University from 1904 to 1921. (Wilkinson, *Brigham Young University,* 1:382, 519.)
14. See Matthew 18:21–35.

15. See Matthew 6:12; Luke 11:4; and 3 Nephi 13:11.
16. The *paternoster* is the Lord's Prayer, as recorded in Luke, chapter 11, and Matthew, chapter 6. A version of this quotation similar to the one Knight used can be found in J. R. Miller, *The Golden Gate of Prayer: Devotional Studies on the Lord's Prayer* (New York: Thomas Y. Crowell, 1900), 185.
17. William Shakespeare, *Merchant of Venice,* act 4, sc. 1, ll. 192–193.
18. See Matthew 18:3; and 3 Nephi 11:38.
19. Doctrine and Covenants 64:9.

CHAPTER 30: AMY BROWN LYMAN, "THE VALUE OF FAITH"

1. Amy Brown Lyman, *In Retrospect: Autobiography of Amy Brown Lyman* (Salt Lake City: General Board of Relief Society, 1945), 36, 42; Belle S. Spafford, "In Memoriam: President Amy Brown Lyman," *Relief Society Magazine* 47, no. 1 (Jan. 1960): 47. The Relief Society offices were housed on the second floor of the Bishop's Building from 1909 until 1956, when the Relief Society Building was dedicated. (Relief Society General Board Minutes, vol. 2, 1892–1910, Dec. 3, 1909, 183, Jan. 27, 1910, 191, CHL; Jill Mulvay Derr, Janath Russell Cannon, and Maureen Ursenbach Beecher, *Women of Covenant: The Story of Relief Society* [Salt Lake City: Deseret Book, 1992], 174–177, 197.)
2. Lyman, *In Retrospect,* 42–43, 89. Joseph F. Smith served as the sixth president of the church from 1901 to 1918. Smith's request that Lyman modernize the Relief Society offices was part of a wider trend within the church to align with Progressive-era practices. (Dave Hall, *A Faded Legacy: Amy Brown Lyman and Mormon Women's Activism, 1872–1959* [Salt Lake City: University of Utah Press, 2015], 64–65; Matthew Bowman, *The Mormon People: The Making of an American Faith* [New York: Random House, 2012], 152–183.)
3. Spafford, "In Memoriam," 5; [Vera White Pohlman], "In Memoriam: Amy Brown Lyman, 1872–1959, Biographical Summary and Funeral Services," 10–11, CHL.
4. Lyman, *In Retrospect,* 30.
5. David Hall, "Anxiously Engaged: Amy Brown Lyman and Relief Society Charity Work, 1917–45," *Dialogue: A Journal of Mormon Thought* 27, no. 2 (Summer 1994): 76–77; Hall, *A Faded Legacy,* 48–50; [Pohlman], "In Memoriam," 12–13.
6. Lyman, *In Retrospect,* 63; Spafford, "In Memoriam," 46.
7. Joseph F. Smith, "Elder Richard R. Lyman Chosen to Fill the Vacancy in the Council of Twelve," in *Eighty-Eighth Annual Conference of the Church of Jesus Christ of Latter-day Saints,* Apr. 5–7, 1918 (Salt Lake City: Deseret News, 1918), 51; Amy Brown Lyman, "Social Service Work in the Relief Society, 1917–1928," Sept. 1928, 4–7, CHL; [Pohlman], "In Memoriam," 13.
8. Lyman, *In Retrospect,* 64–65, 84; Derr, Cannon, and Beecher, *Women of Covenant,* 236. For more on the development of Social Service Institutes, see chapter 31 herein.
9. Lyman, *In Retrospect,* 83; Derr, Cannon, and Beecher, *Women of Covenant,* 231.
10. *The Promotion of the Welfare and Hygiene of Maternity and Infancy* (Washington DC: United States Government Printing Office, 1931), 134, 138; Loretta L. Hefner, "The National Women's Relief Society and the U.S. Sheppard-Towner Act," *Utah Historical Quarterly* 50, no. 3 (Summer 1982): 263–264.
11. Relief Society General Board Minutes, vol. 15, 1926–1927, Apr. 3, 1926, 21, 29.
12. For a contemporary discussion of the plan of salvation and premortal life, see James E. Talmage's popular treatment of Mormon theology, *The Vitality of Mormonism: Brief Essays on Distinctive Doctrines of the Church of Jesus Christ of Latter-day Saints* (Boston: Gorham Press, 1919), 48–51, 256, 236–238.
13. Urbanization, industrialization, and disillusionment with World War I led Americans to question the Victorian ideal of order and rationality in which they had previously taken comfort. For a discussion of the new ways Americans were seeing the world at this time, see Lynn Dumenil, *The Modern Temper: American Culture and Society in the 1920s* (New York: Hill and Wang, 1995), 145–200.
14. See James 2:18.
15. See Romans 1:16; and 1 Peter 1:5.

16. See Genesis 25:29–34.

CHAPTER 31: LALENE H. HART, "SENSING RESPONSIBILITY OF OFFICE"

1. "Mrs. Lalene H. Hart," *Relief Society Magazine* 8, no. 7 (July 1921): 394. Brigham Young College and the Cassia Stake Academy were church schools. The Church Board of Education decided to close the Cassia Stake Academy by 1925, and Brigham Young College was closed in May 1926. (Arnold Kent Garr, "Brigham Young College," in *Encyclopedia of Mormonism,* ed. Daniel H. Ludlow, 5 vols. [New York: Macmillan, 1992], 1:219; William E. Berrett, *A Miracle in Weekday Religious Education* [Salt Lake City: Salt Lake Printing Center, 1988], 36–37; "Cassia Stake Academy to Have New Building," *Deseret News,* May 23, 1908.)
2. See, for example, "Of Interest to Women," *Relief Society Magazine* 10, no. 1 (Jan. 1923): 35.
3. "Lalene H. Hart," obituary, *Deseret News,* July 28, 1972; Elaine Justesen, *Treasures in Heaven: A Biography of Charles Henry Hart, 1866–1934* (Salt Lake City: Charles Henry Hart Family Organization, 1999), 38–39.
4. Justesen, *Treasures in Heaven,* 77, 83.
5. Justesen, *Treasures in Heaven,* 80. During this period, women married to mission presidents served as "Relief Society mission presidents." In this capacity, they organized Relief Society conferences and visited individual units of the Relief Society, oversaw record keeping, coordinated Relief Society activity with missionary work, communicated and established Relief Society policy, and reported to church headquarters. The practice of appointing Relief Society mission presidents began by 1916 and lasted until 1964, when the title of the position changed to "Relief Society mission supervisor." Relief Society mission supervisors were appointed until at least 1973. (Amy Brown Lyman, "General Conference of the Relief Society," *Relief Society Magazine* 3, no. 12 [Dec. 1916]: 663; "Mrs. Lalene H. Hart," *Relief Society Magazine* 18, no. 6 [June 1931]: 335–338; Relief Society Annual General Conference Program, 1963, 18; 1964, 16; 1973, 21, Relief Society Conference and Convention Programs, 1916–1975, CHL.)
6. "Mrs. Lalene H. Hart," *Relief Society Magazine* 14, no. 6 (June 1927): 312.
7. Lalene H. Hart, "The Social Service Institute," *Relief Society Magazine* 19, no. 1 (Jan. 1932): 33–36; Relief Society General Board Minutes, vol. 19, 1932–1933, Dec. 7, 1932, 72, CHL.
8. David Hall, "Anxiously Engaged: Amy Brown Lyman and Relief Society Charity Work, 1917–45," *Dialogue: A Journal of Mormon Thought* 27, no. 2 (Summer 1994): 82, 85.
9. *Handbook of the Relief Society of the Church of Jesus Christ of Latter-day Saints* (Salt Lake City: General Board of the Relief Society, 1931), 55, 178–180; Mayola R. Miltenberger, *Fifty Years of Relief Society Social Services* (Salt Lake City: The Church of Jesus Christ of Latter-day Saints, 1987); Jill Mulvay Derr, "A History of Social Services in the Church of Jesus Christ of Latter-day Saints, 1916–1984" (Salt Lake City: LDS Social Services, 1988), 38–62.
10. Relief Society Annual General Conference Program, 1933, Relief Society Conference and Convention Programs.
11. The term *officer* referred to Relief Society members in leadership positions. Stakes and wards had executive officers (president, first and second counselors, and secretary-treasurer), and other officers, including chorister, teacher, organist, and magazine representative. (*Handbook of the Relief Society of the Church of Jesus Christ of Latter-day Saints* [Salt Lake City: General Board of the Relief Society, 1931], 134, 141.)
12. The meeting in which Hart gave this talk was specifically for Relief Society officers, not for the general membership. In 1933, officers' meetings occurred twice a year and were held the day before the two general sessions of the Relief Society general conference. ("Officers' Meeting," *Relief Society Magazine* 4, no. 6 [June 1917]: 323–324.)
13. Ben Jonson, *Catiline,* act 3, sc. 1, ll. 1–4.

CHAPTER 32: ELSIE TALMAGE BRANDLEY, "THE RELIGIOUS CRISIS OF TODAY"

1. Merry May Booth Talmage Papers, 1–2, CHL; Andrew Jenson, *Latter-day Saint Biographical Encyclopedia: A Compilation of Biographical Sketches of Prominent Men and Women in the Church of Jesus Christ of Latter-day Saints,* 4 vols. (Salt Lake City: Andrew Jenson History Co., 1901–1936), 4:267. James E. and May Booth Talmage had eight children, but one died in infancy. (John R. Talmage, *The Talmage Story: Life of James E. Talmage—Educator, Scientist, Apostle* [Salt Lake City: Bookcraft, 1972], 241.)
2. Talmage, *Talmage Story,* 124, 176, 181.
3. Clarissa A. Beesley, "Elsie Talmage Brandley," *Improvement Era* 38, no. 9 (Sept. 1935): 558.
4. The *White and Blue* was published between 1897 and 1923. (Beesley, "Elsie Talmage Brandley," 558.)
5. Jenson, *LDS Biographical Encyclopedia,* 4:254.
6. She often also turned household tasks into games to engage her children in the work. (Beesley, "Elsie Talmage Brandley," 559.)
7. Jenson, *LDS Biographical Encyclopedia,* 4:254; Harrison R. Merrill, "Elsie Talmage Brandley—Editor and Friend," *Improvement Era* 38, no. 9 (Sept. 1935): 560. Brandley died of a sudden illness a few weeks before her thirty-ninth birthday; her youngest daughter was four years old. (Talmage, *Talmage Story,* 241.)
8. Mattie Horne Tingey was YLMIA general president from 1905 to 1929. Ruth May Fox served as general president of the YLMIA (later YWMIA) from 1929 to 1937.
9. Beesley, "Elsie Talmage Brandley," 559; Jenson, *LDS Biographical Encyclopedia,* 4:254; Thomas C. Romney, "Representative Women of the Church: Elsie Talmage Brandley," *Instructor* 85, no. 11 (Nov. 1950): 324.
10. Jenson, *LDS Biographical Encyclopedia,* 4:254.
11. "Funeral Services in Honor of Elsie Talmage Brandley," Twentieth Ward Chapel, Salt Lake City, UT, Aug. 5, 1935, in family possession. E. E. Ericksen collaborated with Brandley through his position on the YMMIA general board. Brandley worked for the new Senior department (for young adults ages 23–35), of which Ericksen was made chair on April 8, 1931. (Scott Kenney, "The Mutual Improvement Associations: A Preliminary History, 1900–1950" [unpublished manuscript, Jan. 1976], 37, CHL; Romney, "Representative Women of the Church: Elsie Talmage Brandley," 324; E. E. Ericksen, *Memories and Reflections: The Autobiography of E. E. Ericksen,* ed. Scott G. Kenney [Salt Lake City: Signature Books, 1987], 93–94.)
12. Elsie Talmage Brandley, "Peace on Earth," *Improvement Era* 33, no. 2 (Dec. 1929): 102.
13. Jon Savage, *Teenage: The Prehistory of Youth Culture, 1875–1945* (New York: Penguin Books, 2007), 277–280.
14. Young Women General Board Minutes, vol. 13, 1934–1937, Mar. 28, 1934, 26, CHL.
15. Melvin J. Ballard, "Morality and the New Day," *Improvement Era* 37, no. 9 (Sept 1934): 515.
16. Marba C. Josephson, *History of the YWMIA* (Salt Lake City: Young Women's Mutual Improvement Association, 1955), 174–199, 201–202.
17. Kenney, "The Mutual Improvement Associations," 28–31.
18. Young Women General Board Minutes, Mar. 28, 1934, 25, and enclosed letters for May 24, 1934, and May 29, 1934.
19. *Improvement Era,* Special June Conference Issue (June 1934): 7; Young Women General Board Minutes, Jan. 24, 1934, 10; Feb. 7, 1934, 13–14; Feb. 21, 1934, 17; Mar. 14, 1934, 19; Mar. 21, 1934, 21; Young Men's Mutual Improvement Association General Board Minutes, vol. 28, 1933–1935, Feb. 21, 1934, 106–111; Feb. 28, 1934, 111, 135–136; Mar. 7, 1934, 154–156, CHL; Elsie T. Brandley, Journal, Feb. 24, Mar. 16, 1934, in family possession; see Elsie Talmage, KWCF-N9P, Memories, accessed Feb. 1, 2016, familysearch.org.
20. Young Women General Board Minutes, May 2, 1934, 39; May 9, 1934, 43. See *Improvement Era* 37, no. 8 (Aug. 1934), as follows: Henry A. Smith, "Glimpses of June Conference," 454; Oscar A. Kirkham, "Latter-day Saint Youth and the New Day," 463–464, 497; Joseph F. Smith, "The Glorious Possibilities for Us of the Religious Crisis," 465–466, 495–496; and Elsie Talmage Brandley,

"The Religious Crisis of Today," 467–468, 496–497; see also Ballard, "Morality and the New Day," 515–516, 527.

21. Brandley wrote, "After the meeting at least 50 people (I counted 34) stopped me to ask where they might get copies of the talks. . . . Over 85 people, by actual count, came or phoned into the office to get copies of the Saturday morning speeches." (Brandley, Journal, June 9, 11, 1934; see Talmage, Memories.)
22. Elsie Talmage Brandley, "The Religious Crisis of Today," *Latter-day Saints' Millennial Star* 96, no. 36 (Sept. 6, 1934): 561–566; Melvin J. Ballard, "Morality and the New Day," *Latter-day Saints' Millennial Star* 96, no. 39 (Sept. 27, 1934): 609–612.
23. Brandley wrote in an editorial, "To be a leader of youth is to be a kind of creator, for new vision, new determination, new activity and inspiration and ambition come to life in the presence of real leadership." (Elsie T. Brandley, "The Art of Leadership," *Improvement Era* 33, no. 12 [Oct. 1930]: 790.)
24. See James Russell Lowell, *The Vision of Sir Launfal* (Cambridge, UK: John Bartlett, 1849), 26.
25. The three generations Brandley references seem to be the youth, participants and leaders in their twenties and thirties, and older leaders. At this time the YWMIA had the following departments, distinguished by age groups: Bee-Hive Girls (12–14), Junior Girls (15–16), Gleaners (17–23), and Seniors (24–35). ("Report of the Committee on M.I.A. Survey," in Young Women General Board Minutes, Mar. 1934, 10.)
26. Joseph Fielding Smith, who became a member of the Quorum of Twelve Apostles in 1910 and would serve as church president from 1970 to 1972, spoke after Brandley. He taught, "The very genius of Mormonism is its interpreting truth for immediate human welfare and the supplying of technics for making the interpretations practicable. This is the essence of revelation: to interpret truth in terms of present world conditions for the immediate benefit of mankind. . . . Truth must forever receive fresh interpretation." Many prominent church members emphasized correspondence between Latter-day Saint practice and developments in the contemporary world. (Smith, "The Glorious Possibilities for Us of the Religious Crisis," 466; see also, for example, John A. Widtsoe and Leah D. Widtsoe, *The Word of Wisdom: A Modern Interpretation* [Salt Lake City: Deseret Book, 1937]. For more on how church members saw their faith connected with the ideas of the era, see Matthew Bowman, *The Mormon People: The Making of an American Faith* [New York: Random House, 2012], 152–183.)
27. See Doctrine and Covenants 1:24.
28. For an explanation of the changes in the 1920s and 1930s, see Lynn Dumenil, *The Modern Temper: American Culture and Society in the 1920s* (New York: Hill and Wang, 1995).
29. See, for example, Isaiah 11:12. Later twentieth-century scholarship determined that Columbus's educated contemporaries believed the earth to be round, although framings of the Columbus story similar to Brandley's had been widely accepted for many years. (William D. Phillips Jr. and Carla Rahn Phillips, *The Worlds of Christopher Columbus* [New York: Cambridge University Press, 1992], 140.)
30. See, for example, Genesis 3:16. Religious concerns over the use of anesthetic arose among some believers when it was first given to women in childbirth during the 1840s. By the early twentieth century, many women and Progressive-era reformers called for hospital births because they believed they could be safer for mother and child and provide more pain relief, though this was not always the case. There was still some discussion of religious opposition to anesthesia during the 1920s. (Richard W. Wertz and Dorothy C. Wertz, *Lying-In: A History of Childbirth in America,* expanded ed. [New Haven, CT: Yale University Press, 1989], 116–117, 133–135; Howard Wilcox Haggard, *Devils, Drugs, and Doctors: The Story of the Science of Healing from Medicine-Man to Doctor* [London: William Heinemann, 1929], 97–98, 116.)
31. James E. Talmage, *The Earth and Man: Address Delivered in the Tabernacle, Salt Lake City, Utah, Sunday, August 9, 1931* (Salt Lake City: The Church of Jesus Christ of Latter-day Saints, 1931), 6.
32. Chicago held a world's fair from 1933 to 1934. It was a centennial celebration of Chicago and was dubbed "A Century of Progress." (Cheryl R. Ganz, *The 1933 Chicago World's Fair: A Century of Progress* [Chicago: University of Illinois Press, 2008].)

33. Robert Morss Lovett, "Progress—Chicago Style," *Current History* 39, no. 4 (Jan. 1, 1934): 434–435, 437–438. Brandley's quotation does not match Lovett's article word for word.
34. Albert Edward Bailey, "New Churches for Old," *Christian Century* 51 (Jan. 24, 1934): 116–118. Brandley's quotation does not match Bailey's article word for word.
35. Glenn Frank, "The Will to Doubt," *Deseret News,* July 20, 1928. Brandley failed to insert ellipses when skipping portions of Frank's article. The article was published in various venues on this date through the McClure Newspaper Syndicate.
36. A 1950 article summarized Brandley's sentiments thus: "She insisted that they be permitted and even encouraged to think for themselves, and not to accept as a truth an assumption made by others without investigation." (Romney, "Representative Women of the Church: Elsie Talmage Brandley," 324.)
37. Talmage, *Earth and Man,* 14.
38. In an editorial, Brandley wrote, "Though the old way has its faults and its advantages, as has the new, the beauties of both outweigh the negative features by all odds. One of the finest courses in school or out of school one can take is a course in appreciation of other generations." (Elsie T. Brandley, "Autumn Color," *Improvement Era* 35, no. 12 [Oct. 1932]: 706.)
39. Bryant S. Hinckley, "James E. Talmage," *Latter-day Saints' Millennial Star* 94, no. 30 (July 28, 1932): 468. Brandley's quotation does not match Talmage's original word for word.
40. Edward W. Tullidge, "Daniel Spencer," in *History of Salt Lake City,* biographies section (Salt Lake City: Star Printing, 1886), 168. Brandley's quotation does not match Tullidge's original word for word.
41. "Challenge to Middle-Age," *Harper's Magazine* 169 (June 1934): 113–119.
42. Brandley wrote in an editorial, "The Church of Jesus Christ of Latter-day Saints holds within itself the truth which is all of beauty. The light of revelation has dispelled the mists which for so long enshrouded mankind, and has explained the whence and whither of our lives. Greater than all the material possessions of earth is the knowledge that Jesus is the Christ and that he so loved his fellow men that he gave his life that they might live eternally. With this knowledge as a candle to light the way come all the color and rhythm and symmetry which make of life a purposeful harmony, and of salvation a glorious surety." (Elsie Talmage Brandley, "What Is Beauty?" *Improvement Era* 33, no. 3 [Jan. 1930]: 182.)
43. Elsie Talmage Brandley stated in an editorial, "Live today with hope for tomorrow and faith in the future. Day by day extract from life all that life has to offer, and if it is not as sweet to the taste as you would have it, find in its bitterness the medicinal quality of herbs. Few experiences in life are devoid of possibilities for developing growth; and in looking for them day by day, satisfaction will come. If it comes not because of ease and happiness, it will come in spite of them." (Elsie T. Brandley, "Day by Day," *Improvement Era* 35, no. 9 [July 1932]: 515.)

CHAPTER 33: LEONE O. JACOBS, "PREPARE THY HEART"

1. Joseph Jacobs's Armenian parents, Armenag and Osanna Hagopian, were among the first converts in Aleppo, Syria, joining in 1893 and 1896, respectively. ("The Joseph Jacobs Story," Jan. 4, 2006, 2, CHL; Leone O. Jacobs, "Palestine-Syrian Mission History," n.d., 1, 4–5, CHL; Alice B. Steinicke, "Leone Openshaw Jacobs," *Relief Society Magazine* 32, no. 7 [July 1945]: 406–407.)
2. Jacobs, "Palestine-Syrian Mission History," 1.
3. These activities were recorded repeatedly in two diaries Jacobs kept while on her mission. (See Maud Leone Openshaw Jacobs, Diary, Dec. 5, 1938–Feb. 26, 1939; Feb. 27–June 28, 1939, CHL.)
4. Jacobs, "Palestine-Syrian Mission History," 7A; Jacobs, Diary, Feb. 27, June 28, 1939.
5. Steinicke, "Leone Openshaw Jacobs," 406–407; Jacobs, "Palestine-Syrian Mission History," 8–10.
6. Leone Openshaw Jacobs, "To the Land of Our Savior," *Deseret News,* Apr. 5 and 26, 1941.
7. Steinicke, "Leone Openshaw Jacobs," 407; Maud Leone Openshaw Jacobs, "Autobiography of Maud Leone Openshaw Jacobs," 1979, 40–41, CHL.
8. Jacobs, "Autobiography," 40.

9. "Leone O. Jacobs Resigns from the General Board," *Relief Society Magazine* 43, no. 4 (Apr. 1956): 241; Jacobs, "Autobiography," 41–42, 48, 51.
10. Jacobs, "Autobiography," 47, 51. Relief Society conventions were held at the stake level and were also called Relief Society stake conferences. During the 1940s, attendees listened to such talks as "Strengthening Community Virtues" (1946), "Why Relief Society Membership Is Vital to Latter-day Saint Women" (1947), and "How I Co-operate with the Bishop in Ward Welfare Activities" (1949). The meetings also included time for discussion led by a general board member. (Annual Group Stake Conventions, 1946, 5; Annual Group Stake Conventions, 1947, 5; and Annual Relief Society Conventions, 1949, 5, Relief Society Conference and Convention Programs, 1916–1975, CHL.)
11. The Utah Safety Council began in 1939 to promote traffic safety in Utah. By 1945 it expanded its safety efforts beyond traffic to broader safety concerns in the community. The Women's Legislative Council of Utah formed in 1920 to promote legislation instigated by either political party that would benefit the state of Utah. Jacobs served on the council for six years. ("Utah Safety Council," Annual Report, 1958–1959, in editors' possession; Eileen Hallet Stone, "Living History: Utah Women's Group Still Political after 90 Years," *Salt Lake Tribune,* Mar. 2, 2010; Jacobs, "Autobiography," 47.)
12. J. Reuben Clark Jr., a member of the First Presidency, attended the meeting. ("Verbatim Report of the General Relief Society Conference of the Church of Jesus Christ of Latter-day Saints in Salt Lake City, Utah, September 28 and 29, 1949," 230, Relief Society Annual Conference Proceedings, 1945–1975, CHL.)
13. Bridge was a popular card game in the United States during the mid-twentieth century and often a crucial aspect of social life. (Ely Culbertson and Peter F. O'Shea, "Civilization at the Bridge Table," *North American Review* 229, no. 2 [Feb. 1930]: 141–147; Robert D. Putnam, *Bowling Alone: The Collapse and Revival of American Community* [New York: Simon and Schuster, 2000], 102–104.)
14. Ezra 7:10.
15. Doctrine and Covenants 132:3.
16. Ella Wheeler Wilcox, "The Winds of Fate," in *World Voices* (New York: Hearst's International Library, 1916), 51.

CHAPTER 34: MARY J. WILSON, "CULTIVATING LIFE'S ETERNAL VALUES"

1. Relief Society General Board Minutes, vol. 26, 1946–1947, Nov. 13, 1946, 137–138, CHL.
2. Maurine C. Neilsen, "Mary Jacobs Wilson Called to General Board," *Relief Society Magazine* 34, no. 1 (Jan. 1947): 23.
3. Mary and David married on May 31, 1916. ("Death: Mary J. Wilson," *Deseret News,* May 31, 1990.)
4. Neilsen, "Mary Jacobs Wilson Called to General Board," 24.
5. Neilsen, "Mary Jacobs Wilson Called to General Board," 23.
6. *Relief Society Magazine* 34, no. 1 (Jan. 1947): masthead.
7. Relief Society General Board Minutes, vol. 26, 1946–1947, Dec. 11, 1946, 155, and list of general board standing committees, 169, 403–404; vol. 27, 1948–1949, Oct. 5 and Nov. 9, 1949, 340, 365, and list of standing committees, 211–212, 401–402. The 1948–1949 minutes also contain an early family hour pamphlet; see page 30a. Family hour was renamed family home evening around 1965. (Matthew O. Richardson, "Family Home Evening," in *Encyclopedia of Latter-day Saint History,* ed. Arnold K. Garr, Donald Q. Cannon, and Richard O. Cowan [Salt Lake City: Deseret Book, 2000], 360–361.)
8. Relief Society General Board Minutes, Jan. 5, 1949, 224.
9. Elaine Tyler May, *Homeward Bound: American Families in the Cold War Era* (New York: Basic Books, 1988), xviii–xx; Robert J. Norrell, *The House I Live In: Race in the American Century* (New York: Oxford University Press, 2005), 162–186.
10. The first line of the original reads, "Heaven is not reached by a single bound." (Josiah G. Holland,

"Step by Step," in *Hymns for All Christians,* comp. Charles F. Deems and Phoebe Cary [New York: Hurd and Houghton, 1869], 195.)

11. Henry Wadsworth Longfellow, "Builders," in *The Seaside and the Fireside* (Boston: Ticknor, Reed, and Fields, 1850), 56.
12. Another early-twentieth-century translation renders the line thus: "He is that without which one cannot live." (Leo Tolstoy, *My Confession: Critique of Dogmatic Theology,* trans. Leo Wiener [Boston: Dana Estes, 1904], 69.)
13. Marie Curie made crucial theoretical breakthroughs in her studies of radioactivity, a term she coined. Her work resulted in the isolation of two new elements, polonium and radium. She shared the 1903 Nobel Prize in physics with Henri Becquerel and Pierre Curie, her husband. The Nobel committee also awarded her a prize for chemistry in 1911. (Marilyn Bailey Ogilvie, *Marie Curie: A Biography* [Westport, CT: Greenwood Press, 2004], ix–xiii.)
14. 1 Nephi 17:50.
15. Wilson's parents were Emma Rigby and Henry Charitan Jacobs. (Neilsen, "Mary Jacobs Wilson Called to the General Board," 23.)
16. James 2:26.
17. See Mosiah 2:17; and Matthew 25:40.
18. See Acts 10:38.
19. "Acres of diamonds" refers to a famous speech in which Russell H. Conwell told of numerous enterprising men who sold their homes and land in search of wealth elsewhere, only to learn that the land they sold had been worth millions because of the oil, or gold, or diamonds they had failed to recognize in their own backyards. This speech, one of the most popular in American history, was a seminal work in the prosperity gospel tradition. Conwell repeated it thousands of times throughout his life. (Agnes Rush Burr, *Russell H. Conwell and His Work: One Man's Interpretation of Life* [Philadelphia: John C. Winston, 1917], 313.)
20. Michael Pupin, "From Immigrant to Inventor," *Scribner's Magazine* 72, no. 3 (Sept. 1922): 264. The original quote reads, "My boy, if you wish to go out into the world about which you heard so much at the neighborhood gatherings, you must provide yourself with another pair of eyes; the eyes of reading and writing. There is so much wonderful knowledge and learning in the world which you cannot get unless you can read and write."
21. Benjamin Franklin reworded common sayings and then published them in *Poor Richard's Almanack.* This saying is from Richard Saunders, *Poor Richard, 1746: An Almanack for the Year of Christ 1746,* June 1746. (J. A. Leo Lemay, *The Life of Benjamin Franklin, Volume 2: Printer and Publisher, 1730–1747* [Philadelphia: University of Pennsylvania Press, 2006], 194.)
22. Charles William Eliot began publishing a fifty-volume library of world literature, the Harvard Classics, in 1909, toward the end of his tenure as president of Harvard. Eliot believed that anyone who could read these classics for fifteen minutes a day would have a sound substitute for a liberal education. (John T. Bethell, *Harvard Observed: An Illustrated History of the University in the Twentieth Century* [Cambridge, MA: Harvard University Press, 1998], 41.)
23. See 1 Nephi 2:20; and 2 Nephi 1:5.

CHAPTER 35: MARIANNE C. SHARP, "GAINING KNOWLEDGE AND INTELLIGENCE"

1. Marianne Clark Sharp, interview by Jessie L. Embry, May–June 1977, 14, James Moyle Oral History Program, CHL.
2. "Marianne C. Sharp Dies, Ex-Relief Society Leader," *Deseret News,* Jan. 3, 1990.
3. Amy Brown Lyman, "Marianne Clark Sharp: First Counselor in General Presidency, April 1945," *Relief Society Magazine* 32, no. 5 (May 1945): 263.
4. Sharp, interview, 60–64; "New Titles for Lesson Courses," *Relief Society Magazine* 53, no. 5 (June 1966): 460.
5. Sharp, interview, 14–16.
6. Sharp, interview, 16.

7. Amy Brown Lyman, "Marianne C. Sharp Appointed Associate Editor of Relief Society Magazine," *Relief Society Magazine* 30, no. 10 (Oct. 1943): 593, 613; "Death: Marianne C. Sharp," *Deseret News,* Jan. 4, 1990.
8. Lyman, "Marianne C. Sharp Appointed," 613.
9. Jennifer M. Proffitt, "War, Peace, and Free Radio: The Women's National Radio Committee's Efforts to Promote Democracy, 1939–1946," *Journal of Radio and Audio Media* 17, no. 1 (2010): 2; Cindy C. Welch, "Broadcasting the Profession: The American Library Association and the National Children's Radio Hour" (PhD diss., University of Illinois at Urbana-Champaign, 2008), 152–153; Donna L. Halper, *Invisible Stars: A Social History of Women in American Broadcasting* (Armonk, NY: M. E. Sharpe, 2014), 82; Kathy M. Newman, *Radio Active: Advertising and Consumer Activism, 1935–1947* (Berkeley: University of California Press, 2004), 139–140.
10. Sharp, interview, 33.
11. Sharp, interview, 46; "Marianne Clark Sharp," *Relief Society Magazine* 30, no. 10 (Mar. 1940): 153; Lyman, "Marianne C. Sharp Appointed," 593.
12. "Biographical Register of General Church Officers," in *Encyclopedia of Mormonism,* ed. Daniel H. Ludlow, 5 vols. (New York: Macmillan, 1992), 4:1645. J. Reuben Clark Jr., who had been a counselor in the First Presidency since 1933, was initially reluctant for Sharp to assume this role. Sharp also felt discomfort over having a father famous in Mormon circles: "I had been so happy all my life to live . . . where nobody knew who my father was. . . . That way you feel as if you're accepted for yourself instead of for who your parents are. So that was a blow to me, in a way, to come out here [to Salt Lake City] and get into that." (Belle S. Spafford, interview by Jill Mulvay [Derr], 1975–1976, 50, 79–80, 90–91, CHL; Sharp, interview, 44.)
13. Spafford, interview, 110.
14. Sharp, interview, 51, 54–64. Contributions for the construction of the Relief Society Building continued to come after 1948. Ground was broken for the building in 1953, and construction was completed in 1956. Sharp felt this presidency was able to develop and make the substantial contributions it did because of their long tenure in office. Since Spafford's presidency, no general president has served longer than ten years. Recent presidents Mary Ellen W. Smoot, Bonnie D. Parkin, and Julie B. Beck each served for five years. (Jill Mulvay Derr, Janath Russell Cannon, and Maureen Ursenbach Beecher, *Women of Covenant: The Story of Relief Society* [Salt Lake City: Deseret Book, 1992], 308–310, 327–329; Sharp, interview, 47.)
15. In Latter-day Saint thought, an individual's "second estate" refers to life on earth. (See, for example, Rulon S. Wells, in *One Hundred Eleventh Semi-annual Conference of the Church of Jesus Christ of Latter-day Saints,* Oct. 4–6, 1940 [Salt Lake City: The Church of Jesus Christ of Latter-day Saints, 1940], 69.)
16. Doctrine and Covenants 93:36.
17. Lorenzo Snow spoke often on this theme. (See Lorenzo Snow, *The Teachings of Lorenzo Snow: Fifth President of the Church of Jesus Christ of Latter-day Saints,* ed. Clyde J. Williams [Salt Lake City: Bookcraft, 1984], 1–9.)
18. Doctrine and Covenants 130:18–19.
19. Anthon was a classics professor at Columbia College. He and Harris reported their interactions differently. Harris recalled that Anthon confirmed the characters were of ancient origin, while Anthon reported refusing to help with the characters because he suspected fraud. (Royal Skousen and Robin Scott Jensen, eds., *Revelations and Translations, Volume 3, Part 1: Printer's Manuscript of the Book of Mormon, 1 Nephi 1–Alma 35,* vol. 3 of the Revelations and Translations series of *The Joseph Smith Papers,* ed. Ronald K. Esplin and Matthew J. Grow [Salt Lake City: Church Historian's Press, 2015], xvii–xviii.)
20. Citation in original: "2 Nephi 27:20." These verses are Book of Mormon prophet Nephi's clarification and prophecy about Isaiah 29:11–12.
21. Sharp's source for this statement was most likely Joseph Smith et al., *History of the Church of Jesus Christ of Latter-day Saints,* ed. B. H. Roberts, 7 vols. (Salt Lake City: Deseret News, 1902–1912 [vols. 1–6], 1932 [vol. 7]), 4:588. Wilford Woodruff gave a contemporary report of this April 10,

1842, discourse by Joseph Smith in Nauvoo, Illinois. (Wilford Woodruff, Journal, Apr. 10, 1842, CHL.)

22. Doctrine and Covenants 131:6.
23. Doctrine and Covenants 88:77–79.
24. Citation in original: "1 Cor. 13:20."
25. Citation in original: "Matt. 22:37–39."
26. Sharp likely read this quotation in Brigham Young, May 18, 1873, in *Journal of Discourses,* 26 vols. (Liverpool: Various publishers, 1855–1886), 16:40; see also Brigham Young, "Discourses," *Deseret News,* June 11, 1873.

CHAPTER 36: MARGARET C. PICKERING, "UNTO THE LEAST OF THESE"

1. Latter-day Saints University was a predecessor of LDS Business College. Utah Agricultural College was a forerunner to Utah State University. (Ernest L. Wilkinson, ed., *Brigham Young University: The First One Hundred Years,* 4 vols. [Provo, UT: Brigham Young University Press, 1975], 2:592–595; Alice H. Songe, *American Universities and Colleges: A Dictionary of Name Changes* [Metuchen, NJ: Scarecrow Press, 1978], 230.)
2. Amy Brown Lyman, "Margaret Cummock Pickering," *Relief Society Magazine* 33, no. 1 (Jan. 1946): 5. *Improvement Era* content for 1913–1914 included articles and talks by members of the Quorum of the Twelve Apostles and First Presidency, mission reports, fiction, poetry, and columns about priesthood quorums, the Young Men's Mutual Improvement Association, and Scouting. (See individual issues of *Improvement Era,* vols. 16–17 [1913–1914].)
3. "Margaret Aird Cummock Pickering," *Deseret News,* Oct. 11, 1976.
4. Lyman, "Margaret Cummock Pickering," 4; Leone O. Jacobs, "Margaret C. Pickering Resigns as General Secretary-Treasurer," *Relief Society Magazine* 44, no. 3 (Mar. 1957): 159.
5. Lyman, "Margaret Cummock Pickering," 4; Jacobs, "Margaret C. Pickering Resigns," 159. The Salt Lake City Woman's Civic Center offered adult education classes for women in academic and domestic subjects from 1919 to 1961. The Relief Society partnered with the Utah Mental Hygiene Society from its founding in 1925. The society contributed substantially to the establishment of a training school for the mentally disabled in 1929, the appointment of a trained psychiatrist at the state hospital in 1933, and the establishment of the State Department of Public Welfare in 1935. The community chest movement raised funds to support a federation of social service agencies, thereby saving individual agencies from duplicating each other's fund-raising efforts and minimizing inconveniences to donors. Community chests became a very popular means of supporting social work, particularly during the 1920s. In 1945, the Salt Lake County Community Chest represented twenty-four different agencies. A Utah chapter of the American Red Cross developed to support troops during the Spanish-American War in 1898. Red Cross chapters proliferated in Utah during World War I, when Relief Society general president Emmeline B. Wells encouraged Relief Society cooperation with the Red Cross. Pickering received her Red Cross pin marking twenty-five years of service in 1962. (Salt Lake City Women's Civic Center records, collection summary, UU; Beth Frandsen Hartmann, "Mental Health Association: An Historical Overview of the Utah Association for Mental Health" [master's thesis, University of Utah, 1968], vi–vii, 1, 8; Stanley Wenocur and Michael Reisch, *From Charity to Enterprise: The Development of American Social Work in a Market Economy* [Urbana: University of Illinois Press, 1989], 108–110; "Officials of Chest Drive Urge Support of Citizens," *Deseret News,* Oct. 4, 1945; "Editorial Notes," *Woman's Exponent* 27, nos. 1 and 2 [June 1 and 15, 1898]: 292, 293; "Margaret Aird Cummock Pickering"; see also Carol Cornwall Madsen, *Woman Triumphant: An Intimate History of Emmeline B. Wells* [Salt Lake City: University of Utah Press, 2016]; and Kerry William Bate, "Kanarraville Fights World War I," *Utah Historical Quarterly* 63, no. 1 [Winter 1995]: 39–42.)
6. Jacobs, "Margaret C. Pickering Resigns," 159. Local stake Relief Society leaders conducted stake conventions where stake Relief Society and priesthood leaders instructed officers, and general board members spoke and led discussion groups. Most often the conventions included more than one

stake. (*Annual Relief Society Conventions,* 1950, pamphlet, CHL; *Handbook of Instructions of the Relief Society of the Church of Jesus Christ of Latter-day Saints* [Salt Lake City: General Board of Relief Society, 1949], 67–68.)

7. Andrew J. Dunar, *America in the Fifties* (Syracuse, NY: Syracuse University Press, 2006), 54.
8. Steven Casey, *Selling the Korean War: Propaganda, Politics, and Public Opinion in the United States, 1950–1953* (New York: Oxford University Press, 2008), 186.
9. Dunar, *America in the Fifties,* 51. By February 1950, Wisconsin senator Joseph McCarthy had claimed anticommunism as his major political platform and inaugurated a highly publicized period of persecution against many people with leftist political leanings. (Richard M. Fried, *Nightmare in Red: The McCarthy Era in Perspective* [New York: Oxford University Press, 1990].)
10. See Matthew 25:36–40.
11. Service has been a significant part of Relief Society work since the organization's founding and has been called by different names. At the founding meeting, president Emma Hale Smith spoke about the society's object "to seek out and relieve the distressed." Relief Society service work was not consistently called *compassionate service,* as it is today, until the 1940s. David O. McKay's use of the phrase during a 1939 Relief Society general conference may have inspired its official adoption. By 1942, *compassionate service* was the official term used to reference Relief Society charitable service. (Nauvoo Relief Society Minute Book, Mar. 17, 1842, 13, in Jill Mulvay Derr, Carol Cornwall Madsen, Kate Holbrook, and Matthew J. Grow, eds., *The First Fifty Years of Relief Society: Key Documents in Latter-day Saint Women's History* [Salt Lake City: Church Historian's Press, 2016], 36; David O. McKay, "The Highest and Best in Woman's Realm," *Relief Society Magazine* 27, no. 1 [Jan. 1940]: 18; Vera White Pohlman, "Annual Report—1942," *Relief Society Magazine* 30, nos. 6–7 [June–July 1943]: 420.)
12. The official church welfare program began in 1936. For histories of the program's development, see Jill Mulvay Derr, "Changing Relief Society Charity to Make Way for Welfare, 1930–1944," in *New Views of Mormon History: A Collection of Essays in Honor of Leonard J. Arrington,* ed. Davis Bitton and Maureen Ursenbach Beecher (Salt Lake City: University of Utah Press, 1987); and Garth L. Mangum and Bruce D. Blumell, *The Mormons' War on Poverty: A History of LDS Welfare, 1830–1990* (Salt Lake City: University of Utah Press, 1993).
13. Nauvoo Relief Society Minute Book, Apr. 28, 1842, [40], in Derr et al., *First Fifty Years,* 59.
14. From the earliest days of the Relief Society, leaders tracked charitable service statistics in their organizational minute books. Here, Pickering is referencing service recorded by the general board. Service activities were recorded under different categories over time. For the year 1914, for example, service statistics were organized according to the following categories: money distributed to the poor, visits to the sick, families helped, bodies prepared for burial, and days spent in temple work. Gradually the general board stopped recording temple work, and after establishment of the church welfare program in 1936, the Relief Society no longer directly distributed money to the poor. Thus the 1949 report on compassionate service tracked these categories: visits to sick and homebound, days caring for the sick, number of funerals at which the Relief Society assisted, and dressing for burial. (Amy Brown Lyman, "General Conference of the Relief Society," *Relief Society Magazine* 2, no. 12 [Dec. 1915]: 527–528; "Compassionate Service Annual Report—1949," *Relief Society Magazine* 37, no. 9 [Sept. 1950]: [610].)
15. Belle S. Spafford, "Report of Activities and Official Instructions," *Relief Society General Conference,* Salt Lake City, UT, Oct. 3–4, 1945, A-10, CHL.
16. Versions of this quotation appeared in various newspapers, including Louis E. Bisch, "The Magic of Giving," *Dixon (IL) Evening Telegraph,* July 17, 1950. The quotation originally came from a pocket magazine entitled *Your Life: The Popular Guide to Desirable Living.*
17. Psalm 56:3.

CHAPTER 37: LOUISE W. MADSEN, "UNION OF FEELING"

1. "Louise W. Madsen, Former Relief Society Officer, Dies at 78," *Deseret News,* Oct. 6–7, 1987.
2. LDS High School, also called LDS College, offered courses on the high school and college levels.

(Lillie C. Adams, "Elen Louise Wallace Madsen Called to the General Board," *Relief Society Magazine* 35, no. 2 [Feb. 1948]: 81; "Louise W. Madsen.")

3. "Louise W. Madsen."
4. Adams, "Elen Louise Wallace Madsen Called to the General Board," 81. Madsen taught not long after the Latter-day Saint seminary program first began.
5. "Louise W. Madsen."
6. Marianne C. Sharp, "Elen Louise Wallace Madsen Appointed Second Counselor in the General Presidency of Relief Society," *Relief Society Magazine* 45, no. 10 (Oct. 1958): 651–652. Madsen served on the Christmas party, educational helps, literature, Relief Society conference, poetry, short story, social science, and stake conventions committees, among others. (Relief Society General Board Minutes, vol. 27, 1948–1949, 211–212, 401–402; vol. 28, 1950–1951, 243–244, 444–445; vol. 29, 1952–1953, 211–212, 473–474; vol. 30, 1954–1955, 239–241, 507–509; vol. 31, 1956–1957, 251–252, 289–290; vol. 32, 1958–1959, 196–197, CHL.)
7. "New Titles for Lesson Courses," *Relief Society Magazine* 53, no. 6 (June 1966): 460; "Louise W. Madsen."
8. Relief Society General Board Minutes, vol. 33, 1960, Jan. 6, 1960, 10; "Louise W. Madsen." The Red Cross began a program of instruction on home nursing in 1908, and the Relief Society sponsored Red Cross home nursing courses as early as the 1920s. (Lavinia L. Dock et al., *History of American Red Cross Nursing* [New York: Macmillan, 1922], 1352–1354; Jill Mulvay Derr, Janath Russell Cannon, and Maureen Ursenbach Beecher, *Women of Covenant: The Story of Relief Society* [Salt Lake City: Deseret Book, 1992], 233–234.)
9. "Need for Relief Society Nurseries," 2, Louise W. Madsen Papers, CHL. The earliest Relief Society nursery manual is from 1963. The Primary had nursery curriculum for children aged four and younger starting in 1951 and a class for children three and younger starting in about 1956. ("Nursery Committee Report," 1, Louise W. Madsen Papers, CHL; Derr, Cannon, and Beecher, *Women of Covenant,* 345; Carol Cornwall Madsen and Susan Staker Oman, *Sisters and Little Saints: One Hundred Years of Primary* [Salt Lake City: Deseret Book, 1979], 208.)
10. "Louise W. Madsen." During the middle of the twentieth century, the National Council of Women (NCW) was a moderate organization that supported peace and strongly supported the United Nations. Belle S. Spafford, who began holding office in the NCW in 1948 and would serve as president from 1968 to 1970, reported after the 1952 meetings that the council was most concerned with declining moral standards, the breakdown of family life, increasing secularism and materialism, and inadequate educational systems. (Margaret Nunnelley Olsen, "One Nation, One World: American Clubwomen and the Politics of Internationalism, 1945–1961" [master's thesis, Rice University, 2007], 73–76; Belle S. Spafford, "The National Council of Women," *Relief Society Magazine* 40, no. 4 [Apr. 1953]: 217; Priscilla L. Evans, "President Belle S. Spafford Elected to Office in the National Council of Women," *Relief Society Magazine* 36, no. 1 [Jan. 1949]: 20–21; Derr, Cannon, and Beecher, *Women of Covenant,* 337.)
11. "Louise W. Madsen."
12. These incidents included the beating and murder of fourteen-year-old African American Emmett Till; the shootings and bombings of buses, African American homes, and churches following the Montgomery bus boycott; and white adults threatening and taunting African American children during the desegregation of Central High School in Little Rock, Arkansas. (Robert J. Norrell, *The House I Live In: Race in the American Century* [New York: Oxford University Press, 2005], 174–186.)
13. For more information on the Cuban Missile Crisis, see Len Scott and R. Gerald Hughes, eds., *The Cuban Missile Crisis: A Critical Reappraisal* (London: Routledge, 2015).
14. John 17:1.
15. David O. McKay, "Unity in the Church," *Instructor* 87, no. 8 (Aug. 1952): 225.
16. John 17:20–21.
17. Nauvoo Relief Society Minute Book, June 9, 1842, [61], in Jill Mulvay Derr, Carol Cornwall Madsen, Kate Holbrook, and Matthew J. Grow, eds., *The First Fifty Years of Relief Society: Key Documents in Latter-day Saint Women's History* (Salt Lake City: Church Historian's Press, 2016), 78.

18. See Micah 6:8.
19. See Moroni 7:47.
20. See "Know This, That Every Soul Is Free," *Hymns, Church of Jesus Christ of Latter-day Saints* (Salt Lake City: The Church of Jesus Christ of Latter-day Saints, 1948), no. 90; see also *Hymns of the Church of Jesus Christ of Latter-day Saints* (Salt Lake City: The Church of Jesus Christ of Latter-day Saints, 1985), no. 240.
21. Relief Society members took monthly courses in literature, social science, homemaking (work meeting), and theology. At this time, experts in the relevant fields wrote the lessons, including lessons meant to be shared through visiting teaching, which appeared in the *Relief Society Magazine.* Relief Society board members read and critiqued all of the lessons before publication. The goals of the curriculum included increasing members' appreciation for literature, their sense of social obligation and knowledge about how to serve more effectively, their spirituality and understanding of church doctrines, and their civic awareness. ("Lesson Department," *Relief Society Magazine* 48, no. 6 [June 1961]: 411–420; Alice C. Smith, interview by Harvard Heath, Oct. 25, 1985, 42, BYU; *Handbook of Instructions of the Relief Society of the Church of Jesus Christ of Latter-day Saints* [Salt Lake City: General Board of Relief Society, 1962], 92.)
22. Romans 1:12.
23. Romans 15:30.
24. Romans 16:17.
25. Citation in original: "Romans 16:1–4, 6, 12." For more on these women, see Peter Lampe, *From Paul to Valentinus: Christians at Rome in the First Two Centuries* (Minneapolis: Fortress Press, 2003); and Elisabeth Schüssler Fiorenza, *In Memory of Her: A Feminist Theological Reconstruction of Christian Origins* (New York: Crossroad, 1994).
26. Romans 16:12.

CHAPTER 38: ALICE C. SMITH, "MY YOKE IS EASY AND MY BURDEN IS LIGHT"

1. W. Whitney and Alice C. Smith, interview by Christen L. Schmutz, July 12, 1979, preface, James Moyle Oral History Program, CHL.
2. Alice C. Smith, interview by Harvard Heath, Oct. 25, 1985, 73, transcript, BYU.
3. W. Whitney and Alice C. Smith, interview, preface; "Alice Colton Smith," *Relief Society Magazine* 51, no. 12 (Dec. 1964): 897.
4. W. Whitney and Alice C. Smith, interview, preface; "Alice Colton Smith," 897.
5. Peter J. Rabe, "A Conversation with Sister Smith," Austrian Mission Memories, 1960–1963, [13–14], CHL.
6. W. Whitney and Alice C. Smith, interview, preface.
7. "Alice Colton Smith," *Deseret Morning News,* Aug. 3, 2006. Belle S. Spafford was the ninth Relief Society general president, from 1945 to 1974, and Barbara B. Smith was the tenth, from 1974 to 1984.
8. Smith, interview, 29.
9. Smith, interview, 41–42.
10. After reading Smith's first lesson, Harold B. Lee of the Quorum of the Twelve Apostles wrote Marianne C. Sharp that no one was to alter Smith's style or change what she wrote. (Smith, interview by Heath, 42–43.)
11. Smith, interview by Heath, 74. The term *Patty Perfect* first appears in print in 1939 in reference to the perfect secretary. It has been used since the middle of the twentieth century to refer to stereotypical, idealized women in general—including those in the church. (*Business Education World* 20 [1939]: 761.)
12. W. Whitney and Alice C. Smith, interview, 14–15.
13. Jill Mulvay Derr, Carol Cornwall Madsen, Kate Holbrook, and Matthew J. Grow, eds., *The First Fifty Years of Relief Society: Key Documents in Latter-day Saint Women's History* (Salt Lake City: Church Historian's Press, 2016), 8, 288.

14. Jill Mulvay Derr, Janath Russell Cannon, and Maureen Ursenbach Beecher, *Women of Covenant: The Story of Relief Society* (Salt Lake City: Deseret Book, 1992), 244, 288; Belle S. Spafford, interview by Jill Mulvay Derr, Jan. 12, 1976, 29, CHL.
15. Alice Colton Smith, "Visiting Teacher Messages," *Relief Society Magazine* 56, no. 6 (June 1969): 469–471.
16. Citation in original: "Matt. 11:28–30."
17. Citation in original: "D&C 20:17."
18. Citation in original: "Former Relief Society Handbook, p. 29." See *Handbook of the Relief Society of the Church of Jesus Christ of Latter-day Saints* (Salt Lake City: The General Board of the Relief Society, 1931), 29; see also Nauvoo Relief Society Minute Book, July 28, 1843, [101–102], in Derr et al., *First Fifty Years,* 110. Annie Wells Cannon and Vera White Pohlman assisted Amy Brown Lyman in producing the 1931 handbook, which was intended to inform Relief Society members and officers about the organization's history, regulations, and procedures. The authors relied heavily on records from past general secretaries, including Eliza R. Snow, Sarah M. Kimball, Emmeline B. Wells, Olive D. Christensen, Amy Brown Lyman, and Julia A. F. Lund. The book was first issued at the April 1931 Relief Society conference. (Amy Brown Lyman, *In Retrospect: Autobiography of Amy Brown Lyman* [Salt Lake City: General Board of Relief Society, 1945], 84; *Handbook of the Relief Society of the Church of Jesus Christ of Latter-day Saints,* 12–13; "Relief Society Handbook," *Relief Society Magazine* 18, no. 5 [May 1931]: 297.)
19. Visiting teacher meetings at this time took place the first week of each month—excluding four months each summer—immediately before the spiritual living meeting. During each thirty- to forty-five-minute meeting, visiting teachers reported on home visits, an officer presented the visiting teaching message for the new month, and the Relief Society president gave instructions as she saw necessary. (*Handbook of Instructions of the Relief Society of the Church of Jesus Christ of Latter-day Saints* [Salt Lake City: General Board of Relief Society, 1968], 32.)
20. Smith here refers to her time in Austria, during which she presided over the Relief Society and her husband was mission president. (Rabe, "A Conversation with Sister Smith," [13].)
21. In 1942, art professor Jack Sears designed the Relief Society emblem familiar to church members today. It includes two sheaves of wheat, representing Relief Society members' labors to save wheat against times of famine. (Connie Lamb, "Symbols of the LDS Relief Society," *Mormon Historical Studies* 14, no. 1 [Spring 2013]: 115–116, 118–120; see also Jessie L. Embry, "Relief Society Grain Storage Program, 1876–1940" [master's thesis, Brigham Young University, 1974]; and Jessie L. Embry, "Grain Storage: The Balance of Power between Priesthood Authority and Relief Society Autonomy," *Dialogue: A Journal of Mormon Thought* 15, no. 4 [Winter 1982]: 59–66.)
22. Nauvoo Relief Society Minute Book, July 28, 1843, [101–102], in Derr et al., *First Fifty Years,* 110.
23. See Luke 10:34. On April 1, 1842, the *Times and Seasons* published an article on the newly founded Nauvoo Relief Society that stated that one of the purposes of the society was to "pour in oil and wine to the wounded heart of the distressed." Though this article was attributed to the newspaper's editor, Joseph Smith, it was likely authored by John Taylor. Based on the original attribution, the compilers of the manuscript history of the church indicated that Joseph Smith had spoken these words at the Relief Society meeting held on March 24, 1842. The statement was then included in the *History of the Church,* where Alice C. Smith would likely have read it. The original minutes of that meeting do not contain this statement. (Nauvoo Relief Society Minute Book, Mar. 24, 1842, 21, and "Ladies' Relief Society," *Times and Seasons* 3, no. 11 [Apr. 1, 1842]: 743, in Derr et al., *First Fifty Years,* 42, 132–133; Joseph Smith, History, 1838–1856, vol. C-1 [Nov. 2, 1838–July 31, 1842], Mar. 24, 1842, 1302, accessed Feb. 3, 2016, josephsmithpapers.org; Joseph Smith et al., *History of the Church of Jesus Christ of Latter-day Saints,* ed. B. H. Roberts, 7 vols. [Salt Lake City: Deseret News, 1902–1912 (vols. 1–6), 1932 (vol. 7)], 4:567–568.)
24. Likely Nancy Colton. One of Nancy's children reported in a 1977 family history, "In the early years Mother had countless opportunities to give full play to the philanthropic characteristics she had inherited from her mother. There were no doctors in the Valley then and Mother went far and near to help people in times of sickness. No road was too long or too rough, no night was too dark, and

no weather too inclement to keep her from answering the call of someone in need of help." (Miriam C. Perry, ed., *An Historical and Biographical Record of the Sterling Driggs Colton Family, Descendants and Related Families* [Logan, UT: Educational Printing Service, 1977], 23, FHL.)

25. Women fed the hungry both on their own and through organized Relief Society efforts. (Derr, Cannon, and Beecher, *Women of Covenant,* 250, 257–258.)
26. See Doctrine and Covenants 115:5.
27. Citation in original: "Matt. 11:28–30."
28. See John 13:35.

CHAPTER 39: LUCRECIA SUÁREZ DE JUÁREZ, "RELIEF SOCIETY BRINGS HAPPINESS"

1. By 1971 the church had begun to hold area conferences to give members outside of the United States the chance to meet with and learn from general church leaders. This area conference was held in Mexico a year later, August 25–27, 1972. Area conferences were a response to the expansion of church membership around the globe. (Joseph Fielding Smith, Harold B. Lee, and N. Eldon Tanner, "First Presidency Issues Statement on Conference," *Church News,* Feb. 27, 1971; N. Eldon Tanner, in *Official Report of the One Hundred Forty-Sixth Semi-annual General Conference of the Church of Jesus Christ of Latter-day Saints,* Oct. 1–3, 1976 [Salt Lake City: The Church of Jesus Christ of Latter-day Saints, 1977], 119–121.)
2. For more on the Mexican Revolution, see Héctor Aguilar Camín and Lorenzo Meyer, *In the Shadow of the Mexican Revolution: Contemporary Mexican History, 1910–1989,* trans. Luis Alberto Fierro (Austin: University of Texas Press, 1993).
3. Romero was born in 1974. (Miguel A. Romero, emails to Kate Holbrook, Aug. 14, Sept. 2, 2015.)
4. Rex E. Lee reportedly was speaking of Suárez de Juárez when in a later speech he described teaching "a widow and her daughters." After his mission to Mexico, Lee was the founding dean of Brigham Young University's J. Reuben Clark Law School in 1971, served as the thirty-seventh United States solicitor general from 1981 to 1985, and served as the tenth president of Brigham Young University from 1989 to 1995. (Rex E. Lee, "By Study and Also by Faith," in *Educating Zion,* ed. John W. Welch and Don E. Norton [Provo, UT: BYU Studies, 1996], 137–139; Romero, email to Holbrook, Aug. 14, 2015.)
5. "Historia de la Escuela 'Moctezuma Xocoyotzin,'" Mexico, Distrito Federal, 1961–1972, 1, CHL; Paul Swenson, "Thousands Come to Share Peace," *Deseret News,* Oct. 4, 1968.
6. Ammon M. Tenney, Journal, no. 3, Feb. 22, 1903, 66, CHL; Mexican Mission, Historical Record, Mar. 4–15, 1903, CHL. The first Relief Society meeting in Mexico occurred on February 22, 1903. For more information on the establishment of the Relief Society in Mexico, see Jared M. Tamez, "'Our Faithful Sisters': Mormon Worship and the Establishment of the Relief Society in the Mexican Mission, 1901–1903," in *Just South of Zion: The Mormons in Mexico and Its Borderlands,* ed. Jason H. Dormady and Jared M. Tamez (Albuquerque: University of New Mexico Press, 2015), 73–88.
7. F. LaMond Tullis, *Mormons in Mexico: The Dynamics of Faith and Culture* (Logan: Utah State University Press, 1987), 101–104, 110–112, 119–121.
8. In 1975, apostle Howard W. Hunter established eleven new stakes in the Mexico City area. (Boanerges Rubalcava, "Mexico and Central America, the Church in," in *Encyclopedia of Mormonism,* ed. Daniel H. Ludlow, 5 vols. [New York: Macmillan, 1992], 2:900.)
9. Jay M. Todd, "The Remarkable Mexico City Area Conference," *Ensign* 2, no. 11 (Nov. 1972): 89–90.
10. Todd, "The Remarkable Mexico City Area Conference," 93.
11. Todd, "The Remarkable Mexico City Area Conference," 95.
12. In 1972, stake Relief Societies existed in North, Central, and South America, as well as Great Britain, western Europe, Asia, the South Pacific, and Africa. (Relief Society Annual General Conference Program, 1972, 21, in Relief Society Annual Conference Proceedings, 1945–1975, CHL.)
13. In the 1970s, the Relief Society produced a manual in Spanish, as they did in English, which included visiting teaching messages and homemaking lessons. Relief Society instructions for

homemaking meetings in 1972 explain, "The homemaking meeting provides an opportunity for meeting the homemaking needs of the sisters through diversified activities and should be adapted to local conditions and cultures." (*Manual de Lecciones de la Sociedad de Socorro,* 1971, CHL; *1971–72 Relief Society Courses of Study* [Salt Lake City: Relief Society of the Church of Jesus Christ of Latter-day Saints, 1971]; *Handbook of Instructions of the Relief Society of the Church of Jesus Christ of Latter-day Saints* [Salt Lake City: General Board of Relief Society, 1972], 64–65.)

14. Citation in original: "David O. McKay, *Gospel Ideals* (Salt Lake City: An Improvement Era Publication, 1953), p. 449."
15. Visitors at the women's session included church president Harold B. Lee and Freda Joan Lee; Lee's first counselor, N. Eldon Tanner, and Sara Isabelle Merrill Tanner; Amelia Smith McConkie and Helen Kearnes Richards (wives of visiting authorities); Relief Society general board member Leanor J. Brown; Young Women's Mutual Improvement Association general board member Sharon Lee Staples; and Primary general board member Fulvia Call Dixon. ("Women's Session Saturday Evening," *Official Report of the First Mexico and Central America Area General Conference of the Church of Jesus Christ of Latter-day Saints* [Salt Lake City: The Church of Jesus Christ of Latter-day Saints, 1973], 79–80, 85, 87.)

CHAPTER 40: BELLE S. SPAFFORD, "LATTER-DAY SAINT WOMEN IN TODAY'S CHANGING WORLD"

1. Belle S. Spafford, interview by Jill Mulvay [Derr], Nov. 17, 1975, 1–3, 6, James Moyle Oral History Program, CHL.
2. Spafford, interview by Derr, 6–9.
3. "Belle Spafford, Dies at 86, LDS Matron," *Salt Lake Tribune,* Feb. 4, 1982.
4. *A Centenary of Relief Society, 1842–1942* (Salt Lake City: General Board of Relief Society, 1942); Janet Peterson and Connie Lewis, "Making a Difference for Women: Belle S. Spafford," *Ensign* 36, no. 3 (Mar. 2006): 47. For more information on the process of compiling the Relief Society history, see Marianne Clark Sharp, interview by Jessie L. Embry, May–June 1977, 48–51, James Moyle Oral History Program, CHL.
5. "Belle Smith Spafford, Leader of Women, Dies at 86 in Salt Lake," *Deseret News,* Feb. 3, 1982. Relief Society membership shifted from voluntary to automatic during Spafford's presidency. (Peterson and Lewis, "Making a Difference for Women," 49; Spafford, interview by Derr, 99–100.)
6. Under this new arrangement, a member of the stake Relief Society presidency was responsible for single women in the stake aged eighteen and older and was a member of the stake Melchizedek Priesthood Mutual Improvement Association (MIA) committee. The Melchizedek Priesthood MIA was formed to replace previous MIA organizations that had overseen single adults in the church. A counselor in the ward Relief Society presidency was responsible for single women in the ward, including adapting Relief Society meetings and curriculum to their needs. (Harold B. Lee, N. Eldon Tanner, and Marion G. Romney, "To All Stake and Mission Presidents, Bishops, District and Branch Presidents," Apr. 16, 1973, in Relief Society General Board Minutes, vol. 41, 1972–1973, 183, CHL; Harold B. Lee, N. Eldon Tanner, and Marion G. Romney, "To All Stake and Mission Presidents, Bishops, District and Branch Presidents," Apr. 17, 1973, Relief Society General Board Minutes, 185.)
7. Spafford, interview by Derr, 52.
8. In 1982, the University of Utah endowed a chair in Spafford's name in the Graduate School of Social Work—the first chair at the university named for a woman. ("U. Chair Fetes Belle Spafford," *Salt Lake Tribune,* Feb. 4, 1982; Belle S. Spafford, *Women in Today's World* [Salt Lake City: Deseret Book, 1971], x–xi.)
9. Spafford, interview by Derr, 88–90.
10. Spafford, *Women in Today's World,* x; "Belle Smith Spafford, Leader of Women."
11. Spafford, interview by Derr, 36.
12. Construction of the Marriott Center was completed in 1972. The structure initially seated over twenty-three thousand and held basketball games and other university and church events, including

devotionals. (Ernest L. Wilkinson and W. Cleon Skousen, *Brigham Young University: A School of Destiny* [Provo, UT: Brigham Young University Press, 1976], 589–591.)

13. "Equal Rights Amendment," *Church News,* Jan. 11, 1975; J. B. Haws, *The Mormon Image in the American Mind: Fifty Years of Public Perception* (New York: Oxford University Press, 2013), 86–96; Martha Sonntag Bradley, *Pedestals and Podiums: Utah Women, Religious Authority, and Equal Rights* (Salt Lake City: Signature Books, 2005), 141–154. Barbara B. Smith was the tenth general president of the Relief Society from 1974 to 1984.
14. Belle S. Spafford, "The American Woman's Movement" (The Church of Jesus Christ of Latter-day Saints, 1974), 15–20, CHL.
15. The unnamed man who introduced her said, "We are grateful today that we have a lovely young woman to be with us to be our speaker." (Belle S. Spafford, "Latter-day Saint Women in Today's Changing World," audio recording, accessed Oct. 14, 2015, speeches.byu.edu.)
16. N. Eldon Tanner was first counselor in the First Presidency at the time of Spafford's release; Tanner and Spafford were good friends. He joined the Quorum of the Twelve Apostles in 1962 and became a counselor in the First Presidency the following year. ("Sustaining of Church Officers," *Ensign* 4, no. 11 [Nov. 1974]: 36; Spafford, interview by Derr, 237.)
17. BYU sponsored several themed weeks during the 1960s and 1970s, including History Week, Agriculture Week, and Mental Health Week. These weeks were to "provide students and faculty the opportunity for cultural and intellectual growth." Presentation topics varied from spiritual to academic to temporal. Women's Week ended by 1977, and an annual Women's Conference began in 1976, initially as a mother-daughter event. ("'Special' Weeks Emphasize Groups," *Daily Universe* [Provo, UT], Feb. 14, 1975; Carol Lee Hawkins, "Brigham Young University Women's Conference: A History," 1992, 1–4, in editors' possession; "Women's Week, 1966," Register of the Associated Women Students of Brigham Young University, BYU; Nancy Hinsdale Wilcox, "Women's Week: No More Cookie Baking," *Daily Universe,* Feb. 17, 1978.)
18. Citation in original: "'A Centenary of Relief Society,' p. 15"; see also Nauvoo Relief Society Minute Book, Mar. 17, 1842, 8, in Jill Mulvay Derr, Carol Cornwall Madsen, Kate Holbrook, and Matthew J. Grow, eds., *The First Fifty Years of Relief Society: Key Documents in Latter-day Saint Women's History* (Salt Lake City: Church Historian's Press, 2016), 31.
19. Citation in original: "'A Centenary of Relief Society,' p. 16." Spafford's centennial history quoted from the *History of the Church,* whose compilers had changed the original text. The original minute entry that recorded Joseph Smith's words reads: "This Society is to get instruction through the order which God has established—through the medium of those appointed to lead—and I now turn the key to you in the name of God, and this Society shall rejoice, and knowledge and intelligence shall flow down from this time." (Joseph Smith et al., *History of the Church of Jesus Christ of Latter-day Saints,* ed. B. H. Roberts, 7 vols. [Salt Lake City: Deseret News, 1902–1912 (vols. 1-6), 1932 (vol. 7)], 4:607; Nauvoo Relief Society Minute Book, Apr. 28, 1842, [40], in Derr et al., *First Fifty Years,* 59. For more on the change in wording, see Derr et al., *First Fifty Years,* 198–200, 207.)
20. For information on Watergate, inflation and recession, the energy crisis, and oil-producing nations, see Thomas Borstelmann, *The 1970s: A New Global History from Civil Rights to Economic Inequality* (Princeton, NJ: Princeton University Press, 2012), 38–41, 54–58; on food shortages, see "The World Food Crisis," *Time* 104, no. 20 (Nov. 11, 1974): 66–76.
21. The National Women's Political Caucus was formed in 1971 to promote the election to political office of women who would support women's rights. (Janet A. Flammang, *Women's Political Voice: How Women Are Transforming the Practice and Study of Politics* [Philadelphia: Temple University Press, 1997], 189.)
22. Citation in original: "'The Case Against the ERA,' *Nation's Business,* January 1975, pp. 9–10."
23. Citation in original: "[1] Samuel 9:1–3."
24. Citation in original: "see 1 Samuel 10."
25. Citation in original: "1 Samuel 13:13–14."
26. Citation in original: "1 Samuel 15:24."
27. Citation in original: "Mosiah 29:26."

28. Citation in original: "Matthew 5:14–16."
29. Spafford is referring to Relief Society general conference.
30. "Notes to the Field: April General Conference of Relief Society Not Scheduled," *Relief Society Magazine* 29, no. 2 (Feb. 1942): 112.
31. The territorial legislatures of Utah and Wyoming granted women the right to vote in February 1870 and December 1869, respectively. Utah women actually voted first, on February 18, 1870; Wyoming women voted for the first time on September 6, 1870. ("Daily Leader," *Cheyenne Leader,* Dec. 11, 1869; "The Woman Suffrage Bill," *Deseret News,* Feb. 16, 1870; "Local and Other Matters," *Deseret News,* Feb. 19, 1870; "Daily Sentinel," *Laramie Daily Sentinel,* Sept. 7, 1870.)
32. Nauvoo Relief Society Minute Book, Apr. 28, 1842, [40], in Derr et al., *First Fifty Years,* 59.
33. Because of "increasing difficulty in transportation," general conference attendance between 1942 and 1945 was restricted to priesthood leaders—sometimes only general authorities and stake presidencies, sometimes also including bishoprics, branch presidencies, stake high councils, temple presidencies, and mission presidents. Relief Society general conference was not held from 1942 to 1944. (Circular Letters of the First Presidency, Mar. 14, 1942; Sept. 12, 1942; Mar. 17, 1943; Sept. 10, 1943; Mar. 10, 1944; Sept. 13, 1944; Mar. 3, 1945; Sept. 28, 1945, CHL; "Notice to Church Officers," Circular Letter of the First Presidency, Jan. 17, 1942, CHL; Belle S. Spafford, "Report and Official Instructions," *Relief Society Magazine* 32, no. 12 [Dec. 1945]: 725.)
34. Citation in original: "'Address to the Members of Relief Society,' 4 October 1945, *Relief Society Magazine* 32 (1945): 716, 717, 719."
35. Spafford's black notebooks were legendary among those who worked with her; she destroyed them after her release from the presidency. (Belle S. Spafford, interview by Maren Mouritsen and Tamara Quick, ca. 1980, 9, CHL.)
36. Spafford also described this incident in her 1976 oral history interview. (Spafford, interview by Derr, 86.)
37. Rebekah J. Ryan, "In the World: Latter-day Saints in the National Council of Women, 1888–1987," in *Summer Fellows' Papers 2003: Latter-day Saint Women in the Twentieth-Century,* ed. Claudia L. Bushman (Provo, UT: Joseph Fielding Smith Institute for Latter-day Saint History at Brigham Young University, 2005), 131–147; "Winning on the Homefront," *Ensign* 9, no. 7 (July 1979): 78–79.
38. The Relief Society was established on the BYU campus by 1956. (Relief Society Annual General Conference Program, 1956, 10, Relief Society Conference and Convention Programs, 1916–1975, CHL.)
39. Spafford announced that the Relief Society would now be responsible for all single women in the church at the April 1973 Relief Society general conference officers' meeting. Women aged eighteen to twenty-five were called "young adults"; those twenty-six and older were "special interest." ("Relief Society Annual General Conference Officers Meeting," Oct. 3, 1973, 8–9, Relief Society Annual Conference Proceedings, 1945–1975, CHL.)
40. Citation in original: "*Gospel Doctrine,* 3rd ed. (Salt Lake City: Deseret Book, 1919), p. 484." John A. Widtsoe led the effort to compile extracts from Joseph F. Smith's published writings and speeches, organized by subject, for a book titled *Gospel Doctrine.* The book served as the text for priesthood meetings in 1919. (Joseph F. Smith, *Gospel Doctrine: Selections from the Sermons and Writings of Joseph F. Smith,* 2nd ed. [Salt Lake City: Deseret News, 1919], v–vi.)
41. Stephen L Richards joined the Quorum of the Twelve Apostles in 1917.

CHAPTER 41: ARDETH G. KAPP, "DRIFTING, DREAMING, DIRECTING"

1. "Ardeth Greene Kapp, Young Women General President," *Ensign* 14, no. 5 (May 1984): 98; Ardeth G. Kapp, interview by Gordon Irving, Dec. 1978–Sept. 1979, 4–7, James Moyle Oral History Program, CHL; Karen Thomas Arnesen, "Ardeth Greene Kapp: A Prairie Girl, a Young Woman Still," *Ensign* 15, no. 9 (Sept. 1985): 35.
2. Arnesen, "Ardeth Greene Kapp," 36.

3. Anita Thompson, *Stand as a Witness: The Biography of Ardeth Greene Kapp* (Salt Lake City: Deseret Book, 2005), 68–70.
4. Thompson, *Stand as a Witness,* 82–84.
5. Arnesen, "Ardeth Greene Kapp," 37.
6. Thompson, *Stand as a Witness,* 107–108, 114, 141.
7. Arnesen, "Ardeth Greene Kapp," 39.
8. Arnesen, "Ardeth Greene Kapp," 38–39.
9. Kapp, interview, preface, 196; "Ardeth Greene Kapp, Young Women General President," 98.
10. Kapp, interview, preface, 198.
11. "Ardeth Greene Kapp, Young Women General President," 98; Kapp, interview, preface, 196.
12. Kapp, interview, 49–54. This committee was established in 1961 as part of the church's broader correlation movement. (Carol H. Cannon, "Correlation Chronology, as Reflected in Minutes of Correlation Executive Committee Meetings, 1960–1971," 1, CHL; Michael A. Goodman, "Correlation: The Turning Point [1960s]," in *Salt Lake City: The Place Which God Prepared,* ed. Scott C. Esplin and Kenneth L. Alford [Provo, UT: Religious Studies Center, Brigham Young University, 2011], 263–264.)
13. Kapp, interview, 58A, 61.
14. Kapp, interview, 50, 52, 56.
15. "Ardeth Greene Kapp, Young Women General President," 98; Kapp, interview, preface. Kapp would serve as Young Women general president from 1984 to 1992. Under her presidency, the organization revamped the Personal Progress program, defined the Young Women values and motto, and instituted the Young Women theme, which young women and their leaders still recite each week at the beginning of their Sunday meeting. (Ardeth G. Kapp and Carolyn J. Rasmus, interview by Gordon Irving, Apr.–June 1992, 174–175, 200–214, James Moyle Oral History Program, CHL.)
16. Kapp, interview, 197.
17. Kapp, interview, 23–27, 190–192. The *Encyclopedia of Mormonism* says of patriarchal blessings, "As the patriarch seeks the Spirit he may be moved to give admonitions, promises, and assurances. . . . One's spiritual gifts, talents, skills, and potentials may be specified with their associated obligations of gratitude and dedication." (William James Mortimer, "Patriarchal Blessings," in *Encyclopedia of Mormonism,* ed. Daniel H. Ludlow, 5 vols. [New York: Macmillan, 1992], 3:1066.)
18. A. C. Smyth, "Never Be Late," in *The Children Sing* (Salt Lake City: Deseret Book, 1951), 119.
19. See Articles of Faith 1:4.
20. Citation in original: "Alma 17:2–3."
21. Citation in original: "Quoted by Harold B. Lee, in *Conference Report,* October 1955, p. 56."
22. Citation in original: "See Spencer W. Kimball, *My Beloved Sisters,* p. 20."
23. Citation in original: "'Let Us Move Forward and Upward,' *Ensign,* May 1979, p. 83."
24. This is a nineteenth-century translation of Virgil's phrase from Eclogue 8, "*Ipsi sibi somnia fingunt.*" (See, for example, *The Works of Joseph Addison,* 3 vols. [New York: Harper and Brothers, 1845], 1:179.)
25. This lyric is from the song "Happy Talk." *South Pacific* was written by Richard Rogers and Oscar Hammerstein and first performed in 1949. (Jim Lovensheimer, *South Pacific: Paradise Rewritten* [New York: Oxford University Press, 2010], xv, 215–216.)
26. Kapp's graduation was from Brigham Young High School in 1949. Oscar A. Kirkham was a member of the First Quorum of the Seventy from 1941 until his death in 1958. (Thompson, *Stand as a Witness,* 72, 84–87; "He Taught with Trees," *Instructor* 93, no. 5 [May 1958]: 148–149.)
27. Citation in original: "See D&C 11:16."
28. Citation in original: "John 7:16–17."
29. Citation in original: "Ether 12:6"
30. Citation in original: "See Ephesians 4:11–14."
31. See Mosiah 3:14–15.
32. Citation in original: "Moses 5:6."
33. Citation in original: "Moses 5:7."
34. Citation in original: "Joseph Fielding Smith, comp., *Teachings of the Prophet Joseph Smith* (Salt Lake

City, Utah; Deseret Book Co., 1969), p. 54." See "The Elders of the Church in Kirtland, to Their Brethren Abroad," *Evening and Morning Star* 2, no. 18 (Mar. 1834): 284.

35. Kapp repeated this story again at a BYU devotional on February 1, 1987. (Ardeth G. Kapp, "Your Inheritance: Secure or in Jeopardy?" in *Brigham Young University 1986–87 Devotional and Fireside Speeches* [Provo, UT: Brigham Young University, 1987], 102.)
36. Citation in original: "'Prayer and the Prophet Joseph,' *Ensign*, January 1976, p. 23." Truman Madsen was a well-known professor of philosophy at BYU. He also served as director of the Jerusalem Center for Near Eastern Studies. (Lynn Arave, "Former BYU Professor Truman Madsen Dies," *Deseret News*, May 29, 2009.)
37. Citation in original: "*My Beloved Sisters*, p. 44."
38. Citation in original: "*Hymns: The Church of Jesus Christ of Latter-day Saints* (Salt Lake City: Deseret Book Co., 1976), no. 301."
39. Citation in original: "*Church News*, 5 January 1970, p. 28." Neal A. Maxwell was a member of the Quorum of the Twelve Apostles from 1981 until his death in 2004.
40. Citation in original: "*My Beloved Sisters*, p. 37."
41. This quotation is popularly attributed to Joseph F. Smith, but the specific source is unknown. Smith spoke of Elmina S. Taylor in similar terms at her funeral: "Most people of my acquaintance . . . walk very largely in a light that is borrowed. . . . She was one of the few in the world who had the light within her . . . and she walked in it." ("Death of Elmina S. Taylor," *Improvement Era* 8, no. 3 [Jan. 1905]: 221; see also Joseph F. Smith, *Gospel Doctrine: Selections from the Sermons and Writings of Joseph F. Smith* [Salt Lake City: Deseret Book, 1978], 87–88.)
42. Citation in original: "Acts 2:18."

CHAPTER 42: ELAINE A. CANNON, "SEASON OF AWAKENING"

1. Holly C. Metcalf, *Love's Banner: Memories of the Life of Elaine Cannon* (Kenmore, WA: Lamb and Lion, 2011), 21. Metcalf is Elaine Cannon's youngest daughter. (Janet Peterson, "Love's Banner: Memories of the Life of Elaine Cannon," *Meridian Magazine*, June 14, 2012, accessed Dec. 22, 2015, ldsmag.com.)
2. Metcalf, *Love's Banner*, 37–38.
3. "A Wonderful Adventure: Elaine Cannon," *New Era* 13, no. 3 (Apr. 1983): 6.
4. Arlene B. Darger, interview by Marsha G. Richards, Nov. 3, 2003, [2], CHL; Metcalf, *Love's Banner*, 138. For more on the youth correlation committee and the curriculum planning and writing committee, see chapter 41 herein.
5. Elaine A. Cannon, interview by Gordon Irving, 1979–1990, preface, James Moyle Oral History Program, CHL.
6. Cannon, interview, 104.
7. Cannon, interview, 104.
8. Cannon, interview, 105.
9. Cannon, interview, preface, 103–105.
10. Cannon, interview, 100–104. First published in January 1971, the *New Era* is the official English-language church magazine for young people aged twelve to eighteen, along with their parents, teachers, and church leaders. (Jay M. Todd, "The New Era," *New Era* 1, no. 1 [Jan. 1971]: 3.)
11. Cannon, interview, preface. Ardeth G. Kapp and others also supported this idea at the time. (Ardeth G. Kapp, interview by Gordon Irving, 1978–1979, 49–51, James Moyle Oral History Program, CHL.)
12. Cannon, interview, 111–112.
13. Prior to 1980, Relief Society, Primary, Young Men, and Young Women meetings took place during the week. Members attended Sunday School and priesthood meetings on Sunday mornings, then returned in the afternoon for sacrament meeting. The consolidated Sunday meeting schedule meant that members would attend all of their meetings during a three-hour block on Sundays. Young men and young women would continue to have a weeknight evening activity each week. ("Church Consolidates Meeting Schedules," *Ensign* 10, no. 3 [Mar. 1980]: 73.)

14. See Mary Jane Woodger, "Elaine Anderson Cannon, Young Women General President: Innovations, Inspiration, and Implementations," *Journal of Mormon History* 40, no. 4 (Fall 2014): 192–197; see also Elaine Anderson Cannon, Journal, Sept. 1, 1979, Elaine A. Cannon Papers, BYU.
15. Cannon, interview, 182.
16. Metcalf, *Love's Banner,* 195.
17. Cannon, interview, preface.
18. Marvin J. Ashton, "Yellow Ribbons and Charted Courses," *New Era* 11, no. 6 (July 1981): 14.
19. Spencer W. Kimball, "In Love and Power and without Fear," *New Era* 11, no. 6 (July 1981): 8.
20. Spencer W. Kimball joined the Quorum of the Twelve Apostles in 1943 and then served as twelfth president of the church from 1973 to 1985. Camilla E. Kimball taught in various settings throughout her life. (Carol Cornwall Madsen, "In Memoriam: Camilla Eyring Kimball," *Sunstone* 11, no. 4 [July 1987]: 48.)
21. "Young Women Fireside," *New Era* 11, no. 6 (July 1981): 6–17. Marvin J. Ashton was a member of the Quorum of the Twelve Apostles from 1971 to 1994.
22. Citation in original: "Moses 1:39." Arlene B. Darger and Norma B. Smith were Cannon's counselors. (*Official Report of the One Hundred Fiftieth Semiannual General Conference of the Church of Jesus Christ of Latter-day Saints,* Oct. 4 and 5, 1980 [Salt Lake City: The Church of Jesus Christ of Latter-day Saints, 1981], 26.)
23. During the April 1976 priesthood session of general conference, Spencer W. Kimball spoke of the current generation of young people as a "royal generation." (Spencer W. Kimball, "Boys Need Heroes Close By," *Ensign* 6, no. 5 [May 1976]: 45; see also Victor L. Brown, "Follow the Living Prophet," *Ensign* 7, no. 5 [May 1977]: 37.)
24. Citation in original: "Elaine A. Cannon and Margaret Cornwall Richards, 'The Awakening.'" The *New Era* published this song the following year. (Elaine Cannon and Margaret Cornwall Richards, "Awakening," *New Era* 12, no. 2 [Mar. 1982]: 28–29.)
25. Citation in original: "Rom. 8:16."
26. Genesis 12:1–3.
27. Citation in original: "'There Was a Child Went Forth,' in Bruce B. Clark and Robert K. Thomas, *Out of the Best Books,* Deseret Book Co., 1966, 2:363." The American poet Walt Whitman included this poem in his collection *Leaves of Grass* (Brooklyn, NY: printed by the author, 1855), 90–91. The Relief Society commissioned Clark and Thomas to produce *Out of the Best Books* as a text for Relief Society literature classes. (Marian W. Jensen and Alice W. Anderson, "Alice Ludlow Wilkinson," in *Women of Commitment: Elect Ladies of Brigham Young University,* ed. Marian Wilkinson Jensen [Bountiful, UT: Horizon Publishers, 1997], 22.)
28. See chapter 41, note 17, herein.
29. South of Ensign Peak and north of downtown Salt Lake City, the Capitol Hill neighborhood slopes down from the state capitol building with its formal gardens and cherry trees. Streetcars traveled up and down the hill, and a canyon framed one side of the neighborhood. ("A Wonderful Adventure," 9–10; Metcalf, *Love's Banner,* 22–23.)
30. From this same fireside, see Camilla E. Kimball, "We Are His Children," *New Era* 11, no. 6 (July 1981): 7.
31. Cannon and Richards, "Awakening," 28–29.
32. Citation in original: "Jer. 17:7–8."

CHAPTER 43: FRANCINE R. BENNION, "A LATTER-DAY SAINT THEOLOGY OF SUFFERING"

1. Francine Russell Bennion, interview by Kate Holbrook, Apr. 21, 2015, 16, CHL.
2. Bennion, interview, 15–16.
3. "Miss Francine Russell Engaged; Pamela Russell, Mr. Clark to Wed," *Deseret News,* May 30, 1956.
4. Francine Russell Bennion, Curriculum Vitae, Oct. 6, 2012, in editors' possession.
5. Bennion, interview, 4. Established in 1978, the Women's Research Institute was "intended to emphasize the concern for women held by the church and Brigham Young University, by seeking

solutions to women's unique challenges, and by acknowledging women's significant contributions in all disciplines." ("A Farewell Salute to the Women's Research Institute of Brigham Young University," *Square Two* 2, no. 3 [Fall 2009]: 1; "The Women's Research Institute," unpublished manuscript, Oct. 2008, Brigham Young University, 3.)

6. "Five Called to Young Women General Board," *Church News,* May 28, 1977; Francine Bennion, "Encounter in Ammonihah," *Ensign* 7, no. 4 (Apr. 1977): 25–29; Francine Bennion, "Stone or Bread?" *Ensign* 6, no. 1 (Jan. 1976): 38–42.
7. Bennion, interview, 3, 12, 14; "Five Called to Young Women General Board," 5.
8. Bennion, interview, 5–6; Aileen Clyde, email to Kate Holbrook, May 14, 2015.
9. Bennion, interview, 14; "Six Are Called to Serve on Relief Society Board," *Church News,* Dec. 25, 1983.
10. Bennion, interview, 17–18; Francine Bennion, email to Kate Holbrook, Apr. 14, 2016.
11. Mary E. Stovall and Carol Cornwall Madsen, Preface, in *A Heritage of Faith: Talks Selected from the BYU Women's Conferences,* ed. Mary E. Stovall and Carol Cornwall Madsen (Salt Lake City: Deseret Book, 1988), vii; Brigham Young University Women's Conference, Mar. 27–28, 1986, Program, Women's Office History, BYU.
12. Bramhall and Bennion were walking partners and close friends. (Bennion, interview, 2.)
13. Bramhall lived in the Pacific for many years; Kerr became Bramhall's friend during that time. (Bennion, interview, 2.)
14. Citation in original: "From a personal letter to the author."
15. See *Poverty and Hunger: Issues and Options for Food Security in Developing Countries* (Washington DC: World Bank, 1986), 1.
16. Drought caused famine in Ethiopia from 1984 to 1985, and government corruption amplified the disastrous effects of the famine. (Harold G. Marcus, *A History of Ethiopia* [Berkeley: University of California Press, 2002], 205–208.)
17. Bennion here refers to the *Challenger,* a NASA space shuttle that exploded on January 28, 1986, killing everyone on board. (Julianne G. Mahler, *Organizational Learning at NASA: The Challenger and Columbia Accidents* [Washington DC: Georgetown University Press, 2009], 5.)
18. Note in original: "Individual interpretation and breadth of context affect the model to be drawn from any specific verse of scripture."
19. Citation in original: "Judges 11:9–11; 29–39."
20. Citation in original: "Numbers 30:2."
21. Note in original: "Compare the story of Jephthah with Greek accounts of Iphigenia and King Midas. Though plots in the stories are similar, the tellers' contexts, focuses, and theologies differ, as will those of their readers."
22. Citation in original: "Judges 11:1–3."
23. Citation in original: "Genesis 28:20."
24. Citation in original: "Hebrews 11:32–34."
25. Citation in original: "e.g., Moses 4:1–3."
26. Citation in original: "e.g., Matthew 5."
27. Citation in original: "e.g., Isaiah 1:11–17."
28. During the 1980s, Northern Ireland was engaged in the Troubles, a violent conflict over sectarian disagreements and the question of whether Northern Ireland ought to remain in the United Kingdom or join the Republic of Ireland. Beginning in 1982, Iran helped to fund the Lebanese militant group Hezbollah, which killed hundreds of people through suicide bombings throughout the early 1980s and used hostages to barter for weapons for Iran. In July 1984, a boy and two girls were removed from the house of their mother and her boyfriend in Ontario, Canada. Among other abuses, the boyfriend had punished the boy, about six years old, for eating candy by scalding his hands to the point that the skin was coming off. (Andrew Sanders and Ian S. Wood, *Times of Troubles: Britain's War in Northern Ireland* [Edinburgh: Edinburgh University Press, 2012]; Thomas R. Mattair, *Global Security Watch—Iran: A Reference Handbook* [Westport, CT: Praeger

Security International, 2008], 35–36; Janet Bagnall, "How the System Failed 3 Children," *Montreal Gazette,* Jan. 18, 1986.)

29. Citation in original: "Job 4:3–5."
30. Citation in original: "Giordano Bruno, *The Heroic Frenzies,* trans. and ed. Paul Eugene Memmo, Jr. (Chapel Hill: University of North Carolina Press, 1965), p. 122."
31. Note in original: "One of many reasons for this is that humans have traditionally been considered to have no existence except that given them here by God—i.e., they are new creatures with no prior existence, created by God from nothing, and different from him *in kind.* It would therefore be unthinkable that a human might become as he is, might make a leap from one species of creature to another, so to speak. It would be pretentious and prideful for the created to claim true kinship with the Creator. Compare John 5:18."
32. The French essayist, philosopher, poet, novelist, and playwright Voltaire was a preeminent thinker of the eighteenth century. His famous novella *Candide* (1759) satirized the Leibniz philosophy of optimism, which suggested that while the world was not perfect, it was the best of all possible worlds that God could have created. (Nicholas Cronk, ed., *The Cambridge Companion to Voltaire* [New York: Cambridge University Press, 2009], x, xiii, 1–5, 125.)
33. Citation in original: "Such an exercise must of necessity be limited in scope. In 'Science and the Citizen,' *Scientific American,* August 1986, page 62, a discussion of events preceding the *Challenger* explosion begins with this paragraph:

    "'In its final report the presidential commission charged with examining the explosion of the space shuttle *Challenger* identifies the design flaw that caused the accident and describes in detail the events leading up to the tragedy. It does not describe the underlying causes, within the organization of the National Aeronautics and Space Administration, that made it possible for serious dangers to be ignored.'

    "Nor does the report describe underlying causes of the particular organization and decision-making processes at NASA.

    "If one takes a linear view of 'causes' and 'effects,' one must go far beyond recorded history to discover all steps which have affected any subsequent event in any way. One must examine a more complex array of interactions than any human can catalogue. Consider, for example, the difficulty of tracing a traffic accident back to the invention of the wheel and then trying to figure out all that helped get the wheel invented. Then consider all interactions with other factors—for example, the morning toothbrushing that affected the time, to the second, that one of the affected persons reached the intersection at which the accident occurred."
34. Citation in original: "See 1 Corinthians 13:9–12 in context."
35. Citation in original: "See, for example, Doctrine and Covenants 93:29–30; Abraham 3:18, 26–28; Moses 4:1–4; Revelation 12:7–9; Doctrine and Covenants 29:36; and Wilford Woodruff's record of Joseph Smith's King Follett Discourse, available in *The Words of Joseph Smith,* comp. and ed. Andrew F. Ehat and Lyndon W. Cook (Salt Lake City, Utah: Bookcraft, 1981), pp. 343–348.

    "If it were God who originally created our personal capabilities and quiddities, or if they originally came about by any kind of 'chance,' then any differences among us, and results of them, must ultimately be attributed to God or to chance. We could not be responsible for what we are or what we do. If we are choosers now, we must always have been choosers, within the constraints that current knowledge, understanding, or abilities would allow."
36. Note in original: "'What kind of weapons did they use in the war in heaven?' a nine-year-old girl once asked in a Sunday School class I was teaching."
37. A reference to Peter Pan's home, Neverland, in J. M. Barrie's 1904 play *Peter Pan; or, The Boy Who Wouldn't Grow Up,* published as a novel in 1911 as *Peter and Wendy.* Since Peter Pan never grew up, "never-never land" is often used to refer to unending childhood or to an imaginary Utopian society. (*Oxford English Dictionary,* s.v. "never-never land"; J. M. Barrie, *Peter and Wendy* [London: Hodder and Stoughton, 1911].)
38. Citation in original: "See Alma 14:11 in context."
39. See Joseph Smith—History 1:17; Moses 1:3, 6–7; John 20:16; Abraham 1:16; John 21:15; and

Doctrine and Covenants 25:1. The example of Helaman likely was intended as a reference to Nephi, son of Helaman. Latter-day Saints use Elohim as a name for God the Father and Jehovah as a name for Jesus Christ. (See Helaman 7:1; 10:3–6; Keith H. Meservy, "Elohim," and David R. Seely, "Jehovah, Jesus Christ," in *Encyclopedia of Mormonism,* ed. Daniel H. Ludlow, 5 vols. [New York: Macmillan, 1992], 2:452, 720.)

40. Note in original: "Consider the model for Judgment Day suggested by such verses as Alma 29:4–5. If we are to be capable of choosing to become more like God, then we must also know enough to reject it if we do not want what godhood actually is."
41. See Luke 4:1–4, 9–12.
42. See Doctrine and Covenants 88:42–43.
43. Citation in original: "D&C 93:30."
44. Citation in original: "Isaiah 28:9–13."
45. Citation in original: "Compare this concluding paragraph from the unsigned introductory note in *Japanese Haiku* (Mount Vernon, New York: Peter Pauper Press, 1955):

    "'One final word: The *haiku* is not expected to be always a complete or even a clear statement. The reader is supposed to add to the words his own associations and imagery, and thus to become a co-creator of his own pleasure in the poem. The publishers hope their readers may here co-create such pleasure for themselves!'"
46. See Deuteronomy 4:29.
47. Psalm 22:1; Matthew 17:46; Mark 15:34.
48. Citation in original: "This is suggested by such verses as: 2 Nephi 31:3; Isaiah 55:8–9; Doctrine and Covenants 29:31–34; Doctrine and Covenants 130:16–17."
49. Citation in original: "Romans 8:38–39."
50. Citation in original: "Hebrews 4:15–16."
51. Citation in original: "D&C 93:23–24; italics added." See also Doctrine and Covenants 93:25.
52. Citation in original: "2 Nephi 26:24, 33."
53. Citation in original: "See 1 Kings 18."
54. Citation in original: "See, for example, Jacob 4:6; Enos [1:]8; 3 Nephi 17:8; Ether 3, 12:12–21; Moroni 7:37; 10:7."

CHAPTER 44: JUTTA B. BUSCHE, "THE UNKNOWN TREASURE"

1. Jutta Baum Busche, interview by Kate Holbrook, July 14, 2015, 9, 12, CHL; Jutta B. Busche, "The Unknown Treasure," in *Women and the Power Within: To See Life Steadily and See It Whole,* ed. Dawn Hall Anderson and Marie Cornwall (Salt Lake City: Deseret Book, 1991), 21.
2. Busche, interview, 11–12.
3. Busche, interview, 10, 12.
4. Jan Underwood Pinborough, "Elder F. Enzio Busche: To the Ends of the Earth," *Ensign* 15, no. 2 (Feb. 1985): 34–35; "News of the Church: Elder F. Enzio Busche," *Ensign* 7, no. 11 (Nov. 1977): 100.
5. Overseeing church geographical units that existed between the area and stake levels, regional representatives trained the stake presidencies in their regions. The position of regional representative ended in 1995, when regional representative duties were assumed by area authorities, renamed area authority seventies in 1997. (Douglas L. Callister and Gerald J. Day, "Region, Regional Representative," in *Encyclopedia of Mormonism,* ed. Daniel H. Ludlow, 5 vols. [New York: Macmillan, 1992], 1:1198; Gordon B. Hinckley, "This Work Is Concerned with People," *Ensign* 25, no. 5 [May 1995]: 51–52; Gordon B. Hinckley, "May We Be Faithful and True," *Ensign* 27, no. 5 [May 1997]: 5–6.)
6. "News of the Church: Elder F. Enzio Busche," 99; Busche, interview, 2–3.
7. Busche, interview, 8–9.
8. Pinborough, "Elder F. Enzio Busche," 36.
9. Busche, interview, 7.
10. F. Enzio Busche, *Yearning for the Living God: Reflections from the Life of F. Enzio Busche,* ed. Tracie A. Lamb (Salt Lake City: Deseret Book, 2004), 206. Generally appointed for three years, the temple matron and president oversee the functioning of the temple. In addition to supervising temple

workers, sacred ceremonies, and the physical building, they are responsible for the spiritual tone of the temple. (David H. Yarn Jr. and Marilyn S. Yarn, "Temple President and Matron," in Ludlow, *Encyclopedia of Mormonism,* 4:1445–1446.)

11. Busche, interview, 3. Hinckley was first counselor in the First Presidency at this time.
12. Busche, interview, 3–4. Temple recommends are documents from a member's local ecclesiastical leaders certifying that the member is worthy to enter the temple. Worthiness is based on the member's belief in specific doctrines and adherence to basic commandments, such as the law of chastity and being honest in dealings with others. (Robert A. Tucker, "Temple Recommend," in Ludlow, *Encyclopedia of Mormonism,* 4:1446–1447.)
13. Busche, interview, 1–2.
14. Busche, interview, 4.
15. Busche, interview, 5.
16. Busche, interview, 5.
17. Busche, interview, 2.
18. World War II began for Germany on September 1, 1939, with the invasion of Poland. It ended with Germany's unconditional surrender on May 8, 1945. (See Evan Mawdsley, *World War II: A New History* [Cambridge, UK: Cambridge University Press, 2009], 96, 403–404.)
19. See Elisabeth von Berrinberg, *The City in Flames: A Child's Recollection of World War II in Würzburg, Germany* (Minneapolis: Berrinberg Publications, 2013); and Kjersti Ericsson and Eva Simonsen, eds., *Children of World War II: The Hidden Enemy Legacy* (Oxford: Berg, 2005).
20. See Joseph Fielding Smith, *Doctrines of Salvation: Sermons and Writings of Joseph Fielding Smith,* comp. Bruce R. McConkie, 3 vols. (Salt Lake City: Bookcraft, 1954), 1:56–57.
21. See Luke 11:37–54; and Matthew 23:1–39.
22. Citation in original: "As quoted in *TNT: The Power within You,* ed. Claude M. Bristol and Harold Sherman (New York: Prentice-Hall, 1987), p. 52." See also George Long, trans., *The Thoughts of the Emperor Marcus Aurelius Antoninus* (Boston: Little, Brown, 1891), 32.
23. Marcus Aurelius was a Roman emperor and a well-known Stoic philosopher. (See Frank McLynn, *Marcus Aurelius: Warrior, Philosopher, Emperor* [London: Bodley Head, 2009].)
24. F. Enzio Busche was in the First Quorum of the Seventy from 1977 to 2000.
25. Latter-day Saints in Utah typically had larger families than residents who were not Mormon. Utah church members also generally had larger families than other Latter-day Saints in the United States. (Tim B. Heaton, "The Demography of Utah Mormons," in *Utah in Demographic Perspective: Regional and National Contrasts,* ed. Thomas K. Martin, Tim B. Heaton, and Stephen J. Bahr [Salt Lake City: Signature Books, 1986], 181–193.)
26. Spencer W. Kimball, twelfth president of the church, frequently urged members to grow their own gardens. (See, for example, Spencer W. Kimball, "The True Way of Life and Salvation," *Ensign* 8, no. 5 [May 1978]: 4.)
27. Heart fund drives were fund-raisers aimed at educating the public about heart disease and raising money for research to combat the disease. "PTA" stands for parent-teacher association; such associations organize parent volunteers to support schools through fund-raising, classroom volunteering, additional educational programming, and social events. (See, for example, "Heart Association Plans Drive to Raise $200,000," *Deseret News,* Feb. 26, 1981.)
28. A well-known local landmark and the location of multiple hiking trails, Mount Timpanogos is directly north of Provo, Utah, with a summit about 11,750 feet above sea level. The average person takes seven to ten hours to hike to the summit and back. (See Michael R. Kelsey, *Climbing and Exploring Utah's Mt. Timpanogos* [Provo, UT: Kelsey Publishing, 1989], 7, 46, 136.)
29. Temple work includes performing saving ordinances vicariously on behalf of the dead. Spencer W. Kimball encouraged members to keep a personal history and journal. (See *Gospel Principles* [1978; repr., Salt Lake City: The Church of Jesus Christ of Latter-day Saints, 2009], 233–238; Kimball, "True Way of Life and Salvation," 4.)
30. Citation in original: "As quoted in *Great Books of the Western World,* vol. 12, ed. Robert Maynard Hutchins (Chicago: University of Chicago Press, 1952), p. 283."

31. Citation in original: "Romans 12:2."
32. Abraham's posterity (literal or adopted) are considered the children of the covenant. Those who make covenants through church ordinances are counted Abraham's adopted descendants. (See Marion G. Romney, "The Covenant of the Priesthood," *Ensign* 2, no. 7 [July 1972]: 98–99; and Eldred G. Smith, "All May Share in Adam's Blessing," *Ensign* 1, no. 6 [June 1971]: 100–101.)
33. The Frankfurt temple was the second temple dedicated in Germany, in 1987, after the Freiberg temple was dedicated in 1985. ("Temple Time Line—1980–1989," *Church News,* Sept. 2, 1989.)
34. Citation in original: "1 Corinthians 2:12." See also 1 Corinthians 2:9.

CHAPTER 45: ELAINE L. JACK, "GET A LIFE"

1. "New Relief Society General Presidency Called," *Ensign* 20, no. 5 (May 1990): 110; Janet Peterson and LaRene Gaunt, *Faith, Hope, and Charity: Inspiration from the Lives of General Relief Society Presidents* (American Fork, UT: Covenant Communications, 2008), 224–225; Elaine L. Jack, interview by Kate Holbrook, July 21, 2015, 1, CHL.
2. Peterson and Gaunt, *Faith, Hope, and Charity,* 225.
3. "New Relief Society General Presidency Called," 110; "Elaine L. Jack, Second Counselor in the Young Women Presidency," *Ensign* 17, no. 5 (May 1987): 100. The Jacks returned to the Cardston temple to serve as president and matron, and to mark their fiftieth wedding anniversary, in 1998. (Jack, interview by Holbrook, 2; "Appointments," *Ensign* 27, no. 11 [Nov. 1997]: 111; "New Temple Presidents," *Church News,* Sept. 23, 2000; Peterson and Gaunt, *Faith, Hope, and Charity,* 226, 239.)
4. Relief Society General Board Minutes, vol. 41, 1972–1973, 231–232; vol. 42, 1973–1974, 220; vol. 43, 1974–1975, 244–246; vol. 44, 1975–1976, 263; vol. 45, 1977, 242–243; vol. 46, 1978, 236–239; vol. 47, 1979, 202–203; vol. 48, 1980, 204–205; vol. 49, 1981, 163–164; vol. 50, 1982, 261; vol. 51, 1983, 201–202, CHL.
5. "Elaine L. Jack," 100; Ardeth G. Kapp and Carolyn J. Rasmus, interview by Gordon Irving, Apr.–June 1992, 144, James Moyle Oral History Program, CHL.
6. "Elaine L. Jack," 100.
7. For more on Okazaki, see chapter 46 herein. Clyde taught English at Brigham Young University for ten years, then worked as a certified construction flagger, helping other flaggers keep their jobs when they had to miss work for a personal or family illness. She chaired the Utah Task Force on Gender and Justice from 1987 to 1990 and was citizen chair of the Utah Commission on Criminal and Juvenile Justice until 1988, when she began twelve years of service on the Utah State Board of Regents. (Aileen Clyde, emails to Kate Holbrook, July 21, 2015, and Jan. 20, 2016; Aileen H. Clyde 20th Century Women's Legacy Archive, accessed Dec. 8, 2015, lib.utah.edu.)
8. Before updating the purpose statement, Jack and her counselors reviewed earlier statements—paying particular attention to the purpose as recorded in the Nauvoo Relief Society minutes and to statements written by previous presidencies—and then developed their own, which emphasized action and the individual woman. They wanted to create a statement that would be meaningful for women around the world. (Cherry B. Silver, *History of the Relief Society: The Elaine Jack Administration* [Salt Lake City: Relief Society of the Church of Jesus Christ of Latter-day Saints, 2000], 5–6, CHL; Jill Mulvay Derr, Janath Russell Cannon, and Maureen Ursenbach Beecher, *Women of Covenant: The Story of Relief Society* [Salt Lake City: Deseret Book, 1992], 401–403.)
9. Elaine L. Jack, interview by Brian D. Reeves, Jan.–June 1991, 18, James Moyle Oral History Program, CHL.
10. Jack, interview by Reeves, 18–19; Elaine L. Jack, "Women's History Committee Birthday Celebration with Sister Elaine L. Jack," audio recording, Mar. 13, 2013, 14:30, CHL; see also Elaine L. Jack, "Them and Us," Brigham Young University fireside address, June 2, 1991, accessed Dec. 8, 2015, speeches.byu.edu.
11. Jack, "Women's History Committee Birthday Celebration," 17:00; Silver, *History of the Relief Society,* 6.
12. *Relief Society Sesquicentennial Celebration* (Salt Lake City: The Church of Jesus Christ of Latter-day Saints, 1991), 1.
13. Relief Society Sesquicentennial Histories, 1992, Cergy-Pontoise Ward, Paris France Stake, CHL.

14. Relief Society Sesquicentennial Histories, 1992, Magrath, Alberta, CHL.
15. Jack learned of projects both through letters and by visiting Relief Societies around the world. (Elaine Jack, Chieko Okazaki, Aileen Clyde, and Ellen Allred, interview by Brian D. Reeves and Pauline K. Musig, Mar. 20, 1996, 24, James Moyle Oral History Program, CHL; Jack, interview by Holbrook, 5; "Relief Society Sesquicentennial Histories," CHL.)
16. Jack, Okazaki, Clyde, and Allred, interview, 24; Jack, interview by Holbrook, 4.
17. Jack, Okazaki, Clyde, and Allred, interview, 25; *History and Summary of the Gospel Literacy Effort* (Salt Lake City: The Church of Jesus Christ of Latter-day Saints, 1997), 22; Jack, interview by Reeves, 16.
18. The Priesthood Executive Council directed the Curriculum Department and church auxiliaries, including Primary, Young Men, Young Women, Relief Society, and Sunday School. This council was composed of members of the Quorum of the Twelve Apostles, the Quorums of the Seventy, and the Presiding Bishopric. Auxiliary presidencies attended frequently to report and discuss issues related to their spheres of responsibility. (Lee Tom Perry, Paul M. Bons, and Alan L. Wilkins, "Contemporary Organization," in *Encyclopedia of Mormonism,* ed. Daniel H. Ludlow, 5 vols. [New York: Macmillan, 1992], 3:1046.)
19. Jack, "Women's History Committee Birthday Celebration," 40:05; Jack, interview by Holbrook, 7–8. On August 18, 2015, the church designated the presidents of the women-led organizations as official members of general leadership councils. (See "Women Church Leaders Appointed to Leadership Councils," Newsroom Blog of the Church of Jesus Christ of Latter-day Saints, Aug. 19, 2015, accessed Feb. 4, 2016, mormonnewsroom.org.)
20. Citation in original: "Deuteronomy 30:19–20."
21. Citation in original: "Moses 7:28–33."
22. Citation in original: "Bruce Sylvester, 'Making Room,' *Christian Science Monitor,* 25 August 1992, p. 19." This story is also published as Bruce Sylvester, "Family Accommodations," *Christian Science Monitor,* Aug. 25, 1992.
23. According to a national study, 12.1 percent of adult Latter-day Saints in the United States were single in 1990. (Barry A. Kosmin and Seymour P. Lachman, *Research Report: The National Survey of Religious Identification, 1989–90,* Graduate School and University Center of the City University of New York, Mar. 1991, 6, accessed Dec. 9, 2015, jewishdatabank.org.)
24. Citation in original: "1 Nephi 17:6."
25. Citation in original: "1 Nephi 17:2."
26. Citation in original: "1 Nephi 17:3."
27. Gordon B. Hinckley, "Building Your Tabernacle," *Ensign* 22, no. 11 (Nov. 1992): 50–52.
28. Citation in original: "Leo Tolstoy, *Anna Karenina,* trans. Constance Garnett (New York: Random House, 1939), p. 301."
29. See 1 Nephi 15:1–16:5.
30. During the early 1990s, chapels throughout the Philippines had sewing machines to help Relief Society members learn to sew. Many members used these skills to earn money for their families. (See Marvin K. Gardner, "Philippine Saints: A Believing People," *Ensign* 21, no. 7 [July 1991]: 37.)
31. Road shows were short musical programs that local Mutual Improvement Association (MIA) groups wrote and performed in their wards and stakes. These began by the 1920s. Laurel is the name given to the group of young women aged sixteen to eighteen years. ("M. I. A. Notes: Stake Happenings," *Young Woman's Journal* 34, no. 7 [July 1923]: 393; Elaine Anderson Cannon, "Young Women," in Ludlow, *Encyclopedia of Mormonism,* 4:1617–1618.)
32. The Relief Society general board adopted the motto "Charity Never Faileth," from 1 Corinthians 13:8, in 1913. (Jill Mulvay Derr, Janath Russell Cannon, and Maureen Ursenbach Beecher, *Women of Covenant: The Story of Relief Society* [Salt Lake City: Deseret Book, 1992], 194.)
33. Citation in original: "1 Nephi 17:8."
34. Citation in original: "1 Nephi 17:9."
35. Citation in original: "1 Nephi 17:17–18."
36. See 1 Nephi 3:28–4:4; 17:48–55.

37. Citation in original: "George Q. Cannon, *Gospel Truth,* comp. Jerreld L. Newquist (Salt Lake City: Deseret Book Company, 1987), p. 165." Cannon was first counselor in the First Presidency under church presidents John Taylor, Wilford Woodruff, and Lorenzo Snow from 1880 to 1901.
38. Citation in original: "1 Corinthians 13:4."
39. Citation in original: "Moroni 7:45."
40. Citation in original: "D&C 121:41–42."
41. Edgar Lee Masters, "Lucinda Matlock," in *Spoon River Anthology* (New York: Macmillan, 1921), 230.
42. Citation in original: "1 Nephi 19:9."
43. Citation in original: "Deuteronomy 31:6."
44. Bruce R. McConkie served in the Quorum of the Twelve Apostles from 1972 to 1985.
45. Citation in original: "see Marvin J. Ashton, 'Stalwart and Brave We Stand,' *Ensign,* Nov. 1989, p. 36."

CHAPTER 46: CHIEKO N. OKAZAKI, "BASKETS AND BOTTLES"

1. "Obituary: Okazaki, Chieko," *Deseret News,* Aug. 7, 2011.
2. "New Relief Society General Presidency Called," *Ensign* 20, no. 5 (May 1990): 111; "Obituary: Okazaki, Chieko"; Chieko N. Okazaki, interview by Brian D. Reeves, Feb.–Apr. 1991, 33–35, CHL.
3. Gregory A. Prince, "'There Is Always a Struggle': An Interview with Chieko N. Okazaki," *Dialogue: A Journal of Mormon Thought* 45, no. 1 (Spring 2012): 113; "New Relief Society General Presidency Called," 110; Chieko N. Okazaki, *Lighten Up!* (Salt Lake City: Deseret Book, 1993), 29–30.
4. Peggy Fletcher Stack, "Beloved Mormon Women's Leader Chieko Okazaki Dies," *Salt Lake Tribune,* Aug. 5, 2011; Okazaki, *Lighten Up!,* 7, 29. The attack on Pearl Harbor also occurred when she was fifteen. (Okazaki, *Lighten Up!,* 7.)
5. Stack, "Beloved Mormon Women's Leader Chieko Okazaki Dies."
6. "New Relief Society General Presidency Called," 111; "Obituary: Okazaki, Chieko."
7. "Obituary: Okazaki, Chieko"; Okazaki, *Lighten Up!,* 36; "New Relief Society General Presidency Called," 111.
8. Okazaki, *Lighten Up!,* 7.
9. "Obituary: Okazaki, Chieko."
10. Stack, "Beloved Mormon Women's Leader Chieko Okazaki Dies."
11. Okazaki, *Lighten Up!,* 8.
12. See Okazaki, *Lighten Up!,* 48–50; Prince, "There Is Always a Struggle," 114–115.
13. Sunae Mackelprang, telephone interview by Kate Holbrook, Dec. 18, 2015.
14. Chieko N. Okazaki, *What a Friend We Have in Jesus* (Salt Lake City: Deseret Book, 2008), 10–13.
15. Relief Society General Board Minutes, vol. 62, 1995–1997, Jan. 10, 1996, CHL.
16. The number of church members outside of the United States exceeded the number inside as of February 25, 1996. (Jay M. Todd, "More Members Now outside U.S. Than in U.S.," *Ensign* 26, no. 3 [Mar. 1996]: 76; see also Matthew Bowman, *The Mormon People: The Making of an American Faith* [New York: Random House, 2012], 217–222.)
17. Citation in original: "Gal. 3:28."
18. Citation in original: "1 Cor. 12:13."
19. Susan Lillywhite Warner served as the second counselor in the Primary general presidency from 1994 to 1999.
20. Citation in original: "D&C 124:18"; see also Exodus 19:4.
21. Citation in original: "Moro. 10:31."
22. See Galatians 3:28.
23. Gordon B. Hinckley was president of the Church of Jesus Christ of Latter-day Saints at this time, with Thomas S. Monson and James E. Faust as his counselors in the First Presidency.
24. Citation in original: "Gal. 3:27."
25. Citation in original: "2 Ne. 26:33."
26. Citation in original: "Gal. 5:22–23."
27. Citation in original: "Matt. 7:25."

28. See Prince, "There Is Always a Struggle," 121. Gordon B. Hinckley was first counselor in the First Presidency when Okazaki was called in 1990.
29. The church's Translation Department was organized in 1946 and is responsible for translating church material and messages into foreign languages. (See Justus Ernst, "Every Man . . . in his Own Language . . . ," *Ensign* 4, no. 7 [July 1974]: 23.)
30. Citation in original: "Gal. 5:22."
31. Citation in original: "see D&C 38:27."

CHAPTER 47: IRINA KRATZER, "DECISIONS AND MIRACLES: AND NOW I SEE"

1. Irina Kratzer, interview by Kate Holbrook, July 3, 2015, 1, CHL; Irina Kratzer, emails to Kate Holbrook, Sept. 1, 4, 2015.
2. Kratzer, interview, 2; Kratzer, email to Holbrook, Sept. 1, 2015. Kratzer's mother also gave birth to a son, Dmitry, in Barnaul.
3. Kratzer, interview, 13–15.
4. Kratzer, interview, 3; Mark G. Field and Judyth L. Twigg, eds., *Russia's Torn Safety Nets: Health and Social Welfare during the Transition* (New York: St. Martin's Press, 2000), 88, 95.
5. Kratzer, interview, 3, 13–14; Kratzer, email to Holbrook, Sept. 4, 2015.
6. Kratzer, emails to Holbrook, Sept. 1, 4, 2015.
7. Kratzer, interview, 14.
8. The Kratzers would eventually adopt four additional children, raising a total of eight. (Kratzer, interview, 1–2.)
9. Kratzer, interview, 10–11.
10. For more on the Russian Revolution in 1917, see Sheila Fitzpatrick, *The Russian Revolution* (Oxford: Oxford University Press, 2008).
11. Vladimir Ilyich Lenin. (Robert Service, *Lenin: A Biography* [Cambridge, MA: Harvard University Press, 2000].)
12. See Tatiana A. Chumachenko, *Church and State in Soviet Russia: Russian Orthodoxy from World War II to the Khrushchev Years,* ed. and trans. Edward E. Roslof (Armonk, NY: M. E. Sharpe, 2002), 122.
13. "The light of Christ refers to the spiritual power that emanates from God to fill the immensity of space and enlightens every man, woman, and child." (C. Kent Dunford, "Light of Christ," in *Encyclopedia of Mormonism,* ed. Daniel H. Ludlow, 5 vols. [New York: Macmillan, 1992], 2:835.)
14. Citation in original: "M. Russell Ballard, 'Like a Flame Unquenchable,' *Ensign,* May 1999, 85." M. Russell Ballard became a member of the Quorum of the Twelve Apostles in 1985.
15. Citation in original: "Alma 30:17."
16. Citation in original: "2 Nephi 2:25."
17. Kratzer lived in the city of Barnaul. (Kratzer, email to Holbrook, Sept. 1, 2015.)
18. Woodmansee lived from 1918 to 2006. ("Obituary: Terrell Raymond Woodmansee," *Deseret News,* Oct. 28, 2006.)
19. Ray Beckett Jr. was retired and volunteering as a church service missionary for the church's Priesthood Department when Woodmansee asked him for help in obtaining Kratzer's visa. A career as program manager for the University of Utah College of Engineering had taught Beckett how to work with government agencies. Beckett wrote to Utah senator Orrin Hatch requesting help, and Hatch wrote directly to the American ambassador in Moscow. The ambassador in Moscow interviewed Kratzer and warned her that if she went to Utah she would be surrounded by Mormons. Kratzer assured him that was acceptable and obtained her visa. Beckett also obtained church permission to use its mail pouch for transferring travel-related documents back and forth. The church operates a pouch mail system in countries where mail delivery is often unreliable. (Ray Beckett Jr., telephone interview with Kate Holbrook, Jan. 19, 2016.)
20. Kratzer had to travel four hours by bus to retrieve the items from the mission office in Novosibirsk. The Novosibirsk Mission officially opened with the arrival of President Jerald and Sister Mona

Sherwood on July 4, 1994. Missionary work in Russia began in 1990. (Kratzer, email to Holbrook, Sept. 4, 2015; "Russia Novosibirsk Mission History," 1994, July 3–9, 1994, CHL; "New Mission Leaders Assigned," *Church News,* Mar. 26, 1994; Kahlile Mehr, "1989–90: The Curtain Opens," *Ensign* 23, no. 12 [Dec. 1993]: 36–37.)

21. The *Ensign,* which started in January 1971, is the official English-language magazine for adult members of the Church of Jesus Christ of Latter-day Saints.
22. Citation in original: "Thomas S. Monson, 'They Will Come,' *Ensign,* May 1997, 44." Thomas S. Monson joined the Quorum of the Twelve Apostles on October 4, 1963. When this talk was given, he was the first counselor in the First Presidency of the church.
23. Citation in original: "Alma 36:12–13, 17–21."

CHAPTER 48: SHERI L. DEW, "KNOWING WHO YOU ARE—AND WHO YOU HAVE ALWAYS BEEN"

1. Sheri L. Dew, interview by Brittany A. Chapman and Kiersten Olson, Oct. 8, 2010, 2, 3–4, 11, 13, 20, 32, James Moyle Oral History Program, CHL.
2. Sheri L. Dew, interview by Christine R. Marin, Feb. 26, 2002, 2, James Moyle Oral History Program, CHL.
3. Dew, interview by Marin, 2; "Deseret Book Appoints New President," *Church News,* Mar. 2, 2002; "News of the Church," *Ensign* 27, no. 5 (May 1997): 109.
4. Sheri L. Dew, interview by Kate Holbrook, Apr. 25, 2016, 8–9, CHL.
5. Dew served on the Relief Society general board from 1989 to 1990. (Sheri L. Dew, email to Kate Holbrook, May 11, 2016; Dew, interview by Marin, 2.)
6. Dew, interview by Chapman and Olson, 34.
7. Like many children born to Mormon parents, Dew was baptized at age eight. With the ordinance of confirmation, she was invited to receive "the gift of the Holy Ghost," meaning the Holy Ghost would be with her to offer guidance and comfort as long as she led a worthy life.
8. Dew, interview by Holbrook, 5–6.
9. Dew, interview by Holbrook, 6–7.
10. Dew, interview by Marin, 15, 21.
11. Dew, interview by Marin, 15.
12. "I Am a Child of God," *Hymns of the Church of Jesus Christ of Latter-day Saints* (Salt Lake City: The Church of Jesus Christ of Latter-day Saints, 1985), no. 301.
13. "The Family: A Proclamation to the World" was first presented in the general Relief Society meeting in 1995 by Gordon B. Hinckley, soon after his call as the fifteenth president of the church. The proclamation was issued by the First Presidency and Quorum of the Twelve Apostles as a "declaration and reaffirmation of standards, doctrines, and practices relative to the family." (Julie A. Dockstader, "'Best Season,' but Also a Time of Turmoil," *Church News,* Sept. 30, 1995; Gordon B. Hinckley, "Stand Strong against the Wiles of the World," *Ensign* 25, no. 11 [Nov. 1995]: 98–101.)
14. The Young Women values were defined in 1985 while Ardeth G. Kapp was general president of the Young Women organization. In 2001, the values included faith, divine nature, individual worth, knowledge, choice and accountability, good works, and integrity. The Young Women manual in use at the time of this talk said of the value of divine nature, "I have inherited divine qualities which I will strive to develop." (*Personal Progress* [Salt Lake City: The Church of Jesus Christ of Latter-day Saints, 1989], 7; "News of the Church: Young Women Counseled to Stand for Truth and Righteousness," *Ensign* 16, no. 1 [Jan. 1986]: 75–76.)
15. The Relief Society Declaration was issued by the Relief Society presidency on September 25, 1999, during the general Relief Society meeting. The declaration was presented by Mary Ellen Smoot, Relief Society general president. (Julie A. Dockstader, "Declaration Reaffirms Roles, Values of Women in Church," and "Truly a Day to Lift up Our Hearts," *Church News,* Oct. 2, 1999; Mary Ellen Smoot, "Rejoice, Daughters of Zion," *Ensign* 29, no. 11 [Nov. 1999]: 92–94.)
16. Citation in original: "Office Journal of Lorenzo Snow, 8 October 1900, 181–82, Archives of the Church of Jesus Christ of Latter-day Saints, Salt Lake City, Utah." See also Truman G. Madsen, *The*

Highest in Us (Salt Lake City: Bookcraft, 1978), 9. Lorenzo Snow was fifth president of the church from 1898 to 1901. Snow expressed similar ideas in his April 1901 general conference address: "When Jesus lay in the manger . . . he knew not that he was the Son of God, and that formerly he created the earth. . . . He grew up to manhood, and during his progress it was revealed unto him who he was." (Lorenzo Snow, in *Seventy-First Annual Conference of the Church of Jesus Christ of Latter-day Saints,* Apr. 5–7, 1901 [Salt Lake City: Deseret News, 1901], 3.)

17. Citation in original: "Lorenzo Snow, Conference Report, April 1901, 3; emphasis added."
18. Citation in original: "D&C 138:56."
19. See Abraham 3:22–28. Joseph Smith stated in an 1841 address that "we were all present and saw the Savior chosen and appointed, and the plan of salvation made, and we sanctioned it." (Joseph Smith, Discourse, [Jan. 5, 1841], Nauvoo, IL, Joseph Smith Collection, CHL, accessed May 9, 2016, josephsmithpapers.org; see also Doctrine and Covenants 138:55–58; and Alma 13:3–4.)
20. Citation in original: "Job 38:7."
21. Citation in original: "George Q. Cannon, *Gospel Truth: Discourses and Writings of President George Q. Cannon,* sel. Jerreld L. Newquist (Salt Lake City: Deseret Book, 1987), 7; emphasis added." George Q. Cannon was a member of the Quorum of the Twelve Apostles from 1860 to 1901 and served in the First Presidency under four church presidents.
22. Citation in original: "Harold B. Lee, 'Understanding Who We Are Brings Self-Respect,' *Ensign,* January 1974, 5. Bruce R. McConkie, *A New Witness for the Articles of Faith* (Salt Lake City: Deseret Book, 1984), 512." Harold B. Lee was the eleventh president of the church from 1972 to 1973. Bruce R. McConkie was a member of the Quorum of the Twelve Apostles from 1972 to 1985.
23. Latter-day Saints believe that the earth is in its last dispensation before the return of Jesus Christ and call this the dispensation of the fulness of times because of a belief that the gospel knowledge and authority of all previous dispensations would be brought together before Christ's Second Coming. The phrase itself is found throughout the scriptures, particularly in revelations to Joseph Smith. (See Ephesians 1:10; and Doctrine and Covenants 27:13; 112:30; 121:31; 124:41; 128:18, 20; see also Rand H. Packer, "Dispensation of the Fulness of Times," in *Encyclopedia of Mormonism,* ed. Daniel H. Ludlow, 5 vols. [New York: Macmillan, 1992], 1:387–388.)
24. Citation in original: "D&C 33:3–4."
25. Citation in original: "Abraham 2:8."
26. Citation in original: "George Q. Cannon, *Journal of Discourses,* 26 vols. (London: Latter-day Saints' Book Depot, 1852–81), 11:230."
27. Citation in original: "Abraham 3:22–23."
28. Citation in original: "D&C 138:53, 55." Joseph F. Smith was the sixth president of the church from 1901 to 1918 and had this vision shortly before his death. (See Robert L. Millet, "The Vision of the Redemption of the Dead [D&C 138]," in *Sperry Symposium Classics: The Doctrine and Covenants,* ed. Craig K. Manscill [Provo, UT: Religious Studies Center, Brigham Young University, 2004], 314–331.)
29. Citation in original: "*Doctrines of the Restoration: Sermons and Writings of Bruce R. McConkie* (Salt Lake City: Bookcraft, 1989), 197–98; emphasis added."
30. Citation in original: "Joseph Smith, *History of the Church of Jesus Christ of Latter-day Saints,* edited by B. H. Roberts, 2d ed. rev., 7 vols. (Salt Lake City: The Church of Jesus Christ of Latter-day Saints, 1932–51), 6:364." See also Joseph Smith, History, 1838–1856, vol. F-1 [May 1, 1844–Aug. 8, 1844], May 12, 1844, 18, CHL, accessed Apr. 25, 2016, josephsmithpapers.org.
31. Citation in original: "Spencer W. Kimball, 'The Role of Righteous Women,' *Ensign,* November 1979, 102." Spencer W. Kimball was the twelfth president of the church from 1973 to 1985.
32. Citation in original: "Moses 6:31."
33. Citation in original: "Moses 7:21."
34. Citation in original: "Acts 9:5; 22:15."
35. Within the church, the "noble birthright" often refers to those who are heirs of the promises made to Abraham (see Genesis 13:14–16; 17:7; 22:18), particularly those born at this time in the earth's history. The phrase "youth of the noble birthright" is in a Latter-day Saint hymn written in 1930 by

Ruth May Fox, who was the general president of the Young Women organization from 1929 to 1937. The phrase has been used in church discourses including Ardeth G. Kapp, "Youth of the Noble Birthright," *Ensign* 14, no. 5 (May 1984): 77; Ezra Taft Benson, "To the 'Youth of the Noble Birthright,'" *Ensign* 16, no. 5 (May 1986): 43–46; and L. Tom Perry, "Youth of the Noble Birthright," *Ensign* 28, no. 11 (Nov. 1998): 73–74. ("Carry On," *Hymns,* no. 255; J. Spencer Cornwall, *Stories of Our Mormon Hymns* [Salt Lake City: Deseret Book, 1963], 48–52.)

36. Deborah. G. Felder, *The 100 Most Influential Women of All Time: A Ranking Past and Present* (Secaucus, NJ: Carol Publishing Group, 1996).
37. See Genesis 3:20; and Moses 4:26.
38. Citation in original: "1 Samuel 16:7."
39. Citation in original: "Moses 1:12–13."
40. Citation in original: "Moses 1:4, 6."
41. Citation in original: "Joseph F. Smith, *Gospel Doctrine: Sermons and Writings of Joseph F. Smith* (Salt Lake City: Deseret Book, 1986), 14."
42. Citation in original: "D&C 109:15."
43. Citation in original: "See D&C 8:2."
44. Citation in original: "3 Nephi 19:9."
45. Citation in original: "2 Nephi 32:5."
46. See 1 Peter 2:9.
47. Citation in original: "Lee, 'Understanding Who We Are,' 5."
48. Citation in original: "D&C 121:40."
49. Citation in original: "Alma 46:15."
50. Dew, interview by Holbrook, 5.
51. Citation in original: "Gordon B. Hinckley, 'Find the Lambs, Feed the Sheep,' *Ensign,* May 1999, 110."
52. Margaret D. Nadauld was general president of the Young Women organization from 1997 to 2002.
53. Citation in original: "Kimball, 'Righteous Women,' 104."
54. Citation in original: "Gordon B. Hinckley, 'Our Responsibility to Our Young Women,' *Ensign,* September 1988, 11."
55. Citation in original: "Gordon B. Hinckley, 'Live Up to Your Inheritance,' *Ensign,* November 1983, 84."

CHAPTER 49: BONNIE D. PARKIN, "WITH HOLINESS OF HEART"

1. "Bonnie D. Parkin, Relief Society General President," *Liahona* 26, no. 7 (July 2002): 124; Bonnie D. Parkin, interview by Kate Holbrook, Sept. 10, 2015, 1–2, 6, 8, in editors' possession.
2. James L. Parkin studied otolaryngology. (Parkin, interview, 2–4.)
3. Parkin, interview, 3–4; Bonnie D. Parkin, "Fat-Free Feasting," *Ensign* 25, no. 5 (May 1995): 90.
4. Parkin, interview, 3.
5. Parkin, interview, 9.
6. "Bonnie D. Parkin, Relief Society General President," 124; Gordon B. Hinckley, "The Solemn Assembly Sustaining of Church Officers," *Ensign* 24, no. 11 (Nov. 1994): 6.
7. Bonnie D. Parkin, "Celebrating Covenants," *Ensign* 25, no. 5 (May 1995): 78–79.
8. Parkin, interview, 13.
9. Parkin, "Celebrating Covenants," 78.
10. "History of the Relief Society: The Bonnie Parkin Administration, 2002–2007," 2012, 2–3, CHL.
11. "History of the Relief Society," 14; Parkin, interview, 15.
12. Parkin, interview, 15.
13. "Bonnie D. Parkin, Relief Society General President," 124.
14. Parkin, interview, 12–13.
15. Parkin, interview, 17.
16. Thomas S. Monson, "The Sustaining of Church Officers," *Ensign* 32, no. 5 (May 2002): 22.
17. Twenty women gathered for the first Relief Society meeting in Nauvoo, Illinois, on March 17, 1842.

By the last Nauvoo meeting on March 16, 1844, approximately 1,336 women had joined the organization. (Jill Mulvay Derr, Carol Cornwall Madsen, Kate Holbrook, and Matthew J. Grow, eds., *The First Fifty Years of Relief Society: Key Documents in Latter-day Saint Women's History* [Salt Lake City: Church Historian's Press, 2016], 24–26.)

18. Citation in original: "'Walking in the Light of the Lord,' *Ensign,* Nov. 1998, 97; *Liahona,* Jan. 1999, 115." Gordon B. Hinckley became church president in March 1995.
19. This phrase appears multiple times in Latter-day Saint scripture; see, for example, Isaiah 6:8; 2 Nephi 16:8; Moses 4:1; and Abraham 3:27.
20. Staines was born in 1823 and died in Salt Lake City in 1899. (Edward W. Tullidge, *Women of Mormondom* [New York: Tullidge and Crandall, 1877], 285; Priscilla M. Staines, Jan. 4, 1899, in "Utah, Salt Lake County Death Records, 1849–1949," accessed July 22, 2015, familysearch.org.)
21. Tullidge, *Women of Mormondom,* 287–288. For more information on the beginnings of missionary work in England, see James B. Allen, Ronald K. Esplin, and David J. Whittaker, *Men with a Mission, 1837–1841: The Quorum of the Twelve Apostles in the British Isles* (Salt Lake City: Deseret Book, 1992).
22. Citation in original: "Quoted in Edward W. Tullidge, *The Women of Mormondom* (1877), 287; see also 285–86, 288."
23. See Leviticus 19:28; Deuteronomy 6:5; Matthew 22:37–39; and Mosiah 18:8–10.
24. See James E. Talmage, *The House of the Lord* (Salt Lake City: Deseret News, 1912), 100.
25. "New Mission Presidents," *Church News,* Apr. 5, 1997.
26. Citation in original: "3 Nephi 27:21."
27. Gordon B. Hinckley, "The Times in Which We Live," *Ensign* 31, no. 11 (Nov. 2001): 73.
28. Citation in original: "D&C 20:77, 79."
29. See, for example, Edward Leo Lyman, Susan Ward Payne, and S. George Ellsworth, eds., *No Place to Call Home: The 1807–1857 Life Writings of Caroline Barnes Crosby, Chronicler of Outlying Mormon Communities* (Logan: Utah State University Press, 2005), 69–86; Maurine Carr Ward, ed., *Winter Quarters: The 1846–1848 Life Writings of Mary Haskin Parker Richards* (Logan: Utah State University Press, 1996), 13–15; and Patricia H. Stoker, "'The Lord Has Been My Guide': Cordelia Calista Morley Cox," in *Women of Faith in the Latter Days: Volume Two, 1821–1845,* ed. Richard E. Turley Jr. and Brittany A. Chapman (Salt Lake City: Deseret Book, 2012), 45–60.
30. Citation in original: "Ephesians 4:14."
31. See Isaiah 5:20; and 2 Nephi 15:20.
32. Citation in original: "*Ensign,* Nov. 1998, 99; *Liahona,* Jan. 1999, 117." The Hinckley talk referenced here was titled "Walking in the Light of the Lord."
33. Mary Twinberrow Wattis Bennett [Kay]. (Jay Greaves Burrup, "Mary's Altar," *Pioneer* 47, no. 1 [Spring 2000]: 10–16; "Mary T. Kay," *Ogden Standard,* Sept. 27, 1896, 7; Tullidge, *Women of Mormondom,* 291.)
34. Citation in original: "See Tullidge, *Women of Mormondom,* 289, 291."
35. Citation in original: "D&C 46:7."
36. Citation in original: "'More Holiness Give Me,' *Hymns,* no. 131."
37. Citation in original: "Tullidge, *Women of Mormondom,* 288."
38. Church president Gordon B. Hinckley attended this meeting, though he did not speak. (James E. Faust, "You Are All Heaven Sent," *Ensign* 32, no. 11 [Nov. 2002]: 110.)

CHAPTER 50: VIRGINIA H. PEARCE, "PRAYER: A SMALL AND SIMPLE THING"

1. Gordon B. Hinckley was a member of either the Quorum of the Twelve Apostles or the First Presidency of the Church of Jesus Christ of Latter-day Saints for most of Pearce's life. Hinckley became an Assistant to the Twelve in 1958, a member of the Quorum of the Twelve Apostles in 1961, a member of the First Presidency in 1981, and church president in 1995. ("LDS President Gordon B. Hinckley Dies at Age 97," *Deseret News,* Jan. 28, 2008.)
2. Virginia H. Pearce, interview by Kate Holbrook, Aug. 21, 2015, 6, CHL.

3. Pearce, interview by Holbrook, 7.
4. "James Richard McGhie Pearce," *Deseret News,* Oct. 27, 2009; Pearce, interview by Holbrook, 1.
5. Pearce, interview by Holbrook, 11–12.
6. Pearce, interview by Holbrook, 1–2.
7. Pearce, interview by Holbrook, 2; "New Young Women Presidency Is Called," *Church News,* Apr. 11, 1992.
8. "New Young Women Presidency Is Called."
9. Pearce, interview by Holbrook, 2.
10. Virginia H. Pearce, interview by Susan W. Tanner, Oct. 27, 2003, 8, CHL.
11. Bryant Stringham Hinckley worked as a teacher at Brigham Young Academy, as the head of LDS Business College, and as superintendent of the church-owned Deseret Gym. (Sheri L. Dew, *Go Forward with Faith: The Biography of Gordon B. Hinckley* [Salt Lake City: Deseret Book, 1996], 18, 29.)
12. Virginia H. Pearce, ed., *Glimpses into the Life and Heart of Marjorie Pay Hinckley* (Salt Lake City: Deseret Book, 1999). Pearce has written multiple books for children and adults.
13. Gerry Avant, "Leader Hungers, Thirsts for Knowledge," *Church News,* Apr. 25, 1992; Pearce, interview by Holbrook, 3.
14. Pearce, interview by Holbrook, 8.
15. See Words of Mormon 1:7.
16. Pearce, interview by Holbrook, 6.
17. Citation in original: "Alma 37:6."
18. Citation in original: "Wells, Emmeline B., *Musings and Memories,* SLC, UT: *Deseret News,* 1915, 221." Emmeline B. Wells edited the *Woman's Exponent* semimonthly newspaper from 1877 until it ceased publication in 1914. She was general president of the Relief Society from 1910 to 1921. (Carol Cornwall Madsen, *An Advocate for Women: The Public Life of Emmeline B. Wells, 1870–1920* [Provo, UT: Brigham Young University; Salt Lake City: Deseret Book, 2006].)
19. Marjorie Pay Hinckley died in 2004. ("Marjorie Hinckley Dies," *Deseret News,* Apr. 7, 2004.)
20. Citation in original: "Personal history in author's possession."
21. Citation in original: "Bible Dictionary, pp. 752–753."
22. Citation in original: "Isaiah 26:9."
23. Citation in original: "Christus Consolator, *The Master's Hand, the Art of Carl Heinrich Bloch,* Figure 61, p. 114, by Dawn C. Pheysey and Richard Neitzel Holzapfel, Brigham Young University Museum of Art, Provo, UT, Deseret Book Company, Salt Lake City, UT, 2010." Carl Bloch was a Danish painter who often examined religious subjects in his paintings. The Museum of Art at Brigham Young University exhibited his work from November 2010 to May 2011, and copies of his paintings are frequently published in Latter-day Saint materials. (Amy McDonald, "Mormon-Owned BYU Acquires Long-Lost 'Mysterious' Bloch Painting of Jesus," *Salt Lake Tribune,* June 4, 2015; Jason Swensen, "'The Master's Hand' Has Attracted More than 230,000 Visitors to BYU Exhibit," *Church News,* Apr. 22, 2011.)
24. Citation in original: "Ibid., p. 33." At this point in the presentation, Pearce showed an image of a painting by Carl Bloch titled *Landscape from Hellebaek.*
25. Citation in original: "Ibid., p. 55."
26. Citation in original: "D&C 112:10."
27. Citation in original: "Alma 34:27."
28. Citation in original: "Philippians 4:7."
29. Citation in original: "Mosiah 27:26."
30. Citation in original: "Moses 7:21."
31. Citation in original: "D&C 98:1–3."
32. Citation in original: "2 Nephi 32:9."
33. Citation in original: "Moroni 7:48."
34. Citation in original: "2 Nephi 33:2–4."
35. See 2 Nephi 32:9.

36. Julie B. Beck was Relief Society general president from 2007 to 2012.
37. Citation in original: "Beck, Julie B., 'What Latter-day Saint Women Do Best: Stand Strong and Immovable,' *Ensign,* Nov. 2007, p. 110."
38. See Mosiah 18:21.
39. Citation in original: "Bible Dictionary, p. 753."
40. Citation in original: "Maxwell, Neal A., *That Ye May Believe,* Bookcraft, 1992, p. 178." Neal A. Maxwell served in the Quorum of the Twelve Apostles from 1981 to 2004.
41. Citation in original: "Scott, Richard G., 'Using the Supernal Gift of Prayer,' *Ensign,* May 2007." Richard G. Scott served in the Quorum of the Twelve Apostles from 1988 to 2015.
42. Citation in original: "Dew, Sheri, *Go Forward With Faith,* Deseret Book 1996, p. 423." Pearce was the third of Hinckley's five children. ("LDS President Gordon B. Hinckley Dies.")
43. Citation in original: "Journal of Discourses, V. 3:205. Brigham Young taught: 'If I ask him to give me wisdom concerning any requirement in life, or in regard to my own course, or that of my friends, my family, my children, or those that I preside over, and get no answer from him, and then do the very best that my judgment will teach me, he is bound to own and honor that transaction, and he will do so to all intents and purposes.'"
44. Citation in original: "Lund, Gerald, *Divine Signatures: The Confirming Hand of God,* Deseret Book, 2010."
45. Citation in original: "Bible Dictionary, pp. 752–753."
46. James R. M. Pearce practiced internal medicine for thirty-four years; he died of amyotrophic lateral sclerosis (ALS), commonly known as Lou Gehrig's disease. ("James Richard McGhie Pearce.")
47. Citation in original: "Uchtdorf, Dieter F., 'Of Things That Matter Most,' *Ensign,* Nov. 2010." Dieter F. Uchtdorf served in the Quorum of the Twelve Apostles from 2004 to 2008, when he was called to serve in the First Presidency of the church.
48. Citation in original: "Words of Mormon 1:7."
49. See Alma 37:6.

CHAPTER 51: JULIE B. BECK, "WHY WE ARE ORGANIZED INTO QUORUMS AND RELIEF SOCIETIES"

1. Sarah Jane Weaver, "She Will Draw Strength from Childhood Experience," *Church News,* Nov. 30, 2002.
2. Julie B. Beck, interview by Gordon Irving and Justin R. Bray, Feb. 2012, 4, CHL.
3. Beck, interview, 3.
4. Weaver, "She Will Draw Strength from Childhood Experience," 6; Lynn Arave, "Elder William Grant Bangerter Dies at 91," *Deseret News,* Apr. 19, 2010.
5. Beck, interview, 27.
6. Beck, interview, 28.
7. Beck, interview, 30.
8. Beck, interview, 36; "New Board Members," *Church News,* Feb. 21, 1998. Margaret D. Nadauld was the eleventh president of the Young Women organization from 1997 to 2002.
9. Julie Dockstader Heaps, "Divine Identity Is Central to Her Heart," *Church News,* May 19, 2007. Susan W. Tanner was the twelfth president of the Young Women organization from 2002 to 2008.
10. Beck, interview, 30.
11. "Frequently Asked Questions, History—*Daughters in My Kingdom,*" accessed May 18, 2016, lds.org; see also "Preserving the Heritage of Latter-day Saint Women," Church History Symposium, June 3, 2016, accessed July 12, 2016, history.lds.org.
12. Beck, interview, 83. Beck has given multiple addresses about the process of working on *Daughters in My Kingdom.* (See, for example, R. Scott Lloyd, "'Faith Is an Alignment' of Role, Purpose and Priorities," *Church News,* Mar. 24, 2013; and Rachel Sterzer, "Spiritual Legacy of Relief Society," *Church News,* Mar. 13, 2016.)
13. See Nauvoo Relief Society Minute Book, June 9, 1842, [63], in Jill Mulvay Derr, Carol Cornwall

Madsen, Kate Holbrook, and Matthew J. Grow, eds., *The First Fifty Years of Relief Society: Key Documents in Latter-day Saint Women's History* (Salt Lake City: Church Historian's Press, 2016), 79.

14. "The Purpose of the Church," 2.2, *Handbook 2: Administering the Church* (Salt Lake City: The Church of Jesus Christ of Latter-day Saints, 2010), 9.
15. Julie B. Beck, "The Vision of Prophets regarding Relief Society: Faith, Family, Relief," *Ensign* 42, no. 5 (May 2012): 83–85; see also Julie B. Beck, "'Daughters in My Kingdom': The History and Work of Relief Society," *Ensign* 40, no. 11 (Nov. 2010): 112–115.
16. Sarah Jane Weaver, "Visiting Teaching: Opportunity to 'Minister as the Savior Did,'" *Church News,* Mar. 11, 2012.
17. Beck, interview, 8.
18. The Church Board of Education is composed of the First Presidency and other general authorities and officers, including the presidents of the Relief Society and Young Women organizations. This board oversees all of the church schools, including universities, seminaries, institutes, and other schools. (William E. Berrett, "Church Educational System [CES]," in *Encyclopedia of Mormonism,* ed. Daniel H. Ludlow, 5 vols. [New York: Macmillan, 1992], 1:275.)
19. W. Grant Bangerter served his first mission to Brazil from 1939 to 1941 and was president of the Brazilian Mission from 1958 to 1963. He joined the First Quorum of the Seventy in 1975 and served twice in its presidency, from 1978 to 1980 and from 1985 to 1989. (Arave, "Elder William Grant Bangerter Dies at 91.")
20. Citation in original: "Joseph Smith, quoted in Sarah M. Kimball, 'Auto-Biography,' *Woman's Exponent* 12, no. 7 (1 September 1883): 51; cited in *Daughters in My Kingdom: The History and Work of Relief Society* (Salt Lake City: The Church of Jesus Christ of Latter-day Saints, 2011), 12."
21. Citation in original: "See D&C 107:21."
22. The consolidated meeting schedule was implemented in 1980; it grouped sacrament, Sunday School, Melchizedek and Aaronic Priesthood, Relief Society, Young Women, and Primary meetings into a three-hour time block on Sunday. (Hal Knight, "Meeting Schedule Approved," *Church News,* Feb. 2, 1980.)
23. Citation in original: "Boyd K. Packer, 'What Every Elder Should Know—and Every Sister as Well: A Primer on Principles of Priesthood Government,' *Ensign,* February 1993, 9." Boyd K. Packer was a member of the Quorum of the Twelve Apostles from 1970 to 2015, acting president of the quorum from 1994 to 2008, and president from 2008 to 2015.
24. Citation in original: "Boyd K. Packer, 'What Every Elder Should Know,' 9."
25. Citation in original: "Boyd K. Packer, in 'Supplemental Readings, Section B,' *A Royal Priesthood,* Melchizedek Priesthood study guide, 1975–76 (Salt Lake City: The Church of Jesus Christ of Latter-day Saints, 1975), 131."
26. Citation in original: "Spencer W. Kimball, 'First Presidency Message: Relief Society—Its Promise and Potential,' *Ensign,* March 1976, 4; quoted in *Teachings of Presidents of the Church: Spencer W. Kimball* (Salt Lake City: The Church of Jesus Christ of Latter-day Saints, 2006), 217." Spencer W. Kimball was the twelfth president of the church from 1973 to 1985.
27. Citation in original: "*Merriam-Webster's Collegiate Dictionary,* 11th ed. (2003), s.v. 'society,' 1184."
28. Citation in original: "Joseph Smith, in Relief Society Minute Book, Nauvoo, Illinois, 30 March 1842, 22; spelling, punctuation, and capitalization standardized as needed in all excerpts from this minute book; quoted in *Daughters in My Kingdom,* 15." See also Derr et al., *First Fifty Years,* 43.
29. Citation in original: "Joseph F. Smith, in Minutes of the General Board of Relief Society, 17 March 1914, Church History Library, 54–55; quoted in *Daughters in My Kingdom,* 66." Joseph F. Smith was the sixth president of the church from 1901 to 1918.
30. Citation in original: "See *Handbook 2: Administering the Church* (2010), 9.1.1 (p. 64), 9.4.1 (p. 67); http://lds.org/bc/content/shared/content/english/pdf/language-materials/08702_eng.pdf?lang=eng."
31. Citation in original: "See *Handbook 2,* 7.1, 7.1.2 (p. 40); 8.1, 8.1.2 (pp. 50, 51)."
32. Citation in original: "See Boyd K. Packer, 'The Circle of Sisters,' *Ensign,* November 1980, 110."
33. Citation in original: "David O. McKay, in *CR,* October 1968, 84." David O. McKay was the ninth president of the church from 1951 to 1970.

34. Citation in original: "See *Daughters in My Kingdom,* 12."
35. Citation in original: "See Dallin H. Oaks, 'The Relief Society and the Church,' *Ensign,* May 1992, 35."
36. Citation in original: "See Joseph Fielding Smith, 'The Relief Society Organized by Revelation,' *Relief Society Magazine,* January 1965, 5."
37. Citation in original: "Articles of Faith 1:5."
38. Citation in original: "See 'preside,' http://dictionary.reference.com/browse/preside."
39. Citation in original: "Relief Society Minute Book, Nauvoo, Illinois, 28 April 1842, 37." See also Derr et al., *First Fifty Years,* 57.
40. Citation in original: "Joseph Smith, Relief Society Minute Book, Nauvoo, Illinois, 28 April 1842, 40; quoted in *Daughters in My Kingdom,* 14." See also Derr et al., *First Fifty Years,* 59.
41. Citation in original: "See D&C 107:99."
42. Citation in original: "First Presidency message, 3 July 1942, 'To the Presidency, Officers and Members of the Relief Society,' in *A Centenary of Relief Society, 1842–1942* (Salt Lake City: General Board of Relief Society, 1942), 7; quoted in Boyd K. Packer, 'The Circle of Sisters,' 111."
43. Citation in original: "John A. Widtsoe, *Evidences and Reconciliations,* arr. G. Homer Durham (Salt Lake City: Bookcraft, 1987), 308." John A. Widtsoe was a member of the Quorum of the Twelve Apostles from 1921 to 1952.
44. Citation in original: "John A. Widtsoe, *Evidences and Reconciliations,* 308."
45. Citation in original: "*Handbook 2,* 6.1.3 (p. 35)."
46. Citation in original: "D&C 82:19."
47. Citation in original: "Matthew 5:44–47; JST, Matthew 5:50."
48. Citation in original: "Henry B. Eyring, 'The Enduring Legacy of Relief Society,' *Ensign,* November 2009, 123." Henry B. Eyring became a member of the Quorum of the Twelve Apostles in 1995 and a member of the First Presidency in 2007.
49. Citation in original: "Bruce R. McConkie, 'Speaking Today: Only an Elder,' *Ensign,* June 1975, 66, 68, 67." Bruce R. McConkie was a member of the Quorum of the Twelve Apostles from 1972 to 1985.
50. Citation in original: "Thomas S. Monson, 'Home Teaching,' 46–47; quoted in *Teachings of Thomas S. Monson,* 139." Thomas S. Monson became the sixteenth president of the church in 2008.
51. Citation in original: "Henry B. Eyring, 'The Enduring Legacy of Relief Society,' 123."
52. Citation in original: "Spencer W. Kimball, 'A Vision of Visiting Teaching,' *Ensign,* June 1978, 24; see also D&C 20:53; quoted in *Daughters in My Kingdom,* 113."
53. Each Relief Society and priesthood quorum tracks visiting teaching and home teaching performed in its ward on a monthly basis.
54. Citation in original: "Thomas S. Monson, 'Prophets Speak—The Wise Obey,' general conference leadership session, Friday, 3 April 1987; quoted in *Teachings of Thomas S. Monson,* 140."
55. Citation in original: "See *Handbook 2,* 9.5–9.5.4 (pp. 69–70)."
56. Citation in original: "D&C 84:106."
57. Citation in original: "Thomas S. Monson, 'Correlation Brings Blessings,' *Relief Society Magazine,* April 1967, 247."
58. Citation in original: "See Alma 30:17."
59. Citation in original: "2 Timothy 3:1."
60. Citation in original: "Dallin H. Oaks, 'The Relief Society and the Church,' 37." Dallin H. Oaks became a member of the Quorum of the Twelve Apostles in 1984.
61. Citation in original: "*Daughters in My Kingdom,* 86."
62. Citation in original: "Boyd K. Packer, 'The Circle of Sisters,' 110; quoted in *Daughters in My Kingdom,* 86."
63. Citation in original: "Boyd K. Packer, *CR,* April 1998, 97; or 'The Relief Society,' *Ensign,* May 1998, 74; quoted in *Daughters in My Kingdom,* 87."
64. D. Todd Christofferson became a member of the Quorum of the Twelve Apostles in 2008.
65. Citation in original: "See D. Todd Christofferson, 'The Priesthood Quorum,' *Ensign,* November

1998, 40–41, quoting from Vaughn J. Featherstone, in *CR,* April 1973, 46–48; or 'Now Abideth Faith, Hope, and Charity,' *Ensign,* July 1973, 36–37."

66. Citation in original: "D&C 84:110."
67. Citation in original: "Joseph Smith, in *HC* 4:605."
68. The Relief Society adopted this motto in 1913. (Jill Mulvay Derr, Janath Russell Cannon, and Maureen Ursenbach Beecher, *Women of Covenant: The Story of Relief Society* [Salt Lake City: Deseret Book, 1992], 194.)
69. Citation in original: "Eliza R. Snow, address to Lehi Ward Relief Society, 27 October 1869, Lehi Ward, Alpine (Utah) Stake, in Relief Society, Minute Book, 1868–79, Church History Library, Salt Lake City, 26–27."
70. Citation in original: "'Rise Up, O Men of God,' *Hymns,* 2002, no. 323."
71. Citation in original: "Harold B. Lee, 'First Presidency Message: Preparing Our Youth,' *Ensign,* March 1971, 3; emphasis added."
72. Citation in original: "D&C 25:10, 13, 15."
73. Citation in original: "*Handbook 2,* 4.1 (p. 16)."
74. Citation in original: "See *Handbook 2,* 4.3 (p. 16)."
75. Citation in original: "Gordon B. Hinckley, 'Welfare Responsibilities of the Priesthood Quorums,' *Ensign,* November 1977, 86." Gordon B. Hinckley was the fifteenth president of the church from 1995 to 2008.
76. Citation in original: "Boyd K. Packer, 'The Power of the Priesthood,' *Ensign,* May 2010, 9."
77. Citation in original: "*Daughters in My Kingdom,* 169, 171, quoting Joseph Smith, in Relief Society Minute Book, Nauvoo, Illinois, 28 April 1842, Church History Library, 38." See also Derr et al., *First Fifty Years,* 57.
78. Citation in original: "Boyd K. Packer, 'The Circle of Sisters,' 111."
79. Citation in original: "D&C 43:8, 9."
80. Citation in original: "See Joseph F. Smith, in Minutes of the General Board of Relief Society, 17 March 1914, Church History Library, 54–55; quoted in *Daughters in My Kingdom,* 180."
81. Citation in original: "Joseph Smith, in Relief Society Minute Book, Nauvoo, Illinois, 28 April 1842, 38; quoted in *Daughters in My Kingdom,* 181." See also Derr et al., *First Fifty Years,* 57.

CHAPTER 52: JUDY BRUMMER, "OUR FATHER IN HEAVEN HAS A MISSION FOR US"

1. Judy Brummer, email to Kate Holbrook, Aug. 17, 2015.
2. Judy Brummer, email to Kate Holbrook, Dec. 18, 2015; André Brummer and Judy Brummer, interview by Edith Baker and Dan Baker, Apr. 26, 2012, 16, James Moyle Oral History Program, CHL; Karen Trifiletti, "Methodist to Mormon: An Interview with Judy Brummer," *Up Close and Mormon,* accessed July 15, 2016, youtube.com.
3. Brummer's younger brother, Norman Bester, who inherited the ranch, bought homes for Maggie, Jane, and Lizzie when he sold the land. (Judy Brummer, interview by Kate Holbrook, July 1, 2015, 6–7, CHL.)
4. Brummer, interview, 7; André Brummer and Judy Brummer, interview, 18; Judy Brummer, email to Kate Holbrook, Jan. 20, 2016.
5. Jeffrey G. Cannon, "Mormonism's Jesse Haven and the Early Focus on Proselytising the Afrikaner at the Cape of Good Hope, 1853–1855," *Dutch Reformed Theological Journal* 48, nos. 3 and 4 (Sept. and Dec. 2007): 446–456; E. Dale LeBaron, "Africa, the Church in," in *Encyclopedia of Mormonism,* ed. Daniel H. Ludlow, 5 vols. (New York: Macmillan, 1992), 1:22–24.
6. LeBaron, "Africa, the Church in," 24.
7. R. Val Johnson, "South Africa: Land of Good Hope," *Ensign* 23, no. 2 (Feb. 1993): 36.
8. Brummer arrived at mission headquarters in Johannesburg on September 27, 1980, and served in Queenstown for eighteen months. The entire Book of Mormon was first published in Xhosa in 2000. (Queenstown Branch, South African Mission, Annual Historical Reports, Sept. 27, 1980,

CHL; Trifiletti, "Methodist to Mormon"; Johnson, "South Africa," 39; Brent Meisinger, email to Matthew J. Grow, Jan. 26, 2016.)

9. Trifiletti, "Methodist to Mormon"; André Brummer and Judy Brummer, interview, 2–3.
10. The company became Ancestry.com. (Brummer, interview, 12–13; André Brummer and Judy Brummer, interview, 15.)
11. At her bishop's request, she limited her speaking engagements to once a month while she was president of her ward Young Women organization. (Brummer, interview, 1.)
12. Brummer, interview, 2–3.
13. Brummer, interview, 3.
14. The Karoo is an arid region in southwest Africa in the countries of South Africa, Namibia, and Botswana. It includes the Namib desert and the Kalahari savanna. (W. Richard Dean and Suzanne J. Milton, *The Karoo: Ecological Patterns and Processes* [Cambridge, UK: Cambridge University Press, 2004], xxi.)
15. The private school was Diocesan School for Girls in Grahamstown, South Africa. Rhodes University is also in Grahamstown. Gwenna Bester earned a bachelor of science in mathematics and a University Education Diploma. (Brummer, email to Holbrook, Aug. 17, 2015.)
16. Gwenna Bester lived from 1923 to 2008. (Brummer, email to Holbrook, Aug. 17, 2015.)
17. Moroni 10.
18. Moroni 10:7, 32–33.
19. Blacks and whites lived separately in South Africa from the time Jan van Riebeeck established a Dutch outpost in 1652. Apartheid was the extensive government system of racial segregation from 1948 to 1994. (Patti Waldmeir, *Anatomy of a Miracle: The End of Apartheid and the Birth of the New South Africa* [New York: W. W. Norton, 1997], 10.)
20. *Australia,* directed by Baz Luhrmann (Beverly Hills, CA: Twentieth Century Fox, 2008).
21. Nelson Mandela and Thabo Mbeki were the first post-apartheid presidents of South Africa. Mandela was president from 1994 to 1999, and Mbeki was president from 1999 to 2008. The word for the language of Xhosa in the Xhosa language is *isiXhosa.* (Sharlene Swartz, *The Moral Ecology of South Africa's Township Youth* [New York: Palgrave Macmillan, 2009], 188.)
22. David R. Wilkerson, with John Sherrill and Elizabeth Sherrill, *The Cross and the Switchblade* (New York: B. Geis Associates, 1963). *The Cross and the Switchblade* is an autobiographical account written by David Wilkerson about his experiences in New York City starting in 1958, where he preached about God's love and the power of the Spirit to young people who were gang members, drug addicts, prostitutes, and teenage runaways.
23. On June 9, 1978, the First Presidency and Quorum of the Twelve Apostles of the church released a letter announcing that every worthy male member was now eligible to be ordained to the priesthood. (See Doctrine and Covenants, Official Declaration 2; see also Edward L. Kimball, *Lengthen Your Stride: The Presidency of Spencer W. Kimball* [Salt Lake City: Deseret Book, 2005], 215–235; and Richard E. Turley Jr. and Jeffrey G. Cannon, "A Faithful Band: Moses Mahlangu and the First Soweto Saints," *BYU Studies Quarterly* 55, no. 1 [2016]: 8–38.)
24. The farm boy was Joseph Smith. For an account of his "First Vision" see Joseph Smith—History 1:14–20.
25. First convening in Amsterdam in 1948, the World Council of Churches (WCC) is a coalition of churches that "confess the Lord Jesus Christ as God and Saviour." Although it collaborates with the WCC on specific projects, the Catholic church is one of only a few Christian churches that are not official members. The Church of Jesus Christ of Latter-day Saints also is not a member. (E. A. Livingstone, *Concise Dictionary of the Christian Church* [Oxford: Oxford University Press, 2013], 617.)
26. James 1:27.
27. Brummer arrived in her first area on September 27, 1980. She was originally assigned to work with a missionary couple, Don Eugene and Virginia Poppleton, as their translator. (Queenstown Branch Annual Historical Reports, Sept. 27, 1980.)
28. Goliat Kowa took Brummer and her companions to visit the congregations he had established and

encouraged his members to join the official church. Often a missionary would say words of the baptismal prayer in English while Brummer stood nearby and translated the ordinance into Xhosa. Kowa decided to break with the church in December 1982. (Judy Brummer, unrecorded interview by Kate Holbrook, Jan. 28, 2016; André Brummer and Judy Brummer, interview, 20; Illinge Branch, South Africa Johannesburg Mission, Annual Historical Report, Dec. 30, 1982, CHL.)

29. These are areas and cities with Xhosa populations in South Africa's Eastern Cape.
30. Peter Boyton and Nigel Wrench "established contact with several black people in scattered areas and were teaching these the discussion lessons." Kowa is not mentioned by name. (Queenstown Branch Annual Historical Reports, June 2, 1980.)
31. Xhosa people lived in Transkei and Ciskei, two of ten "tribal homelands" that had been contrived by apartheid commissioners during the 1950s and 1960s to force all black South Africans out of urban centers. The ultimate goal was to make the homelands, called Bantustans, into independent entities and leave South Africa a white republic. Apartheid supporters hoped the Bantustans would foster tribal loyalties while decreasing intertribal cooperation; the homelands were arid and crowded. (Kusum Datta, "Bantustans," in *Encyclopedia of the Developing World,* ed. Thomas M. Leonard [New York: Taylor and Francis, 2006], 152–154.)
32. Alfred James Corrigan and Rita Helena Corrigan arrived in Queenstown on June 2, 1980. Brummer's companion was Vivienne Howes. (Queenstown Branch Annual Historical Reports, June 2, 1980.)
33. District headquarters were in East London. On November 21, 1981, a total of fifty-seven converts were interviewed, baptized, and confirmed at Illinge. Additional elders were sent to help Alfred Corrigan with this work. Brummer and Augustine Mjeba translated for the interviews. (Queenstown Branch Annual Historical Reports, Nov. 21, 1981.)
34. *The Gods Must Be Crazy,* directed by Jamie Uys (Culver City, CA: Columbia, 1980).
35. Retention rates are high in Africa. (Sarah Jane Weaver, "LDS Leaders Visit Africa, Say 'Progress Is Remarkable,'" *Church News,* Nov. 7, 2014; Tad Walch, "Major LDS Growth in Africa Unaffected by Priesthood Restriction, Elder Sitati Says," *Deseret News,* Oct. 9, 2015.)
36. Brummer's boss was Andre Wasseman, and Wasseman's boss, who sent the telegram, was Alec Vella. (Brummer, email to Holbrook, Aug. 17, 2015.)
37. This is a reference to the pamphlet *The Prophet Joseph Smith's Testimony* (Salt Lake City: The Church of Jesus Christ of Latter-day Saints), which was first printed in English in 1970 and was used by missionaries to teach about Joseph Smith's first encounter with God the Father and Jesus Christ. Brummer's translation was published in 1982.
38. This quotation of Joseph Smith is in the introduction to the Book of Mormon and was taken from the *History of the Church*: "I told the brethren that the Book of Mormon was the most correct of any book on earth, and the keystone of our religion, and a man would get nearer to God by abiding by its precepts, than by any other book." (Joseph Smith et al., *History of the Church of Jesus Christ of Latter-day Saints,* ed. B. H. Roberts [Salt Lake City: Deseret News, 1902–1912 (vols. 1–6), 1932 (vol. 7)], 4:461; Wilford Woodruff, Journal, Nov. 28, 1841, CHL; see also Scott C. Esplin, "Getting 'Nearer to God': A History of Joseph Smith's Statement," in *Living the Book of Mormon: Abiding by Its Precepts,* ed. Gaye Strathearn and Charles Swift [Provo, UT: Religious Studies Center, Brigham Young University, 2007], 47–49.)
39. Robert Eppel, who was raised in South Africa and in Zimbabwe, became a regional manager for the church in Johannesburg in 1981. (Karen Belliston, "New President Called for Johannesburg South Africa Temple," *Church News,* Oct. 14, 2013.)
40. Gene R. Cook became a seventy in 1975; he was granted emeritus status in 2007.
41. *Gospel Principles* (Salt Lake City: The Church of Jesus Christ of Latter-day Saints, 1978).
42. See Moroni 10:27–28, 32–34; see also, for example, 1 Nephi 19:17; Mosiah 3:20; Mosiah 15:28; and Revelation 14:6.

CHAPTER 53: LINDA K. BURTON, "OUR SABBATH DAY GIFTS"

1. "Linda Kjar Burton: Sixteenth General President of the Relief Society," accessed May 2, 2016, lds.org; "Morris Ashton Kjar," *Salt Lake Tribune,* June 25, 2014.

2. Linda K. Burton, interview by Kate Holbrook, Apr. 20, 2016, 1–2, CHL; "Linda Kjar Burton: Sixteenth General President of the Relief Society."
3. Burton and her fellow board members taught workshops from morning to night for three days during the week before general conference. They taught ideas for teaching lessons to children, for teaching songs to children, and for doing both in Spanish. (Burton, interview, 5–6.)
4. "Linda Kjar Burton: Sixteenth General President of the Relief Society"; "New Mission Presidents," *Church News,* Apr. 14, 2007.
5. Burton, interview, 2–4. Missionaries have one preparation day per week for doing laundry, cleaning, buying groceries, and corresponding with loved ones.
6. "New Relief Society General Board Members," *Church News,* Jan. 8, 2011.
7. Burton, interview, 8–9.
8. "Purposes," 9.1.1, *Handbook 2: Administering the Church* (Salt Lake City: The Church of Jesus Christ of Latter-day Saints, 2010), chapter 9, "Relief Society," accessed May 2, 2016, lds.org. In an interview, Burton mentioned that as Beck studied the history of the Relief Society, she also worked to redefine its purpose statement for the church's *Handbook 2,* published in 2010. In May 2016, the online version of *Handbook 2* was updated to reflect Burton's further refining of the purpose statement. (Burton, interview, 11; Julie B. Beck, interview by Gordon Irving and Justin R. Bray, Mar. 2012, 67, 69, 82–90, CHL; Julie B. Beck, "Fulfilling the Purpose of Relief Society," *Ensign* 38, no. 11 [Nov. 2008]: 109; *Handbook 2,* "Relief Society," accessed Aug. 17, 2016, lds.org.)
9. "Women Church Leaders Appointed to Leadership Councils," Newsroom Blog of the Church of Jesus Christ of Latter-day Saints, Aug. 19, 2015, accessed May 2, 2016, mormonnewsroom.org.
10. Burton, interview, 11–12; Linda K. Burton, "I Was a Stranger," *Ensign* 46, no. 5 (May 2016): 13–15.
11. Elder M. Russell Ballard of the Quorum of the Twelve Apostles explained that church leaders felt it was important that families and individuals reconsider their approach to the Sabbath day. "Our whole desire is that throughout the church, we focus our Sabbath day worship on the Lord," he said. ("Church Leaders Call for Better Observance of Sabbath Day," Newsroom of the Church of Jesus Christ of Latter-day Saints, June 30, 2015, accessed May 2, 2016, mormonnewsroom.org.)
12. Linda K. Burton, email to Kate Holbrook, Apr. 28, 2016.
13. Russell M. Nelson, "The Sabbath Is a Delight," *Ensign* 45, no. 5 (May 2015): 129–132; Burton, interview, 18–19.
14. M. Russell Ballard joined the Quorum of the Twelve Apostles in 1985. Donald L. Hallstrom became a member of the Quorum of the Seventy in 2000 and a member of the Presidency of the Seventy in 2009. Dean M. Davies became second counselor in the Presiding Bishopric in 2012 and first counselor in 2015.
15. Citation in original: "Russell M. Nelson, 'The Sabbath Is a Delight,' *Ensign* 45, no. 5 (May 2015): 129." See also Mark 2:27. Russell M. Nelson became a member of the Quorum of the Twelve Apostles in 1984 and president of the Quorum of the Twelve Apostles in 2015.
16. Morris Ashton Kjar died in 2014. ("Morris Ashton Kjar"; "Linda Kjar Burton: Sixteenth General President of the Relief Society.")
17. Citation in original: "D&C 59:8–9."
18. Citation in original: "Julie Thompson, 'Unspotted from the World,' *Ensign* 42, no. 7 (July 2012): 80."
19. Robert D. Hales was a member of the First Quorum of the Seventy from 1976 to 1985. He joined the Presiding Bishopric in 1985 and became a member of the Quorum of the Twelve Apostles in 1994.
20. Citation in original: "Robert D. Hales, 'Stand Strong in Holy Places,' *Ensign* 43, no. 5 (May 2013): 49."
21. See Mark 2:23–28; 3:1–6; Luke 13:11–16; 14:1–6; and John 5:8–16; 9:14–16.
22. Citation in original: "Spencer W. Kimball, 'The Sabbath—A Delight,' *Ensign* 8, no. 1 (Jan. 1978): 4." Spencer W. Kimball served as twelfth president of the church from 1973 to 1985.
23. Reeves made these comments as a panelist at a general authority training meeting that included the Quorum of the Twelve Apostles and members of the Quorums of the Seventy the week before the April 2015 general conference. (Linda Reeves, email to Kate Holbrook, Apr. 30, 2016.)

24. Citation in original: "Neal A. Maxwell, 'Swallowed Up in the Will of the Father,' *Ensign* 25, no. 11 (Nov. 1995): 24." Neal A. Maxwell was a member of the Quorum of the Twelve Apostles from 1981 to 2004.
25. Citation in original: "M. Russell Ballard, 'Finding Joy through Loving Service,' *Ensign* 41, no. 5 (May 2011): 49."
26. Moroni 4:3; 5:2; Doctrine and Covenants 20:77, 79.

CHAPTER 54: GLADYS N. SITATI, "RESOLVING CONFLICTS USING GOSPEL PRINCIPLES"

1. Jason Swensen, "Full Joy Found in Principles of the Gospel," *Church News,* May 23, 2009.
2. Gladys Sitati, interview by Kate Holbrook, May 5, 2016, 1–3, CHL; Gladys Sitati, email to Kate Holbrook, May 18, 2016.
3. Sitati attended Lugulu Girls High School for her secondary education and Butere Girls High School to prepare for university entrance. (Sitati, interview, 2, 4–5; Sitati, email to Holbrook, May 18, 2016.)
4. Sitati, interview, 1–4, 6–8.
5. Swensen, "Full Joy Found in Principles of the Gospel," 11; Sitati, interview, 1.
6. Sitati, interview, 9. A fireside address Benson gave on February 22, 1987, was published and widely distributed in pamphlet form. (Ezra Taft Benson, *To the Mothers in Zion* [Salt Lake City: The Church of Jesus Christ of Latter-day Saints, 1987].)
7. Sitati, interview, 9–10.
8. Julie Dockstader Heaps, "Serving in Africa," *Church News,* May 31, 2003; E. Dale LeBaron, "Pioneers in East Africa," *Ensign* 24, no. 10 (Oct. 1994): 22; Gerald W. Jensen and Carolyn Jensen, "First Stake in Kenya Created," *Church News,* Sept. 29, 2001; "Sunday School, Young Men Receive New Presidencies," *Deseret News,* Apr. 4, 2004; "New Mission Presidents," *Church News,* Apr. 28, 2007; Swensen, "Full Joy Found in Principles of the Gospel," 11; Peggy Fletcher Stack, "Africa's 'Mormon Superstar' Is First Black African LDS General Authority," *Salt Lake Tribune,* Apr. 20, 2009; Gladys Sitati, "Gospel Growth in Kenya," *Ensign* 28, no. 8 (Aug. 1998): 77–78; Sitati, interview, 21; Sitati, email to Holbrook, May 18, 2016.
9. Sitati, interview, 17–20; see also T. J. Fitikides, *Common Mistakes in English* (London: Longman, 2000).
10. Sitati, interview, 12–13, 23–25; Gladys Sitati, email to Kate Holbrook, May 17, 2016.
11. Citation in original: "3 Nephi 11:29."
12. Citation in original: "Moroni 7:3; Mosiah 18:9."
13. Citation in original: "4 Nephi 1:15–18."
14. Citation in original: "Hebrews 11:1."
15. Citation in original: "Moroni 7:33."
16. See *Lectures on Faith,* Lecture One, in Doctrine and Covenants, 1835 ed., 7 [Lecture First 1:13], in Robin Scott Jensen, Richard E. Turley Jr., and Riley M. Lorimer, eds., *Revelations and Translations, Volume 2: Published Revelations,* vol. 2 of the Revelations and Translations series of *The Joseph Smith Papers,* ed. Dean C. Jessee, Ronald K. Esplin, and Richard Lyman Bushman (Salt Lake City: Church Historian's Press, 2011), 317.
17. This church unit, the Parleys Creek Branch, was created in January 2009. ("Swahili Branch Created in Salt Lake," *Church News,* Jan. 8, 2009; see also Peggy Fletcher Stack, "LDS Swahili Branch Unites African Mormons," *Salt Lake Tribune,* Apr. 17, 2009.)
18. This choir for the women's session included girls and women in Primary, Young Women, and Relief Society from stakes in Salt Lake City. They came from fifty-two countries, speaking twenty different languages. (Rachel Sterzer, "'Sisters in the Gospel' Unified through Music," *Church News,* Mar. 20, 2016; *Ensign* 46, no. 5 [May 2016]: 2.)
19. Citation in original: "'For Peace at Home,' *Ensign* or *Liahona,* May 2013, 31." Richard G. Scott was a member of the Quorum of the Twelve Apostles from 1988 to 2015.
20. Citation in original: "D&C 84:106."

21. Citation in original: "Moroni 10:5."
22. Citation in original: "D&C 9:7–8." Oliver Cowdery served as a scribe to Joseph Smith as he translated the Book of Mormon. This revelation, dictated by Joseph Smith in April 1829, was in response to Cowdery's unsuccessful attempt to translate the book himself, a gift promised to him in an earlier revelation. (See Doctrine and Covenants 8; Revelation, April 1829–D [D&C 9], in Michael Hubbard MacKay, Gerrit J. Dirkmaat, Grant Underwood, Robert J. Woodford, and William G. Hartley, eds., *Documents, Volume 1: July 1828–June 1831,* vol. 1 of the Documents series of *The Joseph Smith Papers,* ed. Dean C. Jessee, Ronald K. Esplin, Richard Lyman Bushman, and Matthew J. Grow [Salt Lake City: Church Historian's Press, 2013], 48–50.)
23. Citation in original: "Romans 8:26, 28, 31."
24. Citation in original: "See Luke 18:1–7."
25. Citation in original: "Matthew 5:43–44."
26. See Clyde J. Williams, ed., *The Teachings of Howard W. Hunter* (Salt Lake City: Bookcraft, 1997), 39–40, quoting Hunter, "Unity Brings Peace," Australia Area General Conference, Nov. 29, 1979, typescript, 6–7, CHL. Howard W. Hunter was the fourteenth president of the church from 1994 to 1995.
27. Citation in original: "D&C 121:45."
28. Citation in original: "See 'Praying Together to Stay Together? The Role Prayer Plays in Relationship Conflict,' *Deseret News,* February 16, 2016."
29. Citation in original: "Matthew 18:21–22."
30. Citation in original: "'Of You It Is Required to Forgive,' *Ensign,* June 1991, 2." Gordon B. Hinckley was the fifteenth president of the church from 1995 to 2008.
31. Citation in original: "'Love—the Essence of the Gospel,' *Ensign* or *Liahona,* May 2014, 91, 94." Thomas S. Monson became the sixteenth president of the church in 2008.
32. Citation in original: "Matthew 5:46–48."
33. Citation in original: "Philippians 2:2–4."
34. Citation in original: "See 'Loving Others and Living with Differences,' *Ensign* or *Liahona,* Nov. 2014, 25–28." Dallin H. Oaks became a member of the Quorum of the Twelve Apostles in 1984.
35. Citation in original: "Mosiah 4:11–13."
36. Citation in original: "Moroni 8:26."
37. Citation in original: "Moroni 8:26."
38. Citation in original: "2 Nephi 32; see 3 Nephi 11:29–30." See also 2 Nephi 31:20.

INDEX

◇◇◇

T

U

V